ASIAN AMERICAN

HISTORY AND CULTURE

AN ENCYCLOPEDIA

VOLUME TWO

EDITED BY HUPING LING AND ALLAN AUSTIN

SHARPE REFERENCE

an imprint of M.E. Sharpe, Inc.

SHARPE REFERENCE

Sharpe Reference is an imprint of M.E. Sharpe, Inc.

M.E. Sharpe, Inc.
80 Business Park Drive
Armonk, NY 10504

Cover photos by Getty and the following (clockwise from top left corner): Nicholas Kamm/AFP; Alex Wong; Hulton Archive/Stringer; MPI/Stringer/Hulton Archive; Max Whittaker/Stringer; David Paul Morris/Stringer.

Library of Congress Cataloging-in-Publication Data

Asian American history and culture: an encyclopedia / Huping Ling and Allan Austin, editors.
    p. cm.
Includes bibliographical references and index.
ISBN 978-0-7656-8077-8 (hardcover : alk. paper)
  1. Asian Americans—Encyclopedias. 2. Asian Americans—History—Encyclopedias.
I. Ling, Huping. II. Austin, Allan W.

E184.A75A8287 2010
973′.0495—dc22
                                                    2009011926

Printed and bound in the United States

IBT (c) 10 9 8 7 6 5 4 3 2 1

Publisher: Myron E. Sharpe
Vice President and Director of New Product Development: Donna Sanzone
Vice President and Production Director: Carmen Chetti
Executive Development Editor: Jeff Hacker
Project Manager: Eileen Chetti
Program Coordinator: Cathleen Prisco
Assistant Editor: Alison Morretta
Text Design and Cover Design: Jesse Sanchez
Typesetter: Nancy Connick

Contents

The Korean American Experience: History and Culture

ASIAN AMERICAN
HISTORY AND CULTURE

AN ENCYCLOPEDIA

VOLUME TWO

The Indian American Experience:

History and Culture

Although Asian Indian Americans have been arriving in the United States in measurable numbers since at least the late nineteenth century, they constitute one of the newer Asian American immigrant groups. (For simplicity's sake, this group is referred to as Indian Americans or Indians in this article.) Of all the major Asian American groups (Chinese, Filipino, Indian, Japanese, Korean, and Vietnamese), Indian Americans are the most likely to have arrived in the United States since the 1980s. At the same time, Indian Americans are the most successful of immigrants in terms of education and income. The third-largest Asian immigrant group after Chinese and Filipinos, Indian Americans tend to settle in large urban areas, though they are relatively well dispersed across the United States.

As in many other Asian American groups, the extended family is an important component in Indian American life, as is faith, though the population—like the home country from which it comes—falls into many religious communities. Indian Americans have long been active in U.S. politics. The first Asian American congressman was an Indian named Dalip Singh Saund, a Democrat from California elected to the first of three terms in 1956, and many Indian Americans provided financial and other forms of support to the independence movement in their native country during the first half of the twentieth century. In the arts and scholarship, Indian Americans have made outsized contributions, particularly in literature, film, and the hard sciences.

Immigrant History

The vast majority of early immigrants to the United States from the Indian subcontinent were Sikhs—members of a syncretic faith that blends elements of Hinduism and Islam, largely based in the Punjabi province in the northwest region of what was then British India. (Today, Punjabis live on both sides of the India-Pakistan border.) In the late nineteenth and early twentieth centuries, the Punjab region was undergoing the most rapid modernization in India, and many of its people were displaced from their traditional lands and occupations.

Some went to British Columbia in the late nineteenth century, then headed south of the border in search of land and job opportunities. By 1900, about 2,000 Sikhs lived in the Pacific Northwest, working in logging, construction, and agriculture. Several thousand more came in the first few years of the twentieth century. By 1907, roughly 2,000 Indians, mostly Sikhs and virtually all of them men, were working on railway projects across the American West. While the vast majority of Indians in America in these years were laborers, a few merchants could be counted among them, largely providing groceries and other supplies to their countrymen. In addition, about 100 students were studying at American colleges and universities in the early twentieth century.

Members of the Sikh faith—who dominated early U.S. immigration from the Indian subcontinent—attend the Annual Sikh Parade in Yuba City, California. Sikhs now constitute a relatively small segment of the overall Indian American population. *(Max Whittaker/Stringer/Getty Images)*

During the agricultural boom of the 1910s, thousands migrated to California and found paid employment, though a few owned their own farms. This was not easy to achieve. In 1913, California passed the Alien Land Law, prohibiting noncitizens from owning land. Since all nonwhites—with the exception of persons of African and Mexican descent—were barred from becoming citizens, this effectively prevented Indians from owning land. Still, enough Indians were able to get around the law, often by marrying Mexican women and putting the deeds in their names. By 1920, Indian farmers owned nearly 40,000 acres (16,200 hectares) in California's agriculturally rich Imperial and Sacramento Valleys. In 1923, the U.S. Supreme Court heard the case of Bhagat Singh Thind, a light-skinned, high-caste Sikh immigrant who claimed that, anthropologically speaking, he was a member of the Caucasian race and thus had the right to become a citizen and own land in California. But the court held against him in *United States v. Bhagat Singh Thind*, ruling that he was not a Caucasian in the "common understanding" of the term. The discrimination experienced by Indian Americans in these years was not just legal. Indeed, many faced hostility and prejudice from government officials and the majority white community. And while such groups as the Asiatic Exclusion League, established in 1905, were largely organized to turn back East Asian immigrants, particularly the Chinese and Japanese, they also targeted Indian Americans, many of whom chose to return to their native land in the first two decades of the twentieth century to escape harassment and persecution.

Between the 1920s and the 1960s, virtually no Indians immigrated to the United States, though Congress passed the Luce-Celler Act in 1946 allowing for them to become citizens. Between the end of World War II and 1965, when the Immigration and Nationality Act effectively ended national quotas, just 6,000 Asian Indians immigrated to the United States. As with other Asian groups, the Indian American population began to grow significantly in the 1970s and dramatically in the 1980s—spurred by the 1965 law, which gave priority to immigrants with useful skills or who had family in the United States. Whereas just over 31,000 Indians immigrated to the United States from 1961 to 1970, the figure for 1971–1980 was nearly 177,000, and for 1981–1989 nearly 292,000. By 1990, the Indian American population stood at roughly 815,000 and by 2000 reached almost 1.65 million, with an additional 210,000 Americans claiming some Asian Indian descent. As of 2005, the Indian American population was estimated at just under 2.32 million, a growth rate of about 41 percent

over five years, the fastest of any major immigrant group in the country. This helps to explain why Asian Indians, at 54 percent, are the least likely to have U.S. citizenship of any Asian American group, though the high percentage of those coming in on temporary worker visas also contributes to this statistic.

While Indian immigrants have settled throughout the United States—just under a third in the Northeast, just under a quarter in both the South and the West, and just under 20 percent in the Midwest—they tend to move to large urban areas. There are major Indian American communities in the New York metropolitan area (largely in the borough of Queens and the cities of northern New Jersey), the Los Angeles metropolitan area (with the heart of the community in the suburban town of Artesia), Chicago, and the San Francisco Bay Area, with a large concentration in the San Jose/Silicon Valley region.

Education and Economics

Indian Americans are a uniquely successful community socioeconomically, arguably the best-educated and most prosperous of all recent immigrant groups, Asian or otherwise—this in spite of the fact that they are also among the most recent to arrive. Of the foreign-born Indian American population, according to the 2000 U.S. Census, more than half arrived in the 1990s, the highest percentage of any major Asian American immigrant group. Of the other 46 percent, more than 60 percent came in the 1980s. (All figures in this section come from the 2000 census, unless otherwise noted.)

Part of what has helped Indians succeed so well in America is their English-language abilities, a legacy of centuries of British rule and an educational system since independence that has been partially modeled after England's. Roughly 77 percent of Indian Americans speak English as their first language or speak it "very well" as a second language, the highest of all Asian American immigrant groups and fully one-fourth more than Asian Americans generally. Asian Indians are also well educated. Nearly two-thirds of the community over the age of twenty-five have a bachelor's degree or higher, by far the highest percentage of any major Asian immigrant group (followed by the Chinese at 48 percent) and roughly 260 percent above that of the U.S. population as a whole. Only about 14 percent of adult Indians do not have a high school diploma, nearly one-third lower than the Asian American community as a whole. While many Indians obtain their education in the United States, significant numbers come with higher degrees. It is estimated that nearly half of the persons entering the country in the early 2000s on H-1B visas, allowing persons with special training or skills to immigrate for work, were persons from India.

Indian Americans are also far more likely to use that education in their work. Nearly 60 percent of the group who had jobs worked in the professions or management positions. Many of these professionals work in the high-tech industry. More than 30,000 Indians worked in Silicon Valley in 2000, including more than 1,000 who had started their own businesses there—roughly 10 percent of the total—and generated nearly $50 billion in revenue. Overall, approximately one-third of the computer engineers in Silicon Valley in the early 2000s were of Indian descent. The Indian American presence in the high-tech industry helps explain their remarkable economic success, as do the large numbers of doctors, engineers, and other professionals in the community and the high rate of entrepreneurialism. To take just one niche industry, about 50 percent of the motels in America are owned by Indian American immigrants. With a median household income of $70,708, Indians were second among all Asian American groups, behind the well-established Japanese American community by a negligible $141. In fact, median household income among Indian Americans was nearly 20 percent higher than for Asian Americans generally and more than 40 percent higher than for U.S. households generally. At the same time, Indian Americans, at 9.7 percent, had a poverty rate more than 20 percent lower than that of all Asian Americans or, for that matter, the U.S. population as a whole. At the other end of the scale, nearly one in twenty-five adult Indian Americans is a millionaire—10 percent of the U.S. total, for only 1 percent of the national population.

The only major socioeconomic index in which Indians lag is in home ownership. While about 66 percent of the country as a whole lived in owner-occupied housing according to the 2000 census, the figure for Indian Americans was about 47 percent—somewhat below the 53 percent for Asian Americans overall. The lag may be explained by three factors—the relatively high proportion of Indians in the country on temporary work visas, the relative newness of the community, and the costliness of housing in the major metropolitan areas where Indian Americans tend to settle.

Family and Faith

The vast majority of Indian Americans live in nuclear households, though the size of their households has been gradually shrinking. In 1990, the median Indian American household included 3.8 persons; by 2000, the figure had fallen to just over three persons. Fully two-thirds of Indian Americans lived in households with two parents in 2000, either with or without children. The percentage of divorced Indian Americans (2.4) was the lowest of any Asian American group and more than 40 percent lower than for Asian Americans generally (and just one-quarter of the rate for Americans overall).

Although Indian Americans typically live in two-parent nuclear households, the extended family remains important to the community. Indian Americans frequently open their households to long visits from grandparents, and well-off members of the household are expected to financially care for the recently arrived or those in need of help—a major explanation for the significantly lower rate of poverty among Indian Americans.

Indian parents expect their children to heed their advice, and while the home-country practice of arranged marriages is fading among second-generation Indian Americans, it still remains strong, with many children still being paired off by parents and other family members, often by bringing in brides or grooms from India. Indeed, Indian Americans stress marrying among their own religious and social networks, including caste. Among all major Asian groups, only Vietnamese Americans are less likely to marry outside their community. Indian Americans also place great importance on the rituals of marriage. Weddings are often elaborate, multiday affairs that relatives and friends travel great distances to attend and in which parents try to outdo one another in expense and lavishness.

India is one of the most religiously diverse countries in the world. While the predominant religion is Hinduism, there are many Muslims, along with significant minorities of Christians, Sikhs, Jains, Zoroastrians, and Buddhists. All major Indian religions are represented in the Indian American community. Whatever the faith, religion is central to the lives of Indians in the home country and in America. The very first Hindu temple in America, located in San Francisco, was built in 1920. By 2000, the number of Hindu places of worship was well into the hundreds. Less organized than Western faiths, Hinduism does not call on adherents to attend services regularly, though many Indian Americans—particularly more elderly or traditional ones—visit temples often for prayer, to mark holidays, or to make offerings to the many deities of the faith. Key Hindu religious institutions with a presence in America—and sometimes with a significant following of non-Indians—are the International Society for Krishna Consciousness (ISKCON, whose members are popularly known as Hare Krishnas), founded in 1966;

the Swaminarayan Sampraday, a Hindu sect dating to the early nineteenth century; Bochasanwasi Akshar Purushottam Swaminarayan Sanstha, a sect begun in the early twentieth century; the Chinmaya Mission, founded in 1953; and Svadhyaya, an ancient orthodox sect of the Brahmin caste. With the exception of ISKCON, which was founded by a Hindu religious leader in New York City, all of these sects are transplants from the home country.

As with Buddhists, members of India's second- and third-largest faiths—Islam and Christianity—usually practice their religion in multiethnic houses of worship, though many of the former belong to the Indian Muslim Council–USA. Members of India's fourth-largest faith, Sikhs, also worship in temples of their own, known as *gurdwaras.* Observant male Sikhs are required to wear turbans and never cut their hair. Because of this, in the wake of the September 11 terrorist attacks in 2001, some Sikhs were mistaken for Arab Muslims. In the weeks and months following the events of that day, there were reports of several violent assaults on Sikh Americans. Among these was the murder by white supremacists of an Arizona gas station owner named Balbir Singh Sodhi.

Civics and Politics

Indian Americans have a long tradition of organizing within their community. Under the leadership of Taraknath Das, a radical scholar from Bengal, Indian Americans on the West Coast organized themselves into the Hindi Association of the Pacific Ocean to fight back against whites attacking their communities in the early twentieth century. In 1913, Punjabi and other Indian workers on the American and Canadian Pacific Coast formed the Ghadar ("mutiny" in Urdu, the language of the Punjab) Party, headquartered in San Francisco and dedicated to overthrowing British rule in India and remaking the country along socialist lines. Hostile to British interests, the party expressed sympathy for Germany in World War I and was crushed by U.S. and Canadian authorities.

With the decline in Indian immigration in the middle years of the twentieth century, Indian American involvement in politics faded. And while Punjab-born Dalip Singh Saund, the Sikh American who represented California's Imperial Valley in Congress from 1957 to 1963, made a name for himself advocating the extension of U.S. citizenship to Indian immigrants—a cause realized with passage of the Luce-Celler Act of 1946—he was elected largely by the votes of Anglo- and Mexican-Americans. Fifty years later, American-born Piyush

"Bobby" Jindal, also of Punjabi descent, would achieve the same cross-ethnic support in his successful run for the governorship of Louisiana in 2007, becoming the highest-ranking elected government official of Indian heritage in U.S. history.

As a relatively new community in the late twentieth century, however, Indian Americans are not particularly active politically. Because of their relatively low rates of citizenship, just 25 percent of the community is registered to vote. Of those who are registered, the vast majority are Democrats. But there are signs that Indian American involvement in politics is growing. Coming from a country with a rich and lively democratic tradition, many younger Indians are entering politics by joining the staffs of state and federal elected officials. In addition, many Silicon Valley entrepreneurs are using their wealth to secure the election of officials friendly to both the computer industry and the Indian American community. Indians also follow the politics of their homeland, and many lobby Congress and write letters to the editor whenever an international crisis affects their homeland. This most often occurs when India is in conflict with archrival Pakistan, as was the case in the nuclear showdown between the two countries in the late 1990s. The most important of the lobbying groups is the U.S. India Political Action Committee, which not only advocates stronger bilateral trade and military relations between the two countries, but also promotes a more open immigration policy and a tougher government line against ethnic discrimination in the United States.

Indians in America have organized hundreds of local civic and business organizations, many of them focusing on specific communities from different regions or religions in India. Among the Pan-Indian organizations are the New York–based Association of Indians in America, promoting political and civic participation among Indian Americans; the National Association of Americans of Asian Indian Descent, headquartered in Nebraska and dedicated to advancing political and social rights among Indian Americans; and the National Federation of Indian American Associations, located in Connecticut and focusing on the promotion of Indian culture. The Network of Indian Professionals, based in San Francisco, is dedicated to aiding the careers of the many Indian Americans in the professions, especially those in the high-tech industry.

Arts and Culture

For such a new community, Indian Americans have had a substantial impact on arts, scholarship, and culture in America. In the first case, Indian American accomplishments have been particularly noteworthy in literature and film. Leading authors include Ved Mehta, a McArthur Foundation "genius" fellowship winner and author of the autobiography *Face to Face* (1957); Anita Desai, author of *In Custody* (1984); Bharati Mukherjee, author of *The Middleman and Other Stories,* 1988 winner of the National Book Critics Circle Award; and Vikram Seth, author of *A Suitable Boy* (1993). Younger writers of note include the London-born, U.S.-raised daughter of Indian immigrants, Jhumpa Lahiri, author of the Pulitzer Prize–winning short story collection *Interpreter of Maladies* (1999).

Though based in London, the late film producer Ismail Merchant was responsible, along with his American-born director-partner James Ivory, for a slew of well-received Hollywood and independent films, including *A Room with a View* (1985), *Howards End* (1992), and *The Remains of the Day* (1993). While Merchant generally stayed away from explicit Indian themes in his productions, that has not been the case for Indian-born, New York–based Mira Nair, the director of *Salaam Bombay!* (1988), an Oscar-nominated documentary about street children in the Indian metropolis. Nair has also directed popular fiction films, including *Mississippi Masala* (1991) and *Monsoon Wedding* (2001).

In classical music, the Mumbai-born conductor Zubin Mehta led several major American orchestras, including the Los Angeles Philharmonic from 1962 to 1978 and the New York Philharmonic from 1978 to 1991. In the culinary arts, the award-winning, best-selling Madhur Jaffrey, also a veteran theater and film actress, has helped introduce the rich tradition of Indian cooking to America and the West in books and on television shows since the 1980s. Self-help guru New Delhi–born Deepak Chopra has sold millions of books that apply Indian philosophical and medical traditions to the health and personal problems facing ordinary Americans. The public intellectual Dinesh D'Souza, originally from Bombay, is a leading conservative thinker and author. The Indian American community also numbers two Nobel Laureates in the sciences—Har Gobind Khorana, winner of the medicine award in 1968, and Subrahmanyan Chandrasekhar, the physics award winner in 1983.

Leading Indian American media outlets include *India Abroad,* a New York–based weekly newspaper focusing on issues of concern to the Indian American community.

Founded in 1970, it is the oldest still-operating Indian publication in the country. The San Jose–based *India Currents* is a monthly magazine with an emphasis on arts and lifestyle topics, while *News India-Times,* out of New York, is, as its name implies, more oriented toward hard news.

While the Indian American community has really come of age only since the 1970s—prior to that it was small and largely rural—it has been remarkably successful in many respects. While Asian Americans generally surpass the U.S. population as a whole in education and income, Asian Indian Americans lead the Asian American populations, with the highest rate of college graduation and the second-highest median household income. The community has also contributed in a major way to American arts, literature, and science, forming the largest and most influential ethnic community in the cutting-edge high-tech and computer sectors of the economy. These accomplishments are only bound to expand, as the Indian American community was the fastest-growing of any major immigrant group in the United States in the early 2000s.

James Ciment

Further Reading

Bhatia, Sunil. *American Karma: Race, Culture, and Identity in the Indian Diaspora.* New York: New York University Press, 2007.

Fenton, John Y. *Transplanting Religious Traditions: Asian Indians in America.* New York: Praeger, 1988.

Helweg, Arthur W. *Strangers in a Not-So-Strange Land: Indian American Immigrants in the Global Age.* Belmont, CA: Wadsworth, 2004.

Helweg, Arthur, and Usha Helweg. *An Immigrant Success Story: East Indians in America.* Philadelphia: University of Pennsylvania Press, 1990.

Jensen, Joan M. *Passage from India: Asian Indian Immigrants in North America.* New Haven, CT: Yale University Press, 1988.

Joshi, Khyati Y. *New Roots in America's Sacred Ground: Religion, Race, and Ethnicity in Indian America.* New Brunswick, NJ: Rutgers University Press, 2006.

Rudrappa, Sharmila. *Ethnic Routes to Becoming American: Indian Immigrants and the Cultures of Citizenship.* New Brunswick, NJ: Rutgers University Press, 2004.

U.S. India Political Action Committee. http://www.usinpac.com.

Indian Americans
Alphabetical Entries

Acculturation and the Indian American Community

A small permanent community of Indian Americans —the first in the United States—was formed in California during the early years of the twentieth century. Nearly all of its members were single men hired as agricultural laborers, who faced great racial discrimination and were legally barred from becoming U.S. citizens. Subsequent immigration, largely confined to manual laborers in the West, remained limited. Those who did remain attempted to fit into American society as best they could. The Immigration and Nationality Act of 1965, which lifted national-origin quotas, opened the way for a heavier influx, especially for individuals with professional training and higher education. As a result, a new wave of Indian immigrants—made up largely of educated professionals—began entering the United States. At first, they downplayed their Indian ethnic heritage. Their children, however, have sought to reclaim their Indian identity while adapting it to conditions found in the United States. The degree of acculturation and accommodation accepted among second-generation Indian Americans has varied from group to group.

Early Immigrants and Acculturation

Most early Indian immigrants were Sikh farmers driven by economic difficulties at home to look for new opportunities overseas. Arriving in the late 1890s and early 1900s, they numbered less than 3,000; many worked as agricultural laborers in California's Central Valley. Known as "Hindoos," the Sikhs were obvious outsiders to American society. Their religious beliefs required that they refrain from cutting their hair and beards, and wear a turban. Their dark complexions also marked the Sikhs as outsiders. Anti-Asian feelings culminated in the 1923 U.S. Supreme Court decision in *United States v. Bhagat Singh Thind,* which declared that Indians could never become citizens because they were not white. As a result, strict limits were imposed on the immigration of additional Indians; virtually none arrived from the early 1920s to the mid-1960s. Since few Sikh women had entered the country at all, many of the men intermarried with Mexican women. Excluded from mainstream American society, they formed their own cultural enclave, founding the first Sikh temple, or *gurdwara,* in Stockton, California, in 1912. Early Indian Americans generally kept a low profile and adapted to conditions around them. The children of the Mexican-Sikh marriages tended to marry non-Indians, leading to the gradual disappearance of the first Indian American community.

Other Indians came to the United States as students and were able to stay. One was Dalip Singh Saund, who earned a PhD in mathematics from the University of California, Berkeley. In July 1946, Congress passed legislation that allowed Indians to become naturalized citizens. Saund did so in 1949; seven years later, he became the first Indian American—indeed, the first Asian American—elected to the U.S. Congress, as a Democrat from California.

Post-1965 Immigration

Most Indian Americans in the United States in the early 2000s either immigrated after 1965 or are the descendants of those who did. In 1965, the Immigration and Nationality Act raised immigration limits, giving preference to those individuals who had training or education needed in the United States. During the next decade, the immigration rate from India increased faster than that of any other nation. By 1975, more than 100,000 new Indian Americans were living in the United States, and most became naturalized citizens.

The new wave of immigrants differed from the earlier ones in background as well as number. They tended to be educated professionals, including doctors, lawyers, and businessmen. Many found jobs in higher education or research. Others opened their own businesses or went to work for American corporations. Unlike the farmers, railroad workers, and other manual laborers who preceded them, these Indian Americans tended to settle in urban areas, especially large multiethnic communities like the ones they had left behind in India. Newer immigrants have also tended to be more scattered, settling less often in confined ethnic neighborhoods. This physical integration has helped the acculturation process.

By 2000, nearly 2 million Indian Americans were living in the United States. As an identifiable minority group, they have a number of traits that reflect the values and culture they brought from India. An emphasis on education, hard work, and family has been clear from the outset. Indian Americans also tend to be more upwardly mobile than other Asian immigrants and the U.S. population at large. As of 2000, the median household income was $48,320—more than 50 percent higher than that of Americans born in the United States. Two-parent households made up 89 percent of the families, and 65 of Indian Americans held a bachelor's degree or higher, compared to 20 percent of native-born Americans. All of these factors have helped Indian Americans fit the image of mainstream American culture.

Four basic patterns of acculturation and assimilation have been identified by sociologists. One is integration, in which one identifies biculturally, with both the culture of one's homeland and that of one's adoptive nation. In this case, individual immigrants value and identify with both Indian and American culture. Another pattern is assimilation, or in this case identifying with American culture while rejecting ties to India. The third is marginalization, rejecting both American and Indian cultures. The final approach, separation, is to identify entirely with one's native culture (Indian) and reject the way of life of one's new home (American culture). According to researchers, integration tends to be the course followed by individual immigrants who face the least difficult economic and social problems. Assimilation or separation results in acculturation with fewer problems. Marginalization often produces individuals who have great trouble with acculturation.

Cultural Change and Modification

Acculturation to American life and modifications to Indian culture can be seen in several aspects of Indian American life. One such area is food. Surveys have found that Indian Americans tend to base their diets on what was common to their region of origin or what is acceptable to their faith. Many Hindus avoid beef, and Muslims will not eat pork; others are vegetarian. Traditional dishes and spices remain popular. Depending on their heritage, Indian Americans enjoy such popular dishes as tandoori (clay-baked chicken or fish in yogurt sauce), *biryani* (flavored rice with vegetables or meat for festive occasions), and *dosai* (crepe-like pancakes filled with spiced potatoes or other vegetables). Special occasions

and holidays are usually marked by festive meals and dishes from a family's Indian background. Compromises with American ways include greater dependence on prepared foods, which require less preparation time. Meals are often less formal than in Indian culture, and men participate more in the meal preparation.

Clothing is another significant area of compromise with American culture. Traditional clothing for women includes a sari (draped dress) and a *bindi* (ornamental forehead dot). Indian American women born in the United States, however, tend to wear this clothing only on special occasions or family events.

Indian dance and music in America have been influenced by, and have influenced, American music and dance. Elements of rap, hip-hop, and reggae have been fused with traditional music and dance and have become popular with younger Indian Americans, as well as with non-Indians. Bands such as Alaap and Dhamak, composed of Indian Americans, have moved into mainstream culture.

Indian Americans celebrate holidays accepted by other Americans, such as Independence Day and Labor Day. Most Hindus also celebrate Diwali, the festival of lights, marked by parades organized by local Indian American organizations. Resolutions have been introduced in Congress to recognize Diwali as a holiday equivalent to Kwanzaa. Muslim and Christian Indian Americans also celebrate the traditional religious holidays of their faiths. One additional holiday celebrated by most Indian Americans is Navaratri, or nine nights. It takes place in the fall and is usually marked by folk dancing.

Indian Americans accept the importance of modern Western medicine, but traditional Indian medical practice is also seen as important. Known as *ayurveda* medicine, it emphasizes preventive care and spiritual as well as physical healing. Particular herbs and natural foods play an important role. Many elements of ayurveda medicine are finding their way into Western medicine as well. A prominent practitioner, Dr. Deepak Chopra, has become a popular advocate in the U.S. mass media.

The family remains the most important part of Indian American life. Traditionally, members of the family perform many important rituals, from birth to death, such as scattering one's ashes in the Ganges River. More and more, however, gender-based roles are being adapted, with women now performing duties once reserved for men. Younger generations of Indian Americans are more likely than their parents to marry outside their own group, whether with Indian Americans from different regions or ethnic groups, or even with non-Indian Americans.

A number of organizations have been established to help Indian Americans to become acculturated to American society, while still retaining their Indian identity. The most prominent is the India League of America, founded in 1964 in Madison, Wisconsin, and now with local chapters throughout the United States. Its stated purpose is to work with immigrants to promote a common heritage and to help one another to become part of the mainstream of American life.

Tim J. Watts

Further Reading

Anderson, Wanni W., and Robert G. Lee. *Displacements and Diasporas: Asians in the Americas.* New Brunswick, NJ: Rutgers University Press, 2005.

Bhatia, Sunil. *American Karma: Race, Culture, and Identity in the Indian Diaspora.* New York: New York University Press, 2007.

Maira, Sunaina. *Desis in the House: Indian American Youth Culture in New York City.* Philadelphia: Temple University Press, 2002.

Warner, R. Stephen, and Judith G. Wittner. *Gatherings in Diaspora: Religious Communities and the New Immigration.* Philadelphia: Temple University Press, 1998.

Anglo-Indians

Anglo-Indians—people of British and Indian descent—were prominent on the subcontinent during the period of British rule, from the mid-nineteenth century to the mid-twentieth century. An estimated 200,000–400,000 still live in India; however, since Indian independence in 1947, many have left the country and settled overseas. The exact number in the United States is not known for sure, but it is certainly in the thousands. Indeed the group is difficult to quantify or locate, as Anglo-Indians often identify as British when in India but tend to be regarded as Indian when overseas. Their shared heritage includes an emphasis on education and Christianity.

Two of the earliest connections between Anglo-Indians and the United States date to the eighteenth century. Elihu Yale, an East India merchant who had been born in Boston, Massachusetts, married an Anglo-Indian, Catherine Hynmers. In 1718, Yale received a request for a donation to a small college in New Haven, Connecticut. He made a sizable donation, and the institution renamed itself after its benefactor, becoming Yale College, now Yale University. Another wealthy East India merchant, Thomas "Diamond" Pitt, also married an Anglo-Indian. Their grandson, William Pitt "the Elder," was the British prime minister during the Seven Years' War and the namesake of Pittsburgh, Pennsylvania.

In India during the period of British rule, many members of the Anglo-Indian community were employed on the railways, in the post office or telegraph offices, in schools, and in clerical positions. As a result, during the twentieth century, many were well educated and able to settle in the United States relatively easily; many prospered. Some assimilated, while others retained their Anglo-Indian identity. Most lived in urban areas, especially the major U.S. cities. Among the early Anglo-Indians to gain prominence in the United States was the film actress Merle Oberon, the daughter of an Indian mother and a British army officer who moved to England in the late 1920s and to Hollywood in the 1930s. Another prominent actress of Anglo-Indian origin was Vivien Leigh, who was born in Darjeeling, India; she moved to Hollywood in 1938 and is best known for her role as Scarlett O'Hara in *Gone with the Wind*. The Anglo-Indian tennis player Betty Nuthall Shoemaker became the first non-American to win the U.S. Nationals (now the U.S. Open), in 1930, eventually moving to the United States.

Justin Corfield

Further Reading

Moore, Gloria Jean. *The Anglo-Indian Vision.* Melbourne, Australia: AE, 1986.

Association of Indians in America (AIA)

The Association of Indians in America, headquartered in New York City, is the oldest national association of Indians in the United States. Founded on August 20, 1967, it was incorporated in 1971 as a tax-exempt, nonpartisan, nonpolitical organization with the goal of providing a "forum of common action to all whose Indian heritage and common commitment offer a bond of unity." Its seventeen chapters, concentrated mainly in the eastern and midwestern states, constitute a loose federation, with members representing all regions and religions of India and coming from varied professional and socioeconomic backgrounds. It considers its main achievements—all through vigorous lobbying efforts—to be the classification of immigrants from India as Asian Indians by the U.S. Census Bureau; the establishment of minority status for Indian Americans under civil rights law in the 1970s; and, beginning in 1980, the enumeration of Indian Americans as an independent category in the U.S. Census.

It was during the mid-1970s that the Indian American community took up the issue of self-representation in a serious way—how they wished to see themselves and how they wished to be regarded collectively by others: as white, black, or in between. In the mid-1960s and early 1970s, when Indian immigrants were comparatively few in number, they had eagerly pressed their claim to be considered white, checking off the "White" or "Other" box in census forms. As their numbers expanded, however, they increasingly saw the need to claim both minority status and their fair share of government programs and benefits. Taking on the mantle of community representative, AIA became actively engaged in this effort. It initiated dialogue with the federal agencies in Washington responsible for deciding which ethnic groups constitute minorities. It wrote to the U.S. Civil Rights Commission in 1975, "Indians are different in appearance; they are equally dark-skinned as other nonwhite individuals and are, therefore, subject to the same prejudices. . . . Indians are disadvantaged, we believe, for reasons of racial discrimination." AIA's successful bid for minority status and separate enumeration for Asian Indians in the U.S. Census enabled them to gain visibility and seek social justice. They could now use demographic and socioeconomic profiles from the U.S. Census to document their claims on a wide range of issues, from underrepresentation in legislatures to underfunding for community programs.

The AIA today conducts voter registration drives, urges Indians to fill out census forms, and educates the community on the advantages of being counted and on the need for organized participation in civic duties and political processes. It also represents Asian Indians on issues of bias and discrimination, setting up legal aid funds for the victims of ethnic and religious bigotry and violence. An ongoing activity of AIA is the distribution of National Honor Awards to individuals in recognition of their contributions to arts and letters and to a greater understanding between the peoples of India and America. In addition to celebrating festivals such as Diwali, it also commemorates national events, such as the independence days of both India and America, for mutual understanding between the communities. It has raised millions of dollars for charity and relief projects in India and around the world, such as drives for blood donation or for earthquake and tsunami relief. In 1997, to commemorate the fiftieth anniversary of India's independence, AIA sponsored the publication of *Ananya: A Portrait of India,* a collection of essays by scholars on Indian history, culture, and society.

Amid the rise of many associations in the Indian American community based on narrower religious, regional, and professional identities, AIA has projected itself as a broad-based, grassroots organization, and has managed to survive on a secular platform where all Indians can speak with one voice.

Padma Rangaswamy

Further Reading

Association of Indians in America. http://www.aiausa.org.

Fisher, Maxine P. *The Indians of New York City: A Study of Immigrants from India.* Columbia: South Asian Books, 1980.

Bose, Sudhindra (1883–1946)

Sudhindra Bose was a champion of Indian independence and self-rule in the United States during the 1920s and 1930s. As a professor at the University of Iowa, he developed and taught courses on Asian politics, imperialism, and Asian culture. He also authored a number of books that outlined Indian history and culture to American readers and served on the advisory board of the Watumull Foundation, campaigning for Indian independence. Bose challenged the American practice of denying citizenship to Asians.

Bose was born in 1883 in Keotkhali, near Dhaka, the capital of what is now Bangladesh. At the time, his home was in Bengal, a province of India, which was ruled by the British. After attending Victoria College in Calcutta (1901–1903), he received permission to study in the United States. He was a student at Park College in Parkville, Missouri, between 1904 and 1906, transferred to the University of Illinois in 1906, and received his BA in 1907. Two years later, he earned his MA in English from the same university and then transferred to the University of Iowa, where he received his PhD in political science in 1913.

Bose began his academic career as an instructor in political science at the University of Iowa in 1913, becoming a lecturer in oriental politics in the department and soon establishing himself as a national authority on the subject. Despite his professional prominence, Bose was never tenured; he remained on the faculty at Iowa until his death. His professional memberships included the American Political Science Association and the Iowa State Historical Society.

Like other Indian Americans of the time, Bose faced discrimination and prejudice. His eloquence and ability to explain the situation in India made him a natural representative for the community. In 1915, Bose was asked to represent Indian Americans to federal authorities in Washington, D.C. He appeared before the House Committee on Immigration and unsuccessfully requested immigration rights for Indians seeking to move to the United States. In the aftermath of World War I, American public opinion turned against immigrants. Although Bose was a naturalized citizen, that status was revoked in 1923, after the U.S. Supreme Court ruled in *United States v. Bhagat Singh Thind* that Asian Indians were ineligible to become American citizens. Bose went to court and won back his citizenship in 1927.

Bose became a well-known advocate for equality and Indian nationalism. He reported on events in America for *The Hindu* in Madras and *Amrita Bazar Patrika* in Calcutta. He also was a correspondent for the *Des Moines Register* while on a world tour. Bose wrote a number of books, articles, and pamphlets that outlined the Indian American immigrant experience and argued against British rule of India. The books included *Some Aspects of British Rule in India* (1916), *Fifteen Years in America* (1920), *Glimpses of America* (1925), and *Mother America* (1934). While Bose loved his adopted country, his books did not ignore its flaws, including racism and discrimination against nonwhites. He traveled widely across the United States, speaking to civic and university groups, and worked with the India League of America to secure legislation allowing Indians to become citizens. He also served on the advisory board of the Hawaii-based Watumull Foundation, which tried to rally American support for Indian independence. Bose died in Iowa City on May 26, 1946, a year before his homeland gained independence from the British.

Tim J. Watts

Further Reading

Bose, Sudhindra. *Fifteen Years in America.* New York: Arno, 1974 [1920].
"Papers of Sudhindra Bose." Special Collections Department, University of Iowa Libraries. http://www.lib.uiowa.edu/speccoll/archives/guides/RG99.0147.htm.

Business and Entrepreneurship, Indian American

The talent and resources required to organize, operate, and assume the risks associated with big business ventures did not become widely available to the Indian American community until the 1990s. During the course of that decade, the information technology boom in the United States, the liberalization of the Indian economy, and the trend toward globalization combined to create an environment in which some Indian Americans built extremely successful enterprises and attained great wealth. Armed with little more than an engineering or business degree, and networking through their professional and ethnic connections, they seized new business opportunities in a range of industries, mostly information technology. According to a Duke University study of engineering and technology companies started in the United States from 1995 to 2005, 90 percent of Indian immigrant-founded companies are in just two industries: software and innovation/manufacturing-related services. The study also found that Indians have founded more companies than immigrants from the United Kingdom, China, Taiwan, and Japan combined. Indian entrepreneurs tend to be dispersed around the country, with key concentrations in California and New Jersey. Indian entrepreneurs can also be found in franchising, global manufacturing, insurance and health services, biotechnology, construction, retail, distribution, transportation, and real estate.

Indian immigrants who arrived in the United States during the 1960s and 1970s were mostly professionals who worked hard to establish themselves in safe, secure, well-paying jobs. The 1980s saw the establishment of many mom-and-pop establishments, grocery stores, sari shops, travel agencies, and eateries, located mostly in ethnic neighborhoods of large cities. These were generally family-owned enterprises, started by Indian immigrants facing a dearth of jobs in an economic recession or lacking the professional and language skills required to succeed in corporate America. Many of these early family-owned enterprises went on to spawn empires of their own, comprising chains of grocery, jewelry, and clothing stores in far-flung locations. For example, Rajbhog Foods started as a mom-and-pop sweets shop in Jackson Heights, Queens (New York City), and by 2007 had grown to an enterprise with seventy employees, three plants, and stores in forty-one states and Canada.

By the 1990s, Indian Americans had amassed the capital and resources to invest in big business enterprises. The Indian government wooed them to invest in their home states in India by giving them priority allotment of sites in export processing zones, reduced tariffs on import of equipment, exemption from duties on imported technology, and other incentives. At the same time, younger Indian Americans, newly graduated from top business schools, became investment bankers and venture capitalists, while fresh immigrants from the top engineering schools in India used their technical expertise to launch new ventures. Some 200,000 Indian Americans were members of the millionaire club in the mid-2000s, more than 20,000 of them in Silicon Valley alone. According to a Dun & Bradstreet study, Indians had started 778 Silicon Valley start-ups by 1998, generating a total of 16,598 jobs.

The success that Indian Americans achieved through intelligence, hard work, persistence, and willingness to take risks is all the more remarkable because it is not based on continuity of entrepreneurial experience from India or carryover of economic practices and preferences. Indeed, in the beginning, they were shunned by venture capitalists and banks, who doubted their ability to head businesses. Many were refused loans because of the belief that Indians lacked leadership and management skills. One after another, however, they proved to possess the ability to bring together ideas, expertise, innovation, and capital, nurture them through rocky starts, and grow them into global businesses. Sabeer Bhatia, born into a middle-class family of civil servants in India, was refused funding several times before he was able to raise the money to pursue his vision; he cofounded the Hotmail Corporation in 1996.

The most common path for Indian American entrepreneurs, most of whom came to the United States between 1970 and 1980, was to start as a consultant or software engineer at a major high-tech corporation, such as Microsoft, Intel, Texas Instruments, or Motorola. Then, pursuing original and innovative ideas in technology applications, they set up their own start-up companies, many of which grew into successful global enterprises. Among the most famous names regularly listed by *Forbes* and *Fortune* magazines in their lists of the most successful and richest American entrepreneurs are Vinod Dham, called the "Father of the Pentium Processor" at Intel Corporation, where he worked before cofounding an Indo-U.S. venture fund; Vinod Khosla, cofounder of Sun Microsystems; Naveen Jain, founder and president of InfoSpace.com and a former vice president at Microsoft; Kanwal Rekhi, whom *Forbes* called "the dominant investor in Silicon Valley and sage to Silicon Valley's affluent Indian community"; Gururaj Deshpande, whose company Sycamore Networks made a splash on the Nasdaq Stock Exchange and grew to a net worth of $3.2 billion; and Sanjiv Sidhu, cofounder and CEO of i2 Technologies. Most of these billionaire entrepreneurs are graduates of Indian Institutes of Technology, now widely acknowledged as among the world's preeminent engineering finishing schools.

Besides Silicon Valley, other regions have also seen the rise of successful entrepreneurs. In the Midwest, for example, Indian Americans are the dominant entrepreneurs among Dunkin' Donuts franchises. Nationwide, the members of the extended Patel family, from Gujarat, own more than 50 percent of the economy lodging in the hospitality industry. Leading a list of top 100 Indian-owned companies in the United States in 2006 was Ducon Technologies, Inc., an environmental products company in New York with more than $328 million in revenues.

One of the hallmarks of Indian American entrepreneurs is a belief in their capacity to do social good. An *India Abroad* survey of the top 100 Indian American companies in October 2000 reported that the CEOs considered their most important role as investors to be creating jobs, developing exports, helping local economies, promoting new business, and supporting start-ups.

Raised in a culture that encourages businessmen to go beyond profit making, they believe in social entrepreneurship and remain convinced that the best solutions to the world's problems of pure drinking water, consistent food supply, universal education, access to raw materials, and environmentally friendly use of energy will come through widespread use of technology. Toward that end, they have established networks and invested their resources in their home country and other parts of the developing world. Indian American entrepreneurs have also been instrumental in making positive changes in governmental economic policies in some of the global emerging markets. Specifically, they have influenced liberalization of key sectors in the Indian economy, including telecom and venture-capital investment.

The best known organization for supporting Indian American entrepreneurs through networking, mentoring, and education is called The Indus Entrepreneurs, or TiE—for Technology, Ideas, Enterprise. TiE was started by South Asian professionals in Silicon Valley in 1992 to share and give back to society. In the years since, it has grown to forty chapters in nine countries with a membership of 8,000. TiE has established chapters in the United States, India, Canada, Great Britain, Pakistan, Singapore, Dubai, Australia, and Malaysia. Thanks to such networking, the aggressive pursuit of innovative ideas, and the financial backing to support them, Indian American entrepreneurs have earned a reputation as the most integrated, successful, and active business minority segment in the United States.

Padma Rangaswamy

Further Reading

Bernstein, Nina. "Immigrant Entrepreneurs Shape a New Economy." *New York Times,* February 6, 2007.

Light, Ivan, and Parminder Bhachu. *Immigration and Entrepreneurship: Culture, Capital and Ethnic Networks.* New Brunswick, NJ: Transaction, 1993.

Rajghatta, Chidanand. "The Billionaires." *Indian Express North American Edition,* September 29, 2000.

Rangaswamy, Padma. *Indian Americans.* New York: Chelsea, 2007.

Chandrasekhar, Subrahmanyan (1910–1995)

Astrophysicist Subrahmanyan Chandrasekhar, a Nobel Prize winner best known for his work on white dwarf stars, was born October 19, 1910, in Lahore, India

Subrahmanyan Chandrasekhar, who was born in India and spent his working life in America, shared the 1983 Nobel Prize in Physics for theoretical studies regarding the structure and evolution of stars. He spent nearly sixty years at the University of Chicago. *(William Franklin McMahon/Time & Life Pictures/Getty Images)*

(now Pakistan). His education and work took him from India to England and on to the United States (1937), which he called home for the fifty-eight years before his death. His notable career spanned several research areas and earned him a share of the Nobel Prize in 1983.

The third of ten children, Chandrasekhar was home tutored until age twelve and attended high school in Madras, British India. While studying physics at Presidency College in Madras, he wrote a paper that was published in the journal *Proceedings of the Royal Society*. It was the success of this paper that helped him secure a scholarship to do graduate work at Cambridge University's Trinity College. He left for England in 1930.

Chandrasekhar quickly developed an interest in astrophysics. While at Trinity College, he did coursework on a variety of topics, including quantum mechanics and relativity theory. After receiving his PhD in 1933, he was accepted for a fellowship at Trinity College. In 1934, Chandrasekhar began working on what would eventually become the Chandrasekhar mass limit, a theory regarding the death of stars with large masses. He presented a paper on the subject to the Royal Astronomical Society, but the theory was challenged by several others in the

scientific community, and Chandrasekhar moved on to different research.

While at Presidency College, Chandrasekhar had become close to a student named Lalitha Doraiswamy. He returned to India in 1936, and they were married that September. Although there was little chance of his finding decent work in India or England, he had employment offers in the United States. Chandrasekhar accepted a position at the University of Chicago's Yerkes Observatory in Williams Bay, Wisconsin, where he began work in January 1937.

While at Yerkes, Chandrasekhar developed a graduate astrophysics program that required him to teach multiple courses each term, in addition to his own research and mentoring students. After the attack on Pearl Harbor in December 1941, Chandrasekhar, like many other scientists at the time, began contributing his skills to the war effort, conducting ballistics research at Maryland's Aberdeen Proving Ground. (He alternated between Aberdeen and Williams Bay, working three weeks at a time in each location.) In 1952, Chandrasekhar chose to move to the physics department at the University of Chicago, where he also began his nineteen years as managing editor of the school's *Astrophysical Journal*.

Chandrasekhar's research and publications covered a variety of astrophysical topics, including white dwarves, stellar dynamics, relativity, and black holes. In 1983, he was awarded the Nobel Prize in Physics, chiefly based on the white dwarf work he began in the 1930s; the prize was shared with American astrophysicist William Alfred Fowler. In his later years, Chandrasekhar set to work translating portions of Newton's work on gravity for a publication titled *Newton's Principia for the Common Reader*. Chandrasekhar continued to work at the university until his death from heart failure on August 21, 1995.

Leah Irvine

Further Reading

Cropper, William H. *Great Physicists: The Life and Times of Leading Physicists from Galileo to Hawking.* New York: Oxford University Press, 2001.

Weber, Robert L. *Pioneers of Science: Nobel Prize Winners in Physics.* Philadelphia: A. Hilger, 1988.

Demographics, Indian American

In the questionnaires and reports of the U.S. Census Bureau, Indian Americans are classified as "Asian Indians" in the general category of Asian Americans.

Demographic findings from the 2000 census reveal a largely foreign-born population that is predominantly male, comparatively young, and with high educational, occupational, and income levels, but also with certain shortcomings, such as relatively weak English language skills and significant poverty levels.

Population Growth

Asian Indians were identified as a separate population group for the first time in 1980, as a result of intense lobbying by the Association of Indians in America. Until that time, they had been submerged under the "Other" category in the decennial census. After 1980, it was possible to obtain detailed demographic and socioeconomic data on Asian Indians. The importance of this classification cannot be overemphasized, as it affirmed their need to be recognized as a separate and distinct group, neither black nor white; enabled them to track their own growth; and allowed them to participate in the American political process based on their growing numbers and socioeconomic strengths.

Demographic data on Indian Americans before 1980 are available in records of the Immigration and Naturalization Service (INS). According to these figures, Indian American immigration increased from one person in 1820 and a total of 716 arrivals from 1820 to 1900. The 1900 census counted 2,050 Indians, based on place of birth rather than ethnic identity. More than 8,500 Indians were admitted to the United States between 1900 and 1930, mostly Punjabi laborers and farmers arriving in California, but restrictive immigration laws and anti-Asian sentiment that fueled return migration caused their numbers to dwindle to a mere 1,500 by 1946. Not until after the Immigration and Nationality Act of 1965, which eliminated racial quotas and admitted Asians based primarily on their skills and family connections, was there a significant increase.

The 1980 census showed an Asian Indian population of 387,223, which more than doubled to 815,447 in 1990 and doubled yet again to 1,678,765 in 2000—the highest growth rate of any major Asian American group. Asian Indians thus make up 16.4 percent of the Asian American population and 0.6 percent of the general population. According to the 2000 census, Asian Indians are spread throughout the United States, with 33 percent in the Northeast region, 26 percent in the South, 23 percent in the West, and 18 percent in the Midwest. The five leading states—California (with an Asian Indian population of 314,819), New York (251,724), New Jersey (169,180), Texas (129,365), and Illinois (124,723)—account for nearly 60 percent of the total Asian Indian population. Other states with high populations are Florida (70,740),

Pennsylvania (57,241), and Michigan (54,631). Southern and eastern states such as Connecticut, Georgia, Maryland, Massachusetts, North Carolina, Ohio, and Virginia, where there has been a boom in hi-tech industries, have also attracted Indians in large numbers. Each of the central and mountain states—Idaho, Montana, Nebraska, New Mexico, North Dakota, South Dakota, Wyoming, and Utah—as well as Hawaii and Alaska, has fewer than 5,000 Asian Indians.

Demographic Profile

Asian Indians prefer to live in major metropolitan areas where jobs are to be found and there are already established Asian Indian immigrant populations. The top six metropolitan statistical areas for the Asian Indian population in 2000 were New York (400,194), San Francisco (144,231), Chicago (116,868), Los Angeles (104,482), Washington, D.C. (88,211), and Philadelphia (53,280). Given this pattern of settlement, urban issues are of particular importance in the lives of Asian Indians. Because of these concentrations, they are able to interact with other ethnic groups, congregate for social, cultural, and religious purposes, build houses of worship, form professional organizations, and develop strong commercial infrastructures that enable them to follow a distinctly ethnic lifestyle.

Asian Indian men outnumber women by 53 percent to 47 percent, which is typical of a heavily immigrant population. (More than 75 percent of Asian Indians are foreign-born.) One-quarter of the population is under eighteen years of age, and nearly three-quarters (71 percent) is eighteen to sixty-four years old—the age-group most likely to be in the workforce. The proportion of elderly (sixty-five years and over), is still small, only 4 percent. The median age is thirty, compared to thirty-five for the general U.S. population; the average family size is 3.8, compared to 3.14 for the general U.S. population.

Some 67 percent of the Asian Indian population fifteen years and over is married, and the divorce rate is very low (2 percent) compared to that of the U.S. population overall (10 percent). Asian Indians are very well educated, with 64 percent holding a bachelor's degree or higher. More than one-third (34 percent) of Asian Indians have a graduate or professional degree. Asian Indian women, too, are much better educated than women in the general population. About 57 percent of Asian Indian women have a bachelor's degree or higher, compared to only 23 percent of women in the general population; 27 percent of Asian Indian women have a graduate or professional degree.

Asian Indians also have a high employment rate (64 percent), and about half the female population is employed. A majority (60 percent) of the Asian Indian workforce is in management and professional occupations; 21 percent work in sales and office positions, and 7 percent in service occupations. Other categories, especially farming, construction, and production, account for the remaining 12 percent of the Asian Indian workforce.

In keeping with their high educational and occupational levels, Asian Indians also have relatively high income levels. According to the 2000 census, the median family income is $70,708 (compared to the U.S. median of $50,046); the Asian Indian median per capita income is $27,514, compared to the U.S. median of $21,587. Nearly one-half (47 percent) of the Asian Indian population has realized the American dream of owning their own home. At the same time, there is also significant poverty among Asian Indians: 7 percent of families, 10 percent of individuals, 22 percent of families with a female householder, 9 percent among the elderly (sixty-five years and over), and 9 percent among children (eighteen years and younger).

Of foreign-born citizens, 39 percent have acquired citizenship. More than half of the foreign-born (54 percent) are comparatively recent immigrants, having entered the United States between 1990 and March 2000. An overwhelming majority (80 percent) speak a language other than English at home. Nearly one in four Indians (23 percent) cannot speak English very well, so low levels of English proficiency are a problem in the community.

Padma Rangaswamy

Further Reading

Bharadwaj, Surinder M., and N. Madhusudana Rao. "Asian Indians in the United States." In *South Asians Overseas: Migration and Ethnicity,* ed. Colin Clarke, Ceri Peach, and Steven Vertovec. Cambridge: Cambridge University Press, 1990.

Saran, Paramatma, and Edwin Eames, eds. *The New Ethnics. Asian Indians in the United States.* New York: Praeger, 1980.

U.S. Census Bureau. http://www.census.gov.

Education, Indian American

Among the most highly educated of all immigrant groups, Indian Americans frequently cite educational opportunities—for themselves and their children—as the main reason for coming to America. Most of those who came in the first post-1965 wave were highly educated professionals who were fluent in English. In the United States, they quickly established a reputation as an elite group of academic achievers. Even with the influx of somewhat less-educated relatives in the 1980s and 1990s, Indian Americans retained their ranking as the best educated of all Americans, regardless of birthplace or ethnicity. Outstanding academic achievements have contributed to their image as a "model minority" and raised the bar for Indian American children, many of whom feel pressured by their parents to excel. The notion of Indian Americans as academic achievers is so pervasive that there is little recognition, even within the community, of a growing number (especially among women) who lack basic literacy and who have limited access to much-needed resources for better education.

According to the 2000 U.S. Census, 64 percent of Indians twenty-five years and older have at least a bachelor's degree; 34 percent have a graduate or professional degree; and 7 percent of males and 3 percent of females have doctorate degrees. A large majority of the advanced degrees are in medicine, engineering, computer science, and biological and health sciences. Indian Americans have tended to concentrate on technical fields, which have the best prospects for high earnings, but an increasing number of students have been turning to law, business, journalism, and social sciences, as these fields are also considered promising for financial stability and professional progress. Indian American parents generally discourage their children from going into such fields as primary or secondary education, social services, entertainment, and other professions they consider low-income or risky.

The emphasis on education begins at a young age in Indian American families, many of whom send their children to private schools to ensure the best schooling. Indian Americans are chosen in disproportionately high numbers as class valedictorians or on honor rolls or dean's lists, and are often seen among the finalists in state and national spelling bees, science fairs, and other academic competitions. While Indian American parents value the merits of U.S. public school education, they are also concerned that there is not enough discipline or moral instruction and worry that their children will lose traditional values. To counteract such influences, many of them send their children to the equivalent of Sunday school for religious education in temples, mosques, or *gurdwaras* (Sikh temples). In the Muslim community, one of the highest priorities is the religious education of the second generation. Thus, many K–12 Islamic schools follow the regular public school curriculum but also teach Arabic and Urdu and the importance of Islamic tenets.

In India, it is not the norm to work one's way through college; it is expected that all schooling will be completed before employment or marriage. A bachelor's degree is considered a basic requirement, so parents plan early to finance their children's college education. At the university level, there is a growing population of second-generation Indian Americans, but there are also increasing numbers of Indians who come as foreign students. Indian Americans registering in American universities recorded an impressive growth of more than 10 percent annually in the early 2000s. According to data released by the American Universities Education Program, nearly 50,000 Indian students, representing more than 15 percent of all foreign students, were admitted to U.S. universities during this period. Even those who have already acquired advanced degrees in India feel the need to obtain American degrees, which are perceived to be more valuable. For females, especially, an American education is viewed as offering more opportunities and incentives, a wider range of academic and career choices, and a greater emphasis on individual freedom. In keeping with their concept of education as a major investment, Indian Americans tend to favor prestigious Ivy League schools or major postdoctoral institutions.

Indeed, the emphasis on education has paid off in many respects. Indian Americans have won professional awards and teaching honors and attained the highest positions in academia. Among the best known are two Nobel Prize winners, Har Gobind Khorana of MIT for physiology or medicine (1968) and Subrahmanyan Chandrasekhar of the University of Chicago for physics (1983). Other notable figures in higher education include A.K. Ramanujan, a University of Chicago translator of poems and folk tales from Tamil and Kannada into English, who was awarded the title of Padma Shri by the Government of India for his contributions to Indian literature and linguistics. There is also a tradition of Indian scholars at the top level of management studies in the United States, among them Dipak Jain, dean of Northwestern University's Kellogg School of Management, the first Asian Indian dean of a major U.S. business school, and Padma Shri Bala Balachandran, a professor at the same institution.

Many Indian Americans believe that they owe much of their success in America to the fine and comparatively inexpensive education they received in India, making them keen to give back to the homeland. Organizations such as ASHA for Education, Pratham USA, and the American India Foundation raise funds for schools operating in the villages and slums of India. At another level, alumni associations of prestigious higher-education institutions such as the Indian Institutes of Technology (IIT) have donated millions of dollars to upgrading their alma maters and turning them into world-class institutions. Thousands of IIT graduates who have achieved huge success in U.S. companies such as Microsoft, Intel, and Sun Microsystems recognize that they obtained one of the best educational bargains in the world because IITs are subsidized up to 80 percent by the Indian government.

Indian Americans have also donated generously to funding "India chairs" at a number of U.S. universities. In short, the modern Indian American experience reflects the globalization of education and the intersection of public policy and private interests at the international level.

Padma Rangaswamy

Further Reading

Helweg, Arthur, and Usha Helweg. *An Immigrant Success Story: East Indians in America.* Philadelphia: University of Pennsylvania Press, 1990.

Rangaswamy, Padma. *Namasté America: Indian Immigrants in an American Metropolis.* University Park: Pennsylvania State University Press, 2000.

Rudrappa, Sharmila. *Ethnic Routes to Becoming American: Indian Immigrants and the Cultures of Citizenship.* New Brunswick, NJ: Rutgers University Press, 2004.

Family Life, Indian American

A strong family ethos and the merging of Indian traditions with American customs in everyday life have proven effective for the social stability and well-being of the Asian American community. Among Asian Americans, Indian Americans have one of the lowest rates of divorce; most families are still headed by two parents. Like most American families, Indian American families are relatively small, at least compared to those India, with an average of 3.8 persons per household. Ethnographic studies indicate that among Indian immigrant families, leisure time is spent primarily with extended family members and other Indian families on the weekends, which creates strong peer groups for the second generation (children). Research on Indian American families documents an emphasis on academic and professional achievement, transnational family ties, the maintenance of cultural and religious traditions, and intergenerational change.

Education and the Family

Census data and demographic studies indicate the high levels of education attained by the Indian immigrant population in the United States, as well as the large numbers of second-generation Indian Americans who have entered scientific and entrepreneurial professions, regardless of whether their parents worked in white-collar jobs or in service or agricultural sectors. Educational achievement is one of the strongest points of emphasis in Indian

American family life. Indian American parents often undertake research to find schools with rigorous academic curricula and gear their children toward the study of math and science, since these subjects are viewed as leading to professional opportunities and economic stability. Parents also send their children to after-school programs that cover other skills and interests to expand their children's abilities and boost their standardized test scores. In urban areas in particular, parents have the opportunity to enroll their children in community programs that offer Indian language instruction and cultural activities, such as lessons in traditional Indian musical instruments (such as the tabla, harmonium, and sitar) and dance (such as *bharata natyam* and *kathak*). Families in less populated areas rely on parents and grandparents to impart heritage language proficiency and cultural practices.

Culture, Language, and Religion in Family Life

India has a rich array of languages, cultures, and religions, and Indian American families reflect this high degree of diversity. The transmission of cultural values and practices occurs in numerous ways in Indian American family life, from cooking Indian meals, listening to Indian music, and watching Bollywood films, to attending Indian weddings, religious events, and cultural festivals. Families who can afford to travel to India visit extended family members who still reside there. Whether on a regular basis or for special occasions such as weddings and funerals, traveling to India allows immigrant parents to introduce their children to the villages and cities in which they were raised and allows them to maintain familial and cultural ties.

The languages most often spoken at home among Indian American families usually reflect the region of origin of older family members—Hindi, Urdu, Punjabi, Gujarati, Bengali, Tamil, and other South Indian languages. Since English language education has been mandatory in most Indian states since the nation's independence in 1947, most immigrants and their families speak English along with their native languages. The second generation often comprehends the language of their parents but may not have the same degree of spoken fluency. Native languages may be used exclusively by some of the elderly immigrants who move to the United States to live in retirement with or near their adult children.

In many Indian American families, language use plays a role in religious practices. While some religious services may be conducted in the congregation's heritage language, other groups prefer to use English for the benefit of the second generation. The majority of Indian Americans are Hindu, but the range of religious affiliations among families reflects the diversity of the population. Numerous temples, mosques, churches, and other religious organizations serve the needs of the Hindu, Sikh, Muslim, Christian, and Buddhist Indian American families in the United States. These institutions provide centers for religious events as well as for social networking and children's religious education. Families who are particularly religious dedicate an area of the home for worship and prayer, and possess religious texts that are printed in the family's ancestral language as well as in English. Traditional clothing and accessories, such as the turban for males in the Sikh religion or the head scarf for women in the Muslim religion, symbolize religious affiliation, and pictures of divine figures, gurus, or holy places may be found in the home.

Intergenerational Continuity and Change

Parents and children face challenges as they attempt to reconcile Indian and American values, especially with respect to issues of sexuality, dating, academics, career choice, and family responsibilities. Dating or marrying outside one's ethnic or religious group is often cited as a divisive issue in Indian American families. While many first-generation immigrants relied on their families to find a spouse, an increasing number of second-generation marriages are not arranged by parents. Indian matrimonial Web sites, such as Shaadi.com, have become a popular way for Indian American singles to meet others from the same cultural background—with or without parental involvement. Another source of tension is the completion of higher education and choice of profession. Parental expectations for their children's academic achievement and pursuit of high-status careers are difficult to manage for some members of the second generation who have different goals. Second-generation women have voiced opposition to traditional gender roles and generally prefer more egalitarian relationships with men. Finally, the shift from the extended family structure in India to the nuclear family unit in the United States has affected elderly family members. Some no longer feel that they can rely on their children to care for them, while others are welcome to reside with their children even after their children have families of their own.

Wendy L. Klein

Further Reading

Gupta, Sangeeta R., ed. *Emerging Voices: South Asian American Women Redefine Self, Family, and Community.* Walnut Creek, CA: AltaMira, 1999.

Khandelwal, Madhulika S. *Becoming American, Being Indian: An Immigrant Community in New York City.* Ithaca, NY: Cornell University Press, 2002.

Leonard, Karen Isaksen. *The South Asian Americans.* Westport, CT: Greenwood, 1997.

First Indo-American Bank

Established in 1986, the First Indo-American Bank was the first bank formed specifically for lending to the Indian American community. Its specific market was Indian American businesses and professional individuals starting out in the Bay Area. The First Indo-American Bank changed its name to the Millennium Bank in 1995 and later merged with other small lending institutions to appeal to a wider community.

The idea of a bank created by and for Indian Americans in the San Francisco Bay Area was first discussed in 1982, as members of the Indian American business and professional communities were concerned that fellow immigrants were finding it difficult to get loans from mainstream banks to establish their businesses. The situation was somewhat unique for Indian Americans. Most had come to the United States for an education and, after earning their degrees, often set up a small business or a professional office. To do so, they needed loans from banks that sometimes were not sympathetic to them.

To receive a charter from the state of California, the founders had to meet two requirements. The first was to show that a need existed. They convinced regulators that Indian Americans who had recently graduated from universities generally had no credit history and that large banks were therefore not likely to make business loans to them. Instead, they maintained, a bank organized by people who had immigrated would be better able to judge the individuals' likelihood of success and to help them create a business plan.

The second requirement was to show that the community to be served was large enough to support a bank. At first, the Indian American founders had trouble proving that the immigrant community was cohesive. Although approximately 30,000 Indian Americans lived in the Bay Area, they were spread throughout the region. Because so many were newly trained doctors, lawyers, engineers, and businessmen, they had settled in a variety of places where their professional services would be in demand. Indeed, the Indian American community in general had successfully integrated into the population at large. To meet the regulators' concerns, founders such as Haresh Shah, an engineering professor at Stanford University, demonstrated that the Indian American community was bound not by geographic proximity but by professional organizations, charitable activities, and family associations.

After years of deliberation, state regulators granted a charter for the First Indo-American Bank. It began operations in December 1986 with $7.6 million in capital, raised from 600 shareholders in California, Asia, and Europe. It had a single location in San Francisco but served its customers with a courier service, online communications, and bank officers willing to travel. The bank's stated purpose was to concentrate on small and medium-sized businesses and professionals, especially those in the Indian American community. Edward Grubel was hired as the bank's first chief executive officer.

The First Indo-American Bank nearly doubled its capital to $14.7 million in 1987 but still showed a loss of $381,000. Assets doubled again in 1998 to $30.1 million, but losses climbed to $829,000—a source of concern to stockholders. As a consequence, the board of directors hired Rob Evans, formerly with the American Asian Bancorp, to turn things around. And indeed earnings improved under Evans's management. In 1989, First Indo-American Bank made a profit of $107,323, and earnings more than doubled the following year. Evans's philosophy was that the bank needed to grow, while still retaining its niche role of serving the Indian American community.

The bank's transition into a mainstream lending institution that concentrated on small business lending continued over the next decade. In 1995, the name was changed to Millennium Bank, primarily to attract customers who were not Indian American. In 2001, Millennium Bank was sold to First Banks America. It had assets of $104.5 million at the time.

Tim J. Watts

Further Reading

Carlsen, Clifford. "First Indo-American Bank Seeks Merger to Add Capital, Earnings." *San Francisco Business Times* 8 (March 22, 1991).

Howe, Kenneth. "Indo-Americans Form New Bank to Serve a Growing Community." *San Francisco Business Times* 6 (February 23, 1987).

Levine, Daniel. "First Indo-American Bank Changes Moniker, Seeks Broader Clientele." *San Francisco Business Times* 10 (August 4, 1995).

Ghadar Movement

During the early 1900s, Indian immigrants living on the West Coast of the United States—most of them Punjabis—started an expatriate movement called

Ghadar (which means "mutiny" in the Urdu/Punjabi language) to throw the British out of India. What began in 1907 as loose party meetings among Indian migrant workers and graduate students grew into a small but significant movement that advocated violent anticolonial measures against the British. The movement touched various parts of the British Empire, established a partnership with Germany during World War I, and helped mobilize anti-British sentiment among Indians in the United States.

Beginning in the late nineteenth century, Indian laborers—primarily agricultural and timber workers—migrated to the Pacific Coast. Many emigrated from India to British Columbia and then migrated southward across the U.S. border, motivated by reports of higher wages and plentiful work in California's booming agricultural sector.

These immigrants, along with growing numbers of other Asian groups, including the Chinese and Japanese, were often met with hostility, discriminatory legislation, exclusionary practices, and violent attacks. The Immigration Act of 1917 (also called the Asiatic Barred Zone Act) and the Exclusion Acts of 1882–1924 expressly excluded immigration of Asians, including those from India. California's Alien Land Law of 1913 prohibited Asians from owning land in the state, and in 1906 the legislature there passed an antimiscegenation law that initially prohibited "Mongols" from marrying whites and was later expanded to include other Asians.

Unlike Chinese and Japanese nationals, Indians—in both the United States and Canada—found that they had no national government to turn to when they needed assistance, as the British consulates refused to help Indian nationals. Increasingly, Indian immigrants began to think of themselves as a stateless people, making them ripe for political action. Along with immigrants in these circumstances were Indian revolutionaries who came to the United States seeking asylum, including incipient Ghadar Party leaders Lala Har Dayal and Bharkatullah. These men settled in Berkeley, California, in the early twentieth century, providing the link between activist Indian students and laborers, many of whom would meet at various "Indian halls" that served as boardinghouses and community centers.

These informal social and political gatherings eventually led to the more overt project of expelling the British from India. The Ghadar Party—its official name was the Hindu Association of the Pacific Coast—officially began on April 21, 1913, in Astoria, Oregon, though meetings had been going on loosely from 1907, and continued into the 1930s. Meetings generally took place in the Pacific Northwest, and the headquarters of the movement was in San Francisco. According to the party's resolutions, its objective would be "to end British rule through armed revolution and to set up a Republican Government based on liberty and equality." In San Francisco, the party began a newspaper called *Ghadar* that was published in Punjabi, Urdu, and Gujarati.

One of its most controversial efforts involved procuring and shipping arms to revolutionaries in India during World War I, an effort aided by the Germans, who were fighting Britain. In a two-pronged effort both to destabilize Britain and to garner support of other anti–British Empire groups, such as Irish Americans, Germany provided strategic advice and arms to the party. In October 1914, Germany authorized the purchase of 10,000–20,000 rifles and their shipment to India on the *Maverick,* apparently bought from a private steamship company for $27,000, and the *Annie Larson,* a German vessel, via the Pacific. The plan was thwarted at various points due in large part to the gross overstatement of the number of Ghadar activists in India by Ghadar leader Ram Chandra, and to the incompetence of German organizers, who were unable to secure working ships and maintain a schedule. Crew members were eventually arrested by U.S. authorities. A second shipment of arms was attempted on June 15, 1915, via New York aboard the *Djember,* but British agents in New York discovered and foiled the plan early on.

Beginning in 1916, the Ghadar Party experienced internecine fighting stemming from accusations of misappropriation of funds as well as religious differences among Sikhs, Muslims, and Hindus. The organization splintered into factions, suffering a fate similar to that of many other radical groups throughout history. In April 1917, U.S. federal agents began arresting various Ghadar members for seditious activities. Their trial in federal court, *U.S. v. Franz Bopp, et al.,* began in November 1917 and ended in April 1918, with all of the accused pleading not guilty. The trial exposed the infighting within the party and ended with one member, Ram Singh, shooting Ghadar leader Ram Chandra to death in the courthouse in San Francisco. Ram Singh, in turn, was immediately shot by a U.S. marshal. All of the accused except one American were found guilty and given sentences ranging from thirty days to two years.

Malini Cadambi

Further Reading

Brown, Giles. "The Hindu Conspiracy, 1914–1917." *Pacific Historical Review* 17:3 (August 1948).

Deol, G.S. *The Role of the Ghadar Party in the National Movement.* Delhi, India: Sterling, 1969.

Fraser, Thomas G. "Germany and Indian Revolution, 1914–1918." *Journal of Contemporary History* 12 (1977): 255–72.

Hoover, Karl. "The Hindu Conspiracy in California, 1913–1918." *German Studies Review* 8:2 (May 1985).

Mathur, L.P. *Indian Revolutionary Movement in the United States of America.* New Delhi: S. Chand, 1970.

Health and Medicine, Indian Americans in

Among the first group of professionals to arrive in the United States from India after 1965 were members of the medical community, who were actively recruited to fill vacancies in hospitals in metropolitan areas and to serve in remote areas where other American doctors were not willing to work. Indian Americans also came as medical academics and researchers, pharmacists and nurses. Despite the hurdles of stringent and often discriminatory legislation, Indian Americans in health and medicine continue to enter the United States in large numbers and fulfill what many health care experts say is a vital need in American society.

Before India's independence in 1947, England was considered the mecca of higher education in medicine. Thereafter, more and more Indians turned to the United States, with its much larger higher education system, to pursue advanced medical degrees. At the same time, the medical colleges of India became modeled after American universities or had American university affiliations, so Indian medical graduates, with their ready command of English and prior exposure to Western ways, achieved rapid success in the United States. Sometimes entire graduating classes from major medical institutions such as the All India Institute of Medical Sciences in New Delhi and Baroda Medical College in Gujarat came to the United States in pursuit of higher education, professional satisfaction, or a better life. Some Indian American physicians have been so successful that they have branched out as entrepreneurs, setting up their own clinical and laboratory services. The medical profession continues to attract Indian American health professionals to the present day.

U.S. Census figures for Asian Indians in health care professional and service occupations in 2000 indicate that nearly one in four Indian American professionals and nearly one in five service providers is in the health care industry. Women outnumber men in all categories in health care occupations. According to community sources, Asian Indians constitute 10–12 percent of the student body in U.S. medical schools, ensuring growing participation in the United States, so their participation is expected to continue growing in this field.

Professional Associations

The medical profession is probably the best organized among all the professional groups in the United States. Not only are there medical school alumni associations with thousands of members across the country, but they are even organized along regional affiliations—such as the Association of Tamil Nadu Medical Graduates, which brings together medical professionals from the south Indian state of Tamil Nadu. Specialty subgroups, such as radiologists, neurologists, ophthalmologists, and pathologists of Indian origin, have their own associations.

The most prominent and effective of all is the American Association of Physicians of Indian Origin (AAPI). The association was established in 1982 in Dearborn, Michigan, as a national umbrella organization, comprising local medical associations that had organized to fight discrimination against physicians in residency requirements. Foreign medical graduates, or FMGs, protested discriminatory laws that set tougher licensing standards for them than for domestic medical graduates. Taking inspiration from the American Medical Association, AAPI grew to be a powerful lobbying group, constantly monitoring policy changes that could affect the practice of its members. In the mid-1990s, changes in managed care intended to slow rapidly rising costs had significant effects on physicians and their practices. The safeguarding of their interests acquired new urgency, which helped AAPI grow in size and importance. The association moved its headquarters to Chicago in 1994, and in the course of the next ten years acquired a direct individual membership base of 35,000 physicians and 10,000 medical students and residents. Despite internal wrangling, the organization has worked successfully to win favorable legislation on issues that affect Indian American medical professionals and to secure federal grants for research on diseases that affect South Asian Americans in particular. (Indian Americans are believed to be four to five times more likely to develop Type 2 diabetes than members of the general U.S. population. They also have a higher mortality rate from cardiovascular disease.)

The uninsured rate among South Asians is said to be 21 percent, roughly twice the national rate, so the medical profession has recognized and responded to the need for charitable work in their own community. The AAPI Charitable Foundation, established in 1989, raises funds for ongoing charitable work in the United States and India, and facilitates donation of supplies and equipment as well as transfer of the latest medical technologies to the homeland. Indian Americans have helped build and staff world-class hospitals in India, such as the Apollo Hospitals and Escorts Institute. Another umbrella organization, the South Asian Public Health Association (SAPHA), undertook the first national initiative to evaluate and summarize existing knowledge about several key health indicators for South Asian Americans.

Nursing

As reflected in 2000 census data, women favor the medical field in both professional and support service occupations. An acute shortage of nurses in the United States has resulted in hospitals scrambling to recruit nurses from abroad, and India is fertile recruiting ground because of its highly trained, English-speaking nursing force. They are fast replacing the nurses who were recruited from the Philippines, Ireland, and Canada in the past. India graduates about 30,000 nurses per year, many of whom are eager to migrate and earn an increase in wages from less than $100 per month in India to $4,000 per month or more in the United States. A number of nursing schools and colleges have sprung up in India to meet the demand, as U.S. recruiting firms travel regularly to India to interview prospective hirees. One state in India, Kerala, supplies an especially high percentage of nurses, many of whom are Christians and raised in the missionary tradition of service to others. Keralites even have their own Malayalee Nurses Association in the United States.

Another area in which there is a shortage of U.S.-trained professionals and an increasing foreign demand due to an aging population is the field of pharmacy. Here, too, Indian Americans have stepped in to fill the gap. India is one of the countries the United States has targeted for increased efforts to hire pharmacists by issuing H1-B visas.

In the twenty-first century, information technology has revolutionized the role of Indians and Indian Americans in health care. In a procedure known as clinical process outsourcing, for example, radiologists working in India are examining scans of patients seeking care within the United States. Other ways in which Indian Americans are affecting the American medical landscape is through the introduction of alternative medicine such as ayurveda, which relies on natural herbs and healthy lifestyle, and yoga and meditation, which take a holistic approach to healing.

Despite the widespread presence of Indian Americans in the fields of health and medicine, recognition from the mainstream, especially the media, has been slow in coming. Television medical dramas now portray Indian American physicians on the staffs of hospitals. Dr. Sanjay Gupta has attained celebrity status as a medical correspondent on the CNN network, and prominent Indian American doctors have been appointed to the President's and Governor's Advisory Commissions on Asian American Affairs.

Padma Rangaswamy

Further Reading

American Physicians of Indian Origins. http://www.aapiusa .org.

David, Stephen. "Sisters to the Rescue." *India Today International,* February 2, 2004, 35–37.

South Asian Public Health Association. "A Brown Paper: The Health of South Asians in the United States." July 2002.

Homosexuality in the Indian American Community

Like members of all immigrant communities, Indian Americans must contend with the broader currents of American culture, including ideals of sexuality. Historical views of sexuality and the primacy of idealized Western values have caused homosexuality to be heavily stigmatized within the Indian American community. Older-generation Indian immigrant parents wish for their children marriage, prosperity, and success. According to many Indian Americans, homosexuality and its lifestyle do not reflect these ideals. Nevertheless, in the United States today, there is a growing number of lesbian, gay, and bisexual (LGB) Indian Americans who seek, from their cultural roots, ways to express their sexuality. Through a number of approaches—exploring homosexuality in South Asian culture, finding a definition within the non-Asian LGB community, and giving LGB Indian Americans a public voice—the Indian American LGB community seeks to establish its strength in the greater ethnic community.

History of Homosexuality in South Asian Cultures

Gay, lesbian, and bisexual Indian Americans today tend to seek acceptance from the mainstream LGB community in the United States rather than seek roots in their own culture. This is in large part due to the homophobia that characterizes colonial South Asian cultures as well as a desire to move toward a more mainstream American identity. However, in an attempt to establish an LGB Indian American community, many South Asian American community leaders point to a long history of same-sex unions in South Asian societies. Ancient Sanskrit texts such as the *Rig Veda* and *Kama Sutra* as well as

Tantric practices all embrace same-sex unions. In traditional Indian society, there is a socially sanctioned identity for transsexuals, intersexuals (hermaphrodites), and homosexuals, the last being known as the *hijras.* While remaining marginalized, the *hijras* perform dances and blessings at family rituals such as births and weddings.

British colonialism undermined the practice of same-sex unions in the mid-nineteenth century. In 1860, British officials passed Section 377 of the Indian Penal Code, under which sexual practices regarded as "offenses against nature" were criminalized. These included sodomy, a practice associated with homosexuality. Section 377 was enacted for all of Britain's colonies, including Pakistan, Bangladesh, Nepal, and Bhutan. Moreover, as South Asian cultures began to modernize, ancient practices were seen as primitive and at times gave way to Christian beliefs and ideals of heterosexual union. Other cultural factors that have prevented homosexuality from being a viable public lifestyle are South Asian priorities of strict obedience to social and familial norms, and arranged marriages. The culture of Indian immigrant communities reflects these internalized beliefs.

Indian American Homosexuality

Homosexuality is seen by many South Asians and Indian Americans who oppose it as a Western practice that has been adopted by South Asian cultures only in modern times. Many feel that one cannot be both LGB and South Asian. Lesbian, gay, and bisexual Indian Americans face a daily struggle to establish a community in which they can confront Westernized stereotypes and prejudices and focus on creating an identity of their own. In many instances, language has been viewed as a barrier to establishing such a community. For example, LGB Indian Americans have appropriated terminology such as "kush" to express a South Asian gay or lesbian orientation.

South Asian homosexuals are confronted with the fear of humiliating and alienating their families. First-generation Indian Americans are concerned that their children will become too Americanized, as reflected in changing gender roles, and that they will not be successful or accepted into mainstream society. Indeed, the second generation is challenging the norms set by their parents with regard to arranged marriages, education, and ethnic identity. Moreover, at the same time that LGB Indian Americans have had difficulty identifying with their parents' cultural identities based on familial and heterosexual norms, they are often marginalized and racialized by the mainstream LGB community itself. Since ethnic stereotypes prevail in American society and subcultures, many LGB Indian Americans feel that their culture and

history are ignored in the mainstream LGB community. LGB Indian Americans find that the mainstream LGB community often attributes American cultural norms and understandings of "gay" and "lesbian" to South Asians, overlooking the cultural diversity within the greater LGB community itself. For example, South Asian lesbians must contend with "white lesbian androgyny." Specifically, South Asian lesbians, many of whom opt to wear their hair long and dress in feminine clothing, are often labeled "femmes," as they contradict the masculine image of white mainstream lesbians. Indian American lesbian identity has been politicized through feminist thought, requiring Indian women not only to seek liberation in a homophobic society, but also to define themselves as women in a patriarchal community where the norm for women is to marry and have children.

Organizations, Publications, and Community Leaders

The South Asian American LGB community has made great strides in establishing itself in the pubic realm. Although "coming out" has been difficult—as prejudice in both South Asian and mainstream communities acted as a deterrent—nevertheless, since the mid-1980s, a number of organizations, publications, community leaders, and other role models have given the South Asian LGB community public expression. Trikone (from the Sanskrit, meaning "triangle"), established in 1986 in San Francisco, is an organization that supports the LGB community and publishes a newsletter of the same name. The organization has a number of satellite groups across the United States and Canada. Shamakami (from Bengali, meaning "the love of an equal") was founded in 1990 in San Francisco specifically on behalf of South Asian lesbians. These organizations provide a network for members worldwide as well as a culturally relevant forum for expressing their identities. Additionally, regional groups such as the South Asian Lesbian and Gays of New York and the Alliance of Massachusetts Asian Lesbian and Gay Men (AMALGAM) provide support, educational resources, publications, and a foundation for dialogue among community members.

Lesbian, gay, and bisexual Indian Americans have confronted racism and heterosexism by increasing their visibility. They continue to march in San Francisco's Gay Pride parade and Chinese New Year's parades. Role models and community leaders include Kashish Chopra, an "out" lesbian, who in 2003 was crowned Miss Congeniality in the Miss South Asian Pageant and has utilized her public role to support the South Asian gay and lesbian community. Urvashi Vaid, a lawyer, author, and social activist who was the executive director of the National Gay and Lesbian Task Force for three years in the 1980s, remains a prominent advocate of gay and lesbian rights.

Publications and films from the United States, Canada, and South Asia focusing on South Asian sexualities have begun to flourish. Published works include *The Golden Gate: A Novel in Verse* (1986) by Vikram Seth and Gayatri Gopinath's *Impossible Desires: Queer Diasporas and South Asian Public Cultures* (2005). Notable films include Nidhi Singh's *Kush Refugees* (1991), Pratibha Parmar's *Kush* (1991), and, more recently, *South Asian, Happy and Gay—VOICES: Gay Identity in South Asian Society* (2003), directed by Darshana Dave.

South Asian American lesbians, gays, and bisexuals seek to establish a community in which they may affirm their identities in a relevant cultural context. This community is being established with a renewed appreciation for South Asian traditions of same-sex unions and is beginning to speak with a strong public voice through publications, films, and political and social organizations.

Erika A. Muse

Further Reading

Ratti, Rakesh, ed. *A Lotus of Another Color: An Unfolding of the South Asian Gay and Lesbian Experience.* Boston: Alyson, 1993.

Roy, Sandip. "The Call of Rice: (South) Asian American Queer Communities." In *A Part, Yet Apart: South Asians in Asian America,* ed. Lavina Dhingra Shankar and Rajini Srikanth, 168–85. Philadelphia: Temple University Press, 1998.

Seshadri P., and L. Ramakrishnan. "Queering Gender: Trans-liberation and Our Lesbigay Movements." *Trikone Magazine,* July 1999, 6–8, 18.

Hotel and Motel Business, Indian Americans in the

The Indian American community today is known for, among other things, its extensive holdings in the hotel and motel industry, ranging from small economy lodges to luxurious high-end hotels. In fact, as of the early 2000s, roughly 50 percent of the assets of the U.S. lodging industry was in the hands of Indian immigrants or their families. One unusual characteristic of the Indian American involvement in this industry is the concentration of people with the last name of Patel, a common surname in Gujarat meaning "village head." (This has led to many quips in the popular media about the Patel/motel connection.) Although Asian Indians represent only a small proportion of the U.S. immigrant population, they control an estimated 65 percent of budget hotels and 40 percent of all hotels and motels nationwide. They have built up the businesses largely through a system of extensive chain migration of family members. Their domination in this industry has led many researchers and journalists to ask who they are, how they entered this niche market, and what factors are responsible for their phenomenal success.

Patels are an agricultural caste from Gujarat in western India who play a prominent role in the social and economic hierarchy of the region. Although they are credited with having an inherent flair for business, they entered the U.S. niche hotel market more by accident than by design, helped along by a combination of cultural, social, political, and legal forces that worked in their favor. In the 1960s and 1970s, the U.S. government granted residency not only for skilled professionals but also for new arrivals who invested $10,000 to run a business in the United States. Gujaratis scraped together the money needed for this initial investment and purchased cheap motels in rundown areas. There were many bargains to be had in motel properties that were being abandoned by white Americans across the country, particularly in smaller towns and cities because domestic road travel had dropped due to the high price of gasoline.

Appeal of the Lodging Industry

The motels were attractive to Indians for many reasons. It gave them an immediate roof over their heads, and the entire family could be employed in the business. They could live on the premises and be available day and night for the kind of upkeep required to run a motel. The nature of motel work was such that women could continue in their traditional role as housewives but also be employed full-time and contribute to the family finances. Entering the United States under the family reunification rules of the 1965 Immigration and Nationality Act enabled all family members to escape labor certification laws, even though they were brought in primarily to work in the family business. It appeared to be a win-win situation since the hotel owner got cheap labor simply by sponsoring relatives, while the relatives got a decent start in the United States as start-up costs were met by their sponsors. Although sometimes it resulted in exploitation, on the whole it helped the community get a strong foothold in the industry.

Financing of the motel and hotel purchases, at least in the beginning, was a community affair. When a property appeared to be a good investment, word spread through the community network, and family resources were pooled for a down payment. Although immigrants were considered thrifty and a low credit risk, many had little collateral, making it impossible to borrow money in the formal banking sector. Instead, the immigrants themselves supported their family members and invested in real estate, since it was something tangible and gave them a sense of security and stability.

Legislation, too, was a factor in the success of the Patels in the motel and hotel business, specifically the family-friendly immigration law of 1965, which allowed Indian immigrants to enter the country through chain migration. Cultural values, which promoted hard work and the involvement of entire families in small business enterprise, also helped in the success.

Challenges

Among the challenges faced by Indian Americans in the hotel and motel business are the long hours and isolation of living in motels located mostly off highway exits, far from middle-class suburban or urban neighborhoods where other immigrants live. They have also experienced discrimination and hostility from competitors who placed "American owned" signs outside their properties in an effort to discredit and take business away from them. Many were denied coverage by insurance companies, who considered them high-risk clients. Indian Americans fought back by organizing and forming their own association, called the Asian American Hotel Owners Association (AAHOA). Founded in 1989 and based in Atlanta, AAHOA has become a powerful advocacy group, championing the rights of Asian American hoteliers and instituting educational programs to help them succeed. With a membership of more than 8,000, and a healthy bottom line (nearly $5 million in assets as of 2006), it has fought for tougher legislation to combat blatantly discriminatory practices and done much to help its members flourish.

Among the leaders of AAHOA are members of the second generation, children of the hotel and motel owners who have stayed in the business but moved up to more upscale facilities than these of their parents. Many graduated from renowned hotel or business schools and used their education to get them to the next level, while others have moved away from the business due to long hours and hard work. Still, the industry continues to attract Indian Americans from all walks of life. Many hotel owners are professionally qualified engineers, chemists, and insurance agents who go into the hospitality business to make more money and to escape the glass ceiling or other forms of discrimination in the corporate world. They may start off with a small investment but quickly become owners of several properties across many states.

Some Indian Americans work as night clerks and managers before taking the plunge into motel ownership.

The role of women in the success of Indian Americans in the hotel and motel business is vital. Many have contributed their labor full-time, in addition to fulfilling their roles as wives and mothers, even though their work was not formally recognized in the labor economy. Their experience has transformed relations within the family and community, and empowered them to question traditional gender hierarchies and social norms.

Indian American involvement in the hotel industry has also changed well-established practices. For instance, hotels now routinely feature Indian catering for special occasions, especially for the booming South Asian wedding industry. The most important issues facing Indian hoteliers today, according to AAHOA, are negotiating franchise agreements and resolving franchise disputes; obtaining financing for new construction, acquisition, and renovation; and finding affordable insurance. AAHOA acts as an insurance agent for its members by providing special group rates.

Padma Rangaswamy

Further Reading

Asian American Hotel Owners Association. http://www.aahoa.com.

Assar, Nandini Narain. "Indian-American Success Story of 'Potel'-Motels: Immigration, Traditions, Community, and Gender." *Current Research on Occupations and Professions* 10 (1998): 67–86.

Herskoovitz, Jon. "U.S. Hotel Dreams and Barons Born in India." *India Bulletin* 15 (May 2004).

Johnson, Douglas P. "Individual Strength, United Voice—Theme of AAHOA Convention." *India Tribune*, May 1, 2004.

Varadarajan, Tunku. "A Patel Motel Cartel?" *New York Times Magazine*, July 4, 1999, 36–39.

Immigration, Indian American

Indians have been emigrating to the United States since the late nineteenth century, but their reasons for, and circumstances of, leaving India and settling in America have changed radically in the ensuing decades. Like members of other nationalities, Indians who have immigrated to the United States since the late twentieth century have done so for a variety of reasons—professional (the opportunity for career advancement), family reunification (the desire to join a spouse or other family members), and economic opportunity (the possibility of making more money). While these are not entirely different from the factors that motivated their predecessors in the early twentieth century, the "push" and "pull" factors have changed radically.

While there are commonalities and differences in motives between the early-twentieth-century immigrants from Punjab who concentrated in California and the post-1965 immigrants who came from all over India and settled throughout the United States, a whole other set of issues is represented by Indians who came to America not from India directly, but from other parts of the world—such as Great Britain, East Africa, Fiji, and the Caribbean—for political and economic reasons. Since modern India has been a flourishing democracy where individual freedom is guaranteed by the national constitution, there have been few refugees from India seeking political asylum in the United States.

Early Twentieth Century

Early Indian settlers, about 7,000 of whom came to the United States between 1904 and 1920, were sojourners who left their villages in Punjab in search of personal fortune. Displaced by British land policies and hard hit by drought and famine, landless younger sons in Sikh farming families were lured by the economic opportunities in the Pacific Northwest, where employers were looking for cheap labor for their lumber mills. Indians also came to work on the railroads and in the fruit orchards, beet farms, and vineyards of California. Though Indian immigrants to the United States were not indentured or bonded labor, as were Indian immigrants to other countries of the British Empire in the Caribbean, Africa, and the Pacific Islands, they faced anti-Asian discrimination and violence and were subject to such discriminatory laws that their condition was often little better than servitude. For example, California's 1913 Alien Land Law prevented noncitizens from owning property; since it was virtually impossible for Indians or other Asians to become citizens, the law was effectively aimed at them. Without the ability to own land, many Indians were forced either to work as agricultural laborers or to lease their property at exorbitant prices from white landlords. Meanwhile, immigration laws against Indians became increasingly restrictive until Congress passed the Immigration Act of 1917—also called the Asiatic Barred Zone Act—which effectively cut off immigration from India entirely.

Immigration from India was also affected by the various interpretations given by U.S. courts with respect to the rights to citizenship for Indians. The United States Naturalization Law of 1790, which reserved citizenship for "whites only," prevented many Indians from becoming citizens, but the U.S. Supreme Court ruled in such cases as *United States v. Balsara* (1910) and *In re Ajkoy Kumar Mazumdar* (1913) that Indians indeed were eligible for citizenship because they were anthropologically "Caucasian" even if their skin color was often significantly darker. About 100 Indians were naturalized between 1913 and 1923. Then, in a dramatic reversal, the Supreme Court ruled in *United States v. Bhagat Singh Thind* (1923) that Indians were not "free, white persons" and were therefore ineligible for citizenship. Aware that they were unwelcome in the United States, some 3,000 Indians left for India between 1920 and 1940.

It was not until after World War II, when Indians gained the right to American citizenship and India itself became free of British rule, that Indians started coming again to the United States, usually as students or as sponsored family members. After 1965, when the United States dropped national quotas and instituted a system of preferences for highly skilled personnel needed in the American labor market, a whole new group of Indians started immigrating—urban, middle-class professionals in their twenties and thirties, doctors, engineers, scientists, and academics. They came with a sense of adventure, not entirely ready to leave their homeland permanently. As they stayed on and prospered, however, it became harder and harder to return. For them, immigration did not happen at a single point in time but

Immigrants Admitted from India to the United States, 1820 to 2005

Period	Number of Immigrants Admitted
1820	1
1821–1830	8
1831–1840	39
1841–1850	36
1851–1860	43
1861–1870	69
1871–1880	163
1881–1890	289
1891–1900	68
1901–1910	4,713
1911–1920	2,082
1921–1930	1,886
1931–1940	496
1941–1950	1,761
1951–1960	1,973
1961–1970	31,200
1971–1980	176,800
1981–1990	261,869
1991–2000	382,969
2001–2005	345,915
Total	1,212,380

Source: U.S. Immigration and Naturalization Service Annual Report, 1975. Table 8a. Immigrants, by Country of Birth: 1961–2005.

through a process that often took years until—without knowing how, why, or when—they became permanent immigrants. In that regard, they are the very antithesis of the mythic American immigrant of yore—neither poor nor oppressed, fleeing neither war nor famine, and certainly not ready to reject the past or the motherland.

For others, immigrating to America was a conscious decision, usually taken after exhaustive consultation with senior family members. Sometimes, the eldest son of the family was sent abroad to make his fortune and send money home so the younger siblings could stay behind and take care of family business or aging parents. In other cases, women come as the vanguard family member, especially if they had the skills traditionally developed among women in India and in demand in the United States, such as teaching, nursing, and physical therapy. Other reasons that immigrants often cite for leaving India have been frustration with conditions of corruption, poor infrastructure, and perennial shortages of basic amenities such as water and electricity; the prospect of better educational opportunities for their children; and the desire to escape religious conflicts that erupt suddenly and make life insecure for minority groups such as Muslims, Sikhs, and Christians. While restrictive controls and cumbersome bureaucracy were oft-cited reasons in the 1980s by Indians seeking a new home in the United States, those reasons have largely vanished since the economic liberalization in India in the 1990s. Thus, many Indians have found new reasons to stay home.

Immigration from the Diaspora

Motivations for immigration also vary based on the diverse geographical origins of immigrants. Besides the émigrés from practically every state in India, many have lived on two or three continents before finding a home in America. The Indian American community thus includes those who fled the tyranny of Uganda's Idi Amin in the early 1970s, those who escaped racial conflict and discrimination under black dictatorships in the Caribbean in the 1960s and 1970s, and those who sought refuge from politically sanctioned discrimination in Fiji since the 1980s. They also include immigrants from England, where Indians may have experienced institutionalized racism and hostility, and Canada, where economic opportunities are not as attractive as in the United States. The motives for immigration are often different for those who come directly from India.

In the 1980s, more than 80 percent of Indian immigrants to the United States were admitted under the "Relative Preferences" category, which meant that they came to join family members who had arrived earlier.

An Indian family in Florida attends the swearing-in ceremony to become U.S. citizens. Barred from naturalization until 1946, Indian Americans—one of the fastest growing of all Asian immigrant groups—are becoming U.S. citizens at a rising rate as well. *(Robert Nickelsberg/Getty Images)*

Brothers and sisters came to join their siblings and seek a better life; elderly parents came to live with their sons, following an age-old Indian tradition that calls upon sons to care for their parents in old age. In the 1990s, the number who arrived under the relative preferences category dropped in comparison to those under occupational preferences. With the boom in the U.S. information technology sector, more Indians came as H1-B temporary visa workers to fill a void in the computer industry. According to U.S. State Department figures, the number of H1-B visas issued to people from India jumped from 2,697 in 1990 to 15,228 in 1995 and 55,047 in 2000.

By the beginning of the twenty-first century, a confluence of factors put a damper on immigration from India. The dot-com bust, tightening visa restrictions after the September 11, 2001, terrorist attacks, and the phenomenon known as "outsourcing" (whereby white-collar customer service jobs are performed by Indians in India at a fraction of the cost in the United States) all have contributed to limit immigration in unprecedented ways. Thanks to satellite technologies, Indians can now work for U.S. companies at lucrative salaries without leaving their homeland. Advances in transportation and telecommunications have also contributed to transnationalism, whereby people live and work in more than one country, and constantly shuttle back and forth between global centers of manufacture and consumption. Still, the United States continues to serve as a beacon for Indian immigrants, and their numbers continue to grow steadily.

Padma Rangaswamy

Further Reading

Chandrasekhar, S. "A History of United States Legislation." In *From India to America. A Brief History of Immigration: Problems of Discrimination, Admission and Assimilation,* ed. S. Chandrasekhar, 11–28. La Jolla: Population Review, 1982.

Helweg, Arthur, and Usha Helweg. *An Immigrant Success Story: East Indians in America.* Philadelphia: University of Pennsylvania Press, 1990.

Rangaswamy, Padma. *Namasté America: Indian Immigrants in an American Metropolis.* University Park: Pennsylvania State University Press, 2000.

U.S. Census Bureau. http://www.census.gov.

Khalsa Diwan Society

The Khalsa Diwan, or Free Divine, Society was the first social and political organization in North America for immigrants from South Asia, organized by Sikhs in Vancouver, British Columbia, Canada, in 1906. The society campaigned to preserve Indian cultural heritage and to have political restrictions placed on Indian immigrants removed. The Khalsa Diwan Society also promoted the cohesiveness of the Sikh community in North America and served as a surrogate family for social occasions.

Among the first South Asians to come to North America were Sikhs serving in the British army, in 1897. After participating in Queen Victoria's Diamond Jubilee, they returned to India via Canada. Impressed by the country, they told other Sikhs, and a number decided to immigrate. The first immigrants arrived in 1904 and soon established a thriving community in Vancouver. Many whites regarded them with suspicion, especially regarding their faith. The Sikhs were discriminated against and had difficulty practicing their religion. When a member of the community died in 1907, authorities would not allow his body to be cremated, per Sikh custom. Christian missionaries tried to convince the Sikhs that he should be buried. Instead, the Sikhs sneaked into the woods at night to carry out their religious rituals and cremate the body at dawn.

The incident highlighted the difficulties faced by Sikhs in following their customs and traditions. As a result, they formed the Khalsa Diwan Society in Vancouver on July 22, 1906, though it was not officially recognized until March 13, 1909. The society was formed as a mutual aid organization, intended to support the Sikh community. It opened the first *gurdwara,* or Sikh temple, in North America in Vancouver in 1908. The *gurdwara* housed a copy of Sikh sacred writings and had a hall for worship and meetings. A school and kitchen that provided free meals were also included.

The Khalsa Diwan Society soon spread to the United States. The first Sikhs had landed in San Francisco in 1899, followed by others seeking agricultural jobs in the farming valleys of California. In 1912, a chapter of Khalsa Diwan was formed in Stockton. Known as the Pacific Coast Khalsa Diwan Society, the organization set out its goals at its first meeting. Key among them was providing for the welfare of South Asian immigrant students and workers. The chapter was incorporated in California and soon acquired land for its own *gurdwara.*

The Khalsa Diwan Society came to operate *gurdwaras* throughout North America. While the temples were the centers of Sikh religious and cultural life, they also played a role in political action. Newspapers were published in the *gurdwaras,* keeping members of the Sikh community in touch with one another and providing insights for non-Sikhs. The society also promoted public celebrations and demonstrations that displayed Sikh culture for those who wanted to learn. Protests over discrimination faced by Sikhs were organized by the society, as well as demands for full citizenship rights. Although as many as 3,000 Sikhs had immigrated to the United States by 1930, national quotas reduced immigration until 1945 to just a handful. By 1950, fewer than 2,700 Sikhs remained. Laws against interracial marriages were enforced in many states, especially California. Pressure to assimilate to American society caused many Sikhs to remove their turbans, shave their beards, and cut their hair. The Khalsa Diwan Society protested these formal and informal attacks on Sikh culture, and by 1970 their demands resulted in laws guaranteeing minority rights. The society was also active in promoting Indian independence from Great Britain. In that campaign, it was aligned with the Ghadar (Revolution) Party, active in India and the United States before independence in 1947.

Tim J. Watts

Further Reading

Khalsa Diwan Society in Vancouver. http://www.sikhpioneers.com.

Singh, Bhai Jodh, and Teja Singh. *The Message of the Sikh Faith.* Stockton, CA: Pacific Coast Khalsa Diwan Society, 1929.

Singha, Bhagata. *Canadian Sikhs Through a Century, 1897–1997.* Delhi: Gyan Sagar, 2001.

Labor and Employment, Indian American

Like a number of American immigrant groups, Asian Indians first came to the United States as laborers, many coming via Canada to the Pacific Northwest in the early twentieth century to work in the timber, railroading, and agricultural industries of that region. Gradually, members of this rather small group moved into the entrepreneurial ranks in the middle years of the twentieth century. Passage of the 1965 Immigration and Nationality Act, which ended national quotas, opened the gates for large-scale Asian Indian immigration to America, with people coming in the hundreds of thousands per decade. While some members of this group were poor and forced to work in low-paying service- and manufacturing-sector jobs, many were well-educated professionals, notably in the health care and high-tech fields. Others came with some capital or could tap into financial resources among extended kin networks, enabling them to open up businesses of their own, particularly in the tourism and retail sectors.

Early Labor in Agriculture and Extractive Industries

Beginning in the early twentieth century and continuing through the late 1910s, when restrictive immigration laws went into effect, roughly 2,000 Indian immigrants, predominantly men from the Punjab region of British India, arrived in California and the Pacific Northwest. This early wave of immigration coincided with the escalation of widespread hostility and institutionalized discrimination against Asian immigrants, particularly Chinese and Japanese. The Immigration Act of 1917, which extended the Chinese Exclusion Act to all other Asians, established that Indian laborers, as immigrants from one of Asia's "barred zones," were no longer able to enter to the United States. The Indian immigrant population thus declined from approximately 6,000 in the early 1920s to approximately 1,000 by 1945. Following World War II, new immigration policies rejuvenated these established communities, especially in the agricultural valleys of central and southeastern California, with the arrival of persons of both sexes and as well as through natural increase.

Rapid economic deterioration in the Punjab prompted the first wave of migration, as the capitalist agricultural economy instituted by the British created a series of lasting economic problems, including water shortages, famines, and severe epidemics, that threatened to impoverish rural villages. Small landowning and peasant families encouraged their younger sons, in particular, to migrate abroad, work as laborers, and send money home to solidify the economic base of the communities and contribute to the maintenance of extended households. These men were generally in their early twenties, some with wives and children who were left behind in the protective care of other family members. The majority were members of the Sikh religious faith, physically distinguishable by their turbans, along with a relatively small number of Punjabi Hindus and Muslims. Some of them, particularly the earliest Sikh immigrants to Canada, were veterans of the British army who had become disillusioned with their treatment by officers during China's Boxer Rebellion and had refused to reenlist or sought discharge soon thereafter. These men tended to hold positions of leadership within the immigrant communities.

Indian immigrants arriving in British Columbia and the Pacific Northwest typically took jobs in the lumber and sawmill industries. The millwork was hard, seasonal, and poorly compensated. Mill owners recognized that Indian American laborers were willing to work in the mills for lower wages than their Euro-American counterparts, who were struggling to maintain high wage levels and decent working conditions through organized labor unions. Concerned by their replacement, Euro-American laborers treated the Indian laborers with open hostility. The tension escalated into violence at several mill sites, as groups of Euro-American laborers threatened the Indian laborers with violence. In Bellingham, a mill town in Washington State, a mob of 500 workers attacked the Indians in their bunkhouse and forcibly expelled them from town on September 5, 1907. This organized riot was followed by similar episodes in Everett, Washington, in the fall of 1907, and in smaller towns along the Pacific coast as well as Juneau, Alaska, and Live Oak, California, in the winter of 1907–1908. The episodes of violence, along with the realization that local courts and police would not protect their rights and that the British government would not press for damages, forced the Indian laborers to move from one mill town to another. They relocated farther south to California in the 1910s, where they found work in the railroad and farming industries.

Indian laborers made up a significant portion of the workforce on the Western Pacific Railway, the last transcontinental line of the Pacific Railroad, in Northern California from 1907 to 1909. Contractors for this project typically employed ethnic laborers, including Italians, Greeks, Austrians, Swedes, and Norwegians, as well as Chinese, Japanese, Koreans, and Indians, for the difficult construction work. As many as 2,000 Indians were working on the railway by 1907. When the railroad project was completed in November 1909, it opened a new network of interstate railroad lines for the transportation of crops from ranches in California to markets in Chicago. The boom in California agribusiness increased both the competition for labor and the wages for that labor. Indians who had previously worked on the railway lines began moving into the agricultural industries.

At first, Indians took jobs as day laborers on existing farms, engaging in activities such as digging potatoes, picking grapes and melons, transplanting celery seedlings, hauling sugar beets, and clearing land and ditches. Once they secured some capital and established their reputations as hard workers, the workers sought loans for agricultural speculation, sometimes pooling their money, in order to buy or lease small farms. By 1914, they were beginning to establish themselves as leaseholders, land tenants, and farm operators. Most of these agriculturalists eventually settled in the older farmlands of the San Joaquin and Sacramento valleys in Central California as well as in the newly developed Imperial Valley in southeastern California. According to the 1919 census of land occupancy in California, Indians owned 88,000 acres (35,600 hectares) in the state; slightly more than half the land was located in the Sacramento Valley and 33,000 acres (13,400 hectares) in the San Joaquin Valley. While some of the agriculturalists prospered, sold their holdings, and returned to India, many chose to remain in California.

The Indian agriculturalists who settled in California established distinctive social networks. Immigrant males could not embark on extended trips abroad in order to find wives or reunite with their existing wives in India, because they might not be allowed back, under the 1917 Immigration Act. Beginning in the second decade of the twentieth century, many of these men began marrying women from Mexico who had migrated to the United States in the aftermath of the Mexican Revolution. These women, who may have worked on the men's farms, moved into the homes that their husbands had established with other Indian immigrants. The descendents of these unions, commonly referred to as "Mexican-Hindus," managed their dual identities in these agricultural communities throughout the second half of the twentieth century.

A number of legislative acts framed the struggle of Indian laborers for eligibility for naturalization during the period 1907–1924. In 1913, the California legislature passed the Alien Land Law, which barred Asians from owning land in the state. In November 1923, the U.S. Supreme Court upheld this law in a case brought by the Sikh American writer and spiritualist Bhagat Singh Thind. In the landmark case of *United States v. Bhagat Singh Thind* (1923), the high court ruled that Indians were not "white persons" but aliens, making them ineligible for citizenship. The decision effectively stripped citizenship rights from some Indians who had already been naturalized. It also meant that the Alien Land Law would apply to Indian agriculturalists, including those who had already leased or purchased land. Thus, some who had moved up to tenant and land-owning farmer status were forced back into the ranks of laborers. Nevertheless, many Indian immigrants found ways to circumvent the legislation by arranging for white landowners, lawyers, and judges, and in some cases, their own wives, to hold the lease contracts in their names.

Post–World War II Professionals

Institutional discrimination continued to create hardships for Indian immigrants and, along with the harsh restrictions on entry, contributed to the sharp decline in population until a bill allowing Indian naturalization and immigration, the Luce-Celler Act, was passed in July 1946. But it was the Immigration and Nationality Act of 1965 that truly changed the labor and employment profile of the Indian American community. By ending national quotas and emphasizing family reunion, education, and professional training as acceptance criteria, the law both greatly expanded the Asian Indian population—from roughly 30,000 in 1960 to more than 2.3 million by the early 2000s—and increased the number of professionals and entrepreneurs among the ranks of the Indian American community.

Well educated and with a strong grasp of English—the latter a legacy of British colonial rule—Asian Indian immigrants have entered the professions in unprecedented numbers since the 1970s. At 64 percent, according to the 2000 U.S. Census, Asian Indian Americans over the age of twenty-five were more likely to hold a bachelor's degree or higher than any other Asian American group and were an astonishing 260 percent more likely to hold such a degree than the American population as a whole. Nearly 60 percent of employed Asian Indian Americans over the age of sixteen were working in managerial or professional positions, the highest proportion of any Asian American community. In addition, Asian Indians were nearly 80 percent more likely to be in such positions than the U.S. working adult population as a whole.

Of the remaining 40 percent of the Indian American workforce, just over half worked in sales or offices, about 20 percent in construction and transportation, 14 percent in the service sector, about 4 percent in construction, and less than 1 percent in farming, fishing, and forestry. The last figure underscored the great distance Asian Indian immigrants had come since the early twentieth century. (The remaining 10 percent worked in miscellaneous or unspecified fields.)

Given this high-status job profile, Asian Indian males earned more than their counterparts in all other Asian American groups, $51,904 annually—nearly $15,000 more than the American male working population as a whole. Asian Indian women also did well, lagging behind only Japanese American women in income, and that by less than $1000 annually. With median earnings of $35,173, the median Asian American female worker earned roughly $8,000 more than American women generally.

At 79 percent, Asian Indian adult males also had the highest rate of labor force participation of any Asian American group—and some nine points higher than adult American males in general. Perhaps reflecting the relatively high earning potential of their husbands, Asian Indian females, at 54 percent, had a labor force participation rate somewhat below that of Asian Americans as a whole and the American population generally—57.5 and 56.4, respectively. Given all of these figures, it is not surprising to find that Asian American Indians, at 9.7 percent, have the lowest poverty rates of any Asian American group except Filipinos, and are about 25 percent less likely to live in poverty than the American population as a whole.

Few immigrant groups have seen their labor and employment fortunes turn more dramatically over the course of the twentieth century than Asian Indian Americans. Once largely confined to low-paying jobs in agriculture and the extractive industries of California and the Pacific Northwest, Indian Americans have become a community of professionals, with their presence in the high-tech sector particularly striking. As of the early 2000s, it was estimated that fully one-third of software engineers in Silicon Valley were of Asian Indian descent, having achieved an upper-middle-class lifestyle just miles from the produce fields where their fellow countrymen once worked for a pittance.

Haley Duschinski

Further Reading

Helweg, Arthur W. *Strangers in a Not-so-Strange Land: Indian American Immigrants in the Global Age.* Belmont, CA: Wadsworth, 2004.

Jensen, Joan M. *Passage from India: Asian Indian Immigrants in North America.* New Haven, CT: Yale University Press, 1988.

Lal, Vinay. "A Political History of Asian Indians in the United States." In *Live Like the Banyan Tree: Images of the Indian American Experience,* ed. Leela Prasad, 42–48. Philadelphia: Balch Institute for Ethnic Studies, 1999.

Leonard, Karen Isaksen. *Making Ethnic Choices: California's Punjabi Mexican Americans.* Philadelphia: Temple University Press, 1992.

———. *The South Asian Americans.* Westport, CT: Greenwood, 1997.

Takaki, Ronald. *Strangers from a Different Shore: A History of Asian Americans.* Rev. ed. Boston: Little, Brown, 1998.

U.S. Census Bureau. "The Asian Population: 2000." Report C2KBR/01–16, February 2002.

Lahiri, Jhumpa (1967–)

A best-selling and award-winning Indian American writer of the late twentieth and early twenty-first centuries, Jhumpa Lahiri is the author of numerous short stories and at least one novel that explore the conflicted identities and intergenerational tensions in transnational Indian American communities.

Born in London on July 11, 1967, Lahiri moved to the United States as a young child, her family settling in South Kingston, Rhode Island, where her father worked as a librarian and her mother as a schoolteacher. Her mother, in particular, was interested in exposing Lahiri to her family's homeland—the Bengal region of India—and so, as a young girl, Lahiri traveled frequently to India.

Highly educated, Lahiri received her bachelor's degree from Barnard College in 1989, and earned master's degrees in English, creative writing, and comparative literature, as well as a PhD in Renaissance studies from

Jhumpa Lahiri burst onto the literary scene with the short-story collection *Interpreter of Maladies* (2000), which won a Pulitzer Prize. In that and later works, she explores identity issues and intergenerational tensions in the Indian American community. *(G. Gershoff/WireImage/Getty Images)*

Boston University, the last in 1997. But it was only during a two-year fellowship at the Provincetown Fine Arts Work Center in Massachusetts in 1997 and 1998 that she committed herself to fiction writing, though she had written stories since grade school.

Lahiri's first published work was *Interpreter of Maladies* (2000), a collection of short stories. The nine pieces in the collection cover a wide range of topics and characters, though all but one of them focus on diasporan Bengalis trying to adjust—with varying degrees of success—to their new life in the United States. Many of her characters, like the homebound Indian woman arraying herself in an elegant sari to babysit her children, illustrate the isolation of the immigrant in a strange land. The title of the book comes from a term invented by a Russian American friend of Lahiri's to explain her profession: she helped immigrants from her country explain their ailments at an American doctor's office. Immediately acclaimed by critics, *Interpreter of Maladies* was bestowed with numerous awards, including the Pulitzer Prize for Fiction in 2000, the first ever for an Indian American woman.

Lahiri's second work, the 2003 novel *The Namesake*, explores many of the same themes as *Interpreter of Maladies,* focusing on thirty years of intergenerational conflict between Indian-born parents and American-born children in a Bengali American family named the Gangulis. The namesake in the book's title refers to the eldest son, Gogol, who, after rebelling against his parents and rejecting his Indian heritage, eventually comes to realize that, though of a different culture, he and his parents experience many of the same emotions and share many of the same values. In 2007, *The Namesake* was released as a feature film directed by the acclaimed Indian American director Mira Nair.

Unaccustomed Earth, another short-story collection about conflicts of culture and generations, appeared in 2008. Lahiri has also published several stories in the *New Yorker*—which, in 1999, named her one of the "20 best writers under the age of 40"—and has taught creative writing at Boston University and the Rhode Island School of Design. Other honors include the 1999 O'Henry Award for the short story "Interpreter of Maladies" and a Guggenheim Fellowship in 2002. Lahiri was married in 2001 and has two children.

James Ciment

Further Reading

Chotiner, Isaac. "Interview with Jhumpa Lahiri." *The Atlantic,* March 18, 2008.

Kaur, Tejinder. "Cultural Dilemmas and Displacements of Immigrants in Jhumpa Lahiri's *The Namesake.*" *Journal of Indian Writing in English* 32:2 (2004): 34–44.

Shah, Purvi. "Interpreter of Maladies." *Amerasia Journal* 27:2 (2001): 183–86.

Literature, Indian American

Since the U.S. immigration reforms of the mid-1960s and the great rise in Indian American immigration that followed, Indian American literature likewise has expanded greatly in variety and maturity. The new wave of immigrants and their children have written extensively and vividly about their experiences and identities as strangers in a strange land and the difficulties of bicultural life.

Several recurring themes have emerged. Among the most important, overarching them all, are transnationalism and transculturalism. An increasingly global society has made it more common for people to move from one country to another, finding themselves caught between cultures, unable to fully integrate into their new homes and unwilling to let go of their old. This relocation also makes it difficult for a person to determine what his or her identity is. For Indian American immigrants, the question has always been whether they were Indian or American or some hybrid of the two. Their children wrestle with a somewhat different problem. Raised in an American culture, they often regard India as an alien world and find they cannot relate to their parents. For both, one recurring theme is the search for belonging, set amidst intergenerational conflicts that pit individual desires and aspirations against family traditions and demands.

Another significant theme is the conflict between immigrant parents and Americanized children. The literature often describes children's rejection of their parents' social expectations, based on Indian standards, particularly those involving the choosing of the mates and the career paths of their offspring. Parents, on the other hand, have their own conflicts, since their immigration indicates they have broken with the society in which they were raised; there is much longing in Indian American literature for an idealized homeland and regrets about choices made. Indian American writing about family conflicts takes varying viewpoints, as well. A central point in this theme is the importance of family among Indian Americans—in all its conflict and complexity.

A third significant theme that emerges in Indian American literature is the tension between genders and gender roles. While Indian society is patriarchal, gender roles in American society tend to be more fluid. This added element of conflict between men and women is a significant element in the literature.

The first Indian immigrants to the United States were from Punjab and were predominately male farmers. Immigration restrictions in the early twentieth century made it difficult for Indians to settle in the United States. As a result, very few works appeared by Indian Americans before the 1960s. The earliest Indian American writer was Dhan Gopal Mukerji (1890–1936). Mukerji graduated from Stanford University and married an American schoolteacher. He was a prolific writer, popular during the 1920s. Mukerji specialized in writing about Indian fables and folktales, usually using animals as his protagonists. Only in his autobiography, *Caste and Outcast* (1923), did Mukerji aim at capturing the sense of not belonging common among immigrants.

While Mukerji was popular among American readers as an exotic outsider writing stories with animal heroes, later Indian American writers were more eager to write about their experiences and their homelands. The first wave of Indian American literature appeared during the 1950s. One of the most common themes was the sense of disruption and fracturing caused by the partition of India. The loss of a homeland and the cultural rootedness that goes with it and the sense of exclusion from the culture left behind and the culture of the new home also appears in these writings. One of the most prolific writers of this generation was Ved (Parkash) Mehta (1934–). Mehta was an outsider in many ways. A blind child, he was sent to the School for the Blind in Arkansas when he was fifteen. Despite his lack of sight, Mehta graduated from college and established himself as a writer in the United States. Except for some short stories and one novel, most of Mehta's writings have been nonfiction. He was a contributor to the *New Yorker* for thirty-three years. His series of autobiographies, known as the *Continents of Exile*, stretched over eleven volumes and appeared between 1972 and 2004. Mehta's commentary on society in both India and the United States often reveals the darker undertones of each while allowing for their complexity as well. He recognized the shortcomings and advantages in both societies to which he has roots. Other Indian American writers of this first generation include Raja Rao (1908–2006), whose writing has its roots in Brahmanism and Hinduism. Rao's books include *The Serpent and the Rope* (1960), about a search for spiritual truth, and *Cat and Shakespeare* (1965), in which a cat symbolizes karma.

A majority of the most noted Indian American writers in recent years have been women. One of the most prolific is Anita Desai (1937–). Desai was born to an Indian mother and German father. She published her first novels while living in India, and they focused on tensions faced by women who tried to balance tradition with modern society. By the 1990s, however, Desai had

moved to the United States. Her novels during this time explored the relationship between India and Western culture. In *Journey to Ithaca* (1995), the reader follows a young American couple making their way through India. In contrast, *Fasting, Feasting* (1995) tells the story of an Indian exchange student trying to cope with his abnormal American host family.

Another outstanding Indian American woman author is Bharati Mukherjee (1940–). Mukherjee moved to the United States in the early 1960s, where she received her PhD in English and married an American. After a time in Canada, Mukherjee moved to California, where she teaches at the University of California, Berkeley. Mukherjee's first novel was *The Tiger's Daughter* (1972), which explored the ideas of exile, displacement, and search for identity as they affected the female characters. Later novels such as *Wife* (1975) and *Darkness* (1985) dealt with the discrimination experienced by immigrants in America. Mukherjee's later novels include *Middleman* (1988) and *Jasmine* (1989). They contain themes illuminating how different cultures can be blended, through characters that are more integrated into their worlds and more positive in outlook.

A more recent woman writer is Chitra Bannerjee Divakaruni (1956–). She writes primarily about Indian American women and the transformations in their lives because of living in America. Divakaruni's novels range from the magical realism of *The Mistress of Spices* (1997) in which the owner of spice shop has the power to prescribe spices that will cure the needs of her clients, to the realistic fiction of *Sister of My Heart* (1999), about two close cousins whose lives are separated by marriage.

Many other Indian American writers are active today. These include such authors as Meena Alexander, Gita Mehta, Vijay Lakshmi, and Amitav Ghosh. While the most respected writers have dealt in fiction, a fair number of Indian American poets have also made an impact. Among these are Agha Shahid Ali, Aimee Nezhukumatathil, and Vikram Seth. As a result, Indian American literature is now a highly regarded genre, with a loyal readership that consists of more than just one ethnic group. The writers share with many others a sense of searching for an identity and a place in the world, with the special concerns of blending their Indian and American heritages.

Tim J. Watts

Further Reading

Brians, Paul. *Modern South Asian Literature in English.* Westport, CT: Greenwood, 2003.

De Courtivron, Isabelle. *Lives in Translation: Bilingual Writers on Identity and Creativity.* New York: Palgrave Macmillan, 2003.

Kafka, Phillipa. *On the Outside Looking In(dian): Indian Women Writers at Home and Abroad.* New York: P. Lang, 2003.

Verma, K.D. *The Indian Imagination: Critical Essays on Indian Writing in English.* New York: St. Martin's, 2000.

Media and Visual Arts, Indian American

Media and visual arts created by Indian Americans are as diverse as the backgrounds of the individuals who created them. At the same time, one theme that unites all of these works is the blending of American and Indian cultures and the tensions that this can cause. Many early works of Indian American art were ignored or tried to fit into the Western tradition without regard for the artists' Indian roots. More recent works, by artists such as Natvar Bhavsar, tend to combine Western and Indian techniques and draw on both cultures for their inspiration. Films such as *Mississippi Masala* (1991), directed by Mira Nair, and *The Namesake* (2007), directed by Nair and based on the novel by Jhumpa Lahiri, dramatize the difficulties Indian Americans may face in trying to fit into American society. In recent years, artists working in the visual arts have been aided by a growing worldwide appreciation for Indian art and the diffusion of Indian works throughout the world.

Art

Indian art draws upon thousands of years of tradition. Focusing on religious themes, traditional art can be noted for its use of symbols and motifs to represent the various moods and aspects of deities. Most surviving works from the past two millennia are stone statues intended to inspire devotion in temples. Other works are sculptures intended for private devotion in homes. These were the art works that American visitors brought back from India. Early immigrants from India also brought devotional art to the United States. The works they produced were often copies of what they had left behind.

The influx of Indian immigrants after the U.S. legislative reforms of 1965 largely consisted of highly educated and professional individuals. This generation of immigrants and their descendants have regarded themselves as Americans and readily embraced the new culture they found. Over time, however, Indian roots became increasingly important to community identity and creative expression. By the beginning of the twenty-first century, more than 20 million people of Indian origin lived outside India—more than 1 million of them in the United States. In the meantime, Americans had increasingly embraced the idea of multiculturalism, creating an unprecedented interest in, and audience for, visual art created by Indian Americans. Organizations such as the Indo-American Arts Council have assisted in promoting works by Indian American artists by arranging exhibitions across the country.

Several forms of visual art illustrate the new acceptance. In the realm of painting, works by Indian American artists convey the feelings of many immigrants—a mixture of loneliness and loss, along with hope for the future. Among the best-known contemporary Indian American artists is Natvar Bhavsar, who was born in Gujarat in 1934. After studying at different schools in India, he attended the Graduate School of Fine Arts at the University of Pennsylvania and later moved to the SoHo District of New York City. Bhavsar was associated with many American avant-garde artists of the 1960s, especially the Abstract Expressionists and Color Field painters. His work, which has been described as "lyrical abstractionism," appears in major art museums across the United States. While distinctly modern, using vivid colors and subtle shadings to evoke a mood or emotion, his technique also draws on his Indian roots—especially a decorative sandpainting technique known as *rangoli*. To create his works, Bhavsar strains pigments through a screen onto a prepared canvas, taking care with virtually every particle to ensure the emotional quality he is seeking. The use of color is especially important to his work, evoking his Hindu faith and celebrations of religious holidays in his home province. American cities, he has observed, are especially lacking in color—one explanation for the attraction of his work among U.S. audiences.

Another notable Indian American artist is Salma Arastu, born in 1950 in Rajasthan. After receiving a bachelor of fine arts degree from Jawaharlal University and a master's degree from the University in Baroda, Arastu relocated to Bethlehem, Pennsylvania. In addition to painting, she has worked in clay, papier-mâché, and other media; her pieces have been exhibited from Asia to Europe and widely in North America. Although many of her works are distinctly abstract, Arastu specializes in figurative paintings based on Indian religious and spiritual themes—executed with Western techniques, such as acrylic paints on paper.

Tara Sabharwal, another female Indian American artist of note, is known for her miniature watercolors, oils, and mixed media. Born in 1957 and educated at the New Delhi Royal College of Art, Sabharwal draws on themes from both Indian and European culture. While many of her subjects come from nature, a recurring theme is the breakdown of family and society, loss of purpose, and sense of loneliness associated with the immigrant experience.

Sculpture has become especially popular among contemporary Indian American artists. Ravinder Reddy, for example, has produced statues and busts of women that clearly draw on those sculpted for Indian temples in the past. Reddy, in contrast to other sculptors, uses polyester resin fiberglass instead of natural materials. Each larger-than-life work is covered with thick layers of car paint to produce the effects that he wants. Although he uses Indian women as his models, their poses and settings are distinctly Western.

Traditional Indian arts and crafts, meanwhile, have entered or influenced mainstream American culture. One is the custom of using henna to produce temporary designs, especially on the human body. Intricate designs produced by henna were used by Indian American women performing traditional Indian dances. Henna designs likewise have been adopted by American body painters and tattoo artists. Indeed, some Indian American women who felt self-conscious in the past about their henna tattoos have felt increasingly at home in mainstream American culture.

Likewise, fine art by Indian Americans has become more popular with the non–Indian American public. Sotheby's and Christie's now hold regular auctions of works by these artists. Even more significantly, second- and third-generation Indian American artists are attracting attention when they exhibit in India, where audiences appreciate the successful blending of Indian and American cultures.

Film

Not to be overlooked among the Indian American visual arts in contemporary American culture are Indian-produced and Indian-influenced films. Bollywood, as the Indian film industry is called, is second only to the American film industry in the quantity and international appeal of its output. Traditional Indian movies, however, were long difficult for Americans to accept. Even those produced in English tended to follow genres or to have religious and cultural themes that were alien to U.S. audiences. Some Indian Americans, however, have successfully made the transition to works that appeal to mainstream American moviegoers. The best known is Mumbai-born Ismail Merchant, famous for his collaborations with American director James Ivory. Their works include *A Room with a View* (1985), *Howards End* (1992), and *The Remains of the Day* (1993). While these films have little to do with Indian themes, other Hollywood releases with strong Indian American connections have also been successful. The films of director Mira Nair, such as *Salaam, Bombay* (1988), *Mississippi Masala* (1991), and *The Namesake* (2007) deal directly with Indian Americans adjusting to life in the United States.

Films made in India are also being made with the goal of appealing to Indian Americans who have become acculturated. *American Desi* (2001), for example, has proved to be very popular with Americans as well as Indians. Music featured in these films has also become popular with Indian American audiences and is sometimes produced by Indian American bands. More often than not, this music is a blend of traditional Indian music with Western popular music.

Tim J. Watts

Further Reading

Helweg, Arthur, and Usha Helweg. *An Immigrant Success Story: East Indians in America.* Philadelphia: University of Pennsylvania Press, 1990.

Eck, Diana L. *Darsán: Seeing the Divine Image in India.* New York: Columbia University Press, 1996.

Rajan, Gita, and Shailja Sharma, eds. *New Cosmopolitanisms: South Asians in the U.S.* Palo Alto, CA: Stanford University Press, 2006.

Takaki, Ronald. *India in the West: South Asians in America.* New York: Chelsea House, 1995.

Mehta, Zubin (1936–)

Zubin Mehta is a world-renowned India-born conductor of classical music who has led several of the world's great orchestra companies. He was born on April 29, 1936, in Bombay (now Mumbai), India, to violinist and conductor Mehli Mehta and Tehmina Mehta. The family is Parsi, a religious minority in India. His father was the founding conductor of the Bombay Symphony, and the teenage Mehta would sometimes conduct the orchestra for his father.

Mehta did not hear a major Western orchestra until moving to Vienna in 1954 to attend school, and he later described his musical influence as being chiefly Viennese. After training under Hans Swarowsky at the Vienna Academy of Music, Mehta made his conducting debut in that city in 1958. Also that year, he won the International Conducting Competition and became assistant conductor of the Royal Liverpool Philharmonic Orchestra. In 1960, Mehta joined the Montreal Symphony Orchestra as music director, a post that he would hold until 1967. He made several conducting debuts in 1961, including performances with the Berlin Philharmonic, Israel Philharmonic, and Los Angeles Philharmonic, as well as the Vienna Philharmonic.

Himself the son of a symphony conductor, Mumbai-born Zubin Mehta has served as music director of both the Los Angeles Philharmonic and the New York Philharmonic. *(Liu Jin/Stringer/AFP/Getty Images)*

A rising star, Mehta in 1962 became the youngest music director of the Los Angeles Philharmonic, which he elevated to international prominence. Mehta would later express regret that he did not spend enough time with famed Russian composer Igor Stravinsky, the conductor of the Los Angeles orchestra at the time. Still, Mehta valued his sixteen years in Los Angeles for the opportunity to learn from musicians who had worked with conductors Stravinsky, Otto Klemperer, and Bruno Walter. Mehta became known for his solicitude of soloists and his patience with all of the musicians. Critics faulted him for being theatrical and seeking the limelight.

Named the Israel Philharmonic's music adviser in 1969, Mehta became music director for life in 1981. The Israelis and the Israel Philharmonic became his great love. Israel, he said, reminds him of his home because both Israelis and Indians possess what he describes as the Asiatic characteristic of formulating an opinion and speaking at the same time. The Yiddish-speaking conductor is the only non-Israeli to receive the coveted Israel Prize (1991), awarded by the state.

In an age of peripatetic conductors, Mehta has stayed in place—but not without leading some of the world's great orchestras at the same time, both as guest conductor and as musical director. In addition to his sixteen years with the Los Angeles Philharmonic, he was the longest-serving music director of the New York Philharmonic (1978–1991). During his years in New York, Mehta conducted with such voice and instrumental luminaries as Leontyne Price, Kathleen Battle, Jessye Norman, Isaac Stern, and Itzhak Perlman. From 1998 to 2006, Mehta also ran Munich's Bavarian State Opera. Among his career highlights, he lists a 1996 production of Richard Wagner's Ring Cycle with the Lyric Opera of Chicago, the Wolf Foundation Prize for music, the Vienna Philharmonic Ring of Honor, the Berlin Philharmonic Hans van Bulow Medal, and India's Order of the Lotus. His brother, Zarin, became executive director of the New York Philharmonic in 2000.

Caryn E. Neumann

Further Reading

Bookspan, Martin, and Ross Yockey. *Zubin: The Zubin Mehta Story.* New York: Harper and Row, 1978.

Mexican-Indian Marriages

The term "Mexidus" was used in the early decades of the twentieth century to signify the ethnoracial group composed of Indian men and Mexican women on the West Coast of the United States. A combination of "Mexicans" and "Hindus," the word actually misrepresented the identity of the Indian immigrant men who married Mexican women, since these immigrants were primarily Sikh. At the time, however, all South Asian immigrants were classified as "Hindoos" in the census and by American society at large. In any event, these Punjabi-Mexican marriages, which led to the formation of a vibrant hybrid community, stand as a testament to the ability of early Asian immigrants to survive in a hostile social environment. Moreover, these relationships, forged in the crucible of anti-immigration laws, alien land law acts, and antimiscegenation policies, highlight the dynamics of racial formation in the United States.

Most of the men from the Punjab region in north India came as sojourners intending merely to work, make money, and return home, often to the families they had left. Many, however, ended up deciding to stay in America. The Immigration Act of 1917, however, barred immigration from India and effectively stopped Indian women (and men) from emigrating to the United States until passage of the Luce-Celler Act in 1946. The Indian men who were able to emigrate and who wanted to start families generally married Mexican women. Since many of these women worked alongside Punjabi men as farmers in cotton fields, they became the obvious choice on a practical level. Sometimes a set of Mexican sisters married Sikh brothers or business partners, forming joint-family households. The marriages led to the formation of a culture with a distinctive flavor—whether in its mixed cuisines, the naming of children, or religious practices and social customs. In her extensively researched book, *Making Ethnic Choices: California's Punjabi Mexican Americans* (1992),

Karen Isaksen Leonard reports that the Punjabi-Mexican marriages began in Southern California in 1916, with a couple named Sher Singh and Antonia Alvarez. According to historian Ronald Takaki, these unions increased steadily between 1913 and 1946: 47 percent of the wives of several thousand Sikh men in Northern California were Mexican; 76 percent were Mexican in Central California; and 92 percent of the spouses were Mexican in Southern California. It has been suggested that about 500 of such unions took place in the early twentieth century. Capturing the violent prejudice against these mixed marriages, which came from both Mexican and Punjabi men, writer Chitra Banerjee Divakaruni in her poetic narrative "Yuba City Wedding" details the experience of an immigrant Sikh protagonist who cannot sleep the night before his wedding. He remembers both being attacked by his Mexican bride's brother and provoking the discontent of the Punjabi elders who bar him from coming to the *gurdwara* (Sikh temple) because of marriage outside his ethnoreligious community.

Like Divakaruni, who fictionalizes the experiences of these South Asian immigrants, film-maker Jayasri Mazumdar-Hart's documentary film *Roots in the Sand* (1998) uses archival footage, family photographs, legal documents, and interviews to focus on the formation and survival of this bi-ethnic community. While the Punjabi-Mexican community continues to survive in California, it is minuscule in comparison with newer South Asian immigrants to the country, and its members have faced the prejudice of recent (post-1965) Asian Indian immigrants who fail to view them as ethnically "Indian." Still, Indian-Mexican marriages constitute an important chapter in the history of early South Asian immigrants, highlighting the conscious decision to form communities in defiance of the laws of their adoptive homeland.

Anupama Arora

Further Reading

Leonard, Karen Isaksen. *Making Ethnic Choices: California's Punjabi Mexican Americans.* Philadelphia: Temple University Press, 1992.

Shankar, Lavina Dhingra, and Rajini Srikanth, eds. *A Part, Yet Apart: South Asians in Asian America.* Philadelphia: Temple University Press, 1998.

Mukherjee, Bharati (1940–)

A prolific Indian American writer of Bengali origin, Bharati Mukherjee has published numerous novels and short-story collections, as well as a memoir and several nonfiction works, including a book-length account of a 1985 terrorist bombing of an Air India jet. Much of her fiction focuses on the struggles of identity among Indian American immigrants and their descendants caught between two cultures.

Mukherjee was born in Calcutta on July 27, 1940, the daughter of upper-middle-class, high-caste Brahmin parents. She spent her first eight years in India, living in an extended family household of several dozen relatives. A child prodigy, she learned to read and write by the age of three, before moving with her family to Great Britain in 1947. Returning to India, she earned a bachelor's degree from the University of Calcutta in 1959 and a master's degree in English and Ancient Indian Culture from the University of Baroda two years later. Awarded a scholarship to the University of Iowa, she received her master's of fine arts in creative writing from the prestigious Writer's Workshop there in 1963, followed by a PhD in English and comparative literature in 1969. From 1968 to 1980, she lived in Canada, before moving back to the United States.

Mukherjee's first three novels—*The Tiger's Daughter* (1971), *Wife* (1985), and *Jasmine* (1989)—all take as their protagonists contemporary young Indian women who find themselves struggling to make sense of their lives in the unfamiliar landscape of American culture. The two latter books also explore the meaning of arranged marriages in the modern world of the transnational Indian diasporan community. Later novels have been more wide-ranging in their locale and timeframes. Based on *The Scarlet Letter,* the nineteenth-century novel by American author Nathaniel Hawthorne, *The Holder of the World* (1993) is a time-travel tale that jumps back and forth between life in India and America in the seventeenth and twentieth centuries, examining the themes of adultery and societal norms. The 1997 novel *Leave It to Me* explores the mythology surrounding the Hindu mother goddess Durga. *Desirable Daughters* (2002) and its sequel, *The Tree Bride* (2004), tell the story and family history of Tara Chatterjee, the narrator of both novels and the daughter of a wealthy Calcutta family who ends up married to an Indian American Silicon Valley billionaire. While the former work focuses on Tara's life in the multicultural environs of the San Francisco Bay Area, the latter goes back in time to explore the life of an ancestor who fought against British rule in India.

Mukherjee, who won the National Book Critics Circle Award in 1988 for her short-story collection *The Middleman and Other Stories* (1988), is known for her lush prose and sharply drawn female characters, many of whom suffer greatly at the hands of hostile bureaucracies, abusive husbands, and hostile American and Canadian societies but somehow manage to survive and forge an identity for themselves that bridges the cultural divide in which they find themselves. Mukherjee, who is married to a Canadian writer and has two children, is a distinguished professor of English at the University of California, Berkeley.

James Ciment

Further Reading
Alam, Fakrul. *Bharati Mukherjee.* New York: Twayne, 1996.
Chua, C.L. "Passages from India: Migrating to America in the Fiction of V.S. Naipaul and Bharati Mukherjee." In *Reworlding: The Literature of the Indian Diaspora,* ed. Emmanuel S. Nelson. Westport, CT: Greenwood, 1992.
Nelson, Emmanuel S., ed. *Bharati Mukherjee: Critical Perspectives.* New York: Garland, 1993.

Newsstands, Indian

The prominence of Indian Americans in the U.S. newsstand business became a highly visible phenomenon in the 1980s, as recognizable as Koreans in grocery retailing. The newsstands, however, are not just shops run as self-employment enterprises in the classic small-family business model. Instead, many require heavy capitalization and the use of low-wage workers to make them profitable. A complex set of social and economic factors made both capital and labor available within the Indian American community in the 1980s and created their dominance in the newsstand industry.

According to the 1997 U.S. Economic Census, there were 2,313 news dealers and newsstands with paid employees in the United States. New York, California, Pennsylvania, New Jersey, and Illinois, all states with large Indian American populations, accounted for about 50 percent, while New York alone accounted for 25 percent of the total. Like most newsstands, those owned and/or operated by Indian Americans tend to be located on busy street corners, in train and bus stations, on subway platforms, and in the lobbies of large buildings in metropolitan areas. In addition to newspapers and magazines, they offer the general public such sundries as candy, gum, and cigarettes, and sometimes even coffee and sandwiches. The capital required to purchase long-term commercial leases for these newsstands may run into millions of dollars and is usually beyond the capacity of a single family or investor. Much of the capital has come from within the Indian American community. By the 1980s, well-paid Indian American professionals who had arrived in the 1970s had built up substantial savings and access to bank credit and other informal loans. They formed complex investment groups and saw an

opportunity in the newsstand business. The 1980s also saw the arrival of large numbers of new immigrants from India who came on family preference quotas, without the professional and English language skills required to find jobs easily in a difficult economic climate. They formed a ready pool of labor for operating the newsstands. Even those who were educated but had no marketable skills took up newsstand work in sheer desperation when they failed to find other employment.

The work was usually arduous, with some newsstands open for twenty-four hours a day. Typically, an operator (who may call himself owner but is often only a lessee) pays a fixed rent to the investor and hires relatives or friends to work shifts. While some owners/operators no doubt exploited the readily available ethnic labor, even hiring illegal workers at below-minimum wages, the workers themselves saw their employment, at least temporarily, as a survival strategy in the absence of other options. Many Indian Americans who started out operating newsstands hoped to become owners or investors themselves, while for others it was dead-end, low-paying work.

Notwithstanding the harsh working conditions and the low status associated with newsstand work, the presence of Indian Americans in the industry can be seen as an example of how an immigrant community carves out a niche for itself in the U.S. marketplace by providing profits and wage work to fellow ethnics and important services to the host society.

Padma Rangaswamy

Further Reading
Nair, Mira. *So Far from India.* Mirabai Films: 1982.

Pandit, Sakharam Ganesh (1875–1959)

Sakharam Ganesh Pandit was a Hindu immigrant and California lawyer whose forceful legal arguments in favor of Indian Americans' right to citizenship won him the right to remain a naturalized citizen in 1927. His victory in the Supreme Court case of *United States v. Sakharam Ganesh Pandit* also stopped the government from revoking the citizenship of other naturalized Indian Americans.

Born a high-caste Hindu on November 1, 1875, Pandit arrived in California in 1909, became a citizen in 1914, and was admitted to the California State Bar as a practicing attorney on December 20, 1917. In spite of prevailing antimiscegenation laws that prohibited interracial marriage, Pandit wed a white woman early in

1920. During the course of the next decade, the question of who was eligible for naturalization among Asians was taken up by the federal courts, which loosely interpreted the terms "free white persons" and "Caucasian" to either grant or deny Asian Indians citizenship. Following adverse U.S. Supreme Court verdicts in the *Takao Ozawa v. United States* (1922) and *United States v. Bhagat Singh Thind* (1923) cases, which made it clear that Asians of any color could not be naturalized, federal authorities began proceedings to revoke nearly seventy naturalization certificates previously granted to Asian Indians. Between 1923 and 1926, the government succeeded in revoking some fifty naturalization certificates on the grounds that since Indians were ineligible for citizenship in the first place, the certificates had been obtained "fraudulently."

Pandit championed the cause of Indian Americans caught in the thick of this naturalization debate. In a 1926 publication, coauthored with Raymond Eugene Chase, titled "An Examination of the Opinion of the Supreme Court of the United States Deciding Against the Eligibility of Hindus for Citizenship," Pandit analyzed the *Ozawa* and *Thind* decisions. Pandit concluded that the two rulings were inconsistent: the determination in the *Ozawa* case was based on race rather than color, while the ruling in the *Thind* case was based on color, not race.

When the U.S. Justice Department filed a petition to denaturalize Pandit, he argued his own case before a federal court in 1924. Holding himself up as a responsible member of society who had practiced law for ten years in California and owned a home in Los Angeles, he argued that cancellation of his citizenship would deprive him of his livelihood and property, place the legality of his marriage in question, and under then-current law (the Cable Act of 1922) cause his wife to lose her citizenship. The judge agreed with Pandit that his citizenship had been granted by a proper court and procured legally, and ruled that the government could no longer challenge the decision because it had waited too long. The case went up to district court, the circuit court of appeals, and finally the U.S. Supreme Court, where the government lost its case on March 14, 1927. Following Pandit's victory, the U.S. commissioner of naturalization and the Labor Department grudgingly cancelled all pending denaturalization cases.

Although the U.S. government continued its discriminatory and restrictive policies toward Asians through World War II, the efforts of Sakharam Ganesh Pandit and other Indian Americans like him went a long way in combating the government's racist ideology and enabled countless numbers to enjoy the rights of citizenship. Pandit died on August 7, 1959.

Padma Rangaswamy

Further Reading

Chandrasekhar, S. "A History of U.S. Legislation with Respect to Immigration from India." In *From India to America: A Brief History of Immigration; Problems of Discrimination; Admission and Assimilation,* ed. S. Chandrasekhar. La Jolla, CA: Population Review, 1982.

Jensen, Joan M. *Passage from India: Asian Indian Immigrants in North America.* New Haven, CT: Yale University Press, 1988.

United States v. Sakharam Ganesh Pandit, 273 U.S. 759 (1927).

Political and Social Empowerment, Indian American

Like several other Asian immigrant groups, Indian Americans are often tagged with the label "model minority." Indeed the characterization holds true to a certain extent, as Indian Americans are well represented among the entrepreneurs and high-paid workers of California's high-tech Silicon Valley. Moreover, aside from Japanese Americans, Indian Americans have the highest per capita income of any South or East Asian American community, at more than $27,500 according to the 2000 census. Despite this relative economic success, however, Indian Americans likewise share with many other Asian communities a distinctly low profile in U.S. political life. A number of factors help explain this phenomenon, including relatively low citizenship rates among Indian Americans, an emphasis among many immigrants on entrepreneurial activity over political involvement, and ethnic and religious divisions within the community.

Indian immigrants have been coming to the United States in significant numbers since the late nineteenth and early twentieth centuries, many of them Sikhs coming from Canada, where they had been brought in as railroad workers. Most of the early Indian immigrants were poor and focused on surviving economically in their new land; many turned to farm labor, logging, and railroad construction in Northern and Central California. Indian Americans in the early years faced the same discrimination confronting other Asian immigrant groups. Anti-Hindu housing covenants, forbidding members of that religion—as well as Sikhs—from buying homes in certain neighborhoods, became common in communities where Indians settled. In 1913, California passed the Alien Land Law, prohibiting noncitizens from acquiring land. Since nonwhite immigrants were barred from citizenship, this effectively—and purposefully—banned Indians and other

Asians from acquiring land. A 1923 Supreme Court challenge to the ban (*United States v. Bhagat Singh Thind*)—based on the anthropological argument that Indians were, despite their usually dark skin tones, technically Caucasian—proved unsuccessful. And while members of the Indian community won another key case—*United States v. Sakharam Ganesh Pandit* (1927)—halting denaturalization of existing Indian American citizens, it was not until passage of the Luce-Celler Act of 1946 that new Indian immigrants would regain the right to become citizens and own land. In 1917, meanwhile, the United States imposed a ban on all immigration from Asia—except for immediate family members. However, while such as groups the Indo-American Association helped fight these legal battles, much Indian American politicking in the first half of the twentieth century concerned the status of the homeland. While the bulk of early Indian immigrants were poor farmers and laborers, a small contingent were nationalists in exile from British-occupied India. These politically active Indians organized groups such as the Home Rule League, founded in New York in 1910, and the Ghadar (Revolution) Party, established in San Francisco in 1913.

Until passage of the Immigration and Nationality Act of 1965, which ended national immigrant quotas and laid the foundation for mass immigration from the developing world, the Indian American community remained small in numbers and thus politically weak. In the years since that act, the Indian population in the United States has soared, from roughly 5,000 in 1960 to more than 1.6 million in 2000. New institutions emerged as well. In 1967, the first of the post-1965 Indian American political organizations formed in New York. Known as the Association of Indians in America (AIA), it addressed issues of immigration law, racial discrimination, economic development, political representation, lobbying, and promoting Indian American cultural events. Among its first efforts was to get Indians recognized as a distinct ethnic group under the U.S. census, part of a broader effort to get Indians covered under existing civil rights statutes. Other organizations arose as the Indian population grew rapidly in the 1980s, including the National Federation of Indian American Associations (1980) and the Federation of Indian Associations, an umbrella organization of local political and social empowerment groups, founded in the middle years of the decade.

Meanwhile, the large numbers of professionals within the Indian American community has led to the formation of organizations dedicated to advancing their interests, including the Network of Indian Professionals—founded in Chicago in 1990—dedicated to raising political and cultural awareness, as well as to providing professional development help and community service, among Indi-

Piyush "Bobby" Jindal served two terms as a U.S. congressman before winning election as governor of Louisiana in 2007. At age thirty-six, the young Republican became the first Indian American to win statewide office in U.S. history. *(Karen Bleier/AFP/Getty Images)*

ans in the professions and business. Specific professional groups have founded their own organizations, which are dedicated to professional development, education, political involvement, and community service. Among these are the Association of Physicians from India, located in metropolitan Chicago, and the Indian Dentists Association, located in New York. Likewise, nonprofessionals in the Indian American community have founded their own organizations to push for political and social empowerment, including the Leased Drivers Coalition, a taxi-driver group that has organized protests against cab companies.

Most of these organizations, much of whose membership is first-generation immigrant, are dedicated to economic improvement. However, as second- and third-generation Indian Americans become assimilated into American culture, issues that were taboo for first-generation immigrants—such as racial discrimination, gender bias, sexual abuse, homosexuality, domestic violence, and cross-racial marriage—have become an integral part of community discourse. Organizations such as Sakhi, Maitri, Pragati, Manavi, Narika, and Asian Indian Women in America (AIWA) are dedicated to the cause of women who are abused physically or psychologically. Organizations such as the Alliance of South Asians Taking Action (ASATA), the South Asian Lesbian and Gay Association (SALGA), and Concerned South Asians (CSA) are engaged in combating discrimination against gays and lesbians, exploitation of immigrant workers, and unfair immigration policies of the U.S. government, both inside and outside the Indian American community. In that sense, they hearken back to the organizations of the early part of the twentieth century, fighting against pervasive discrimination. The difference is that many of these groups also struggle to fight discrimination within their own Indian American communities.

Sudarsan Padmanabhan and James Ciment

Further Reading

Kalita, S. Mitra. *Suburban Sahibs: Three Immigrant Families and Their Passage from India to America.* Piscataway, NJ: Rutgers University Press, 2003.

Khandelwal, Madhulika S. *Becoming American, Being Indian: An Immigrant Community in New York City.* Ithaca, NY: Cornell University Press, 2002.

Kumar, Amitava. *Bombay, London, New York.* New York: Routledge, 2002.

Press, Indian American

The Indian American press, like the community itself, has undergone fascinating transformations in the course of recent decades. In the early years of large-scale immigration from India during the late 1960s and early 1970s, Indian American newspapers and radio broadcasts devoted most of their columns or airtime to relaying news and programs from India. As the Indian American community grew to some 1.6 million by the early 2000s, its newspapers, magazines, radio broadcasts, television programs, and eventually Web sites underwent a significant metamorphosis by focusing on issues of concern to the Indian diaspora in the United States—including politics, business, and social and cultural issues—while simultaneously keeping them abreast of the social, political, and cultural events taking place in India.

Newspapers

The vernacular Indian American press plays an important role in maintaining community cohesion among Indian Americans, who come from distinct linguistic-geographical regions in the homeland. Nevertheless, the important function of facilitating the formation of an effective Pan-Indian cultural network is carried out by the English-language Indian American press. Indeed, the vernacular Indian American press is overshadowed by English-language newspapers, television programs, and radio broadcasts, a situation diametrically opposite to that in India. Founded in New York in 1970 and with some 70,000 subscribers, *India Abroad*—to take the most popular of these English-language newspapers—has a relatively large circulation for an immigrant press organ. Originating as a biweekly newsletter, *India Abroad* expanded to become a forty-page weekly newspaper with a wide readership in North America, Canada, and other parts of the world. As scholars of the immigrant press point out, newspapers such as *India Abroad* act as community forums for the cultural expression of Indian Americans in the United States.

By the 1980s, the Indian American community had grown large enough to support competition to *India Abroad. News India,* the first major rival, was also published out of New York, as that city's metropolitan area was home to more Indian Americans than any other. The two newspapers offered similar coverage, including news from India, reports on the Indian American community, and a host of services, including matrimonial classified advertisements. In 1991, these weeklies were joined by the New York–based monthly *Little India.* Aimed at a somewhat younger audience, *Little India* offers articles on lifestyle, youth culture, fashion, and education, alongside more conventional pieces on American, Indian, and international affairs.

In the 1990s and 2000s, other newspapers sprang up in various cities around the country where large concentrations of Indian Americans live, among them *India Post, India Monitor, The Asian Reporter, Atlanta Samachar, East-West Times, Express India, India Bulletin, India West,* and *Asia Online,* a Web-based publication. The magazines *SiliconIndia* and *Siliconeer,* both published in California's Silicon Valley, focus on the large and influential Indian American high-tech community.

Indian Americans, of course, also read the international editions of major press organs from the home country. Perhaps the most popular is the weekly newsmagazine *India Today.* Founded in 1975 and published in New Delhi, *India Today* is considered one of the most respected weekly magazines in India. It launched an international edition in the 1990s and has gained thousands of subscribers in the United States, most of whom read it in English. (It is also offered in Hindi and three other major Indian vernacular languages.)

Some Indian regional newspapers, such as the *Gujarat Samachar,* also have extensive readerships in the Gujarati community of the United States. *Gujarat Samachar* is originally published in the state of Gujarat in India and reprinted in New York City. Other bilingual newspapers, in Punjabi and English, are printed in Vancouver and Toronto and sold in Indian shops and newsstands in the United States. In addition, a number of publications in Indian vernacular languages are based in the United States and serve regional Indian American communities. High-quality publications in Tamil, Telugu, Gujarati, Kannada, Malayalam, and other Indian languages have increased in recent years. Among the most important of these publications are the California-based *Tenral* and the Florida-based *Khassbaati,* serving the Gujarati American community.

Thus, the Indian American press has grown up with the Indian American community itself. Starting out with a single New York–based publication in 1970, the Indian press has grown in two ways commensurate with the immigrant community: competition with the general-interest newspaper and magazine market, and diversification of readership as publications emerged to cater to regional Indian groups and the important high-tech sector. So important has the Indian American press become that it has generated its own professional group, the New York–based South Asian Journalists Association (SAJA). Founded in 1991 to provide networking resources for Indian American and Indian Canadian journalists, as well as to promote accurate coverage of South Asian Americans in the mainstream press, the nonpartisan SAJA has chapters in nine U.S. cities and Toronto.

Sudarsan Padmanabhan

Further Reading

Cropp, Fritz, Cynthia M. Frisby, and Dean Mills, eds. *Journalism Across Cultures.* Ames: Iowa State Press, 2003.

Das, Gurcharan. *India Unbound.* New Delhi: Penguin Books, 2002.

Hsu, Hua. "Ethnic Media Grows Up." *Colorline* 5:3 (Fall 2002): 7–9.

Khandelwal, Madhulika S. *Becoming American, Being Indian: An Immigrant Community in New York City.* Ithaca, NY: Cornell University Press, 2002.

South Asian Journalists Association. http://www.saja.org.

Punjabi Americans

Punjabi Americans are immigrants and the descendants of immigrants originating from the Punjab region of northwestern India and, to a lesser extent, Pakistan. They are largely identified linguistically, as speakers of the Punjab language. The first wave of Pun-

jabi immigrants arrived in North America in the late 1800s and early 1900s; it effectively ended with the Immigration Act of 1924. Many had served in the Indian army and had heard tales about life in America. Aside from a minor influx of students from India, the majority of the first wave was made up of male Sikhs who came to America to make money in agriculture. Many had been involved in farming back home, and the Californian landscape was similar to that of the Punjab. Some also found jobs with railroads, factories, and lumber mills. Most came with the intention of returning home, but as they grew more successful in America, they began to consider staying. For many, the success has continued. According to the U.S. Census Bureau, the average annual income for Indian American households was more than $68,000 in 2004.

Although many of the men in the first wave of Punjabi immigrants had been married young in India, their wives did not come with them to America. Once the men settled, mostly in the western states, a significant number chose to remarry. Barred by law from marrying white women, many Punjabis married Hispanic women, which resulted in a new ethnic subculture, known as Punjabi Mexican. Children of the marriages would generally be raised Catholic and Spanish speaking. Thus, a new cultural identity developed among subsequent generations of Punjabi Mexicans.

The first wave of Punjabi immigrants, for the most part, adjusted well and experienced limited conflict with life in America. The men retained their language and religion, but they also adopted American cultural attributes and were often committed to becoming citizens. They lobbied for that right until the Luce-Celler Act of 1946 made it possible, after which many of them took the opportunity. The same measure also reopened U.S. borders to a limited number of new immigrants.

The second wave of immigrants from the Punjab differed from the first in that entire families were immigrating together. The new group did not blend well with the Punjabi Mexican community, as their assimilation into American culture and the fact that they had no practical knowledge of Punjabi culture made many new immigrants feel that Punjabi Mexicans were not truly Indian. The uneasiness went both ways, as first-wave immigrants felt the newcomers were too resistant to American culture. In 1965, the Immigration and Nationality (Hart-Celler) Act loosened immigration restrictions even further. Unlike earlier immigrants, who settled mainly in the West, those who have come since 1965 have spread out across the country. Although specific numbers are difficult to determine, many of the 1 million to 1.6 million Indian Americans are of Punjabi origin. The U.S. Census Bureau projects a 213 percent increase in the Asian American population by the year 2050, likely ensuring the future of the unique Punjabi American culture.

Leah Irvine

Further Reading

Leonard, Karen. "Historical Constructions of Ethnicity: Research on Punjabi Immigrants in California." *Journal of American Ethnic History* 12:4 (Summer 1993): 3–27.

Leonard, Karen Isaksen. *Making Ethnic Choices: California's Punjabi Mexican Americans.* Philadelphia: Temple University Press, 1992.

Ramakrishna Mission

The Ramakrishna Mission is the Hindu monastic order and service organization that came into being after the passing away in 1886 of Sri Ramakrishna, a temple priest and devout worshipper of the goddess Kali. Ramakrishna's ideas would provide the philosophical and theological foundation of the mission, established in Calcutta (now Kolkata) by his principal disciple, Swami Vivekananda, who also translated the mystical and Vedantic ideas expounded by Ramakrishna. Beginning with his address at the first World's Parliament of Religions in Chicago in 1893, Vivekananda emerged as the most inspiring awakener of Hinduism, and in particular of Vedanta, in the West. Derived from the Vedas, the ancient Hindu scriptures, the core idea of Vedanta is that God, the underlying reality, exists in every being. The divinity in everyone can be realized through the practice of the four *yogas: Bhakti yoga,* or the path of devotion; *Jnana yoga,* or the path of knowledge; *Karma yoga,* or the path of selfless service to others, and *Raja yoga,* or the path of meditation. Vivekananda played the important role of simplifying and adapting the yogas to make them understandable to Westerners and promoting East-West understanding through his lectures, while remaining firm in his defense of traditional Hindu practices.

The Ramakrishna Math and the Ramakrishna Mission represent the two main organs of the movement. The former, founded by Ramakrishna in 1886, functions as the monastic organization of the order; the latter, founded by Vivekananda in 1897, oversees the educational and humanitarian programs of the order. Sarada Math, established in 1954 in honor of Ramakrishna's wife, Sarada Devi, is the sister monastic institution. From their headquarters at Belur Math outside Kolkata, the swamis, or religious masters, are responsible for the spiritual decisions in the order. Day-to-day operations of the centers in the United States are overseen by the American Board of Trustees. As of May 2004, the Ramakrishna order managed 135 centers throughout the world, of which twelve are located in the United States. Of its 2 million worldwide followers, several thousand are in the United States. The three principal centers in America are the Vivekananda Vedanta Society in Chicago, the Vedanta Society of Northern California in San Francisco, and the Vedanta Society of Southern California in Hollywood. The movement is kept alive in the West by a steady flow of swamis sent by the Belur Math headquarters.

Prior to World War II, the centers in America attracted Western followers primarily. Since passage of the Immigration and Nationality Act of 1965, which opened the doors to waves of new immigrants, the centers have begun to attract Indian-born members, whose presence has led to a revival of Hindu traditions. Consequently, American devotees have been calling for a return to the Western Vedanta as envisioned by Vivekananda. In addition, the Ramakrishna Mission, with its message of tolerance and a return to ancient Hindu teachings, has served as a bridge within the disparate Indian American community, uniting Hindu Indian Americans of different regional and linguistic backgrounds who come to worship and serve together, particularly in relief missions. Albeit in a state of transformation, the Ramakrishna Mission continues to carry the banner of Vedanta in the West as it continues to grow, adapting and encouraging Western interest in this ancient philosophy of the East.

Yosay Wangdi

Further Reading

Burke, Marie Louise. *Swami Vivekananda in the West: New Discoveries.* 4th ed. 6 vols. Calcutta: Advaita Ashrama, 1983.

Jackson, Carl T. *Vedanta for the West: The Ramakrishna Movement in the United States.* Bloomington: Indiana University Press, 1994.

Religion, Indian American

India is a multicultural country whose people practice a variety of different faiths. The major ones—Hinduism, Islam, Buddhism, Sikhism, and Jainism—have all found a place in Indian American culture. From the beginning, immigrants to the United States have brought their beliefs and practices with them, and these faiths constitute a vital part of the Indian American identity. Early immigrants downplayed their non-Christian religions and made accommodations borrowed from American culture. After 1965, however, when immigration limits were raised, more Indian Americans have displayed their faiths more openly. In addition, a growing number of non-Indian Americans have been attracted to those traditions and beliefs.

Hinduism

In its various sects and schools of thought, Hinduism is the most widely practiced religion in India. Hinduism reached the United States before any Indian immigrants. During the eighteenth century, European scholars translated Hindu religious texts and made them available to Western scholars. American transcendentalists such as Henry David Thoreau and Ralph Waldo Emerson became familiar with Hindu teachings and incorporated some of its concepts in their thinking. The first Hindu teacher in the United States was Swami Vivekananda, who introduced the faith to America at the World's Parliament of Religions, held as part of the Columbian Exposition in Chicago in 1893. Vivekananda's intellect and command of English attracted large audiences at lectures he gave across the United States.

A relatively limited number of Indians immigrated to the United States before 1965, primarily due to limits on Asian immigration. Most of the early arrivals were Sikhs or Muslims but were commonly referred to by Americans as "Hindoos." As the objects of racial discrimination, they kept their religious beliefs largely to themselves. After 1965, however, strict national quotas on immigration were lifted with the passage of the Immigration and Nationality Act, and hundreds of thousands of Indians began entering the United States every year. By the 2000 census, more than 1.5 million people were identified as Indian Americans. Most were Hindus and came from the educated classes.

The new generation of Indian Americans at first practiced their faith quietly in small groups. By the 1970s, however, their large numbers and economic security encouraged Hindus to build their own temples along the model of those in India. The first were consecrated in 1977. Among them was the Sri Ganesha Temple (now the Maha Vallabha Ganapati Devasthanam) in Flushing, Queens (New York City). Originally a Russian Orthodox church, the temple became symbolic of the changing ethnic mixture in New York. Another notable Hindu temple opened that year was the Sri Venkateswara Temple in Pittsburgh, Pennsylvania. The sites in Flushing and Pittsburgh set the standard for 150 or more Hindu temples that followed in virtually every major American city. Unlike those in India, Hindu temples in America perform multiple functions and often serve as cultural centers. While most Hindu worship in India is done individually, American temples have sanctuaries for congregational worship. Unlike Indian temples, some also have chairs, and men and women are more likely to be integrated during worship. American temples typically have institutional-quality kitchens and meeting rooms for social gatherings; some have classrooms for teaching children about the faith. Facilities such as those in Flushing have been made available to other secular and religious groups for weddings and events. Thus, in many ways, Hindu temples are not unlike large American Christian churches.

American Hindus have made concessions in observance and practice as well. While Indian temples may be dedicated to a single deity, American ones generally honor multiple deities. Differences in language and ethnic background are more likely to be accommodated, but traditions such as the caste system are less often upheld by second-generation Indian Americans. The second generation is also more likely to marry non-Hindus. Ironically, even as Indian American parents struggle to keep their children faithful to Hinduism, Americans in increasing numbers have been attracted to the faith. As of 2007, Hinduism was the fifth-largest religion in the United States.

Islam

Muslims make up the second-largest religious group of Indian Americans. Of the approximately 6 million Muslims in the United States, immigrants from South Asia number about 1.2 million, or nearly a quarter. Like other minority religious groups, Muslims have faced various forms of discrimination for more than century. After the terrorist attacks of September 11, 2001, however, they have been regarded with particular suspicion by many mainstream Americans. Like Hindu Indian immigrants, Muslim Indian Americans tend to be better educated and to hold better jobs. They follow the teachings of the various sects of Islam and share the same concerns about raising their children in their faith. Muslim Indian Americans have been more likely to build schools to instruct their children than other Indian American religious groups. By the early 1990s, more than 150 Islamic schools were operating across the United States. According to a survey in 2000, approximately 2,000 mosques were in use as well. Like Hindu temples, most mosques serve as educational and cultural centers as well as places of worship. African American Muslims, whose practices vary somewhat from those of their South Asian counterparts, represent a growing segment of the Islamic faithful in America.

Buddhism

Buddhism is found primarily among Indian Americans from Sri Lanka or Tibet, though the practices of those subgroups also vary. The first Buddhists to come to the United States were from China and Japan; those from India made their first appearance at the World's Parliament of Religions in Chicago in 1893. Among the Indian Buddhists attending that event was Anagarika Dharmapala from Sri Lanka. A few days after the meeting, he conducted the rite for the first American to convert to Buddhism. Most Indian American Buddhists adhere to the more conservative Theravada ("Way of the Elders") branch of the religion, which encourages enlightenment through experience and study, not faith alone. American followers put less emphasis on monasticism than their counterparts in India, and women play a greater leadership role in Indian American Buddhism. Religious organizations in America have also adopted more democratic administrative practices than those in India. Americans of non-Indian descent have been attracted to Buddhism partially because of the high regard in which Tibet's exiled Dalai Lama is held. There are an estimated 1.5 million Buddhists in the United States today, of which Indian Americans constitute a minority.

Sikhism and Jainism

Sikhism is more tied to an ethnic identity than any of the other Indian American religions. Male adherents can be identified by their turbans and uncut hair, as well as other religiously mandated characteristics. The first Sikh immigrants to North America were farmworkers who settled in western Canada and then migrated to California in the early twentieth century. The first *gurdwara,* or Sikh temple, was founded in Stockton, California, in 1912. When immigration quotas were lifted in 1965, many more educated Sikhs relocated to the United States for economic reasons. By 2000, the Sikh population in America was estimated at 250,000–500,000. At least 127 *gurdwaras* have been founded on U.S. soil, each containing a copy of their sacred scriptures, the *Guru Granth Sahib. Gurdwaras* also function as social and cultural centers, with many offering classes in Punjabi for the children of Sikh Americans.

Religious devotion among Sikhs in the United States intensified in 1984, when the Indian army attacked the Golden Temple in the Punjabi city of Amritsar, the most sacred shrine among Sikhs. In America, adherents of the faith openly expressed pride in their religion as well as outrage against the attack, and organized parades and other public events to educate the American public. As

The Guru Granth Sahib, or Sikh holy scripture, is recited in 2006 ceremonies to mark the opening of the National Gurdwara (temple) and Sikh Cultural Center in Washington, D.C. Sikhism is one of several faiths that have found a place in Indian American life. *(Chip Somodevilla/Getty Images)*

a result, growing numbers of Americans have been attracted to Sikhism. This development has raised an issue in the Sikh community as to whether converts can be treated as full members of the faith.

The most recent Indian American religion to appear in the United States is Jainism. The first Jain temple in America was built at the 1904 St. Louis World's Fair, then dismantled and reassembled in Las Vegas. The first Jain immigrants did not arrive until 1944, however, and even then there were very few. In the early 1970s, Jain merchants were expelled from several countries in Africa, and many relocated to the United States. At first they joined with Hindus in building temples that were used by both. In 1973, the first Jain-only temple opened in Boston. Other temples and cultural centers followed in urban centers across the country. Today, up to 100,000 Jains are estimated to live in the United States. Their teachings of nonviolence, vegetarianism, and self-denial have appealed to many Americans, such as members of the animal-rights movement.

Tim J. Watts

Further Reading

Carnes, Tony, and Fenggang Yang, eds. *Asian American Religions: The Making and Remaking of Borders and Boundaries.* New York: New York University Press, 2004.

Min, Pyong Gap, and Jung Ha Kim. *Religions in Asian America: Building Faith Communities.* Walnut Creek, CA: AltaMira, 2002.

Prasad, Leela, and David H. Wells. *Live Like the Banyan Tree: Images of the Indian American Experience.* Philadelphia: Balch Institute for Ethnic Studies, 1999.

Williams, Raymond Brady. *Religions of Immigrants from India and Pakistan: New Threads in the American Tapestry.* New York: Cambridge University Press, 1988.

Restaurants and Cuisine, Indian American

Like other immigrant groups from other parts of the world, Indian Americans have sought to preserve many of the cultural traditions and customs of their homeland—not least in the form of cuisine. Indian cuisine, world famous for its unique blend of spices and aromatic flavors, is as diverse as the geography, languages, cultures, and climate of India. It has become very popular in the United States, thanks mainly to the immigrant population. While chicken tikka has yet to supplant the hamburger as the national dish (as it has replaced fish 'n' chips in England), more and more Americans have discovered the joys of Indian cooking. Today, restaurants serving fare from diverse regions of India are to be found not only in major metropolises, but also in smaller towns where Indians have settled, and many where they have not. Once nostalgic outlets for homesick Indians, they are now frequented by Americans from virtually every walk of life. The restaurants themselves, in many cases, have evolved from small, family-owned businesses to chain holdings in locations nationwide. The industry has diversified as well, branching out into catering for weddings, conventions, Indian heritage festivals, and other large gatherings.

Origins

In the decades before 1965, when the Indian immigrant population was still small, few restaurants served authentic Indian fare, and the only way to cook Indian food at home was to send for spices and special ingredients from a mail-order outfit in New York or make do with substitutes. Even during the 1970s, as the first Indian restaurants began opening in major cities such as New York and Chicago, the choice was largely limited to North Indian or Mughlai food. In the years since, however, restaurants have sprung up that specialize in the diverse regional cuisines of India. In the New York area alone, one can find more than 100 Indian restaurants with names that reflect a regional specialty—such as Tandoor Oven, Shalimar, Dosa Hut, Annapurna, Chola, Biryani, and Madras Café. Many Indian restaurants serve a twelve- or fourteen-course Northern Indian style buffet seven days a week. The dishes typically include pulao rice, Indian breads such as naans and parathas, vegetarian dishes, daal (lentil soup), tandoori chicken (marinated in a blend of yogurt and spices and seared over high heat in a clay oven called the tandoor), salads, and kheer (usually a rice pudding).

Many Indian restaurants in America are still family-owned enterprises. Others have grown because of the demand for caterers for big social events such as weddings, graduations, and theme parties. Indeed the industry has become so lucrative that restaurants are now run by people who have given up successful careers in banking, finance, and other professional fields. The style varies—from simple rustic, in family restaurants, to trendy, in bistros catering to young sophisticates. Diner-style, fast-food eateries in ethnic neighborhoods are a favorite place to meet friends and take a break from shopping. Upscale restaurants in more chic downtown locations feature fancy décor and chefs brought in from five-star hotels in Mumbai or New Delhi. Some restaurants offer "fusion food," a mix of Eastern cuisines that preserves the delicate balance of herbs and spices but modifies it to suit the American palate. The continuously evolving Indian American restaurant industry has even spawned "Indian Chinese" restaurants that serve Chinese food spiced for the Indian palate, with dishes such as Gobi (cauliflower) Manchurian and Chili Chicken.

Broadly speaking, Indian cuisine is distinguished by its use of spices, chief among which are cumin, coriander, cardamom, clove, cinnamon, black pepper, red chilies, turmeric, aniseed, and asafetida, to name only a few. The rice used in North Indian cooking is called basmati and has a unique flavor. Indian cuisine is also characterized by its use of a wide variety of vegetables. Every state and region brings its own touch to popular dishes, based on local conditions. North Indian cuisine uses more wheat, while South Indian cuisine is based on rice as the staple, but the distinctions go further than that. For instance, dishes from the southern states of Tamil Nadu and Andhra Pradesh make generous use of red-hot chilies and tamarind, while those from Goa and Kerala (and other coastal states) rely heavily on coconut. There are strong central Asian influences in the cuisines of northern states, such as Kashmir and Punjab, while the cuisine of desert states such as Gujarat and Rajasthan rely heavily on dry daals (lentils) and achars (pickles and preserves) to compensate for the relative lack of fresh vegetables. Dishes in eastern states such as Bengal and Assam, often including fish, are influenced by the cuisine of the Far East.

Ingredients and Preparation

Many of the spices used in Indian food have medicinal properties and are used as much for their healing qualities as for their flavor and taste. Ginger, for instance, which is believed to have originated in India, is often added to tea to relieve sore throats and the common cold. Turmeric is known to have antiseptic qualities and is used routinely in Indian cooking to protect against skin diseases. Some foods are shunned by certain religious groups as having undesirable qualities. Jains, for example, who believe in nonviolence and avoid harming even the tiniest of insects, are strict vegetarians and refrain from eating onions, garlic, and root vegetables, whose harvesting might incur loss of life.

Most Indian dishes require a good deal of planning and preparation. Many Indian American housewives have little time or inclination to go through the multistep processes demanded of Indian cooking—soaking, marinating, grinding, fermenting, frying, or stirring a dish for hours over a slow fire. They tend to prefer simpler dishes suited for everyday eating (and quite different from restaurant fare) or patronize the frozen-foods and ready-to-eat sections of Indian grocery stores. What was a cottage industry in the 1970s and 1980s—the supply of ready-to-eat chappatis (unleavened bread), pickles, and papads (lentil crisps)—has turned into a multinational enterprise, with such foods being made in factories and imported from India, Great Britain, and Africa.

The popularity of Indian American restaurants has helped make Indian cooking increasingly popular in mainstream American culture. Indian cookbooks can be found in virtually any bookstore, and spices and canned and frozen products are now widely available in supermarkets. Indian cuisine has also made major inroads in the restaurant menus and catering business of major hotel chains. Many restaurateurs have made it their mission to educate non-Indian customers about Indian cuisine and bring it fully into the American mainstream. Already such Indian favorites as mangoes, spicy chai (masala tea), samosas (potato turnovers), and tandoori chicken are familiar to many Americans. It may be not be long before they are embraced by Americans as widely as pizza, tacos, and other foods introduced by previous immigrant groups.

Padma Rangaswamy

Further Reading

Balagopal, Padmini, ed. *Indian and Pakistani Food Practices, Customs, and Holidays.* Alexandria, VA: American Dietetic Association, 1996.

Bladholm, Linda. *The Indian Grocery Store Demystified.* Los Angeles: Renaissance Books, 1999.

Jaffrey, Madhur. *An Invitation to Indian Cooking.* New York: Alfred A. Knopf, 1973.

San Francisco Radical Club

The San Francisco Radical Club was a community organization founded in the early part of the twentieth century, consisting of South Asian immigrants, expatriates, exiles, and students committed to the cause of militant nationalism on the Indian subcontinent. One of the first organizations of its kind, it established the foundation for more well-known community organizations, such as the Ghadar Party, which launched the radical nationalist movement espousing and advocating violence and armed struggle against British colonial rule in India.

Some of the earliest immigrants from South Asia to North America at the beginning of the twentieth century were political dissidents and nationalist activists from the Indian subcontinent who were seeking safe places to pursue their revolutionary agenda. Particularly on the Pacific coasts of the United States and Canada, these political dissidents joined with Punjabi agriculturalists, mostly Sikhs, and South Asian students enrolled at local universities, especially the University of California, Berkeley, and Stanford University, to mobilize in support of their primary political cause of Indian independence.

While immigrant and student activists were united by their common grievance against British colonial rule on the Indian subcontinent, they were also bound together by their resistance to the immigration restrictions imposed by the governments of the United States and Canada and by the discriminatory practices of anti-immigration organizations such as the Asiatic Exclusion League. Many of their activities focused on matters of social concern, such as immigration rights, labor rights, and welfare issues. The failure of the British Indian government to support aggressively the rights of its own citizens in North America only served to firm up the immigrants' militant political agenda against the forces of colonial domination.

One of the most powerful leaders of the militant nationalist movement at this time was Har Dayal, a Punjabi Hindu by birth who had become radicalized through his association with V.D. Savarkar, a prominent Hindu militant nationalist, during his period of postgraduate study at Oxford University, England, from 1905 to 1907. After his arrival in San Francisco in 1911, Dayal briefly taught Indian philosophy as an unpaid instructor at nearby Stanford University and established relationships with members of the flourishing intellectual radical movement in the Palo Alto area.

Initially undetected by British surveillance, Dayal became secretary of the Socialist Radical Club, an organization formed to study, write, and speak about issues such as socialism, feminism, and social change, with a membership including Manuel Larkin (an economics professor at Stanford), defense attorney Clarence Darrow, journalist John D. Barry, author Cora Older, and anarchist Emma Goldman. Dayal sketched his vision of world solidarity among workers in a 1911 lecture delivered before the International Workers of the World in Oakland, and he began to develop plans for a fraternity of anarchists, including men as well as women, committed to the goals of moral, intellectual, and economic emancipation. In 1912, he established the San Francisco Radical Club as a venue for the circulation of his revolutionary ideas through writings and lectures. An informal gathering of like-minded intellectuals, the club proved short-lived, fading away as Dayal turned to more explicitly Indian nationalist causes.

The following year, Dayal established the Hindu Association of the Pacific Coast and began printing a weekly newspaper called the *Ghadar* (which means "mutiny" in Hindi, Urdu, and Punjabi). Soon renamed the Ghadar Party, it became the most well-known and far-reaching organization coordinating nationalist activities among South Asian immigrant and student activists on the West Coast for the next three decades. Although the British government in India thwarted the movement's attempted revolt on the subcontinent in 1915, the Ghadar Party's revolutionary activities continued throughout World War I and, more sporadically, in the 1920s and 1930s.

Haley Duschinski

Further Reading

Brown, Emily C. *Har Dayal: Hindu Revolutionary and Rationalist.* Tucson: University of Arizona Press, 1975.

Jensen, Joan M. *Passage from India: Asian Indian Immigrants in North America.* New Haven, CT: Yale University Press, 1988.

Puri, Harish. *Ghadar Movement: Ideology, Organisation, and Strategy.* 2nd ed. Amritsar, India: Guru Nanak Dev University, 1993.

Saund, Dalip Singh (1899–1973)

The first Asian American, as well as the first person to practice a non-Western faith, to serve in the United States Congress, Dalip Singh Saund represented the Twenty-ninth Congressional District of California, serving three terms from 1957 to 1963. A liberal Democrat, but also a staunch anti-Communist, Saund

Born in the Indian Punjab, Dalip Singh Saund came to America to complete his education and went on to become a successful farmer and judge. In 1956, he won election as the first Asian American member of Congress, representing California's Imperial Valley. *(Library of Congress)*

advocated antidiscrimination legislation, help for small farmers, and U.S. foreign aid, which he believed would help counter the appeal of Communism in a developing world emerging out of the dying European empires.

Saund was born on September 20, 1899, in the Punjab region of what was then British India. Born into an uneducated but prosperous Sikh family, Saund received his bachelor's degree from the University of Punjab in 1919. Like many educated Indians, Saund was active in the Gandhian movement for independence and was deeply disappointed when Britain failed to liberate his country following World War I. At the age of twenty-two, he moved to the United States to study at the University of California, Berkeley, where he received a doctorate degree in mathematics in 1924.

During his time at Berkeley, Saund worked in the canneries of California's Central Valley and lived at a Sikh temple in nearby Stockton. There, and as a member of the Hindustani Association of America, Saund became active in Indian and Indian American politics. While having promised his parents that he would return to Indian after receiving his degree, and despite receiving offers to teach at various Indian universities, Saund decided to stay on in America after being offered a job as a foreman on an Indian American–owned farm in the Imperial Valley of Southern California, home to a small but thriving community of Hindus and Sikhs that included his maternal grandparents and other relatives. There, he also met and married Marian Kosa, the daughter of Czech immigrants, with whom he would have three children.

In the mid-1930s, Saund became active in local social organizations, including the Social Events Club, and would tour the region making speeches about various liberal political causes and introducing locals to Indian culture. He also became involved in the effort to lift the ban on the naturalization of Indian immigrants, in place since the *United States v. Bhagat Singh Thind* Supreme Court decision of 1923. When that was achieved with the Luce-Cellar act of 1946, Saund applied for citizenship, which he received in 1949. In 1950, he ran successfully as justice of the peace for Westmorland. When the election was overturned after local businessmen protested that he had not been a citizen for a full year before running— a legal requirement—he was appointed by the Imperial County Board of Supervisors as soon as he qualified. Saund emphasized cleaning up vice in the area, including shutting down the town's brothels.

Meanwhile, Saund was becoming active in local Democratic politics, becoming chair of the Imperial Country Democratic Central Committee in 1951, where he ran the unsuccessful campaigns of Democratic candidates attempting to unseat the long-serving Republican congressman John Phillips. When Phillips announced he would not run for reelection in 1956, Saund threw his hat into the ring and won both the Democratic primary and the general election—the latter against famed aviatrix Jacqueline Cochran Odlum—in campaigns where his opponents emphasized his exotic foreign origins and the fact that he was not white and not a Christian.

Representing a largely agricultural district, Saund made aid to small farmers a key part of his agenda, winning passage of a law limiting federally subsidized irrigation to farmers with less than 160 acres (65 hectares). Supporting most liberal Democratic legislation, Saund was also a strong believer in foreign aid and traveled extensively on fact-finding missions, particularly to Asia. Although his district was conservative and he barely squeaked to victory in his first election, he easily won reelection twice by margins of more than 60 percent, largely because of his efforts to help farmers. During his second term, in 1960, Saund published his memoir, *Congressman from India.*

Crippled by a stroke in May 1962, Saund was forced to give up campaigning for a fourth term, though he won the Democratic primary. But news that he could not speak or even stand up cost him the general election. Cared for by his wife, Saund eventually recovered his ability to walk but remained unable to speak the rest of his life. He died in Los Angeles on April 22, 1973.

James Ciment and Anupama Arora

Further Reading

McCaye, Milton. "U.S. Congressman from Asia." *Saturday Evening Post,* August 2, 1958.
Patterson, Tom. "Triumph and Tragedy of Dalip Saund." *California Historian* (June 1992).
Saund, Dalip Singh. *Congressman from India.* New York: Dutton, 1960.

Seattle Exclusion League

The Asiatic Exclusion League was an early-twentieth-century organization, made up largely of native-born whites, that sought to prevent the immigration of Asians to the United States, promote discriminatory laws against Asians already in the country, and keep them from taking jobs in industries dominated by white workers. To achieve these ends, the league lobbied city and state governments, primarily on the West Coast, where most Asian Americans lived at the time, and organized public demonstrations, some of which led to mob violence against Asian American neighborhoods.

Led by white labor leaders, some of whom were European immigrants themselves, the Asiatic Exclusion League was formed in San Francisco on May 14, 1905. Originally called the Japanese and Korean Exclusion League, it soon changed its name to include Indians among its targets. According to its stated policies, the organization sought to promote hostile sentiment against Asians in order to exert pressure on the U.S. government to restrict Asian immigration. The organization's tactics, including marches and public demonstrations, often incited outbreaks of violence, including riots, ransackings, beatings, and attacks on personal property. Its exclusionist activities, including lobbying and political organizing, had a significant effect on official U.S. immigration policy, which became increasingly restrictive from 1910 to 1924.

Among the most active of the Asiatic Exclusion League branches was the Seattle Exclusion League, which focused its activities in the Pacific Northwest and British Columbia during the period from 1904 to 1911. Organized by A.E. Fowler in 1907, the Seattle Exclusion League focused its efforts on Indian immigrants, thousands of whom were entering the labor force of the Pacific Northwest as lumber mill workers. The Seattle Exclusion League played an important role in mobilizing popular sentiment and action against immigrant labor-ers throughout the region, in towns such as Bellingham, Washington, and Vancouver, British Columbia.

Fowler, the secretary of the Seattle Exclusion League, was particularly adept at mobilizing crowds of white workers through fiery rhetoric that identified Asian im-migrants as a threat to the white labor force. Having settled in Seattle sometime after 1901 and launching a magazine called *The Yellow Peril* in 1906, Fowler began to deliver lectures and circulate pamphlets against Asian immigra-tion. He organized the Seattle Exclusion League as race and class antagonisms were escalating in the mills in the state. On September 5, 1907, the agitation against Indian immigrants came to a head in the mill town of Bellingham, where an angry mob of 500 white workers attacked Indian laborers by dragging them from their beds and driving them out of the city. Although not directly responsible for organizing the Bellingham riots, Fowler indicated in the press soon afterward that they had been a successful if regrettable way of excluding the Asians from the town.

In the days and weeks following the Bellingham riots, tensions spread throughout the region as Indian laborers relocated to other towns in search of work. The Seattle Ex-clusion League actively sought to influence popular opinion and police action, with varying degrees of success. When conflict flared in Seattle, the *Post-Intelligencer* played a role in defusing the work of the exclusion league by publicly condemning it as an "un-American" organization. The league found greater success in British Columbia, where it encouraged the Vancouver branch of the organization to coordinate protests against Asian immigration. Fowler himself incited a crowd to riot in Vancouver's Chinatown on September 7, 1907. As a result of these kinds of epi-sodes, Indian laborers increasingly relocated farther south along the Pacific Coast, finding work in the railroading and farming industries of California.

Haley Duschinski

Further Reading

Daniels, Roger. *History of Indian Immigration to the United States: An Interpretative Essay.* New York: Asia Society, 1989.

Jensen, Joan M. *Passage from India: Asian Indian Immigrants in North America.* New Haven, CT: Yale University Press, 1988.

Takaki, Ronald. *Strangers from a Different Shore: A History of Asian Americans.* Rev. ed. Boston: Little, Brown, 1998.

Self-Realization Fellowship

The Self-Realization Fellowship (SRF) is an interna-tional Hindu organization based in Los Angeles. Founded in 1920, it represented one of the first highly visible, Asian-derived meditation movements attractive to white Americans in the early to mid-twentieth cen-tury. Its founder was a Bengali yogi and guru named Paramahansa Yogananda (1893–1952), who taught *kriya* yoga, a meditation discipline that promises quick achievement of enlightenment, or sense of oneness with the divine. This approach to meditation became attrac-tive to many spiritual seekers in the United States in the early decades of the twentieth century.

Yogananda grew up during a period in Indian his-tory when British-educated Indians, especially in Ben-gal, were combining Western values and science with traditional Hindu texts and teachings. Due to his family connections and social status, Yogananda was exposed to Western values and education at an early age; he was also introduced to several famous yoga teachers. He had barely finished high school when he moved to the sacred Hindu city of Benares (or Varanasi) to study and prac-tice meditation. In 1917, he established a boys' school in Bengal—an event said to mark the beginning of the Yogoda Satsanga Society (YSS), the sister organization in India to the SRF.

A yoga teacher of renown by his twenties, Yogananda was invited to address a congress of religious liberals in Boston in 1920, beginning his long-term relation-ship with American devotees. The SRF also claims that year as the official founding of the organization. Given his background in Bengal, where British influence was not uncommon among Bengalis of his social class, Yo-gananda's move to the United States was consistent with his ability to communicate traditional Indian spiritual values to Westerners. He gave lectures and yoga work-shops throughout the country.

In 1925, a group of his followers bought an estate called Mount Washington in Los Angeles, which be-came the headquarters of SRF. Yogananda traveled back to India in 1935 but returned to the United States the following year and lived there until his death, teaching disciples and writing books and lessons. According to Yogananda and the SRF, *kriya* yoga enables the meditator to achieve liberation more quickly than with other forms of yoga. He also insisted that the results of *kriya* yoga could be scientifically verified. By means of particular breath techniques and meditative exercises, *kriya* yoga is said to transform the practitioner's physical body, mind, and soul by the infusion of universal, divine energy. Yo-gananda's religious background was heavily influenced by the goddess-oriented forms of bhakti, or theistic devotionalism, characteristic of Bengal in his time. Like bhakti, *kriya* yoga emphasizes loving submission to one's guru (or yoga teacher) and to the all-pervasive divine force or energy in the universe, which Yogananda called

The Self-Realization Fellowship Lake Shrine in Pacific Palisades, California, is one of a number of facilities maintained by the fellowship across America. The Hindu meditation organization was founded in Los Angeles by a Bengali yogi in 1920. *(Andrew Shawaf/Getty Images)*

God. Those who wish to follow *kriya* yoga as a way of life take monastic vows; monks and nuns are the core of SRF leadership.

Many people were introduced to *kriya* yoga through Yogananda's enormously popular *Autobiography of a Yogi* (1946), in which he presents readers with a world of visions, dreams, and miraculous events. Yogananda claimed to have met Jesus Christ, whom he identified as an avatar of the divine, like Krishna before him and like Babaji, the founder of Yogananda's yoga lineage, after him. After Yogananda's death, he was succeeded as leader of the SRF by an American named James Lynn (1892–1955), whose yoga name was Rajarsi Janakananda. Janakananda was succeeded by another American and SRF's current president, Sri Daya Mata (born Faye Wright). Today the SRF continues to provide inquirers with Yogananda's teachings through mail-order yoga lessons, publication of Yogananda's books, and maintenance of nearly 500 SRF centers worldwide. SRF's official Web site lists more than fifty temples, centers, and meditation groups in the United States. Participants in the SRF include Indians and Indian Americans, as well as people from many other countries.

Although the SRF is the primary vehicle for Yogananda's teachings, other movements also claim to represent him. One of the most well-known is Ananda, begun by Yogananda disciple Swami Kriyananda (born J. Donald Walters). Ananda has six intentional communities worldwide, the first established by Kriyananda in Northern California in 1968.

W. Michael Ashcraft

Further Reading

The Second Coming of Christ: The Resurrection of the Christ Within You. Los Angeles: Self-Realization Fellowship, 2004.

Self-Realization Fellowship. http://www.yogananda-srf.org.

Trout, Polly. *Eastern Seeds, Western Soil: Three Gurus in America.* Mountain View, CA: Mayfield, 2000.

Yogananda, Paramahansa. *Autobiography of a Yogi.* Los Angeles: Self-Realization Fellowship, 1993.

Shridharani, Krishnalal (1911–1960)

A close collaborator of Indian nationalist leader and pacifist Mohandas K. Gandhi, Krishnalal Shridharani carried the Mahatma's message of nonviolence to the United States. For twelve years beginning in 1934, Shridharani tried to explain Gandhi's movement and to garner support for Indian independence. In the process, he directly influenced members of the American civil rights movement, who adopted nonviolence in pursuing their cause.

Shridharani was born on September 16, 1911, in Umrala, Gujarat, India. His father was a successful lawyer who died when Shridharani was only eight. His mother, occupied with business interests and raising four other children, sent Shridharani to live with her brother and mother. Later, Shridharani's mother became an enthusiastic follower of Mahatma Gandhi and enrolled the boy in a nationalist boarding school. She died when he was fourteen, but Shridharani went on to study at the Kashi Vidyapitha (later Mahatma Gandhi Kashi Vidyapitha) nationalist university.

Shridharani was one of sixty followers chosen by Gandhi in 1930 to join him on the March to the Sea, from Ahmedabad to the Arabian Sea, to protest the monopoly on salt held by the colonial government. Despite his youth, Shridharani was selected to make speeches explaining the protest to farmers and workers along the way. Along with tens of thousands of others, Shridharani's group was arrested and jailed for the protest. Following his release, Shridharani studied at the International University in Ahmedabad and earned degrees in history and philosophy.

In 1934, Shridharani received a scholarship to study in the United States and went on to earn a PhD in sociology from Columbia University. During the course of his studies, however, he spent much of his time talking to groups about Indian independence. And he was well suited to winning Americans to his point of view. Known for dressing well and smoking cigars, he did not apologize for eschewing the ascetic life led by Gandhi. Indian people, he explained, were not the exotic characters of popular Western imagination, but individuals just like the Americans to whom he spoke. Shridharani was a well-respected writer as well. Even before leaving India, he had published novels, plays, and poems in his native tongue of Gujarati.

Shridharani's most important and enduring activities during his stay in the United States were his writings. In 1939, he published *War Without Violence,* an explanation of Gandhi's philosophy of satyagraha ("determined pursuit of truth"). Militant nonviolence in the pursuit of a specific goal was an important part of satyagraha, which Shridharani explained in pragmatic terms that resonated with his audiences. Criticizing American pacifists for regarding peace as an end in itself, Shridharani argued for militant nonviolence as a method of social change to achieve justice. He discounted the spiritual elements of satyagraha as being important to Gandhi but not necessarily central to its effectiveness. In Part 1 of *War Without Violence,* he describes the various stages of a campaign of militant nonviolence, including demonstrations, strikes, and civil disobedience. In Part 2, he illustrates each stage with real-life examples from India. In the final section, he compares and contrasts satyagraha with pacifism, internationalism, and war as a method of social change.

Shridharani followed his first book with *My India, My America* (1941) and *The Mahatma and the World* (1946). The former work is a witty comparison of life in both countries through Shridharani's eyes. In the latter work, he offers a clear portrait of Gandhi as a man. For many Americans, *The Mahatma and the World* was their first chance to understand what inspired Gandhi's campaign for independence.

Shridharani's works inspired many Americans who believed nonviolent social change was possible. Among the groups directly affected by his explanation of Gandhi's movement were the Fellowship of Reconciliation and the Congress of Racial Equality (CORE). The leaders of CORE, in particular, were inspired by Shridharani to take their first nonviolent steps along the road to racial equality immediately following World War II. Shridharani returned to India in 1946 and died in New Delhi on July 23, 1960.

Tim J. Watts

Further Reading

Shridharani, Krishnalal. *The Mahatma and the World.* New York: Duell, Sloan and Pearce, 1946.

———. *My India, My America.* New York: Duell, Sloan and Pearce, 1941.

Sibley, Mulford Quickert, ed. *The Quiet Battle: Writings on the Theory and Practice of Non-Violent Resistance.* Garden City, NY: Doubleday, 1963.

Singh, Jawala (1859–1938)

Born in 1859 to a poor, peasant family in the village of Thatian, in the Amritsar District of Punjab, Jawala Singh left British India for North America in 1905 in search of better economic opportunity. He emerged as one of the wealthiest farmers in America, as well as a dedicated activist for social justice and a revolutionary Indian patriot.

The timing of Jawala Singh's arrival in California enabled him to take advantage of the low price of land. Joining with another Sikh immigrant in a joint farming venture, a common practice among early Indian Americans, he began leasing and then purchasing land. His remarkable success in agriculture earned him the nickname the "Potato King."

In 1912, Singh collaborated with other Sikh settlers in the area in organizing construction of the first *gurdwara* (Sikh temple) in the United States, in Stockton, California. The temple, known as the Stockton Gurdwara Sahib, was particularly important as a community institution to early South Asian American settlers, serving as a focus of both political solidarity and religious faith. It offered Sikh, Muslim, and Hindu migrants a community center in which to discuss affairs of interest to the small community as its members adjusted to life in a hostile, alien environment.

Jawala Singh was among the founders and leaders of the Ghadar Party, a United States–based revolutionary organization that sought to liberate India from the yoke of British imperialism. It was a remarkable collective venture, which bridged the divisions among Sikhs, Hindus, and Muslims in the South Asian American community. Publishing a widely distributed newsletter and uniting South Asian migrants in the United States with supporters throughout Europe and Asia, the group sought to foment armed rebellion in an effort to liberate their subjugated homeland. Eventually, the Ghadar leadership was able to acquire weapons from Germany, which sought to weaken its enemy, Great Britain, during World War I. Despite his wealth and status, Jawala Singh joined the group of Ghadar revolutionaries that engaged in a doomed armed invasion of India in 1914. The British were aware of the plot, and most of the revolutionaries were arrested immediately upon arrival in Calcutta.

For his part in the uprising, Jawala Singh was arrested by British authorities in India and sentenced to life in prison. He served eighteen years, obtaining his release in 1933. While in jail in the Andaman Islands, then a British possession off the coast of India, he went on a hunger strike in protest of the cruel treatment of prisoners there. Upon returning to India in 1933, he again ran afoul of British authorities as a result of his work on behalf of peasant farmers. Due to these activities, he served another year in jail. He remained an activist until his death in 1938. Among the more lasting of Jawala Singh's contributions was the establishment of the Guru Gobind Singh Sahib scholarship at the University of California, Berkeley, which brought numerous students from India to the United States to study.

Jaideep Singh

Further Reading

Angelo, Michael. *The Sikh Diaspora: Tradition and Change in an Immigrant Community.* New York: Garland, 1997.

Jensen, Joan M. *Passage from India: Asian Indian Immigrants in North America.* New Haven, CT: Yale University Press, 1988.

Subba Row, Yellapragada (1895–1948)

Largely unknown in both his native India and the United States, where he did his major work, physician and medical researcher Yellapragada Subba Row did groundbreaking work in the study of tropical diseases and helped develop cures for several during the first half of the twentieth century. Subba Row and his researchers isolated vitamins, developed financially profitable antibiotics, and laid the foundation for future medical researchers.

Subba Row was born on January 12, 1895, in what is now Andhra Pradesh, India. His father had been forced by ill health to give up a government position, leaving the family with little money. Resisting his mother's encouragement of higher education, Subba Row felt drawn to serving his fellow man. When he was twenty-two, however, his brother died of tropical sprue, an intestinal disease that Western medicine was powerless to treat. Subba Row vowed to dedicate his life to finding a cure for this and other tropical diseases. He enrolled at the Madras Medical School, where he studied traditional Ayurvedic drugs derived from plants. After obtaining both master of science and medical degrees in 1951, he became a teaching assistant at the university. Subba Row's sympathy for Gandhi's independence movement, however, angered British medical authorities and limited his career in India.

After studying at the School of Tropical Medicine at London University, Subba Row accepted an offer to assist in medical research at the Harvard School of Medicine in the United States. With less than $100 in his pocket, Subba Row arrived in Boston on October 26, 1923. He worked for a year in the tropical diseases laboratory of Dr. Richard Strong, supporting himself with work as an orderly, night librarian, and janitor. He later collaborated with Dr. Cyrus Fiske, with whom he developed a widely used system to measure the phosphorus in body fluids and tissues. Subba Row and Fiske also discovered the phosphocreatine and adenosine triphosphate (ATP) molecules and showed that they provided the energy for muscular activity.

After completing his PhD in biochemistry in 1930, Subba Row continued his studies in phosphorus compounds in the liver and muscles, vitamin chemistry, and nutrition. In 1933, he met Dr. G.W. Clark, who was doing research at Lederle Laboratories in Pearl River, New York, a division of American Cyanamid Company. Clark invited Subba Row to join his research team, and from 1933 to 1940 he spent four days a week at Harvard and the other three at Lederle. His discoveries at Lederle included folic acid and methods to synthesize it—yielding a cure for tropical sprue. He also discovered other vitamins in the B series and determined their medical uses.

Subba Row left Harvard in 1940 and became the research director at Lederle by 1942. Known for hiring and inspiring talented young researchers, Subba Row was determined to find cures for other diseases. Among his many accomplishments were the development of such antibiotics as teropterin, used in cancer treatment, and aminopterin, the first effective drug in helping people with leukemia. He also discovered hetrazan, used internationally to treat filariasis, a parasitic disease common to millions of people. In 1945, Subba Row and his associates developed aureomycin, the first tetracycline antibiotic and the basis for many of the antibiotics that followed over the next sixty years. He allowed credit for most of these discoveries to go to his associates.

Subba Row proudly retained his Indian citizenship, even after he could have become a naturalized U.S. citizen. His dedication to work led to declining health. Subba Row was working to develop a cure for cancer when he died in his sleep on August 9, 1948.

Tim J. Watts

Further Reading

Gupta, S.P.K., and Edgar L. Milford. *In Quest of Panacea: Successes and Failures of Yellapragada SubbaRow.* Nanuet, NY: Evelyn, 1987.

Narasimham, Raji, and S.P.K. Gupta. *Yellapragada SubbaRow, a Life in Quest of Panacea: An Album in Words and Pictures.* New Delhi: Vigyan Prasar, 2003.

Torgersen, Gordon M. *A Ten Talent Christian from India: The Story of Yellapragada Subbarow.* New York: American Baptist Foreign Mission Society, 1952.

Theosophical Society

The Theosophical Society is an organization founded in New York City in 1875 to promote the philosophy of its founders, the Russian spiritualist Madame Helena Petrovna Blavatsky (1831–1891) and the American Civil War officer, lawyer, and journalist Henry Steel Olcott (1832–1907). The Theosophical movement was organized to promote universal brotherhood, the study of spiritual truths that underlie all religions, the rejection of materialism, and public service by all members and followers for the betterment of humankind, especially the establishment and operation of schools and efforts to improve social conditions for women.

Madame Blavatsky, the author of *Isis* (1877) and the *The Secret Doctrine* (1888), claimed her books were the result of mystical revelations. Henry Steel Olcott, a Buddhist convert interested in experimental psychology, met Blavatsky while researching articles on séances and Spiritualism. Both were fascinated with the occult. In 1875, they joined with an Irish occultist name William Quan Judge in founding the Theosophical Society, and in December 1878 they set sail for India to move their headquarters. Arriving the following month, they set up in Bombay and later moved to Adyar in Madras.

Over the course of the next two years, they established 100 branches in India and several in the United States and Europe. In 1888 they started a school, followed by a journal, *The Theosophist,* to publicize their views. Katherine Tingsley, an associate of Judge, became president of the society until 1929, followed by Gottfried de Purucker from 1929 to 1942 and James A. Long from 1951 until his death in 1971. Long also founded *Sunrise: Theosophic Perspectives,* a bimonthly magazine aimed at bringing theosophist teachings to the general public. Grace F. Knoche took over as leader of the Theosophical Society in 1971, followed by the present-day leader, Randell C. Grubb.

The Theosophists developed a body of eclectic teachings based on the Hindu idea of reincarnation and the belief that one could escape from it. At the same time, theosophists believe in the idea of working toward a higher spiritual plane, both for the individual and for humanity. They also advocate the integration of religion, science, and philosophy along the lines of the Hindu spiritual belief in the atman, the One, the universal soul that pervades the universe and unites all things. This esoteric, highly spiritual, mystical body of teaching resonated with the spiritually minded in both India and the West. In addition, the theosophists valued indigenous religious traditions, especially among urban Westernized Indians.

The Theosophical Society also advocated independence for India from British rule. Annie Besant was a social reformer in England before becoming attracted to theosophy and joining the society in 1889. She traveled to India in 1893 and made Benares her home from 1895 to 1907. In 1907 she became president of the Theosophical Society and in 1918 set up the Central Hindu College, later Banares Hindu University, and the National University at Adyar. She advocated home rule for India as early as 1914 and established a weekly magazine, *Commonwealth*, and a daily newspaper, *New India,* to promote the cause. In 1916 she established a Home Rule League and was briefly interned by the British. She chose Jiddu Krishnamurti as her successor, but he left the movement in 1929.

The Theosophical Society in the United States today is an international organization based in Pasadena, California, that promotes the ideas of the theosophists through its publications, especially the online magazine *Sunrise,* a lecture series, correspondence courses, Friday evening meetings, a book-publishing business, and a Web site. The society is not a mass organization but its followers are devoted Theosophists, who enjoy the sense of spirituality the society fosters. Founded by non-Indians for a largely Western audience, the Theosophical Society does not have deep roots in the Indian American community, though some immigrants of South Asian descent are members.

Roger D. Long

Further Reading

Cranston, Sylvia. *HPB: The Extraordinary Life and Influence of Helen Blavatsky, Founder of the Modern Theosophical Movement.* New York: G.P. Putnam, 1993.

Johnson, K. Paul. *Initiates of Theosophical Masters.* Albany: State University of New York, 1995.

Taylor, Anne. *Annie Besant: A Biography.* New York: Oxford University Press, 1992.

Theosophical Society. http://www.theosociety.org.

United States v. Bhagat Singh Thind (1923)

In a precedent-setting decision in 1923, the U.S. Supreme Court in *United States v. Bhagat Singh Thind* offered a reinterpretation of the Naturalization Act of 1790, which had declared that only "free, White persons" could become citizens of the United States. When Bhagat Singh Thind, an Indian immigrant, claimed that, anthropologically speaking, he was a member of the Caucasian race and therefore eligible for citizenship, the court rejected his claim, saying that the "White" person qualification of the 1790 act should be understood in the commonsense meaning of the term, an interpretation that excluded persons of South Asian descent.

The *Thind* decision was not the first time the 1790 law had been revisited. Amendments to the legislation in the 1860s and 1920s had granted formal citizenship rights to African and Native Americans, but immigrant groups from Asia, the Middle East, and other parts of the world could not be naturalized unless they were considered white. The racial prerequisite cases were a series of suits brought between 1878 and 1944 to determine which of these ethnic groups were eligible for U.S. citizenship. Federal courts used various standards, ranging from congressional intent to scientific knowledge to skin color, to determine who was and was not white.

Bhagat Singh Thind was born in Punjab (India) in 1892 and settled in Seattle, Washington, in 1912. He served in the U.S. Army during World War I and went on to receive a PhD in philosophy from the University of California, Berkeley. In 1920, Thind sought U.S. citizenship in Oregon and was challenged by the U.S. Bureau of Naturalization. This was a time of rising anti-immigrant sentiment. Congress had passed the Immigration Act of 1917, which barred further immigration from India. Prior racial prerequisite cases involving Asian Indians had yielded mixed results; some courts classified as them as white, while others did not.

The federal district court in Oregon granted citizenship to Thind, but the decision was appealed. Meanwhile, the U.S. Supreme Court heard its first racial prerequisite case, *Takao Ozawa v. United States* (1922). In that decision, the Court denied naturalization to Japanese immigrant Takao Ozawa, ruling that "white" was synonymous with "Caucasian." This seemed to bode well for Thind's chances, since most authorities considered Asian Indians, unlike Japanese, to be Caucasian.

In 1923, however, the Supreme Court rejected Thind's citizenship bid, amending its prior definition of white. Writing for a unanimous court, Justice George Sutherland declared that "Caucasian" was equivalent to "white" only in accordance with common understanding. Since Asian Indians were not commonly understood to be white, the justices reasoned, they did not qualify for citizenship. As a consequence of the ruling, numerous Asian Indians were stripped of their citizenship between 1923 and 1927, and other racial prerequisite cases followed the *Thind* precedent for the next two decades. Thind himself was granted citizenship in New York in 1936, where naturalization examiners chose not to challenge his application. He would go on to become a Sikh spiritual leader and author of numerous books; he died in 1967.

The *Thind* decision became obsolete in 1946, when the Luce-Celler Act created a small immigration quota of Asian Indians and permitted their naturalization; in 1965, the quota was essentially dropped. The 1952 McCarran-Walter Act completely supplanted the 1790 Naturalization Law, removing all race restrictions to citizenship. Nevertheless, the *Thind* case portended future controversy about classification of Asian Indians. In 1970, the U.S. Census Bureau classified Asian Indians as white, denying them protected minority status. After much internal debate, Indian American organizations successfully lobbied to change this classification to Asian Indian, which later fell under the Asian and Pacific Islander category. All of these events illustrate the inherently political nature of racial categorization.

Vinay Harpalani

Further Reading

Haney-López, Ian F. *White by Law: The Legal Construction of Race.* New York: New York University Press, 1996.

Koshy, Susan. "Category Crisis: South Asian Americans and Questions of Race and Ethnicity." *Diaspora* 7:2 (1998): 285–320.

United States v. Bhagat Singh Thind, 261 U.S. 204 (1923).

Watumull Foundation

The Watumull Foundation was established in Honolulu, Hawaii, by businessman and Indian immigrant G.J. (Gobindram Jhamandas) Watumull in 1942 to promote a better quality of life in India, to advance goodwill and understanding between the peoples of India and the United States, and to support cultural, educational, and philanthropic activities in Hawaii. Thousands of individuals and institutions have directly benefited from grants and scholarships from the foundation.

The foundation was the brainchild of G.J. Watumull, who moved from Hyderabad, India, to Honolulu in 1917 to help an older brother with his retail business. Known as the East India Store, the company grew from a small bazaar to a modern department store that specialized in products from India and Asia. By 1937, Watumull had built an impressive new building in downtown Honolulu. Branch stores around Oahu followed. Although hampered by the interruption in supplies during World War II, Watumull continued to expand. By 1947, the business grossed $2.6 million annually.

Although Watumull found financial success in the United States, he never lost his love for his native India. He was an active supporter of Mohandas Gandhi and the Indian independence movement. Before the end of British rule in 1947, Watumull lobbied lawmakers in Washington, D.C., and sponsored speaking tours by distinguished Indians such as Krishnalal Shridharani.

To improve the quality of life in India into the future, Watumull realized that education would play an important role. The foundation therefore established scholarships for worthy Indian students to study at U.S. colleges and universities. Initially, Watumull and his wife, Ellen Jensen Watumull, selected the students with input from distinguished Indian scholars in the United States. The students' areas of study were important in deciding who would be selected. Because Watumull wanted to help those who would return to India and use their knowledge to build a modern state, fields such as medicine, agronomy, economics, and engineering received priority. For every ten applicants, only one was chosen.

The foundation also supplied direct aid to Indian institutions. Books were collected and donated to Indian schools and public libraries. Medical equipment was provided to hospitals as well. Assistance to ordinary people was included, such as digging wells to increase agricultural production and providing funds for resettling and retraining individuals who were displaced by the partition of India into two countries. Famine relief was provided through the Cooperative for American Relief to Everywhere (CARE) and Meals for Millions Foundation.

Birth control was an important aspect of the aid given to India. Ellen Watumull was especially interested in making sure that every child born was wanted. She arranged for Margaret Sanger, matriarch of the American birth control movement, to speak in India. The first International Planned Parenthood Conference was held in India in 1952. The foundation also provided contraceptives and information about birth control to family planning centers in India.

To promote understanding between the two countries, the Watumull Foundation has financed visiting professorships for American and Indian scholars to teach in each others' countries. Funds were provided for American libraries to purchase books about India and South Asia. Working with the American Historical Association, the foundation offers a biennial prize for the best book about Indian history. The foundation remains well-known in Hawaii for its financial assistance to organizations such as the YMCA, YWCA, hospitals, and the Honolulu Academy of Arts.

Tim J. Watts

Further Reading

Clark, Blake. "G.J. Shows That East and West Can Meet." *Reader's Digest* 51 (December 1947): 73–77.
Kamath, M.V. *The United States and India, 1776–1976.* Washington, DC: Indian Embassy, 1976.

Women, Indian American

The strong family values and stability for which Indian Americans are renowned can be attributed in large part to the significant presence of women (47 percent) in the population. By contrast, the first wave of Indian migration at the turn of the twentieth century from Punjab to California contained hardly any women due to restrictive immigration laws. The dearth of Indian women was largely responsible for the transient lives of the men, returning to India or marrying Mexican women (since antimiscegenation laws prevented them from marrying white women). It was not until 1946 that Indian women were permitted to enter the United States under a quota system that allowed men already in the country to send for their families. After 1965, Indian women were admitted in numbers that were nearly as large as—and in some years larger than—those of the men. They came as professional primary immigrants in their own right, as students, or as accompanying family members.

Indian American women do not conform to the stereotype of submissive and oppressed Asian women. Their experience in the United States is heavily influenced by their background in India, which could be rural or urban, small town or cosmopolitan. If they arrived as single women, they are likely to be much more independent and career minded than if they came as married women, already committed to husband and children. For some women, migration has meant an increase in social mobility, economic independence, and relative autonomy. Their educational level is one of the most significant factors affecting the quality of their lives. A majority of those who came in the first post-1965 immigration wave are highly educated. Many chose to pursue professional careers in medicine, education, and business. Others who found their Indian education inadequate for the American marketplace retrained in American universities. According to the 2000 U.S. Census, 57 percent of Indian American women have bachelor's degree or higher, 54 percent have management and professional jobs, and 28 percent work in sales and office occupations. Their median earnings, at $35,173, are also much higher than those of the average U.S. woman ($27,184). Among the most prominent Indian American women in recent years are corporate manager Indra Nooyi, the head of PepsiCo; Kalpana Chawla, the astronaut who died tragically in the 2003 *Columbia* space shuttle disaster; and Pulitzer Prize–winning author Jhumpa Lahiri. During the 1990s and after, many women immigrants have been physical therapists, nurses, and teachers. The 2000 census showed 97,611 Indian American women in educational, health, and social services, a number far greater than in any other industry.

Hidden behind the story of prosperity and high achievement among professional and well-qualified women is the parallel growth of an undocumented, unprotected, and exploited labor sector, where females work under difficult conditions at poorly paid jobs. Some women came as dependent spouses or family members

A native of the Punjab, Kalpana Chawla came to the United States to study aeronautical engineering and joined the NASA astronaut corps in 1995. She flew her first space shuttle mission two years later and died tragically in her second, aboard *Columbia*, in 2003. *(Tony Ranze/Stringer/ AFP/Getty Images)*

straight from the villages of India without so much as a basic education. They work in production jobs in factories or in family-owned establishments or are hired in the back rooms of Indian American restaurants or in the unorganized sector as babysitters, domestics, or self-employed providers of goods and services to the Indian community. Another disadvantage suffered by many Indian American women is dependence on husbands, fiancés, or other male family members for visas. Such women may find themselves stranded when they are estranged from or lose their husbands, such as the widows of Indian Americans who died in the World Trade Center terrorist attack on September 11, 2001.

Indian American women raised in India carry a mixed cultural baggage. Whereas they had enjoyed equal rights in the home country—the right to inherit property, vote, divorce, remarry, and get an abortion—many succumbed to the unspoken laws governing Indian society whereby the woman is primarily homemaker, wife, and mother. Chastity, obedience to husband, and unflinching loyalty to family represent the ideal path for many Indian women—an ideology that survives to some extent even among modern, upper-class women who have migrated to the United States. Many go through an identity crisis trying to reconcile the different worlds in which they live—a traditional, male-dominated, patriarchal world within the family and the more egalitarian world outside, where they pursue careers and make a living. Religion can become a further complicating factor. Women from devout Muslim or Hindu families have to find their place in American society, which often views their religious upbringing with hostility. At the same time, they have to carve out a space for themselves in an Indian culture that is suspicious of corrupting Western values. Trying to bridge the gap between these worlds has resulted in strained family relationships and personal hardship for many Indian American women.

In the ranks of second-generation Indian women, there is a measure of rebelliousness among those who demand more equal participation from men in home life, housework, and caring for children. Many are choosing more adventurous careers than their mothers did, venturing into theater, cinema, television, journalism, broadcasting, and the fine arts. They are also protesting the undue burden placed on them as "keepers of the cultural flame" and "preservers of ethnic community honor." Indian American women, both first and second generation, often resent attitudes that deny the existence of problems in their midst and have organized effectively to tackle such problems. Sakhi is an organization started in 1989 in New York by a group of committed South Asian American women to help survivors of domestic violence and is part of a network of such organizations that have sprung up throughout the United States and Canada to cater to the culturally specific needs of South Asian women in distress, especially low-income, new immigrant women ignorant of their basic rights.

As immigrants, Indian American women have experienced unique challenges and opportunities. They have banded together to pursue their traditional ideals, as in the Chicago-based Club of Indian Women, whose mission is to promote the "self-growth" of its members. They have organized to help the disadvantaged and draw attention to their problems. Like other American women, they walk a tightrope, trying to balance family obligations, career interests, and social responsibilities—only, in their case, between two cultures and across generations.

Padma Rangaswamy

Further Reading

Abraham, Margaret. *Speaking the Unspeakable: Marital Violence Among South Asian Women in the United States.* New Brunswick, NJ: Rutgers University Press, 2000.

DasGupta, Shamita Das, ed. *A Patchwork Shawl: Chronicles of South Asian Women in America.* New Brunswick, NJ: Rutgers University Press, 1998.

Gupta, Sangeeta R., ed. *Emerging Voices: South Asian American Women Redefine Self, Family, and Community.* Walnut Creek, CA: AltaMira, 1999.

Women of South Asian Decent Collective, ed. *Our Feet Walk the Sky.* San Francisco: Aunt Lute, 1993.

Yuba City, California

Located forty miles (sixty kilometers) north of Sacramento, California, Yuba City is home to the largest Sikh community in the United States. The state of California is home to an estimated 250,000 Sikhs, of, which about 10,000 reside in the Yuba City metropolitan area. The largest group of Indian Americans in the Yuba City area is Punjabi and predominantly Sikh, with some Hindus and Muslims as well.

Yuba City began as a mining distribution center during the gold rush of the mid-nineteenth century. Situated in Northern California's fertile Sacramento River Valley, Yuba City developed into an agricultural hub. Sikhs originally began coming to the Sacramento Valley in the early twentieth century, primarily between 1907 and 1911. Many had originally migrated to British Columbia and moved southward along the coast, drawn by word of higher wages and eager to escape repressive Canadian immigration laws. The land in California was also said to resemble that in the Punjab, and Sikh farmers were able to grow crops similar to those in their homeland.

Beginning in 1913, however, California barred Asians from owning or leasing property in the state under what become known as the Asian Land Laws. Some Indians were able to get around the restriction by partnering with whites to purchase land. The laws were finally repealed in 1952, opening the way for Sikhs and other Asians to openly and independently own land in California. In the meantime, some early Sikh farmworkers were able to save their earnings either individually or by pooling them to purchase land in the Yuba City area, where they remain prominent as farm owners into the early twentieth-first century. Didar Singh Bains, whose great grandfather migrated to Canada in 1890 and then to California in 1920, still owns large tracts of land just outside of Yuba City and supplies peaches to the Del Monte fruit company. Singh Bains is also a founder of Yuba City's annual Sikh parade.

Due to restrictive immigration laws, Indian American men in the early years were unable to bring their wives or potential brides from the home country, while antimiscegenation laws did not permit them to marry Anglo-American women. Thus, until the second half of the twentieth century, nearly 50 percent of marriages in Yuba City involving Indian men were to Mexican women. Indian American men married Mexican or Mexican American women for a variety of reasons, including similarities of complexion, class, and racial status, the sheer availability of marriageable women, and certainly companionship. These relationships, which anthropologist Bruce LaBrack has characterized as a "unique and transitory phenomena," produced offspring who were referred to as "Mexican-Hindus." Such bi-ethnic families tended to remain somewhat isolated, not entirely accepted by either the Mexican or the Indian community.

Asian Indian immigration into the United States all but ceased from the 1917 to 1945. The Luce-Celler Act of 1946 allowed 100 Indians to immigrate annually but granted naturalization rights to Indian and Filipino Americans. The immigrants, moreover, were allowed to bring their spouses and children from India. After passage of the Immigration and Nationality Act of 1965, which effectively eliminated national immigration quotas, Sikh families who had not been allowed to come to the United States were now able to join male family members who had settled in California. The reunifications were often difficult, however, as the Sikhs who came prior to 1965 were primarily agricultural workers who may have married outside their religious community, while the new immigrants were often more educated or professionally trained and tended to look down on the agricultural workers' intermarriages with Mexican women.

Yuba City opened its first *gurdwara* (Sikh temple) in 1969 and is now home to three. The Sikh community also maintains a cultural school, while the Punjabi-American Day parade—marking the birthday in 1469 of Sikh founder Guru Nanak—was started in 1979 and is held annually on the first Sunday in November. As of the early twenty-first century, Sikhs were represented in any number of occupations in the Yuba City area, from small business owners to medical professionals and politicians.

Malini Cadambi

Further Reading

Gonzales, Juan L., Jr. "Asian Indian Immigration Patterns: The Origins of the Sikh Community in California." *International Migration Review* 20:1 (Spring 1986).

LaBrack, Bruce, and Karen Leonard. "Conflict and Compatibility in Punjabi-Mexican Immigrant Families in Rural California, 1915–1965." *Journal of Marriage and the Family* 46:3 (August 1984): 527–37.

Leonard, Karen. "Ethnicity Confounded: Punjabi Pioneers in California." In *Sikh History and Religion in the Twentieth Century,* ed. Joseph T. O'Connell. Toronto: Centre for South Asian Studies, University of Toronto, 1988.

Melendy, Brett. *Asians in America: Filipinos, Koreans, and East Indians.* Boston: Twayne, 1977.

The Indonesian American Experience: History and Culture

Indonesia is the fourth most populous nation in the world (nearly 240 million people as of mid-2008), consisting of more than a dozen major ethnolinguistic groups and about 100 smaller ones living on more than 13,000 islands. It is also the world's largest majority Muslim country, though it also has sizable groups of Christians, Hindus, Buddhists, and animists. Few Indonesians came to the United States before changes in federal immigration law in 1965—specifically, the lifting of national quotas—and little has been written about them.

Immigration History

From the late sixteenth century through the middle of the twentieth century, Indonesia was a colony of the Netherlands. Indonesians served aboard Dutch ships and a few are believed to have jumped ship and settled in American ports in the nineteenth and early twentieth centuries, though there is little documentation on this. During World War II, some were stranded in the United States after their homeland was occupied by the Japanese and remained there after the war.

Beginning in 1953, the International Cooperation Agency, the precursor to the United States Agency for International Development, began giving out scholarships for medical students to the University of California, Berkeley, and followed three years later with a program to bring engineering students of the Bandung Institute of Technology to study at the University of Kentucky. Most of these students were government employees and their offspring. Meanwhile, following independence from the Netherlands in 1950—after a long and brutal national liberation struggle—tens of thousands of "Indos," or mixed Indonesian-Europeans, fled their homeland. While most settled in the Netherlands, several thousand came to the United States as refugees.

Political turmoil in the 1960s and a bloody 1965 coup sent several thousand more Indonesians to the United States, many of them of Chinese descent. Chinese Indonesians, though prosperous, were much despised by native Indonesians and, with nationalist sentiments rising, many were persecuted or physically attacked, or had their property seized.

Though diverse ethnically, these post–World War II groups shared certain socioeconomic characteristics. Most were well educated and came from propertied families. With the reform of U.S. immigration law in 1965—which ended national quotas and emphasized family reunification—the number of poorer and less well-educated Indonesians began to rise. Still, Indonesians represent a drop in the bucket of Asian American immigration, as most who relocate to the West choose the Netherlands and other European countries as their new homes. Thus, the Indonesian American population, just 9,618, according to the 1980 census, has grown modestly. In 1990, there were little more than 30,000; ten years later, that population was just under 40,000. This represented just 0.4 percent of the overall Asian American population, though it is estimated that another 30,000 to 70,000 undocumented Indonesians currently reside in the United States.

Demographics, Culture, and Way of Life

Like many Asian American immigrant groups, the largest portion—about 45 percent—has made its home in California, particularly the southern half of the state. Small in number and diverse in culture, language, religion, and ethnicity, Indonesian Americans have not developed their own enclaves in California or elsewhere. However, as a good number of Indonesian Americans are of Chinese descent, many have settled in areas with large Chinese American populations, especially the San Gabriel Valley and eastern San Fernando Valley areas of the Los Angeles metropolitan region. There are also numerically significant Indonesian American populations in the New York and Washington, D.C., metropolitan areas.

Again, because of their diversity, it is difficult to generalize about Indonesian American immigrants, though it is safe to say that, because of past ethnic and religious persecution at home, minorities are more represented among Indonesian Americans than they are in their homeland. This includes not just Indonesians of Chinese descent but also those of the Christian and Buddhist persuasions. Still, the majority of Indonesian Americans practice the Islamic faith of the vast majority of their compatriots back home. Like most Indonesian Muslims, however, Indonesian Americans practice a more liberal form of the faith, and women rarely cover their heads.

Despite not having enclaves of their own, Indonesian Americans have been able to preserve many of the customs of their homeland. These include the batik method of cloth dyeing, the dance dramas of the island of Bali, the shadow puppet shows, or *wajang,* of Java, and their distinctive cuisine. Rice based and resembling other Southeast Asian cuisines, Indonesian cooking employs large amounts of coconut milk and palm oil, with vegetables and meats often slow-baked in banana leaves. Both at home and in the few Indonesian American restaurants, diners often eat with their fingers from large collective platters set in the middle of the table. While most Indonesian Americans don Western clothing for work and everyday use, on special occasions men and women will put on wraparound sarongs, many of them dyed in batik patterns. Of diverse religious and ethnic background, Indonesian Americans observe various Muslim, Christian, Hindu, and Chinese holidays. The languages spoken by Indonesian Americans are diverse, too; the majority speak Bahasa Indonesian, a modified form of Malay largely spoken on the main island of Java that was adopted as the national language of Indonesia during the last years of Dutch rule.

As with most Asian American groups, the family is central to Indonesian American life, with children expected not only to respect their parents and elders but to accept their advice in major life decisions. While most Indonesian Americans live in nuclear households, extended family networks are more important to them than they are to the general American populace; extended kin often celebrate major holidays and family events together and are knit together by financial obligations to each other. Because of their small numbers, Indonesians often marry outside their ethnic group, especially with Chinese and other Asian Americans.

Since many Indonesians came to the United States as students or as members of well-educated and better-financed minorities, such as Chinese Indonesians, their socioeconomic indices are among the highest for Asian Americans. It is estimated that roughly two-thirds of working-age Indonesian Americans are in either managerial or professional positions. There are roughly 800 Indonesian American–owned businesses in the United States, many of them specializing in the import of the many artisan crafts—including wood sculpture and batik textiles—native to their homeland.

While participating in many Pan-Asian organizations, the national Indonesian American community is linked together through several media outlets and cultural and political organizations. Of the former, the most important is the *Indonesian Journal.* Founded in 1988 and published out of West Covina, a suburb of Los Angeles, the monthly magazine—written largely in Bahasa Indonesian and featuring articles on the culture, society, and politics of Indonesia and the Indonesian American community—is distributed free at Indonesian restaurants, churches, and social organizations. The American Indonesian Chamber of Commerce, founded in 1949 and headquartered in New York, has roughly 150 members and promotes economic links between and among Indonesians, Indonesian Americans, and the American business community as a whole. The Indonesian Community Association, headquartered at the Indonesian embassy in Washington, speaks for Indonesian Americans to the nation's lawmakers while supporting social and cultural events throughout the country.

James Ciment and Clark E. Cunningham

Further Reading

Allen, James P., and Eugene Turner. "Indonesians." In *The Ethnic Quilt: Population Diversity in Southern California.* Northridge: California State University, Northridge, The Center for Geographical Studies, 1997.

Cunningham, Clark E. "Indonesians." In *American Immigrant Cultures: Builders of a Nation*, ed. David Levinson and Melvin Ember. New York: Macmillan Reference USA, 1997.

———. "Unity and Diversity Among Indonesian Migrants to the United States." In *Emerging Voices: The Experiences of Underrepresented Asian Americans*, ed. Huping Ling. Piscataway, NJ: Rutgers University Press, 2008.

Gall, Susan B., and Irene Natividad, eds. "Who are the Indonesian Americans?" In *Asian American Almanac: A Reference Work on Asians in the United States.* Detroit: Gale Research, 1995.

Society for Indonesian Americans. http://www.sianews.org.

The Japanese American Experience: History and Culture

The history of the Japanese in the United States is relatively brief compared to that of other immigrant groups, but their presence had a powerful influence on political and social developments in the country over the course of the twentieth century. Although there were some Japanese living in the United States and Hawaii in the mid-nineteenth century, the first significant immigration occurred in the 1880s. Japan's rapid modernization during the Meiji period (1868–1912) took land out of cultivation and displaced thousands of people, prompting the government to lift emigration restrictions and allow Japanese laborers to work on Hawaiian plantations in 1884. Businesses on the U.S. mainland also encouraged Japanese immigration after the Chinese Exclusion Act of 1882 stopped the influx of much-needed workers. Labor agents recruited Japanese workers to sign limited contracts for agricultural employment in the United States. Most contract labors were "sojourners," or young men intending to work overseas temporarily and return to Japan with their earnings.

This combination of "push" and "pull" factors brought more than 2,000 Japanese to the United States by 1890. The number exceeded 24,000 in 1900 and jumped to more than 72,000 by 1910. Most of the newcomers settled along the Pacific Coast after being processed at the Angel Island immigration station in San Francisco Bay. (Seattle and Portland were also key ports of entry.) In 1900, 18,629 of the 24,326 Japanese in the United States lived in Pacific states; this trend continued over the next forty years, with 71,952 of 111,010 living on the West Coast in 1920, and 112,353 of 126,948 in the region in 1940. Only in Colorado, Utah, and New York did the Japanese population reach 1,000. Clearly, not every sojourner returned to Japan. Some stayed to pursue further opportunities in the United States, while others found their wages insufficient to return home. For all who stayed, the transformation from sojourner to citizen was an arduous struggle against the nativist belief that to be American meant to be white.

Exclusion, Resistance, and Community Development: 1880–1940

New arrivals from Japan were immediately confronted with racism on the part of established anti-Asian groups who had targeted Chinese immigrants for decades. Laborers, entrepreneurs, and city dwellers developed an array of strategies for challenging discriminatory laws and practices. Hundreds of Japanese sugar-beet workers in Oxnard, California, joined their Mexican counterparts to form the Japanese-Mexican Labor Association (JMLA) in 1903. The JMLA organized a successful strike to protest 50 percent wage cuts. JMLA leaders approached the American Federation of Labor to charter the group as the Sugar Beet Farm Laborers' Union of Oxnard, but the union would admit only Mexican members—Asians were excluded. Absent the support of organized labor, the JMLA disbanded within a few years.

Labor unions were among the staunchest opponents of Japanese inclusion, and their members were active in anti-Japanese organizations such as the Asiatic Exclusion League. The league's purpose was to exclude all Japanese and Koreans from the United States, allegedly to protect jobs for white workers. Similar groups, such as the Native Sons of the Golden West, the Grange Association, and the American Legion, pressured politicians to deport Asians en masse or to segregate them into a noncitizen laboring underclass. Newspapers such as the *San Francisco Chronicle* bolstered anti-Japanese sentiment with warnings of a "yellow peril," whereby Asians would destroy American society with disease, crime, "backward" cultural practices, "theft" of economic opportunity from whites, and the seduction or rape of white women. As these racial stereotypes took hold, public opinion largely supported the anti-Asian policies and practices.

This is not to say that discrimination went unchallenged. When the city of San Francisco ordered Japanese into segregated Chinese schools in 1906, the Japanese government denounced the measure as a humiliation to a modern military power. President Theodore Roosevelt demanded that city officials reverse the policy before it strained relations between Washington and Tokyo. Roosevelt entered the so-called Gentlemen's Agreement with the Japanese government in 1907, whereby Japan ceased granting passports to laborers as long as Roosevelt blocked passage of anti-Japanese legislation. Roosevelt also issued Executive Order 589, however, prohibiting Japanese from entering the United States through Hawaii, Canada, or Mexico. From 1908 to 1924, most Japanese newcomers were the wives and children of immigrants who were permitted to reunite with their families. Among them were some 20,000 "picture brides," or women who married by proxy in Japan before joining their new husbands in the United States. Still, the flow of female Japanese immigrants diminished after the Japanese government signed the so-called Ladies Agreement in 1920, in which they agreed to block such emigration. Overall Japanese immigration came to a near-complete halt when the Immigration Act of 1924 barred all "aliens ineligible for citizenship" from entering the United States, which according to the Naturalization Act of 1870 meant anyone who could not be classified as "white" or "black."

The fortunes of the established Japanese community varied greatly in the 1910s and 1920s. A number of Japanese agriculturalists amassed considerable wealth and influence within and outside the Japanese community. George Shima's abundant yields on his 10,000 acres (4,000 hectares) of reclaimed land earned him distinction both as the "Potato King" and as America's first Japanese millionaire in the first decades of the twentieth century. Seito Saibara raised Japanese seed on a 1,000-acre (400-hectare) lease in Texas, launching a multimillion-dollar industry that continues to sustain the Gulf Coast. Masuo Yasui, a successful orchardist and retailer in Hood River, Oregon, became a leader among agriculturalists by starting the Mid-Columbia Vegetable Growers Association and assisted Japanese settlers in central Oregon, becoming a pillar of both the business and immigrant communities.

Residents of Los Angeles, San Francisco, Portland, Seattle, and smaller cities developed self-sustaining enclaves called Nihonmachi (or "Japantowns"), where residents lived in a culturally familiar setting relatively free of white racism. Nihonmachi were bustling business centers where entrepreneurs opened hotels, grocery stores, restaurants, barbershops, and laundries that catered to and employed other Japanese—men and women alike. Business leaders founded Japanese civil rights organizations, the most prominent being the Japanese American Citizens League (JACL) organized in Seattle in 1929 to support Japanese economic and educational initiatives, promote American principles, and fight discrimination. JACL chapters were founded in several states and rose to national prominence during World War II.

The range of institutions in Nihonmachi reflects the religious and cultural diversity within Japanese American communities. Buddhist, Shinto, and Christian churches offered newcomers room and board, English lessons, job placement, and social activities. Japanese language schools provided immigrant children instruction in Japanese culture to preserve language and traditions in their new homeland. Prefectural associations, organized by immigrants from the same localities in Japan, oriented new arrivals to American life, provided financial aid, and administered social services. Yet, despite the comforts of a thriving Japanese community, some found life in Nihonmachi constraining. Young professionals unable to be hired in their fields found themselves underemployed in Japanese enterprises. Japanese residents had little contact with non-Japanese, fostering isolation. White Americans found the "exotic" qualities of Nihonmachi intriguing, yet held up the enclaves as proof that the Japanese were "clannish" and not capable of assimilation into American society, thus legitimating exclusionist sentiment.

Race, Citizenship, and the Law: 1913–1925

Given that many of the most successful Japanese immigrants made their fortunes in agriculture, it is not surprising that the anti-Japanese movement sought to prevent them from holding land as well as citizenship. Even small Japanese family farms had proven astonishingly prosperous. Their labor-intensive, high-yield techniques produced 10 percent of California's agricultural value on the 1 percent of California's Japanese-owned land in the 1910s and 1920s. Anglo-Americans, long concerned that Japanese immigrants plotted to conquer the Pacific states, demanded the state government stop the "Japanese invasion" of California agriculture. The result was California's Alien Land Law of 1913, prohibiting "aliens ineligible for citizenship" from buying or leasing land for longer than three years. Arizona, Idaho, Wyoming, Kansas, Louisiana, Florida, Minnesota, Missouri, Nebraska, New Mexico, Oregon, Texas, and Washington passed similar laws by 1914, and California amended its law in 1920 to close remaining loopholes. By the 1920s, Japanese families routinely converted ownership of their land to their American-born children, whom the Constitution defined as citizens.

The U.S. Supreme Court upheld the classification of "alien ineligible for citizenship" in the case of *Takao Ozawa v. United States* (1922). The plaintiff, Takao Ozawa, argued that he should be naturalized because he lived as an American citizen—he spoke English, wore Western dress, practiced Christianity, and was even light-skinned. But the Court held that citizenship was open only to Caucasian or African Americans, and that Asians (or "Mongolians") were neither. Ozawa's permanent status, therefore, was "alien ineligible for citizenship." The high court made a related ruling in the case of *Toyota v. United States* (1925), declaring that Hidemitsu Toyota, a Japanese who served in the U.S. Coast Guard during World War I, remained an alien ineligible for citizenship because demonstrations of loyalty could not alter one's race.

Incarceration: 1941–1946

Absent the protections of citizenship, the Japanese were subject to arbitrary treatment at the onset of World War II. Japan's attack on Pearl Harbor in December 1941 reinvigorated fears that the Japanese—with the aid of their American children—plotted to conquer the West. Of particular concern was the concentration of Japanese communities in the far west; the 1940 census showed that 88.5 percent of all Japanese lived in the Pacific states. As Japan made military gains across the Pacific, the leadership of the Japanese American Citizens League (JACL) issued statements of Japanese Americans' loyalty to the United States, in Congress, to military officials, and to the public. These statements proved unconvincing in the face of rumors that Japanese Americans aided in the bombing of Pearl Harbor. Federal officials were pressed to make a visible response. On December 7, the Federal Bureau of Investigation began a roundup of hundreds of Issei (first-generation immigrant) community leaders, who were held in Department of Justice incarceration camps without formal charges.

The Nisei (second-generation Japanese Americans) were equally surprised at President Franklin Roosevelt's Executive Order 9066. The order, issued February 19, 1942, designated Washington, Oregon, California, and portions of Arizona as a military zone from which all people of Japanese ancestry—whether alien or citizen—were eventually restricted. Roosevelt cast the forced removal as a military necessity, though officials in law enforcement and military intelligence expressed doubts about this behind closed doors. Even those advocating the evacuation granted that there was no evidence of widespread disloyalty among the Japanese community and

Japanese Americans in San Francisco assemble for forced removal to a military "relocation center" in spring 1942. In the aftermath of Pearl Harbor, more than 112,000 West Coast Japanese were evacuated to ten isolated camps for the duration of the war. *(Library of Congress)*

that in casting a wide net to catch a few potential spies or saboteurs, the federal government would be detaining a population of almost entirely innocent people.

The federal government established first a military agency, the Wartime Civil Control Adminstration (WCCA), and then a civilian agency called the War Relocation Authority (WRA) to oversee the evacuation and detention of more than 112,000 West Coast Japanese Americans. The evacuation began with removal of the fishing community on Terminal Island in Los Angeles Harbor and continued along the West Coast. Groups of several hundred Japanese were moved to local "assembly centers," which were fairgrounds or race tracks whose animal stalls had been hastily painted to serve as housing units. Internees were not allowed to leave the centers without permission and were held under military guard. The WRA assured the Japanese that their cooperation with the incarceration would stand as proof of their loyalty to the United States. Many hoped that this wartime sacrifice would lead to full inclusion in American society when the fighting was over.

The WRA transferred the internees from assembly centers to semipermanent "relocation centers" in the interior during the spring and summer of 1942. The ten centers were located at Manzanar and Tule Lake, California; Amache, Colorado; Minidoka, Idaho; Topaz, Utah; Heart Mountain, Wyoming; Rohwer and Jerome, Arkansas; and Gila River and Poston, Arizona. In these isolated locations, the Japanese community lived behind barbed wire in substandard barracks under armed guard and constant surveillance. Although the WRA referred to the camps as "barbed-wire democracies," internees lost their freedoms of movement, association, and, to a great degree, political expression. The WRA provided jobs and a camp government, but the wages were meager and political decisions were subject to WRA veto. Meanwhile, internees were unable to continue their educations, practice their professions, maintain their property, or participate in the life of their chosen communities. In spite of these hardships, most Japanese internees worked to improve their circumstances by starting hobbyist clubs, planting gardens, hosting social events, organizing mutual assistance networks, and developing vibrant communities within the camps.

Internees hoping to pass the WRA's loyalty test were horribly disappointed in February 1943, when the agency distributed questionnaires to determine and document who was loyal enough to be resettled outside relocation centers. Question 28 asked the Japanese to sever all ties to Japan. For Issei, "aliens ineligible for citizenship" under the 1924 immigration law, compliance would render them stateless. Nonetheless, federal officials interpreted "no" as a statement of disloyalty, which subjected the respondent to segregation at the high-security detention facility at Tule Lake. Equally troubling was question 27, which asked whether respondents would serve in the U.S. armed forces. For those whose parents agonized over how to answer question 28, the request seemed outrageous. Many concluded that the "loyalty test" that the government administered in the assembly centers would ultimately prove impossible to pass.

There was little the Japanese community could do to stop the incarceration or shape WRA policy, yet a number of individuals challenged the constitutionality of their forced evacuation. Fred Korematsu of San Leandro, California, Gordon Hirabayashi of Seattle, and Minoru Yasui of Portland (the son of Oregon agriculturalist Masuo Yasui) refused to comply with curfew and evacuation orders. The three were jailed, convicted, and sent to incarceration camps. Citing government powers in national emergencies, the U.S. Supreme Court upheld all three convictions in the following cases: *Hirabayshi v. United States* (1943); *Yasui v. United States* (1943); and *Korematsu v. United States* (1944). A fourth petitioner, Mitsuye Endo, received a more favorable decision. Endo had followed evacuation orders to the letter, yet when the American Civil Liberties Union demanded a writ of habeas corpus, the U.S. District Court ruled that she was not entitled to such protection. The Supreme Court ruled

in *Ex parte Endo* (1944) that no constitutional basis existed for incarcerating citizens such as Endo, whom the government itself defined as loyal. The *Endo* decision spurred the WRA to hasten the release of all internees.

Wartime Patriotism and the Dilemmas of Military Service: 1943–1945

In 1944, the Nisei in incarceration camps were reclassified by the military as eligible for the military draft. Although some Nisei had volunteered for military service in 1943, for many potential draftees, the arrival of recruiters posed a difficult dilemma. Military service could provide the ultimate proof of loyalty, yet it was difficult for many to leave their families to fight a war for global democracy when they themselves had been stripped of their freedoms. The Nisei expressed their fidelity to American values in a variety of ways that generated conflict both within and outside the Japanese community.

The Heart Mountain Fair Play Committee organized a draft resistance movement that resulted in the imprisonment of eighty-five resisters and charges of conspiracy against the Fair Play leadership. President Harry S. Truman pardoned all Nisei draft resisters in 1947, including hundreds in other relocation centers who had joined the widening protest. Nisei who complied with the draft were inducted into the 442nd Regimental Combat Team, a segregated unit activated in February 1943. They joined the 100th Infantry Battalion, an all-Nisei unit from Hawaii. Both units fought in the European theater and sustained high casualty and low desertion rates, winning numerous citations in their relatively short period of combat. The best-known campaign was the late 1944 rescue of the Texas "Lost Battalion" from behind enemy lines in France in which 184 of the "fighting Nisei" were killed. President Truman joyously proclaimed to Nisei veterans in 1946, "you have fought against prejudice, and you have won"—yet decades would pass before Japanese Americans enjoyed full legal and social equality.

Resettlement and Postwar Politics (1946–1970)

WRA officials worked assiduously from 1943 to 1946 to resettle inmates in states outside the restricted zone on the West Coast. The immediate aim was to close the camps, but the long-term goal was to disperse the "clannish" Japanese from West Coast cities into communities across the country. College students were placed in universities in New England, the Midwest, and the South, and laborers were scattered among farms and factories. In many towns, particularly in the South, resettlement brought their first Japanese residents. The largest contingent resettled in Chicago, where Issei bachelor communities grew most noticeably. Resettlement continued through 1946 as officials struggled to place Japanese Americans suffering from advanced age, mental illness, lack of family, or poverty. President Truman made the first gesture toward reparations by signing the Japanese American Evacuation Claims Act in July 1948, providing $38 million to compensate Japanese Americans for property losses resulting from forced evacuation. This amounted to a fraction of the estimated $6 billion–$10 billion losses actually sustained and did not constitute a formal apology.

The combination of changing attitudes toward the Japanese and the work of Japanese American activists brought changes in longstanding policies on immigration, land tenure, and citizenship in the postwar era. The Supreme Court weakened the Alien Land Laws in 1948 in its ruling in *Oyama v. California,* which concluded that Japanese parents, despite being "aliens ineligible for citizenship," had the right to purchase land for a child without running afoul of the law. While the judiciary loosened barriers to Japanese land ownership, Congress and the White House cracked open the doors to immigration and citizenship. The War Brides Act of 1945 allowed 2,000 Japanese spouses and adopted children of U.S. military personnel to enter the United States. The McCarran-Walter Act of 1952 set a quota of 105 immigrants from every Asian country and—most significantly—made Japanese immigrants eligible for citizenship. The next critical change came when President Lyndon Johnson signed the Immigration and Nationality Act in 1965, which set immigration quotas without regard to race and distributed visas on a first-come, first-served basis. Emigrants from across Asia responded to this newly opened border, spurring the growth of Asian American communities across the United States.

The 1960s and 1970s expanded Japanese American political participation in electoral politics and grassroots activism. Daniel K. Inouye of Hawaii, a veteran of the 442nd Regimental Combat Team, was the first Japanese American elected to the U.S. House of Representatives in 1959 and became the first Japanese American senator in 1963. Spark Matsunaga of Hawaii was elected to the House in 1962 and to the Senate in 1976, and Representative Patsy Takemoto Mink, from the same state, became the first Asian American congresswoman in 1965. Norman Y. Mineta of California won election

as the first mainland Japanese American in Congress in 1974, the same year that Hawaii elected the first Japanese American governor, George R. Ariyoshi. S.I. Hayakawa, of California, joined the Senate in 1977, and Representative Robert Matsui represented constituents in the Sacramento area from 1979 until his death in 2005. (Except for Hayakawa, all of these Japanese American politicians were Democrats.)

At the same time, grassroots activists organized to promote the inclusion and visibility of the Japanese in American society. In 1968, a coalition of students of color at San Francisco State University—including a number of Nisei and Sansei (third-generation Japanese Americans)—called for the creation of an ethnic studies program. Students responded to the university's refusal with a six-month strike that effectively shut down the campus. Despite violent confrontations with police, students persisted until university officials established what would be the first department of ethnic studies at an American university. The Asian American Pacific Alliance at the University of California at Berkeley joined in similar actions to establish its ethnic studies department in 1969. By the 1980s, most universities in America not only had ethnic studies departments but had integrated ethnic studies into the standard curriculum.

A quieter but no less significant movement began in December 1969, when a group of Japanese Americans of all ages made a trip to the site of the Manzanar incarceration center, which became the first of a series of annual pilgrimages. The following years saw pilgrimages to other former incarceration sites, which encouraged reflection on the enduring significance of the Japanese in American life and the meaning of their incarceration. The Manzanar Committee and the JACL persuaded officials to name Manzanar a national historic landmark in 1985. Similar designations have been granted for other sites or are under consideration, thus preserving the historical memory of the incarceration for all Americans.

Redress, Remembrance, and Racial Equality: 1976–2001

Americans everywhere engaged in collective historical reflection during the 1976 bicentennial. President Gerald R. Ford called for an "honest reckoning" of mistakes as well as accomplishments and began by rescinding Executive Order 9066 on February 19—the date President Roosevelt issued it in 1942. In 1977, Ford granted a presidential pardon to Ikuko "Iva" Toguri (D'Aquino), who was convicted of treason in 1949 for her wartime broadcasts as "Tokyo Rose" for Japanese state radio. Her

Members of the Japantown community in San Francisco carry a *mikoshi* (portable Shinto shrine) in the Cherry Blossom Festival parade. The annual spring event features a street fair, a food bazaar, arts and crafts displays, and cultural entertainment. *(Michael S. Yamashita/National Geographic/Getty Images)*

ten-year sentence was reduced to six after investigators became convinced that Toguri had been held by Japan as an enemy alien and attempted to sabotage the broadcasts to reduce their impact on U.S. troops.

President Ford's reversal of these wartime measures suggest lessened fears of Japanese treachery, but they did not address the damage wrought by the incarceration. The federal government had yet to make a formal apology for the incarceration, despite numerous references to the evacuation as a "wartime mistake." The 1978 national convention of the Japanese American Citizens League resolved to seek redress and reparations for former internees. The combined efforts of the JACL, the National Coalition for Redress/Reparations, and other activist groups broke the silence surrounding the incarceration and garnered allies in Congress. In 1981, Congress established the Commission on Wartime Relocation and Internment of Civilians to conduct hearings to determine whether additional compensation was warranted. Testimony from more than 750 witnesses led the committee to conclude that the incarceration had not been a military necessity but the result of "race prejudice, war hysteria and a failure of political leadership."

The House of Representatives voted in 1987 to extend an official apology to Japanese Americans and to pay reparations to each surviving internee. The Senate followed suit in 1988. Despite objections to redress and reparations, President Ronald Reagan signed the Civil Liberties Act of 1988, providing $20,000 to each surviving internee and a $1.25 billion education fund, among other provisions. Disbursements began shortly after President George H.W. Bush signed the appropriations bill in 1989, and continued over a ten-year period.

The success of the redress movement created a favorable climate for revisiting the *Yasui, Hirabayashi,* and *Korematsu* cases in the early 1980s. The three men petitioned the Supreme Court to reverse their wartime convictions based on recent acknowledgments that the incarceration had not been a military necessity and revelations of prosecutorial misconduct (error *coram nobis*) in the wartime trials. Yasui's and Hirabayashi's convictions were overturned by federal courts in 1985 and 1986. While the federal district court reversed Korematsu's conviction in 1984, it affirmed the 1944 ruling legitimating racially based detention, leaving legal precedent for future incarcerations. For his decades-long struggle, Korematsu was awarded the Presidential Medal of Freedom by President Bill Clinton in 1998.

Following al-Qaeda's terrorist attacks of September 11, 2001, on the Pentagon and the World Trade Center, Fred Korematsu joined hundreds of Japanese Americans at the forefront of campaigns to protect Arab Americans and American Muslims from blanket restrictions on civil liberties. One such group was the National Coalition for Redress/Reparations (NCRR), founded in 1980 by Japanese activists seeking redress. Instead of disbanding after passage of the Civil Rights Act, the NCRR changed its name to the Nikkei Committee for Civil Rights and Redress and continued work on a broad civil liberties agenda. The NCRR's September 11 Committee was formed in 2001 out of concern that Muslims, Arabs, and South Asians would be treated as enemies after the September 11 attacks, just as Japanese Americans had been after Pearl Harbor. The Japanese American Citizens League, the NCRR, the Japanese American National Museum, and numerous other Japanese organizations united with Muslim American and Arab American groups to remind the public of the dangers of using racial profiling in national security policy. In this way, the Japanese American community assumed an essential leadership role in American society at a critical moment in the nation's history.

Heather Fryer

Further Reading

Chan, Sucheng. *Asian Americans: An Interpretive History.* New York: Twayne, 1991.

Daniels, Roger. *Asian America: Chinese and Japanese in the United States Since 1850.* Seattle: University of Washington Press, 1988.

———. *Prisoners Without Trial: Japanese Americans in World War II.* New York: Hill and Wang, 2004.

Daniels, Roger, Sandra C. Taylor, Harry H.L. Kitano, and Leonard J. Arrington. *Japanese Americans: From Relocation to Redress.* Seattle: University of Washington Press, 1992.

Harth, Erica. *Last Witnesses: Reflections on the Wartime Incarceration of Japanese Americans.* New York: Palgrave MacMillan, 2001.

Japanese American Citizens League. http://www.jacl.org.

Takaki, Ronald. *Strangers from a Different Shore: A History of Asian Americans.* Rev. ed. Boston: Little, Brown, 1998.

Japanese Americans
Alphabetical Entries

Acculturation and the Japanese American Community

The acculturation of the Japanese American community is often singled out as a prime example of immigrant assimilation because of the rapidity and totality with which the Japanese Americans have integrated themselves into mainstream American culture and society. Historically, the Japanese American community in the United States moved from an inward-looking orientation, during the period when the Issei (first generation) were immersing themselves in their new lives, to a much greater degree of integration during the era of the Nisei (second generation). The gulf between the Issei and the Nisei was due in large part to the racism and anti-Japanese discrimination that the first generation encountered, but which they vowed their children would not have to face.

Japanese immigration to the United States was negligible until just before the turn of the twentieth century. Most left Japan to work on the sugar plantations of Hawaii or in agriculture or railroads on the U.S. Pacific Coast. Many left home with the objective of making their fortune and later returning to Japan. When the Issei first arrived on the mainland, they tended to live in groups and were mostly men. When it became evident that they were in the country to stay, they sent home to Japan for their wives or asked their families to arrange a marriage to a "picture bride." It was at this point that Japanese women started to come to the United States in significant numbers. Thus, it was not until the early twentieth century and the arrival of women that there was any real family life in the Japanese American community.

The number of Japanese in the United States stood at just over 2,000 in 1890, rising to 72,257 by 1910. As of 1930, the Japanese and Japanese American community in the United States numbered 138,834. The vast majority were concentrated either in the Hawaiian Islands or in the Pacific states of California (home to some 42 percent of the mainland Japanese population), Oregon, and Washington. There was also a sizable Japanese community that spread east into Montana, Idaho, Utah, and Colorado. This first generation of Japanese immigrants is referred to as the Issei, which would face the greatest challenges in settling into the United States.

Cultural Roots of Acculturation

In terms of acculturation, many historians point out that Japanese culture historically has adopted foreign elements to rejuvenate and modernize itself. Typically this involved the adaptation of Asian elements (usually Chinese). Thus, it has been argued, the Japanese in the United States were more inclined to selectively adopt certain aspects of American culture and integrate these into their own traditions as a means of adapting to the times.

In the early twentieth century, the Hawaiian Islands were the main destination for many Japanese. By 1890, the islands were home to 12,610 Japanese migrants, a number that jumped to 61,111 in 1900 and 109,274 by 1920. The Japanese in Hawaii found it easier to integrate into the island's culture in part because they were the largest minority group (43 percent of the total population). Because there was relatively little anti-Japanese discrimination in Hawaii, the Japanese integrated smoothly into the island's economy, not only on the plantations, but also in the service and business sectors.

The mainland Issei faced more widespread and virulent anti-Japanese sentiment than their counterparts in the Hawaiian Islands. For this reason, mainland Japanese formed a greater degree of ethnic solidarity than their Hawaiian counterparts. As few Caucasian stores or services would welcome Japanese business, Issei on the mainland formed their own parallel economy that provided for their growing community. Japanese businesses ranged from hotels to tailor and barber shops to supply houses. For the Issei, this tended to discourage assimilation into the American mainstream. The segregation of the Japanese community, in turn, fueled further anti-Japanese sentiment among Anglo-Americans as well.

The Japanese and Japanese American community on the Pacific Coast bore the brunt of discrimination and racism. Japanese Americans were spit at in the street, taunted on playgrounds for having "slanty eyes," and beat up by non-Japanese Americans, among other things. Cries of "the Japs must go," were familiar to many in the community.

Some of the earliest advocates against the Japanese presence on the Pacific Coast were agricultural laborers and farmers, many of whom were jealous of the Japanese success in agriculture. It was well documented that the Issei were adept at taking barren land and cultivating it to breed prosperous fruit and vegetable crops, notably strawberries.

One of the more infamous anti-Japanese discriminatory measures taken on the U.S. mainland was a 1906 ruling by the San Francisco School Board, which attempted to segregate all children of Asian descent—Chinese and Koreans as well as Japanese—by sending them to a specifically designated "Oriental School." The decision was played up in both the U.S. and the Japanese press; only with the intervention of President Theodore Roosevelt and considerable pressure from Japanese authorities was the decision rescinded.

Another notable anti-Japanese act was the California Alien Land Act of 1913, which was significant in that it was the first law on the books to deprive the Japanese of landownership rights—the essence of the American Dream. Loopholes in the law allowed the Issei to transfer title to their land to their children, who, thanks to *jus solis* ("right of the soil," or automatic citizenship for persons born in a country), were American citizens. Still, the legislation was important in that it actively sought to halt Japanese upward mobility into the managerial and ownership class of the California agricultural industry. Still, the most blatantly anti-Japanese measure was the U.S. Immigration Act of 1924—also referred to as the Asian Exclusion Act—which all but cut off Japanese immigration into the United States and Hawaii.

Political Activism

To combat the discriminatory measures enacted against them, the Issei and Nisei became increasingly politically active, forming unions and organizations to work for improved conditions and legislation. Indeed it was not only in California that the Japanese American community encountered formal discrimination. Several other Western states, such as Oregon, Nevada, and Montana, considered or passed anti-Japanese or anti-Asian legislation in the wake of the California laws in the early 1900s.

The most potent and widespread measure to combat discrimination and racism was assimilation into mainstream American society. The Nisei were crucially important in that process. Not only were they the genera-

tion that grew up in American schools, learned English, and were able to transmit and explain American customs and habits to their parents, but the Nisei also had many non–Japanese American friends. By inclusion in American youth culture at large—attending community center programs, high school dances, sporting events, and the like—the Nisei quickly absorbed mainstream society and culture. Language was one means of acculturation available to at least some members of every generation. Even Issei knew some English, as it was a required subject in all middle schools in Japan. In addition, many sought to improve their English once they arrived in the United States. However, it was the Nisei who fully mastered the English language, speaking it in public and in school, reverting to Japanese only at home with their family and parents, if at all. Many Nisei did attend special schools to learn the language, customs, and traditions of Japan, though many fewer Sansei (third generation) attended such schools. Statistics on Japanese-language fluency is a telling indicator of acculturation and assimilation from generation to generation: 100 percent the Issei were fluent in Japanese, compared to only 19.3 percent of Nisei and 2.4 percent of Sansei.

Education

Based on their experiences with discrimination and racism, Issei believed that their children would overcome these obstacles and be accepted as "American" if they did well in school and were able to enter better-paid and more influential professions. This, at least in part, explains the great emphasis in the Japanese American family on higher education and learning. Many Issei scrimped and saved in order to send their children to university. Over time, the Japanese American community had a consistently higher percentage of adults who completed four or more years of college, exceeding the overall U.S. average.

Through schooling, especially at the university level, many of the Nisei gained access to the majority mainstream. Their friends and companions tended to be of mixed background, and many Japanese Americans quickly assimilated themselves into university culture and life. Upon graduating, if they were able to obtain a position worthy of their degrees—by no means automatic given discriminatory practices in hiring—the Nisei tended to live in mixed or non-Japanese communities. By literally moving into mainstream society, Japanese Americans were able to facilitate the acculturation and assimilation process. Of the Issei prior to 1908, 48 percent lived in Japanese communities, 21 percent lived in mixed neighborhoods, and 31.5 percent lived in mostly non–Japanese American communities. This trend changed quickly, as Issei and Nisei moved to mixed or non–Japanese American neighborhoods in the period 1910–1941, finally accounting for 70 percent of the Japanese American population. The internment camp experience of World War II accelerated the trend, so by the post-1945 period, only 10 percent of the Japanese American community lived in insular communities.

One indication of how quickly the Japanese American community sought to integrate and assimilate itself into American culture was the patterns and continuities seen in child rearing. The traditional Japanese approach was based on *shushin,* the cultural transmission of traditional moral and social values, including an emphasis on proper behavior, the primacy of the family, and subordination to authority. According to a study in the early 1980s, some 98 percent of the Issei were raised in the *shushin* tradition, declining to 69 percent of the Nisei and 56 percent of the Sansei. For all generations, maintaining family connections remained a core value even in America. The Issei tended to visit with relatives at a rate of 57 percent, rising to 72 percent among the Nisei and dipping only slightly to 69 percent for the Sansei—reflecting the fact that parents and grandparents were more likely to be in the United States than in Japan and therefore easier to visit. Another indication was assistance from a community member in securing employment. For the Issei, such connections were crucial in obtaining a job, as an estimated 96 percent went through Japanese American community channels. Among their children, however, only about 50 percent relied on community ties to secure employment, rising to 59 percent among the Sansei.

Lindsay Sarah Krasnoff

Further Reading

O'Brien, David J., and Stephen S. Fugita. *The Japanese American Experience.* Bloomington: University of Indiana Press, 1991.

Takaki, Ronald. *Strangers from a Different Shore: A History of Asian Americans.* Rev. ed. Boston: Little, Brown, 1998.

Woodrum, Eric. "An Assessment of Japanese American Assimilation, Pluralism, and Subordination." *American Journal of Sociology* 87:1 (July 1981): 161.

Agriculture, Japanese Americans in

The history of Japanese American agriculture is an account of ongoing struggle over land between white "natives" and Japanese immigrants and their children. The earliest immigrants came from Japan as con-

tract laborers to Hawaii in the late nineteenth century, with the possibility of higher wages and more work luring many to California shortly thereafter. On the Pacific Coast, despite alien land laws and recurring anti-Asian violence, many moved up the agricultural ladder, from laborer to farm operator. At the same time, many whites were fearful that the Japanese farmers were becoming too dominant in the state's agricultural business, a fear that abated only with their incarceration during World War II. Following the war, many Japanese rebuilt their agricultural businesses, demonstrating the persistence of this long-standing Asian American group.

Early History

The majority of Japanese emigrants after 1885 came from southwestern Japan, including the Fukuoka, Kumamoto, Hiroshima, Nagaski, Okayama, Saga, and Wakayama prefectures. Many came as a result of the relationship that began in the 1870s linking American businessman Robert Walker Irwin, Japanese finance ministry official Takashi Masuda, and Kaoru Inouye, a reformist minister of finance in the Meiji regime. Under a legal arrangement between the U.S. and Japanese governments, and through Irwin's arrangements with the Hawaiian regime and agricultural interests, Japanese laborers were being recruited for Hawaiian sugar plantations under three-year contracts. A total of 23,071 men, 5,487 women, and 133 children traveled to Hawaii before 1894. Of that group, 46 percent returned to Japan, 7 percent died, and 3 percent traveled to the continental United States. According to historian Sucheng Chan, about 125,000 Japanese migrated to Hawaii from 1894 to 1908, mainly with private companies originally established by Irwin and the Japanese government. More than half came from Fukuoka, Kumamoto, Hiroshima, and Yamaguchi.

Even before mass Japanese migration, large-scale and efficient "industrial plantations" had emerged throughout Hawaii, and the Japanese were brought in to work them. First-generation Japanese immigrants (Issei) then followed in the footsteps of Chinese immigrants, carving out a niche as agricultural laborers and, increasingly, tenant and land owning farmers. After the Chinese Exclusion Act of 1882 barred the arrival of further Chinese laborers in the United States, Japanese plantation workers soon came to outnumber both Chinese and Hawaiian laborers.

After 1900, mainland labor recruiters worked with Japanese boardinghouse owners to entice Japanese laborers from Hawaii by offering them higher wages. Farm owners, railroad companies, and lumber mills in the Pacific Northwest and California all sought Japanese laborers because they could no longer find sufficient numbers of low-paid Chinese workers. Thus, from 1902 through 1906, some 34,000 Japanese left Hawaii for the U.S. mainland. In order to stop the further exodus of their workers, plantation owners in Hawaii won 1905 legislation that required recruiters to pay a $500 license fee. Thus, by the 1910s, most Japanese leaving Hawaii went back to Japan and not the American mainland.

California Agriculture

Compared to Hawaii, California had the advantage of greater crop variety, as well as differing landownership patterns and crop marketing. Because each harvest lasted from two to six weeks, and because the crops were so varied, farm laborers could obtain work year-round by migrating. Thus, despite harsh labor conditions and low pay for migrant farm workers, many Issei saved enough money to become tenant farmers and ultimately landowners themselves.

Specialty crops became the backbone of the Issei ethnic economy in agriculture. The earliest migrant laborers had been students who arrived in California in 1888 and harvested corn in the Vaca Valley. By saving and pooling wages and resources, they could buy or lease land and grow labor-intensive crops such as strawberries, tomatoes, celery, onions, and other vegetables and fruits. When Japan stopped issuing passports to workers as part

A Japanese American farm family returns to the land in Washington state after release from an internment camp in 1945. Many others lost their land and equipment during the war and resettled in cities and suburban areas across the country. *(J.R. Eyerman/Stringer/Time & Life Pictures/ Getty Images)*

of the Gentlemen's Agreement (1907–1908) with the Theodore Roosevelt administration, Issei farmers sent for their wives, prospective brides, and younger relatives to ensure a steady labor supply.

Despite the immigration restrictions, anti-Japanese sentiment was growing in the agricultural regions of the Golden State. In 1913, the California legislature passed the Alien Land Law, which prohibited "aliens ineligible for citizenship" (most nonwhites) from purchasing land or leasing it for more than three years. At the time, there were an estimated 6,000 Japanese tenant farmers in California. Loopholes in the legislation—by which the Issei could transfer land titles to their U.S.-born children or transfer them to a corporation—generally negated the effects of the Alien Land Law, so that four years later there were 8,000 Issei tenant farmers in the state. (Oregon, Washington, and other parts of the West showed similar patterns.) Thus, by the time the United States entered World War I, the Issei in California produced about 90 percent of the state's berries, cantaloupes, tomatoes, onions, asparagus, and celery. Other crops largely grown by Japanese farmers included sugar beets, grapes, leafy vegetables, and floricultural products.

Anti-Japanese groups finally succeeded in closing the loopholes in the Alien Land Law that had allowed these increases. In 1920, Californians voted to prohibit Asian aliens from leasing land altogether and to bar ownership of corporations by stockholders who were more than 50 percent Issei or by their American-born children (Nisei). In 1923, the U.S. Supreme Court upheld the Alien Land Law in the cases of *Webb v. O'Brien* and *Frick v. Webb,* affirming the bans on cropping contracts and purchasing shares in land companies by "aliens ineligible for citizenship." In the wake of the California legislation, Arizona, Washington, Louisiana, New Mexico, Idaho, Montana, Oregon, and Kansas passed similar alien land laws.

Denied a political voice because they were ineligible for citizenship, Japanese and other Asian farm laborers were also subject to violent attacks. In 1921, after the local chamber of commerce and American Legion's post in Turlock, California, censured landowners who hired Japanese workers in the San Joaquin Valley, fifty to sixty white American workers surrounded a store owned by a Japanese immigrant, broke in, and drove out eighteen Japanese farmworkers—threatening to lynch them should they return. Later that night, the mob forced another forty Japanese laborers out of town. The perpetrators were arrested, tried, and ultimately acquitted. Nor were these the only spontaneous eruptions of violence against Japanese and other Asian laborers. Even in the so-called progressive political and social movements of the late nineteenth and early twentieth centuries—from organized labor and Populism to early twentieth-century progressivism and the Socialist Party—anti-Asian sentiment was rampant. Many reformers believed that by attacking Asian immigrant laborers they were containing monopoly capitalists. Only with the forced removal of Japanese Americans during World War II did it become clear that they were in fact small farmers surrounded by white American-owned corporate giants and could have easily continued agricultural production during the war.

Impact of World War II

After the Japanese bombing of Pearl Harbor on December 7, 1941, more than 40,000 Issei living on the Pacific Coast, along with 70,000 Americans of Japanese descent, were forcibly removed to ten "relocation camps" throughout the West. When President Franklin Roosevelt signed Executive Order 9066 on February 19, 1942, Japanese Americans had approximately one week's notice to decide what to do with their property and vacate. At the time, Japanese and Japanese Americans in California owned as much as 200,000 acres, or 80,000 hectares, of land in the state. Many sold their property for far less than its actual value. Determining the amount of property owned by Japanese Americans prior to internment remained an important issue into the late twentieth century, as it was critical in calculating the economic toll of incarceration and the extent of reparations.

Although most Japanese and Japanese American farming communities did not rebuild following the war, at least two communities in California, Cortez and Livingston, did. By establishing collective arrangements that consisted of an operations manager, an advisory board, and a board of trustees—as well as obtaining a sizable loan of approximately $2 million from the Bank of America—the Japanese farmers of Cortez had managed to hold onto their land during the war. Cortez agriculture has clearly changed over the course of the decades, and the future of the community remains in the hands of third- and fourth-generation Japanese Americans. Nevertheless, the golden age of Japanese agriculture on the U.S. mainland had come to an end as the vast majority of Japanese Americans, returning from incarceration camps during World War II, opted instead to settle in urban and suburban communities, where they achieved unprecedented prosperity and gradual acceptance by the larger society.

Jeannie Shinozuka

Further Reading

Chan, Sucheng. *Asian Americans: An Interpretive History.* New York: Twayne, 1991.

Lye, Colleen. *America's Asia: Racial Form and American Literature, 1893–1945.* Princeton, NJ: Princeton University Press, 2005.

Matsumoto, Valerie J. *Farming the Home Place: A Japanese American Community in California, 1919–1982.* Ithaca, NY: Cornell University Press, 1993.

Anti-Japanese Movement

Although racist acts and comments were directed at Japanese Americans as early as the 1860s, an organized anti-Japanese movement did not take shape in the United States until the 1890s. The movement that developed in the last decade of the nineteenth century was built in part on the anti-Chinese crusade that preceded it and originated in San Francisco, where some laborers feared economic competition from the newly arrived racial outsiders. A brief flurry of anti-Japanese activity, inspired by an economic recession and the arrival of Japanese laborers, followed between 1891 and 1893. Newspapers played a central role by suggesting that Japanese immigrants were simply replacing their Chinese predecessors and warning that Japanese were coming into contact with white women. Dennis Kearney, a populist political and labor leader, resuscitated his anti-Chinese campaign by altering his famous slogan from "The Chinese Must Go" to "The Japs Must Go." As a result of this agitation, the San Francisco School Board voted to send Japanese students to a segregated Chinese school. The board eventually rescinded this decision, however, after protests from the Japanese government helped convince President Theodore Roosevelt to pressure the board members to change their policy.

The anti-Japanese movement of the 1890s ultimately failed to sustain itself for two reasons. First, the small number of Japanese immigrants—the 1890 U.S. census recorded only slightly more than 2,000 Japanese in the United States—limited the appeal of the movement. Furthermore, most Americans did not yet perceive that Japan was a rising world power so they did not yet feel threatened by it. However, the two mitigating conditions changed significantly in the early decades of the twentieth century, when Japan won the Russo-Japanese War in 1905 and Japanese immigration to the United States began to increase considerably—to 24,326 in 1900, 72,157 in 1910, and 111,010 in 1920.

The West Coast

A sustained and organized anti-Japanese movement led by the press and local labor organizations began in San

Francisco in the early 1900s, initially building on the West Coast campaign to make Chinese exclusion "permanent." The press promoted the image of inassimilable Japanese invaders who threatened white women, bred crime and poverty, and burdened public schools. As time passed, both public and private anti-Japanese agitators increasingly focused their arguments on racial concerns, although reflexive economic worries did not disappear. Two Californian congressmen, for example, introduced bills in 1905 to end Japanese immigration that did not pass. In the same year, labor leaders met in San Francisco to form the Asiatic Exclusion League, the first anti-Japanese pressure group. The organization used propaganda and boycotts against Japanese businesses to rally support while lobbying politicians to restrict immigration.

The anti-Japanese movement gained national (and even international) notoriety in 1906, when the San Francisco School Board again attempted to force Japanese students to attend segregated schools already in place for Chinese students. The resulting diplomatic crisis with the Japanese government prompted President Theodore Roosevelt to intervene. Roosevelt convinced the board to rescind its decision in return for his promise to end Japanese immigration. As a result of his pledge, Roosevelt negotiated the Gentlemen's Agreement (1907–1908) with Japan. The arrangement, which consisted of a series of notes exchanged between the U.S. and Japanese governments, led Japan to agree to restrict immigration by refusing to issue passports to Japanese laborers. Both sides agreed to allow wives and family members of Japanese already in the United States to immigrate. As a result, despite the U.S. government's presentation of the Gentlemen's Agreement as tantamount to exclusion, many Japanese, particularly women, continued to arrive in the United States over the next sixteen years. An unintended consequence of the restriction was that the balanced gender ratio in the Japanese American community resulted in its continued growth.

Californian politicians, feeling betrayed by federal promises and reflecting the prejudice of their constituents, continued to push an anti-Japanese agenda focused on preventing landownership that drew strong support from the South as well as increasing support from the Midwest and Northeast. Republican control of the presidency and western governorships, however, prevented the passage of discriminatory measures that would embarrass the president until the election of Democrat Woodrow Wilson in 1912. During his presidency, West Coast politicians moved forward with their anti-Japanese agendas, most notably with California's Alien Land Laws of 1913 and 1920. Based on the federal Naturalization Act of 1870, which limited naturalization to "white

A cartoon from 1913 depicts Uncle Sam banishing a Japanese soldier fishing with a bayonet in Magdalena Bay off the Pacific Coast of Mexico. Japan was barred from any presence in the U.S. sphere of influence, and Japanese immigrants were barred from owning land. *(MPI/Stringer/Hulton Archive/ Getty Images)*

persons and persons of African descent" (and thus made Japanese "aliens ineligible for citizenship"), the land laws attempted to prevent Japanese Americans from owning land, in the process highlighting the alien nature of Japanese Americans and encouraging further discrimination against them. The 1913 legislation failed to meet expectations, however, because Japanese Americans could increase their land tenure by leasing land or avoiding the laws, which they could do by forming corporations or transferring ownership to their American-born children. The complaints of white farmers that Japanese Americans were running them out of the business were unfounded; in fact, most Japanese American farmers were engaged in complementary economic activities, raising vegetables for the Asian American market, for example, that did not compete with white-owned businesses. Still, Californians successfully lobbied for a more stringent alien land law in 1920 that closed the loopholes in the 1913 act. The

Japanese Exclusion League, made up of farmers, laborers, and members of middle-class patriotic and fraternal organizations, led the push for the new law. It, too, failed to live up to expectations, since a large number of native-born Japanese Americans could now own land.

The National Level

At the same time that Californians were debating and passing the alien land laws, other forms of anti-Japanese prejudice and discrimination flourished throughout the United States. Although school segregation of Japanese American children was rare, state legislatures passed laws prohibiting the marriage of whites and Asians. Restrictive covenants in real estate deeds made it illegal to sell property to nonwhites. Theaters commonly seated Asian patrons either in the balcony or to the side. Some pools and beaches were even barred to Asians. Furthermore, many Californians began to worry about the alleged high birth rate of Japanese Americans, a figure artificially inflated by skewed statistics published in newspapers.

The federal government resisted anti-Japanese legislation prior to the 1920s. For example, the Immigration Act of 1917 (or Asiatic Barred Zone Act) excluded all Asians except Filipinos, who were American nationals, and Japanese, who were exempt under the terms of the Gentlemen's Agreement. Nevertheless, the federal government finally gave in to the rising nativist and anti-Japanese sentiments of the 1920s. Under pressure from constituents, the press, and private organizations—as well as from *Sacramento Bee* publisher V.S. McClatchy's accusation that Japanese American language schools (attended in the evening by Japanese American children to learn the Japanese language and culture) were actually promoting Japanese ideals and loyalty—Congress denied immigration quotas in the Immigration Act of 1924 (or National Origins Act) to all "aliens ineligible for citizenship." Although not specifically named, the legislation affected only the Japanese and effectively abrogated the Gentlemen's Agreement. With passage of the 1924 legislation, Congress met the primary demand of the anti-Japanese movement and condoned ongoing discrimination against Japanese Americans. Anti-Japanese sentiment would resurface in the future, most notably during World War II and in the "Japan-bashing" phenomenon of the 1980s.

Allan W. Austin

Further Reading

Daniels, Roger. *Asian America: Chinese and Japanese in the United States Since 1850.* Seattle: University of Washington Press, 1988.

———. *The Politics of Prejudice: The Anti-Japanese Movement in California and the Struggle for Japanese Exclusion.* 2nd ed. Berkeley: University of California Press, 1977.

Ichioka, Yuji. *The Issei: The World of the First Generation Japanese Immigrants, 1885–1924.* New York: Free Press, 1988.

Kitano, Harry H.L., and Roger Daniels. *Asian Americans: Emerging Minorities.* 3rd ed. Upper Saddle River, NJ: Prentice Hall, 2001.

Arai, Clarence Takeya (1901–1964)

Clarence Takeya Arai was a founding member and the first president of the Japanese American Citizens League (JACL), an organization that has advocated since 1930 for the inclusion of Japanese in American society, the restoration of Asian American civil rights, and the Japanese American redress claims of 1948 and 1988. Arai was also a well-known labor attorney in Seattle and a community leader during the Japanese American incarceration of World War II.

Born in 1901 in Seattle, Washington, Arai received his law degree from the University of Washington in 1924 and began his career as a lawyer in Seattle. From 1928 to 1930, he traveled up and down the West Coast with George Ishihara on behalf of the Seattle Progressive Citizens League to promote the formation of a regional Nisei citizens league. His visit to California in 1928 re-energized the American Loyalty League, a statewide Nisei citizens organization led by Thomas T. Yatabe, a Fresno dentist. It was on a trip to Los Angeles in 1930 that he met his future wife, Yone Utsunomiya. At a meeting in San Francisco that year, Arai proposed the formation of a national council of Japanese American Citizens Leagues to take place in Seattle.

At the August 1930 council in Seattle, delegates debated at length over what to call the new organization—whether they should refer to themselves strictly as "Japanese," or whether "Japanese" should be used as an adjective to modify "American"; and if the latter, whether a hyphen should be used between "Japanese" and "American." The debate reflected the group's emphasis on promoting assimilation for second-generation Japanese immigrants into American society and their goal of educating American society about the Japanese community. The JACL strongly advocated patriotism, self-improvement, and self-reliance as the keys to acceptance by U.S. society at large. Arai was an early president of the newly formed organization. In the ten years between its founding and 1940, the ranks of the JACL expanded to nearly 6,000 members, made up primarily of young Nisei professionals and small business men who felt a sense of responsibility to their communities. Arai also served as president of the Seattle chapter of the JACL five times. In Washington State politics, he was a Republican precinct committeeman, vice president of the Thirty-seventh Legislative District Republican Club, and delegate to the state Republican convention. He also launched an unsuccessful bid for a seat in the Washington State legislature in 1934.

World War II changed the life of the Arai family. After Pearl Harbor, the JACL encouraged its members to cooperate with the government's request for information and with Executive Order 9066, which removed Japanese Americans from the West Coast and placed them in concentration camps inland. In accordance with the evacuation order in April 1942, the Arai family was sent to the Puyallup Assembly Center in Washington, nicknamed "Camp Harmony." Selected JACL members were allowed to take part in the day-to-day governance of Camp Harmony. James Y. Sakamoto, the former JACL national president, was the chief supervisor; Clarence Arai played an active role in camp life as judge advocate; and his wife, Yone, served as an assistant chief interpreter. The Arai family, along with 7,200 others, were moved to Minidoka Internment Camp, Idaho, in August 1942. While in Minidoka, Arai suffered a mild stroke due to high blood pressure. The Arais returned to Seattle when the war was over; shortly thereafter, their only son died of cancer at the age of nine. As Clarence's health continued to decline, he ended his law career and took up photography. He died in 1964.

Emily Hiramatsu Morishima

Further Reading

Niiya, Brian, ed. *Encyclopedia of Japanese American History Updated Edition: An A-to-Z Reference from 1868 to the Present.* New York: Facts on File, 2001.

Takaki, Ronald. *Strangers from a Different Shore: A History of Asian Americans.* Rev. ed. Boston: Little, Brown: 1998.

Taylor, Quintard. "Blacks and Asians in a White City: Japanese Americans and African Americans in Seattle, 1890–1940." *Western Historical Quarterly* 22:4 (November 1991): 401–29.

Asiatic Exclusion League

On May 14, 1905, white residents concerned with the growing Asian immigrant population met in San Francisco to demand policies to exclude immigrants from Japan and Korea. Reviving objections similar to those voiced against Chinese immigration, they formed a pressure group called the Japanese and Korean Exclusion League. In 1907, the league changed its name to the Asiatic Exclusion League (AEL), in part to include immigrants from India among its targets. By this time, the league claimed to have as many as 200,000 total members in California, Oregon, Washington, Idaho, Colorado, and Nebraska—110,000 in California alone. Besides insisting that Asian immigrant labor depressed wages and degraded working conditions, the league argued that Asian immigrants could not safely assimilate into the nation's culture and political institutions, and warned against the dangers of miscegenation and disease. From 1905 through 1913, the AEL distributed anti-Asian propaganda, endorsed immigration restriction legislation, and supported boycotts to undermine Asian immigrant livelihood. It also played a role in the campaign to force Japanese and Korean students to attend a racially segregated public school in San Francisco.

Labor organizations, particularly the San Francisco Building Trades Council, were the driving force behind the AEL and provided financing and leadership for its activities. Unions represented 195 out of 231 groups affiliated with the league in 1908, and labor leaders dominated its top positions. Olaf Tveitmore, for example, was not only president of the AEL but also secretary of the Building Trades Council and editor of *Organized Labor.* He used the newspaper to spread anti-Asian sentiment, once declaring in print that the Japanese were "the most dangerous spies that have ever been allowed to exist this side of HELL."

Throughout most of its existence, the AEL actively engaged in mobilizations against Asian immigrants. As the number of Japanese restaurants increased in the period following the 1906 San Francisco earthquake and fire, the league called for a boycott of these establishments. The protest movement included the circulation of matchboxes carrying the message "White men and women, patronize your own race." Similar calls for racial solidarity surfaced in 1908, when Tveitmore helped unionize laundry workers and their employers to form the Anti-Jap Laundry League. An ensuing boycott against Japanese laundries included billboards chastising Japanese laundry customers. "Foolish woman!" one sign read. "Spending your man's Earnings on Japs. Be Fair, patronize Your Own." Around the same time, the league denounced immigrants from India for "their lack of cleanliness, disregard of sanitary laws, petty pilfering, especially of chickens, and insolence to women" and began pressuring immigration officials and legislators to protect Americans against what they considered a new racial menace.

The AEL continued to lobby for anti-Asian policies until 1911, when powerful supporters, one of whom,

E.E. Schmitz, had become mayor of San Francisco, started opposing such legislation in the hope of strengthening San Francisco's bid to host the 1915 Panama-Pacific International Exposition. After these defections, the Asiatic Exclusion League declined in influence and ultimately disintegrated in 1913.

Scott H. Tang

Further Reading

Daniels, Roger. *The Politics of Prejudice: The Anti-Japanese Movement in California and the Struggle for Japanese Exclusion.* 2nd ed. Berkeley: University of California Press, 1977.

Jensen, Joan M. *Passage from India: Asian Indian Immigrants in North America.* New Haven, CT: Yale University Press, 1988.

Buddhist Churches of America

The Buddhist Churches of America (BCA) is an incorporated religious organization affiliated with the Jodo Shinshu Honganji-ha sect founded on the teachings of Shinran (1173–1262), a Japanese cleric. Since the arrival of the Reverends Sonoda Shuye and Nishijima Kakuryo in San Francisco on September 1, 1899, the faith and its institution have continually adapted to their American experience.

Jodo Shinshu (Shin or Pure Land) Buddhists maintain that Shinran's thoughts, contained in the *Kyogyoshinsho, Tan'nisho,* and other writings, crystallize the spiritual vision articulated in the *Muryojukyo* (*Larger Sukhavativyuha-sutra*), *Kammuryojukyo* (*Amitayurdhyana-satra*), and *Amidakyo* (*Smaller Sukhavativyuha-sutra*). Most important, the *Muryojukyo* lists forty-eight vows that Dharmakara fulfilled to become Amida Buddha (the Buddha of Everlasting Light) and to establish the Pure Land with the intent to save all beings. Of the forty-eight vows, the eighteenth is central: "If sentient beings hear [Amida's] name and quicken faith and joy, with even a single thought [of the Amida Buddha]; and if they offer their spiritual merit to others with a sincere heart; and if they desire to be born in [Amida's] Pure Land, they will attain birth there and reside in the stage of nonretrogression. Only those who commit the five damning offenses or slander the true teaching will be excluded."

Over the course of the development of Japanese Pure Land thought, the ideas in this passage were broadened to ensure spiritual release for all beings. The expression "a single thought" evolved to mean uttering the Amida's name in the form *Namu Amida Butsu*—"I take refuge in Amida Buddha." The *Amidakyo* states that sentient beings can be born in the Pure Land by simply hearing and by being sincerely mindful of Amida's name. Carrying this idea further, the *Muryojukyo* expounds that even evil persons on their deathbeds who utter Amida Buddha's name with utmost sincerity will be received in Pure Land.

The insights from these three sutras provided Shinran with the rationale for dispensing with rigorous spiritual discipline and highlighting the centrality of *shinjin,* the true or sincere faith espoused by Nagarjuna (ca. 150–250 C.E.), Vasubandhu (ca. fifth century C.E.), and others. The centrality of faith ensures spiritual release when the devotee appreciates his or her inadequacies and surrenders to the absolute Other Power (*tariki*) of Amida Buddha. *Shinjin,* the prime condition for birth in the Pure Land, is a gift from Amida Buddha; and the sincere utterance of the *nembutsu* is an invocation of gratitude and joy for Amida's compassion. Birth in the Pure Land is the most conducive way station for the ultimate realization of enlightenment (*bodhi*) or *nirvana.*

The Honganji-ha sect, headquartered in Kyoto, dispatched the first priests to serve the growing Japanese immigrant community in America, which had grown tenfold from 2,039 in 1890 to 24,327 in 1900. From 1905 to 1923, Bishop Uchida Koyu established thirteen temples throughout the Western and Mountain states and laid the foundations for a national organization. The sixth bishop, Masuyama Kenju, began the shift to an English-speaking institution by enlisting the assistance of Robert Clifton, Julius A. Goldwater, Sunya Pratt, and other European Americans, and encouraged American-born and educated Noboru Tsunoda and Masaru Kumata to become priests.

With the outbreak of World War II, the U.S. government shuttered the temples in the Pacific Coast states and incarcerated most of their leaders, who continued their activities in the internment camps. At Topaz Relocation Center in Utah, Bishop Matsukage Ryotai met with clerics and lay leaders in late April 1944 to incorporate the Buddhist Churches of America. Beginning in 1959, Bishop Hanayama Shinsho and his successor, Kenryu Tsuji, the first American bishop, initiated innovative educational, outreach, ministerial, and financial programs in an attempt to nurture a new generation of leaders and devotees. In 1954, the BCA established the Buddhist Study Center in Berkeley, California, to instruct ministerial aspirants in English. Renamed the Institute of Buddhist Studies (IBS) in 1966, it became an affiliate of the Graduate Theological Union in 1985.

Beginning in the mid-1970s, the BCA's vitality began to wane, due in part to dwindling membership, financial difficulties, an aging clergy, and uninspiring leadership. Declining from a peak of approximately 100,000 devotees in the early 1930s, the BCA as of 2006 administered sixty-one temples and six fellowships, with approximately 17,000 devotees and an annual budget of approximately $2 million from its headquarters in San Francisco. Of its eight administrative districts, six are located in the Pacific states. The Mountain States District serves Colorado, Wyoming, and Nebraska; the Eastern District stretches from Minnesota to the Eastern seaboard. The BCA is governed by a board of directors made up of the bishop, elected clerics, and lay representatives. Annual meetings are held in February. The individual temples support the national organization through an annual assessment based on their respective membership rolls. The bishop represents the BCA, oversees the IBS, appoints ministers to the local temples, and mediates problems. Shin Buddhists in the state of Hawaii have a separate organization that traces its beginnings in 1889 to the Kingdom of Hawaii. Canadian Shin Buddhists also have a separate organization, which began in 1905.

Ronald Y. Nakasone

Further Reading

Buddhist Churches of America. *Buddhist Churches of America*. 2 vols. Chicago: Nobart, 1974.

———. http://buddhistchurchesofamerica.org.

———. *2006 Annual Report*. San Francisco: Buddhist Churches of America, 2007.

Business and Entrepreneurship, Japanese American

Entrepreneurship has played a vital role in the lives of Japanese Americans since virtually the beginning of their immigration in the late nineteenth century. Although the majority of early Japanese Americans arrived as laborers employed by others, largely working in the agricultural fields of Hawaii and California, their thirst for upward mobility was strong. Many struggled to overcome popular and official discrimination—the Japanese were barred from owning land in California after 1913, for instance—which kept a large portion of the community in low-paying jobs.

At the same time, many early Japanese American immigrants recognized the business opportunities of catering to the needs of their marginalized countrymen. The spirit of cooperation—strong in Japan and among Japanese American immigrants—thus fostered early efforts at entrepreneurship, as business owners could rely on their fellow immigrants to obtain financing and customers. Japanese Americans by the 1920s became involved in a wide variety of entrepreneurial activities, particularly in Hawaii and on the West Coast. These activities included farms and agricultural enterprises, hotels, restaurants, boardinghouses, grocery and supply stores, gardening services, laundries, food wholesalers and distributors, flower shops, tailor shops, shoe repair, pharmacies, bars, pool halls, trading companies, medical clinics, and even newspapers.

Among the more successful of these early entrepreneurs was Harry Sotaro Kawabe, a first-generation Japanese immigrant (Issei) who went into the laundry business in Alaska in 1915 and made a small fortune through contracts with railroad companies, steamship lines, and the U.S. military. Another was Keisaburo Koda, who started out as a migrant farm worker in the early 1900s and opened laundries and a wholesale fish business in California before going into rice growing. By the eve of World War II, Koda was one of the largest growers of rice in the country, earning the sobriquet "Rice King." Kyutaro Abiko, another Issei, was a fluent English speaker when he arrived in San Francisco in the 1880s. After running a laundry and a restaurant, he purchased two struggling Japanese-language newspapers, merging them in 1899 to form the *Nichibei Shimbun,* which soon became the most successful Japanese newspaper in the country.

While Kawabe, Koda, and Abiko saw great success, most of the Japanese American–owned businesses were small and labor-intensive. The owner would often work hard and employ family members, all of whom lived simply and frugally so that savings could be used to further expand the business. Cooperation was also important, as businesses relied on the Japanese American community to raise funds through locally run mutual aid societies and locally owned savings institutions. The spirit of cooperation among Japanese American immigrants, or at least among those from the same prefecture in Japan, also assisted many Japanese Americans in forming businesses and obtaining the necessary credit. Immigrants from the same prefecture often loaned money among themselves informally.

Moreover, as normal channels for credit were closed to Japanese Americans, locally based Japanese American civic groups pooled funds to help strengthen new and expanding businesses. Tanomoshi, or rotating credit associations, developed to pool money and provide rotating loans to their members. Japanese American entrepreneurs could also find employees in the community whom they could pay low wages, often in exchange for room and board and always with a sense of belonging.

The prevalence of Japanese American entrepreneurs is further explained by the fact that many came to the United States specifically for business opportunities. As immigrants, they were ambitious and willing to take challenges and accept risks. Even if economic conditions forced them to begin their careers as laborers, they had aspirations to own their own laundry establishments, restaurants, grocery stores, or farms. An additional source of entrepreneurship came as a response to the discrimination faced by many Japanese Americans, both official and unofficial. Japanese and other Asian Americans were barred from owning land in California in 1913, while many professional associations and industry trade groups barred Japanese members. From time to time, white business owners angry at Japanese American competition would organize community boycotts against them.

Discrimination forced Japanese Americans to develop an alternative approach to business. Because they were barred from owning land, for example, many leased small plots from other farmers and went into truck farming—growing small but valuable vegetable and fruit crops for local markets, many of them in Japanese American communities. Vertical integration became an important part of this industry, as Japanese Americans developed businesses to control the production, distribution, and sale of their crops, as many white distributors and wholesalers would not buy from them.

Entrepreneurship thus was an essential part of the early Japanese American experience, without which it would have been difficult under prevailing conditions to rise from contract laborer to business owner. During World War II, however, the incarceration of more than 112,000 Japanese Americans forced many to abandon private businesses. Because of the need to vacate their homes and businesses quickly, they often had to sell their assets and accept large losses. When the war was over, many families relocated to new places and had to start from scratch. After World War II, however, mainstream American society was generally more tolerant of Japanese Americans, which made it possible not only to restore previous ventures but to pursue business and occupational opportunities that were previously unavailable. Indeed, the new avenues made entrepreneurship itself perhaps less essential than before the war for upwardly mobile Japanese Americans. At the same time, the improving situation also allowed entrepreneurs to expand their businesses beyond the Japanese American community itself.

Although most entrepreneurs were content to run small businesses, a number of Japanese Americans have gained widespread recognition for their success. For instance, the image of Naoichi Hokazono graces a stained glass window in the Colorado State Capitol to recognize his contribution in bringing contracted Japanese laborers to Colorado in the early twentieth century to work in agriculture, transportation, and infrastructure development, including irrigation and dam construction. George Shima (Ushijima) became known as the "Potato King" in the 1910s for work on reclaiming and leasing land in the San Joaquin Delta near Sacramento, California; he grew enough potatoes on leased land to leave a $15 million estate when he died in 1926. In Florida, Sukeji Morikami developed a fortune through land investments in the mid-twentieth century, later donating the acreage for a park in Palm Beach County that houses the Morikami Museum and Japanese Gardens. A more recent Japanese American entrepreneur of note is Hiroaki "Rocky" Aoki, who came to America in 1964 and developed a nationwide chain of Benihana Steak Houses.

Wade Pfau

Further Reading

Bonacich, Edna, and John Modell. *The Economic Basis of Ethnic Solidarity: Small Business in the Japanese American Community.* Berkeley: University of California Press, 1980.

Kitano, Harry H.L. *Japanese Americans: The Evolution of a Subculture.* Englewood Cliffs, NJ: Prentice Hall, 1969.

Wilson, Robert A., and Bill Hosokawa. *East to America: A History of the Japanese in the United States.* New York: William Morrow, 1980.

Civil Liberties Act (1988)

Congress passed the Civil Liberties Act of 1988, also known as the "Redress Bill," to make amends to Japanese Americans and Aleuts who were forced by the federal government to relocate or live in concentration camps during World War II. President Ronald Reagan signed the bill into law on August 10, 1988. The legislation compensated Japanese Americans who survived the camps with $20,000 and called for a formal written apology from the president. The legislation also demanded that the U.S. government pay each surviving Aleut Indian, forced to relocate from the Pribilof and Aleutian islands during World War II, up to $12,000.

Japanese Americans had fought for decades to make the Civil Liberties Act a reality. In 1948, the Japanese American Citizens League (JACL) had successfully lobbied Congress to pass the Evacuation Claims Act, which called for restitution to Japanese Americans for economic losses resulting from wartime relocation. The measure was relatively narrow in scope, however, with the government paying for property losses only—averaging just $340 per internee. Twenty-two years later, the Seattle JACL, reinvigorated by the Asian American civil rights movement of the 1960s and 1970s, urged the national organization to renew its efforts to get Congress to enact a redress bill—to no avail. In 1976, the JACL established the National Committee for Redress and in 1978 adopted a proposal demanding $25,000 in reparations for each Japanese American forced to move during World War II. Two other organizations emerged from the Japanese American community during the late 1970s to seek redress and reparations: the National Council for Japanese American Redress and the National Coalition of Redress/Reparations (NCRR).

In 1980, largely in response to the growing political influence of the JACL and NCRR, President Jimmy Carter created the Federal Commission on Wartime Relocation and Internment of Civilians (CWRIC), which held public hearings to investigate the concentration camps and their effects on prisoners. The hearings proved to be a turning point of the redress movement. In 1983, the CWRIC concluded that the camps had not been a military necessity and that the "historical causes" shaping the decision to incarcerate Japanese Americans were the result of "race prejudice, war hysteria and a failure of political leadership." It also recommended that the federal government make a formal apology and compensate each survivor with a onetime, tax-free payment of $20,000.

The CWRIC's recommendations formed the basis of the Civil Liberties Act of 1988, which was sponsored in Congress by Representative Norman Mineta, a California Democrat who had been interned as a boy, and Senator Alan Simpson, a Wyoming Democrat. Payment to all surviving Japanese American citizens or permanent legal residents who had been incarcerated in the camps began in October 1990. Between 1990 and 1993, more than 79,000 former internees each received $20,000 in compensation. When the last of the payments were made in the early 1990s, however, nearly half of those who would have been entitled to compensation were no longer alive.

Bruce E. Stewart

Further Reading

Kitano, Harry H.L., and Roger Daniels. *Asian Americans: Emerging Minorities.* Englewood Cliffs, NJ: Prentice Hall, 1988.

Wei, William. *The Asian American Movement.* Philadelphia: Temple University Press, 1993.

Collins, Wayne M. (1918–1974)

San Francisco civil rights attorney Wayne Mortimer Collins built a career defending the rights of people regardless of race or public popularity, including persons of Japanese descent during and immediately after World War II. Collins's clients included the unpopular "Tule Lake renunciants," internees who renounced their U.S. citizenship while in World War II detention camps, and Ikuko "Tokyo Rose" Toguri, who broadcast anti-American propaganda from Tokyo during the war. Collins also defended Japanese Peruvian internees and Japanese Americans stranded in Japan during the war who were viewed by the U.S. government as collaborators with the enemy.

Of the more than 112,000 Japanese Americans interned during World War II, the U.S. government placed more than 18,000 at Tule Lake Segregation Center in Northern California. As a sign of protest against the incarceration, more than 5,000 native-born citizens of Japanese ancestry renounced their U.S. citizenship. The federal government thereupon classified them as "enemy aliens," rendering them deportable under Public Proclamation No. 2655.

The Tule Lake Defense Committee, representing the renunciant group, asked Collins in August 1945 to be their legal representative. The young attorney began advising them of their rights from that moment and continued to do so until 1960. On behalf of the 4,754 persons he represented, Collins wrote an appeal to U.S. Attorney General Tom Clarke in 1945 withdrawing their renunciation and expressing their desire to remain in the United States. According to his appeal, the renunciation had been made under duress and was a direct result of actions by the U.S. government rather than any true wavering of allegiance. On November 13, 1945, Collins proceeded to file two mass class equity suits on their behalf, *Abo v. Clark* and *Furuya v. Clark,* and two mass class habeas corpus proceedings, *Abo v. William* and *Furuya v. Williams,* all in federal district court. The filings immediately halted the deportation orders and forced mitigation hearings for the plaintiffs. The hearings took place at three enemy alien camps (Tule Lake, California; Bismarck, North Dakota; and Santa Fe, New Mexico) and resulted in the release of most of the internees from either their removal orders or the internment camp itself. Those who remained in the camps were paroled into Collin's custody, and their removal orders were permanently canceled soon thereafter. The U.S. government rescinded the renunciations of approximately 1,000 internees and agreed to administrative remedies for the remaining parolees.

Collins also helped stay the deportation orders of Japanese Latin Americans, most of whom had been removed from Peru and placed in enemy alien camps in the United States and were subject to deportation to Japan after the war. The U.S. government intended to trade these internees for Americans stranded in Japan during the war, but the plan was never realized. When the war was over, the Latin American governments were unreceptive to the return of their citizens and permanent residents of Japanese descent, so the United States began to deport them to Japan. Collins first assisted the internees in fighting the deportation orders and then helped them gain the right to reside legally in the United States.

In 1949, Collins also served as the principal defense attorney for Ikuko "Iva" Toguri in her trial on eight counts of treason for alleged broadcasts as Tokyo Rose on Radio Tokyo during World War II. Toguri, a U.S. citizen of Japanese descent who found herself in Japan at the time of the Pearl Harbor attack, was recruited by the Japanese government to broadcast propaganda to American troops during the war in an effort to undermine military morale. Toguri was found guilty on one count, sentenced to ten years in prison and a $10,000 fine, and released on parole after six years, in January 1956. Collins characterized the verdict as "guilty without evidence," and the case did not come to an end until three years after his death, with a presidential pardon of Toguri by Gerald Ford in 1977 (after it was revealed that key witnesses in the trial had lied). Wayne Collins was also active in the fight against the Levering Act of 1950, a California law during the McCarthy era requiring state government employees to take loyalty oaths, and the Berkeley Free Speech Movement of 1964.

Jane J. Cho

Further Reading

Gardiner, C. Harvey. *Pawns in a Triangle of Hate: The Peruvian Japanese in the United States.* Seattle: University of Washington Press, 1981.

Wayne M. Collins Papers, BANC MSS 78/177 c, Bancroft Library, University of California, Berkeley.

Commission on Wartime Relocation and Internment of Civilians

The Commission on Wartime Relocation and Internment of Civilians (CWRIC) was formed on July 31, 1980, when President Jimmy Carter signed Public Law 96-317. The CWRIC was asked to study the mass removal and internment of Japanese Americans during World War II and recommend an appropriate remedy. The formation of the CWRIC and the bill sponsoring its creation were indicative of the ideological split between

activists in the redress movement. Formed in 1976, the Japanese American Citizens League (JACL) National Committee for Redress switched its support from reparation payments to the creation of a government committee in May 1979. Members of the committee split from the group that formed the National Council for Japanese American Redress (NCJAR), which focused on getting Congress to pass a bill seeking direct reparations rather than instituting a committee to study the matter. The National Coalition of Redress/Reparations (NCRR) served as a kind of independent watchdog of the CWRIC and its hearings.

The CWRIC was chaired by Joan Z. Bernstein, a lawyer from Washington, D.C. Other committee members included Daniel E. Lungren, Edward Brooke, Rev. Robert Drinan, Arthur S. Flemming, Arthur Goldberg, Ishmael V. Gromoff, William Marutani, and Hugh B. Mitchell. Beginning in 1981, the CWRIC held hearings in cities across the country, at which 750 Japanese Americans testified about their wartime experience. Hearings were held in Washington D.C., Los Angeles, San Francisco, Seattle, Alaska, Chicago, New York City, and Cambridge, Massachusetts. Witness testimony revealed innumerable examples of uncompensated loss and emotional injury. The CWRIC also hired an independent contractor, IFC Incorporated, to determine the economic damage caused by the internment. The company reviewed settlements from the 1948 Evacuation Claims Act, which granted reimbursement for properly documented material losses and concluded that the $37 million then disbursed was grossly inadequate.

After eighteen months of research, the CWRIC published its report, *Personal Justice Denied,* on February 22, 1983. The final document combined the testimonies at the hearings and the research of former internee and Japanese American activist Aiko Yoshinaga-Herzig. The CWRIC found that the internment of civilians was not a military necessity but a result of "race prejudice, war hysteria and a failure of political leadership." Economic losses were estimated at between $1.2 billion and $3.1 billion (as high as $6.2 billion when adjusted for inflation). The CWRIC's report provided essential validation for the Japanese Americans' struggle for redress. John Tateishi, redress director for the JACL, believes that the CWRIC findings swayed public support toward redress, that they raised public awareness of the incarceration and its injustice, and, perhaps most important, that the testimony was cathartic for the Japanese American community.

On June 16, 1983, the CWRIC recommended to Congress that individual payments of $20,000 be paid to the more than 60,000 survivors of the camps and that the government issue a formal apology. In addition, the CWRIC proposed the issue of presidential pardons to Fred Korematsu, Gordon Hirabayashi, and Minoru Yasui, whose *coram nobis* cases (petitions to overturn previous convictions) were before U.S. district courts. The CWRIC recommendations formed the basis for the redress bills presented to the House and Senate in 1983, which eventually resulted in passage of the Civil Liberties Act of 1988, providing monetary compensation to survivors of the incarceration and a formal apology from the U.S. government.

Emily Hiramatsu Morishima

Further Reading

Ng, Wendy. *Japanese American Internment During World War II: A History and Reference Guide.* Westport, CT: Greenwood, 2002.

Tateishi, John. "The Japanese American Citizens League and the Struggle for Redress." In *Japanese Americans: From Relocation to Redress,* ed. Roger Daniels, Sandra C. Taylor, and Harry H.L. Kitano. Seattle: University of Washington Press, 1991.

Taylor, Sandra C. "Evacuation and Economic Loss: Questions and Perspectives." In *Japanese Americans: From Relocation to Redress,* ed. Roger Daniels, Sandra C. Taylor, and Harry H.L. Kitano. Seattle: University of Washington Press, 1991.

Coram Nobis Cases (1943, 1944)

The Latin term *coram nobis* means "before us." In law, *coram nobis* refers to cases in which a court is petitioned for a "writ of error" to overturn previous convictions. Specifically, the term is often applied to the reopening of three U.S. Supreme Court cases pertaining to the incarceration of American citizens and residents of Japanese descent during World War II: *Hirabayashi v. United States* (1943), *Yasui v. United States* (1943), and *Korematsu v. United States* (1944). A writ of error *coram nobis* was filed in U.S. district courts on behalf of the respective plaintiffs in January 1983. A relatively obscure form of petition, the writ of *coram nobis* applies only to cases in which a defendant has been convicted and released from custody and to raise errors of facts knowingly withheld by the prosecution.

Convictions and Appeals

On May 9, 1942, Japanese American welder Fred Korematsu did not report to the Tanforan Assembly Center in California with his parents and three brothers as or-

dered by the U.S. Army. Korematsu was arrested three weeks later and charged with violating Public Law 503, requiring adherence to military directives under Executive Order 9066. Found guilty in federal court in September 1942, Korematsu was approached by the American Civil Liberties Union (ACLU) and two other Nisei held in the San Francisco County Jail looking for volunteers to test the exclusion order. Wayne Collins, the attorney assigned to Korematsu's case, filed a demurrer, or request for dismissal of the case, based on a lack of legal foundation. The demurrer charged the government with sixty-nine violations of Korematsu's rights. The judge denied the demurrer and, in a second case, Korematsu was found guilty.

Gordon Hirabayashi, a Seattle-born student pacifist, began his challenge of the exclusion order on May 16, 1942, when he went to the city's Federal Bureau of Investigation office with his lawyer, Arthur Barnett, to deliver a statement titled "Why I Refused to Register for Evacuation." In addition to violating the exclusion order, Hirabayashi was also charged with violating the curfew order imposed on people of Japanese ancestry. He was found guilty of both charges.

A Nisei attorney living in Portland, Oregon, Minoru Yasui deliberately violated the curfew. When his case was brought before Judge James Fee, the court ruled that such a curfew was unconstitutional for American citizens. But because Yasui was an employee of the Japanese consulate, the judge ruled, he had forfeited his U.S. citizenship and was therefore guilty of violating the curfew and classified as an "enemy alien."

Represented by Collins, Fred Korematsu, Gordon Hirabayashi, and Minoru Yasui appeared before the federal court of appeals on February 19, 1943. Collins argued that the civil rights of the Japanese Americans had been violated, lost the appeal, and filed for another appeal to the Supreme Court. In June 1943, the high court issued its ruling against Hirabayashi and Yasui, followed by one against Korematsu in December 1944.

Writs

In 1981, while examining archival documents for his book on *Ex parte Endo,* another World War II Japanese American incarceration case, Peter Irons, a legal historian, discovered that complaints that had been filed in the Korematsu, Hirabayashi, and Yasui cases had been ignored, and he became convinced that a writ of *coram nobis* could get the wartime convictions of Korematsu, Hirabayashi, and Yasui overturned. Their lawyers then filed suit charging that evidence had been suppressed and that the government had "lied" to the Supreme Court in all three cases.

As part of its June 1983 recommendations, the federal Commission on Wartime Relocation and Internment of Civilians (CWRIC) suggested that President Ronald Reagan issue pardons for the *coram nobis* plaintiffs. The CWRIC report proved instrumental in the overturn of their convictions. Judge Marilyn Hall Patel, who granted Korematsu's petition, cited the CWRIC report as justification for her response on October 4, 1983. Yasui's case was the second to be heard, on January 16, 1984. The judge granted the government's request to vacate the original conviction and deny the petition, but Yasui—seeking a finding of government misconduct—appealed that ruling. He died before the arguments could be heard (on November 12, 1986), which rendered the case moot. Gordon Hirabayashi's *coram nobis* petition was heard on May 18, 1984, one month after Patel issued her written opinion on *Korematsu v. United States*. After a two-week hearing, Judge Donald Voorhees ordered that Hirabayashi's evacuation conviction be erased but not the curfew order conviction. Both sides of the case appealed the ruling. Ninth Circuit Court of Appeals Judge Mary Schroeder overturned Voorhees's ruling on the curfew order and ordered him to vacate both convictions; Hirabayashi's curfew order conviction was overturned on January 12, 1988.

Emily Hiramatsu Morishima

Further Reading

Irons, Peter. *Justice at War: The Story of the Japanese-American Internment Cases.* Berkeley: University of California Press, 1993.

Irons, Peter, ed. *Justice Delayed: The Record of the Japanese American Internment Cases.* Middletown, CT: Wesleyan University Press, 1989.

Day of Remembrance

The Day of Remembrance (DOR) is observed in many Japanese American communities across the United States on February 19, the anniversary of President Franklin Roosevelt's signing of Executive Order 9066. Effective February 19, 1942, Executive Order 9066 served as the legal basis for the mass removal and incarceration of more than 112,000 Japanese Americans during World War II. Ceremonies are held across the United States to remember the event and ensure that it never occurs again.

The first Day of Remembrance was held in Seattle on November 25, 1978, conceived by local residents—many of Japanese descent—to attract media attention and develop public support for redress (financial compensation

Members of the Northern California Okinawa Kenjinkai dance troupe get ready to march in a Day of Remembrance parade. Every February 19, Japanese communities across America recall the signing of Executive Order 9066 in 1942, which called for the wartime incarceration of Japanese Americans. *(Associated Press/Marcio Jose Sanchez)*

to survivors and a formal government apology). At the suggestion of Frank Chin, a Chinese American activist, the organizers agreed to hold the event in November rather than February to capitalize on public interest and combat the damage done by Senator S.I Hayakawa (R-CA), who spoke against redress. Chin pitched the event to the ABC's news magazine *20/20* as a "homecoming" story of Japanese Americans returning to the Puyallup fairgrounds, south of Seattle, where their internment began. ABC filmed the event but did not air the footage.

Chin worked with reporter and film producer Frank Abe, Japanese American Citizens League member Henry Miyatake, Kathy Wong of the Seattle Evacuation Redress Committee, and others to plan the day's events. More than 2,000 participants met at Sick's Stadium in Seattle and rode buses to Puyallup, the former site of "Camp Harmony," an assembly center where Japanese Americans were ordered to report before being sent to incarceration camps in other parts of the country. The attendees each donned a yellow tag with their name and family number, replicas of the ones internees wore in 1942. Speakers included incarceration camp memoirists Monica Sone and Shosuke Sasaki; actors and former internees Pat Morita and Mako; Washington State Supreme Court justice Charles Z. Smith, who overturned a decision against a Japanese American lawyer who was refused the right to practice law in the early twentieth century; Gordon Hirabayashi, the plaintiff in a 1943 U.S. Supreme Court case challenging the incarceration order; and former internee Amy Uno Ishii. Having pledged support for redress in October, Mike Lowry, the

Democratic winner of a close contest for a Seattle-area seat in the U.S. House of Representatives, attended the Seattle portion of the event.

Participants could also view arts and crafts made at the camps, take a tour of the site, watch dance performances, observe a slide show, and attend a play. The event received a great deal of positive press coverage and brought the issue of redress back into public discourse. It was the largest gathering of Japanese Americans since the incarceration and served as a powerful mobilizing force for the Japanese American community and the redress movement. By the end of 1978, several other West Coast cities were planning their own Days of Remembrance.

Over the years, communities across the country have held DOR events including lectures, plays, reenactments, and candlelight vigils. Some states and counties have officially recognized February 19 as the Day of Remembrance, and activists have lobbied to make the Day of Remembrance recognized nationally. More recently, on February 5, 2003, Representative Mike Honda of California introduced House Resolution 56 to "support the goals of the Japanese American, German American, and Italian American communities in recognizing a National Day of Remembrance to increase public awareness of the events surrounding the restriction, exclusion, and internment of individuals and families during World War II." On February 13, 2007, the House of Representatives unanimously passed Resolution 122, calling for the National Day of Remembrance as proposed in Honda's resolution.

Emily Hiramatsu Morishima

Further Reading

Niiya, Brian, ed. *Encyclopedia of Japanese American History Updated Edition: An A-to-Z Reference from 1868 to the Present.* New York: Facts on File, 2001.

Shimabukuro, Robert Sadamu. *Born in Seattle: The Campaign for Japanese American Redress.* Seattle: University of Washington Press, 2001.

Diaspora, Japanese

The term "Japanese diaspora" refers to Japanese émigrés and their descendants living abroad—also called Nikkei. Between 1868—the year when Japan ended its 250 years of self-imposed isolation—and 1941—the year World War II began in the Pacific—an estimated 1.65 million people left Japan. As of the early 2000s, some 2.5 million Nikkei resided outside Japan. The largest Japanese populations outside Japan today are located in Brazil (1.5 million), the United States (850,000), Peru (85,000), and Canada (68,000). If less well known than the peoples who made some of the other great movements in world history, overseas Japanese have nonetheless represented an important presence in their home nations.

After opening the country in the late nineteenth century, the Meiji imperial government of Japan sought desperately to industrialize, develop a conscript army, and revamp its economy by means of a draconian tax system. This was to avoid becoming a Western colony, like India or China after the Opium Wars in the 1840s. Instant modernization put great pressure on many segments of society, especially farmers in poor areas who were already struggling to make ends meet. These forces—along with a succession of earthquakes and other natural disasters, several nationwide famines, and fear of the newly instituted military draft—caused many Japanese to seek new homes overseas. Although most planned on returning to Japan after becoming wealthy overseas, few who left actually did come back, as the lives of the first-generation immigrants abroad generally did not turn out to be as prosperous as expected.

Hawaii

Japanese migration to Hawaii began 1868 when the American businessman Eugene M. Van Reed brought 149 Japanese (141 men, six women, and two children) to work on sugar plantations. This marked the beginning of the modern Japanese diaspora. Since these people left in the first year of the Meiji Era (1868–1912), they were called *gannen-mono* ("first-year persons"). Later that year, forty-two Japanese also went to Guam.

In both locations, the migrants were treated little better than slaves, so many ran away before their contracts ended. Thus, the Japanese government halted further labor migration for nearly two decades. Massive Japanese migration to Hawaii did not start until after 1885, when the Japanese government assumed the right to directly protect its immigrants in Hawaii. These workers, often working long hours for low pay, sought better working conditions elsewhere.

North America

After Hawaii was annexed by the United States in 1898, many Japanese re-migrated to the U.S. mainland. In 1900 alone, more than 12,000 Japanese left Hawaii for California and other parts of the mainland, where about 61,000 Japanese were already living. The rapid growth of the Japanese population accelerated anti-Asian discrimination on the West Coast, where feelings against Chinese immigrants already ran deep.

The history of the Japanese in Canada began in 1877, when the young Japanese sailor Manzo Nagano first landed and became a permanent resident. In 1897, a year before the massive influx into California, the Japanese Fishermen's Association was established in Steveston, British Columbia. By the turn of the century, almost 5,000 Japanese were living in Canada. Initially, Japanese migration to Canada was seasonal, as Japanese came to Steveston during the salmon-fishing season and returned to Japan after their catches were processed. However, Japanese workers gradually began taking jobs in the Canaries in British Columbia instead of returning to Japan, becoming de facto permanent residents.

In the early part of the twentieth century, both the United States and Canada signed a number of accords—such as the Gentlemen's Agreement between the U.S. and Japanese governments in 1907–1908—and passed a series of laws that effectively eliminated new Japanese immigration to North America.

During World War II, 112,000 Japanese and their American-born children were relocated to ten internment camps, where they were confined by barbed wire and watchtowers. By the end of the war, some 8,000 Nisei (second-generation) children had been born in the camps. In Canada, more than 21,000 Japanese were moved to isolated locations in the nation's interior. Although the camps were not the prisonlike facilities of those in the United States, some had only tents and no heat during the harsh Canadian winters. In 1988, Japanese Americans and Canadians who were interned during the war received an official apology from their respective governments. Those who were incarcerated and still living received US$20,000 (for Americans) and CD$21,000 (for Canadians).

Latin America

Significant Japanese communities are also found in other parts of the Americas. The Japanese Mexican community began in 1897 with the first group of thirty-five migrants who established the Enomoto colony in Chiapas. The area was purchased by Takeaki Enomoto, creator of the Department of Migration in the new Meiji government (established to promote Japanese emigration to other nations from an overpopulated Japan), as well as the founder of the Japanese-Mexican Colonizer's Company. The Japanese Peruvian community started with 790 Japanese arrivals at the Callao seaport in 1899. This immigration was the result of the Treaty of Peace, Friendship, Commerce, and Navigation between the Peruvian and Japanese governments.

Although the Japanese Peruvian community has suffered great racial discrimination in the decades since, it also produced the first president of a Latin American country of Japanese descent, Alberto Fujimori (served 1990–2000). The Japanese Chilean community began with 120 coal miners in 1903, and the Japanese Argentinean community began with fifty re-migrants from Brazil in 1909.

The Japanese Brazilian community can be traced to the arrival of 781 coffee plantation workers in 1908. In Brazil, Japanese largely took over the jobs held by Afro-Brazilians in the decades after slavery was abolished in 1888. Yet many Japanese were disappointed by life in Brazil, as they found vast differences in terms of working conditions and wages between what they were promised by emigration agents in Japan and what life was actually like on the plantations.

Although most Japanese originally came to Latin America as plantation and agricultural laborers, many in Peru, Argentina, and Chile eventually moved to the cities and developed urban Japanese diasporic communities in the period before World War II. Those who could raise enough capital gravitated toward certain types of business enterprises. In the "Japan towns" of Lima, for example, many Japanese opened barbershops; in Buenos Aires, many became involved in the laundry business.

The growth and development of Japanese communities in Latin America were directly connected to racial discrimination in North America. When Asian immigration to Canada and the United States was outlawed, Japanese emigrants turned to South America and Mexico for new places to settle. For example, the Japanese government started aggressively sending families to Brazil in the 1920s and 1930s, especially to four Japanese government-sponsored villages in São Paulo and Paraná. By the time Brazil closed its doors to Japanese immigrants in 1941, more than 188,000 had entered the country.

Dekasegi Descendants in Japan

The Japanese diaspora includes not only Japanese emigrants who left the country and stayed away permanently, but "returnees" who went back to the homeland after varying periods of time. In the late 1980s, while the Japanese economy was booming, inflation in Latin America was running as high as 1,500 to 2,000 percent in nations such as Brazil and Peru. But an ever-declining birth rate since the 1970s left Japan with a serious labor shortage, especially in the so-called three-k occupations—jobs that were dirty (*kitanai*), dangerous (*kiken*), or difficult (*kitsui*). Government policy makers, believing that Nikkei shared race, language, and culture with Japanese in Japan, concluded that the perfect solution was to let Latin Americans of Japanese ancestry come in to work on temporary visas for one or two years. These people are called *dekasegi* workers, and the vast majority are from Brazil.

It did not take long, however, for both the *dekasegi* workers and the local Japanese to realize that there were clear ethnic differences between these populations. Nonetheless, because of the high wages relative to their home countries, *dekasegi* workers continue to come to Japan, though at a noticeably lower rate than at the height in the early to mid-1990s. (The peak increase, 13.4 percent, was recorded in 1991.) In the first decade of the twenty-first century, there were an estimated 1.3 million *dekasegi* workers in Japan.

Nobuko Adachi

Further Reading

Adachi, Ken. *The Enemy That Never Was: A History of Japanese Canadians.* Toronto: McClelland and Stewart, 1991.

Discover Nikkei. http://www.discovernikkei.org/en.

Gardiner, Harvey C. *Pawns in a Triangle of Hate: The Peruvian Japanese and the United States.* Seattle: University of Washington Press, 1981.

Okihiro, Gary Y. *Cane Fires: The Anti-Japanese Movement in Hawaii 1865–1945.* Philadelphia: Temple University Press, 1991.

Draft Resistance, World War II

Following the Japanese attack on Pearl Harbor in December 1941, Americans of Japanese descent, both alien and citizen, were forced to resettle in ten "War Relocation Camps" under President Franklin Roosevelt's Executive Order 9066. The government issued the directive on the belief that Japanese Americans might harbor loyalty to their home country rather than to the United States and therefore constituted a threat to national security. In 1943, the War Department responded to requests by the Japanese American Citizens League (JACL) to allow Japanese Americans to fight in the U.S. armed forces.

Later, the government instituted a military draft to organize a 5,000-member all-Nisei (second generation) combat unit. Thus, all draft-age Nisei men at the camps were asked to complete a questionnaire that would test their willingness to serve. In particular, questions 27 ("Are you willing to serve in the armed forces of the United States on combat duty, wherever ordered?") and 28 ("Will

you swear unqualified allegiance to the United States of America and faithfully defend the United States from any and all attack by foreign or domestic forces, and foreswear any form of allegiance to the Japanese Emperor, or any other foreign government, power, or organizations?") were phrased to coerce "yes" answers of loyalty or else brand the respondents as traitors. As a result, three separate groups emerged: those answering "no-no," those answering "yes-yes," and those answering "yes-no."

The only relocation center to organize a resistance movement to the military draft was Heart Mountain, in northwestern Wyoming. Formed in February 1943, an internee group called the Heart Mountain Congress of American Citizens protested the registration of Nisei for the U.S. military and objected to the JACL's obvious cooperation with the government. Of the 2,300 eligible men, 126 refused to respond to question 28, 104 provided qualified answers, and 278 replied negatively. The rest who answered "yes" did not intend to comply but campaigned to resist on principle: they had never violated their loyalty to the United States and ought not to have been deprived of their freedom. Ultimately, only thirty-eight Heart Mountain Nisei volunteered, of whom half failed their physical examinations.

The organized resistance at Heart Mountain began with internee Kiyoshi Okamoto, the "Fair Play Committee of One," who, later joined by six other men, conducted "open forums" in the camp to persuade new followers. Ironically, four of the men were ineligible for the draft because they were overage or had families. Nevertheless, they joined the protest with Okamoto and James Omura, editor of the Denver-based newspaper *Rocky Shimpo.* In addition to eighty-five other draft resisters at Heart Mountain, the seven leaders of the Fair Play Committee and Omura were arrested for resisting the draft, but only Omura was found innocent. The seven convictions of the Fair Play Committee leaders were overturned in December 1945.

Draft resisters did surface in other camps, although they were not as effectively organized as the Heart Mountain group; all were duly punished. At Minidoka, Idaho, forty-four draft resisters were tried individually and given two- to three-year sentences at McNeil Island Federal Penitentiary as well as $2,000 fines. At Amache, Colorado, thirty-six resisters were tried individually and sent to Catalina Federal Honor Camp, along with 111 from Poston, Arizona, and five from Topaz, Utah. In addition, there were four from Rohwer and Jerome, Arkansas, eleven from Hawaii, and five from other locations.

Executive Order 9814, issued on December 23, 1946, by President Harry S. Truman set in motion the pardon of 284 Nisei who had violated the Selective Training and Service Act of 1940. Surviving resisters have questioned this total, however, claiming that some names were omitted from the official list. Thus, the total of 315 draft resisters—not all of them officially pardoned—has become the most current estimate.

Gabriella Oldham

Further Reading

Daniels, Roger. *Concentration Camps, North America: Japanese in the United States and Canada During World War II.* Malabar, FL: Robert E. Krieger, 1981.

Hayashi, Bruce Masaru. *Democratizing the Enemy: The Japanese American Internment.* Princeton, NJ: Princeton University Press, 2004.

Kashima, Tetsuden. *Judgment Without Trial: Japanese American Imprisonment During World War II.* Seattle: University of Washington Press, 2003.

Education, Japanese American

The importance placed on education by Japanese Americans has long been recognized by scholars and even the public at large. The first immigrants from Japan understood that education was a key to improving the lives of their children and they pursued that goal vigorously. Cultural factors in Japanese American society—including the emphasis on hard work, sacrifice, and filial obligation—also led to exceptional educational achievements among American-born Japanese. As a result, Japanese Americans came to be seen by the American population at large as a "model" minority group—hardworking, eager to succeed, and wanting to fit into American society. While some of this is stereotype, educational statistics bear out the image of the well-educated Japanese American. According to the 2000 census, roughly 42 percent of Japanese Americans over the age of twenty-five had a college degree or higher, compared with less than 25 percent for the American population as a whole.

Japanese Americans first began arriving in significant numbers in Hawaii and the West Coast in the late nineteenth century; most of them were agricultural laborers and few had much formal education. As with many immigrant groups, Japanese American parents recognized that a better life for their children in America could come only through education. But, like other Asian Americans, the Japanese faced prejudice and discrimination in their first decades in America. In 1906, the San Francisco Board of Education ordered that all Japanese children were to attend segregated schools with Chinese and Korean children. But Japanese Americans had one advantage these other groups did not; their homeland was a rising power in the world, able to better look out for its people living abroad. Japanese American parents petitioned the Japanese government, which protested in turn to the U.S. government. President Theodore Roosevelt forced the San Francisco authorities to back off from their demand and allow Japanese American children to attend normal schools. In return, however, Roosevelt negotiated the Gentlemen's Agreement of 1907–1908, by which the Japanese government stopped allowing laborers to immigrate to the United States.

By the 1920s, many American educators believed that public schools had a duty to integrate immigrant children into American society and to instill the values of democracy. Courses such as history, civics, and geography were the core of these efforts, but informal Americanization attempts were also made. Schools in California and other states with significant Japanese American populations produced patriotic plays and sponsored such events as "Better English Week," to encourage Japanese American students—along with other foreign-born students or students with foreign-born parents—to become more fluent in English, instead of their native language.

Although Japanese American parents generally supported education for their children, they were also concerned about their becoming too "Americanized." As a result, Japanese language schools were opened in many Japanese American communities, beginning with the first in Hawaii in 1892. Intended to supplement the public school curriculum with lessons in written and spoken Japanese, homeland cultural values, and loyalty to Japan and its emperor, the schools conducted most of their classes in evenings and on weekends. By 1920, roughly 20,000 Japanese American students were attending those schools in Hawaii alone, along with smaller numbers on the U.S. mainland.

During the 1920s, many whites saw the schools—with their Japanese nationalist curriculum—as a threat, especially as America began to see Japan as a strategic threat to its power in the Pacific. Municipal and state laws were introduced to close the Japanese language schools, with opponents claiming that the schools interfered with the public school's Americanization mission. Supporters fought back, declaring that the schools promoted family values and other characteristics that made students good American citizens. In 1927, the U.S. Supreme Court in *Farrington v. T. Tokushige* upheld a Hawaiian court decision that declared the anti-Japanese school legislation unconstitutional.

The reprieve was temporary. When American went to war with Japan in December 1941, the schools were closed down and new ones were prohibited from opening in the incarceration camps where West Coast Japanese had been sent for the duration. After the war ended, many, but not all, of the schools reopened. By that time, however, fewer students enrolled. The third generation of Japanese Americans, the Sansei, was more Americanized than their parents, and many of them were anxious to separate themselves from being identified as Japanese. Another factor was the dispersal of Japanese American communities. More and more moved to the suburbs, where they became dispersed, making it more difficult for them to attend the Japanese language schools. The decline continued as newer generations were born, though a modest reversal occurred from the 1960s onward as many Japanese Americans became interested in learning the language of their parents and grandparents to take advantage of Japan's emergence as an economic superpower and major trading partner of the United States.

Meanwhile, public schools were maintained in the incarceration camps of World War II. As the Sansei came of age after the war, their parents continued to stress the importance of education. Although many Nisei (second generation) had attended college before World War II, racial discrimination kept many of them underemployed. The economic boom after the war opened new opportunities for their children. The civil rights movement helped to end discriminatory admittance policies at schools and universities toward Japanese Americans. Many colleges and universities, especially on the West Coast, had significant numbers of Japanese American students in the postwar years. The breakdown of racial barriers extended as well to employment. Japanese Americans with professional and advanced degrees were more likely to become employed at a level appropriate to their education.

By the end of the twentieth century, Japanese Americans were far better educated than the U.S. population as a whole. Yet, at the same time, this most assimilated of Asian American communities was falling behind newer Asian American communities in terms of educational achievement. According to the 2000 census, the 41.9 percent figure for Japanese Americans with college degrees or higher put them no higher than sixth among all major Asian American groups, and several points below the Asian American average of 44.1 percent.

Tim J. Watts

Further Reading

Adler, Susan Matoba. *Mothering, Education, and Ethnicity: The Transformation of Japanese American Culture.* New York: Garland, 1998.

Austin, Allan W. *From Concentration Camp to Campus: Japanese American Students and World War II.* Urbana: University of Illinois Press, 2004.

Morimoto, Toyotomi. *Japanese Americans and Cultural Continuity: Maintaining Language and Heritage.* New York: Garland, 1997.

Yoo, David. *Growing Up Nisei: Race, Generation, and Culture Among Japanese Americans of California, 1924–49.* Urbana: University of Illinois Press, 2000.

Emigration Companies

In the mid-1880s, to relieve the pressures of overpopulation and economic difficulties in rural areas, the Meiji imperial government of Japan actively began encouraging its citizens to work overseas. Indeed, to promote emigration, the government established several quasi-official agencies to help Japanese find employment abroad. Several *toriasukainin* (private immigration agents) in Yokohama and Kobe helped the majority of potential emigrants complete their legal paperwork and obtain passports to migrate to various countries, including the United States and Canada.

In 1891, recognizing the increasing number of Japanese who wanted to work in the new American colony of Hawaii, Taijiro Yoshikawa, vice president of the Nihon Yusen Kaisha steamship company, and Teiichi Sakuma, a prominent Tokyo businessman, established the first private sponsoring firm, called the Nippon Yoshisa Emigration Company. Unlike government agents, the private recruiters not only identified emigrants and processed their papers; they also offered lower fares than the government for passage overseas. Thus, the Japanese government ended its labor emigration efforts in 1894, and a number of private emigration companies immediately sprang up. There were a total of fifty-one by the time the Gentlemen's Agreement of 1907–1908 prohibited further Japanese immigration to the United States.

Besides recruiting from local farms and villages, emigrant companies negotiated with foreign employers regarding jobs and working conditions, and processed all government documents. Thus, agents who had connections with Japanese and foreign officials were able to send their clients abroad quickly and easily. The majority of successful companies, then, had some level or form of involvement from *shizoku* (former samurai) or local politicians. Some emigration agents also published guidebooks about the host nations. For example, Ryo Mizuno, president of the Kokoku Shokumin Emigration Company, wrote *Nambei Toko Annai* (Guide for Moving to South America) in 1906. By 1908, Japanese emigration companies had sent more than 125,000 workers to Hawaii and initiated the first Japanese migrations to Latin America.

Since emigration companies were not regulated, at least at first, some regularly defrauded their clients or put them in difficult or dangerous situations. In 1894, therefore, the Japanese government passed the Emigrant Protection Ordinance (Imin Hogokisoku), followed two years later by the Emigrant Protection Law (Imin Hogoho). These measures placed constraints on the more obvious recruitment abuses by emigration companies, including overcharging on fares to America and misleading immigrants on the kinds of work they could expect to do. Nevertheless, since the legislation focused more on governmental, political, and economic regulations than on emigrant protection, many problems with emigration companies persisted. In 1908, for example, 781 emigrants were recruited by the Kokoku Shokumin Emigration Company to work in Brazil. Being unable to post bond to the Japanese government for their safe passage, the company required the emigrants to do so. Ryo Mizuno collected the funds in Kobe before their departure, telling them that the money would be returned after arriving in São Paulo. These funds were never returned, and the workers were sent to the plantations without any money of their own.

The majority of emigration companies closed after 1908, except for a few that continued to send workers to South America. In 1916, the Morioka Emigration Company, the Toyo Emigration Company, and the Nambei Emigration Company merged to become the Brazil Imin Kumiai (the Brazilian Emigrant Cooperative). It later became a quasi-governmental organization and controlled all Japanese migration to Brazil until World War II.

Nobuko Adachi

Further Reading

Ichioka, Yuji. *The Issei: The World of the First Generation Japanese Immigrants, 1885–1924.* New York: Free Press, 1988.

Moriyama, Alan Takeo. *Imingaisha: Japanese Emigration Companies and Hawai'i 1894–1908.* Honolulu: University of Hawai'i Press, 1985.

Ex parte Endo (1944)

Mitsuye Endo, a government clerk and American-born woman of Japanese descent from Sacramento, California, never appeared at her court trial, but her name is recorded in history as the woman who filed a writ of habeas corpus for release from the relocation camp where she had been imprisoned during World War II based only on her Japanese ancestry. Her case was appealed to the U.S. Supreme Court, which ruled in her favor in a unanimous decision on December 14, 1944. As opposed to other cases regarding the World War II internment camps, such as *Korematsu v. United States* (handed down on the same day in 1944), in which the high court ruled that the incarceration of Japanese Americans was constitutional as a wartime security measure, the justices in *Ex parte Endo* ruled unanimously that the government could not incarcerate someone whose loyalty the government had effectively conceded.

Endo was a twenty-two-year-old civil service stenographer for the California State Highway Commission in Sacramento, when she was ordered, under the provisions of Executive Order 9066, to leave her home and her job on May 15, 1942, and be removed to the Tule Lake Relocation Camp in Northern California. Under Public Proclamations No. 1 and 2 of the order, the capital of the state was classified as a sensitive military zone. All Japanese nationals and Japanese Americans within the zone were put under dusk-to-dawn curfew and ordered to areas deemed less security-sensitive.

Although Mitsuye Endo was an American citizen and her brother a member of the U.S. Army, she was still viewed as a military risk. After waiting to see the outcome of the new law, she filed a writ of habeas corpus (a demand for the government to present the evidence for an arrest) while in detention in July 1942, asking the court to grant her freedom and release from the camp. Two earlier cases had been filed in California state courts citing the same grounds for release; in both cases, the petitioners were American citizens of Japanese descent who had never been charged with a crime. The American Civil Liberties Union filed petitions for release on behalf of other internees, but it was unable to bring the cases to trial. Endo would be the federal test case.

Endo's attorney argued that her detention was illegal due to the length of time she had been detained without charges filed, the lack of due process during the evacuation, federal abuse of the War Powers Act in creating the detention facilities, and finally, violation of the Equal Protection Clause of the Fourteenth Amendment (because German Americans and Italian Americans, members of other ethnic groups whose home countries were officially at war with the United States, had not been detained in the same manner). The lower courts denied Endo's petition, but the Supreme Court agreed on all counts. Endo then launched the formal process to show that, indeed, she was a citizen whose loyalty could not be questioned. Before the Supreme Court ruling could be put in effect, the camp ordered Endo released based on the citizenship review. The high court ruling nevertheless provided a strong legal precedent for subsequent court challenges.

Pamela Lee Gray

Further Reading

Irons, Peter, ed. *Justice Delayed: The Record of the Japanese American Internment Cases.* Middletown, CT: Wesleyan University Press, 1989.

Rehnquist, William H. *All the Laws but One: Civil Liberties in Wartime.* New York: Alfred A. Knopf, 1998.

Executive Order 9066 (1942)

Executive Order 9066 was signed into law by President Franklin D. Roosevelt on February 19, 1942, two months after the Japanese attack on Pearl Harbor. The order gave broad powers to the federal government to create military zones, as well as the authority to remove individuals—largely American citizens and residents of Japanese descent—from these areas based on alleged threats to national security.

Even before the order was issued, the government was targeting persons of Japanese descent as potential national security threats. In the immediate aftermath of Pearl Harbor, the Federal Bureau of Investigation (FBI) had begun identifying Japanese American community leaders in California, Oregon, and Washington—states designated as critical national security zones. The leaders included editors, teachers, church officials, and community organizers, who were promptly arrested and taken to U.S. Department of Justice detention centers, where they were held without bail, without formal charges, and without knowing what crime they were accused of committing.

Once the order was issued, the Western Defense Command and Lieutenant General John L. DeWitt, under delegated authority of the secretary of war, issued a series of public proclamations that instituted a curfew and placed travel restrictions on all Japanese Americans in Washington, Oregon, and California. The long Pacific coastline—exposed to potential Japanese attack and with its many defense and weapons industries, key military installations, deep harbors, and abundant natural resources needed for war industries—made these states a region of strategic military importance. By public proclamation, notices were ordered posted in these states requiring all Japanese aliens and Japanese Americans to report to assembly areas called "relocation centers." During the "evacuation," families were allowed to bring only personal goods that could be carried. The evacuation of Japanese nationals and Japanese Americans began in the spring of 1942 and eventually placed more than 112,000 people in ten camps located in remote regions: Manzanar and Tule Lake, California; Amache, Colorado; Minidoka, Idaho; Topaz, Utah; Heart Mountain, Wyoming; Rohwer and Jerome, Arkansas; and Gila River and Poston, Arizona. All facilities were surrounded by barbed wire and military guard towers.

The Western Growers Protective Association and the White American Nurserymen of Los Angeles, hoping to eliminate competition from Japanese farmers and nursery owners, were major proponents of the government's actions. Notably, Executive Order 9066 was not utilized to relocate Hawaiian Japanese, who made up nearly one-third of the population on the islands where the initial military attack had occurred.

Within a few years, U.S. public opinion began to change about the need for and justice of incarcerating persons who had demonstrated no disloyalty to the United States. Secretary of War Henry Stimson, for one, withdrew his support of the order in 1944, blaming the program on inaccurate and misleading information and public hysteria. In the decades after the war, the order came to be seen as a blot on America's reputation for civil liberties and personal freedom. The Japanese American Citizens League (JACL) began a campaign in 1978 to redress the loss of freedom and property during the relocation. The nine-member federal Commission on Wartime Relocation and Internment of Civilians (CWRIC) met from 1980 to 1982 to investigate the effects of the order, conditions in the camps, and appropriate remedies. In 1988, President Ronald Reagan signed the Civil Liberties Act (also called the Redress Act), which provided monetary compensation of up to $20,000 for the remaining survivors of the camps, as well as an official apology from the federal government. As enacted on August 10, 1988, the text of the legislation read as follows:

> The Congress recognizes that, as described in the Commission on Wartime Relocation and Internment of Civilians, a grave injustice was done to both citizens and permanent residents of Japanese ancestry by the evacuation, relocation, and internment of civilians during World War II.
>
> As the Commission documents, these actions were carried out without adequate security reasons and without any acts of espionage or sabotage documented by the Commission, and were motivated largely by racial prejudice, wartime hysteria, and a failure of political leadership.
>
> The excluded individuals of Japanese ancestry suffered enormous damages, both material and intangible, and there were incalculable losses in education and job training, all of which resulted in significant human suffering for which appropriate compensation has not been made.

For these fundamental violations of the basic civil liberties and constitutional rights of these individuals of Japanese ancestry, the Congress apologizes on behalf of the Nation.

Pamela Lee Gray

Further Reading

Conrat, Maisie. *Executive Order 9066: The Internment of 110,000 Japanese Americans.* Los Angeles: University of California Press, 1992.

Daniels, Roger. *Concentration Camps, North America: Japanese in the United States and Canada During World War II.* Melbourne, FL: Robert E. Krieger, 1993.

Robinson, Greg. *By Order of the President: FDR and the Internment of Japanese Americans.* Cambridge, MA: Harvard University, 2001.

Exile and Incarceration: Japanese Americans in World War II

In December 1941, American's abrupt entry into World War II led to one of the largest programs of forced removal and incarceration of individuals in the nation's history. More than 112,000 persons of Japanese ancestry were removed from their homes in the states of California, Oregon, Washington, and western Arizona to ten "internment camps" located in isolated, desolate areas of the United States. Two-thirds of those individuals who were forced to move were U.S. citizens.

Within days of the bombing of Pearl Harbor, the Federal Bureau of Investigation arrested more than 1,000 Japanese community leaders, Buddhist priests, and Japanese language teachers. Without due process, they were imprisoned in Department of Justice Internment Camps and Detention Centers located in Idaho, Montana, North Dakota, New Mexico, and Texas. In addition, the U.S. government ordered a nighttime curfew and enacted measures to restrict the movement of persons of Japanese ancestry in the Western area of the United States. On February 19, 1942, President Franklin D. Roosevelt issued Executive Order 9066, which authorized the Department of War to take steps necessary to provide for the national security of the United States while the country was at war. The order eventually led to the development of an evacuation and removal program for all persons of Japanese ancestry residing on the West Coast of the United States.

The Japanese American population on Hawaii, a U.S.

territory since 1900, was not subject to the incarceration. Japanese accounted for 37 percent of the population in the islands, and almost 75 percent had been born in Hawaii. Although martial law was imposed on the islands, and Hawaii's Japanese were watched closely, military officials there did not believe a mass evacuation program would be possible for the islands. Moreover, Hawaii's Japanese population was needed to help rebuild the islands, and there was fear that the economy would collapse if the entire population was removed.

Causes of Evacuation

The mass evacuation and incarceration program was preceded by long-standing anti-Asian sentiment that had its early beginnings with Chinese immigrants, resulting in the Chinese Exclusion Act in 1882. Japanese immigrants began arriving in larger numbers beginning in the 1880s, and initially they were welcomed and viewed more favorably than the Chinese. Within a short period of time, however, Japanese immigrants experienced various forms of discrimination that included the inability to obtain naturalized U.S. citizenship, formal and informal segregation, and prohibitions against interracial marriage. In 1907–1908, the Gentlemen's Agreement was negotiated between Japan and the United States, effectively halting any new immigration of Japanese laborers to the mainland. In 1913, California passed the nation's first alien land law, which prohibited any "alien ineligible for citizenship"—including Japanese and other Asian farmers—from buying or leasing land. Nine other states followed with similar land laws in subsequent years. By 1924, U.S. immigration laws prohibited further Japanese immigration, thereby curtailing the growth of the Japanese American community. Nevertheless, Japanese immigrants were able to form substantial settlements throughout the western United States and in Hawaii.

Despite the limitations on alien land ownership, a substantial number of Japanese on the West Coast made their living in agricultural work. Many grew labor-intensive specialty crops such as strawberries, deciduous fruits, and cut flowers. They were highly successful in these markets, which incurred the intense hostility of competing white growers. As stated by a spokesman for a group called the Grower-Shipper Vegetable Association, "If all the Japs were removed tomorrow, we'd never miss them in two weeks, because the white farmers can take over and produce everything the Japs grow. And we don't want them back when the war ends, either."

Popular anti-Japanese sentiment fueled the movement toward enacting a removal and evacuation program for Japanese aliens and U.S. citizens who lived on the

The Manzanar War Relocation Center, located in the Owens Valley of Southern California, was one of ten incarceration sites for Japanese Americans during World War II. Manzanar housed up to 10,000 detainees from March 1942 to November 1945. *(Library of Congress)*

West Coast. The region was viewed as particularly vulnerable to possible invasion by Japan. At the same time, government intelligence reports conducted before Pearl Harbor suggested that the Japanese in the United States did not represent an internal military threat. According to the 1941 Munson Report (named after Curtis Munson, the State Department official who wrote it), "For the most part the local Japanese are loyal to the United States or, at worst, hope that by remaining quiet they can avoid concentration camps or irresponsible mobs. We do not believe that they would be at least any more disloyal than any other racial group in the United States." The Munson Report was largely ignored by the higher military officials who advised President Roosevelt and his cabinet and supported the removal of all Japanese to a type of concentration camp.

Decades later, in the 1980s, the U.S. government appointed a commission to investigate the World War II evacuation and internment program. According to the Commission on Wartime Relocation and Internment of Civilians (CWRIC), the underlying causes of the evacuation were race prejudice fueled by wartime hysteria and a failure of leadership at the top levels of government. More recent research has revealed that plans for the evacuation and imprisonment of Japanese Americans had been considered long before the outbreak of World War II.

Evacuation and Assembly Centers

By March 1942, Japanese throughout California, Oregon, and Washington were ordered to leave their homes. They first reported to an evacuation center and then were moved to a short-term facility called an as-

sembly center. They were allowed to bring two suitcases and bedding items; everything else they owned had to be either stored or sold. Some communities were given as little as twenty-four to forty-eight hours to dispose of their property, pack their clothes, and report to an evacuation center.

By May 1942, most of the West Coast Japanese were either living in assembly centers or had voluntarily relocated to areas outside the region to avoid being relocated. The assembly centers were built at fairgrounds and racetracks; stalls once occupied by horses and other livestock now housed families. The conditions were barely adequate in terms of housing and food. Attempts to establish schools and other activities for adults and children proved short-lived, as there was a great deal of uncertainty as to how long they would be confined there. Within a few months, people began to leave the assembly centers, moved by bus and train to the more permanent relocation centers. By the fall of 1942, all of the assembly centers were closed.

Life in the Camps

Ten internment camps were erected in the states of Arizona, California, Colorado, Idaho, Arkansas, Utah, and Wyoming. Selected for their geographic isolation, these facilities were the size of small cities and towns. Attempts were made to settle entire communities in the same camps. Thus, for example, most of the Japanese

Assembly Centers, 1942

Assembly Center	Population	Dates Open, 1942
Puyallup, Washington	7,390	April 28 to September 12
Portland, Oregon	3,676	May 2 to September 10
Marysville, California	2,451	May 8 to June 29
Sacramento, California	4,739	May 6 June 26
Tanforan, California	7,816	April 28 to October 13
Stockton, California	4,271	May 10 to October 17
Turlock, California	3,661	April 30 to August 12
Salinas, California	3,586	April 27 to July 4
Merced, California	4,508	May 6 to September 15
Pinedale, California	4,792	May 7 to July 23
Fresno, California	5,120	May 6 to October 30
Tulare, California	4,978	April 20 to September 4
Santa Anita, California	18,719	March 27 to October 27
Pomona, California	5,434	May 7 to August 24
Mayer, Arizona	245	May 7 to June 2
Manzanar, California*	9,837	March 21 to June 2

*Manzanar was transferred to the War Relocation Authority for use as an internment camp.

Source: Commission on Wartime Relocation and Internment of Civilians 1982:138.

Relocation Centers, 1942–1945

Center	Location	Population	Date Opened	Date Closed
Topaz	Utah	8,130	September 11, 1942	October 31, 1945
Poston	Arizona	17,814	May 5, 1942	November 28, 1945
Gila River	Arizona	13,348	July 20, 1942	November 10, 1945
Granada	Colorado	7,318	August 27, 1942	October 15, 1945
Heart Mountain	Wyoming	10,767	August 12, 1942	November 10, 1945
Jerome	Arkansas	8,497	October 6, 1942	June 30, 1944
Manzanar	California	10,056	June 1, 1942	November 21, 1945
Minidoka	Idaho	9,397	August 10, 1942	October 2, 1945
Rohwer	Arkansas	8,475	September 18, 1942	November 30, 1945
Tule Lake	California	18,789	May 27, 1942	March 20, 1946

Source: War Relocation Authority, U.S. Department of Interior 1946:197.

Americans living in the San Francisco Bay Area were relocated to Topaz in Utah; those living in Los Angeles were sent to Manzanar; and those living in Oregon or Washington State were sent to Tule Lake in Northern California, or Minidoka, Idaho.

The facilities at the relocation centers were spartan at best. Living quarters consisted of barracks built according to army specifications: 20 feet (6 meters) by 100 feet (30 meters) long and divided into four to six rooms. Each family lived in a single room with a coal-burning stove for warmth; there were no walls or separate bedrooms for individuals or couples. Food was served in communal mess halls throughout the camp complex. Laundry washrooms, shower facilities, toilets, and a recreational hall were also communal. In a number of ways, the experience disrupted traditional family life and personal privacy, as internees no longer ate meals together as a family and lacked privacy in their living quarters and surroundings. Their homes were now surrounded by a barbed-wire fence, with armed military guards in towers looking over them.

Over time, however, internal self-government bodies emerged, schools were established, daily newspapers published, and Buddhist and Christian religious services conducted, as internees tried to make their lives as "normal" as possible. Community councils, made up of Nisei (second-generation) internees, were set up to help distribute supplies and act as liaisons with military authorities. Issei (those born in Japan) were barred from leadership but, as respected elders, had a role to play as well, serving as unofficial advisers to the community councils. Meanwhile, some individuals began to work for the U.S. government as teachers in the schools and medical personnel in the hospital and infirmary. Others were hired to work outside the camps as agricultural field workers because of the shortage of labor due to the war.

In 1943, the U.S. government initiated a program to review the loyalty of Japanese Americans by means of a questionnaire administered to all adults in the camp. Two questions among many would serve as the test: "Are you willing to serve in the armed forces of the United States on combat duty, wherever ordered?" and "Will you swear unqualified allegiance to the United States of America and faithfully defend the United States from any or all attack by foreign or domestic forces, and forswear any form of allegiance or obedience to the Japanese Emperor, or any other foreign government, power, or organization?" The responses would be used to determine loyalty, willingness to serve in the military, and freedom to leave camp to settle elsewhere. The questionnaire naturally generated a great deal of controversy among the inmates. Those who did not respond affirmatively to the questionnaire (referred to as "no-nos") were moved to the Tule Lake camp, redesignated as a segregation center.

The internment camps were not without their internal conflicts and problems. Several experienced riots and uprisings (Manzanar, Tule Lake). An internee was shot at Topaz (Utah) and at Gila River (Arizona). Camp living was not without conflict as tensions erupted over the living conditions, shortage of food and supplies, and general leadership within the community. Disruptions continued as the months and years of imprisonment took their toll on the morale of many of those incarcerated.

The U.S. armed forces reinstated the draft for Nisei men, some of whom had earlier volunteered for the all-Japanese 442nd Regimental Combat Team. The government's initial hopes of finding thousands of volunteers were never realized, however, as only about 1,000 camp Nisei signed up. In the end, nonincarcerated Hawaiian Nisei, recruited into the 100th Army Battalion, which was later incorporated into the 442nd, were needed to create a full regiment. Members of both units received special awards and citations for bravery in combat. In addition, Nisei served in military intelligence, working as translators and interrogators of Japanese prisoners of war. Many Japanese American soldiers served while their families remained in relocation centers.

Others resisted the draft. At the Heart Mountain Relocation Center in Wyoming, eighty-five Nisei resisted conscription—the largest number of draft resisters from all ten internment centers. Although many felt a patriotic duty to their country, they felt they could not serve in the armed forces while their families remained incarcerated in camps. The men were tried in federal court, found guilty of avoiding the draft, and sentenced to three years of federal prison. Although they received a pardon from President Harry S. Truman after the war, they were stigmatized as unpatriotic within the Japanese American community for decades longer.

By the last years of the war, with some Nisei men having joined the military or been drafted, and many whose loyalty questionnaires had been cleared having left for jobs or college, camp populations had dwindled. Only young children, their parents, and elderly people were left in the camps; many of the able-bodied had left.

Camp Closing, Resettlement, and Redress

By late 1944, several cases challenging the legality of the evacuation and curfew orders were heard by the U.S. Supreme Court. Three individuals—Gordon Hirabayashi, Minoru Yasui, and Fred Korematsu—challenged the legality of the Japanese American internment and relocation program. Although the cases were complex and differed in several aspects, the court essentially ruled that the curfew laws, as well as the evacuation orders, were necessary as national security in wartime and trumped individual rights. In the case of *Ex parte Endo* (1944), however, the high court ruled that the government could not keep a U.S. citizen in camp if that person had signed a loyalty review affirmatively, since the government had already declared that someone who signed such an oath was, by definition, not a security threat. Shortly thereafter, the War Relocation Authority announced that the internment camps would be closing. Tule Lake was the last to close, in March 1946.

The government plan for resettlement encouraged many Japanese Americans to move to communities where they could assimilate and blend in easily. Thus, during and after the war, Japanese American communities grew in places such as Chicago, Denver, and other midwestern and East Coast cities. Still, many Japanese Americans returned to the West Coast homes and communities they had left at the outbreak of war. Prejudice against the Japanese was evident in many of these communities, and those who returned had to rebuild their lives with few resources and in a resistant atmosphere.

Within a few years after the end of World War II,

scholars began to analyze the causes and consequences of the mass evacuation and removal program. It was clear that politicians, media, and economic interests fostered an anti-Japanese climate that contributed to the support of the evacuation program. More than that, however, Japanese Americans themselves were limited in their ability to voice their concerns and resistance to the government's policy. Though the vast majority of the population cooperated with the removal, some did challenge the program. Their resistance, whether in the form of court challenges, resistance to the draft, or reluctance to respond affirmatively to the loyalty questionnaire, suggests that there were many who understood that their personal rights and civil liberties were at stake. Later, in the 1960s, Japanese American advocacy organizations such as the Japanese American Citizens League (JACL) would cite the incarceration program to protest cold war laws that called for the detention of alleged subversives, ultimately leading to the 1971 repeal of part of the Internal Security Act of 1950.

After the war, Japanese Americans received financial compensation for their material and economic losses resulting from the evacuation. In reality, the actual dollar amount was nowhere near the real cost of the losses. In the 1970s, a movement began to call for an investigation and study of the Japanese American internment camp experience. During the 1980s, the Commission on Wartime Relocation and Internment of Civilians (CWRIC) heard testimony from Japanese Americans and Alaskan natives who were moved and incarcerated in camps during World War II. As a result of their study, the commission recommended some form of redress and compensation from the federal government for those who had been forcibly relocated during the war. In addition to reparations of $20,000 per surviving person, the commission recommended a formal apology from the U.S. government. The Redress Bill made its way through Congress and was signed into law as the Civil Liberties Act of 1988 by President Ronald Reagan. Thus, Japanese Americans succeeded in mobilizing and using the very system that had imprisoned them to redress the wrongs of the past.

While the Redress Bill offered a sense of closure for many, the emotional and social effects of incarceration would take much longer to resolve. In the decades since, as a community and as individuals, Japanese Americans have had to rebuild their sense of identity and cultural pride shattered by physical dislocation and the stigma associated with incarceration.

Wendy Ng

Further Reading

Commission on Wartime Relocation and Internment of Civilians. *Personal Justice Denied*. Washington, DC: Government Printing Office, 1982.

Crost, Lyn. *Honor by Fire: Japanese Americans at War in Europe and the Pacific.* Novato, CA: Presidio, 1994.

Daniels, Roger. *Concentration Camps U.S.A.: Japanese Americans and World War II.* New York: Holt, Rinehart, and Winston, 1971.

Grodzins, Morton. *Americans Betrayed: Politics and the Japanese American Evacuation.* Chicago: University of Chicago Press, 1949.

Hatamiya, Leslie T. *Righting a Wrong: Japanese Americans and the Passage of the Civil Liberties Act of 1988.* Palo Alto, CA: Stanford University Press, 1993.

Irons, Peter. *Justice at War.* New York: Oxford University Press, 1983.

Kashima, Tetsuden. *Judgment Without Trial: Japanese American Imprisonment During World War II.* Seattle: University of Washington Press, 2003.

Ng, Wendy. *Japanese American Internment During World War II: A History and Reference Guide.* Westport, CT: Greenwood, 2002.

War Relocation Authority, U.S. Department of Interior. *WRA: A Story of Human Conservation.* Washington, DC: Government Printing Office, 1946.

Family Life, Japanese American

In the late nineteenth century, when the first Japanese immigrants began arriving in America, Japan was the most modernized and Westernized country in Asia. Coming from such a country, Japanese American families, from the beginning, tended to be more like mainstream American families than did other immigrant Asians, and acculturated more quickly to the nuclear family household norm. Nevertheless, there were subtle differences between Japanese and mainstream American households in the early years of Japanese immigration. Parents tended to exercise more control over their children, for example, and husbands tended to hold more authority over their wives. As one of the oldest immigrant communities—albeit one that has seen less immigration of newcomers in recent years—Japanese American families, along with the large number of American families that mix Japanese with non-Japanese, have become perhaps the most Americanized and acculturated of all Asian American families in the early twenty-first century.

Social modernization began in Japan long before it did in other Asian countries, as the importance of lineage-based clans—largely confined to single villages—abated by the sixteenth century and gave way to smaller extended kin families living in more dispersed locations. By the late nineteenth century, under the impact of rapid urbanization and industrialization, the nuclear family had become the norm in Japanese culture, with only the eldest son and his family living in the parental household or on parental land. Thus, most Japanese immigrants found it easy to acculturate to American family norms—at least once they were able to establish families.

Most early Japanese immigrants were single males who came to Hawaii and the West Coast in the late nineteenth and early twentieth centuries and did manual farm labor. Once settled down and making enough money to marry, they began to look to the homeland for a spouse; most turned to their families to find brides for them in the Japanese tradition. Because it was risky to go back—for fear of being drafted into the Japanese military or being denied reentry into the United States—a variant on the arranged marriage system evolved, whereby pictures were exchanged between America and Japan. The flow of so-called picture brides corrected an early gender imbalance in the Japanese American community much sooner than similar imbalances were overcome in other major Asian immigrant groups—the Chinese and Filipinos—and hastened the development of a full family life. By 1930, more than half of all Japanese Americans were members of the Nisei generation—the second generation, or those born in America.

As was the case for most American immigrant groups, an estrangement emerged between more traditional-minded Japanese-born parents and their more individualistic American-born or American-raised children. The estrangement was particularly acute among teenagers. While Japanese parents traditionally dote on their young children, they often demand a high level of obedience and achievement from their older children. Indeed, Japanese culture places great emphasis on four virtues: respect toward elders; humility; helping others, particularly family members; and determination to achieve one's goals despite hardships and obstacles. Japanese teenagers saw their white compatriots enjoying a carefree life—but often found it denied to *them*.

Exacerbating tensions in the emerging Japanese family of the 1930s was the political climate. As World War II approached, relations between the United States and Japan grew more hostile. Many Japanese parents felt that they might have to return their families to the homeland and told their children not to become too attached to the American way of life. Many enrolled their children in Japanese language schools to inculcate not just the Japanese tongue but Japanese culture and values as well. But the emphasis placed on tradition and homeland values in these schools rubbed many Americanized children the wrong way, and Japanese parents began complaining of disrespect and the lack of a sense of duty among their teenaged children.

Internment during World War II only added to the

tensions, as families were forced to live together in barracks with numerous other families. Many older Japanese American children blamed their parents for the incarceration. Many of the youth felt it was their parents' seeming unwillingness to acculturate to American values that had gotten the whole community into trouble in the first place. Youths also tended to socialize with their peers in the camps, engaging in sports and other activities rather than staying in crowded barracks with their families.

Upon release from the camps near and after the end of World War II, Japanese Americans of all ages were eager to blend in, especially as they tended to settle not in traditional Japanese enclaves but in mixed neighborhoods. Education and acculturation were emphasized. As the Nisei generation came of age to marry, many chose romantic partners rather than spouses chosen by their parents. Thus, by the time the Sansei—third generation—came of age in the 1950s and 1960s, Japanese families were among the most acculturated and accepted of all racial minorities, especially because their high levels of education and income placed them solidly in the middle class. Like their Nisei parents, many Sansei, too, were eager to blend into the larger American culture, especially in the conformist 1950s. But among the Yonsei—fourth-generation Japanese Americans—there has been a new desire to reconnect with cultural roots, though most thoroughly accept mainstream American values about the family, including more autonomy for children and more decision-making power for wives.

James Ciment and Chellammal Vaidyanathan

Further Reading

Fukei, Budd. *The Japanese American Story.* Minneapolis, MN: Dillon, 1976.

Kitano, Harry H.L. *Japanese Americans: The Evolution of a Subculture.* 2nd ed. Englewood Cliffs, NJ: Prentice-Hall, 1976.

Peterson, William. *Japanese Americans: Oppression and Success.* New York: Random House, 1971.

Simpson, Caroline Chung. *An Absent Presence: Japanese Americans in Postwar American Culture, 1945–1960.* Durham, NC: Duke University Press, 2001.

Spickard, Paul R. *Japanese Americans: The Formation and Transformations of an Ethnic Group.* New York: Twayne, 1996.

442nd Regimental Combat Team

The most decorated unit of its size in the U.S. Army during World War II, the roughly 4,000-strong 442nd Regimental Combat Team consisted of Japanese Americans, mostly from Hawaii and some recruited from the internment camps where Japanese were incarcerated during the war. The existence of the unit, which fought on the European front, was cited by some in the army and the Japanese American community as undermining the legal justification for the camps. That is to say, if Japanese Americans were deemed loyal enough to serve in the military, they should not be considered a threat to national security.

The U.S. government created the 442nd Regimental Combat Team in February 1943, after the fear of Japanese Americans had largely subsided. As an active unit, it was composed of Japanese American citizens who had volunteered to fight or had been drafted from incarceration camps in various parts of the United States. Backing the decision to create an all-Japanese American fighting unit, President Franklin D. Roosevelt declared, "Americanism was not, and never was, a matter of race and ancestry"—a contradiction to his order to incarcerate 112,000 Japanese Americans whose loyalty had never been questioned.

Out of these contradictions, the 442nd emerged from a group of Japanese American National Guardsmen in Hawaii who sought to demonstrate their loyalty by fighting for their country. The idea was promoted by General Delos Emmons, the U.S. Army commander for Hawaii, and on February 1, 1943, the government reversed its previous ban on Japanese American volunteers or draftees. Beginning their recruitment efforts in the

The 442nd Regimental Combat Team, a U.S. Army unit made up primarily of Japanese Americans, trained at Fort Shelby, Mississippi (above), and served with distinction in Europe. Twenty-one members won the Medal of Honor. *(Al Fenn/ Time & Life Pictures/Getty Images)*

internment camps themselves, military officials sought its first enlistees at the facility in Minidoka, Idaho, which had the reputation of a "model camp," in the winter of 1943. Camp administrators encouraged volunteers by suggesting that it would be a way to prove their loyalty. Whereas the government hoped to enlist 3,600 volunteers from the camps, only about 1,000 actually signed up. Thus, the unit was filled largely by Nisei volunteers from Hawaii, who had never been incarcerated, and draftees from the camps.

One of the primary debates concerning the 442nd was segregation. The Japanese American's Citizen's League (JACL) felt Japanese Americans should have the opportunity to serve on an equal basis with white soldiers. Military officials and the Roosevelt administration argued that a separate Japanese American unit would be a better way to demonstrate the community's loyalty to the public at large, as a few thousand Japanese scattered among millions of other soldiers would go unnoticed. The government also had ulterior motives for a segregated unit, as it could, and did, use it to reap positive public relations.

Upon returning from Europe to their shattered communities after the war, the 442nd Regimental Combat Unit received a well-deserved hero's welcome from family members and friends. Members of the unit had fought in grueling campaigns in Italy before moving to combat in France that included the well-known liberation of Bruyères and the battle to save the "Lost Battalion" at Biffontaine. Among the many honors bestowed on the unit were seven Presidential Unit Citations for extraordinary heroism. Indeed, the 442nd earned a reputation as the most decorated unit of its size in the U.S. Army during World War II. It suffered a total of 9,486 casualties in its campaigns in Italy and France. The 442nd and the 100th Infantry Battalion, which the former eventually absorbed, received 18,143 individual decorations, including a Congressional Medal of Honor, forty-seven Distinguished Service Crosses, 350 Silver Stars, and more than 3,600 Purple Hearts.

Nevertheless, the unit's homecoming was not entirely positive. Many of the soldiers resented draft resisters in the camp, whom they felt had undermined their efforts to convince the public that the Japanese American community was loyal to the United States. It would take nearly half a century for a full reconciliation to take place, as veterans of the 442nd issued an official declaration in August 1998 saying the draft resisters had been heroes of another type. By refusing to enter the armed forces of a country that incarcerated them because of their ethnic background, the declaration stated, they had fought an equally important battle to uphold civil rights and liberties.

Renee Lavin

Further Reading

Daniels, Roger. *Asian America: Chinese and Japanese in the United States Since 1850*. Seattle: University of Washington Press, 1988.

Muller, Eric L. *Free to Die for Their Country: The Story of the Japanese American Draft Resisters in World War II*. Chicago: University of Chicago Press, 2001.

Furuya, Masajiro (1862–1938)

Masajiro Furuya was a well-known Issei (first-generation) banker, merchant, and manufacturer in the Pacific Northwest during the early twentieth century. While most Issei businessmen operated on a small scale, Masajiro Furuya built and ran a large enterprise and was considered one of the leading entrepreneurs on the West Coast—important enough to be featured in "Who's Who in Washington State" as early as 1927.

Furuya was born on November 7, 1862, in Yamanashi Prefecture, where he had earned his teacher's credentials, served in the military for three years, and apprenticed as a tailor when he began planning to immigrate to America. In 1890, at the age of twenty-eight, Furuya made his long-awaited journey across the Pacific, landed in Vancouver, British Columbia, and traveled south to Seattle, Washington. During his first year in America, Furuya worked in Seattle as a tailor and then traveled to Chicago and St. Louis, where he took a job in a grocery store. In 1892, he returned to Seattle, where he opened a Japanese grocery store of his own and worked as a tailor out of the back.

As Japanese immigration to the Pacific Northwest increased, Furuya's grocery store grew into a department store in 1900. As he expanded into other retail goods, the M. Furuya Company came to occupy a six-story building in downtown Seattle. At the store, customers could find not only Japanese foods but art objects and other imported goods. Doing business in wholesale as well as retail imports and exports, Furuya employed an army of traveling salesmen to take orders from rural areas in the Pacific Northwest. The Furuya salesmen visited sawmills, railroads, and other facilities that employed Japanese immigrants, taking orders and returning to deliver the goods. As a result of these contacts, Furuya started a labor brokerage business for a local sawmill on Bainbridge Island, Washington, serving as a liaison between the mill and Japanese immigrant labor by recruiting newcomers looking for work.

Furuya's business was profitable in part because he paid his employees inordinately low wages. As members of the Japanese American community, most of his employees were unable to obtain jobs in white-owned companies and were forced to accept the wages Furuya offered. He also exacted strict discipline and loyalty from his employees, who referred to him as "Captain." A devout Christian and member of Seattle First Methodist Church, Furuya strongly encouraged his employees to adopt the Christian faith and conducted daily inspirational meetings. Like Furuya himself, they worked on Sundays and had no vacations. Some employees lived on the first floor of a boardinghouse he operated in Seattle; the Furuya family lived upstairs.

With the number of immigrants from Japan continuing to expand, Furuya's business grew rapidly on both sides of the ocean. By the end of the 1920s, he was a millionaire. Furuya stores opened in Portland and Tacoma, Washington; Vancouver, British Columbia; and Kobe and Yokohama, Japan. Aside from his mercantile trade business, Masajiro Furuya became active in banking as well, establishing the Japanese Commercial Bank in Seattle in 1907, purchasing control of two faltering banks in 1914 and 1923, and in 1928 consolidating the three into the Pacific Commercial Bank—also located in the Furuya Building. Other enterprises included the Gudeware Manufacturing Company, which produced suits and coats for women during World War II, and a popular summer destination for Seattle's Japanese community called the Furuya Resort house, complete with Japanese-style bathhouse and expansive grounds for recreation.

The Great Depression was Furuya's undoing, as his banking and commercial enterprises failed and the business went bankrupt on October 23, 1931. Like other Issei, Furuya was never eligible for U.S. citizenship. Estranged from Seattle's Japanese American community because of money owed after the bank losses, Furuya moved to Los Angeles and then returned to Yokohama, Japan, where he died on February 15, 1938.

Emily Hiramatsu Morishima

Further Reading

Iwamoto, Gary. "Rise and Fall of an Empire." *International Examiner,* August 17–September 7, 2005, 16.

Niiya, Brian, ed. *Encyclopedia of Japanese American History Updated Edition: An A-to-Z Reference from 1868 to the Present.* New York: Facts on File, 2001.

Takaki, Ronald. *Strangers from a Different Shore: A History of Asian Americans.* Rev. ed. Boston: Little, Brown, 1998.

Gentlemen's Agreement (1907–1908)

The Gentlemen's Agreement of 1907–1908 between Japan and the United States—and its counterpart in the latter year between Japan and Canada—curtailed and eventually halted Japanese immigration in North America.

Until large numbers of Japanese plantation workers began arriving in Hawaii in the late 1890s, the vast majority of Japanese in the United States were either government officials or students. The number of passports issued by the Japanese government to students going to the U.S. mainland between 1891 and 1900 was 2,764 (compared to 60,000 Japanese going to Hawaii as plantation laborers by 1898). When Hawaii was annexed as a U.S. territory in 1898, many Japanese re-migrated to California seeking better working conditions and pay. In 1900 alone, more than 12,000 Japanese landed in California, even though anti-Asian sentiment already ran high due to massive numbers of Chinese who had come in the nineteenth century.

Seeing large-scale Japanese immigration taking place in the West Coast, Americans became increasingly discriminatory. In San Francisco, for example, the municipal school board forced Asian students to attend segregated schools in 1906. When the San Francisco Earthquake occurred that same year, incidents of violence erupted between Japanese immigrants and "native" Californians, as false rumors of Japanese looting spread. Amid mounting tensions, the Theodore Roosevelt administration determined that direct consultation between Tokyo and Washington, D.C., was necessary. After a year of difficult negotiations, much of it through the exchange of notes, Japan agreed to cease issuing passports valid for the United States to laborers; the United States would be allowed to deport Japanese who had entered the country from Hawaii, Mexico, and Canada. In return, the U.S. federal government agreed that Japanese already living in America could send for their wives and family members left behind, and the state of California agreed not to pass overtly anti-Japanese legislation or policies.

Meanwhile, Japanese settlers in Canada were also confronting discrimination. By 1901, 4,738 Japanese had settled in the country, 97 percent of them in British Columbia (mostly concentrated around Vancouver). More than 4,000 were engaged in the fishing industry in Steveston, and 570 had small businesses in the Japantown section on Powell Street in Vancouver.

Although the total number of Japanese was much smaller than in the United States, they were becoming a visible and, to established residents, bothersome presence in the small fishing community of Steveston. When the British Columbia Fishermen's Union organized a strike in 1899, some Japanese agreed to work as strikebreakers—further embittering the community. By 1901, the majority of the Japanese in Canada were employed in commercial fishing, holding 1,958 of the 4,722 licenses issued.

In 1908, Canadian minister of labor Rodolphe Lemieux requested that the Japanese government voluntarily restrict emigration to Canada. Although no formal agreement was signed, Lemieux and Japanese foreign minister Hayashi Tadasu agreed that no more than 400 male laborers and domestics could emigrate to Canada. A misunderstanding soon emerged, however, as Hayashi thought the 400 number applied only to new migrants, not returning residents or their close relatives, while Lemieux thought it meant actual physical bodies. The pact—referred to as the Lemieux-Hayashi Agreement or Canadian Gentlemen's Agreement—was amended in 1923 with further restrictions on Japanese emigration.

Both agreements let Japanese men already in North America bring wives and family members from the home country. Since many men were unmarried and could not afford to return to Japan, they sent photos to their relatives back home to choose a wife for them. The women were allowed to marry without their new husbands being present and then travel to America. Regarding "picture-bride immigration," as the practice was called, a violation the Gentleman's Agreement, the United States passed the Immigration Act of 1924 (also called the National Origins Act), which effectively prohibited any Japanese from settling in the United States—and unilaterally ended the Gentleman's Agreement. Canada had taken similar action the previous year. Despite the efforts by the United States and Canada to reduce their respective populations of Japanese, the large influx of women and stabilization of family life nonetheless caused the number of North American–born Japanese to increase significantly and the Japanese American community to thrive.

Nobuko Adachi

Further Reading

Adachi, Ken. *The Enemy That Never Was: A History of Japanese Canadians.* Toronto: McClelland and Stewart, 1991.

Daniels, Roger. *The Politics of Prejudice: The Anti-Japanese Movement in California and the Struggle for Japanese Exclusion.* 2nd ed. Berkeley: University of California Press, 1977.

Ichioka, Yuji. *The Issei: The World of the First Generation Japanese Immigrants, 1885–1924.* New York: Free Press, 1988.

Hawaii Seven

The Hawaii Seven was a group of seven island residents arrested, tried, and convicted of advocating the overthrow of the U.S. government in 1950–1951, amid the anti-Communist hysteria that permeated American society during the early cold war. The U.S. Department of Justice prosecuted the Hawaii Seven defendants for conspiring to violate the Smith Act (also known as the Alien Registration Act) of 1940, which made it illegal to teach, advocate, advise, abet, or encourage the overthrow and destruction of the federal government by force and violence or to organize or affiliate with any organization that teaches, advises, or encourages a forceful or violent overthrow.

The Hawaii Seven case was the Justice Department's second post–World War II prosecution of Communist Party members pursuant to the Smith Act. The prosecution followed the U.S. Supreme Court's decision in *Dennis v. United States* (1951), which upheld the Smith Act convictions of eleven Communist Party USA leaders in New York. The high court ruled that the defendants in *Dennis* had formed "a highly organized conspiracy" that "was ready to make the attempt" to overthrow the federal government.

The Hawaii Seven were International Longshore and Warehouse Union (ILWU) regional director Jack W. Hall; *Honolulu Record* labor newspaper editor Koji Ariyoshi; construction worker Dwight James "Jim" Freeman; Communist Party of Hawaii chair and former University of Hawai'i research chemist Charles K. Fujimoto; ILWU local secretary and former teacher Eileen Fujimoto; *Honolulu Record* circulation manager and former Communist Party of Hawaii chair Denichi "Jack" Kimoto; and former University of Hawai'i adjunct instructor and public school teacher John E. Reinecke. Freeman and Reinecke were also employees of the *Honolulu Record*. In addition, Reinecke worked as a research assistant for ILWU and as a labor negotiator.

In his July 1951 testimony before the House Un-American Activities Committee (HUAC), Hawaii Democratic Party strategist and former ILWU leader Jack Kawano identified each of the Hawaii Seven as Communist Party members. Kawano's decision to cooperate with HUAC came about one year after he had gained notoriety as one of thirty-nine witnesses, including five of the Hawaii Seven, who refused to answer questions at HUAC hearings in Honolulu in April 1950. The witnesses were known as the Defiant 39. In January 1951, the trial judge acquitted all thirty-nine witnesses on contempt of Congress charges, and Kawano abandoned his "defiant" posture the following month. In a February letter to the Hawaii Subversive Activities Commission, Kawano disclosed his past involvement in the Communist Party of Hawaii, explaining why he had joined and then quit the party. On July 6, 1951, Kawano testified in a closed session before HUAC in Washington, D.C., about the history, structure, and activities of the Communist

Party of Hawaii and the relationship between the party and the ILWU. During the course of his testimony, he named several dozen people as party members, including the Hawaii Seven.

On August 28, 1951, FBI agents arrested each of the Hawaii Seven, and a federal grand jury in Honolulu indicted them the next day. The indictment charged the defendants with the commission of eleven "overt acts" to establish that they had conspired to advocate or teach "the duty and necessity of overthrowing" the U.S. government by force and violence in violation of the Smith Act. The alleged overt acts included attending Communist Party conventions, serving on the executive board of the Communist Party of Hawaii, and defendant Koji Ariyoshi's publication of the *Honolulu Record* newspaper.

The trial began more than fourteen months later, on November 5, 1952. The prosecution's case relied largely on witness testimony of former Communists who discussed the objectives and activities of the Communist Party and identified the defendants as party members. On June 19, 1953, the jury found all seven defendants guilty of violating the Smith Act. The six men each received five-year prison sentences and $5,000 fines; Eileen Fujimoto received a three-year prison sentence and a $2,000 fine. When they learned of the guilty verdicts, several thousand ILWU dock and plantation workers walked off their jobs in protest, freezing business on the Honolulu and Hilo waterfronts for several days.

Four years later, in the case of *Yates v. United States* (1957), the U.S. Supreme Court reversed the Smith Act convictions of five California Communist Party leaders. The justices ruled that the Smith Act did not prohibit teaching and advocating the forcible overthrow of government absent "any effort to instigate actions to that end" or "evil intent." Based on that ruling, the Ninth Circuit Court of Appeals reversed the convictions of the Hawaii Seven on January 20, 1958.

Daniel H. Inouye

Further Reading

Holmes, T. Michael. *The Specter of Communism in Hawaii*. Honolulu: University of Hawai'i Press, 1994.

Reinecke, John E. *A Man Must Stand Up: The Autobiography of a Gentle Activist*. Honolulu: University of Hawai'i Press, 1993.

Hayakawa, S.I. (1906–1992)

As president of San Francisco State College during the late 1960s and early 1970s, Samuel Ichiye

Hayakawa earned a reputation as a law-and-order conservative for his tough stance against college protesters. A Canadian-born linguistics scholar of Japanese descent, Hayakawa used that reputation to run successfully for the U.S. Senate from California, where he became an outspoken conservative.

Born in Vancouver, Canada, on July 18, 1906, Hayakawa spent most of his youth in British Columbia, where his father owned a successful import-export business. After twenty-eight years in Canada, his father returned to Japan, but the younger Hayakawa stayed in Canada to pursue a career in academia. He received his bachelor's degree from the University of Manitoba in 1927 and his master's degree in English a year later from McGill University in Montreal. He earned his doctorate in linguistics from the University of Wisconsin in 1935 and went on to teach in the English department after receiving his degree. In 1941, he published *Language in Action,* an exploration of semantic theory that became a standard classroom text. (Retitled *Language in Thought and Action,* it went through several revised editions.) Hayakawa taught at the Armour Institute of Technology (1939–1947) and University of Chicago (1950–1955) before accepting a professorship at San Francisco State College in 1955.

It was during a period of student demonstrations that Hayakawa became the spokesman of the conservative Faculty Renaissance Committee. Hayakawa was opposed to the students' demands for a multicultural curriculum, arguing that being forced to teach courses with an imposed curriculum represented an infringement of his academic freedom. It was during the student strike of 1968 that Hayakawa was selected as the new president of San Francisco State. During his tenure in that capacity (1968–1973), he took a hard-line stance against the student protesters, at one point climbing aboard a demonstrator's sound truck and ripping out the wires from the loudspeakers. On campus, he was a much-disliked figure, especially among the student body and much of the liberal faculty. Among an increasingly conservative public, he was admired for his tough-guy approach to protesters.

After more than four contentious years, Hayakawa resigned as president of San Francisco State and changed his political affiliation from Democrat to Republican. Three years later, in 1976, he ran a successful campaign for the U.S. Senate, becoming the first Japanese American from outside Hawaii to serve in that body. His single term in office was not particularly distinguished for any policy initiatives. Indeed, the press made fun of the aging politician—he was seventy when he first took office—for his alleged propensity to fall asleep in the Senate chamber. In addition, the blunt outspokenness admired by so many Californians when directed at long-haired student protestors soon became a liability, according to political observers, as Hayakawa found himself increasingly isolated in office.

Fellow Japanese Americans had their own issues with Hayakawa. At first proud to see one of their own in the Senate, members of the community were deeply offended when he called them "ridiculous" for demanding reparations for incarceration during World War II—especially since Hayakawa had been living in the Midwest during World War II and thus was not subject to the internment order. In public speeches, he went so far as to claim that the internment was good for the Japanese American community; during the Iranian hostage crisis of 1979–1980, he suggested that Iranian Americans should be put into concentration camps as well. Despite his opposition to redress, Hayakawa agreed to support the formation of the Congressional Commission on Wartime Internment and Relocation of Civilians (CWRIC). In 1981, however, he testified before the CWRIC that the Nisei request for reparations filled him with "shame and embarrassment."

Hayakawa left office in 1983 and became active in the movement to make English the official language of California, founding the organization U.S. English to promote the cause. He believed that English is the way for immigrants to succeed in America and that bilingual voting ballots are racist. S.I. Hayakawa died in Greenbrae, California, on February 26, 1992, at the age of eighty-five.

Emily Hiramatsu Morishima

Further Reading

Barlow, William, and Peter Shapiro. *An End to Silence: The San Francisco State College Student Movement in the '60s.* New York: Pegasus, 1971.

Daniels, Roger. "The Redress Movement." In *Japanese Americans: From Relocation to Redress,* ed. Roger Daniels, Sandra C. Taylor, and Harry H.L. Kitano. Seattle: University of Washington Press, 1991.

Karagueuzian, Dikran. *Blow It Up! The Black Student Revolt at San Francisco State College and the Emergence of Dr. Hayakawa.* Boston: Gambit, 1971.

Heart Mountain Fair Play Committee

The Heart Mountain Fair Play Committee was an organized Japanese American draft resistance organization during World War II, based at the Heart Mountain Internment Camp in Park County, Wyoming.

In January 1944, following the administration of the federal government's loyalty questionnaire, which asked all Japanese American adults to declare their loyalty to the United States and forswear any allegiance to Japan, the War Department instituted the draft for Nisei (second-generation Japanese) men in the concentration camps. Within a week of the War Department's announcement, the internees at Heart Mountain organized the Fair Play Committee (FPC). The draft resistance movement was designed to bring the issue of the Japanese American internment into the court system. Of the ten War Relocation Authority Camps, as they were officially designated, Heart Mountain was the only one with an organized resistance to the draft. The committee was founded by, and began with the efforts of, a single member—Kiyoski Okamoto, a Nisei from Hawaii. Okamoto's original "organization" was formed as the Fair Play Committee of One. He was quickly joined by fellow internees Frank Seishi Emi, Isamu Sam Horino, Paul Takeo Nakadate, Minoru Tamesa, Tsutomu Ben Wakaye, and Guntaro Kubota. Of the FPC members, only Horino, Tamesa, and Wakaye were eligible for the draft; the others were either too old or married with children. Regardless of their draft status, the FPC members refused to cooperate with conscription in any way until they were restored to full rights as American citizens—including their release. The Japanese American Citizens League (JACL) condemned the group's resistance as unpatriotic activity in its newspaper, the *Pacific Citizen.* The FPC was also denounced in the *Heart Mountain Sentinel,* the camp newspaper.

In the government's effort to stem the draft resistance movement, Okamoto and Horino were shipped to Tule Lake Segregation Center in Northern California in April 1944. The seven leaders of the Fair Play Committee and James Omura, English editor of the *Rocky Shimpo,* were arrested and charged with conspiracy to violate the Selective Service Act. Omura was arrested because he had written an article in the *Rocky Shimpo* questioning whether it was fair and just to draft imprisoned men and force them to fight while their families were still held in camps. The seven FPC leaders were convicted in November 1944; Omura was found innocent on First Amendment grounds. The FPC leaders were sent to Leavenworth Federal Penitentiary in Kansas, from which they mounted a legal appeal. The convictions were eventually overturned by the Tenth Circuit Court of Appeals in December 1945.

In addition to the leaders of the FPC, eighty-five other men from Heart Mountain were also arrested and found guilty of violating the Selective Service Act. Sixty-three men were arrested in May 1944 for failing to report for their physicals. They were convicted and sentenced to three years in a federal penitentiary in the largest mass trial in Wyoming history. Twenty-two others were arrested during November and December 1944 and sentenced to two years in federal prison. The single young men were sent to McNeil Island Penitentiary in Washington; the older married men were sent to Leavenworth.

On December 23, 1946, Executive Order 9814 set in motion the pardon of 284 draft resisters, including those from Heart Mountain and the FPC. In California, the FPC was later incorporated as the Fair Rights Committee to seek redress; it disbanded after passage of the Evacuation Claims Act (1948), which provided modest monetary compensation for Japanese Americans with documented claims of property or financial loss caused by the internment.

Despite the executive order, surviving resisters believe that several names were omitted from the pardon. Draft resisters who did receive pardons, as well as their families, were shunned by the JACL and Nisei veterans during and after the war. Many had difficulty finding employment because of their wartime convictions. It was not until July 2000 that the national JACL voted to apologize to the resisters; the apology was made by JACL president Floyd Mori at a formal ceremony in May 2002.

Emily Hiramatsu Morishima

Further Reading

Hohri, William. "Redress as a Movement Towards Enfranchisement." In *Japanese Americans: From Relocation to Redress,* ed. Roger Daniels, Sandra C. Taylor, and Harry H.L. Kitano. Seattle: University of Washington Press, 1991.

Niiya, Brian, ed. *Encyclopedia of Japanese American History, Updated Edition: An A-to-Z Reference from 1868 to the Present.* New York: Facts on File, 2001.

Heco, Joseph (1837–1897)

Joseph Heco was the first Japanese native to become a citizen of the United States (1858) and a key figure in nineteenth-century relations between the United States and Japan, bridging the cultural and linguistic gulf between the two countries in his various roles as newspaper publisher, author, interpreter, government official, and entrepreneur.

Heco was born Hamada Hikozo in Harima Province (in present-day Hyogo Prefecture) on September 20, 1837. His life was forever changed in 1850, while on board a small junk with this sailor stepfather. The ship was cast adrift in a Pacific storm; Heco and the sixteen-member crew spent nearly two months at sea before being rescued in February 1851 by the American merchant vessel *Auckland* and taken to San Francisco. The U.S.

government, seeking a pretext to open trade negotiations with Japan, decided to repatriate the castaways as part of Commodore Matthew Perry's diplomatic mission to Japan in 1853. Upon the mission's arrival in Hong Kong, however, Heco opted to return to the United States rather than finish the final leg of the journey. According to his autobiography, he decided to return to California to "make money . . . that one day we might yet return to our far-distant home with our earnings." Others have speculated that he feared returning to a country that still punished travel abroad with death.

Heco spent the next several years in the United States, during which time he was baptized as a Catholic in 1854, became a naturalized U.S. citizen in June 1858, mastered the English language, and adopted the name "Joseph Heco" (an Anglicized version of the first two syllables of his surname).

In 1859, Heco resolved to return to his homeland. While en route in China, he chanced to meet E.M. Dorr, the newly appointed U.S. consul to Kanagawa, who offered Heco a position as his interpreter. Heco accepted the position but soon resigned to pursue work as a commission agent in Yokohama. But business was poor and *sonno joi* ("revere the emperor, expel the barbarian") xenophobia was reaching its zenith, so Heco returned to the United States in 1861. As he noted in the September 16 entry of his English-language diary/autobiography, "It was a well-ascertained fact that several ronin [masterless samurai] deemed me worthy of their attention, and were on the outlook for me to cut me down."

Heco spent a full year in the United States, using his connections to meet Abraham Lincoln. Returning to Japan the following year, he again found work in the U.S. consulate. In 1865, in response to frequent requests for news of the world outside Japan, he launched a newspaper in Yokohama called *Kaigai Shinbun* ("Overseas News"). Compiled with the help of assistants—Heco had never learned to write in Japanese—the paper featured a mix of international news, American history, and passages from the New Testament. Heco continued publishing the *Kaigai Shinbun* until January 1867, when international commercial interests drew him to the foreign enclaves of Nagasaki, Kobe, and eventually Tokyo. For a time in the early Meiji period (1868–1912), Heco worked for the Ministry of Finance, but he spent the majority of his final years quietly pursuing financial interests. He died in Tokyo in on December 12, 1897.

Todd S. Munson

Further Reading

Heco, Joseph. *Narrative of a Japanese.* Ed. James Murdoch. San Francisco: Japanese Publishing Association, 1950.

Hsu, Hsuan L. "Personality, Race, and Geopolitics in Joseph Heco's Narrative of a Japanese." *Biography* 29:2 (Spring 2006): 273–306.

Oaks, Robert F. "Golden Gate Castaway: Joseph Heco and San Francisco, 1851–1859." *California History* 82:2 (Spring 2004): 38–65.

Hirabayashi v. United States (1943)

*H*irabayashi v. United States (1943) was one of a series of critical U.S. Supreme Court decisions that declared constitutional the incarceration of Japanese American citizens and residents living on the West Coast as a national security measure following the attack on Pearl Harbor in December 1941.

Gordon Kiyoshi Hirabayashi, an American-born student at the University of Washington, refused to obey a World War II exclusion order requiring all persons of Japanese ancestry to remain indoors at defined curfew times between 8 P.M. and 6 A.M. and to report to a Civil Control Center to register for permanent relocation. Hirabayashi's case in 1943 was one of the first challenges to the exclusionary laws based on race, on the grounds that a curfew order applying to only one ethnic group violated the constitutional protection of equal rights under the law. The Supreme Court denied his challenge, ruling that national security was more important than the rights of the individual. This case, along with *Ex parte Endo* (1943), *Yasui v. United States* (1943), and *Korematsu v. United States* (1944), are known as the "Japanese American Cases."

Hirabayashi, a second-generation Japanese American born in Washington, was a senior at the University of Washington when Pearl Harbor was bombed and President Franklin D. Roosevelt issued Executive Orders 9066 and 9102 in February–March 1942, calling for the internment of persons of Japanese descent. Under the first order, the secretary of war was given the power to designate areas in the United States as "military exclusion zones," where people of "Foreign Enemy Ancestry" could be excluded. The West Coast, exposed to a possible Japanese attack, was deemed a protected area and placed under the command of Lieutenant General John L. DeWitt. The second order established the War Relocation Authority and gave it the power to register, remove, maintain, and supervise people within the designated area. Hirabayashi claimed that his Fifth Amendment rights to "due process under the law" were violated by these orders; in filing his claim, he became the first test case against the laws in May 1943. Hirabayshi's attorneys argued that he was a U.S. citizen,

had no ties to Japan, had never been to Japan, and had no association with anyone residing in Japan.

The Court's decision, handed down on June 21, 1943, declared that national security was paramount during wartime. Avoiding the more complex issue of relocation and registration, the Court focused on Hirabayashi's violation of the curfew law. Chief Justice Harlan Fiske Stone wrote the majority opinion, arguing that the violation of rights during wartime was justified due to the risk of Japanese American alliances with the Tokyo government. He also noted that the West Coast of the United States had war industries and facilities that might be subject to sabotage and attack. In a separate concurring opinion, Justice William O. Douglas agreed that the sudden attack required expediency in dealing with a large number of potential security risks. At the same time, Douglas encouraged Hirabayashi to consider challenging the laws requiring registration and relocation. Hirabayashi declined to do so.

In its unanimous decision, the court called the curfew a "protective measure" and allowed Hirabayashi's conviction to stand. He served a total of ninety days in prison; his conviction on the exclusion count was overturned in 1986 and his conviction for the curfew violation was overturned in 1988 under a writ of error called *coram nobis*. His attorney successfully argued that the original court had made factual errors based on inaccurate information regarding the scope of disloyalty among Japanese Americans in Washington State. The Federal Appeals Court agreed and issued formal apologies for the original convictions.

Pamela Lee Gray

Further Reading

Hirabayashi v. United States 320 U.S. 81 (1943).

Irons, Peter. *Justice at War: The Story of the Japanese-American Internment Cases.* Berkeley: University of California Press, 1993.

Urofsky, Melvin I. *100 Americans Making Constitutional History: A Biographical History.* Washington, DC: Congressional Quarterly, 2004.

Hood River Incident

The Hood River Incident took place in the town of Hood River, Oregon, on November 29, 1944, when the local American Legion post removed the names of sixteen Nisei servicemen from a commemorative plaque located in front of city hall. The removal of the names was part of a larger campaign of intimidation, threats, vandalism, and boycotts designed to keep the Japanese from returning to the West Coast after being released from the internment camps where they had been held since early 1942. The *Pacific Citizen,* the newspaper of the Japanese American Citizens League (JACL), reported more than forty incidents of violence or intimidation in California within the first six months of 1945.

The hostility toward Japanese Americans was due in part to their perceived economic success in the Hood River Valley. The number of Japanese immigrants living in Oregon had grown from only twenty-five in 1890 to 2,501 in 1900. As the immigrant population increased, so did anti-Japanese sentiment among the white "native" population in Oregon and throughout the Pacific Northwest and California. The first Oregon law designed to keep Japanese immigrants from buying land was introduced in 1917 by a state senator from Hood River. Issei (first-generation Japanese immigrants) in the region had been working primarily as farm laborers and in logging camps. With their savings or in exchange for work, some bought small tracts of land in the Hood River Valley. Clearing the land and raising crops, they gradually transformed the region into productive farmland with a strong immigrant community. By World War II, Japanese Americans accounted for about 25 percent of the area's total fruit production and 75 percent of its strawberries. In early 1942, American Legion posts in Oregon and Washington passed resolutions urging the government to remove all persons of Japanese ancestry from the West Coast.

Many Nisei soldiers had hoped that by fighting in World War II, they would prove their loyalty to America. The Hood River Incident doused those hopes. By removing the names of Nisei veterans from a plaque honoring Hood River servicemen, the American Legion publicly disavowed the contribution of Japanese Americans who fought in the war and rejected the claims to patriotism on the part of so many. One of the names removed from the plaque was that of Frank Hachiya, who had been killed in action in the Philippines. Indeed the gesture on the part of the American Legion was just one of many acts and expressions of community sentiment over a period of several months intended to intimidate and drive away returning Japanese Americans. Hundreds of valley residents signed five full-page newspaper ads in the first three months of 1945, typified by the headline on the first: "So Sorry! Japs Are Not Wanted in Hood River."

The plaque, carrying the names of every county resident who had served in the war, had been erected by the Hood River American Legion post in 1943. The names were removed for purportedly patriotic reasons—concern over the dual citizenship of the Nisei, who would not be reinstated until their tours of service were complete and a decision rendered on their dual citizenship. The sixteen names removed from the plaque were George Akiyama,

Shoichi Endow, Sumio Fukui, Isao Namba, Mamoru Noji, Billy Yamaki, Masaaki Asai, Tao Asai, Frank Hachiya, George Kinoshita, Seiji Nishioka, Harry Norimatsu, Setsu Shitara, Harry Takagi, Noboru Takasumi, and Harry Tamura.

Several local residents immediately protested the action, and the incident gained national media attention. Coverage of the heroism of Nisei soldiers in the press helped spur public outrage over the local American Legion's act, as newspapers, magazines, and television shows around the country joined in condemnation. Angry letters from servicemen flooded the *Hood River News.* In April 1945, pending an investigation to revoke their charter, the local American Legion restored the names. The furor subsided, but the Hood River Incident was far from the only expression of resistance to returning Japanese Americans at the end of World War II.

Emily Hiramatsu Morishima

Further Reading

Leonard, Kevin Allen. "'Is This What We Fought For?' Japanese Americans and Racism in California, the Impact of World War II." *Western Historical Quarterly* 21:4 (November 1990): 463–82.

Tamura, Linda. *The Hood River Issei: An Oral History of Japanese Settlers in Oregon's Hood River Valley.* Chicago: University of Illinois Press, 1993.

Ichihashi, Yamato (1878–1963)

Yamato Ichihashi was a pioneer in the study of Japanese immigration to the United States, publishing the first major academic study on the subject, *The Japanese in the United States* (1932). One of the first academic scholars of Asian descent in America, he became the first nonwhite professor at Stanford University when he began teaching there in 1913. With a hiatus only during World War II, Ichihashi continued to teach at Stanford until his death in 1963.

Ichihashi was born in 1878 in the city of Nagoya, Aichi Province, to a former samurai family. He left Japan for San Francisco in 1894 on a student visa and attended Lowell High there before entering Stanford University. He received his bachelor's and master's degrees in economics in 1907 and 1908, respectively, before working with economist Harry A. Millis on a project studying Japanese immigration for the U.S. Immigration Commission. He would use this research and his own experience as an immigrant for his PhD dissertation at Harvard University, where he studied with such notables as Frederick Jackson Turner and earned his degree in 1913. He returned to Stanford as the first nonwhite professor on campus and began teaching courses in Japanese history and government, international relations, and the Japanese American experience.

Meanwhile, the anti-Japanese movement was flourishing on the West Coast, resulting in the 1913 Alien Land Law in California, which prevented noncitizens from land or property; the measure effectively barred Issei from land ownership because they were also denied citizenship. In an effort to improve U.S. public opinion, the Japanese Foreign ministry launched a public campaign to educate Americans about Japanese culture and Japanese immigration. As a part of this effort, the ministry funneled $3,000 through dummy private donors (false names) to fund a position at Stanford to teach Japanese history and government. It was this position that Yamato Ichihashi was appointed to fill. This put him in the somewhat difficult position of being employed by Stanford University while earning his salary from the Japanese government at a time when Japanese immigrants were already suspected of having more loyalty to Japan than to America.

In his first year at Stanford, Ichihashi wrote a pamphlet sponsored by the Japanese Association of America titled *Japanese Immigration: Its Status in California*. With this pamphlet and other writings, he attempted to use statistics and other hard information to promote a positive view of Japanese immigration. In October 1920, however, an article in the *Oakland Tribune* by Yoshisaburo Kuno, who taught Japanese at the University of California, Berkeley, accused Ichihashi of being a propagandist for Japan; this brought him under surveillance by U.S. intelligence agencies. After renewing the Stanford professorship for nine consecutive years, the Japanese government established a permanent endowment in 1922—again donating the money through a dummy private donor—in response to the rising anti-Japanese movement. In 1928, after fifteen years at Stanford, Ichihashi was finally granted tenure. In the same year, he published *The Washington Conference and After*, based on his experiences as an interpreter and secretary to Baron Kato Tomosaburo, a senior Japanese delegate, at the Washington Conference on the Limitation of Armaments (1921–1922).

Ichihashi published his landmark work, *Japanese in the United States: A Critical Study of the Problems of the Japanese Immigrants and Their Children*, in 1932. The book, praised for its objectivity, presented statistics and a cultural analysis of Japanese immigration from 1870 to 1930, the rise of California's anti-Japanese legislation,

and the experience of the Nisei (second generation). Like more than 112,000 other Japanese Americans on the West Coast, Ichihashi and his family were forced to leave their home and face incarceration in the early days of World War II. He and his family were transferred from the Santa Anita Assembly Center to the Tule Lake Relocation Center, where they spent the rest of the war years. Ichihashi attempted to document every aspect of his internment experience in correspondence with colleagues and a daily diary. Although he intended to write a book about the experience, he published no further books in the last twenty years of his life.

The Ichihashi family was allowed to return to their home in April 1945, but the internment had taken its toll on the family. Ichihashi himself was deeply depressed and remained estranged from his son until a few years before his death on April 5, 1963. Shortly after his death, his wife, Kei Ichihashi, suffered a nervous breakdown; she died in a mental institution a few years later. Yamato Ichihashi's internment writings were published posthumously in 1997 as *Morning Glory, Evening Shadow: The Internment Writings of Yamato Ichihashi, 1942–1945*. They were compiled by Gordon Chang from Ichihashi's manuscripts in the Special Collections department at Stanford's Green Library.

Emily Hiramatsu Morishima

Further Reading

Chang, Gordon. "We Almost Wept: Professor Yamato Ichihashi was a Respected Scholar and Member of the Stanford Community, but That Wasn't Enough to Spare Him the Humiliation of Internment." *Stanford Today*, November–December 1996.

Ichioka, Yuji. "'Attorney for the Defense': Yamato Ichihashi and Japanese Immigration." *Pacific Historical Review* 55:2 (May 1986): 192–225.

Ichioka, Yuji (1936–2002)

A leading Japanese American historian, activist, and authority on the Issei (first-generation) experience, Yuji Ichioka is known for having coined the term "Asian American" in the late 1960s. A preeminent scholar of Japanese American history, he taught for more than thirty years at the University of California, Los Angeles (UCLA), where he founded the Asian American Studies Center in 1969.

Born on June 23, 1936, in San Francisco, Ichioka was relocated with his family to the Topaz Internment Camp in Utah when he was five years old. After serving in the U.S. Army, he attended UCLA and received a MA in history from UC Berkeley in 1968. A diligent researcher and among the first in America to rely on Japanese-language sources, Ichioka became an expert in early Japanese American history. In the late 1960s, he recognized the power of political alliance amid the antiwar, civil rights, and ethnic pride movements of the time, and he is credited with coining the term "Asian American" to bring together the diverse ethnic groups previously referred to as "Oriental" or "Asiatic." The term was intended to unite these groups politically, drawing on their shared history, experiences, and goals, but at the same time recognizing their differences.

Also in 1968, Ichioka founded the Asian American Political Alliance at San Francisco State College to bring together Asian students who opposed the Vietnam War. The following year, Ichioka returned to UCLA, where he taught the campus's first Asian American studies course and founded the Asian American Studies Center. He also served as a research associate of the center and an adjunct associate professor of history for thirty-three years until his death on September 1, 2002.

As a foremost authority on Japanese American history, Yuji Ichioka testified before the Congressional Committee on Wartime Relocation and Internment of Civilians (CWRIC) in 1981. The hearings would eventually lead to the committee's recommendation to the federal government to compensate Japanese Americans for their forced evacuation and incarceration during World War II. In 1988, Ichioka published *The Issei: The World of the First Generation Japanese Immigrants, 1885–1924,* which won the 1989 U.S. History Award from the National Association for Asian American Studies. Ichioka then shifted his primary focus to the Nisei (second generation), publishing a succession of articles on Nisei politics, the effects of Issei nationalism on the next generation, and Nisei education. He also helped found the Japanese American Research Project Collection at UCLA, the nation's largest archive of Japanese American history. Other published works include *A Buried Past* (1974) and *A Buried Past II* (1999), annotated bibliographies of the collection that are invaluable to Asian American scholars.

Ichioka was among the first American scholars to use Japanese-language sources to reveal the experience of the immigrants, previously understood by historians on the basis of English-language sources only. He began to study Japanese while employed as a parole worker in New York in preparation for a trip to Japan. In 1969, when he began his career at UCLA, he enlisted the help of Yasuo Sakata, then a doctoral candidate in history, to help him translate the Meiji-era Japanese used in some

of the sources used in *The Issei.* He believed his mission was to uncover histories that were yet unwritten and use them to construct new interpretations of the past. In addition, he dedicated his life to social justice in the United States, Japan, and Latin America. Ichioka was honored for his lifelong commitment to labor equity with the 2002 International Longshore and Warehouse Union's Yoneda Award. Upon his death, a fund was initiated to endow the Yuji Ichioka Chair in Social Justice Studies at UCLA to recognize and support the research, teaching, and community service activities of leading scholars in the fields of racial, ethnic, and gender studies. A compilation of his essays, *Before Internment: Essays in Prewar Japanese American History* (2006), was published posthumously by Stanford University Press.

Emily Hiramatsu Morishima

Further Reading

Ichioka, Yuji. *Before Internment: Essays in Prewar Japanese American History.* Ed. Gordon H. Chang and Eiichiro Azuma. Stanford, CA: Stanford University Press, 2006.

Ichioka, Yuji. *The Issei: The World of the First Generation Japanese Immigrants, 1885–1924.* New York: Free Press, 1988.

———. "A Historian by Happenstance." *Amerasia* 26:1 (2000): 32–53.

Kang, K. Connie. "Yuji Ichioka, 66; Led Way in Studying Lives of Asian Americans." *Los Angeles Times,* September 7, 2002.

Inouye, Daniel K. (1924–)

Daniel K. Inouye has represented the state of Hawaii since 1954, when he was elected to the Territorial House of Representatives, and later to the Senate of the same body. When Hawaii entered the union in 1959, Inouye was elected as one of its first members of the U.S. House of Representatives (1959–1962) and later as a U.S. senator (1962–). A Democrat, he is the first Japanese American to serve in either house of the U.S. Congress.

Daniel Ken Inouye was born in Honolulu on September 7, 1924. His life changed in December 1941, when Pearl Harbor was bombed and he volunteered on a first aid crew. Two years later, after the army lifted its ban on recruiting Japanese Americans, the eighteen-year-old Inouye left college and enlisted in the 442nd Regimental Combat Team. Experiencing combat in France and Italy, he survived a bullet wound in the abdomen and lost his right arm in battle. At the end of the war, he held the rank of captain and was awarded the Distinguished Service Cross (upgraded in 2000 to the Medal of Honor, the nation's highest award for service), the Bronze Star, Purple Heart, and twelve other military service medals. After almost two years in military hospitals, Inouye graduated from the University of Hawai'i in 1950 and completed his law degree at Washington University School of Law in 1952. Before entering politics, he worked for a year as deputy public prosecutor in Honolulu.

Inouye received national attention as the keynote speaker at the Chicago Democratic National Convention in 1968. Best known for his work on the Senate Watergate Committee in 1973, he later served on the Kissinger Commission, which investigated U.S. policy in Central America in 1984. Inouye also had a high level of national media exposure when he chaired the 1987 Senate committee investigating secret military assistance to Iran and Nicaragua, also known as the Iran-Contra Hearings. His legislative efforts generally have focused on health and welfare, education, and military defense.

Inouye is also a strong advocate of the rights of Native Hawaiians, and served for extended periods on the Senate Committee on Indian Affairs (1987–1995 and 2001–2003). His successes in that area include efforts to restore and return the small island of Kahoolawe—which had been used as a practice target by the U.S. military for many years—to Native Hawaiians. On an issue of great concern to many Japanese Americans, Senator Inouye was instrumental in acting on the 1983 recommendation of the Commission on Wartime Relocation and Internment of Civilians (CWRIC) to write legislation providing reparations—and a formal government apology—to Japanese Americans who were interned under Executive Order 9066 during World War II. Both recommendations were realized upon the passage and signing of the Civil Liberties Act of 1988. He likewise supported legislation to preserve the World War II internment camps as historic landmarks and make funds available to use the facilities as educational museums. Based on his experience as a veteran of World War II, Inouye has remained keenly interested in military defense appropriations and funding for troop support.

Pamela Lee Gray

Further Reading

Inouye, Daniel K., with Lawrence Elliott. *Journey to Washington.* Englewood Cliffs, NJ: Prentice-Hall, 1967.

Okamura, Jonathan, ed. *The Japanese American Historical Experience in Hawaii.* Dubuque, IA: Kendall/Hunt, 2001.

Interracial Dating and Marriage, Japanese American

Japanese Americans have historically had a high rate of interracial dating and marriage with the non–Asian American population, at least since the coming of age of the Nisei, the American-born generation. The reasons Japanese Americans intermarry or date across racial lines more than other Asian groups—and perhaps more than any other minority—have much to do with their rapid assimilation into mainstream American culture, their tendency to live in non-Asian communities, and their relatively high socioeconomic status.

Due to strong anti-Japanese sentiment among the general U.S. population, as well as their own cultural reservations, it was very rare for the Issei (first-generation Japanese Americans) to marry across racial lines. When they decided to settle permanently in the United States, most Issei sent back to Japan for their wives or asked family members back home to find them wives and send them to America. The Gentlemen's Agreement of 1907–1908 was a direct attempt to shut down most immigration from Japan. Under the accord, the Japanese government would issue passports for travel to the United States only to nonlaborers. The measure did not succeed in stemming the influx of so-called picture brides, and most Issei, if they married at all, tended to do so with other Japanese.

The Issei thus found it more opportune to marry among themselves, especially given the widespread racism and discrimination they encountered on the U.S. mainland from the majority Caucasian population. Many Issei worried that if they produced a biracial child it would not be considered either Japanese or Caucasian, and that it would encounter even more ostracism than a regular American child of Japanese descent.

This attitude began to change with the Nisei generation for a variety of reasons. First, as Japanese American families began to move into mixed or non-Asian communities, their children had more daily contact with non-Asians. Second, with the Japanese American emphasis on education and obtaining a college degree as a path to socioeconomic betterment and social acceptance, more Nisei and Sansei (third generation) went to college. Studies have shown that higher education generally leads to greater intermingling with people of various racial and ethnic groups encountered on campus, or later in the workplace. In the case of Japanese Americans and other groups with relatively high levels of educational achievement, this certainly helps explain the higher rate of interracial dating and marriage. The fact that the Nisei were encouraged so strongly to attend college—and did in large numbers—naturally gave them greater access to interracial relationships that extended to the workplace.

Another factor was the post–World War II Japanese war brides phenomenon. Despite opposition on the part of the general public, military brass, and religious leaders, many American GIs married Japanese women while stationed in Japan after the war. The War Brides Act of 1945 officially allowed the spouses and children of World War II veterans to enter the United States, though there was no specific provision for Japanese or other Asian brides. It was not until after August 1950 that U.S. servicemen in general were officially allowed to marry and reenter the United States with Japanese spouses. At this point, the official military policy was to discourage such unions, requiring GIs to obtain approval from their commander and their chaplain. Despite such prohibitive measures, many GIs returned home with Japanese wives.

In the postwar era, the combination of high educational levels, socioeconomic status, and assimilation into American society at large has contributed to steady increases in Japanese marriages to non-Japanese—from about 10 percent in 1950, to about 30 percent in 1980, to more than 40 percent in 1990. According to the 1990 U.S. Census, the most recent data on the subject, 53.6 percent of Japanese American males and 67.5 percent of Japanese American females were married to Caucasians, in contrast to 6.6 percent each to other Asians. The trend is expected to continue.

Lindsay Sarah Krasnoff

Further Reading

Strauss, Anselm L. "Strain and Harmony in American-Japanese War-Bride Marriages." *Marriage and Family Living* 16:2 (May 1954): 99–106.

Inu (Informants)

Inu is a Japanese American term of insult—it means "dog" in Japanese—used in reference to members of the community who were perceived as cooperating too enthusiastically with government authorities—and receiving preferential treatment in return—during the World War II incarceration.

The term was applied in various ways and to various groups in the Japanese American community. Many used it in reference to the Japanese American Citizens League (JACL). The oldest and most prestigious social

and political institution in the Japanese American community, the JACL was a conservative organization that pleaded with Japanese Americans to accept the incarceration without resistance or protest. Arguing that any such activities would reflect badly on the patriotism and loyalty of the community—and possibly bring on even harsher treatment in the aftermath of Pearl Harbor—the JACL even opposed legal means for resisting internment, actively discouraging Japanese from filing civil liberties lawsuits. In addition, JACL members provided names of "suspects"—usually outspoken critics of the incarceration—to the Federal Bureau of Investigation as possible subversives and repeatedly urged the government to create suicide battalions of Japanese Americans to prove their loyalty. While in the internment and assembly centers, many JACL members worked closely with the War Relocation Authority in the management of camps and inmates. At the Puyallup Assembly Center in Washington, for example, a select group of JACL members were granted the day-to-day governance of what internees came to call "Camp Harmony." The JACL officials received special benefits for their efforts, including better housing and food.

There was also a generational component to the use of the *inu* label. Many Issei (first-generation immigrants) and Kibei (those born in America but sent to Japan for their education) used the term against the Nisei, who were born and raised in America. Being the most assimilated of all Japanese Americans, the Nisei often acted as liaisons between government authorities and internees. The Issei, moreover, because they had been born in Japan, were simply banned by government authorities from leadership positions in the camps, creating further animosity. Nisei were also seen by many Issei and Kibei as not fully Japanese and therefore not entirely loyal to the community.

Notably, incarcerated Japanese Americans directed their anger as much toward people identified as *inu* stooges or traitors as they did toward the authorities who held them prisoner. At the Manzanar Internment Camp in California, Fred Tayama, a member of the JACL and suspected government informant, was severely beaten by other internees in December 1942. The arrest and imprisonment of one of the alleged assailants produced a crowd of protestors that marched on the administration building. Military police ordered them to disperse, the internees refused, and rioting broke out. Two persons were killed and ten wounded when the MPs fired on the crowd; a number of people suspected of being *inu* were removed from the camps for their safety. In similar circumstances, other deadly clashes with authorities took place in Tule Lake, California, and Topaz, Utah.

While Japanese Americans in Hawaii were not

subject to incarceration during World War II, the term *inu* was used there to describe people seen as too quick to hide or ignore their Japanese heritage and those who participated in the jingoistic "Speak American" campaign—an Americanization-through-language program during the 1940s.

Emily Hiramatsu Morishima

Further Reading

Daniels, Roger. *Prisoners Without Trial: Japanese Americans in World War II.* New York: Hill and Wang, 1993.

Kashima, Tetsuden. *Judgment Without Trial: Japanese American Imprisonment During World War II.* Seattle: University of Washington Press, 2003.

Irwin, Robert Walker (1844–1925)

One of the defining characteristics of Japanese migration to Hawaii was its systematic nature. After the first wave of Japanese immigrants, *Gannen-mono*, landed on Hawaiian soil in 1868, immigration was halted for twenty years until the Hawaiian consul general to Japan, Robert Walker Irwin, established a systematic contract labor migration plan. Through this plan, the Japanese and Hawaiian governments oversaw the move of 28,691 Japanese between 1885 and 1894.

Robert Irwin was born in Copenhagen, Denmark, on January 7, 1844. His father, William Wallace Irwin, was a U.S. diplomat and politician; his mother was a fourth-generation direct descendent of Benjamin Franklin. Richard Irwin, one of Robert's four siblings and a member of the Pacific Mail Steamship Company, sent him to Japan in 1866 as the Yokohama agent of the company. Irwin later worked for a Yokohama-based firm called Walsh, Hall and Company in Yokohama, through which he met Japanese government officials Kaoru Inouye and Takashi Masuda and businessman Okada Heizo. In 1876, they established Mitsui Bussan Kaisha (Mitsui Trading Company) together. Irwin, as a counselor of the firm, had privileges and power equal to those of the company president, Masuda.

Irwin entered into Hawaiian affairs when Harlan P. Lillibridge, the U.S. consul general to Japan, took a leave of absence to return to the mainland in 1880. Lillibridge, who valued Irwin's close connection with prominent Japanese businessman and political figures, thought he would be an appropriate acting consul general and had him appointed to the position. The following year, when U.S. officials in Hawaii learned that Lillibridge would not be coming back, they appointed Irwin full consul general in Japan.

With the growth of the sugar plantation industry in Hawaii, the planters on the islands demanded a more stable and dependable labor source. Irwin's connections in Japan proved ideal for establishing a steady source of laborers. Irwin consulted with Inouye and Matsuda regarding the ideal candidates and where to find them. The main criterion for migrant laborer selection would be a temperament of perseverance and obedience, to which Matsuda replied that the people of Yamaguchi and Hiroshima were ideal. Inouye likewise identified Yamaguchi, his home prefecture, as an ideal place to find immigrants. In particular, he pointed to Oshima, a district that had undergone a series of natural disasters (a drought in 1883 and a storm in 1884) and was facing an overpopulation problem. With the help of the Mitsui Bussan Company in advertising and recruiting workers, Irwin was paid a $5 commission plus an additional fee for every adult male immigrant he recruited.

Although Irwin did everything he could to perpetuate the immigration system, the revolution of 1893 and establishment of the Republic of Hawaii the following year brought the system to an end. Irwin went on to establish a sugar refinery in Formosa and later became a Japanese citizen. He died in February 1925 in Tokyo. His summer house was rebuilt in 1986 and is preserved in Ikaho city, Gumma Prefecture.

Toru T. Yamada

Further Reading

Irwin, Yukiko, and Hilary Conroy. "Robert Walker Irwin and Systematic Immigration to Hawaii." In *East Across the Pacific: Historical and Sociological Studies of Japanese Immigration and Assimilation,* ed. Hilary Conroy and T. Scott Miyakawa. Santa Barbara, CA: American Bibliographic Center, 1962, 40–55.

Kotani, Roland. *The Japanese in Hawaii: A Century of Struggle.* Honolulu: Hawaii Hochi, 1985.

Issei

The term Issei refers to the first generation of Japanese immigrants to the United States. For the most part, the Issei were born between 1850 and 1905 and immigrated between 1885 and 1924. Japanese immigrants went first to Hawaii, then on to the West Coast, particularly California, working as migratory seasonal workers. In the early 1900s, those immigrants started settling down and the Japanese American population grew rapidly—from about 25,000 in 1900 to 111,010 in 1920. Los Angeles was home to an especially large Issei community, with 20,000 in 1920. Since the early stages of immigration were primarily labor-related, the vast majority of first arrivals were male. In Los Angeles, for example, there were seven male Issei for every female. In the Gentleman's Agreement of 1907–1908, however, the Japanese government arranged with the Theodore Roosevelt administration to stem the flow of laborers leaving Japan for America. However, women and children were not barred from emigrating to American to join their husbands (many married in absentia), which evened out the gender ratio and allowed the formation of full Issei families in abundance. Between 1910 and 1924, 30,000 Japanese women immigrated to the United States, enough to keep the Japanese American community thriving even after the Asian Exclusion Act of 1924.

The most common source of income among the Issei was farming. The early immigrants who traveled to Hawaii worked on sugarcane plantations. Later immigrants, who came mainly to California and Washington, had great success in farming rice, vegetables, and flowers. By 1913, Issei farmers controlled 282,000 acres (114,000 hectares) of farmland in the United States. Despite California's Alien Land Act of 1913, which prohibited them from owning land in the state, the Issei continued to prosper by transferring their land titles to their American-born children, a generation known as the Nisei. By the time a clause was added to close this loophole, Japanese American farmers were already prospering. The Issei also hoped this would get the Nisei interested in farming and carrying on the family businesses. To help the cause, they ran educational programs aimed at bringing the Nisei back to the farms.

At the outbreak of World War II, anti-Japanese hysteria led to Executive Order 9066, which allowed for the internment of all Japanese Americans. In early 1942, more than 112,000 people were taken from their homes and sent to relocation camps away from the West Coast, where most were kept until the end of the war. Since immigration laws had prevented the Issei from ever becoming naturalized citizens, many were classed as enemy aliens and were not allowed to become citizens until 1952. The Japanese American community in Hawaii was not subjected to the same degree of persecution, as it was more ingrained and because Hawaii was a U.S. territory away from the mainland. In any event, by the time the Issei were released from the internment camps, much of their land and property had been seized and sold. With farming no longer an option for many, the Issei started exploring a wide variety of alternate businesses. Although some filed claims to be reimbursed for their lost property, those who were successful received only a fraction of the full amount. In 1988, the government agreed to pay out $20,000 to each living person who was sent to a camp.

Leah Irvine

Further Reading

Ichioka, Yuji. *The Issei: The World of the First Generation Japanese Immigrants, 1885–1924*. New York: Free Press, 1988.

Kimura, Yukiko. *Issei: Japanese Immigrants in Hawaii*. Honolulu: University of Hawai'i Press, 1988.

Tamura, Linda. *The Hood River Issei: An Oral History of Japanese Settlers in Oregon's Hood River Valley*. Chicago: University of Illinois Press, 1993.

Japan Bashing

Japan bashing is a term used to describe the negative images of Japan perpetuated by the American media and politicians from the late 1970s to the early 1990s, a time when the Japanese economy was growing rapidly and Japanese products began to flood the American marketplace. As early as 1978, *Time* magazine ran an article warning the public about the growing trade deficit with Japan. At around the same time, American automakers and manufacturers were facing massive cutbacks and layoffs in order to streamline their businesses. Japan was blamed for the subsequent rise in unemployment, although other economic issues, including overall global competition and a desire by corporations to make their companies more efficient, were very much involved.

As a sign of their frustration, angry autoworkers began smashing imported Japanese cars in public rallies. The media covered these events without explaining the larger global issues at stake, giving the public the impression that perhaps Japan was indeed responsible for America's economic woes. The result was violence. In 1982, a twenty-seven-year-old Chinese American engineer named Vincent Chin was beaten to death in Detroit by two autoworkers who mistook him for Japanese and blamed him for recent layoffs. Eventually, Chin's killers received a reduced sentence in exchange for a plea bargain. They were given three years' probation and fined $3,780 each, which they never paid.

By the late 1980s, Japan bashing had reached farther inland. Family farmers, particularly in the Midwest, faced an economic crisis themselves as agribusiness began to replace individual families as the most efficient way to work the land. Still, their woes were also blamed on Japan by many in the media. For example, the *Des Moines Register*

Activists commemorate the 1982 murder of Chinese American Vincent Chin in Detroit. Chin was beaten to death by unemployed white autoworkers, who mistook him for Japanese, at a time when U.S. carmakers were losing sales to Japanese imports. *(Associated Press/Paul Sancya)*

in 1989 began running regular columns about the Japanese threat. One column published April 21, 1989, was entitled, "The Latest War with Japan." Another column published on March 22 warned, "We've forgotten Pearl Harbor." While the articles avoided the outright racism of World War II, the gist of much of the writing was that Japan did not practice fair trade, keeping its doors closed to American imports while subsidizing Japanese exports.

Purchases by Japanese corporations of American landmarks and companies, including Columbia pictures by Sony in 1989 and Rockefeller Center by Mitsubishi in 1990, helped fan the flames of fear that Japan would surpass America economically. Ironically, Great Britain and Germany owned more land and companies in the United States at this time than Japan, but this was rarely reported in the media, which chose to focus on Japanese purchases.

Japan bashing may have reached its peak in 1992 with the publication of Michael Crichton's novel *Rising Sun,* which portrayed predatory Japanese businessmen who were not content to wage economic warfare with the United States, but also kidnapped young white women to work in their brothels. In October of that year, a young Japanese high school student was shot and killed by a panicked Louisiana resident when the student knocked on the man's door while looking for a Halloween party. The teenager, Yoshi Hattori, became a symbol of the irrational fear of Japanese in America, and images of his mournful parents were played repeatedly on network television. In the aftermath of this incident, the media began to downplay Japan as a threat to America. Also by the mid-1990s, the Japanese economic bubble had burst and the country fell into a deep recession, from which it was still trying to recover in the early twenty-first century.

By the late 1990s, the Japan-bashing phenomenon had come to an end, especially as America's own economy entered a period of prolonged growth and Japan's experienced a highly publicized slump. Finally, the terrorist attacks of September 11, 2001, focused America's attention on other issues and other enemies.

May-lee Chai

Further Reading

LaFeber, Walter. *The Clash: A History of U.S.–Japan Relations.* New York: W.W. Norton, 1997.

Zia, Helen. *Asian American Dreams: The Emergence of an American People.* New York: Farrar, Straus and Giroux, 2000, 55–81.

Japanese American Citizens League

The Japanese American Citizens League (JACL), founded in 1929, is the oldest national organization advocating for and protecting the rights of Japanese Americans. With headquarters in San Francisco, the organization has 113 branch chapters in a total of twenty-three states. As of the early 2000s, the JACL had a membership of approximately 18,000. The organization is run by a national board consisting of six elected officers and governors representing seven regional districts. Each region has its own board of governors as well, elected by local chapters.

The origins of the JACL are rooted in the influx of Japanese immigrants in the early decades of the twentieth century. The largest groups settled on the West Coast, particularly in California, Oregon, and Washington. From the late 1800s through the mid-twentieth century, laws, policies, and groups of people across the country targeted people of Asian ancestry for myriad forms of discrimination and exclusion. Little effort was made to differentiate between those of Japanese or Chinese ancestry by discriminatory groups, such as the Sons of the Golden West and the Japanese Exclusion League. Passage of the Chinese Exclusion Act of 1882, which all but eliminated Chinese immigration to the United States, paved the way for subsequent legislation—such as the Immigration Act of 1924—targeting all Asian immigration. After its inception in 1929 the Japanese American Citizens League remained small, was based largely in California, and drew upon a limited membership.

After the attack on Pearl Harbor, President Franklin D. Roosevelt signed Executive Order 9066, which began the process of moving Japanese Americans to "relocation" centers. This also had the effect of disabling most of the leadership of the JACL, as many of its members were among those incarcerated. Those remaining outside the camps kept the JACL active during this period but could accomplish little in the face of national anti-Japanese sentiment. After being relocated and classified as enemy aliens, some Japanese Americans joined the armed forces in some capacity, including heavy combat. The JACL played a critical role in this turn of events, lobbying the U.S. government to allow the Japanese American community to demonstrate its patriotism by enlisting for military service. Indeed the 442nd Regimental Combat Team, an army unit made up of 4,000 Japanese from Hawaii and the internment camps themselves, was the most highly decorated unit of its size during World War II. Nevertheless, the JACL was the object of sometimes angry opposition among

Officials of the Japanese American Citizens League in Seattle post signs notifying community members to register for evacuation in 1942. The highly influential, historically conservative civic organization has been in operation for more than eighty years. *(Associated Press)*

some members of the Japanese American community, especially internees, for pandering to government interests, collaborating with the War Relocation Authority, and accepting special benefits for their efforts.

In the decades after the war, the JACL took on some of the most discriminatory laws and policies, with a good measure of success. The JACL had long attacked the California Alien Land Law of 1913 and helped bring about its repeal in 1946. It sought reparations for the losses of the Japanese American community as a result of wartime incarceration, lobbying for the Evacuation Claims Act of 1948 as a first step. The organization also pushed for the right of Japanese Americans to become naturalized citizens and spearheaded the McCarren-Walter Act (also called the Immigration and Nationality Act of 1952), which allowed for expanded, though still strictly limited, immigration from Asia. The JACL also actively lobbied for the landmark Civil Rights Act of 1964, which prohibited discrimination based on race, color, religion, sex, or national origin.

It was not until the presidency of Jimmy Carter that the JACL's efforts to seek redress for the internment of World War II began meeting with real success. In 1980, Carter approved the formation of the Commission on Wartime Relocation and Internment of Civilians (CWRIC), whose report two years later concluded that the government had acted in an unconstitutional manner, that the relocation was not justified by military necessity, that those subjected to it should be paid reparations, and that the federal government should issue a formal apology. The payments—$20,000 for each living former detainee—were formally authorized when President Ronald Reagan signed the Civil Liberties Act of 1988. In 1994, the JACL became the first civil rights organization in America to openly and actively support same-sex marriage.

In the 1980s, meanwhile, the JACL broadened its efforts to protect the rights of everyone in the growing Pacific-Asian community, not just those of Japanese heritage. It remains an active protector of civil liberties to the present day. Early in 2007 it supported the passage of HR 1592, the Local Law Enforcement Hate Crimes Prevention Act. In June 2007, the JACL announced its support of a Muslim high school student in San Francisco who was humiliated in the cafeteria when the principal demanded that she remove her Islamic head scarf. The ongoing mission of the JACL today is "to secure and maintain the civil rights of Japanese Americans and all others who are victimized by injustice and bigotry. The leaders and members of the JACL also work to promote cultural, educational and social values and preserve the heritage and legacy of the Japanese American community."

Antonio Thompson

Further Reading

Hosokawa, Bill. *JACL in Quest of Justice.* New York: William Morrow, 1982.

Japanese American Citizens League. http://www.jacl.org.

Japanese American Evacuation Claims Act (1948)

The Japanese American Evacuation Claims Act, signed into law by President Harry S. Truman in July 1948, provided monetary compensation for property losses incurred during the World War II internment of more than 112,000 people of Japanese ancestry. President Truman had urged the Congress to support the legislation at a ceremony honoring the all–Japanese American 442nd Regimental Combat Team in 1946 and by including the bill in a special civil rights message to Congress in 1948. The Japanese American Citizen's League (JACL), under the leadership of Mike Masaoka, had lobbied for passage of the bill since 1946. Approximately $37 million was appropriated by Congress to pay for the claims, which continued until 1965.

In 1946, two bills were introduced in the Senate and the House (S.R. 2127 and H.R. 6780) with the support of President Truman. The House bill died, but the Senate bill was passed in July of that year. Members of both chambers worried that Japanese citizens who repatriated to Japan would be eligible for compensation and that Italian and German Americans were excluded from the bill. In the next Congress, a new House bill (H.R. 3999) was introduced and passed unanimously in July 1947. During Senate subcommittee hearings of the measure, John J. McCloy, the former assistant secretary of war and supporter of the exclusion order, testified in support of the Evacuation Claims bill. On June 18, 1948, the Senate passed H.R. 3999 with minor amendments that were approved by the House the next day. President Truman signed the act into law on July 2.

Despite the intention of providing redress for property losses, there were several aspects that made the legislation ineffective. For example, the process of filing a claim required documentation and a witness's testimony. Because of the haste with which families were forced to leave their homes, many of the documents needed for the claim process had been lost or destroyed during the war. As a result, many claims were rejected for lack of evidence. Moreover, individual claims were capped at $2,500. Those whose claim exceeded that amount had to wait for Congress to appropriate additional money. In addition, the claims were processed very slowly, while most applicants needed the money quickly to help reestablish their lives. In 1950, only 211 out of 22,903 claims had been processed. Journalist Bill Hosokawa revealed that the government had spent more than $1,000 fighting a single claim for $450. Ultimately, the claim was paid in 1965 to the survivors of rice farmer and entrepreneur Keisaburo Koda; the total of $362,500 was the largest settlement made under the Japanese American Evacuation Claims Act.

In the end, only about one-tenth of the total value of estimated losses incurred by the Japanese American community, $37 million, was paid under the Evacuation Claims Act. Inflation ate into the total value of the payments, which were based on 1942 dollars. Nor did the measure compensate the internees for lost wages and productivity during the war. When the Congressional Commission on Wartime Relocation and Internment of Civilians (CWRIC) reviewed the results of the legislation in 1981, the payments of $37 million were deemed woefully inadequate. Japanese American economic losses due to the internment, adjusted for inflation and including lost income, were estimated to be as high as $6.2 billion.

Emily Hiramatsu Morishima

Further Reading

Maki, Mitchell T., Harry H.L. Kitano, and S. Megan Berthold, eds. *Achieving the Impossible Dream: How Japanese Americans Obtained Redress.* Chicago: University of Illinois Press, 1999.

Taylor, Sandra C. "Evacuation and Economic Loss: Questions and Perspectives." In *Japanese Americans: From Relocation to Redress,* ed. Roger Daniels, Sandra C. Taylor, and Harry H.L. Kitano. Seattle: University of Washington Press, 1991.

Japanese American National Museum

Located in the Little Tokyo section of downtown Los Angeles, the Japanese American National Museum (JANM) is the first such facility dedicated to conveying the experiences of Japanese Americans to the general public.

Efforts to launch the museum began in the early 1980s by two groups: Little Tokyo businessmen and veterans of the 442nd Regimental Combat Team, who sponsored the "Japanese American Soldier" exhibit at the Los Angeles County Museum of Natural History in 1982 and were seeking a permanent site. The JANM was officially established as a nonprofit institute in 1985, with headquarters in the abandoned Nishi Hongwanji Buddhist Temple. The museum project received funding from the city of Los Angeles's redevelopment agency as well as the California State Legislature. In 1986, the Los Angeles City Council approved a fifty-year lease for the temple at the rate of $1 a year. The National Endowment for the Humanities (NEH) then awarded the museum multiple grants to formulate a multiyear exhibit master plan and fund its first exhibit. In addition, the museum launched its own $24 million development campaign to renovate the temple and construct a secondary pavilion. In 1990, a groundbreaking ceremony was held to initiate the temple's renovation into a museum. Two years later, the JANM opened its doors to the public. In 1996, ground was broken on a new 84,000-square-foot (7,800-square-meter) pavilion designed by architect Gyo Obata. Opened in 1999, the pavilion houses the museum's primary exhibits, a resource center, life history studio, staff offices, and a rock and water garden designed by Robert Murase.

The pavilion is also home to the museum's permanent exhibit, "Common Ground: the Heart of Community," which presents an overview of Japanese American history through personal artifacts, film, and photographs. Prominent as well is a presentation of the history of World War II incarceration of Japanese Americans, including videos, letters, a scale model of the Manzanar camp, and a reconstructed barrack from the Heart Mountain camp. The JANM resource center contains one of the most complete collections of histories and literature about the Japanese American experience. Along with a multimedia lab, the resource center also maintains an active Web site, where it provides a variety of fact sheets and a searchable directory of its collection.

The JANM provides a valuable space for exhibitions featuring new interpretations of history. It has attempted to grow beyond its theoretical and physical bounds, coproducing exhibits with other museums and community groups, sponsoring exhibits in Hawaii, and hosting a Smithsonian exhibit titled *September 11: Bearing Witness to History.* The museum hosts a variety of film screenings, conferences, lectures, book signings, and live theater about the Japanese American and Asian American experience. There is strong community support for the facility, with volunteers making most of its programming possible. The JANM has more than 50,000 members and donors in all fifty states and sixteen countries. The museum's declared mission is "to promote understanding and appreciation of America's ethnic and cultural diversity by preserving, interpreting and sharing the experiences of Japanese Americans."

Emily Hiramatsu Morishima

Further Reading

Japanese American National Museum. http://www.janm.org.

Yoo, David. "Captivating Memories: Museology, Concentration Camps, and Japanese American History." *American Quarterly* 48:4 (1996): 680–99.

Japanese Associations

Between the turn of the twentieth century and U.S. entry into World War II in 1941, Japanese communities in North America were partially self-governed by a local Japanese association (Nihonjin-kai), sometimes started by local government officials and sometimes by civic and business leaders. The first was established in August 1891 in San Francisco by the local Japanese consul as the Greater Japanese Association, but it dissolved within a decade. The association was revamped in 1900, and expanded five years later in response to rising anti-Japanese activism.

Japanese associations ran a variety of community activities, from secular language schools to holiday parades, and served as a liaison between the ethnic community and local officials. During the Americanization period in the late nineteenth and early twentieth centuries, when Japanese immigrants were first adjusting to life in the United States, community associations sponsored English classes for Issei (first-generation immigrants) and English-language kindergartens for Nisei (second-generation offspring). Association officers were selected primarily from the Issei business class. Hawaii's Central Japanese League (founded in 1903), for example, reflected a pro-business bias by frequently siding with sugar planters over Japanese workers during labor disputes. Two years later, the workers launched a Reform Association to protest the league's cooperation with planters and a bank that exploited Japanese laborers.

Membership was optional, with annual dues of $3 to $6 per year, but was required in order to secure endorsements for Japanese consular documents. The Japanese consulates allowed registration fees to go to the associations to support community activities. The registration system was part of the Gentleman's Agreement of 1907–1908, in which the Tokyo government agreed to a U.S. State Department request to collect information on Japanese nationals living in the United States. For Issei, the most important functions of the local Japanese association were the family registrations and passport applications that allowed them to bring wives and children to America. Associations were also authorized by the U.S. and Japanese governments to issue identity documents for Issei, as well as Japanese draft deferment cards so that Japanese nationals residing in the United States did not have to return to the homeland to fulfill their military commitment.

Associations tended to be politically and socially conservative, much like Japanese diplomats who tried to avoid conflict, even if it meant avoiding a fight for personal or community rights. According to the noted historian Yuji Ichioka, the system of "endorsement rights" and collecting of information on local Nikkei allowed the associations to "keep track of Japanese immigrants and inform each other of anyone who stepped out of line," such as gamblers, prostitutes, or socialists.

Each local association reported to a regional body corresponding to Japanese consular districts. In 1919, the regional bodies included the United Northwestern Japanese Association, with headquarters in Seattle and fifteen chapters in Washington and Montana; the Japanese Association of Oregon, based in Portland and also covering Idaho; the Japanese Association of America, headquartered in San Francisco and with forty chapters in Northern California, Nevada, Utah, and Colorado; and the Central Japanese Association of Southern California (Los Angeles). All of the West Coast regional associations sent representatives to the Pacific Coast Deliberative Council.

Most Japanese Americans belonged to local associations, at least until 1924, when it no longer became possible to secure visas for immigrants' family members. The virtual cessation of Japanese immigration also meant the end of the main source of association income—the processing fees for family registrations and passports.

Japanese associations might have died out like other Nikkei social organizations, such as *kumiai* (local self-support groups) and *kenjinkai* (prefectural associations), as acculturated Nisei came to lead the ethnic community and began to participate in American economic, political, and social institutions. It was federal suppression during World War II, however, that terminated most associations. Immediately following World War II, association leaders were arrested by the FBI and detained in Immigration and Naturalization Service internment camps because of their ties to Japan. The Japanese American Citizen's League (JACL) took over the role as primary community organization. According to journalist Bill Hosokawa, a longtime observer of the Japanese American community, the JACL spurned Japanese association entreaties to help them resist or protest the internment, despite the fact that several association leaders underwrote early JACL activities before the war. After the war, Japanese American community leadership shifted to JACL chapters, local *kumiai*, or Japanese chambers of commerce. Temples and churches now also fulfill many of these communal roles.

Andrew B. Wertheimer

Further Reading

Ichioka, Yuji. "Japanese Associations and the Japanese Government: A Special Relationship, 1906–1926." *Pacific Historical Review* 46 (1977): 409–37.

Spickard, Paul R. *Japanese Americans: The Formation and Transformations of an Ethnic Group.* New York: Twayne, 1996.

Japanese Language Schools

Beginning in late-nineteenth-century Hawaii and flourishing on the American West Coast in the first half of the twentieth century, Japanese language schools were established by Japanese American community organizations, religious institutions, and other groups to provide language and cultural instruction to Japanese youths born in the United States.

The first Japanese language schools were run by Buddhist temples and Japanese Christian churches in Hawaii in the 1890s. Nonreligious schools appeared in the early twentieth century, and, by 1934, roughly 75 percent of Japanese language schools were not affiliated with religious institutions. Most followed the curriculum used in Japan's own public schools.

On the U.S. mainland, Japanese grade schools were established as early as 1902 and increasingly appeared in the first decade of the twentieth century in cities with high concentrations of Japanese Americans, such as San Francisco, Sacramento, and Seattle. As in Hawaii, the mainland schools utilized curriculum textbooks approved by the Japanese Ministry of Education, which, at the time, emphasized a highly nationalistic course of study. While this included such noncontroversial topics as cultural traditions and values, it also put great emphasis on loyalty to the Japanese emperor and state.

Japanese language schools were rarely a substitute for public education. Issei, or first-generation immigrant Japanese parents, typically sent their children to American public schools—some integrated and some segregated, depending on local law—for a practical education in the sciences, English, and other studies. Most also required their offspring to attend Japanese language schools to provide what many Issei felt was a moral dimension missing from public school instruction.

During and immediately after World War I, in a climate of growing nativism, American educational authorities began to oppose the promotion of Japanese values, particularly the emphasis on loyalty to the emperor. In some localities and states, the government issued regulations restricting the number of hours students could attend foreign language schools and required teachers at those institutions to take proficiency examinations in English and U.S. history. In 1927, however, the U.S. Supreme Court ruled in the case of *Farrington v. T. Tokushige* that Hawaiian legislation restricting private foreign language education was an abridgement of the Equal Rights provisions of the Fourteenth Amendment. The ruling thus overturned the law in Hawaii and any other state that restricted foreign language instruction. As a result, dozens of new Japanese language schools emerged in Hawaii and on the mainland.

The World War II incarceration of Japanese Americans led to the closure of all Japanese language schools in the West Coast region where the internment orders were in effect. But even in Hawaii and the eastern states, the war brought the shutdown of Japanese language schools for fear that they would become targets of violence in the heated wartime climate. As for the relocation camps, many had rules against instruction in Japanese, and many parents did not want to be seen as disloyal for having their children instructed in Japanese culture and values.

Eager to assimilate and put the past behind them, Japanese American communities after the war generally did not attempt to replace the language schools that had been shut down. Moreover, as Japanese Americans

prospered in the postwar economic boom, and as prejudice against them declined, many moved out of their traditional communities into suburban America, where their children became culturally assimilated.

With the Japanese economic boom of the 1970s and 1980s, a new kind of Japanese language school emerged in many cities without traditionally large Japanese American populations. As Japanese businessmen were relocated to corporate sites in America, many sought a traditional Japanese education for their children so they could reenroll in Japanese schools upon returning to the home country. So-called Saturday schools provided a supplementary education to students attending U.S. public school, but few settled Japanese Americans attended them.

Suzuko Morikawa

Further Reading

Asato, Noriko. *Teaching Mikadoism: The Attack on Japanese Language Schools in Hawaii, California, and Washington, 1919–1927.* Honolulu: University of Hawai'i Press, 2006.

Hawkins, John. "Politics, Education, and Language Policy: The Case of Japanese Language Schools in Hawaii." *Amerasia* 5:1 (1978): 39–56.

Ichioka, Yuji. *The Issei: The World of the First Generation Japanese Immigrants, 1885–1924.* New York: Free Press, 1988.

Kumei, Teruko. "'The Twain Shall Meet' in the Nisei? Japanese Language Education and U.S.–Japan Relations, 1900–1940." In *New Worlds, New Lives: Globalization and People of Japanese Descent in the Americas and from Latin America in Japan,* ed. Lane Ryo Hirabayashi, Akemi Kikumura-Yano, and James A. Hirabayashi, 108–25. Palo Alto, CA: Stanford University Press, 2002.

Japanese-Mexican Labor Association

The Japanese-Mexican Labor Association (JMLA), the first organized farmworkers union in California, was formed in 1903 in Oxnard, where some 500 Japanese and 200 Mexican workers joined together to demand better wages from their employers and challenged the exclusion of Asian workers by organized labor.

Japanese immigrant laborers, most of whom were hired by Japanese labor contractors, were first employed in the sugar beet fields of Oxnard in 1899. The local industry grew rapidly, as the American Beet Sugar Company expanded from processing 63,000 tons (57,000 metric tons) of sugar beets in 1900 to 200,000 tons (180,000 metric tons) in 1903. Founded in 1902 to combat Japanese contractors, the Western Agricultural Contracting Company (WACC) began contracting farmworkers to Oxnard sugar beet growers in large numbers. By the following year, 75 percent of the sugar beet crop was harvested by WACC workers, and the piecework rate for thinning beets had dropped from $5 to $3.75 per acre. The labor dispute began when the WACC recruited 120 Japanese workers and assigned them to work for subcontractors at lower wages. The new workers protested against this arrangement and soon organized others to join them, forming the JMLA.

The fledgling union elected labor organizer Kozaburo Baba as its president. Meetings were conducted in English with discussions in Spanish and Japanese. The Cottage Hotel in Oxnard served as union headquarters. The first order of business was to oppose the lower wages offered by the WACC and the entire subcontracting system. Under that system, the workers were required to pay a daily commission to both the WACC and the subcontractor. The union further protested the requirement to shop at the company store, which sold goods at inflated prices and gave kickbacks to the WACC.

The strike began in March, and by the end of the month, 90 percent of the labor force—or about 1,200 workers—were taking part. On March 23, a violent confrontation resulted in the shooting death of Luis Vasquez, a twenty-one-year-old Mexican American farmworker, and injuries to two Japanese American and two Mexican American farmworkers. On March 30, the company and workers reached an agreement that effectively ended the WACC monopoly on labor and its practice of subcontracting. The farm company also agreed to pay union laborers $5 an acre for thinning beets.

The success of the JMLA strike of 1903 led American labor in general to begin reversing its exclusion of racial minorities. The Los Angeles County labor council, for one, voted to include any laborers, including Japanese, on its rolls. J.M. Lizarras, secretary of the JMLA's Mexican branch, sought to build on the growing solidarity and in March 1903 applied for a charter from the American Federation of Labor (AFL), the dominant force in the national labor movement. But the president of the AFL, Samuel Gompers, would agree to a charter only if the JMLA got rid of its Asian members. His position was consistent with the AFL's opposition to Chinese and Japanese immigration, which the federation viewed as a threat to American labor. In June 1903, Lizarras protested the injustice by refusing the charter issued for Mexican members of the JMLA and wrote to Gompers again to ask for a charter under which "we can unite all the Sugar Beet & Field Laborers of Oxnard, without regard to their color or race." The AFL again refused to accept Asians, and the JMLA remained on its own. Without the backing of a powerful national union, however, the Japanese-Mexican Labor Association soon passed from the scene.

Emily Hiramatsu Morishima

Further Reading

Almaguer, Tomás. "Racial Domination and Class Conflict in Capitalist Agriculture: The Oxnard Sugar Beet Workers' Strike of 1903." In *Working People of California,* ed. Daniel Cornford. Berkeley: University of California Press, 1995.

Ichioka, Yuji. *The Issei: The World of the First Generation Japanese Immigrants, 1885–1924.* New York: Free Press, 1988.

Takaki, Ronald. *Strangers from a Different Shore: A History of Asian Americans.* Rev. ed. Boston: Little, Brown, 1998.

Japanese Peruvians

Japanese immigration to Peru began in 1899, when 790 agricultural contract workers from rural Japan—eager to find better job opportunities and the chance to farm their own land—arrived in Callao Seaport near Lima. The new settlers faced not only racial, cultural, and language barriers, but the threat of tropical diseases for which they had no immunity, such as malaria, typhoid, and yellow fever. Within a year, 143 had died and ninety-three had fled to Bolivia (the first Japanese immigrants to that country). As a result of these difficulties, the second wave of immigration from Japan did not occur until years later, beginning in about 1903. Since that time, Japanese have been arriving in Peru on a regular basis, regardless of the rampant discrimination against Asians. Today, the Japanese Peruvian community numbers an estimated 85,000 (about 0.3 percent of the Peruvian population), covering four generations.

Paradoxically, while most of the Japanese came to Peru initially do to agricultural work, most did not settle on farms—making them different from Japanese immigrants to other Latin American countries, such as Brazil. By 1930, 45 percent of all Japanese in Peru ran small businesses in Lima. As a result, the Eighty Percent Law of 1932 required shop owners to have at least 80 percent of their employees be non-Asian Peruvians. The Immigration Law of 1936 prohibited citizenship to any child of alien parents, even if born in Peru.

It was during this period of rising anti-Japanese sentiment, in May 1940, that an earthquake destroyed most of the city of Lima, setting off a wave of anti-Japanese violence. By this time, there were approximately 30,000 Japanese in Peru, who owned a significant number of stores and shops in the capital city. In the aftermath of the quake, with many people facing hunger and home-lessness, rumors began to fly of price gouging on the part of Japanese Peruvians. In the weeks that followed, some 650 Japanese houses were attacked in Lima. Later that year, the government decreed that Japanese Peruvians who went home to pursue their studies would lose their Peruvian citizenship.

When Peru broke diplomatic relations with Japan in 1942 because of World War II, the Peruvian government confiscated all property from Japanese settlers and deported at least 1,800 people of Japanese descent—including some who had been born in Peru—to internment camps in the United States. When the war was over, those detained in the United States were barred from returning to Peru and their belongings were with-held by the Peruvian government. Many were relocated by the American government to towns across the United States, where companies were recruited to hire them. A significant number settled in Bridgeton, New Jersey, and went to work for Seabrook Farms, a frozen foods company with a long history of hiring Japanese American workers. Most Japanese Peruvians had learned enough English in the camps to forge social connections with Japanese Americans and, after the war, blended easily into this larger population.

Unlike the more than 112,000 Japanese Americans who were incarcerated during the war, Japanese Peruvians (and other Japanese Latin Americans) who were interned received no reparations or formal apology. When they had been deported from Peru in 1942, it was the Peruvian government that had taken away their passports. Upon their arrival in the United States, they were technically considered "illegal aliens." Since they were neither U.S. citizens nor permanent residents at the time, they failed to qualify for reparations after the war. Finally, in June 1998, Latin Americans who had been held American internment camps during the war received an official apology from the U.S. government and nominal compensation of $5,000 (compared to $20,000 for Japanese American internees). Some Japanese Peruvians refused the offer and continued the campaign for redress with the Organization of American States, where it is still pending.

Nobuko Adachi

Further Reading

Gardiner, C. Harvey. *The Japanese and Peru: 1873–1973.* Albu-querque: University of New Mexico Press, 1975.

———. *Pawns in a Triangle of Hate: The Peruvian Japanese and the United States.* Seattle: University of Washington Press, 1981.

Takenaka, Ayumi. "The Japanese in Peru: History of Im-migration, Settlement, and Racialization." *Latin American Perspectives* 31:3 (May 2004): 77–98.

Kibei

The term *Kibei* (literally, "returning to America") re-fers to the first American-born generation of Japa-nese immigrants, who were raised in Japan during their adolescent years for education and socialization and later rejoined their immediate families in the United States. Kibei are a subgroup of Nisei (second-generation Japa-nese Americans) and hold a distinctive identity because of their unique two-culture experience in the United States and Japan.

The Kibei were sent by their Issei parents (the first generation of Japanese immigrants) to be raised by their grandparents or other relatives back in Japan because of the child-care problem in the United States—many Japa-nese American women were forced to work long hours to help the family make ends meet—and to help them maintain Japanese culture, especially moral values and the ability to speak both English and Japanese. In the early 1930s, Kibei made up about 13 percent of the total Nisei population and consisted of two basic subgroups: those who received their education mostly in the United States but spent four to five years in Japan, and those who were sent to Japan at an early age and returned to the United States around high school age, after receiving their formative education. Another division was between those who went back to Japan in the early twentieth cen-tury and those who went back in the 1930s. The various groups were not exclusive, of course, as some Kibei fell into more than one category.

Because of their unique experience of education, language, and culture, as well as of discrimination and exclusion in United States and Japanese societies, the Kibei developed an independent identity from the larger Nisei community. Kibei often felt a sense of alienation from Japanese education and culture, especially during the 1930s, when Japanese schools provided military training during the war with China. After returning to the United States, they had difficulty readapting to American society in the midst of anti-Asian agitation. At the same time, they often had trouble fitting into Japanese American society because their command of English was not strong and because they were accultur-ated to Japanese customs more than Japanese American ones. In California, Kibei workers confronted labor dis-crimination much more severe than other Nisei workers did, due to their limited English skills. Amid such mar-ginalization and alienation, the Kibei organized social and political groups that addressed their special interests and needs. Among their community support groups were special divisions within the Japanese American

Citizens League (JACL) and the Kibei Citizens Council of San Francisco.

In 1941, prior to U.S. entrance into World War II, many Kibei were recruited to teach Japanese to Nisei soldiers in the U.S. Military Intelligence Service Language School. Like the Nisei, the Kibei were overrepresented in the Military Intelligence Service during the war, as Japanese language skills were needed to interrogate captured Japanese soldiers, to translate Japanese documents in the Pacific theater, and for countless other purposes. At the same time, the Kibei and Issei were the Japanese American groups most targeted for disloyalty by the Federal Bureau of Investigation and local police during World War II. Between 1942 and 1946, a significant number of Kibei were forcibly relocated to the Tule Lake Segregation Center, an internment camp specifically designated for people of Japanese descent whom the War Relocation Authority deemed loyal to Japan or whose loyalties to the United States were especially suspect. As a result of their pro-Japan sentiment and the humiliation they experienced in the camp, many Kibei repatriated to Japan after the war.

Suzuko Morikawa

Further Reading

Kiyota, Minoru, and Linda Klepinger Keenan. *Beyond Loyalty: The Story of a Kibei.* Honolulu: University of Hawai'i Press, 1997.

Takahashi, Jere. *Nisei/Sansei: Shifting Japanese American Identities and Politics.* Philadelphia: Temple University Press, 1997.

Yoneda, Karl. *Ganbatte: Sixty-Year Struggle of a Kibei Worker.* Los Angeles: Asian American Studies Center, 1983.

Kitano, Harry H.L. (1926–2002)

Harry Kitano was a prominent scholar in Asian American Studies and a leading authority on race and ethnic relations who held joint appointments in the Department of Social Work and the Department of Sociology at the University of California, Los Angeles (UCLA). The author of more than 150 books and articles during the second half of the twentieth century, Kitano pioneered the social scientific approach to studying the Japanese American population and experience.

Kitano was born in San Francisco on February 14, 1926, to Motoji and Kou Yuki Kitano, immigrants from Kyushu, Japan. His parents ran a hotel in Chinatown, where Harry grew up. World War II wrought great changes in his young life, as the internment order of 1942

forced him to leave high school at age sixteen. His father was detained by the FBI, while the rest of the family reported to the Santa Anita Race Track, where they waited for six months before being shipped to the relocation camp at Topaz, Utah. After being released in 1945, Kitano worked briefly as a farmhand before playing trombone in several jazz bands under the alias Harry Lee.

Kitano returned to California in 1946 and immediately resumed his education. He earned his bachelor's degree in 1948, master of social work degree in 1951, and PhD in psychology and education in 1958, all from the University of California, Berkeley. He began his academic career in 1958 at UCLA, where he remained until his retirement in 1995. He served twice as acting director of the Asian American Studies Center and was a codirector of the UCLA's Alcohol Research Center.

Kitano's first book was *Japanese Americans: The Evolution of a Subculture* (1969), a sociological analysis of the Japanese American experience; the book has become a standard in the field and has been translated into many languages. He is also well known for *Race Relations* (1974), which presents an analytical framework for race relations and specific case studies of various racial groups; the sixth edition appeared in 2006. With Roger Daniels, he coauthored *American Racism: Exploration of the Nature of Prejudice* (1970), which explores ideas about superiority and inferiority and their effects on racial attitudes in the United States. *Asian Americans: Emerging Minorities* (1988), also coauthored with Roger Daniels, is an introduction to most of the major Asian American groups from a historical and sociocultural perspective.

Kitano was the first to study interracial marriages, juvenile delinquency, mental health, and alcohol abuse in the Asian American population. He was also among the first to apply social science theory and techniques to understanding the Japanese American and Asian American populations. Among his controversial ideas was his conclusion that the World War II internment camps, because of a unique organizational structure that relied on Nisei participation in governance and communal living arrangements, may have had a positive impact in releasing Nisei children from subservient roles to their parents. The internment camps also allowed them to participate fully in community activities that were closed to them in their home communities, such as cheerleading and student government. Kitano's studies on interracial marriage are among the most widely referenced by scholars studying the process of assimilation because they revealed an outmarriage rate over 50 percent, much higher than for other racial minorities. His studies on juvenile delinquency and alcohol abuse were vital to raising awareness of problems that were obscured by stereotypes of Asian Americans as the model minority.

In 1990, Kitano became the first recipient of the endowed chair in Japanese American studies at UCLA, the first position of its kind at any university in the United States. He finally received his high school diploma in 1997 in a special ceremony organized by the San Francisco School Board. After his retirement, Kitano continued to serve on the Faculty Advisory Committee for the Asian American Studies Center and coauthored *Achieving the Impossible Dream: How Japanese Americans Achieved Redress* (1999) with Mitchell Maki and S. Megan Berthold. He died in Los Angeles on October 19, 2002.

Emily Hiramatsu Morishima

Further Reading

Kang, K. Connie. "Harry Kitano, 76; UCLA Professor, Expert on Race Relations." *Los Angeles Times,* October 24, 2002.

Kitano, Harry H.L. *Japanese Americans: The Evolution of a Subculture.* Englewood Cliffs, NJ: Prentice-Hall, 1969.

———. *Race Relations.* Englewood Cliffs, NJ: Prentice Hall, 1974.

Kitano, Harry H.L., with Roger C. Daniels. *American Racism: Exploration of the Nature of Prejudice.* Englewood Cliffs, NJ: Prentice-Hall, 1970.

———. *Generations and Identity: The Japanese American.* Needham Heights, MA: Ginn, 1993.

Kitano, Harry H.L., and S. Sue. "The Model Minorities." *Journal of Social Issues* 29:2 (1973).

Koda, Keisaburo (1882–1964)

Keisaburo Koda was as a highly successful rice farmer in California's San Joaquin Valley, known among Japanese Americans as "the Rice King." His business survived the incarceration of West Coast Japanese during World War II and is still run by the Koda family in the twenty-first century.

Born in Japan in 1882, Koda was the son of a miller and broker of rice and rice flour. He earned his university degree at Meiji University and worked as a teacher and school principal in rural Japan. He came to America in 1906 to join his brother and worked throughout central California as a migrant farm laborer, laundry worker, oil driller, and hotel employee. Saving his money to open three laundries, he took his earnings and moved to Southern California and opened a successful wholesale fish business with partners, the Tajima brothers, in San Pedro.

At the end of World War I, Koda and the Tajimas sold the business for $250,000, and Koda moved to the San Joaquin Valley to grow rice, a new industry in Califor-nia. From meager beginnings in 1912, the California rice harvest grew from 500,000 pounds (227,000 kilograms) to more than 330 million pounds (150 million kilograms) by 1920. In the early years of California rice production, several Issei (first-generation Japanese) growers together held more than 10,000 acres (4,000 hectares), but the Alien Land Law of 1913—which effectively prohibited Asian Americans from owning real property in the state—led to the abrupt demise of their operations, and some of the growers were imprisoned. To circumvent the law, many Issei—including Koda—purchased land under the names of their American-born children. With his children as stockholders, he formed State Farming Co., Inc., in the late 1920s and began growing rice.

Initially he sharecropped 1,400 acres (570 hectares) and rented an additional 1,800 acres (730 hectares). The first crops failed, and Koda lost his money. After working as a laborer on another rice farm, he tried again with the backing of a non-Japanese friend—and this time proved successful. He made $20,000 to $30,000 per year from his rice crops from 1924 to 1927, earning the nickname "Rice King." An innovator in the field, Koda established a new agricultural technique for rice: using airplanes to sow seeds. Following in his father's footsteps, Koda also opened a rice mill and established the Kokuho brand.

By 1932, Koda was growing more than 10,000 acres of rice, and by the early 1940s he was a millionaire several times over. Like the more than112,000 other Japanese Americans on the West Coast, however, Koda and his family were incarcerated in the months after Pearl Harbor and U.S. entry into World War II. The Kodas were relocated to the Granada concentration camp in Colorado. Upon his departure, he was forced to hand over management of the farm to strangers. When he returned in 1945, he learned that two-thirds of his land and all of his machinery and equipment had been sold.

At the age of sixty-three, with the help of his two sons, William and Edward, Koda began the process of rebuilding the farm and business. First he tried to get his land back through the legal system, filing for a claim under the Japanese American Evacuation Claims Act of 1948. The legislation called for compensation for proven economic losses resulting from the internment, but most internees had a hard time proving their claims because they lacked sufficient evidence. Koda's claim, moreover, exceeded the law's $2,500 maximum and took even longer to process.

Despite the delay with his claim, Koda continued to raise rice on his remaining land and launched the People's Rights Protection Association to lobby against the Alien Land Laws, which were still on the books. He introduced a new strain of rice, a medium grain called Kokuho Rose, that proved highly successful and helped restore his fortune. After retiring from the business and turning it over to his sons, Koda devoted his energies to lobbying for naturalization rights for Issei, supporting the efforts of the Japanese American Citizens League, and convincing the Bank of Tokyo to do business in California. He became a naturalized citizen in 1954.

Koda died on December 16, 1964, while visiting Japan. The following year, his survivors received $362,500 from the U.S. government, the largest settlement from the Japanese American Claims Act. Koda Farms in California's San Joaquin Valley continues to be run by third-generation family members.

Emily Hiramatsu Morishima

Further Reading

Iwata, Masakazu. *Planted in Good Soil: A History of the Issei in United States Agriculture.* New York: Peter Lang, 1992.

Japanese American Curriculum Project. "Keisaburo Koda." *Japanese American Journey: The Story of a People.* Ed. Florence M. Hongo. San Mateo, CA: JACP, 1985.

Koda Farms. http://www.kodafarms.com.

Korematsu v. United States (1944)

Korematsu v. United States (1944) was a landmark U.S. Supreme Court decision on civil liberties. Ruling on the case of Fred Korematsu, a California welder of Japanese descent who refused to obey government orders to relocate to an incarceration camp in 1942, the high court held that national security interests during wartime take precedence over individual liberties and thus the internment of Japanese Americans was constitutional.

In February 1942, President Franklin Roosevelt had issued Executive Order 9066, requiring all persons of Japanese descent living on the West Coast to turn themselves over to local authorities for removal to internment camps the government was building in various states. Korematsu refused to obey the order and was arrested for violating what was known as Civilian Exclusion Order Number 34. He was convicted in federal court on September 8, 1942, and the decision was reaffirmed by the Ninth Circuit Court of Appeals on January 7, 1944. Korematsu then appealed his case to the U.S. Supreme Court.

Two questions were presented to the Court: whether or not the forced relocation of Japanese Americans—citizens and residents alike—to incarceration camps was beyond the wartime powers of the government; and whether or not relocation violated the Constitution. The Court had already upheld the decision to set curfews for Japanese people on the West Coast in the case of *Hira-*

bayashi v. United States (1943) but had not yet determined the constitutionality of relocation. *Korematsu v. United States* was argued on October 11 and 12, 1944, and decided on December 18, 1944. Five justices affirmed the conviction, and the majority opinion of the court, delivered by Justice Hugo Black, expressed the opinion that national security concerns outweighed Korematsu's constitutional rights.

One justice, Felix Frankfurter, concurred with the court's decision but on different grounds. He argued that since the country was in a state of war, the military had a right to enact any "reasonably expedient military precautions," as long as it did not explicitly violate the Constitution. Taking a strict constructionist approach, Frankfurter contended that the relocation was not unconstitutional because the Constitution does not specifically forbid such a military order.

Three justices—Owen Roberts, Frank Murphy, and Robert Jackson—dissented from the majority opinion and wrote opinions of their own. Justice Roberts believed that relocation was analogous to imprisonment. Since no evidence of disloyalty was presented against Japanese Americans and there was no trial, Roberts argued, their Fifth Amendment rights had been violated, rendering the military order unconstitutional. Justice Murphy agreed with Roberts that relocation was a violation of Fifth Amendment rights but also believed that relocation was an act of racism against Japanese Americans. He felt that since there was no real evidence of sabotage or espionage on the part of Japanese Americans, they did not constitute a threat to either the war effort or national security. Justice Jackson dissented on the grounds that, since the military order targeted only Japanese Americans whose parents who were born in Japan, it was unconstitutional because it involved the use of inherited guilt. That is to say, it presumed that the purported disloyalty of foreign-born parents applied to their American-born children as well. Furthermore, Jackson pointed out, the Court had no evidence to support the necessity of relocation and so there was no legal basis for it.

In the years since the war, most constitutional scholars have come to agree that the arguments of the dissenting justices, particularly those of Frank Murphy, were the correct ones and that the majority opinion did, in fact, represent a serious violation of civil liberties. In 1998, President Bill Clinton awarded Korematsu the Presidential Medal of Freedom for his struggle in defense of individual rights.

Nathan Cao

Further Reading

Irons, Peter. *Justice at War.* New York: Oxford University Press, 1983.

Irons, Peter, ed. *Justice Delayed: The Record of the Japanese American Internment Cases*. Middletown, CT: Wesleyan University Press, 1989.

Korematsu v. United States 323 U.S. 214 (1944).

Rehnquist, William H. *All the Laws but One: Civil Liberties in Wartime*. New York: Knopf, 1998.

Urofsky, Melvin I. *100 Americans Making Constitutional History: A Biographical History*. Washington, DC: Congressional Quarterly, 2004.

Labor and Employment, Japanese American

The story of Japanese American labor in the late nineteenth and early twentieth centuries provides a backdrop for many of the subsequent events in Japanese American history. Most early immigrant laborers came with the intention of saving money and returning to Japan to buy land or pay off debts. But the life of the Japanese laborer in Hawaii and on the U.S. mainland proved difficult, and saving enough to return home often proved unrealistic. Many decided to settle and put down roots in America. Japanese laborers in the late nineteenth and early twentieth centuries worked under the labor contracting system, in which they were employed for a set period of time and for a set wage, but found that additional charges made by their contractor for miscellaneous expenses cut deeply into their wages. The conditions were such that an active labor movement soon developed among the immigrants. The movement would find some success, particularly in Hawaii. The large-scale immigration of Japanese laborers occurred between 1886 and 1908, and Japanese American workers contributed to the economic development of the West Coast and Hawaii. Their presence provided the impetus for developing a Japanese American community in the United States as they later formed their own businesses, farms, and community organizations.

Contract Labor

Though there had been a few small prior experiments in which Japanese would come to America to work as laborers—such as the 149 *gannen-mono* ("first-year people") who went to Hawaii in 1868, or the founders of the Wakamatsu Tea and Silk Farm Colony in 1869—the process of Japanese American immigration began in earnest in 1886, when Japan and Hawaii agreed to a system whereby Japanese citizens could work in Hawaii under set labor contracts. The Japanese government had been hesitant to enter into such an agreement for fear that the Japanese workers would be subjected to almost slavelike conditions in Hawaii. But part of the agreement allowed the Japanese government to inspect the working conditions of the laborers and help prevent abuses. Many of the workers who went dreamed of earning enough to buy land or to repay debts in Japan. Often they did not intend to stay permanently, and some would eventually return to Japan.

The motivation from the American side was to find suitable labor to fill the chronic shortages in Hawaii's expanding sugar plantation industry or in West Coast railroad companies, for instance. Employers also sought Japanese workers to fill the gap in immigration created by the Chinese Exclusion Act of 1882. In Hawaii, many of the laborers were exploited, forced to work long and grueling hours under the strict conditions of their three-year contracts. Living conditions were often deplorable, as labor contractors charged high rents and exorbitant prices for goods the workers were obliged to purchase as a part of their contracts.

Laborers also experienced discrimination in the wider society that would limit their opportunities for advancement, which in turn made it more difficult to save the funds necessary to return to Japan. Under the Gentlemen's Agreement between the United States and Japan in 1907–1908, the immigration of Japanese laborers would come to an almost complete halt, and the tenor of life in America shifted as laborers increasingly accepted that they would remain permanently in America. Meanwhile, those in California and other West Coast areas often found work as migrant laborers in a variety of fields, including agriculture, railroads, mining, fishing, and canning. As other Japanese Americans formed their own businesses, laborers could also rely on finding jobs among employers in the Japanese American community.

Organized Labor

Japanese American history includes a number of instances in which organized labor groups fought for better treatment. Japanese Americans were frequently excluded from mainstream American labor unions, as their hardworking nature and willingness to accept low wages made them unpopular with white labor leaders. Nevertheless, Japanese Americans could lead the fight on their own terms. In 1891, for example, the Hawaiian Supreme Court heard a case from a laborer named Mioshi who argued that the labor contract system amounted to a form of slavery. In 1900, Japanese laborers in Hawaii held more than twenty strikes. In the same year, the Japanese Labor League, based in San Francisco, attempted to free workers from the contract system.

Meanwhile, in February 1903, workers in the sugar beet industry in Oxnard, California, came together to form the Japanese-Mexican Labor Association. A month later, a strike ensued in protest against the labor contracting system, and strikers succeeded in ending the monopoly power of the labor contractors. The biggest strike to date occurred in 1909, when 7,000 Japanese agricultural laborers in Oahu struck against the Hawaiian Sugar Planters' Association for four months. Their demands included higher wages and a salary structure that did not discriminate on the basis of race. Again, in 1920, Japanese workers would be joined by Filipino workers on Oahu in a six-month-long strike that sought the same goals as the 1909 action.

Entrepreneurship and the Professional Ranks

Not all Japanese Americans were interested in the labor movement. Many sought to leave organized labor and become independent either as farmers or business owners. The internment of Japanese Americans during World War II caused major disruptions in this upward mobility of Japanese workers and families, most of whom lost their businesses, homes, and other assets during their incarceration in 1942. For many who had once experienced contract labor but went on obtain their own land and start a business, the postwar period required a return to paid labor, at least temporarily. But as conditions improved after the war, Japanese Americans could increasingly find positions in the professional fields, or they could open businesses that were able to interact with the majority society.

By the end of the twentieth century, Japanese Americans had succeeded in climbing to the top ranks of American society in terms of income and occupational status. According to the 2000 census, adult Japanese males had median earnings of $50,876, second only to Asian Indians and significantly higher than Asian Americans generally ($40,650) and the American male population as a whole ($37,057). Japanese women, with median earnings of nearly $36,000, were ahead of all Asian groups and the American adult female population as a whole. These figures put Japanese American household median income at $70,849, the highest of any Asian American group and fully $20,800 more than U.S. households overall. Japanese Americans were also 14 percent more likely to be in managerial and professional positions than the American working population as a whole—50.7 percent versus 44.5 percent. At the other end of the income scale, Japanese Americans were 21 percent less likely to live in poverty than Americans as a whole—9.7 versus 12.4.

One of the first Asian nationalities to immigrate to America, the Japanese are also one of the oldest. That is, compared with other major Asian American groups, they have far fewer persons still coming to live in the United States, a result of their former homeland's mature and developed economy. Thus, Japanese Americans tend to be among the most acculturated of Asian Americans, with higher levels of English language skills and homeownership. This success is testament to the skills, talents, and work ethic of the community, for unlike most other immigrant groups, the Japanese had to climb the socioeconomic ladder twice—once when they first began arriving in the early twentieth century and again when they left the incarceration camps after World War II.

Wade Pfau

Further Reading

Kitano, Harry H.L. *Japanese Americans: The Evolution of a Subculture.* Englewood Cliffs, NJ: Prentice Hall, 1969.

Spickard, Paul R. *Japanese Americans: The Formation and Transformations of an Ethnic Group.* New York: Twayne Publishers, 1996.

Takahashi, Jere. *Nisei/Sansei: Shifting Japanese American Identities and Politics.* Philadelphia: Temple University Press, 1997.

Wilson, Robert A., and Bill Hosokawa. *East to America: A History of the Japanese in the United States.* New York: William Morrow, 1980.

Literature, Japanese American

Japanese American literature over the past century has reflected the vicissitudes of the Japanese American experience. From the late nineteenth century, when Japanese immigrants began to arrive in Hawaii and on the U.S. mainland in significant numbers, through the onset of World War II, the literature was often backward looking, toward Japanese society and culture, with authors attempting to explain their seemingly exotic homeland to American audiences. But with the incarceration of Japanese Americans during World War II, an anger at American racism entered the literature from the 1940s through the 1960s, along with the more traditional immigrant theme of the conflict between traditionalist parents and acculturated and rebellious children. With the civil rights movement and a new emphasis on multiculturalism in the broader society of the 1960s and 1970s, younger Japanese American writers began to emphasize a new bicultural identity for themselves.

Pre–World War II Writing

Two of the most significant writers of the early period of Japanese American letters were Etsu Sugimoto and Jun Fujita. Born to a samurai family in Echigo, Japan, in 1874, Sugimoto authored a number of novels in the 1930s and early 1940s—including *A Daughter of the Narikin* (1932), *A Daughter of the Nohfu* (1935), and *Grandmother O Kyo* (1940)—but is best known for her first book, a 1925 memoir entitled *A Daughter of the Samurai.* In it, she writes of life in a bleak, northern Japanese town barely touched by the new Western-influenced, reformist spirit sweeping her country. When her brother runs off to America rather than submit to an arranged marriage, Etsu is required to carry on the ancient traditions of the family. Like much of early Japanese American literature, Sugimoto's memoir looks back longingly at a homeland left behind even as it tries to explain traditional Japanese culture to an American audience.

Born in a southern village near Hiroshima in 1888, Fujita immigrated to Canada and then the United States in the early twentieth century. Best known as a photojournalist, Fujita was also a well-regarded poet, contributing a number of pieces to the influential magazine *Poetry.* Writing from his retreat in rural Minnesota, Fujita penned spare and minimalist poems on nature, attempting to juxtapose traditional Japanese verse—particularly the five-line tanka verse form—with imagery from his life as a newspaper photographer in Chicago. In one piece from his best-known collection, *Tanka: Poems in Exile* (1923), Fujita writes:

> A sudden caw, lost in the air,
> Leaves the hillside to the autumn sun;
> Save a leaf or two curling
> Not a sound is here.

By the 1930s, a new generation of Japanese, known as the Nisei, had come of age. Born in America to immigrant parents, Nisei writers explored traditional themes of immigrant literature, most notably the tensions between traditional parents and acculturated American-born children. Among the best-known works of this generation is a collection of short stories, *Yokohama, California* (1949), by Toshio Mori. Though published after World War II, many of the stories were written during the 1930s and depicted life in Japanese America before the war. Born in Oakland, California, in 1910, Mori borrowed the title of his book from the popular name for the Japanese American neighborhood where he grew up. The stories cover a host of subjects, with many reflecting on the struggle of Nisei—confined to segregated communities and caught

between two worlds—to understand an America that was both familiar and yet distant. In the story "1936," a struggling young writer notes, "I wanted to do everything, I wanted to know women, I wanted to know the white people, the minds of my generation and people, the Nisei, the nature of our parents, the Issei, the culture of Japan, the culture of America, of life as a whole."

Post–World War II Writing

Monica Sone, born to immigrant parents in Seattle in 1919, wrote what is perhaps the best-known Japanese American memoir of the mid-twentieth century. *Nisei Daughter* (1953) tells the story of Sone and her family as they attempt to make ends meet in the rundown Skid Row neighborhood of the Washington State metropolis. Particularly poignant are the sections where Sone writes about having to overcome her Japanese parents' objections to her participating in such all-American activities as ballet class and dating. She wants to join the larger society while they fear she will grow away from them and her culture. Much of the latter half of the book is devoted to the family's experiences in the Minidoka War Relocation Center in Idaho, where they were incarcerated after Japan's attack on Pearl Harbor in 1941. While these chapters expose the brutality and racism of the American government and public, much of the narrative is about efforts to establish a normal life in the very harsh conditions of the camp.

Farewell to Manzanar (1973), however, is widely considered to be the definitive memoir of life in the incarceration camps. Penned by Jeanne Wakatsuki Houston, it tells the story of her family and her community's efforts to cope with the isolation of the desert camp at Manzanar, California, and their efforts to maintain their dignity and cultural identity against the institutionalized racism of the U.S. military.

Meanwhile, Japanese American writers in Hawaii—living in a more multicultural environment and never forced to undergo the indignities and privations of camp life (Japanese Hawaiians were not incarcerated during World War II)—developed their own unique literature, marked by the use of the pidgin English employed by the diverse peoples of the islands. Milton Murayama's 1959 novel, *All I Asking for Is My Body,* uses such vernacular to explore the racial and class struggles of Hawaii during the 1930s and 1940s.

By the 1970s and 1980s, a new generation of Japanese American writers was coming of age. Raised by American-born parents, who in the wake of their World War II experience did everything they could to Americanize their children, they had little connection to the culture and traditions of the old country. At the same time, many were influenced by the new emphasis on multiculturalism and ethnic pride, which was a hallmark of minority life in the latter part of the twentieth century. These Sansei, or third-generation writers, who include playwright Philip Ken Gotanda, mystery writer Dale Furutani, and novelist Julie Otsuka, worked to resurrect their Japanese identities, even as they recognized that they were essentially shaped by the larger American culture. Although these writers were born after the war, family memories of the internment camps haunt their writings. Otsuka's 2002 novel *When the Emperor Was Divine* and Philip Kan Gotanda's *After the War* (2007) both explore the dynamics of families and communities attempting to recover economically and psychologically from the internment. In Otsuka's work, the plot revolves around a family accepting the fact that their once powerful and patriarchal father has been broken by the camp while Gotanda's drama explores the Japanese American communities' shame over the actions of the "no-no boys," young Japanese men in the camps who refused to sign up for the U.S. military and refused to denounce allegiance to the Japanese emperor.

Japanese American literature has continued to evolve in the late twentieth and early twenty-first century as writers endeavor to fuse American and Japanese themes in their work. Among the most interesting of these efforts are Furutani's mysteries, which attempt to infuse the American hard-boiled detective genre with Japanese characters and storylines, including three interrelated books set in medieval Japan, the Samurai Mystery Trilogy.

James Ciment and Tim J. Watts

Further Reading

Bloom, Harold, ed. *Asian-American Writers.* Philadelphia: Chelsea House, 1999.

Cheung, King-Kok. *An Interethnic Companion to Asian American Literature.* New York: Cambridge University Press, 1997.

Knippling, Alpana Sharma. *New Immigrant Literatures in the United States: A Sourcebook to Our Multicultural Literary Heritage.* Westport, CT: Greenwood, 1996.

Lim, Shirley, and Amy Ling. *Reading the Literatures of Asian America.* Philadelphia: Temple University Press, 1992.

Little Tokyo

Little Tokyo is the area in downtown Los Angeles first settled by Japanese at the end of the nineteenth century and still an ethnic and cultural enclave in the city today. The term is also used loosely in reference to other Japanese American communities in other U.S. cities. Little Tokyo in L.A., also referred to as "Japantown," "J-Town," or "Nihonmachi," was known until the 1950s as "Lil' Tokio" and originally as "Rafu"—the Japanese translation of its Chinese name. Since 1910, more Japanese Americans have lived there than in any other community in the United States. By the early twenty-first century, however, most Japanese had left, leaving behind a residual Japanese American population of about 1,000.

As host to a number of annual cultural events, such as Nisei Week, flower and tofu festivals, and a major New Year's celebration, Little Tokyo serves as a nexus for international tourism but maintains its intimate character with traditional shops such as the Miyakawa Bakery, founded in 1923. The neighborhood is also home to works of public art, including Isamu Noguchi's sculpture *To Issei* and to such institutions as the Japanese American Cultural and Community Center, Japanese American National Museum, and the Union Center for the Arts, home of the East West Players theater group and the LA Artcore gallery. More than a tourist attraction, the neighborhood is an enduring marker of Japanese American history—a century of social and economic change in which individual and collective identities were formed.

Little Tokyo pioneers were *wataridori* (sojourners), who occupied local boardinghouses. The first documented inhabitant was a former seaman named Kame (Hamanosuke Shigeta), the proprietor of one of many restaurants opened in the 1880s that served traditional American fare. Since jobs available to Caucasians were often not accessible to Japanese, many local residents worked as domestics, gardeners, railroad hands, produce workers, and employees

Community leaders in Los Angeles's Little Tokyo are attempting to attract young Japanese Americans with new housing, shops, and public gardens. With many residents having left for the suburbs, Little Tokyo became a chiefly commercial and cultural center. *(Associated Press/Reed Saxon)*

of Japanese-owned bamboo shops, tobacco factories, pool halls, and dry goods stores. They excelled in agriculture and, with Chinese, Russian, and American wholesalers, opened City Market in the community.

With housing discrimination and assaults on Japanese common outside the enclave, local businesses and associations offered stability and safety. In 1903, residents started a newspaper, *Rafu Shimpo,* published in both English and Japanese. To further promote unity, Japanese heritage, and Little Tokyo businesses, the Nisei Week summer festival was organized in 1934, featuring a fashion show, traditional *ondo* dancing, and sports tournaments. Later incorporating an essay contest, baby pageant, and festival queen competition, it became the single largest local attraction, targeting both the general public and Nisei, children of the first generation who had started shopping outside the quarter.

Daily life in Little Tokyo tragically shifted after the Japanese attack on Pearl Harbor in 1941. The Federal Bureau of Investigation arrested community leaders, stores were closed, and bank accounts frozen. Under Executive Order 9066 in February 1942, those of Japanese descent were corralled into ten distant concentration camps or later enlisted in the U.S. military as part of the 442nd Regimental Combat Team of Japanese Americans. The abandoned spaces on East First Street were settled by African Americans, many of whom opened cafés and jazz clubs; Little Tokyo became known as Bronzeville.

It was not until the spring of 1945 that Japanese and Japanese American internees were able to return to their homes. Dry goods merchant Kiichi Uyeda was reportedly one of the first to be released from the Manzanar facility to resume business downtown. More than 25,000 in all returned to the Los Angeles community, notwithstanding reports of a housing shortage and warnings by the War Relocation Authority to not congregate with large groups of Japanese. In 1946, *Rafu Shimpo* presses began rolling again, and in 1949 merchants reinstated the annual Nisei Week festival.

As laws restricting immigration, citizenship, land use, and housing were slowly rescinded, allowing for more mobility, Nisei families moved from the urban center to the suburbs. Thus, by the latter half of the 1950s, the Japanese American population in Southern California became increasingly decentralized. Moreover, the City Planning Commission demolished the entire northwest section of Little Tokyo. During the 1960s and 1970s, however, three buildings and several nursing homes were constructed there, in part the result of social activism— Asian Americans, like other minorities, were taking to the streets to protest the war in Vietnam and call for civil rights. Nevertheless, area development continued for Civic Center expansion, Japanese investments, and

other commercial projects, as tenants were displaced and landmarks, such as the Olympic Hotel and the Sun Building, were leveled.

As defined by the Little Tokyo Redevelopment Project and designated by the City of Los Angeles, Little Tokyo today occupies 67 acres (27 hectares), bordered by Third, Alameda, First, and Los Angeles streets. The scaled-down Little Tokyo remains a symbol for ethnic identity and a link to the past. Although postwar flight to the suburbs and assimilation into mainstream society were viewed as a boon to local race relations, the area continues to unify Southern California's Japanese American community, serving not only as a destination but also as a vital support network throughout the twentieth century. Little Tokyo was designated as a National Historic Landmark District in 1995.

Bruna Mori Darini

Further Reading

Japanese American Historical Society of Southern California. *Nanka Nikkei Voices: Little Tokyo, Changing Times, Changing Faces.* Vol. 3. Los Angeles: Japanese American Historical Society of Southern California, 2004.

Kurashige, Lon. *Japanese American Celebration and Conflict: A History of Ethnic Identity and Festival, 1934–1990.* Berkeley: University of California Press, 2002.

Murase, Ichiro Mike. *Little Tokyo: One Hundred Years in Pictures.* Los Angeles: Visual Communications / Asian American Studies Central, 1983.

Manzanar Incident

The Manzanar Incident was an armed confrontation between Japanese American inmates and guards at California's Manzanar internment camp in December 1942; two inmates were killed and ten wounded. The Manzanar Incident was not the only civil disturbance stemming from inmate resistance at the camps, but it was arguably the most serious conflict at any relocation center during the war. Some historians dispute the term "incident" as a description of what happened, accusing government authorities of using the word to underplay the seriousness of the event. Instead, these historians say, it was an "uprising" on the part of detainees.

Manzanar was the largest of the ten concentration camps, built to house 120,000 Japanese Americans forced from their homes by Executive Order 9066 in February 1942. There are several different accounts of what happened and how many people were involved; estimates range from a few dozen to several hundred. What is known is that on December 6, 1942, inmates at the Manzanar facility gathered to protest camp conditions and the arrest of internee Harry Ueno, who was taken to Inyo County Jail on suspicion of beating Japanese American Citizens League (JACL) leader Fred Tayama the previous night. Ueno was a critic of the JACL and had been trying to unionize the kitchen workers. Crowds gathered to protest Ueno's arrest and his imprisonment in a jail outside of the camp. Members of the group denounced Tayama and several others as traitors and informants (*inu*), who were removed from the camp for their own safety. Military police were called in to quiet the mob that had gathered to demand Ueno's release. The MPs attempted to use tear gas, but the heavy winds common to the area blew it away. The protestors grew angry and unruly, and the MPs fired live ammunition into the crowd. One detainee was killed immediately, ten were injured, and one died of injuries days later. A doctor from Manzanar and several others claim that the injured persons were shot in the back as they fled the MPs. Newspapers of the time reported that the camp's inmates were celebrating the anniversary of Pearl Harbor when the fight broke out, though most inmate accounts dismiss such reporting as biased.

War Relocation Authority investigators sought the cause of the riot and reported their findings in a December 22 memo entitled "The Manzanar 'Incident': December 5 to December 19, 1942." Although the immediate cause was the arrest of Harry Ueno, according to the investigators, numerous other problems lay at the root of the incident. Of the twenty-five reasons they cited for the riot, one of the main causes was the administration's reliance on information about conditions in the camp provided by JACL leaders. Those individuals—who were not even elected by the JACL—were not unanimously respected among the camp's residents, many of whom regarded them as stooges to camp authorities. The presence of informers in the camp and the pro-government Manzanar *Free Press* added to the problem by heightening suspicion of collusion with government authorities. In addition, the Issei were excluded from good jobs and positions of importance in the camp. Rumors about stores of sugar being stolen and the wide variations in food quality among the mess halls fueled inmate disgruntlement. Other factors were said to include inconsistencies in camp policies due to frequent changes in administration; delays in the payment of wages and clothing allowances; and inadequate translations of official notices into Japanese. Many families complained of their Issei loved ones being held in camps far away, while others expressed concern about their future and anger at the loss of income and property as a result of the evacuation.

Emily Hiramatsu Morishima

Further Reading

Garrett, Jessie A., and Ronald C. Larson, eds. *Camp and Community: Manzanar and the Owens Valley*. Fullerton: California State University, Japanese American Oral History Project, 1977.

Houston, Jeanne Wakatsuki, and James D. Houston. *Farewell to Manzanar: A True Story of Japanese American Experience During and After the World War II Internment*. Boston: Houghton Mifflin, 2002.

Unrau, Harlan D. "The Evacuation and Relocation of Persons of Japanese Ancestry During World War II: A Historical Study of the Manzanar Relocation Center." National Park Service, 1996. http://www.nps.gov/archive/manz/hrs/hrst.htm.

Martial Arts, Japanese

The history of Japanese martial arts in the United States began in 1885 on the day the first official immigrants from Japan arrived in Hawaii. A sumo match was held to celebrate their arrival, and sumo quickly became a favorite pastime of plantation workers, with each plantation sending its best wrestlers to regionwide tournaments. Although sumo had deep religious connections in Japan, Japanese American sumo wrestlers de-emphasized its religious symbolism and it became a team sport much like Western wrestling. In the early twentieth century, sumo helped maintain bonds among Japanese American communities.

Judo

Judo, a form of jacket wrestling developed in the late 1880s by a Japanese educator named Jigoro Kano, also spread throughout Japanese communities in Hawaii, California, and the Pacific Northwest. Kano created judo from preexisting forms of jujutsu ("art of yielding," referring to a variety of traditional Japanese martial art styles) and combined them with Western physical education pedagogy (emphasis on health and hygiene, using public lectures and textbooks to promote the art, systemized competition). His ideas on the relationship between physical education and spiritual training influenced the development of other modern Japanese martial arts.

Unlike sumo, which was practiced almost exclusively by Japanese, judo enjoyed a short period of popularity among the Caucasian elite in the early twentieth century. In 1903, prominent Seattle businessman Samuel Hill invited Kano's top student, Yoshiaki Yamashita, to teach judo to his son. After a brief stay in Seattle, Yamashita was taken by Hill to Washington, D.C., in 1904, where both he and his wife began teaching judo to diplomats and other Washington elites. Even President Theodore Roosevelt learned judo from Yamashita in order to lose weight for an upcoming election. Roosevelt became an active promoter of judo and secured Yamashita a position teaching judo at the U.S. Naval Academy. The armed forces continued to employ judo instructors at West Point and the naval academy in the pre–World War II period, and the military incorporated judo techniques into its training curriculum. Still, Japanese Americans made up the bulk of the practitioners and leaders of the art. Judo provided Japanese Americans with cultural and social ties to Japan. Even Kano, the founder of the art, toured judo schools located in Japanese American communities throughout the United States.

World War II changed the organizational development of judo in America. Detainees at the internment centers where more than 112,000 Japanese Americans were incarcerated during World War II practiced sumo, judo, and kendo (sword fighting) along with other sports in the camps, and even held tournaments. The camps provided Japanese American judo practitioners with opportunities to train with people from other regions. These newly formed bonds facilitated the development of a national judo organization. Before the war, judo groups had their own connections to the Kodokan, the headquarters of judo located in Japan, and only occasional, informal connections to each other. Moreover, the U.S. military promoted judo through the auspices of the Strategic Air Command (SAC), which sent military men to Japan to study not only judo, but aikido (a stylized form of jujutsu) and karate as well. From these developments emerged the first national judo organization in 1952, now known as the United States Judo Federation (USJF). One of the many judo personalities active in this period was Fukuda Keiko, the highest-ranking female judo practitioner in the world. She is widely respected not only for her efforts in promoting women's judo in America, but also as one of the few students of Jigoro Kano still alive and active today.

Kendo

A modern form of swordsmanship or fencing, kendo developed in the late nineteenth century from older forms of weaponry but did not enjoy the same level of popularity as did sumo and judo. Only Issei elite, usually those of samurai background or military training, could afford the equipment to practice the art. However, Issei did encourage the next generation of Japanese Americans to practice kendo as a way to learn "proper" Japanese behavior, especially after Japan's defeat of Russia in the Russo-Japanese War and its emergence as a superpower during World War I. The Federal Bureau of Investigation (FBI) was deeply suspicious of kendo because of its association with Japanese militarism. Indeed, the Butokukai (Martial Virtue Association) promoted martial education throughout Japan as part of its war efforts, in particular kendo. Many kendo clubs in the Japanese American communities belonged to the U.S. branch of the Butokukai, and the government feared that its practitioners were spies or saboteurs. Kendo was not the only martial art under suspicion during World War II—many Japanese American martial arts instructors were listed as category "A" in the ABC list. (The U.S. government recorded the names of all Japanese believed to be potentially dangerous to the United States, and those classified in category "A" were considered the most dangerous.) Although some kendo was practiced in the relocation centers, the stigma against the art and its relative lack of popularity among Japanese American youths compared to other sports marked a clear break in kendo history between prewar and postwar periods. While some instructors in Hawaii continued to teach kendo throughout the war, servicemen and Japanese immigrants were the main forces in promoting the art after the war.

Karate, Aikido, and Other Arts

Karate and aikido had only limited existence in the United States before the 1940s but gained popularity after the war. U.S. servicemen brought back knowledge of karate, a native civilian defense art of Okinawa that had not reached the rest of Japan until the 1920s. Karate comprises a number of different hand-and-foot fighting styles, each with distinctive techniques and teachings. Despite certain similarities, it is more fragmented than other martial arts. The most popular styles include *shotokan, goju-ryu shito-ryu,* and *shorin ryu.* Aikido was developed by Ueshiba Morihei during the 1920s and 1930s from a variety of martial arts, mostly jujutsu. He also incorporated spiritual teachings of Omoto-kyo, a type of Shinto developed in the late nineteenth and early twentieth centuries. A famous aikido instructor, Koichi Tohei, is credited with introducing the art to America through the Hawaiian Japanese American community in the early 1950s. The art gained mainstream exposure in the late 1980s through movies starring American-born aikido master Steven Seagal.

Other, less popular Japanese martial arts practiced in the United States include *iaido, kyudo,* and *naginata.* *Iaido* consists of prearranged sword drawing and cutting and is often practiced alongside other arts such as kendo. *Naginata* is the art of fencing with a bamboo halberd and uses much of the same equipment as kendo. *Kyudo* (archery), like kendo, was practiced by elite members of the Japanese community before World War II but was not as popular as sumo, kendo, or judo. *Kyudo* is widely regarded as a spiritual martial art because of its putative connections to Zen Buddhism. The stereotype began with the publication of *Zen in the Art of Archery* (1948) by Eugen Herrigel, a German philosophy professor who studied Zen and kyudo in Japan during the 1930s. Herrigel, who could not speak Japanese, studied with a kyudo teacher named Awa Kenzo, who combined his own spiritual beliefs with kyudo. Herrigel articulated his understanding of kyudo in terms of Zen. His book was translated into English and Japanese in the 1950s and became a best seller.

Michael J. Wert

Further Reading

Brousse, Michel, and David Matsumoto. *Judo in the U.S.: A Century of Dedication.* Berkeley, CA: North Atlantic Books, 2005.

Fukuda, Keiko. *Born for the Mat: A Kodokan kata Textbook for Women.* San Francisco: N.p., 1973.

Green, Thomas A., ed. *Martial Arts of the World: An Encyclopedia.* Santa Barbara, CA: ABC-CLIO, 2002.

Green, Thomas A., and Joseph Svinth, eds. *Martial Arts in the Modern World.* Westport, CT: Praeger, 2003.

Hurst, G. Cameron, III. *Armed Martial Arts of Japan: Swordsmanship and Archery.* New Haven, CT: Yale University Press, 1998.

Niiya, Brian, ed. *More Than a Game: Sport in the Japanese American Community.* Los Angeles: Japanese American National Museum, 2000.

Svinth, Joseph R. *Getting a Grip: Judo in the Nikkei Communities of the Pacific Northwest 1900–1950.* Ontario: Electronic Journals of Martial Arts and Sciences, 2003.

Masaoka, Mike Masaru (1915–1991)

A high-ranking official for many years in the Japanese American Citizens League (JACL)—the oldest and largest Japanese American advocacy group—Mike Masaru Masaoka was instrumental in persuading members of the community to cooperate with government authorities during World War II and accept incarceration for the duration of the war.

He was born Masaru Masaoka in Fresno, California, on October 15, 1915, to Issei (first-generation immigrant) parents. The fourth of eight children, he moved with his family to Salt Lake City, Utah, as a young boy

Mike Masaoka (second from left) and three brothers served in the 442nd Regimental Combat Team in World War II. As a leader of the Japanese American Citizens League, Masaoka urged Japanese Americans to accept internment and persuaded the U.S. military to draft Nisei as a way for them to prove their loyalty. *(Library of Congress)*

and attended public school there. It was in Salt Lake City that he changed his name to "Mike" and became a member of the Mormon Church (Church of Jesus Christ of Latter-day Saints). He graduated from the University of Utah in 1937, with a bachelor's degree in economic and political science. The following year, he attended an annual gathering of the Japanese American Citizens League (JACL) and was moved by the idea of helping fellow Japanese Americans. He joined the organization and rose quickly throughout the ranks, becoming national secretary in 1941. He served in this capacity, and as a field executive, from 1941 through 1943 and again from 1945 through 1946.

The JACL took on special importance during World War II and the internment of West Coast Japanese American citizens and resident aliens. The organization advocated cooperation with the War Relocation Authority, the federal agency responsible for administering the incarceration camps. During the war, the JACL sent Masaoka to Washington, D.C., where he lobbied Congress, military authorities, and the Franklin Roosevelt administration to draft Nisei, or American-born Japanese, into the military, as a way for them to prove their patriotism and loyalty to America. Out of this lobbying came the 442nd Regimental Combat Team, which Masaoka joined and which he served as the unit's publicist.

After his military service concluded in 1945, Masaoka returned to Washington as a lobbyist for the JACL. He successfully fought for the repeal of the 1924 Asian Exclusion Act and lobbied for reparations to Japanese Americans who had been adversely affected by their relocation to internment camps. He served as the national legislative director of the JACL Anti-Discrimination Committee form 1946 through 1952, lobbying successfully for naturalized citizenship for members of the Issei generation of Japanese Americans.

Masaoka continued as a lobbyist for the JACL until 1972. During this time, he also worked to improve immigration and naturalization laws and fought for civil rights, creating alliances with Latino groups and participating in the historic March on Washington for Jobs and Freedom in August 1963. In 1972, Masaoka left the JACL to form his own lobbying firm, Mike Masaoka Associates, representing American, Japanese, and Japanese American business interests. In 1980, he was appointed by Congress to the Commission on Wartime Relocation and Internment of Civilians (CWRIC), charged with addressing the issue of reparations for surviving members of the World War II incarceration camps. His autobiography, *They Call Me Moses Masaoka* (coauthored with Bill Hosokawa), was published in 1987, and Masaoka died of heart ailments on June 26, 1991, in Washington, D.C.

Amelia Maijala

Further Reading

Hosokawa, Bill. *JACL in Quest of Justice.* New York: William Morrow, 1982.

Masaoka, Mike, with Bill Hosokawa. *They Call Me Moses Masaoka: An American Saga.* New York: William Morrow, 1987.

Matsunaga, Spark (1916–1990)

A longtime Democratic member of Congress (1963–1990) from Hawaii who played a critical role in winning statehood for the Aloha state, Masayuki "Spark" Matsunaga was born on October 8, 1916, to immigrant Japanese plantation workers in Kukuiula, Kauai, Hawaii. He legally adopted his childhood nickname "Spark" later in life. During his seven terms in the U.S. House of Representatives (1963–1977) and more than two terms in the Senate (1977–1990), Matsunaga advocated persistently for the rights of immigrants, veterans, Japanese Americans, and other minorities.

Upon graduating from the University of Hawai'i in June 1941, he was commissioned in the U.S. Army Reserve and was serving on Molokai Island, Hawaii, when Pearl Harbor was attacked on December 7. Relieved of his duties because he was Japanese, Matsunaga was sent to Camp McCoy, a military facility in Wisconsin, to await the War Department's decision on his "loyalty."

Once cleared, he joined 1,500 other Japanese Americans for combat duty in the 100th Infantry Battalion. In September 1943, Matsunaga was wounded twice on the same night in a minefield in Italy, later receiving Purple Hearts and the Bronze Star. By the end of the war, his battalion became part of the army's most decorated unit, the all-Japanese American 442nd Regimental Combat Team. Upon returning to the United States after the war, he gave 800 speeches focusing on how Japanese Americans could reintegrate into society upon leaving the internment camps.

After graduating from Harvard University Law School in 1951, Matsunaga became an assistant prosecutor in Honolulu in 1952. He launched his political career two years later and was elected to the Territorial Legislature in 1954. Matsunaga was instrumental in gaining passage of federal legislation granting Hawaiian statehood in 1959, having twice served as a member of the territory's petitioning delegation to Congress.

Matsunaga won election to his first term as a U.S. Representative as a Democrat in 1962, and was returned to office for six more terms. After the retirement of Senator Hiram Fong in 1976, Matsunaga defeated former Hawaii governor William Quinn to earn the seat he would hold until his death. Serving on the Senate Finance Committee and International Trade and Aging subcommittees, among others, he worked for more than two decades to establish what would eventually became the U.S. Peace Institute, a nonpartisan organization funded by Congress and dedicated to the peaceful resolution of international conflict. Other legislation with which he was associated includes the Spark M. Matsunaga Hydrogen Research, Development, and Demonstration Program Act of 1990, a bill he wrote that financed alternative energy studies. In his most significant legislative accomplishment on behalf of the Japanese American community, Matsunaga served as a point man in the Senate for passage of the Japanese-American Redress Bill, which called for $20,000 in reparations to each survivor of internment. Renamed the Civil Liberties Act, the bill was passed by Congress, signed by President Ronald Reagan on August 10, 1988, and disbursed under President George H.W. Bush.

Matsunaga died on Easter Sunday, April 15, 1990; his ashes are interred at Punchbowl National Cemetery in Honolulu. Native Hawaiian and Chinese American Democrat Daniel K. Akaka filled his vacancy in the Senate. Commemorating his lifelong dedication to nonviolent solutions to international disputes, the University of Hawai'i established the Matsunaga Institute for Peace, a conflict resolution organization, shortly after his death.

Gabriella Oldham

Further Reading

Halloran, Richard. *Sparky: Warrior, Peacemaker, Poet, Patriot: A Portrait of Senator Spark M. Matsunaga.* Honolulu: Watermark, 2002.

Matsunaga, Spark M. *The Mars Project: Journeys Beyond the Cold War.* New York: Hill and Wang, 1986.

Matsunaga, Spark M., and Ping Chen. *Rulemakers of the House.* Urbana: University of Illinois Press, 1978.

McClatchy, V.S. (1857–1938)

Valentine Stuart McClatchy was an active member of California's Japanese exclusion movement in the early twentieth century. In the decades leading up to his death, he acted as a financial sponsor, publicist, and mouthpiece for the movement.

Born in 1857, the son of an Irish immigrant newspaper editor—his father, James McClatchy, was an editor of the *Sacramento Bee* and founder of the McClatchy Newspaper Company—V.S. McClatchy and his brother Charles went to work in the family publishing business as young men. At the same time, Valentine became integrally involved in the movement that sought to bar Japanese immigrants from entering America. One of the exclusionist groups with which McClatchy was closely involved was the Japanese Exclusion League, founded in 1920. When the group faced financial difficulties, Mc-Clatchy chose to continue funding it himself. When the name of the group began drawing negative associations for people, the California Joint Immigration Committee (CJIC) was established to absorb the old organization and McClatchy became the secretary.

His main goal in working with the CJIC was making the exclusionist case, particularly to those who supported a possible adjustment to the 1924 immigration law that would allow for a quota on Japanese immigrants like the one in place for immigrants from other countries. McClatchy took it upon himself to visit various areas of California, making speeches and meeting with people whom he might convert to the exclusionist cause. He continually stressed that the CJIC was in favor of the fair treatment of Japanese immigrants already in the United States, but that it simply did not want changes made to the law that had excluded further immigration.

One of McClatchy's main contributions to the exclusionist movement was the writing of a series of pamphlets. Among these was one in 1921 titled "Japanese Immigration and Colonization." In it, McClatchy advanced the theory that the Japanese were attempting to colonize and take over America, beginning with Hawaii and California. He was particularly wary of married couples immigrating because he believed the Japanese to have a more prodigious birth rate than others. He warned that if they were permitted entry, they would reproduce and quickly displace the white population. McClatchy cautioned about Japanese women being allowed to enter the country as wives for the same reason.

McClatchy wrote about other dangers he perceived about immigration as well. For example, he expressed concern that Japanese women were raising their American-born children to serve the emperor rather than America. The same children, he argued, were being used to circumvent the 1913 Alien Land Law, which forbade Japanese immigrants from owning land; instead, first-generation immigrants were buying real property under the names of their American-born children. In addition, McClatchy believed that the Japanese were accustomed to a lower standard of living and could therefore enter American industries for lower wages—and take over from the bottom up. McClatchy supported repealing the law that allowed for wives of Japanese immigrants to join their husbands in America and made every attempt to discourage pro-quota movements.

McClatchy always believed that the anti-quota movement would find success quickly. As it turned out, the pro-quota movement proved just as tenacious, and McClatchy spent the rest of his life making his case. He died on May 15, 1938.

Leah Irvine

Further Reading

Hirobe, Izumi. *Japanese Pride, American Prejudice: Modifying the Exclusion Clause of the 1924 Immigration Act.* Palo Alto, CA: Stanford University Press, 2001.

Midori (1971–)

Midori Goto is a world-renowned classical violinist from Japan who moved to the United States at age eleven to pursue her career as a musician. She was born on October 25, 1971, in Osaka, Japan, and learned to play the violin during infancy from her mother, Setsu Goto. Midori received her first violin at four years old and performed publicly—one of the difficult caprices by Niccolò Paganini—at age seven in Osaka.

In 1981, still only nine, Midori was invited to the Aspen Summer Music School and Festival in Colorado by Dorothy DeLay, a famous violin instructor at New York City's Juilliard School, to whom the girl had sent a recording. Midori impressed the Aspen audience by playing the entire Bach Chaconne, said to be one of the most difficult pieces in the violin solo repertoire. In 1982, Midori and her mother moved to New York City, where she began studying under DeLay. In December of that year, the eleven-year-old Midori made her debut with the New York Philharmonic under the direction Zubin Mehta, with whom she began a career-long friendship and working relationship. Midori's star continued to rise in the course of succeeding years, even as she continued studying with DeLay. She performed with the world-famous Philadelphia Orchestra (1983) and the Toronto Symphony (1985), among others, and then traveled as a member of the European Community Youth Orchestra on the televised "Hiroshima Peace Tour" organized by Leonard Bernstein.

At fourteen, Midori made her recording debut in 1986 on the Philips label, performing Bach and Vivaldi. Later that year she made what would become a legendary debut performance at the Tanglewood Music Festival in Stockbridge, Massachusetts, the summer home of the Boston Symphony Orchestra. Twice during the performance she broke the E string on her violin and had to borrow an instrument from a member of the orchestra.

The Japanese-born violin prodigy Midori moved to New York in 1982, at age eleven, for advanced study at the Juilliard School. She debuted with the New York Philharmonic that same year and went on to international acclaim as a concert and recording artist. *(Marianne Barcellona/Time & Life Pictures/Getty Images)*

Nevertheless, she performed brilliantly, to the great applause of the audience and orchestra and to the awe of conductor Leonard Bernstein.

The next milestone in Midori's career was a recording contract with the Sony Classical label, signed in 1988. Over the course of the next decade, Midori recorded a number of pieces for Sony, including a Grammy-nominated rendition of Paganini's caprice. She continued to record exclusively for Sony and released a total of twelve albums, including her twentieth-anniversary album in 2002.

Midori has won several prestigious awards during her career, including the Japanese Government Best Artist of the Year (1988), the Los Angeles Music Center's Dorothy B. Chandler Performing Arts Award (1990), New York State's Asian-American Heritage Month Award (1991), the Suntory Hall Award (1994), Japan's Crystal Award (1995), and the Avery Fisher Prize in 2001. She followed upon this success by being named the Musical America International Directory of the Arts Instrumentalist of the Year in 2002.

In addition to her work as an award-winning musician, Midori is also active in community service. In 1992 she created the Midori & Friends Foundation, which supports music education in New York City public schools through its charitable activities. The foundation provides opportunities for children to express themselves using musical instruments and offers workshops for students of all ages in music appreciation and performance through hands-on instruction and other activities. Using the money from her Avery Fisher Prize, Midori also founded Partners in Performance in 2001, followed by the University Residencies Program in 2003 and the Orchestra Residencies Program in 2004.

Between performing, recording, and working for her foundations, Midori also enrolled in the undergraduate program of New York University's Gallatin School of Individualized Study in 1995. She graduated magna cum laude in 2000, with a bachelor's degree in psychology and gender studies. She then went on to graduate school, earning her master's degree in psychology in 2005. At the turn of the millennium, Midori also became a professional music teacher, taking positions at the Manhattan School of Music (2001–2006) and the University of Southern California as the Jascha Heifetz Chair at the Thornton School of Music (2004–).

Antonio Thompson

Further Reading

Simon, Charnan. *Midori: Brilliant Violinist.* Chicago: Children's Press, 1993.

Midori official Web site. http://www.gotomidori.com.

Mineta, Norman (1931–)

A longtime Democratic politician of Japanese American descent, Norman Mineta served in Congress as representative from the San Jose, California, area for twenty years (1975–1995). Having made transportation and public works major elements of his legislative agenda, Mineta was chosen by President George W. Bush in 2001 to serve as secretary of transportation, becoming the only Democrat to serve in the Republican president's cabinet.

Norman Yoshio Mineta was born on November 12, 1931, in what was then the small town of San Jose. Mineta and his family were among the more than 112,000 Japanese Americans forced to relocate to internment camps under Executive Order 9066 during World War II. When the war was over, he finished high school in San Jose and went on to attend the University of California, Berkeley, where he graduated in 1953 with a degree in business administration. Following college, Mineta began his career of public service as an intelligence officer in the U.S. Army, serving from 1953 to 1956 in Japan and Korea. After returning to civilian life in 1956 and working for his father's insurance company, he entered local politics in 1962 and won election to the city council of San Jose in 1968. Three years later, Mineta became the first Asian American mayor of a major U.S. city when he was elected mayor of San Jose. Rising in the ranks of the Democratic Party as well, he ran successfully for the U.S. House of Representatives in 1974, part of the wave of Democratic victories following the Watergate scandal.

Reelected ten times, Mineta left office in the middle of his term in 1995 to take a high-level position with the Lockheed Martin aerospace company. While in Congress, he rose to several senior positions, including chairman of the House Public Works and Transportation committee, Surface Transportation subcommittee, and Public Works and Transportation aviation subcommittee. Perhaps his greatest achievement as a congressman was his sponsorship and leadership role in the passage of the Civil Liberties Act of 1988, which offered an official apology and reparations to Japanese Americans for their internment and other injustices committed against them during World War II. Mineta's contributions to Asian American political empowerment also included cofounding the Congressional Asian Pacific American Caucus in 1995, which he served as founding chairman. For his civil rights work, Mineta received the Martin Luther King, Jr., Commemorative Medal from George Washington University in 1995.

Public service did not end there for Mineta, as he went on to become the first Asian Pacific American to serve in the Cabinet when President Bill Clinton named him secretary of commerce in 1993. In the Bush White House, Mineta served as secretary of transportation, from 2001 until his retirement in 2006. The city of San Jose honored its native son for his service to the city, state, and country by naming its airport after him in 2001.

David Hou

Further Reading

U.S. House of Representatives biography. http://bioguide.congress.gov/scripts/biodisplay.pl?index=M000794.

Mink, Patsy Takemoto (1927–2002)

A native of Hawaii, Patsy Takemoto Mink was the first Asian American woman and the first woman of color elected to the U.S. House of Representatives (1964). A Democrat, she won a total of thirteen terms in office, serving from 1965 to 1976 and again from 1991 to 2003. She also served as assistant U.S. secretary of state in the Jimmy Carter administration and as president of the liberal advocacy group Americans for Democratic Action.

Patsy Matsu Takemoto Mink was born to Nisei (second-generation) Japanese American parents on December 6, 1927, in Paia, on the island of Maui. She graduated as valedictorian from Maui High School in 1944 and attended colleges in Hawaii and on the mainland, including the University of Nebraska, where she organized successful protests against the school's segregationist dorm policy. She finally transferred to the University of Hawai'i and received her bachelor's degree in zoology and chemistry in 1948.

Unable to get into medical school because she was a woman, Mink attended law school at the University of Chicago and earned her degree in 1951. Returning to Hawaii in 1953, she became the first Asian American woman to practice law in the territory. She also taught business law at the University of Hawai'i and became involved in Democratic Party politics, organizing a branch of the Oahu Young Democrats in 1954.

Mink entered elective politics two years later, when she won a seat in the Hawaii Territorial House. She was elected to the Hawaii State Senate in 1957, serving until 1959 and again from 1962 to 1964. Hawaii, meanwhile, had been granted statehood in 1959; when it was granted a second seat in the U.S. House of Representatives, Mink was elected to fill it. At the time, there were only twelve women serving in Congress, and Mink became the first

A Sansei (third-generation Japanese American) from Hawaii, Patsy Mink was the first Asian American woman elected to the U.S. House of Representatives. The liberal Democrat served a total of thirteen terms, beginning in 1965. *(Library of Congress)*

female minority to join that body. Her terms of service were highlighted by a staunch commitment to civil rights issues, health care, women's rights, and education. Mink is probably best remembered for her coauthorship of Title IX, Educational Amendment of 1972, which required all institutions of higher education receiving federal money to provide equal spending on female and male students. Title IX revolutionized all aspects of higher education, most conspicuously by supporting women's sports programs equally with men's.

After giving up her seat to run—unsuccessfully—for the U.S. Senate in 1976, Mink stayed in Washington, serving in the Carter administration as assistant secretary of state for oceans and international environmental and scientific affairs from 1977 to 1978 and as president of Americans for Democratic Action from 1978 to 1981.

Returning to her home state in the early 1980s, Mink taught at the University of Hawai'i, practiced law, and became involved in Honolulu politics. She was elected to the Honolulu City Council in 1983 and served two terms but ran unsuccessfully for governor of Hawaii (1986) and mayor of Honolulu (1988).

In the early 1990s, Mink was returned to the U.S.

House of Representatives in a special election held to fill the vacancy created by the resignation of Representative Daniel Akaka. She won reelection to the seven succeeding Congresses—the last one posthumously. Mink died in Honolulu of viral pneumonia on September 28, 2002, at age seventy-four, and won reelection that November. The Patsy Takemoto Mink Education Foundation for Low-Income Women and Children was founded in 2003 in her honor.

Amelia Maijala

Further Reading

Davidson, Sue. *A Heart in Politics: Jeannette Rankin and Patsy T. Mink.* Seattle: Seal, 1994.

Myer, Dillon S. (1891–1982)

Dillon S. Myer is a controversial figure in the tragic history of Japanese incarceration in the United States during World War II. As chief administrator of the War Relocation Authority (WRA) under President Franklin D. Roosevelt, Myer oversaw the evacuation of more than 112,000 Japanese nationals and Japanese Americans to ten internment centers in seven states and visited the camps to negotiate in times of internal crisis. He both supported the establishment of what he called "temporary havens" to handle the risk of disloyalty to the country at war, and later condemned the institutions as "undesirable" and "un-American." Myer's legacy continues to provoke intense debate over his role and responsibility.

Born in Licking County, Ohio, on September 4, 1891, he majored in agronomy at Ohio State University and earned an MA in education from Columbia University, New York. After working at the Department of Agriculture (1933–1942), Myer earned his place in history as director of the WRA (1942–1946). The agency was formed on March 18, 1942, by Executive Order 9102 to implement Executive Order 9066, signed by President Roosevelt, to evacuate all Japanese residents in the western United States to "segregation centers." The first WRA chief, Milton Eisenhower (later president of three major American universities and younger brother of future President Dwight D. Eisenhower) resigned from the post in July. He recommended Myer as his successor but advised him to take the job only if he felt he could sleep at night after incarcerating innocent people. Myer became director of the WRA on July 17, 1942.

Perhaps the most critical event of Myer's tenure occurred in 1943 at the largest internment camp, the Tule Lake Segregation Center in California, which was created specifically to isolate evacuees perceived to be loyal to Japan rather than to the United States. At its peak, from September to October 1943, Tule Lake held 18,000 inmates. The "suspicious" population included those who applied for repatriation to Japan, answered "loyalty questions" negatively or not at all, or had been designated "troublemakers," in addition to family members who expressed loyalty to the United States but wished to accompany relatives to the facility. The day after assuring the San Francisco Press Club that the relocation centers were operating smoothly, Myer visited Tule Lake on November 1, 1944, to meet with camp leaders who, on behalf of the inmates, sought to negotiate with the WRA to improve the camp's squalid housing, inadequate food, poor medical care, and unsafe working conditions. Inmates had begun to protest by calling work stoppages and demonstrations. As Myer met with his staff and camp leaders, thousands of inmates assembled around the building to show their support for the protest. Myer insisted that he would not negotiate under pressure, but announced after the meeting that he would study the group's recommendations in Washington. Meanwhile, the mass assembly had prompted camp administrators to erect barbed wire to protect them from inmates, and the press, misconstruing the situation, reported that militant "Japs" had held Myer captive. Subsequent skirmishes over a truckload of food brought the arrival of army troops to restore order.

Ironically, on May 14, 1943, more than a year before the Tule Lake incident, Myer had recommended to the president that the relocation centers be dismantled as soon as possible since life there was unnatural and un-American. "Keep in mind," he said, "that the evacuees were charged with nothing except having Japanese ancestors." Not until July 13, 1945, however, could Myer announce that all the camps (except Tule Lake) would be closed between October and December of that year; Tule Lake was finally closed on March 20, 1946. Executive Order 9742, signed by President Harry S. Truman, terminated the WRA on June 30, 1946. Later that year, Truman awarded Myer the nation's Medal of Merit, and Secretary of the Interior Harold L. Ickes praised him for setting a precedent "for equitable treatment of dislocated minorities."

After heading the WRA, Myer served as commissioner of the Federal Public Housing Authority (1946–1947), Public Housing Administration (1947), and Bureau of Indian Affairs (1950–1953); executive director of the Group Health Association (1953–1958); and United Nations senior expert in public administration in Caracas, Venezuela (1959–1960). Myer recorded his World War II memoirs in *Uprooted Americans: The Japanese Americans and the War Relocation Authority During World War II* (1971). He died on October 4, 1982, in Silver Spring, Maryland.

Perceptions of Myer's role in the Japanese American internment experience have shifted over time. At a 1946 testimonial dinner, the Japanese American Citizens League (JACL) commended him for "courageous and inspired leadership" as a "champion of human rights and common decency." More recent studies, such as Michi Weglyn's *Days of Infamy* (1976) and, especially, Richard Drinnon's *Keeper of Concentration Camps: Dillon S. Myer and American Racism* (1987), seem to belie his accolades, depicting him as more culpable during his administration of the camps. Drinnon regards Myer's activities with Japanese Americans and his later work with Native Americans as manifestations of the country's ongoing racism against both populations. Myer also firmly opposed the redress movement of the 1960s through 1980s, which called for the government to financially compensate former internees for the loss of their civil liberties and property. Even Mike Masaru Masaoka, a key figure in the JACL, would come to consider Myer a basically well-intentioned individual who was forced by circumstances to be just a "jail-keeper."

Gabriella Oldham

Further Reading

Christgau, John. *"Enemies": World War II Alien Internment*. Ames: Iowa State University Press, 1985.

Daniels, Roger. *Concentration Camps, North America: Japanese in the United States and Canada During World War II*. Malabar, FL: Robert E. Krieger, 1981.

Dillon S. Myer Papers (1934–1966). Including correspondence, memoranda, meeting minutes, newspaper clippings, reports, and speeches. Harry S. Truman Library and Museum, Independence, Missouri. http://www.trumanlibrary.org/hstpaper/myers.htm.

National Japanese American Student Relocation Council

Formed in 1942 by concerned educators and organizations, the National Japanese American Student Relocation Council (NJASRC) was established to help Japanese youth on the West Coast who had been interned during the war continue their education at schools in areas not affected by the relocation orders, largely in the Midwest and Northeast.

About two-thirds of the more than 112,000 Japanese Americans detained during World War II were Nisei, or the offspring of immigrants, with an average age of about seventeen. This included many students at colleges and universities in California, Washington, and Arizona, as well as high schoolers beginning to plan their academic lives. Despite the prevailing anti-Japanese mood across the country, several progressive educators were concerned about the students dispossessed by the forced mass evacuation, and created grassroots connections to send students to schools in the Midwest and East Coast. Educators at Christian schools were especially active in transferring congregants to affiliated schools east of the exclusion zone.

The American Friends Service Committee united most of these grassroots efforts under the NJASRC. The organization helped rescue educational opportunity and hope for more than 3,600 students who were able to begin or resume their higher education by getting them placed in schools and housing and by finding them part-time jobs to pay for their education.

The NJASRC and Nisei students faced many hurdles. The U.S. Army and Navy treated Nisei with much suspicion and initially forbade them from seeking refuge in communities that were close to major railroad stations, ports, or military bases or from campuses themselves if any military research was being conducted there. This ruled out all but small rural colleges. Each student also had to pass War Relocation Authority (WRA) and FBI leave-clearance examinations.

Students also struggled to finance their educations, as they could not live at home and their parents' assets had been frozen since 1941; many family incomes were limited to WRA monthly salaries between $9 and $16. Most students took several jobs while on campus in order to pay for tuition, books, room, and board. The NJASRC helped out by soliciting and managing scholarships, funded primarily by churches to subsidize congregants' tuitions. The council also functioned as a clearinghouse of college information and as placement advisers, informing Nisei which colleges had not yet reached their quota of Japanese American students.

Several midwestern communities, such as Lincoln, Nebraska, formed local organizations to help Nisei students secure housing and part-time employment. Yet not all communities were so supportive. Vigilantes in Moscow, Idaho, threatened six Washington Nisei at the University of Idaho in the spring of 1942, two of whom were placed in jail for their own protection. According to former NJASRC director Robert W. O'Brien, the states that admitted the largest number of Nisei students in 1943 were Utah (224), Colorado (219), and Nebraska (135).

Critics such as historian Gary Okihiro fault the council for cooperating too closely with the War Relocation Authority, rather than opposing the injustice of the detention, and for internalizing WRA thinking that encouraged Nisei to be cultural ambassadors and avoid congregating together. These and other criticisms aside, the NJASRC's achievements are remarkable for a time when so few Americans chose to differentiate between imperial soldiers and Japanese Americans. Combined with the GI Bill (which benefited many Nisei veterans) and the sacrifices of the Issei, the NJASRC assisted in an important stage in the lives of the Nisei generation and fostered a new measure of diversity in American higher education. In 1980, some of the former students assisted by the NJASRC established the Nisei Student Relocation Commemorative Fund, which has given more than $340,000 to Southeast Asian American college students in the spirit of the group's motto, "Extending helping hands once offered to us."

Andrew B. Wertheimer

Further Reading

Austin, Allan W. *From Concentration Camp to Campus: Japanese American Students and World War II.* Urbana: University of Illinois Press, 2004.

Okihiro, Gary Y. *Storied Lives: Japanese American Students and World War II.* Seattle: University of Washington Press, 1999.

Wertheimer, Andrew B. "Admitting Nebraska's Nisei: Japanese American Students at the University of Nebraska, 1942–1945." *Nebraska History* 83 (Summer 2002): 52–78.

Native Sons of the Golden West

Originally a white fraternal and charitable society founded in 1875 to preserve memories of the gold rush and California's early days, the Native Sons of the Golden West (NSGW) by the early twentieth century had become a nativist political group, issuing anti-Japanese literature and advocating tough measures against Japanese immigrants and Japanese Americans, including a bar on further immigration and a ban on Japanese American land ownership.

Japanese immigrants began arriving in California at the end of the nineteenth century, largely to work as laborers in the state's growing agricultural sector. But as the Japanese began to save money and purchase businesses and land of their own, sentiment against the Asian American group began to rise among Anglo Californians. While California passed a law barring the ownership of land by resident aliens—the Alien

Land Law of 1913 was largely aimed at the successful Japanese American community in the state—Japanese Americans got around the law by registering land deeds in the names of their American-born children. Under the U.S. Constitution, persons born on U.S. soil are automatically citizens.

Such tactics angered many white Californians, and stopping further Japanese immigration became a major theme of the NSGW's monthly newspaper, the *Grizzly Bear.* Joining forces with farmer organizations such as the Grange and patriotic groups such as the newly formed American Legion, the NSGW pushed for a total ban on Japanese immigration throughout the period between World Wars I and II.

In the early 1920s, the *Grizzly Bear* regularly featured diatribes by anti-Japanese nativists, such as newspaper magnate V.S. McClatchy's "Indisputable Facts and Figures Proving California Will Become Japanized Unless Yellow Peril Stamped Out," and state senator James Inman's "The Time Has Arrived to Eliminate the Japs as California Landholders." In January 1920, in a characteristic editorial, *Grizzly Bear* editor Clarence M. Hunt wrote: "The Japanese cancer has already taken an almost fatal hold on California, whence it will spread rapidly throughout the United States." He called on the government to pass legislation to halt Japanese immigration, school integration, the right to own property, and other aspects of what he called "'Japanitis' (the yellow cancer)." Hunt's paper also frequently reported on the anti-Japanese campaigns of local parlors (as the NSGW units were called) and gathered news in "Japagraphs." California's political candidates also advertised their anti-Japanese credentials in the *Grizzly Bear.* Governor William Stephens, for example, claimed in 1922 that he "has unswervingly taken a fearless stand against JAPANESE INVASION; Preserving our lands in perpetuity for future Generations of the White Race."

The Immigration Act of 1924, which created national quotas for immigrants and effectively barred the further influx of Japanese, has been called the ultimate triumph of the Native Sons, though forces interested in stopping immigration from Eastern and Southern Europe were a larger factor in the law's passage nationally. Nor did the Asian Exclusion Act, as the 1924 legislation was also called, bring an end to the association's anti-Asian activism. Again after Pearl Harbor in December 1941, the NSGW became a leading proponent—along with the American Legion, Farm Bureau Federation, and Joint Immigration Committee—of "evacuating" Japanese Americans from the West Coast. Even after Japanese Americans were removed from California to wartime internment camps, the NSGW continued to oppose the interests of the community. For example, it supported California's

legal efforts to deprive Nisei (American-born Japanese) of their voting rights. NSGW grand historian Peter T. Conmy was especially proud of this role, publishing a 1942 pamphlet titled, *The History of California's Japanese Problem and the Part Played by the Native Sons of the Golden West in Its Solution.*

In the years since World War II, the organization dropped its nativist advocacy and shifted back to its original focus on patriotism and historic preservation, alongside its sister organization, the Native Daughters of the Golden West, founded in 1886. As of the early 2000s, each group had about 8,000 members and headquarters in San Francisco.

Andrew B. Wertheimer

Further Reading

Daniels, Roger. *The Politics of Prejudice: The Anti-Japanese Movement in California and the Struggle for Japanese Exclusion.* 2nd ed. Berkeley: University of California Press, 1977.

Kimball, Richard C., and Barney Noel. *Native Sons of the Golden West.* Charleston, SC: Arcadia, 2005.

Native Sons of the Golden West. http://www.nsgw.org.

Nisei

The Nisei were second-generation Japanese Americans, the first born in America. They were the children of the Issei, the original Japanese immigrants who arrived on the West Coast in the late 1800s and early 1900s. Most Nisei were adults, or nearly so, by the start of World War II and endured the hardship and humiliation of wartime incarceration. They are the parents of the Sansei (third generation) and grandparents of the Yonsei (fourth generation, or great-grandchildren of the Issei). Unlike their parents, who could not become U.S. citizens because of stringent immigration laws, the Nisei were citizens by virtue of being born on U.S. soil. And not only were the Nisei American-born, they were also American-educated—which sets them apart from the other group of Japanese Americans in their generation, the Kibei, who were born in America but educated in Japan.

A problem unique to the Nisei generation was the need to find a balance between being Japanese and being American. It was important to the Issei that their children be imbued with Japanese values, and they relied on educational programs in Japanese community schools to accomplish this. Some anti-Japanese activists became concerned that a competing cultural education would undermine their American values and allegiance to the

United States, and some states passed laws in the 1920s that limited what Nisei children could be taught about Japanese culture and tradition.

The main source of income among early Japanese immigrants was farming, but 1913 legislation in California called the Alien Land Act barred the Issei from owning real property in the state. But because the Nisei had been born in America, they were not affected by the law. Thus, until another measure was passed in 1920 to close the loophole, Issei farmers simply signed over their farmland to their Nisei children or bought new property under their names. Although the second generation was less interested in agriculture and sought other avenues of success in America, their parents hoped they could be convinced to stay on the farm (or, in the case of the Kibei, return to it). By 1930, there were as many Nisei in the United States as there were Issei, and their numbers continued to increase thereafter. Of the approximately 93,000 Japanese Americans in California at the beginning of World War II, 60 percent were Nisei.

After the 1941 attack on Pearl Harbor, many Anglo Americans on the West Coast—and government officials in Washington—began to question the loyalty of the Japanese American community. In 1942, more than 112,000 of them were removed from their homes and businesses and interned in detention camps at the order of the government. Although their parents were considered enemy aliens, mainland Nisei were declared eligible to join the U.S. armed forces in February 1943, and 17,600 of them did so to prove their loyalty to America. Many were accepted into the Military Intelligence Service because their Japanese language skills allowed them to interpret and interrogate. Others joined frontline units, most notably the 442nd Regimental Combat Team, a highly decorated unit made up entirely of Nisei and Hawaiian Japanese soldiers. While others relocated from the camps during the war to pursue jobs or education, some Nisei in internment camps were not released until 1945, only to find that their farmland and equipment had been sold off during the war. Some later started a movement that resulted in government reparations of $20,000 to each internee who was still alive in 1988 and a formal apology from the federal government.

Leah Irvine

Further Reading

Azuma, Eiichiro. *Between Two Empires: Race, History, and Transnationalism in Japanese America.* Cary, NC: Oxford University Press, 2005.

McGowen, Tom. *Go for Broke: Japanese Americans in World War II.* New York: F. Watts, 1995.

Noguchi, Isamu (1904–1988)

Among the most innovative and influential American sculptors of the twentieth century, Isamu Noguchi—the son of a white American mother and Japanese-born father—is perhaps most celebrated for his monumental outdoor creations, which combine Eastern and Western aesthetic traditions, as well as the many stage sets he designed and built for the dancer/choreographer Martha Graham.

Noguchi was born in Los Angeles on November 17, 1904, to a literary family. His mother, Leonie Gilmore, was a journalist and writer; his father, Yone Noguchi, was one of early-twentieth-century Japan's most influential poets and literary critics. Noguchi moved to Japan when he was three, not returning to the United States until age fourteen. After attending a boarding high school in Indiana, where his talent in sculpting was soon recognized, Noguchi moved to New York. Although he apprenticed with Gutzon Borglum, best known as the sculptor of Mount Rushmore, Noguchi opted for a more practical career path as a premed student at Columbia University. Encouraged by his mother, who had returned from Japan, he enrolled in an evening art academy and had his first exhibit of terra-cotta works. Noguchi soon dropped out of university to sculpt full time.

Noguchi earned a living with commissions for traditional busts but was taken with more modernist works, particularly the semi-abstract busts sculptures of the Romanian-born artist Constantin Brancusi. When Noguchi won a Guggenheim fellowship to study in Paris in 1927, he became Brancusi's assistant and his work came to reflect that influence.

Seeking a new source of inspiration, Noguchi traveled to Asia in the early 1930s, before returning to a Depression-era United States, where he won some minor commissions for the Federal Arts Project, as well as helping his friend and collaborator, the architect and designer Buckminster Fuller, design the innovative Dymaxion car. Noguchi also collaborated with Graham during the 1930s and again after World War II, designing stage sets for her modernist dance productions of *Frontier* and *Appalachian Spring*. In these, Noguchi used simple geometric shapes to complement Graham's spare, free-flowing modernist choreography.

While Noguchi was not incarcerated during the war—living in New York, he was exempt from the internment order—he organized a group of Nisei writers and artists protesting the incarceration, before having himself voluntarily incarcerated at the camp in Poston, Arizona, where he taught arts and crafts.

Although Noguchi sculpted extensively before 1945 and was praised for his busts of Graham and Fuller, it is his postwar work—particularly his monumental abstract outdoor sculpture—that propelled him to the front ranks of twentieth-century American art, though he was also acclaimed for his innovative, free-flowing modernist furniture. Following the war, Noguchi returned to Japan on a Bollingen Fellowship from 1948 to 1952, where he was deeply influenced by the clean and simple sculptural forms found in Japanese architecture and gardens, as well as the purity of Zen thought.

That influence can be seen in some of Noguchi's most celebrated works, including his 1961–1962 fountain for the John Hancock Insurance Building in New Orleans. Like much of Noguchi's later sculpture, it is a simple piece with a Greek Doric column topped by a crescent-shaped capital, evoking the wooden support beams in Japanese temples, both roughly hewn and appearing only half-finished. Together, the two parts juxtapose Western and Eastern influences, even as the uneven surfaces contrast with the smooth lines of the modernist building on whose front plaza the fountain sits.

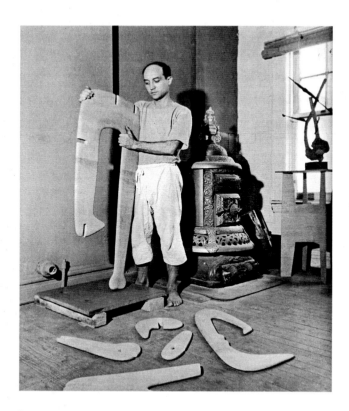

Los Angeles native Isamu Noguchi, the son of a prominent Japanese poet and an American mother, was best known for his abstract sculptures in a variety of materials. His garden designs, stage sets, and furniture pieces were also acclaimed. *(Eliot Elisofon/Stringer/Time & Life Pictures/Getty Images)*

While considered one of Noguchi's finest pieces, the Hancock Insurance fountain is not representative of his work, beyond its simple abstraction and monumental size. Indeed, few works seem representative, as Noguchi's oeuvre is eclectic above all. Another of his most celebrated pieces, the 1968 Red Cube, designed for the Marine Midland Bank Plaza in Manhattan, is simply that: a red-painted steel cube, poised on one of its corners, with an unpainted hole in its center. Once again, Western and Eastern influences are present, the polished steel cube evoking the solidity of Western technology and the emptiness at the center the eternal nothingness that adherents of Zen Buddhism aspire to seek.

Noguchi received numerous accolades during his career, including membership in the American Academy of Arts and Letters and the American Academy of Arts and Sciences, as well as the National Medal of Arts. In 1985, Noguchi turned a former factory building opposite his studio in Long Island City, New York, into a museum to house his work. He died three years later, on December 30, 1988.

James Ciment and Robert J. Maeda

Further Reading

Apostolos-Cappadona, Diane, and Bruce Altshuler, eds. *Isamu Noguchi: Essays and Conversations.* New York: Harry Abrams/Isamu Noguchi Foundation, 1994.

Ashton, Dore. *Noguchi East and West.* New York: Alfred A. Knopf, 1992.

Noguchi, Isamu. *Isamu Noguchi: A Sculptor's World.* New York: Harper and Row, 1968.

Noguchi Museum. http://www.noguchi.org.

Okubo, Miné (1912–2001)

Miné Okubo was a Nisei artist known for her depictions of life in the internment camps of World War II. Her book *Citizen 13660,* combining 206 pen-and-ink drawings and accompanying text, was the first book by an internee to depict life in the camps. Originally published in 1946, it was the first direct account of the relocation and imprisonment, testifying firsthand to the personal and collective effects of the hardships, fear, and deprivation faced by Japanese and Japanese American internees. In print since 1946, translated into multiple foreign languages, and republished in 1983, *Citizen 13660* won the American Book Award for 1984. Testifying to the enduring impact of Okubo's art and book, *Amerasia,* an academic journal on Asian American history and culture, published an entire issue in tribute to her work in 2004.

Okubo was born on June 27, 1912, in Riverside, California, to Issei (first-generation immigrant) parents. Her father worked as a gardener, and her mother was a graduate of the Tokyo Art Institute. Miné Okubo attended Riverside Community College and went on to earn her master's degree in art from the University of California, Berkeley, in 1936. After touring Europe on a Bertha Taussig Traveling Scholarship, she returned to the Bay Area upon the outbreak of World War II in Europe and the illness of her mother. Working for the Federal Arts Program, Okubo explained the work of Mexican artist Diego Rivera to onlookers as he painted the Pan American Unity Mural. Okubo herself was also commissioned by the Federal Arts Program to create murals and mosaics for the U.S. Army at California's Fort Ord, Government Island, Oakland Hospitality House, and Treasure Island.

After President Franklin Roosevelt issued Executive Order 9066 in February 1943, Okubo applied for a special exemption from the government curfew and travel restrictions in order to complete the murals and mosaics in Oakland because she lived in Berkeley. In April, however, she and her brother Toku were sent to the Tanforan Assembly Center in San Bruno, California (their mother had since died), where they lived for half a year in a converted horse stall. Finally moving to the internment camp at Utah, Okubo contributed drawings to the camp's literary magazine, taught art to schoolchildren, and helped edit the camp's newspaper. She also spent time documenting camp life in drawings and paintings (cameras were not allowed). The 250 pen-and-ink drawings she made at the Tanforan Assembly Center and at Topaz became the basis for *Citizen 13660.* Okubo won a drawing contest sponsored by the camp magazine, *Trek,* which led to a contract with *Fortune* magazine to illustrate their articles. With the war winding down, the magazine's editors were able to move her to New York City.

In New York, Okubo emerged as a highly successful commercial illustrator for magazines and books. Her work appeared in such prominent publication as *Time, Life,* and the *New York Times. Citizen 13660,* named for the number assigned to her in camp, began as a way for Okubo to document the camp experience for friends who sent care packages and letters from the outside. Most of her drawings feature Okubo as a participant or observer, making the work essentially autobiographical. Also featured prominently, however, are the numbered tags identifying each family's goods and underscoring the dehumanization of the internee population. Okubo

struggled to find a publisher and finally succeeded in 1946 with Columbia University Press. The book remained in print with a series of small presses until being reissued in 1983 by the University of Washington Press. In 1981, Okubo testified before the U.S. Congressional Commission on Wartime Relocation and Internment of Civilians (CWRIC) and submitted her book for the commission's records.

Having left New York in 1950 to lecture on art at the University of California, Berkeley, Okube returned in 1952 to pursue her own artistic vision in drawing and painting full-time. Exhibitions of her work were mounted in New York, Massachusetts, and Oakland, and a forty-year retrospective was featured at the Catherine Gallery and Basement Workshop in New York in 1986. In the view of artist and professor Betty La Duke, Okubo's work is marked by experimentation with a variety of schools, from "early figurative realism" to "expressionist landscapes," and an evolution into "bolder stylized forms" from the "underlying calligraphy" of her earlier work, indicative of her continued search for simplicity of form. Okubo died in Manhattan on February 10, 2001.

Emily Hiramatsu Morishima

Further Reading

"A Tribute to Mine Okubo." *Amerasia Journal* 30:2 (2004).
Kuramitsu, Kristine C. "Internment and Identity in Japanese American Art." *American Quarterly* 47:4 (December 1995): 619–58.
La Duke, Betty. "On the Right Road: The Life of Mine Okubo." *Art Education* 40:3 (May 1987): 42–48.
Robison, Greg, and Elena Tajima Creef, eds. *Miné Okubo: Following Her Own Road.* Seattle: University of Washington Press, 2007.

Omura, James Matsumoto (1912–1994)

James Matsumoto Omura was a Japanese American journalist whose reputation was tarnished by his outspoken defense of draft resistance during World War II, when Japanese Americans were interned but then asked to prove their loyalty by enlisting in the military.

Born on Bainbridge Island in Seattle, Washington, on November 17, 1912, Omura launched his first publication, *Current Life,* in 1940 with the help of his wife, Fumi Okuma, and his savings from odd jobs since junior high school. Although it lasted only fifteen months, *Current Life* featured news and writings by second-generation (Nisei) Japanese Americans that Omura hoped would reflect their contributions to American society, particularly after the attack on Pearl Harbor aroused a national outcry against individuals of Japanese descent. Unable to continue his publication once the war began, Omura started an employment agency to help Japanese Americans who had been removed to internment camps in the Denver area. To avoid incarceration himself, Omura fled to Colorado, which was not in the West Coast zone (from which, under Executive Order 9066, Americans of Japanese descent were forced to relocate).

Omura's concern for the integrity of Japanese Americans under assault created conflict with members of the community as well as the government. He did not agree with the Japanese American Citizens League (JACL), the largest civil rights organization for the community at the time, which maintained that any opposition to evacuation would uphold the stereotype of "disloyalty." The JACL believed that demonstrating complete loyalty to the United States by complying with evacuation would at least guarantee safety, if not freedom, for Japanese Americans. Testifying to the Tolan Committee, a select congressional committee investigating "National Defense Migration" (that is, the removal of Japanese aliens and citizens), Omura stood alone against the JACL, declaring that evacuation "would not solve the question of Nisei loyalty. If any such action is taken I believe that we would be only procrastinating on the question of loyalty, that we are afraid to deal with it, and at this, our first opportunity, we are trying to strip the Nisei of their opportunity to prove their loyalty."

As editor of the Denver-based Japanese American newspaper *Rocky Shimpo,* Omura published opinion columns advocating the Heart Mountain Fair Play Committee, the only draft resistance group that developed in the ten relocation camps. War Relocation Authority director Dillon S. Myer was advised that Omura's editorials bordered on "sedition" and was urged by other publishers and members of the public to conduct an investigation of the newspaper's assets, since the original Issei owners were considered "enemy aliens." *The Heart Mountain Sentinel,* a rival newspaper, branded Omura "the number one menace to the post-war assimilation of the Nisei" and accused him of "prostituting the privileges of freedom of the press to advocate an un-American stand." In 1944, the seven leaders of the Fair Play Committee and Omura were arrested on charges of conspiracy and aiding, abetting, and counseling the draft resistance. Omura was eventually found innocent, though the seven others were found guilty and sentenced to prison.

After World War II, Omura became a landscaper in Colorado and president of the Colorado Landscape Body for two terms. In an interview forty years later, he remarked, "The *Shimpo* took up the cudgel of Nisei rights under the Constitution." He died in Denver in 1994.

Gabriella Oldham

Further Reading

Daniels, Roger. *Concentration Camps, North America: Japanese in the United States and Canada During World War II.* Malabar, FL: Robert E. Krieger, 1981.

Hansen, Arthur. "James Matsumoto Omura: An Interview." *Amerasia Journal* 13:2 (1986–1987): 99–113.

Takaki, Ronald. *Strangers from a Different Shore: A History of Asian Americans.* Rev. ed. Boston: Little, Brown, 1998.

Ozawa, Seiji (1935–)

Seiji Ozawa is a Japanese conductor of classical music who spent nearly thirty years as music director of the famed Boston Symphony Orchestra. Ozawa was born on September 1, 1935, in Shenyang, China, during the Japanese occupation. Upon graduating from the Toho Gakuen School of Music in Tokyo in 1959, he studied at the Berkshire Music Center (now Tanglewood) and worked under conductor Herbert von Karajan with the Berlin Philharmonic.

Orchestra conductor Seiji Ozawa, who served as music director of the Boston Symphony from 1973 to 2002, accepts an honorary degree from Harvard University at commencement exercises in 2000. *(Darren McCollester/Getty Images)*

In 1961, Leonard Bernstein hired Ozawa to work as his assistant conductor at the New York Philharmonic. Madame Serge Koussevitzky had arranged for Ozawa to meet Bernstein when the New York Philharmonic came on tour to West Berlin, and the meeting served as an impromptu interview. Ozawa later cited Bernstein as one of his major influences. Upon leaving New York in 1962, Ozawa joined the Japan Philharmonic Orchestra before moving to Toronto.

Musicians are notorious for disliking conductors, but Ozawa proved the exception. An extroverted, sports-loving man, Ozawa played Ping Pong with orchestra members during his tenure as music director of the Toronto Symphony Orchestra from 1965 to 1969. In his free time, he played golf. In sharp contrast to the sedate conductors of the past, the colorful Ozawa shocked the classical world by donning white turtlenecks with the traditional black formals worn by conductors. When he left Toronto to lead the San Francisco Symphony Orchestra (1969–1976), the Canadian musicians mourned his departure.

Ozawa became the thirteenth musical director of the Boston Symphony Orchestra in 1973 and held the position until leaving in 2002. The Boston Symphony is widely regarded as one of the leading companies in America, and Ozawa treasured the opportunity to play his Romantic favorites with it, notably Berlioz's *Symphonie Fantastique.* During his tenure there, Ozawa was seen in attendance at Boston Red Sox baseball games and Boston Celtics basketball games. He ended his twenty-nine years (the longest of any musical director of the Boston Symphony) with a spectacular performance of Mahler's Ninth Symphony. Reflecting on his years as a conductor, Ozawa identified scheduling as the major problem facing orchestras and lamented that the fifty-two-week schedule resulted in tired musicians and prevented the highest level of performance.

In his later years, Ozawa devoted himself to opera, a great love. Upon leaving Boston in 2002, he became music director of the Vienna State Opera, a position he was slated to keep until 2010. In addition, in 2005 he conducted the first performance of the Tokyo Opera Nomori, a company he founded. He opened the latter season with the Richard Strauss opera *Elektra,* part of a ten-day, all-Strauss event. Ozawa described the performance as the culmination of a lifelong dream to establish a Western opera company in Japan, with Japanese musicians.

Caryn E. Neumann

Further Reading

Smedvig, Caroline, ed. *Seiji: An Intimate Portrait of Seiji Ozawa.* Boston: Houghton Mifflin, 1998.

Picture Brides

A picture bride was a Japanese woman who immigrated to the United States to join her husband, whom she had married by proxy in Japan and never met before. Often she had seen a photo of her husband-to-be and, conversely, he had seen a photo of her—hence the designation. The institution of the picture bride was important to the early Japanese American community in several ways: it enabled immigrants who had decided to stay in America but could not afford a return trip to Japan a way to marry a Japanese woman; it helped bring parity to the gender ratio of Japanese residing in the United States; and it helped foster a settled, stable family life in the Japanese American community.

Most of the Issei (first-generation Japanese immigrants) were men. Indeed there were very few Japanese women in the United States until after 1905, when the Issei began to put down roots and send home for wives or picture brides. The phenomenon of the picture bride originated from the Japanese concept of marriage, which was based on family connections. Historically, romantic love had little to do with the decision of whom to marry in Japan. Instead, it was common for marriages to be arranged between families through a middleman, known as a *nakodo,* based on each family's ancestry, education, health, and wealth. If the conditions were deemed favorable, the head of the two families would meet in person to arrange the details. The prospective bride and groom often accompanied their fathers (or other head of family) to these meetings, but they rarely had he opportunity to speak or get to know each other before the engagement period and wedding.

For Japanese men who had put down roots in the United States, returning to the homeland to find a wife entailed a considerable expense, not to mention the time (and lost wages) associated with the long journey, the matchmaking process, and the engagement period. Furthermore, returning to Japan to find a bride was risky. At the turn of the twentieth century, Japan had obligatory military service for all male citizens. Japanese men who migrated overseas were given deferments, but if they returned to Japan for a period longer than one month they were eligible to be drafted. As the engagement and wedding period typically lasted longer than thirty days, it was desirable for the men to remain abroad. The system of picture brides (also referred to as "mail-order brides") thus became standard practice.

The phenomenon of the picture bride fit well into the Japanese wedding tradition, as all that was necessary for a marriage to be considered official and legal was a ceremony in which the bride's name and personal information were recorded in her husband's family records. As long as the bride was available to complete the ceremony with a member of the groom's family, the marriage was legal. The groom did not have to be present.

There are no definitive statistics on the number of Japanese picture brides who arrived in the United States between 1905 and 1924. It has been estimated, however, that they accounted for more than half of all married Japanese women who arrived in the United States during this period. According to the U.S. Census Bureau, the number of married Japanese American women in the United States grew significantly during that general period, from 410 in 1900 to 5,581 in 1910, 22,193 in 1920, and 23,930 by 1930.

The Japanese government initially supported the migration of wives and picture brides to the United States, which it regarded as an excellent means of balancing the ratio of Japanese males to females. This mattered to the Meiji regime in Tokyo because it hoped to avoid the problems encountered in Chinese migration to the United States, which was predominantly male and plagued by high rates of gambling, drinking, and prostitution. These were qualities the Japanese wished to avoid for fear that they could sully their reputation with America.

In signing the Gentleman's Agreement of 1907–1908, the Japanese government willingly regulated and reduced the number of Japanese traveling to the United States. One of the tools it used to stem the tide of women émigrés was to require economic proof that the husband had enough money support his wife. Thus, at first, only men employed as professionals could send home for a wife. After 1915, the Japanese extended the privilege to any Japanese male who resided in the United States and could demonstrate that he had a savings of at least $800.

Restrictions were also placed on Japanese women. To ensure that the picture bride system was not being taken advantage of, the Japanese government required that all brides be no more than thirteen years younger than their husbands. It also conducted stringent physical examinations of all women wishing to migrate to the United States, to ensure that they had clean bills of health and would not be turned away by U.S. immigration officials for carrying disease. It was not until the so-called Ladies Agreement of 1920 that the Japanese government declined to issue passports for any more picture brides, largely in reaction to the growing anti-Japanese movement in the United States.

Many of the picture brides were less than enthralled with their husbands upon arrival, finding out that the photos looked quite different from the real men. Others

A 1965 painting by the Japanese American artist Henry Sugimoto depicts the experience of Japanese picture brides—women who marry émigré husbands they have never met and then travel to America to join them. The couples know each other only by photographs. *(Gift of Madeleine Sugimoto and Naomi Tagawa, Japanese American National Museum, 92.97.108)*

found that their new husband had exaggerated his economic status during the wedding negotiations process and were forced to work on his farm or in his shop.

As they brought gender parity to the Japanese American community, so picture brides started families and introduced conventional family life. Their children, the Nisei (second generation), were U.S. citizens and emerged as one of the greatest tools of acculturation and assimilation into American society and culture. The number of Nisei increased from only 269 in 1900 to 4,502 in 1910. Within the next twenty years, the total reached 68,357—or about half the entire Japanese American population in 1930.

Lindsay Sarah Krasnoff

Further Reading

Ichioka, Yuji. "*Amerika Nadeshiko:* Japanese Immigrant Women in the United States, 1900–1924." *Pacific Historical Review* 49:2 (May 1980): 339–57.

O'Brien, David J., and Stephen S. Fugita. *The Japanese American Experience.* Bloomington: University of Indiana Press, 1991.

Press, Japanese American

The Japanese American press has played a key role in the history of the Japanese American community, helping newly arrived immigrants adjust to life in America and survive the deprivations and injustices of internment during World War II. In the postwar era, however, the Japanese American press has been a victim of the community's success at assimilating into and prospering in mainstream American society. The East Asian American community with the highest level of English-language skills, Japanese Americans in the late twentieth and early twentieth-first centuries have generally opted to get their news from English-language newspapers or other forms of non-Japanese-language media.

Origins

Many Nisei (second-generation Japanese Americans) recall their parents reading Japanese-language newspapers. Often their memoirs portray a father reading a paper aloud to them, or summarizing stories. For the immigrant generation, or Issei, Japanese newspapers were their lifeblood, providing news from the homeland and a unifying cultural voice in the community. The first Japanese newspapers in Hawaii and the West Coast during the 1880s were merely handwritten or mimeographed broadsides—many political tracts smuggled from Japan—but they established the foundation of a dynamic ethnic American press. The papers informed immigrant workers of Japan's rapid modernization under the Meiji regime, explained events taking place in their adopted country, and shared news from the local ethnic community. Since Issei were denied the possibility of citizenship (at least until 1952), newspapers also functioned as a voice of community opinion, often competing fiercely in terms of both circulation and ideas. In the territory of Hawaii, for example, Kinzaburo Makino's *Hawaii Hochi* (*Hawaii Post*) and Yasutaro Soga's *Nippu Jiji* (*Japanese Times*) clashed over questions of politics and cultural identity. Like other editors, these men were considered intellectuals and community leaders. Editors and newspapers alike faced hard times during the post–World War I Americanization period, and especially during World War II. During the interwar period, many newspapers also began transforming from purely Japanese-language pages into bilingual ethnic forums.

Golden Years: The 1920s

The 1920s marked the peak of Japanese-language newspaper publishing. In Honolulu, Japanese dailies, including *Hawaii Hochi* and *Nippu Jiji,* exceeded the combined circulation of the city's English-language papers. The latter sometimes printed translations of stories from the Japanese-language press, if not always in context. Indeed, the power of the Japanese press worried territorial leaders during the Americanization period. During the 1920 plantation strike, territorial legislators passed laws to control the Japanese press.

On the continent, Kyutaro Abiko ran the *Nichibei Shimbun* in San Francisco, as well as a model community (Yamato Colony), in his effort to get early immigrants to think of themselves as settlers rather than as sojourners. To the north, Seattle had several Japanese dailies, including the *Hokubei Hochi* (*North American Post*) and *Hokubei Jiji* (*North American Times*). Smaller Japanese communities boasted local newspapers, albeit thinner in size and news than their large urban counterparts. In addition to the major newspapers of Hawaii, California, Washington, and Oregon, Japanese dailies also emerged in Utah, Colorado, Illinois, and New York—such as the *Utah Nippo* (*Japanese Utah*) and the *Rocky Nippon* (*Rocky Mountain Japanese*). Most featured local news and reprinted items from other Japanese papers, along with translations from the local press. Ethnic papers also emerged on Canada's West Coast, such as the *Vancouver Shimpo* (*Vancouver Newspaper*).

Newspapers carried not only news and editorials, but also serializations of Japanese novels and tanka, haiku, and senryu (forms of Japanese verse) by amateur Issei poets. Women's sections featured advice on manners and fashions. Advertisements announced the availability of films, books, and dry goods from Japan along with local hotels and jobs. Some tabloids carried reports of runaway spouses or other scandalous gossip.

Prewar Transformations: Emergence of the Nisei Press

The Gentleman's Agreement of 1907–1908 and the Immigration Act of 1924, which severely limited immigration, foreshadowed a long, gradual decline of the Japanese-language press as the number of readers decreased. As the Nisei generation came of age, however, newspapers began experimenting with English-language pages and news of political events, artistic efforts, and especially Nisei socials. By the 1930s, most ethnic papers featured some English-language pages written by and for Nisei. But the most famous Nisei paper was the Japanese American Citizen's League's house organ, the *Pacific Citizen,* founded in 1929 as a semimonthly called the *Nikkei Shimin* (*Japanese American Citizen*) by the New American Citizens League of

The staff of the *Utah Nippo* poses in the Salt Lake City pressroom in 1917. Local Japanese newspapers helped the early immigrant community adjust to life in America and endure hardships. The *Utah Nippo* was allowed to continue publishing during World War II. *(Taro Yamasaki/Time & Life Pictures/Getty Images)*

San Francisco. Other influential prewar Nisei papers include James Sakamoto's *Japanese-American Courier* and James Omura's literary monthly, *Current Life.* There also was a bilingual socialist newspaper, called *Doho,* which was published in Colorado during World War II by California Kibei (Nisei educated in Japan) who had moved there to avoid the West Coast internment order.

World War II

If the halt to immigration and acculturation had not signaled the end of the Japanese American press, government action during World War II nearly extinguished it. Within days of the attack on Pearl Harbor, FBI agents detained Issei journalists and editors. Although most Japanese-language papers before Pearl Harbor carried Japanese newswire accounts of the victories of "our troops" in China, there was no evidence that any were truly anti-American. In the absence of judicial process, many newspapermen spent the war years in internment camps.

The government also closed most Japanese-language newspapers, especially in the designated relocation areas on the West Coast, causing great confusion and much hardship. Issei without bilingual children were cut off from current events. The JACL volunteered to fill the gap with mimeographed translations of official news releases, delivered by Boy Scouts. Still, confusion reigned and rumors abounded.

The War Relocation Authority (WRA) allowed detainees to publish newspapers in the assembly centers and internment camps, where more than 112,000 Japanese Americans from the West Coast had been incarcerated. The mere existence of newspapers allowed camp officials to claim a free press, but most were mimeographed bulletins carrying little beyond official announcements. Some were actually typeset and printed, and staffed by talented writers, but none carried the opposition opinion of detained Nikkei.

Only a few Japanese American newspapers were allowed to continue in the free zone, albeit heavily censored. A few tried in vain to resettle west of the Exclusion Zone, but the only papers allowed on the mainland were the JACL's *Pacific Citizen* (which moved to Salt Lake City) and several bilingual papers originally in Utah and Colorado, including *Utah Nippo* and the *Rocky Nippon.* Press control over war news was extremely tight in all papers at the time, Japanese American or otherwise, which contributed to Issei cynicism about the freedom of the American press. In 1944, for example, *Rocky Shimpo* editor James Omura was tried for printing columns that recognized the right of Nisei in the Heart Mountain Internment Camp to resist military conscription. Although Omura was found innocent of subverting the draft, the government coerced the publisher to fire him. The lack of a free press has been cited as one cause of the violence that sometimes erupted in the camps, as there were no acceptable forums to express dissent.

From World War II to Today

The Japanese press in postwar America—despite some successes—has declined in the face of a more diverse and complex market. Many Nikkei still receive the weekly *Pacific Citizen* with their JACL membership. For more than fifty years, the *Citizen* featured a column called "From the Frying Pan" by Bill Hosokawa, perhaps the most respected and widely read Japanese American journalist. Meanwhile, magazines such as *Nisei Vue,* which appeared for a brief time in the 1950s, carried creative efforts of Nisei writers. In the 1970s, *Gidra* published the writings of Sansei activists who led the Asian American studies movement. And yet, despite renewed immigration from Japan, the low birthrate among Japanese Americans, rapid assimilation, and divisions in the community all have combined to cause a drop in readership and the number of publications. The last decades of the twentieth century and first years of the twenty-first century, therefore, have seen the demise of many Japanese American newspapers.

Postwar immigrants continue to read the surviving Japanese-language newspapers, a few of which are now owned by Japanese conglomerates. The majority of Japanese Americans, however, turn instead to local ethnic or Pan Asian American media for ethnic news. The handful of surviving Japanese American papers, including San Francisco's *Nichei Bei Times* and Los Angeles's *Rafu Shimpo,* attempt to compete with the electronic media as well as the Pan Asian press featuring articles on the Japanese American community and news from Japan.

Andrew B. Wertheimer

Further Reading

Brislin, Tom. "Weep into Silence/Cries of Rage: Bitter Divisions in Hawaii's Japanese Press." *Journalism and Communication Monographs* 154 (1995): 1–29.

Kessler, Lauren. "Fettered Freedoms: The Journalism of World War II Japanese Internment Camps." *Journalism History* 15 (1988): 60–69.

Kitano, Harry H.L. "The Japanese-American Press." In *The Ethnic Press in the United States: A Historical Analysis and Handbook,* ed. Sally M. Miller, 191–202. Westport, CT: Greenwood, 1987.

Pacific Citizen Web site. http://www.pacificcitizen.org.

Yoo, David. "'Read All About It': Race, Generation and the Japanese American Press, 1925–1941." *Amerasia Journal* 19 (1993): 69–92.

Redress Movement

The redress movement was the long-term struggle by the Japanese American community to obtain an apology and compensation from the U.S. government for incarcerating Japanese American citizens and residents during World War II. Limited reparations for direct property losses were made by the government under the Japanese American Evacuation Claims Act of 1948. The claims process was complicated, however, and many Japanese Americans lacked the required documentation or witness testimony because of the haste with which they had been forced to evacuate their homes and businesses. Moreover, individual claims were capped at $2,500, with additional appropriations from Congress required for any larger amount.

At a 1970 convention of the Japanese American Citizen's League (JACL), former internee and educator Edison Uno was the first to call upon the organization to pursue compensation from the U.S. government specifically for the internment of more than 112,000 Japanese Americans during the war. While Uno was able to get resolutions introduced in Congress, none got out of the subcommittees to which they were assigned. To further the cause, the Seattle Evacuation Redress Committee of the JACL was formed in the early 1970s and developed its own plan for gaining reparations for individuals. Then in 1976, the JACL formed the National Committee for Redress (NCR), which came up with its own recommendations. Meanwhile, local groups emerged around the country to lobby for compensation.

A major split in the national movement occurred when the NCR altered its strategy from direct support for compensation to supporting a government study of the impact of Executive Order 9066. In response, the National Council for Japanese American Redress (NCJAR) was established in 1979. As its first action, the council sought a legislative sponsor to introduce a redress bill in Congress. The first bill, following the Seattle group's plan, was introduced by Representative Mike Lowry, a Democrat from Seattle in 1983. However, the bill did not even receive the support of the four Japanese Americans in Congress (all Democrats), who supported a government study.

Despite the objections of the NCJAR, the Commission on Wartime Relocation and Internment of Civilians (CWRIC) was formed in July 1980 by an act of Congress to study the mass removal and incarceration of Japanese Americans during the war and recommend appropriate remedies. As part of its study, the CWRIC held hearings in twenty cities across the United States. To ensure that the hearings were not a token gesture and that the Japanese American community would be full participants, the independent National Coalition for Redress/Reparations (NCRR) was also formed in July 1980.

The CWRIC published its findings, *Personal Justice Denied,* in December 1982 and issued its formal recommendations in June of the following year: $20,000 in individual compensation to surviving inmates, a formal apology, and the granting of presidential pardons to Fred Korematsu, Gordon Hirabayashi, and Minoru Yasui, whose *coram nobis* cases were before the U.S. district courts. The NCJAR, meanwhile, had filed a class-action lawsuit against the U.S. government that was eventually dismissed, but not before putting significant pressure upon the government to support reparations. The CWRIC recommendations formed the basis of new congressional redress bills, such as H.R. 442 and S. 1009, introduced in both houses in 1987. The NCRR continued to push for the measure through a large lobbying effort, sending delegations on more than 100 congressional visits. Bolstered by the NCRR campaign, H.R. 442 passed the House on September 19, 1987, followed by S. 1009 in the Senate the following April. After more lobbying and a national letter-writing campaign in support of the bills, President Ronald Reagan signed the final measure—the Civil Liberties Act of 1988—on August 10. The first redress payments were made to the oldest survivors on October 9, 1990. By the time the process was completed in 1993, more than 70,000 surviving internees, including several thousand who had returned to Japan, received $20,000 each from the federal government. The legislation also included a formal apology on behalf of the American people for the relocation and internment of Japanese American citizens and Japanese aliens during the war.

Emily Hiramatsu Morishima

Further Reading

Maki, Mitchell T., Harry H.L. Kitano, and S. Megan Berthold, eds. *Achieving the Impossible Dream: How Japanese Americans Obtained Redress.* Chicago: University of Illinois Press, 1999.

Shimabukuro, Robert Sadamu. *Born in Seattle: The Campaign for Japanese American Redress.* Seattle: University of Washington Press, 2001.

Takezawa, Yasuko I. *Breaking the Silence: Redress and Japanese American Ethnicity.* Ithaca, NY: Cornell University Press, 1995.

Religion, Japanese American

The religious faiths of Japanese Americans are based on those that were prominent in Japan, but they have been tailored to fit the demands of American society. The predominant religions are Buddhism, Confucianism, and Shintoism. As practiced by Japanese immigrants and their offspring, these faiths stress the values of moral and ethical living in this world—values such as duty, obligation to family and community, self-restraint, and concern for the collective good—rather than the search for salvation in the next. These qualities have helped immigrants succeed in America despite racial discrimination.

Early Period

The first Japanese to come to American territory in the 1880s were single young men, employed as laborers in Hawaii and on the West Coast. Like most Japanese, these men were Buddhists; most belonged to the reformist Jodo Shinshu school of Buddhism, founded in the twelfth and thirteenth centuries. Sometimes referred to as the "easy path," Jodo Shinshu, or Shin Buddhism, eschews esoteric learning and difficult rituals for the attainment of enlightenment, the highest goal of Buddhists. Because Shin Buddhism does entail some ritual and ceremony, early Buddhist settlers petitioned

the head abbot of the Nishi (Western) Hongwan-ji, or sect, to send priests to the United States to minister to the faithful. A separate missionary branch was set up during the 1880s to take care of the needs of the Buddhists in Hawaii.

The first Japanese Buddhist priests arrived in San Francisco in 1893 but were received coolly by many whites in the city. In an age of strong anti-Japanese prejudice, the priests were accused of seeking to convert white people to Buddhism. Even so, the first official Jodo Shinshu priests, authorized by religious authorities in Japan, arrived in September 1899. They opened the first American Buddhist temple later that year in San Francisco. Other temples followed where Japanese immigrants had settled in considerable numbers, including other cities in the Bay Area, the agricultural Central Valley, and in Southern California. Other agricultural areas, such as Dinuba, Guadalupe, and Sacramento, all had their own temples. Still other temples were built in Seattle and other cities in Washington to serve the Japanese there.

For most Japanese Americans, practicing Buddhism began in the home. They constructed a shrine, or *butsudan,* in their homes. Each day, they would light incense, contemplate the teachings of Buddha, and recite prayers. As followers of Shin Buddhism, they did not regularly attend services in the temples, except for important life-cycle events. The temples were the location of weddings, funerals, and other ceremonial rituals. The Jodo Shinshu temples on the mainland were affiliated with the Buddhist Mission of North America (BMNA). Priests who performed religious ceremonies were trained in Japan and assigned to temples in the United States. They were regarded as community leaders by Japanese Americans, although many did not speak English.

World War II to the Present

World War II marked a turning point religiously for Japanese Americans. The BMNA was replaced on April 6, 1944, by the Buddhist Churches of America (BCA). The meeting that incorporated the BCA took place in the Topaz Relocation Center in Utah. The creation of the BCA largely took control away from the Issei, or immigrants from Japan, and placed it under the Nisei, Japanese Americans born in the United States. The move was part of a campaign to create an American identity to reduce Japanese American connections with Japan.

Even before the war, Japanese American religious activities had been modified to reflect American religious norms. Individual temples were referred to as churches. Regularly scheduled Sunday school and worship services became more typical. Racial discrimination forced the segregation of Japanese Americans, so each temple

Members of the Buddhist Temple of San Diego make traditional Japanese rice cakes called *mochi*. Religious institutions play a vital role in preserving cultural traditions, community ties, and social values, as well as practice of the faith. *(Stan Honda/AFP/Getty Images)*

organized youth groups and sports activities, such as basketball or baseball teams. Temples were built to look like churches, with pews and lecterns instead of prayer mats. Choirs and Western-style musical instruments became standard. Services were often conducted in English, instead of Japanese.

After World War II, Japanese Americans made a renewed effort to make a place for themselves in American society, with many members of the older generation urging their children to play down their Japanese traditions. But with a new emphasis on multiculturalism emerging in the 1960s, many younger Japanese Americans, with fewer ties to the homeland, became more interested in reconnecting to the spiritual path of Buddhism, even as many non-Asian Americans became curious about the alternative belief systems of the East. To that end, the Institute of Buddhist Studies (IBS) Graduate School and Seminary was established by the BCA in 1966 in Berkeley, California. The IBS educates ministers for Jodo Shinshu temples in the United States. The IBS also helps to explain Buddhism to non-Buddhist Americans. Increasing numbers of non-Japanese Americans have become Buddhists in recent years, making Jodo Shinshu less of an ethnic-based faith. By the end of the twentieth century, the BCA had sixty independent temples, mostly in western states, while a separate organization in Hawaii had another thirty-seven. More than 100,000 Japanese Americans are estimated to be Buddhists today.

Other religions practiced by Japanese Americans included Shintoism and Confucianism. The former, an ancient, indigenous faith of Japan—that invested ancestors, nature, and even the Japanese emperor with divine powers—has lost much of its appeal among Japanese Americans since 1945, as it became associated in the home islands with the fascist government that fought against the United States in World War II. While some within the Japanese community continue to adhere to a non-nationalist form of Shintoism, their numbers are few, perhaps 50,000 in all of North America. Confucianism—more of a code of ethics than a religious faith in the Western sense—is often practiced by Japanese in indirect ways, as its stress on proper moral conduct, harmonious social relations, and hard work remains central to the Japanese American ethos.

Two factors have contributed to the decline of traditional religious practices within the Japanese American community in recent decades. First, as members of one of the oldest and most assimilated of Asian American communities, many second-, third-, and fourth-generation Japanese Americans have adopted the more individualist ethos of their adopted homeland, leading many away from the traditional, collectivist values promoted by Buddhism, Confucianism, and Shintoism. This trend is reflected in the declining numbers attending traditional services or practicing traditional faiths at home.

The second factor has been the rise of Christianity within the Japanese American community. Christians represent a very small part of the population in the Japanese home islands and, thus, a small proportion of Japanese immigrants. But they played a disproportionately large role in Japanese American society. Some Japanese Christians emigrated to the United States because they saw it as a Christian country. Other immigrants became Christian when they arrived, thanks to Christian missionaries or because they believed it would help them fit into American society. Some also saw Christianity as a more active and involved religion, more in keeping with American culture than the more passive Buddhism. Because of discrimination, Japanese Americans ordinarily formed their own congregations. In most other ways, they resembled their American Protestant counterparts. Meanwhile, as the community matured in America, some American-born Japanese converted to various, largely Protestant denominations.

Finally, in recent years, increasing integration of Japanese Americans into mainstream U.S. society has caused a decline in unique Japanese American religions. Japanese Americans are less likely to be concentrated in a particular location. Those who want to preserve an ethnic identity are more likely to join Pan–Asian American religious organizations.

Tim J. Watts

Further Reading

Laderman, Gary, and Luis D. Leon. *Religion and American Cultures: An Encyclopedia of Traditions, Diversity, and Popular Expressions.* Santa Barbara, CA: ABC-CLIO, 2003.

Min, Pyong Gap, and Jung Ha Kim. *Religions in Asian America: Building Faith Communities.* Walnut Creek, CA: AltaMira, 2002.

Nakamaki, Hirochika. *Japanese Religions at Home and Abroad: Anthropological Perspectives.* New York: RoutledgeCurzon, 2003.

Tuck, Donald R. *Buddhist Churches of America: Jodo Shinshu.* Lewiston, NY: Edwin Mellen, 1987.

Resettlement, Post–World War II Incarceration

The War Relocation Authority (WRA), the federal civilian agency in charge of the incarceration of Japanese Americans during World War II, used the term "resettlement" to refer to the movement of Japanese Americans out of the internment camps and back into mainstream society in the final years of the war. A related term, "voluntary resettlement," is used in reference to Japanese Americans who chose to leave restricted areas on the West Coast in order to avoid being forced into camps in early 1942.

The WRA allowed some inmates to leave almost as soon as the camps opened. The first allowed to leave were college students. The WRA instructed them to not to complain about their incarceration or to engage in overt displays of ethnic identity, out of fear of anti-Japanese sentiment and potential violence. Other small groups of inmates were allowed to leave the incarceration centers for temporary work camps to help with the agricultural harvest in various western states. In addition, inmates who volunteered left to attend Military Intelligence Specialist School.

By July 1942, the WRA had developed regulations for "leave" and "permanent resettlement," to be applied to those who passed strict guidelines and security clearances. The WRA director, Dillon S. Myer, was reluctant to let Japanese Americans return to the West Coast and the Japantowns and ethnic enclaves that they had been forced to leave. Japanese Americans who qualified and opted for leave or permanent resettlement were directed to settle in the North and East, where, because of wartime labor shortages, jobs could be found. The WRA opened a total of six regional offices and thirty-five subregional offices charged with making arrangements in the local area and preparing the Japanese American arrivals for their new life. The agency also held briefings in the camps and provided information about potential resettlement cities. Independent religious groups set up their own hostels and resettlement programs, including the Committee on Resettlement of Japanese Americans, which published the monthly *Resettlement Bulletin* starting in April 1943.

The WRA had hoped to move 75,000 people out of the camps by 1943, but many internees were reluctant to leave, scared by stories of the hostile environment outside. Thus, by the end of that year, only 17,000 people had left the camps. By January 1945, only one-third of the 112,000 internees had been resettled. The most popular destinations for those who chose to leave were Salt Lake City and Denver because they already had significant communities of Japanese Americans who had not been included in the original West Coast exclusion order. Chicago, Minneapolis–Saint Paul, Cleveland, St. Louis, and New York were other popular destinations. Of the nearly 30,000 traceable people who left the camps before January 1945, 75 percent settled in Illinois, Colorado, Ohio, Utah, Idaho, Michigan, Minnesota, and New York.

In December 1944, the U.S. Supreme Court ruled in the *Ex parte Endo* case that Japanese Americans who had proved their loyalty could return to restricted areas on the West Coast. As a result, nearly two-thirds of the people who left the camps after January 1945 went to that part of the country. By the end of the war in August 1945, the vast majority of the internees had resettled, largely in areas where they had originally lived. Most of the camps closed down that fall. Tule Lake in California was the last to shut down, in March 1946.

Emily Hiramatsu Morishima

A Japanese American family receives a permit to depart the Tule Lake Relocation Center in northern California—the last internment camp to close—in early 1946. Some internees returned to their former communities; others moved to whole new parts of the country. *(Gift of Jack and Peggy Iwata, Japanese American National Museum, 93.102.7)*

Further Reading

Austin, Allan W. "Eastward Pioneers: Japanese American Re-settlement During World War II and the Contested Meaning of Exile and Incarceration." *Journal of American Ethnic History* 26:2 (2007): 58–84.

Daniels, Roger. *Prisoners Without Trial: Japanese Americans in World War II.* New York: Hill and Wang, 1993.

Ng, Wendy. *Japanese American Internment During World War II.* Greenwich, CT: Greenwood Publishing, 2002.

War Relocation Authority, U.S. Department of Interior. *WRA: A Story of Human Conservation.* Washington, DC: Government Printing Office, 1946.

Restaurants and Cuisine, Japanese American

Japanese American cuisine can be defined as a fusion cooking style that synthesizes Japanese food with mainstream American foods. Japanese food was first introduced to the United States by Japanese contract plantation workers who went to Hawaii in the 1880s, as well as Japanese farmworkers who migrated to the U.S. mainland in the 1890s.

With Chinese immigration cut off by the Chinese Exclusion Act of 1882, Hawaiian sugar farmers and California vegetable farmers turned to Japan for workers, leading to large-scale immigration from that country—both Mainland Japan and Okinawa—around the turn of the twentieth century. First-generation Japanese immigrants, or Issei, often formed communal kitchens to make *miso* (a thick fermented paste made of soybeans), *sake* (Japanese house wine), *tofu* (soybean curd), *somen* (Japanese fine noodles), *umeboshi* (pickled red plums), and other staples of their homeland. The early Japanese immigrants also introduced such commonplace Japanese dishes as *sushi* (sliced raw fish on top of vinegary rice), *ton katsu* (deep fried pork), *musubi* (rice ball), *chicken katsu* (deep fried chicken), and *teriyaki chicken* (baked chicken marinated in a sweet soy-sauce-based sauce), as well as traditional New Year's dishes, such as *toshikoshi soba* (buckwheat noodles), *mochi* (rice cake), *kamaboko* (fish cake), and *mame* (beans). In Hawaii, these traditional Japanese foods, along with culinary practices such as *bento* (lunch boxes filled with assorted foods), which plantation workers carried to the fields, became centerpieces of the local cuisine.

On the mainland, Japanese immigrants retained traditional Japanese-style food not just through home cooking but also in the restaurants of the Nihonmachi (Japantown, J-town, or Little Tokyo), where social, cultural, and political events were held. In the 1890s, the Nihonmachi began to prosper in major cities on the West Coast, such as San Francisco, Seattle, Los Angeles, and San Jose, and Japanese restaurants there became popular among immigrants. Even after strict immigration restriction and severe ethnic antagonism against the Japanese in the early twentieth century, Japanese restaurants continued to serve farmers and local residents of the bustling Japantowns until the mass relocation and incarceration during World War II.

Inside the internment camps, Japanese-cooked meals became an important form of cultural identity for displaced and imprisoned families. Internees planted and harvested *daikon* (white radish), *nappa* (Japanese cabbage), and other vegetables and fruits, and constructed modest *tofu* and *shoyu* factories. Japanese Americans also acquired a taste for "war food," that is, canned goods. In Hawaii, SPAM (spiced ham by Hormel) was introduced by military forces during World War II, and Japanese Americans devised a unique local dish by combining this American product with Japanese traditional foods. SPAM *musubi*—sliced, stir-fried SPAM in teriyaki sauce on top of rice wrapped in *nori* (dried seaweed)—which has been a popular Hawaiian finger food for decades, is sold in local grocery stores, convenience stores, and fast-food restaurants throughout the islands.

In the aftermath of World War II, Japanese soy sauce companies tried to expand into the American market. Exports from Japan resumed after the immediate postwar shortages of the late 1940s, and Kikkoman, the country's major soy sauce producer, promoted teriyaki sauce (a soy-sauce-based product that contains *sake* and *mirin*, or sweet cooking wine) in order to expand U.S. consumption beyond the Asian American community and into the mainstream. In the 1960s, teriyaki sauce became widely used in the United States with ingredients such as chicken, salmon, and beef.

In the 1960s and 1970s, with the influx of immigrants after the lifting of national quotas, the United States became more ethnically diverse and ethnic restaurants became a trend in big cities across the nation. The new mainstream American fascination for sushi—seen as a healthy alternative to meat-based American cuisines—contributed to the creation of Japanese American varieties using locally available ingredients. Indeed, perhaps the most well-known and well-accepted example of Japanese American cuisine is the California roll. Invented by Ichiro Mashita, the chef at Tokyo Kaikan restaurant in Los Angeles in the early 1960s, the California roll became widely available in the early 1970s. Mashita, who had noticed the similarity in taste between avocado and tuna, substituted California avocado for the fish when

The chief sushi chef directs his kitchen staff before the debut of a new Japanese restaurant in South Beach, Florida. The mainstream American craze for sushi has given rise to variations based on local ingredients, such as the popular California roll. *(Joe Raedle/Getty Images)*

the latter was out of season and rolled the ingredients with rice in *nori*. The idea was to make the roll more palatable to mainstream Americans unaccustomed to raw fish and seaweed.

Teppanyaki, a stir-fried food preparation method in Japan, is probably the most popular Japanese fusion dining style in the United States. Founded by Rocky Aoki, a Japanese former wrestler, in New York in 1964, Benihana, also known as Hibachi Steak House, first introduced teppanyaki cooking with acrobatic knife skills as restaurant entertainment. In teppanyaki restaurants, customers dine at a communal table in front of a large steel grill while a chef cooks the requested ingredients, such as seafood, noodles, meat, and vegetables, with a demonstration of cutting and slicing showmanship. After its success in U.S. franchise restaurants, teppanyaki has found popularity in Europe and Latin America as well.

Since the late 1990s, several upscale Japanese fusion restaurants owned by "Iron chefs"—famous for their appearances on the popular competitive cooking television show of the same name—have opened in major cities in the United States. Originally broadcast in Japan, *Iron Chef* (*Ryori no Tetsujin*), which found a cult following when it began airing in the United States, introduced more exotic ingredients, such as *fugu* (blowfish), *natto* (fermented soy beans), and river eel—to American audiences. The show also features highly skilled Japanese chefs who specialize in Japanese, Italian, Chinese, or French cuisine.

Suzuko Morikawa

Further Reading

Cwiertka, Katarzyna, and Boudewijn Walraven, eds. *Asian Food: The Global and the Local.* Honolulu: University of Hawai'i Press, 2001.

Dusselier, Jane. "Does Food Make Place? Food Protests in Japanese American Concentration Camps." *Food and Foodways* 10 (2002): 137–65.

Okihiro, Gary Y. "The Japanese in America." In *Japanese American History: An A-to-Z Reference from 1868 to the Present,* ed. Brian Niiya, 1–23. New York: Facts on File, 1993.

Takaki, Ronald. *Pau Hana: Plantation Life and Labor in Hawaii 1835–1920.* Honolulu: University of Hawai'i Press, 1983.

Satow, Masao (1908–1977)

A leader of the Japanese American Citizens League (JACL) before, during, and after the World War II internment of Japanese Americans—which he and the organization told fellow Americans of Japanese descent to accept quietly to prove their loyalty—Masao "Mas" Satow served with the JACL from the 1930s until his death in 1977.

Satow was born in San Mateo, California, in 1908 and moved with his parents—first-generation immigrants (Issei) Shuzo and Kiyose Satow—to Los Angeles when he was a toddler. His father barely earned enough from menial labor to support the family, but Satow managed to find the funds to pay for his education at the University of California at Los Angeles (UCLA). Upon graduating in 1929, he completed a bachelor of theology degree in 1932 from Princeton Theological Seminary.

Also in 1932, Satow joined the JACL, a membership that would consume his life. Founded in 1929, the organization was the largest and most vocal advocacy group for Japanese Americans in the United States, promoting assimilation and Americanization. Its support for internment during World War II was highly controversial in the Japanese American and civil liberties communities. Indeed, some of its leaders who were interned, including Satow, were often removed from camp for their safety from violence by the resisters.

Satow remained a staunch advocate for the JACL platform. Elected as assistant executive secretary in 1936, he was simultaneously appointed chair of the Second General Development Program, whose function was to assist Nisei (second-generation Japanese Americans) with integrating into all aspects of American life. When the forced mobilization of Japanese Americans began in February 1942, Satow and his wife, Chizuko, were interned at the Santa Anita Assembly Center and then moved to the Granada Relocation Center in Colorado. They remained there until December 1944.

During the resettlement period after the war, Satow moved to Milwaukee, Wisconsin, and became a national board field representative for the Young Men's Christian Association (YMCA). As the former general secretary of the YMCA's Los Angeles chapter in Little Tokyo before the war, he was now able to help former internees through the resources of the national organization. He continued his association with JACL as the Eastern-Midwest District representative, and in 1946 agreed to fill the position of national secretary when Mike Masaru Masaoka was transferred to Washington, D.C., as the JACL's full-time lobbyist for Japanese American equal rights legislation. Satow intended to fulfill his obligation for one year, but remained the national secretary—and later national director—for a quarter of a century, aided as well by his wife's close involvement with the organization. Satow presided over a period of growth of the organization in terms of membership, finances, and influence. When his tenure as the national secretary began in 1947, the JACL had 3,100 members in twenty-five chapters (two of which were on the West Coast). By the time he retired in 1972, it had 27,000 members in ninety-four chapters across the country.

Satow also served on the committee for the Japanese American Research Project at UCLA, the nation's largest collection of papers, oral history tapes, photographs, artworks, and survey data on the Japanese American community. After he retired, Satow continued to work as a senior adviser to the president of Sumitomo Bank in California. He died on March 3, 1977. In recognition of his dedication and leadership, the JACL renamed its San Francisco headquarters the Satow Building. In Gardena, a suburb of Los Angeles with a large Japanese American community, the public library was named in his honor.

Gabriella Oldham

Further Reading
Hosokawa, Bill. *JACL in Quest of Justice.* New York: William Morrow, 1982.
Kim, Hyung-Chan, ed. *Dictionary of Asian American History.* New York: Greenwood, 1986.
O'Brien, David J., and Stephen S. Fugita. *The Japanese American Experience.* Bloomington: Indiana University Press, 1991.

"Schoolboy"/"Schoolgirl"

Schoolboy" and "schoolgirl" were terms used for Japanese youths who had immigrated to the United States in the late nineteenth and early twentieth centuries and sought the financial means to support going to school and learning English. Domestic work, which also provided room and board, was frequently the only employment available to these new arrivals. Although the pay was meager—$1.50 a week in 1900—the work provided shelter to a young man with no other attachments in the country and an on-the-spot course in running an American household. Local newspapers abounded with advertisements placed by the Issei (first-generation Japanese) seeking such positions. In the early 1900s, more than 4,000 schoolboys were working in San Francisco alone.

The decade of the schoolboy lasted from approximately the turn of the century until shortly after the Gentleman's Agreement of 1907–1908, which sought to stop Japanese labor migration to the United States. The agreement significantly reduced the number of schoolboys by the end of the 1910s, as many Issei opted for the type of labor that would eventually lead them to procure their own farm or business. Noted Issei who worked as schoolboys before moving into more rewarding positions include Kyutaro Abiko, a newspaper publisher and banker who started three utopian farming colonies for Issei in California's Central Valley in the early twentieth century, and Yonejiro Noguchi, who settled in San Francisco in 1893 and later became the father of world-renowned sculptor Isamu Noguchi.

While the male Issei chose to move on to more lucrative positions, Issei and Nisei women before World War II found that domestic live-in service was a socially acceptable, often long-term occupation. It not only supported their education, but gave them the opportunity to learn American customs and household operations that would serve them in married life. Often their domestic training was complemented by sewing school. As the Nisei women acquired more mobility to middle-class status following World War II, few Sansei (third generation) chose the schoolgirl route.

Despite the more acceptable regard that schoolgirls had as keepers of the home, the positions of schoolboy and schoolgirl spawned stereotypes of docile Japanese servants grunting mangled English—images that would brand themselves on Japanese characters in film, television, and literature. Notable books of the period about the schoolboy experience include *Letters of a Japanese Schoolboy* (1909) by Wallace Irwin and a comic book by first-generation immigrant Henry Kiyama titled *The Four Immigrants Manga: A Japanese Experience in San Francisco, 1904–1924* (1927).

Gabriella Oldham

Further Reading
Irwin, Wallace. *Letters of a Japanese Schoolboy.* Reprint ed. Upper Saddle River, NJ: Literature House, 1969.

Kiyama, Henry. *The Four Immigrants Manga: A Japanese Experience in San Francisco, 1904–1924.* Trans. and ed. Frederik L. Schodt. Berkeley, CA: Stone Bridge, 1999.

Seabrook Farms

Seabrook Farms in Upper Deerfield, New Jersey, was one of the world's largest producers of frozen and canned vegetables from the 1930s through the 1950s. It was also the work site for thousands of resettled Japanese Americans, recruited from the internment camps to which they had been deported during World War II. Through mutual agreement, Seabrook offered work, home, and school for Japanese Americans, who in turn promised six months of labor. While many employees did return to the West Coast after the war, their employment was a significant ingredient in Seabrook's success when steady manpower was scarce.

Charles F. Seabrook bought the sixty-acre (twenty-four-hectare) farm from his father, Arthur P. Seabrook, in 1911. The son, a shrewd businessman, believed in applying factory methods and new technology to farming, earning him the nickname "the Henry Ford of agriculture." On the farm, Arthur had initiated the use of overhead irrigation and gasoline tractors; Charles constructed two railroads as well as canning, ice, and power plants. Accruing political power as well, Charles became a state highway commissioner and was instrumental in building Route 77, a state highway on which he had vegetables trucked to Camden. He reemerged from financial ruin in the 1930s after discovering a quick-freezing technique for vegetables through direct expansion ammonia. He started freezing vegetables for General Foods but began selling under the farm's own label by 1943. During World War II, Seabrook produced an estimated one-fifth of the country's frozen vegetables; by the end of the decade, its output was 10 million pounds (4.5 million kilograms) of canned vegetables and 65 million pounds (29.5 million kilograms) of frozen vegetables.

World War II drained the supply of hired labor, however, and Seabrook Farms was forced to turn to immigrant sources for its workers. Until the 1950s, displaced and jobless Jamaicans, Italians, Germans, Russians, and Americans found work at Seabrook. Japanese Americans were particularly singled out as responsible farmers, and those deemed "loyal" to the United States were invited to work for the company. Seabrook recruiters visited the internment camps and advertised promising work opportunities in camp newspapers, while reassuring nervous locals about the potential influx of Japanese Americans to the community. The first Japanese Americans arrived

Employees of Seabrook Farms pose outside the company's southern New Jersey facility in 1954. A major producer of frozen and canned vegetables, Seabrook hired, transported, and housed more than 2,500 former Japanese internees after World War II. *(Yale Joel/Stringer/Time & Life Pictures/Getty Images)*

in February 1944, and by 1947 they constituted half (an average of 2,500) of the total labor force.

Charles Seabrook erected prefabricated homes for his workers, as well as a Buddhist temple. Wages started at fifty cents an hour, varying according to the nature of the work and union membership. Although a large number stayed on after the war, many Japanese Americans considered Seabrook a transition back to freedom and the Pacific Coast. By 1949, the number of Japanese American company laborers was less than half its peak of two years earlier. Damage caused by a hurricane in 1954 and family disputes led management to sell Seabrook Farms to a wholesale grocery in 1959. Although its final owners closed the plant in 1979 and donated the property to the township, Charles's two grandsons revived the business in 1981 and by 1994 had repurchased the original plant site. A small population of Japanese Americans remains in Seabrook today, and reunions of Seabrook workers are held in the community. In 1994, the Seabrook Educational and Cultural Center was opened to commemorate the multicultural heritage of the farm through oral histories, exhibits, and a large-scale model of Seabrook Village in the 1950s.

Gabriella Oldham

Further Reading

Harrison, Charles H. *Growing a Global Village: Making History at Seabrook Farms.* New York: Holmes and Meier, 2003.

Sawada, Miziko. "After the Camps: Seabrook Farms, New Jersey, and the Resettlement of Japanese Americans, 1944–47." *Amerasia Journal* 13:2 (1986–1987): 117–36.

Settlements, Japanese American

When Japanese immigrants first began arriving on the U.S. mainland in the late nineteenth and early twentieth centuries, they faced rampant discrimination and sometimes violent racism. With many geographic areas and professions closed to them, most Issei (first-generation immigrants) found their greatest opportunities in agriculture. With little other choice, they founded their own settlements in rural areas of California, Oregon, Washington, and other western states. In these colonies, Japanese Americans could participate fully in community life, retain their own ethnic identity, and begin the process of Americanization. Although most of these settlements have long since disappeared or become integrated into larger urban centers, they played an important role in developing what would become a thriving Japanese American culture.

Early Settlements

The earliest Japanese settlement in the United States was located in the El Dorado Hills, not far from Placerville, California, east of Sacramento. In 1869, a group of twenty-two Japanese immigrants traveled from Aizu-Wakamatsu in what is now Fukushima Prefecture to Gold Hill near Placerville and established a colony. Some historians of Japanese American culture refer to the settlement as the Plymouth Rock or Jamestown of Japanese immigration. The new arrivals had been granted permission to leave Japan in the aftermath of the civil war that established the Meiji imperial regime. (At the time, emigration was technically illegal.) The group was led by the adviser to a defeated Japanese lord, a German named John Henry Schnell, and arrived in San Francisco on May 27, 1869. Schnell purchased a 600-acre (240-hectare) ranch on which the settlers established the Wakamatsu Tea and Silk Farm Colony with the 50,000 mulberry trees and silk worms they brought with them, along with tea seeds and a variety of cuttings from plants grown in Japan.

The settlement seemed to prosper at first, but Schnell soon realized that the soil was not well suited to mulberry trees and tea. The California weather was also hotter and drier than in Japan, and irrigation was not available. Schnell ran out of money by the following year and left the settlement with his Japanese wife and two children. The remaining members followed soon thereafter. Their fates are largely unknown, although records show that one member, a man named Kuninosuke Masumizu, married into an interracial family of Native Americans and African Americans; he died in 1915, after working as a court interpreter. In 1969, the state of California placed a historical marker at the site to commemorate the first Japanese settlement in North America.

The first Japanese immigrants to U.S. territory were young men recruited to work and live on plantations in Hawaii during the 1880s. Many later moved to the mainland, with others following directly from Japan. The Meiji regime, newly active in world affairs, believed it was important that Japanese citizens make a good impression on foreign countries to which they moved. As a result, the government screened prospective émigrés to make certain they were educated, healthy, and hardworking. Also realizing that young single men might be seen as potential troublemakers in other countries, the government also encouraged Japanese women to emigrate and form Japanese families overseas.

Nearly all Japanese of the Issei generation worked on farms. By 1909, at least 38,000 Japanese were employed on farms in California and the Pacific Northwest. Strictly migrant workers at first, some later became sharecroppers. Under the latter arrangement, they lived and worked on the farm and split the harvest with the landowner. Because it did not require a large capital investment, sharecropping was an important first step out of migrant labor and toward self-sufficiency. Discrimination and racism generally forced Japanese immigrants to form their own settlements in rural (agricultural) areas of the western United States, especially California, Oregon, and Washington. Afraid of increasing the number of Japanese immigrants and risking competition with nervous white growers, state governments passed laws to prevent people who could not become citizens from owning land. Since Asians could not become citizens by law, the laws were aimed at them. Japanese Americans got around the law by purchasing land in the names of their children (the Nisei, or second generation), who were American citizens by virtue of being born on U.S. soil. Others formed land cooperatives, rather than naming individuals, to purchase the land.

Among the notable Japanese agricultural settlements was the Yamato Colony, near Livingston in the Central Valley of California. The settlement was the brainchild of Kyutaro Abiko, a San Francisco newspaper publisher who purchased 3,000 acres (1,200 hectares) in 1904 and advertised in Japanese-language newspapers for farmers to establish a community. To attract settlers, Abiko sold the land for $35 an acre and financed the purchases. The settlement was slow in building—by 1908, only thirty farm families had settled in Yamato Colony—but others soon followed as the colony became a success. Most farmers bought only a few acres at first and spent their energy converting the land into productive fields. Peaches and grapes were among the first crops planted, but the first harvests would take years. The first cash crops were eggplants grown by a Mrs. Naka, which found a ready market in San Francisco. The next year, other colony members followed with more eggplants, melons, sweet potatoes, and asparagus. Combining knowledge of irrigation and cultivation with hard work, the Japanese American farmers were able to succeed on small plots. In 1910, the settlement established a food-buying cooperative, and in 1914 it launched a marketing cooperative. A Christian church was built in 1917, marking the Yamato Colony as one of the few Japanese American settlements without a Buddhist temple.

Early Japanese settlers were careful to establish businesses that were closely related to their farming activities and not try to compete directly with white businesses. At the Yamato Colony and elsewhere, therefore, enterprises such as dry goods and grocery stores were generally eschewed. But the settlers did form their own educational and social groups. The Japanese Association of America, formed in 1909, served as a general welfare association to help the sick, the injured, and those in need. The Yamato Colony was especially noted by observers for its sports teams. Its baseball, basketball, volleyball, and softball squads, for participants ranging from school age to adults in their thirties, were a source of great civic pride. They normally competed against teams from other Japanese settlements, drawing spectators of all ages and even coverage in local white newspapers.

Other significant Japanese settlements were found in rural Northern California and Washington State, in particular. In the latter, most were located in the White River Valley and grew crops such as strawberries, lettuce, beans, cauliflower, peas, cabbage, celery, and carrots. In fact, much of the fresh produce sold in Seattle at the time was supplied by Japanese American farmers. By the outbreak of World War I, Japanese American farmers occupied 70 percent of the stalls at the Pike Place Market in Seattle.

Impact of World War II

The outbreak of World War II spelled the end of Japanese American agricultural settlements. Beginning in early 1942, most Japanese in the United States—citizens and resident aliens alike—were relocated to internment camps far from their homes. In their absence, their land, buildings, and equipment were either sold or simply taken over by American farmers. After the war, only a few were able to return to their property, restore the land, and rebuild the business. The Americanization of the Nisei generation, new educational opportunities,

and access to the professions helped integrate Japanese Americans into mainstream society. With other opportunities available, many young Japanese Americans left the farms.

Nevertheless, Japanese American farm owners remain responsible for much of the produce grown in the western United States. In the former Yamato Colony, the Farmers' Association has sixty-five members, of which fifty-seven are Japanese Americans. Other changes have taken place as well. Almonds and kiwi fruit have replaced most of the peaches and grapes. Mechanization has replaced much of the manual labor. Many of the uniquely Japanese institutions have merged with mainstream institutions. In 1977, for example, the Japanese Methodist Church merged with the white Methodist Church in Livingston.

Tim J. Watts

Further Reading

Iwata, Masakazu. *Planted in Good Soil: A History of the Issei in United States Agriculture.* New York: Peter Lang, 1992.

Matsumoto, Valerie J. *Farming the Home Place: A Japanese American Community in California, 1919–1982.* Ithaca, NY: Cornell University Press, 1993.

Noda, Kesa. *Yamato Colony: 1906–1960 Livingston, California.* Livingston, CA: Livingston-Merced JACL Chapter, 1981.

United States. Works Projects Administration (California). *The Story of Japanese Farming in California.* San Francisco: R and E Research Associates, 1971 [1957].

Shikata Ga Nai

In Japan, when a child cries for a toy she covets but does not have, her caretaker might well reply with a rhetorical question: *"Shikata ga nai de sho?"* ("It cannot be helped, can it?" or "There is no other choice, is there?") So common is the usage, and the perceived reaction, that the phrase *shikata ga nai* has come to be identified with a particular way the Japanese people are said respond to adverse situations. According to this view, Japanese Americans repeatedly have endured challenging situations with what appears to be the conformist attitude that certain things simply cannot be helped.

While the attitude may seem passive and helpless from a Western perspective, it is not entirely so in the Japanese view. Indeed, the attitude of *shikata ga nai* has been identified as a source of particular perseverance and courage among Japanese Americans during their collective relocation and internment beginning in 1942. The incarceration was devastating not only because of the unjustified imprisonment itself but also because it dissolved Japanese American communities throughout the West Coast. Yet while some members of the internee population actively protested their circumstances, resisted the U.S. military draft, sued the federal government, and otherwise expressed their outrage at the incarceration, others followed the advice of the Japanese American Citizens League (JACL) to accede to the program so as to reassure the government of their "loyalty." To the more vigorous opponents of internment, largely the Nisei (second generation), that response smacked of passivity and *shikata ga nai.*

In any event, at the end of the incarceration, Japanese Americans returned to their old neighborhoods to find their businesses and properties taken over by new owners, vandalized, or in disrepair from sheer neglect. Rather than dwell on what they had lost, however, the Japanese American community devoted its efforts to rebuilding their lives, whether on their old farms or in new locations. Again, the attitude of *shikata ga nai*—that the loss has already taken place and could not be helped—prompted Japanese Americans to bring even greater energy to their new lives and the improvement of their circumstances. Indeed, within a few short decades of their internment, Japanese Americans had become almost uniquely successful among American ethnic groups—academically, professionally, and financially. In 1966, a sociology professor at the University of California, Berkeley, singled out Japanese Americans as the single most successful—no matter how "success" is measured—of all ethnic groups in the United States, including European Americans.

While *shikata ga nai* no doubt has contributed to the success of the Japanese American community, adverse aspects associated with the attitude have also been noted in the postwar era. In his 1969 book *Nisei: The Quiet Americans,* for example, Bill Hosokawa observes that Japanese Americans in the years following the end of internment generally refrained from questioning social injustice or proclaiming their civil rights, instead focusing on gaining acceptance in mainstream society—quietly. By contrast, the generations of Japanese Americans born after the war, who witnessed the civil rights, feminist, gay rights, and other social movements of the 1960s and 1970s, identified less and less with the Japanese philosophy of *shikata ga nai.*

The fading of the attitude among younger and more assimilated generations of Japanese Americans, particularly the Nisei and Sansei (second and third generations, respectively) may certainly have been instrumental in the success of the redress movement, launched in the 1970s to seek compensation and formal government apology for the treatment of Japanese Americans under Executive Order 9066. Many members of these U.S.-born generations had assimilated American ideas about individual rights and the need to participate in the electoral process to achieve political ends. Thus, while the *shikata ga nai* attitude may have facilitated Japanese Americans' efforts to endure the grim realities of relocation and internment, redemption was achieved through a directly contradictory attitude—underscoring the assimilation and acculturation of Japanese Americans into the larger mainstream of U.S. society.

Daisuke Akiba

Further Reading

Fugita, Stephen, and David O'Brien. *Japanese American Ethnicity: The Persistence of Community.* Seattle: University of Washington Press, 1991.

Hosokawa, Bill. *Nisei: The Quiet Americans.* New York: William Morrow, 1969.

Shima, George (1864–1926)

George Shima—born Kinji Ushijima in 1864 in Kurume, Japan—emigrated to the United States in 1887 with less than $1,000. He eventually became one of the most successful agricultural entrepreneurs in the early history of California, with landholdings that exceeded 10,000 acres (4,000 hectares) and the unofficial title of "Potato King."

As a youth, Shima wanted to study Chinese classics but failed the entrance exam to his preferred university in Tokyo because he did not know English. In 1889, on impulse, he left Japan for the United States to study English. Upon arriving in San Francisco, he changed his name to George Shima and worked as a domestic servant—one of the few urban occupations white Americans allowed Asian immigrants to perform at the time—while learning English. Later that year, he left the city for the San Joaquin Valley to become a potato picker and later a labor contractor. These contractors played an important role in the early Japanese American community on the strength of their English-language skills, which allowed them to serve as liaisons with white farmers seeking access to cheap immigrant labor. Passage of the Chinese Exclusion Act of 1882 had made low-wage farm labor scarce in California, and Japanese migrants rushed in to fill the void.

Being a labor contractor afforded Shima higher pay and status, which he parleyed into fifteen acres (six hectares) of leased land in the San Joaquin–Sacramento River delta east of San Francisco. He later had the ingenuity to purchase swampy lowlands and flooded islands in the delta for $3 to $5 per acre, as opposed to the $150 per acre that prime farming land could command. By undertaking the arduous work of draining and diking property eschewed by white farmers, he converted the forbidding terrain into highly productive farmland, in one of the largest land reclamation efforts on the West Coast.

On his developed farmland, Shima took advantage of his experience with labor-intensive, high-yield agricultural methods from his homeland to lucrative effect. Spending a decade mastering how to grow potatoes in the region, Shima made them his primary crop. This was a risk few Japanese Americans were willing to take because it involved selling primarily to white consumers instead of Japanese Americans, in direct competition with white farmers. But Shima saw the great potential of potatoes as a nonperishable product that could be shipped to distant markets. Seeking advice from agricultural experts at Stanford University and the University of California, Berkeley, to improve his crop and yield, Shima became known as the "Potato King" of California by 1909. By 1913, he had 28,000 acres (11,300 hectares) in production, and by the end of the decade his Shima Fancy brand was estimated to be worth $18 million.

His business success translated into a leadership position in the early Japanese American community. Shima served as the first president of the Japanese Association of America, a coalition of more than fifty Japanese immigrant community groups established in 1908. Despite his achievements, influence, and wealth, Shima was told to move to an "Oriental" neighborhood when he bought a home in Berkeley. When he died from a stroke in April 1926, Shima left an estate worth an estimated $15 million to $17 million. Pallbearers at his funeral included the mayor of San Francisco, James Rolph, Jr., and David Starr Jordan, chancellor emeritus of Stanford.

Jaideep Singh

Further Reading

Hasegawa, Yoshino Tajiri, and Keith Boettcher, eds. *Success Through Perseverance: Japanese-Americans in the San Joaquin Valley*. Fresno, CA: Japanese-American Project, San Joaquin Valley Library System, 1980.

Hata, Don, and Nadine Hata. "George Shima: "The Potato King of California." *Journal of the West* (January 1986): 55–63.

Slocum, Tokutaro "Tokie" (1895–1974)

The highest-ranking Japanese American serviceman in World War I, Tokutaro "Tokie" Nishimura

Slocum was a major figure in the fight for naturalized citizenship for Japanese American veterans in the 1920s and 1930s.

Slocum was born in Japan in 1895 and emigrated to North Dakota with his parents when he was ten years old. He received his American surname from the family that adopted him soon thereafter. "Tokie" attended both the University of Minnesota and Columbia University in New York City, but his law studies at the latter school were interrupted by World War I, when he joined the 328th Infantry in France. Exposed to noxious gas during combat, Slocum returned home with medical problems that would plague him for years. Elevated to sergeant major, he became the highest-ranking Asian in the U.S. Army. Under federal legislation in 1918 that opened citizenship to aliens with honorable veteran status, Slocum became a naturalized U.S. citizen at a time when other Japanese immigrants were legally ineligible.

Slocum resumed his law studies but soon felt compelled to campaign, almost single-handedly, for the rights of Issei (first-generation) war veterans to become naturalized. His motivation stemmed from the U.S. Supreme Court decision in *Toyota v. United States* (1925). In this case, the honorably discharged Hidemitsu Toyota, who had served with U.S. forces in World War I, lost his certificate of citizenship when a circuit court overrode a lower court's decision to grant it. The Supreme Court upheld the cancellation, refusing to broaden the definition of "eligible aliens" to benefit the Japanese. Recognizing that he would most likely lose his citizenship, which was required for admission to the bar, Slocum left law school to introduce the cause of naturalization for Issei war veterans to a national audience.

Slocum soon became affiliated with and staunchly supportive of the Japanese American Citizens League (JACL), becoming one of its official lobbyists in 1934. His efforts were rewarded when Congress passed the Nye-Lea Bill, signed into law by President Franklin D. Roosevelt on June 24, 1935. That legislation, sponsored by Senator Gerald Nye of Slocum's home state of North Dakota (and Representative Clarence Lea of California), granted citizenship to some 500 World War I veterans of Asian descent, most of them Japanese. Nevertheless, Slocum's belief that Japanese Americans should demonstrate their loyalty to the United States would earn him a reputation in the Japanese American community as an *inu*, or informant, during World War II. Slocum was among those who called on Japanese Americans to accept their relocation to internment camps, and for some later to answer the military draft, as expressions of such loyalty.

Slocum served as a member of the Southern California JACL committee assisting the federal investigation of Japanese Americans after Pearl Harbor. In testifying before the Tolan Committee (or House Select Committee Investigating National Defense Migration), established to explore the possibility of forcibly removing Japanese Americans, Slocum voiced what he felt was the sentiment of all: "The very fact and very proof of [loyalty] is . . . you don't hear a holler going up when your Commander-in-Chief, through General De Witt says, 'Evacuate.' Everybody is willing. . . . They want to know where to go and how to go, really." He personified his belief in the benefits of evacuation by joining his peers at the Manzanar Relocation Center, where he worked for the camp police. In 1942, Slocum and several other outspoken JACL supporters were targeted by more radical internees in a protest uprising that became known as the "Manzanar Incident" and was removed from the camp for his personal safety.

Gabriella Oldham

Further Reading

Daniels, Roger. *Concentration Camps, North America: Japanese in the United States and Canada During World War II.* Malabar, FL: Robert E. Krieger, 1981.

Hosokawa, Bill. *JACL in Quest of Justice.* New York: William Morrow, 1982.

Takao Ozawa v. United States (1922)

In October 1914, Takao Ozawa, a well-assimilated Japanese immigrant who had lived in the United States or U.S. territory for twenty years, applied for citizenship in U.S. District Court in Hawaii. When the court rejected his application on the grounds that he was of the Japanese race, Ozawa initiated a federal lawsuit that eventually reached the Supreme Court. The high court's ruling in November 1922 clearly stated that first-generation Japanese Americans were not eligible for citizenship.

Takao Ozawa's challenge represented an important test case for the Naturalization Act of 1870, which limited naturalization to "white persons and persons of African descent." Ozawa did not directly challenge the constitutionality of a racially discriminatory law; rather, he sought to have Japanese classified as "white." In fact, Ozawa had been chosen deliberately by the Pacific Coast Japanese Association Deliberative Council, a federation of Japanese Association civic organizations, to test the naturalization law's ambiguous use of the term "white."

Born in Japan in 1875, Takao had emigrated to the United States in 1894, graduated from Berkeley (California) High School, and attended the University of California, Berkeley, prior to settling in Hawaii. Ozawa presented his case directly to the court there, describing himself as an assimilated American and emphasizing his Americanized lifestyle. In his brief, Ozawa stressed that he had no connections to Japan or Japanese organizations and that his children attended an American church. In addition, he stressed that his entire family had been educated in American schools and that English was the primary language in his home. Ozawa hoped that his twenty years in the United States, in combination with his desire to contribute to his new country, would convince the courts to grant him citizenship.

Ozawa suffered a string of judicial defeats as the case moved toward the Supreme Court. The District Court of Hawaii denied his petition on the grounds that, having been born in Japan and "being of the Japanese race," he was not a "white person" under the statute. The ruling was appealed to the Ninth Circuit Court and then the Supreme Court—which agreed that the term "white person" could not be applied literally. Such a test, the justices reasoned, was impractical because color could vary significantly among persons of the same race. Pigmentation, according to the unanimous opinion of Justice George Sutherland, did not necessarily correlate with any specific racial identity. Instead, the justices relied on contemporary scientific definitions of "Caucasian" and "Mongolian" based on physical typologies—and barred Ozawa from citizenship on those grounds. In arguing that the term "white" in the 1870 statute was synonymous with "Caucasian," the court's decision clearly established that first-generation Issei could not become citizens. If not by intention, the ruling implicitly condoned the continuation of anti-Japanese animosity. The Court, it should be noted, altered its position three months later in the case of *United States v. Bhagat Singh Thind* (1923), pertaining to an Asian Indian technically classified as "Caucasian" by anthropologists at the time. While admitting the existence of a scientific link between Europeans and South Asians, the justices insisted that the two groups were distinctly separate in the popular imagination. The Court's decision in *Thind* determined that, in cases involving citizenship, the term "white" was now to be defined as commonly understood by unscientific men.

In conjunction with the Supreme Court's 1923 rejection of challenges to California's Alien Land Law of 1920 and the banning of all Japanese immigration by the Immigration Act of 1924, the *Ozawa* decision clearly established the second-class status of Issei in the United States. The Issei, in fact, would be banned from

U.S. citizenship until the Immigration and Nationality Act of 1952.

Allan W. Austin

Further Reading

Haney-López, Ian F. *White by Law: The Legal Construction of Race.* New York: New York University Press, 1996.

Ichioka, Yuji. *The Issei: The World of the First Generation Japanese Immigrants, 1885–1924.* New York: Free Press, 1988.

Tokyo Rose (Ikuko "Iva" Toguri) (1916–2006)

Caught in Japan at the time of that country's attack on Pearl Harbor in December 1941, Ikuko "Iva" Toguri—an American-born woman of Japanese immigrant parents—was recruited by the Japanese government to make propaganda broadcasts aimed at American troops, earning her the nickname, bestowed on her by those same troops, "Tokyo Rose." The nickname was later applied to other English-speaking Japanese female radio propagandists.

Ikuko "Iva" Toguri was born in Los Angeles on July 4, 1916. She worked in her father's store and graduated from Compton Community College and the University of California, Los Angeles. Visiting a sick aunt in Japan in July 1941, she was detained in the country for failing to carry a valid passport. Five months later, while her passport application was pending, Pearl Harbor was attacked and travel between the United States and Japan was severely restricted. After several efforts to get out of the country legally, Toguri opted to remain in Japan until the war was over. While retaining her U.S. citizenship, she went to work as a secretary at the Domei News Agency and later Radio Tokyo, where, with her fluent English skills, she was pressed into service as an on-air personality.

The show in which she participated, known as *Zero Hour,* was broadcast daily from 1943 through 1945 for the purpose of demoralizing U.S. troops on the Pacific Front. The soldiers were taunted with reminders about loved ones at home and misled by reports of false military defeats. The broadcast included news and a female personality known as "Orphan Annie"—referred to by U.S. troops as "Tokyo Rose"—who introduced popular American music. Toguri was one of many women who played the role of Annie. The success of the broadcasts was limited, say historians of the war, as most soldiers tended to listen to the music and laugh off what they recognized as overt attempts at propaganda.

While in Japan, Toguri married Felipe D'Aquino,

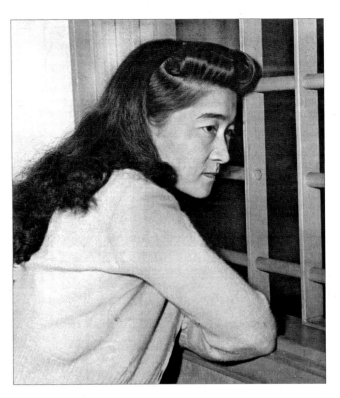

Iva Toguri-D'Aquino—aka Tokyo Rose—looks out of her jail cell in 1945. A Nisei born in Los Angeles, she was arrested, tried, and convicted of treason for making radio broadcasts intended to demoralize U.S. forces in the Pacific during World War II. She was pardoned in 1977. *(Hulton Archive/Stringer/ Getty Images)*

a Portuguese national. When the war was over and with a baby on the way, she claimed to be the voice of Tokyo Rose in order to collect money from an investigative news reporter from the United States. In late 1945, she was imprisoned as a security risk by occupation forces in Japan and then released. But in the wake of a jingoistic media frenzy spearheaded by radio commentator Walter Winchell, she was brought to San Francisco by U.S. authorities and rearrested by the Federal Bureau of Investigation in 1948. Charged with eight counts of treason, she was tried the following year and found guilty on one count—falsely stating that American ships had been destroyed in the Pacific—and sentenced to ten years in prison and a fine of $100,000. Brokenhearted at the loss of her child shortly after its birth in San Francisco, Toguri-D'Aquino did not participate fully in her defense.

After serving six years in a federal prison in Illinois, Toguri-D'Aquino, her lawyer Wayne Collins (who called the verdict a case of "guilt without evidence"), and a group of supporters filed petitions for a presidential pardon in 1954. The request was turned down, but Toguri-D'Aquino persisted, filing new petitions in 1968 and 1976. During the latter petitioning process, it was discovered by her legal team that witnesses had been coerced into false testimony by the FBI and that the judge's instructions to the jury and his rulings on points of law deprived her of a fair trial. She was granted a pardon by President Gerald Ford on January 19, 1977, and died in Chicago on September 26, 2006.

Pamela Lee Gray

Further Reading

Duus, Masayo. *Tokyo Rose: Orphan of the Pacific.* New York: Harper and Row, 1979.

Howe, Russell Warren. *The Hunt for "Tokyo Rose."* Lanham, MD: Madison Books, 1990.

Tolan Committee

The Tolan Committee—officially the House Select Committee Investigating National Defense Migration—was established by Congress in 1940 to investigate the hiring and treatment of migrant labor in American agribusiness, including the roughly 50 percent of migrant workers who were of Japanese ancestry. Following the Japanese attack on Pearl Harbor in December 1941, however, the committee's purposes changed dramatically. Its new mission was to investigate the feasibility and means of relocating tens of thousands of Japanese and Japanese Americans from their residences on the West Coast to internment centers. The findings of the committee did much to justify the enforcement of President Franklin Roosevelt's Executive Order 9066 of February 1942, establishing just such an incarceration policy.

The Tolan Committee—chaired by Representative John H. Tolan, a Democrat from the seventh district of California—was appointed by Speaker of the House Sam Rayburn on April 22, 1940. By the end of 1941, the committee had four additional members from the House of Representatives: Ohio Republican George Bender, Nebraska Republican Carl Curtis, Alabama Democrat John Sparkman, and Illinois Democrat Laurence Arnold. The committee was established in the wake of public outrage over the abuses of migrant farm laborers exposed in the 1940 film *The Grapes of Wrath,* based on John Steinbeck's novel of the previous year. Thus, the original purpose of the committee was to investigate the hiring practices of agribusiness and the treatment of migrant workers (about half of whom were of Japanese ancestry) in the West. By early 1942, however, the committee was conducting hearings in Seattle, San Francisco, Los Angeles, and Portland to address the implications of Executive Order 9066, including what it would mean for American agriculture.

Most of the witnesses at the hearings were fearful of, or antagonistic toward, Japanese Americans. California attorney general Earl Warren, for instance, used maps to show how lands leased by Japanese farmers lay close to defense plants, implying that such proximity left the plants open to sabotage. Secretary of the Navy Frank Knox and groups such as the California Joint Immigration Committee laid out similar scenarios of sabotage.

The Japanese American Citizens League (JACL) did all it could to stop the mass removal of "loyal" Japanese. "As your committee continues its investigations in this and subsequent hearings," National Secretary Mike Masaoka of the JACL testified on February 23, "we hope and trust that you will recommend to the proper authorities that no undue discrimination be shown to American citizens of Japanese descent." Nonetheless, Masaoka and the JACL conceded that if evacuation were deemed "a military necessity," they would comply with Executive Order 9066 and urge members of the Japanese American community to do so as well.

In the end, the Tolan Committee, heeding the warnings of Warren, Knox, and other anti–Japanese American groups, endorsed Executive Order 9066. It did not support blanket incarceration, however, opting to hold hearings at "assembly centers" and allowing Japanese Americans deemed "loyal" to settle in ordinary communities away from the West Coast. At the same time, the Tolan Committee refused to investigate parallel treatment of German and Italian Americans, arguing that this was "out of the question if we intend to win the war." Some historians and contemporaries have contended that the real reason for the difference in treatment was anti-Asian bias.

Bruce E. Stewart

Further Reading

Daniels, Roger. *Asian America: Chinese and Japanese in the United States Since 1850.* Seattle: University of Washington Press, 1988.

Weglyn, Michi. *Years of Infamy: The Untold Story of America's Concentration Camps.* New York: William Morrow, 1976.

Uchida, Yoshiko (1921–1992)

Yoshiko Uchida, a prolific writer for children and young adults, is best known for recounting the evacuation of Japanese Americans and their lives in the internment camps during World War II. Drawing heavily on her personal life and family experiences, she explores such issues as cultural identity, gender boundary, and intergenerational friendship through the eyes of Japanese and Japanese American children. Her thirty-six books include collections of folktales, picture books, young adult books, adult books, and autobiographies.

Born on November 24, 1921, in Alameda, California, to first-generation Japanese immigrants, Uchida grew up in a loving and stable family. Though secure in the Japanese community, she encountered widespread prejudice and discrimination in American society at large and was totally excluded from the social lives of her white peers in school. She was in her senior year at the University of California, Berkeley, when the Japanese attacked Pearl Harbor and President Franklin Roosevelt issued Executive Order 9066 in February 1942, which allowed for the internment of all West Coast Japanese Americans. Uchida and her family were sent to the Tanforan Assembly Center in the San Francisco Bay Area community of San Bruno, where they lived in a horse stall, and later transferred to the internment camp in Topaz, Utah. The miseries of camp life ended for her in 1943, when she was allowed to leave for graduate study at Smith College in Massachusetts.

Uchida began her career writing Japanese folktales. Her first book, *The Dancing Kettle and Other Japanese Folk Tales,* was published in 1949. Three years later, she won a fellowship to study folktales in Japan, which expanded and lent a touch of authenticity to her storytelling. From her experiences in Japan came more books, among them *The Magic Listening Cap: More Folk Tales from Japan* (1955) and *The Sea of Gold and Other Tales from Japan* (1965), which extol Japanese virtues of patience and endurance, respect for the elderly, and the perils of greed.

Most of Uchida's writings are intended for readers aged eight to twelve. *The Forever Christmas Tree* (1963) tells a heartwarming story of two children decorating a Christmas tree to cheer up an old man. In *Sumi's Prize* (1964), *Sumi's Special Happening* (1966), and *Sumi and the Goat and the Tokyo Express* (1969), the main character crosses the gender boundary to enter a kite contest and also ventures beyond her immediate family to the outside world. *Journey to Topaz* (1971) and *Journey Home* (1978) relate the hardship and suffering endured by the fictional Sakane family during the evacuation of 1942, at the internment camp, and in the struggle after being released. In spite of these tragedies, resilience, fortitude, and unity help this family sustain and survive the ordeal. In the trilogy of *A Jar of Dreams* (1981), *The Best Bad Thing* (1983), and *The Happiest Ending* (1985), eleven-year-old Rinko is portrayed as a confident young woman with a sense of her own identity despite being entangled in two different cultures. Uchida's autobiographies, *The Invisible Thread* (1991) and *Desert Exile* (1982), recorded her childhood and the tragic history of Japanese Americans. In *Picture Bride* (1987), based on the experiences of her parents, she portrays the arranged marriages of Japanese Americans in the early years of their immigration to the United States.

Uchida and her books were honored with prestigious awards and citations from a number of professional, literary, and Japanese American civic organizations. She shared her painful experiences in the hope that institutionalized injustice and discrimination would never again happen to any minority group. Yoshiko Uchida died in Berkeley, California, on June 21, 1992.

Shu-Hsien L. Chen

Further Reading

Uchida, Yoshiko. *Desert Exile: The Uprooting of a Japanese American Family.* Seattle: University of Washington Press, 1982.
———. *The Invisible Thread: An Autobiography.* New York: Beech Tree Paperback, 1995.

Uno, Edison Tomimaro (1929–1976)

A teacher, writer, and longtime social and human rights activist, Edison Tomimaro Uno dedicated his efforts to issues of his own Japanese American community, particularly concerning the incarceration of Japanese Americans during World War II and Japanese American educational achievement and political involvement in the postwar era.

A Nisei (second-generation Japanese American, born in the United States), Uno was born in Los Angeles on October 19, 1929, and relocated with his family at age thirteen to the Granada Internment Camp in Utah. His father, George Kimemaro Uno, was sent to a different camp, in Crystal City, Texas, and prevented from communicating with the rest of the family because one of Edison's brothers worked for the Japanese Army Press Bureau in Japan. After four of Edison's other brothers volunteered for service in the U.S. Army in 1943, Edison and his mother moved to Texas to be with George.

When the war was over, Uno returned with his family to Los Angeles, where he graduated from Los Angeles State College (now California State University at Los Angeles) with a degree in political science. After working as an advertising and publicity agent for Japanese American newspapers, he changed career paths in 1964 and became an administrator at San Francisco State University. Rising from operations manager to financial aid officer to assistant dean of students from 1969 to 1974, he was finally dismissed for his strong advocacy for student rights. Meanwhile, he had also begun lecturing on Japanese American history and Asian Studies at Stanford University, California State University, San Francisco, and other area institutions.

Uno is perhaps best known for his community activism, including twenty-two years of service in the Japanese American Citizens League (JACL), the oldest and largest Japanese American advocacy organization in the country. He focused on legal, political, and educational issues, serving as chairman of the Nisei Voters League of San Francisco, vice chairman of the Japanese American Curriculum Project, and cochairman of the JACL's Committee to Repeal Detention Camp Legislation, a federal cold war measure that called for the detention of subversives during national security emergencies. He was an active force in the redress movement of the 1970s, which later succeeded in gaining compensation for more than 70,000 former Japanese internees and an apology from the U.S. government. Uno also helped raise funds and promote awareness for the legal cases involving Wendy Yoshimura, a radical Japanese American artist accused of involvement in bomb plots in the early 1970s, and Ikuko "Iva" Toguri, better known as "Tokyo Rose," a Japanese American woman convicted of aiding the enemy as a radio propagandist during World War II. In the early 1970s as well, Uno helped organize the JACL's controversial exhibition on Japanese American history, which featured a scathing portrait of U.S. government action against Japanese Americans during World War II.

Among his various honors and awards were the San Francisco Bar Association's Liberty Bell Award and the University of California, San Francisco Chancellor's Public Service Award. The JACL Edison Uno Civil Rights Award and Edison Uno Institute at San Francisco State University were also named in his honor. Uno died in 1976, not living to see the culmination of the redress movement with passage of the Civil Liberties Act of 1988.

Amelia Maijala

Further Reading
Edison Uno Papers Web site. Online Archive of California. http://www.oac.cdlib.org/findaid/ark:/13030/ft9t1nb4jd.

War Relocation Authority

Created by Executive Order 9102 in March 1942, the War Relocation Authority (WRA) was a civilian federal agency that oversaw ten permanent "relocation centers" for Japanese Americans evacuated from the West Coast during World War II, and directed the physical removal of more than 112,000 evacuees. Milton S. Eisenhower, a Department of Agriculture (USDA) bureaucrat and the older brother of General Dwight Eisenhower, was the first administrator of the WRA. He was succeeded by another former USDA official, Dillon S. Myer, in early 1942. Myer directed the WRA and oversaw the Japanese Americans it imprisoned without due process for the remainder of World War II.

The creation of the WRA resulted from both fears of Japanese sabotage in the early months of World War II and a long-standing mistrust of Japanese Americans among many other Americans in the West. Nearly 127,000 ethnic Japanese lived in the United States by 1940, overwhelmingly concentrated on the West Coast and predominately in California. While these immigrants and citizens of Japanese descent made up only a tiny fraction of California's population—never more than 2.1 percent—they often engendered hatred among race-conscious Americans, who irrationally saw them, like Chinese immigrants, as the vanguard of an invasion of cheap labor and alien ideals from the Far East.

The onset of war with imperial Japan in December 1941 raised concerns about possible Japanese spies and saboteurs and, despite a dearth of such activity, provided the opportunity for some western politicians, journalists, and others to call for measures to restrict the rights of Japanese Americans. By February 1942, their clamoring reached receptive ears in the federal government; President Franklin Roosevelt signed Executive Order 9066, providing for the forced removal of enemy aliens but was never applied to German and Italian Americans. The WRA was created weeks later to provide for civilian oversight.

Although many WRA officials, including Milton Eisenhower, remained uneasy about the forced relocation and hoped to provide reasonable accommodations for internees, camp life remained unduly harsh. Japanese Americans were herded into crude wooden barracks ringed with barbed wire and devoid of privacy save for the tarpaper walls that segregated families into single-room apartments. Life in the camps was made even more miserable by the cots and blankets that passed as furnishings and the communal bathrooms, dining areas, and laundry facilities.

The WRA did allow some detainees to leave the camps beginning in 1943, mostly American-born Nisei considered adequately loyal to the United States, provided they could find a job elsewhere in the nation or a college to accept them. Whatever benevolence the WRA exhibited quickly faded in 1944, when a significant number of Nisei men refused to renounce imperial Japan and were shipped to an even poorer facility at Tule Lake, California. In early 1945, the WRA began closing the internment camps and aided some Japanese Americans in returning home, but provided little else. Many of the detainees, who had lost their residences and businesses in the forced evacuation, were left in poor economic straits. The WRA released the last inmate from Tule Lake in March 1946, more than seven months after the Japanese surrender that ended the war. The WRA was abolished by Executive Order 9742 that June.

Kevin Bower

Further Reading

Daniels, Roger. *Prisoners Without Trial: Japanese Americans in World War II.* New York: Hill and Wang, 1993.
Irons, Peter. *Justice at War.* New York: Oxford University Press, 1983.

Weglyn, Michi Nishiura (1926–1999)

A historian, activist, and fashion designer, Michi Nishiura Weglyn is best known for her book *Years of Infamy: The Untold Story of America's Concentration Camps* (1976), a thorough, rigorously documented history of Japanese American internment during World War II. The book proved influential as well as highly acclaimed, providing activists with a valuable tool in the fight for redress. Beyond demonstrating with government documents that the incarceration of more than 112,000 persons of Japanese ancestry was unnecessary and unjustified, *Years of Infamy* validated the anger and sadness many in the Japanese American community had kept inside and helped inspire the redress movement itself. So influential was the book that Weglyn came to be referred to as the "mother of redress" or "the Rosa Parks of the Japanese American redress movement." She was highly active in the movement itself, supporting the Heart Mountain draft resisters in their fight for justice and backing plaintiff William Hohri in his class-action lawsuit for redress in the 1980s.

Michi Nishiura was born to Issei (first-generation immigrant) farmers Tomojiro Nishiura and Hisao Yuwasa Nishiura in Stockton, California, on November 29, 1926. In early 1942, she and her family were forced from their California home and sent to the Gila River Relocation Center in Arizona. Her already fragile health deteriorated in the dusty camp environment, where she was infected with tuberculosis. On the strength of her academic promise, however, Weglyn was released from

the camp in 1944 to attend Mount Holyoke College in Massachusetts. Later in the 1940s, she moved to New York City, where she worked as a costume designer on TV's *Perry Como Show* for eight years, and painted and wrote poetry in her spare time. It was also in New York that she met Walter Weglyn, a Jewish Holocaust survivor, whom she married in 1950. Her husband is credited with encouraging her to write about the camp experience.

Michi Weglyn spent eight years researching government documents at the National Archives in Washington, D.C., and the Franklin Delano Roosevelt Library in Hyde Park, New York, before writing *Years of Infamy*. In it, she was able to portray camp life in grim detail and interpret the documents and data without hiding the anger caused by her own imprisonment. She also included government sources and the opinions of prominent citizens with dissenting views on the military necessity of internment. Among these were excerpts from a report for the U.S. State Department *before* Pearl Harbor by an analyst named Curtis Munson, who maintained that the majority of Japanese Americans were loyal to the United States and eager to assimilate. The book also contained an appendix with other government documents that seemed to argue that the internment was unnecessary on national security grounds. Finally the work revealed incidents and aspects of the relocation previously unknown to the public, such as the internment of Japanese in Latin America for prospective hostage exchange with the Japanese regime. Decades after its publication, *Years of Infamy* remains one of the premier sources of modern Japanese American history.

In addition to her activities in the Japanese American redress movement, Weglyn also lent her research and lobbying skills to redress efforts by Japanese Latin American internees and Japanese American railroad and mine workers fired on government orders during World War II. In 1996, she initiated a massive letter-writing campaign to the Office of Redress on behalf of the railroad and mine workers, and her research uncovered government documents supporting the workers' claims. Because the railroad workers were fired from their jobs or forced to relocate during the war, they were declared eligible in 1998 to apply for the same monetary redress as those interned under the Civil Liberties Act of 1988.

Weglyn was awarded honorary doctorates from Hunter College (1990) and Mount Holyoke College (1994) for her service to the Asian American community. She continued to research and write up to her death, working on two books and arranging for a colleague to complete the manuscripts. She died on April 25, 1999.

Emily Hiramatsu Morishima

Further Reading

Nash, Phil Tajitsu. "In Memorium." *Amerasia* 25:1 (1999): iv–viii.

Niiya, Brian, ed. *Encyclopedia of Japanese American History Updated Edition: An A-to-Z Reference from 1868 to the Present.* New York: Facts on File, 2001.

Taguma, Kenji G. "National Redress Activist, Author Michi Weglyn Dies." *Nichi Bei Times,* April 27, 1999.

Yamaguchi, Kristi (1971–)

Kristi Yamaguchi was the first Japanese American to win an Olympic gold medal in figure skating, at the 1992 Winter Games in Albertville, France, making her one of the most recognizable athletes in the world. She also won world championships in women's singles competition in 1991 and 1992, and a U.S. championship in 1992. Yamaguchi was a source of particular pride to her community as an example of achievement, assimilation, hard work, and determination, having overcome a childhood deformity to reach the pinnacle of success in her chosen field.

Born in Hayward, California, on July 12, 1971, Yamaguchi is a Sansei, or third-generation Japanese American. Her paternal grandparents and maternal great-grandparents arrived from Japan in the early twentieth century, and both of her parents were born on U.S. soil—her mother in an internment camp during World War II. Her father served in the U.S. Army as a lieutenant and later became a dentist. Growing up in Fremont and San Jose, California, Kristi suffered from clubbed feet as a young girl and began an exercise program to get her out of her casts, strengthen her legs, and walk without assistance. Dreaming of becoming a figure skater like her childhood idol, 1976 Olympic gold medalist Dorothy Hamill, Yamaguchi took up skating at age ten.

She began her competitive skating career as a young teenager in both pairs and singles events. With partner Rudy Galindo, she won the junior pairs title at the U.S. championships in 1986 and 1988, followed by the senior pairs championship in 1989 and 1990. In the meantime, she had won the junior single's title in 1988. In international competition, Yamaguchi and Galindo placed fifth in the world pair's championships, and Yamaguchi placed fourth as a solo performer in the same competition.

It was not until she began focusing on her solo career that Yamaguchi began to achieve the success for which she is known. Having moved to Canada to train with coach Christy Ness, she won her first major titles in 1991 and 1992—culminating in her sweep of the U.S., world, and Olympic single's titles in the latter year. Turning professional after the 1992 international season, she became a fixture in the Stars on Ice touring show and the competitive pro circuit, winning the World Pro Figure Skating Championship in 1992, 1994, 1996, and 1997.

Yamaguchi was one of the first five inductees into the Japanese Cultural and Community Center of Northern California (JCCCNC)'s Japanese Sports Hall of Fame in November 2002, in acknowledgment of her pioneering work in establishing a place for Japanese American athletes in U.S. sports industries. She has also been inducted into the United States Figure Skating Hall of Fame and the World Skating Hall of Fame.

In 1996, Yamaguchi established the Always Dream Foundation, dedicated to supporting and encouraging the dreams of children. Aside from raising her own children, the foundation has been her major project, raising funds for a range of programs and organizations that seek to make a difference in children's lives in the western United States. Yamaguchi is married to ice hockey player Bret Hedican.

Lindsay Sarah Krasnoff

Further Reading

Hasday, Judy L. *Kristi Yamaguchi.* New York: Chelsea House, 2007.

Savage, Jeff. *Kristi Yamaguchi: Pure Gold.* New York: Maxwell Macmillan, 1993.

Yasui v. United States (1943)

In the 1943 case of *Yasui v. United States,* the U.S. Supreme Court declared constitutional much of President Franklin Roosevelt's Executive Order 9066 (1942), which allowed for the relocation and internment of persons of Japanese descent, whether citizens or resident aliens, for the duration of World War II. One of a trio of related cases that went before the high court (collectively referred to as the *coram nobis* cases), *Yasui* pertained specifically to the constitutionality of the curfew imposed by the government on the Japanese American community.

The plaintiff in the case, Minoru Yasui, was born in Oregon to Issei (Japanese-born, first-generation immigrant) parents. A practicing attorney in Portland, Yasui deliberately broke the curfew on March 28, 1942, by walking downtown after hours and presenting himself to the police station. At the time of his arrest, he had just resigned as a legal counsel for the Japanese consulate in Chicago and resolved to test the constitutionality of the curfew. In addition to being a member of the Oregon bar, Yasui was also an army second lieutenant in the infantry reserve. He had tried to enlist in the regular army in the wake of Pearl Harbor but was refused on the grounds of his ethnicity. His father, once a decorated soldier in the Japanese imperial armed forces, was placed under arrest by the Federal Bureau of Investigation as an enemy of the United States.

Under Executive Order 9066 on February 19, 1942, the U.S. Army established restrictive areas where enemy aliens (non-native-born U.S. residents) were required to observe a curfew from 9 P.M. to 6 A.M. that limited their movement from home to work and back—no more than 5 miles (8 kilometers) each way. Under Public Proclamation Number 3 issued on March 24, 1942, the restrictions were expanded to include Japanese American citizens, citing increased risk of espionage and acts of sabotage. Four days later, Yasui entered a Portland city police station after violating curfew, stating that he was a U.S. citizen. He was immediately arrested. (In what would become a related case, a student in Seattle named Gordon Hirabayashi was arrested for violating the curfew and refusing to register for the relocation.)

Waiving his right to a trial by jury, Yasui was found guilty by a federal judge and sentenced to one year in the Multnomah County Jail in Portland and a fine of $5,000—the strictest penalty allowed under the law. He served nine months of his sentence and then worked at the Minidoka War Relocation Camp in 1944. While serving his sentence, Yasui filed an appeal with the Ninth Circuit Court, which certified two questions to the U.S. Supreme Court. The latter decided to rule on the entire case itself.

The Supreme Court heard the case in May 1943 and issued its ruling, written by Chief Justice Harlan Fiske Stone, on June 21, 1943. In finding against Yasui and upholding his arrest, the court cited the constitutional authority of the U.S. Congress and the president under the War Powers Act. Thus, the court held, the curfew and exclusion orders were constitutional and valid even for U.S. citizens.

A writ of error *coram nobis* (based on alleged errors of fact in the original trial) was filed on behalf of Minoru Yasui in February 1983, citing evidence to the effect that the U.S. Justice Department had purposely destroyed and withheld evidence that undermined the defense in the original trial. Government attorneys asked the court to dismiss the original conviction as well as the petition of error, and the judge so ruled. Yasui appealed the decision to dismiss the petition, seeking a finding of government misconduct, but he died before that issue could be adjudicated. His death rendered the case moot.

Pamela Lee Gray

Further Reading

Hosokawa, Bill. *JACL: In Quest of Justice.* New York: William Morrow, 1982.

Irons, Peter. *Justice at War.* New York: Oxford University Press, 1983.

———. *Justice Delayed: The Record of the Japanese American Internment Cases.* Middletown, CT: Wesleyan University Press, 1989.

Yasui v. United States 320 U.S. 115 (1943).

The Korean American Experience:

History and Culture

The fifth-largest Asian American group after (in descending order) Chinese, Filipino, Asian Indian, and Vietnamese—Korean Americans are both one of the oldest of Asian communities in the United States and one of the newest. Small numbers were recruited by Hawaiian sugar growers at the beginning of the twentieth century. More came as brides of American soldiers stationed in Korea after the Korean War of the early 1950s. But it was only with passage of the Immigration and Nationality Act of 1965, ending national quotas on immigration into the United States, that large numbers of Koreans began moving to the mainland United States. In the years since, hundreds of thousands of Koreans have moved to locations—especially metropolises—across the country. The largest cohort settled in Los Angeles, where, in the Mid-Wilshire district, they established the most populous enclave of Koreans in the world outside the Korean Peninsula itself.

Korean Americans generally lag somewhat behind other major Asian American groups in terms of educational achievement and household income. (Major Asian American groups include Chinese, Filipino, Asian Indian, Vietnamese, and Japanese.) At the same time, they are the most entrepreneurial, with Korean Americans having a business ownership rate far in excess of Americans in general. As relative newcomers, however, many Korean entrepreneurs have established businesses in more economically marginal neighborhoods, which has sometimes sparked clashes with African Americans and Latinos.

As with many other Asian American groups, family—both nuclear and extended—is of great importance to Korean Americans, who often place duty and obligation to relatives above their own individual needs and wants. Korean culture has traditionally been heavily influenced by that of China, with Confucian ideals of learning, harmony, filial duty, and social hierarchy holding sway over many Koreans, both in the home country and in the United States. However, while the majority of Koreans are Buddhist, the vast majority of Korean Americans are Protestant Christians.

Immigration History

While a few Koreans had made their way to Hawaii and mainland America in the late nineteenth century, the first large wave of immigrants did not come until the first decade of the twentieth. Brought by the labor recruiters of major Hawaiian sugar planters—who had lost access to Chinese workers through passage of the Chinese Exclusion Act (1882), which went into effect in Hawaii when the islands were annexed by the United States in the 1890s—some 7,000 Koreans had settled in Hawaii by 1907, lured by the promise of higher wages and fleeing oppression from the Japanese occupiers of their homeland. In 1907, however, Japan, fearing a mass exodus of workers, cut off emigration from Korea. Meanwhile, several thousand Koreans in Hawaii, facing the high cost of living in the islands, either moved back to Korea or relocated to the West Coast of the United States. Most of the workers both in Hawaii and on the mainland were single men, though roughly 1,000 Korean women came to the United States between 1910 and 1924 as "picture brides"—chosen as mates by male workers through photos provided by marriage brokers back in Korea. Early Korean immigrants experienced much of the same prejudice and discrimination facing other Asian Americans, as most white Americans tended to confuse members of the small Korean American community with Chinese or Japanese Americans.

A new restrictive U.S. immigration law in 1924, along with continued Japanese suppression, largely ended Korean immigration to the United States, though several hundred political refugees, fleeing persecution by Japanese occupiers, were admitted. World War II, the Communist takeover of the northern half of the Korean Peninsula, the Korean War, and continued restriction on immigration by the U.S. government kept Korean newcomers to a trickle until the mid-1960s, though several thousand war orphans were adopted by American families and a few thousand brides of American GIs came during these years. By 1960, an estimated 10,000 Koreans were living in the United States.

The 1965 immigration reform law put a premium on family reunification and professional skills. Beginning in the late 1960s, tens of thousands of Koreans took advantage of these aspects of the law to enter the United States. While South Korea began to experience one of the fastest rates of economic growth in world history beginning in the 1970s, it was not enough to provide opportunities for a population that was becoming rapidly educated and urbanized. Hundreds of thousands went abroad, largely to the United States, the country that had done more to protect South Korea from a Communist takeover in the early 1950s than any other and that continued to maintain a major military presence on the peninsula. By the mid-1980s, the Korean American population had soared to roughly half a million, climbing to more than 800,000 by the 1990 census. Over the subsequent years, continued immigration—along with growth in the U.S.-born Korean population—produced a near doubling of the Korean American community, to more than 1.5 million, by 2007. Virtually all of the Koreans entering the United States came from capitalist and increasingly democratic South Korea, as the Communist government of North Korea maintained tightly sealed borders.

Although the vast majority of Koreans were farmers as late as the 1950s, the country has undergone rapid urbanization since. By the early 2000s, less than 25 percent of the population lives in rural areas and small towns. Therefore, Korean immigrants to the United States in recent decades have settled primarily in urban and suburban areas. Today there are major Korean enclaves in New York City, Washington, D.C., Chicago, and Honolulu, but the largest by far is in Southern California. The Koreatown neighborhood of Los Angeles, as it has been officially designated since the 1970s, was home to roughly 200,000 Korean Americans by the early 2000s, or roughly one in seven of all Koreans in the United States. With most, Korean immigrants having come to the United States since the 1970s, the percentage of foreign-born Korean Americans, according to the 2000 census, is the highest among all major Asian American populations.

Education and Economics

In general, Korean Americans fall somewhere in the middle of all Asian Americans on socioeconomic indices. First, they are neither the best- nor the worst-educated of Asian American groups, though their level of educational achievement does exceed that of the U.S. population as a whole. While 19.6 percent of all Asians twenty-five and older have not graduated from high school, the figure for Korean Americans is just 13.7. (All statistics in this section come from the 2000 U.S. Census.) At the same time, only 64.7 percent of Korean Americans have some college education or have earned their bachelor's degree, a figure roughly equal to that for all Asian Americans but substantially higher than the 51.8 figure for the U.S. population as a whole.

The median Korean American household income stood at $47,624 in 2000, lagging somewhat behind that of the U.S. population as a whole ($50,046) and substantially behind that of all Asian American households ($59,324). Indeed, other than the figure for Vietnamese Americans (at $47,103), the median household income for Korean Americans was the lowest of any major Asian American group. Their poverty level (14.8) was also the highest of all major Asian American groups, other than the Vietnamese (16.0), and somewhat higher than that for the U.S. population as a whole (12.4). Korean Americans also have one of the lowest home-ownership rates of any Asian American community, even lower than those of the relatively impoverished Southeast American groups. Only Hmong Americans were less likely to own their own home. While just 40.1 percent of Koreans lived in owner-occupied housing units, the equivalent figure for Asian Americans generally was 53.8 and, for Americans overall, 66.2. The relatively low home-ownership rate may have something to do with the high real-estate prices of the urban areas in which they have tended to settle and the fact that Koreans are relative newcomers compared to all other major Asian American groups, barring the Vietnamese.

Where Korean Americans shine is in entrepreneurship. With roughly one enterprise for every eight adults, Korean Americans had the highest rate of business ownership of any ethnic group in America, Asian or otherwise. This may also help explain the low home-ownership rate, as many Koreans put their capital into their businesses rather than their residences.

Family and Faith

Few countries in modern world history can claim to have undergone as rapid a modernization process as South Korea. Within two generations, a largely rural, impoverished, and war-torn nation has turned itself into an urban and democratic economic powerhouse. Many long-standing Korean customs have wilted in the heat of this transformation. Traditionally, Koreans followed Confucian ideals about the family. The male played the dominant role in the household and, along with the mother, a dominant role in the lives of the children, often choosing their marriage partners and even careers. And while most Korean American parents no longer make such decisions for their offspring, they nevertheless play a larger role in the choices of their children than do non-Asian American parents—insisting, for example, that they get a good education.

Korean families also tend to take care of their own. Among the siblings, the eldest son was traditionally the favored child, receiving much of the family's inheritance. However, he was also obligated to take care of aging parents and come to the aid of younger siblings should they need it. Koreans Americans tend to shun public assistance in times of financial trouble, seeing it as shameful. Instead, they rely on family—both immediate and extended—to help them through hard times.

In other ways, however, modernization and migration have had a major impact on the family. Some sociologists have pointed out that, because of these trends, marriage has become all the more important to Korean Americans. That is, the bonds between husband and wife become stronger as the ties between generations raised in such differing cultures and economic situations weaken. Yet even the institution of marriage has felt the impact of modernization. Korean tradition frowns on divorce and historically—even among the picture brides of early-twentieth-century Korean Hawaii (who had not even met their husbands before the wedding)—few marriages broke up. However, Korean American divorce rates by the early 2000s were approaching those of the American public in general, though the total number of Koreans who were divorced remained less than half that of the U.S. population as a whole (4.6 versus 9.7 percent), according to the 2000 census. Sociologists cite career stress as the major cause of the rapidly rising divorce rate among Korean Americans, who, either as entrepreneurs or as employees of retail and manufacturing establishments, tend to work very long hours.

While many of these trends mark other Asian American groups, there is one social arena in which Koreans remain markedly different—faith. With the exception of Filipinos, who come from a long Catholic tradition, Korean Americans, at 80 percent, are more likely to be followers of Christianity than any other Asian group. Unlike Filipinos, they tend to be Protestant and often evangelical. In Korea itself, Christianity is a fast-growing religion. The Protestant message of individual salvation, say students of Korean society, makes sense in a modernizing Korean culture that is discarding its communal, Confucian past. Moreover, many Korean churches offer social services to families that no longer can rely on their

own and a sense of community in a rapidly urbanizing society. Not surprisingly, given the shock of immigration and the anomie of life in modern urban America, evangelical churches have also found a huge following among Korean Americans. Estimates place the number of churches of all denominations serving the Korean American community at 4,000.

Politics and Civic Culture

Given the high level of entrepreneurial activity in the Korean American community, it is not surprising to find that business groups—of both the traditional and modern varieties—are central to Korean American public life. The ancient Korean system of *kye,* a mutual aid society among small businesspersons, whereby funds are paid in collectively and doled out to one individual to invest each year, continues to thrive in modern Korean America. More modern trade associations—offering expertise, access to bank credit, and other contemporary business assistance—have arisen alongside the traditional *kye* societies. One of the most powerful trade associations is the Korean Produce Association of New York, which serves the thousands of Korean-owned greengrocers in the city.

Traditionally, Koreans have had a high degree of distrust toward government, a legacy of more than fifty years of oppressive Japanese colonial rule through World War II and decades of dictatorship until the 1980s. While Koreans in Hawaii and on the U.S. mainland in the first half of the twentieth century organized to raise awareness and funds for the anti-Japanese struggle in their homeland, many more recent Korean immigrants tend to avoid involvement in U.S. politics. Nevertheless, Korean American groups in Washington, D.C., such as the U.S.-Korea Foundation (now merged into the Korea Society), lobbied the U.S. government to do what it could to aid the transition to democracy in South Korea in the 1980s. At the same time, Korean Americans tend to be more conservative on intra-Korean relations, generally favoring a tougher line with North Korea than do South Koreans.

Polls show that Koreans tend to be more conservative than other Asian American groups, with the exception of the strongly anti-Communist Vietnamese Americans; and Korean American voter registration is about evenly divided between the Democratic and Republican parties. (Most Asian Americans, like immigrant groups generally, tend to lean more to the Democratic side.) Korean conservatism is probably the result of their strong affiliation to evangelical Protestantism and their high level of entrepreneurial activity, both indicators of conservatism in politics.

Korean Americans' general aloofness from U.S. politics is changing, however, particularly as more American-born children of Korean immigrants come of voting age. In the wake of the Los Angeles riots of 1992, when Korean-owned businesses were singled out for burning and looting by African American and Latino rioters angry at perceived economic exploitation of their neighborhoods, community leaders created the National Association of Korean Americans to help bridge the social and cultural gap between an ethnic group often seen as aloof and other communities in the city.

In addition, since the late 1990s, Korean Americans have won positions on city councils in suburban areas, though they had yet to make their presence felt on the Los Angeles City Council as of the early 2000s. The highest elected Korean American was California Republican congressperson Chang-jun "Jay" Kim from suburban Los Angeles, who served from 1993 to 1999. In 1971, Judge Herbert Choy became the first Asian American to sit on the federal bench; thirty years earlier, he became the first American lawyer of Korean ancestry admitted to the bar. More recently, Korean American John Yoo served as deputy attorney general of the United States in the George W. Bush administration, and became the center of controversy for his legal justifications of government surveillance of electronic communications and coercive interrogation techniques that critics claim amounted to torture.

Korean beauty queens ride the lead parade float in the Los Angeles Korean Festival, an annual celebration of community and culture held at Seoul International Park in the heart of the city's Koreatown district. *(Hyungwon Kang/Time & Life Pictures/Getty Images)*

Arts, Media, and Culture

Korean Americans, whether Buddhist or Christian, celebrate a number of traditional holidays. Perhaps the most important is that of *sol,* or Lunar New Year, celebrated in late January or February. Members of the community observe the holiday by dressing in traditional clothes, usually featuring elaborate headdresses, visiting elder members of the extended family, and participating in a variety of feasts, games, and rituals, some of which are intended to ward off evil spirits in the coming year. The first full moon in the calendar is a time to pay homage to ancestors, usually by visiting family gravesites. Christian Koreans, of course, celebrate the major holidays of that tradition, while Buddhists, who represent about 20 percent of Korean Americans, honor the Buddha's birthday on April 8. Secular Korean holidays, such as Constitution Day, June 15, are generally observed by Korean government offices in the United States but ignored by most Korean Americans, though many elderly members of the community remember the lives lost in the Korean War on the Korean Memorial Day of June 6.

A number of Korean Americans have made significant contributions to American arts and popular culture. Korean-born artist Nam June Paik has been a pioneer in the field of video installation, with his pieces on display in major art museums around the world. Violin virtuoso Sarah Chang has been entertaining audiences since childhood. Peter Hyun, who worked in the middle and latter years of the twentieth century, was director of leading theatrical companies, including the Children's Theatre of New York and the Studio Players of Cambridge, Massachusetts. Pianist Myung-whun Chung served as assistant and then associate conductor of the Los Angeles Philharmonic in the late 1970s and early 1980s. Major Korean American cultural associations include the Korean Cultural Center, founded in Los Angeles in 1980, and the academically oriented Association for Korean Studies, also located in the Los Angeles area.

Perhaps best known to the U.S. public at large is American-born actress and comedian Margaret Cho, whose stand-up routines, often poking fun at the disconnect between her own bisexual orientation and the conservative attitudes of her parents, pack concert halls and whose comic recordings have sold in the tens of thousands.

Korean Americans have also made notable contributions to American sports. Diver Sammy Lee won gold medals at the 1948 and 1952 Olympic Games. The first Asian American to win Olympic gold for the United States, Lee was named Athlete of the Year in 1953 by the Amateur Athletic Union and went on to coach the U.S. diving team in the 1960s. More recently, in 2002, Hawaii-born Michelle Wie became the youngest golfer in history to qualify for a Ladies Professional Golf Association event. She was just thirteen.

While Korean Americans have been in the United States in significant numbers longer than any Asian group other than the Chinese and the Japanese, their community is largely the creation of post-1965 immigration policy. Exploding from just 10,000 in 1960 to more than 1.5 million less than a half-century later, they have become one of the most visible of Asian American communities, particularly because of their high levels of business ownership in non-Korean neighborhoods. As in their homeland, Korean Americans have had to make a relatively sudden jump from traditional culture to modern, urban society. In doing so, they have achieved much, establishing thriving businesses, a network of evangelical churches, and vibrant communities, often rescuing inner-city neighborhoods from decay in the process. Perhaps, say students of the Korean community, this success will finally relieve Korean Americans from what Koreans call their national lament of *han*—a feeling of being exploited, wronged, and unable to reverse injustice, the legacy of a long history of oppression at the hands of outside powers.

James Ciment

Further Reading

Chung, Angie Y. *Legacies of Struggle: Conflict and Cooperation in Korean American Politics.* Palo Alto, CA: Stanford University Press, 2007.

Jo, Moon H. *Korean Immigrants and the Challenge of Adjustment.* Westport, CT: Greenwood, 1999.

Kibria, Nazli. *Becoming Asian American: Second-Generation Chinese and Korean American Identities.* Baltimore: Johns Hopkins University Press, 2002.

Kwon, Ho-Youn, Kwang Chung Kim, and R. Stephen Warner, eds. *Korean Americans and Their Religions: Pilgrims and Missionaries from a Different Shore.* University Park: Pennsylvania State University Press, 2001.

Min, Pyong Gap. *Caught in the Middle: Korean Merchants in America's Multiethnic Cities.* Berkeley: University of California Press, 1996.

Song, Min Hyoung. *Strange Future: Pessimism and the 1992 Los Angeles Riots.* Durham, NC: Duke University Press, 2005.

Yoo, David, and Ruth H. Chung, eds. *Religion and Spirituality in Korean America.* Urbana: University of Illinois Press, 2008.

Korean Americans
Alphabetical Entries

Association of Korean Political Studies

The Association of Korean Political Studies in North America (AKPSNA), a nonprofit academic organization dedicated to the promotion and advancement of scholarly exchange in Korea-related political studies, was established in 1973 by a core group of Korean and Korean American political scientists. The first meeting was held in Chicago on March 1, 1973, in conjunction with the annual meeting of the Association for Asian Studies. The founders of the original organization included Chang-hyun Cho, Young Hoon Kang, C.I. Eugene Kim, Han-kyo Kim, and Young Chin Kim—the last of whom was elected first chairman. AKPSNA was officially registered as a nonprofit educational organization on October 18, 1973. Ten years later, with more than 25 percent of members residing outside North America, the group shorted its name to the Association of Korean Political Studies (AKPS; in Korean, *Chaemi hanguk ch'ongji yongu hakhoe*). The name change was further precipitated by a desire to open up and expand organization membership in the age of globalism and create stronger institutional ties with Korean political science scholars—and political scientists studying Korean issues—in Korea and other countries around the world.

The AKPS is managed by a seven-person governing board elected to three-year terms by dues-paying members. The board in turn elects a president, who serves a two-year term. The stated mission of the AKPS is the promotion and advancement of scholarly exchanges in the area of Korea-related political studies. To this end, it holds annual meetings in conjunction with the annual conferences of either the American Political Science Association or the Association for Asian Studies, at which the AKPS routinely sponsors panels and roundtable workshops. In addition, the AKPS holds a biannual conference in Seoul, Korea, in conjunction with the Korean Political Science Association (KPSA). Since 1989, the association also has cooperated with the KPSA to hold the biannual World Conference of Korean Political Studies. As of the early 2000s, the KPSA had well over 200 members, including most of the top scholars on Korea working in North America.

Daniel C. Kane

Further Reading
Association of Korean Political Studies. http://www.akps.org.

Business and Entrepreneurship, Korean American

More than any other Asian American community, Korean Americans have gravitated toward small business. By the early 2000s, it was estimated that there was one Korean American–owned enterprise for every eight members of the Korean American community, the highest rate for any ethnic group in America, Asian or otherwise. Economists and sociologists cite different reasons for this high rate of entrepreneurship. Economists suggest that the highest rates of Korean immigration to the United States, in the late 1970s to early 1990s, corresponded with a time of massive restructuring in the American economy, when there were fewer opportunities for skilled and educated newcomers to find jobs in industry, especially if those persons did not speak English well. Economists also note the Korean tradition of informal credit associations, a key access to capital for immigrants who may not have the credit history or collateral that traditional banks look for when lending money to new businesses. Sociologists point to a cultural emphasis on hard work, a philosophy of self-help, and strong family networks that allow Korean business owners to find low-cost or even no-cost staff.

Statistics and Trends

Prior to the Immigration and Nationality Act of 1965, which ended national quotas and allowed for greatly enhanced immigration from Korea and other Asian countries, few Koreans found their way to the United States. As late as 1960, there were only about 10,000 persons of Korean descent living in the United States. Of the first several thousand who emigrated to Hawaii and the U.S. mainland in the early part of the twentieth century, most came as agricultural laborers. Those who settled in urban areas took low-level jobs in the service sector, as even well-educated immigrants were often informally barred from professions. Still, a small number of these early immigrants were eventually able to found small commercial enterprises—groceries, barbershops, bakeries, and the like—catering primarily to the small Korean American community or other, larger Asian American communities, such as the Chinese and Japanese.

After 1965, immigration increased dramatically, from several thousand per year in the late 1960s to roughly 30,000 per year from the late 1970s to 1990, before falling off to about 15,000 per year in the 1990s and early 2000s. These numbers also reflect conditions in the home country, as South Korea—the source of virtually all immigration from the peninsula—underwent dramatic economic change on its way to becoming the ninth-largest industrial economy in the world. As of 2007, it was estimated that there were roughly 1.5 million Korean Americans, about one-third of whom were American-born.

From the beginning of their large-scale immigration to America, Koreans have gravitated toward small business ownership. As early 1980, it was estimated that 13.5 percent of employed Korean Americans were either business owners or unpaid family workers, roughly double the rate for the U.S. population as a whole. By 1990, it was estimated that roughly 25 percent of employed Korean Americans were self-employed, either as small businesspersons or as professionals in independent practice, the highest rate of any ethnic group. By the 1990s, estimates put the percentage of working Korean Americans involved in small business—either as owners or workers, paid and unpaid—at about 70 percent. In New York City alone, more than 15,000 businesses were owned by Korean Americans in the early 1990s.

According to a 2006 U.S. Census study (with statistics for 2002), Korean Americans owned more than 157,000 businesses, with annual sales and receipts of nearly $50 billion. Of these, about 57,000 employed

Latino workers and leaders of the Korean Immigrant Workers Alliance in Los Angeles join in advocating for immigration reform and rights for low-wage laborers in 2006. In part by necessity, Korean immigrants have gravitated toward private business. (Associated Press/Nick Ut)

persons other than the proprietor, with an annual payroll of just over $6.7 billion. The largest single sector was retail, with about 34,000 of the 157,000 total businesses, followed by professional, scientific, and technical services, and food services and accommodation, with about 14,000 firms each. In addition, Korean Americans owned nearly 10,000 health care and social assistance companies, more than 8,200 real estate and rental firms, nearly 7,500 wholesale trade firms (usually in the import business), nearly 4,000 transportation and warehousing companies, and nearly 4,000 firms in the arts, recreation, and entertainment fields.

The impact of all of this business activity on local economies was equally dramatic. To take one prominent example, in the Los Angeles metropolitan area—whose 200,000–250,000 Korean Americans represented the largest concentration of this ethnic group in the United States—nearly half of all liquor and small grocery stores were Korean American–owned, even though Korean Americans represented just 1.5 percent of the area's total population. Nationally, no less than 20 percent of all dry-cleaning establishments were Korean American–owned by the early 2000s, though Korean Americans represented less than half of 1 percent of the total population. As in the case of many other immigrant groups, Korean American entrepreneurs are concentrated in several core business fields—dry cleaning, small grocery stores, liquor stores, importing (usually of low-cost goods from South Korea), and garment manufacturing.

Explanations

Korean immigrants have gravitated to business ownership for several reasons. One was the deindustrialization of the American economy during the peak years of immigration in the 1970s and 1980s. Blue-collar Koreans could not find employment commensurate with their skills, while white-collar Koreans often ran up against the language barrier. Moreover, many large American enterprises did not recognize university or vocational degrees granted by Korean institutions. But there were positive draws as well. Small business ownership offered more rapid income and social mobility than the low-paid jobs available to immigrants. Fluency in English was not necessary to succeed. Many Koreans dealt with suppliers who were also Korean, and the transactions involved in small retail business generally did not require extensive English-language skills; if they did, the transactions could be conducted by offspring who, being schooled in America, were more fluent in English.

Aside from the emphasis on work in Korean culture—encapsulated in the popular phrase *norokui taekka* (hard work is rewarded)—several other cultural traits aided Korean American business owners. One was family. Korean American entrepreneurs expect to put family members to work, thereby saving on labor costs. Second, Korean Americans have an unusually large informal network of social institutions—including churches, business groups, alumni associations, and others—that allow businesspeople to meet and socialize, establishing relationships that can be transferred to the economic sphere. Finally, there is the Korean tradition of rotating credit societies, or *kyes,* whereby a group of entrepreneurs or would-be entrepreneurs pool their money, each taking out loans in turn. *Kyes* helped Korean Americans overcome a traditional obstacle facing immigrant entrepreneurs—the inability to get credit from traditional banks because of a lack of credit history, collateral, and English-language skills. The inaccessibility of bank credit has eased somewhat since the 1990s, however, with the establishment of Korean American–owned banks or branches of South Korean banks in large Korean American neighborhoods. Such banks in California alone had an estimated $1 billion in assets by the year 2000.

Like other immigrant groups, many Korean Americans have found their business opportunities in poor and inner-city neighborhoods shunned by large corporations. By the early 1990s, it was estimated that Korean Americans owned more than 2,000 businesses in the working-class, predominantly black and Latino neighborhood of South Central Los Angeles (now known as South Los Angeles). This has often put them in a situation—exacerbated by their unfamiliarity with the history of racial tension in America—where they are viewed as exploitive outsiders. Anger at perceived abuse of minority shoppers led to organized boycotts of Korean-owned businesses in New York City in the early 1990s. More devastating to Korean American business owners were the 1992 riots in Los Angeles. Although set off by a perceived failure of the justice system to punish police officers accused of brutality against a black motorist, rioters—many of them African American and Latino—often expressed their outrage at economic inequalities in their communities by burning and looting Korean American–owned businesses. It is estimated that some 2,000 Korean American–owned businesses in South Central Los Angeles, the epicenter of the riots, were destroyed in three days of rioting; only one Korean American lost his life in the violence. In the aftermath, about half of the businesses in the neighborhood permanently shut their doors.

Korean American entrepreneurship is likely to grow and evolve in coming years, for a variety of reasons. As existing firms become better capitalized, they are likely to grow into larger enterprises. Meanwhile, entrepreneurs born and raised in America—or simply acculturated to life in the United States—have moved into nontraditional

Korean American fields, such as computer hardware and software. High-profile firms include All in One (AIO), a manufacturer of semiconductor testing equipment, founded in 1988 by longtime Silicon Valley computer engineer In-kon Kim; and Corio, a computer application service provider established in 1998 by Korean-born, University of California–educated Jonathan Lee.

James Ciment

Further Reading

Ahn, Hyeon-Hyo, and Jang-Pyo Hong. "The Evolution of Korean Ethnic Banks in California." *Journal of Regional Studies* (Korea) 7:2 (2001): 97–120.

Jo, Moon H. *Korean Immigrants and the Challenge of Adjustment.* Westport, CT: Greenwood, 1999.

Light, Ivan, and Steven J. Gold. *Ethnic Economies.* San Diego, CA: Academic, 2000.

Min, Pyong Gap. *Caught in the Middle: Korean Merchants in America's Multiethnic Cities.* Berkeley: University of California Press, 1996.

Park, Lisa Sun-Hee. *Consuming Citizenship: Children of Asian Immigrant Entrepreneurs.* Palo Alto, CA: Stanford University Press, 2005.

Song, Min Hyoung. *Strange Future: Pessimism and the 1992 Los Angeles Riots.* Durham, NC: Duke University Press, 2005.

U.S. Census Bureau. *Asian-Owned Firms: 2002.* Washington, DC: U.S. Department of Commerce, August 2006.

Chang, Sarah (1980–)

The Korean American violinist Sarah Chang is best known for being part of a wave of classical music child prodigies in the 1980s. Like her well-known Japanese-born competitor Midori, Chang seamlessly made the transition from child prodigy to adult musician.

Chang was born on December 10, 1980, in Philadelphia, Pennsylvania, to Korean-born parents who came to America in 1979 to study music. Her father, Min-soo Chang, went on to teach violin at Rutgers University in New Jersey. Her mother, Myoung Jun Chang, is a composer who also teaches. With this background, it is perhaps not surprising that Chang began playing violin at the young age of four, with a one-sixteenth-size instrument her parents bought for her. Tutored by her father, she began appearing with orchestras in Philadelphia at age five. By the following year, she was studying with the well-known violin teacher Dorothy DeLay of the Juilliard School in New York City (where she traveled on Saturdays while attending school in Philadelphia during the week). Chang has also cited the great Yehudi Menuhin as a mentor, from whom she learned to treat the violin like the human voice and slide up to high notes as a singer would. Chang gained national renown at the age of eight, when auditions with music directors Zubin Mehta and Riccardo Muti earned debuts with, respectively, the New York Philharmonic and the Philadelphia Orchestra.

Chang attended the prestigious Germantown Friends School in Philadelphia, in part because it could accommodate her music study and performance schedule. While earning mostly As, she also received bad marks for insufficient attendance. In interviews, Chang also lamented how far ahead her schedule was planned and how she longed for spontaneity. Nevertheless, she showed few signs of the emotional difficulties that have frequently plagued other child prodigies. By all accounts, she had a fairly stable upbringing with one of her parents typically traveling with her on tour. She speaks Korean at home and is fluent in German as well as English.

Chang made her recording debut in 1989 at age nine. The album, titled *Debut,* was not released until three years later, to wide acclaim. Playing an early-eighteenth-century Guarneri violin purchased in her teens, Chang went on to perform with most of the world's great orchestras and conductors. In 1998, she made her debut at the Proms, the fabled London summer concert series in Royal Albert Hall. Also that year, she recorded a concerto by the Hungarian composer Karl Goldmark, with James Conlon conducting the Cologne Philharmonic, before touring Europe with the Czech Philharmonic. She has been a soloist with the London Symphony Orchestra and the Vienna Philharmonic, among others, and she is signed to the EMI Classics recording label. In 1999, she was named the winner of the Avery Fisher Prize, one of the most prestigious awards in music.

Chang has described being onstage as her greatest delight. Addicted to the violin, she once stated that her fingers feel strange if they have not touched the instrument in a few days. She has attributed the plethora of Asian stars in classical music to a cultural ethic that emphasizes the ideals of discipline, family support, and hard work. Resisting commercial pressure to become a crossover artist, she remains loyal to classical music but has also played a dance piece for the American Ballet Theatre in New York City. Chiefly, as she has stated, Chang plays for herself.

Caryn E. Neumann

Further Reading

Levithan, David. *You Are Here This Is Now: The Best Young Writers and Artists in America.* New York: Push, 2002.

Sarah Chang Official Website. http://sarahchang.com.

Cho, Margaret (1968–)

An actress, comedienne, recording artist, memoirist, and political activist, Margaret Cho has made a name for herself in television—starring in the first network sitcom with a predominantly Asian American cast—and on stage, with her sexually provocative stand-up routine, much of it based on her experiences as a bisexual woman in an immigrant Korean American family.

Cho was born in San Francisco, on December 5, 1968, into a family with both literary and comic aspirations. Her Korean-born parents, father Seung-Hoon and mother Young-Hie, ran a bookstore, with her father also authoring joke books and contributing columns to newspapers back in Seoul, South Korea.

Growing up in what she has described as a melting-pot neighborhood of aging hippies, drag queens, and ordinary Asian Americans, the young Cho attended a performing arts high school, where she first got involved with improvisational comedy. She was soon performing stand-up routines in a club next to her parents' bookstore, where she riffed on the traditional immigrant theme of

Margaret Cho, a second-generation Korean American born in San Francisco, achieved mainstream stardom as a stand-up comic and television actress. Her short-lived 1994 sitcom, *All-American Girl*, was the first network series to feature an Asian American cast. *(Kevin Winter/Getty Images)*

the cultural clash between American-born children and straight-laced immigrant parents, who find it difficult to fully comprehend the values of their adopted country or the uninhibited ways of their offspring.

Cho's routine soon caught the attention of the entertainment community; in the early 1990s, she became a regular on "The Arsenio Hall Show," a late-night talk show with a youthful audience, as well as an opening act for popular stand-up comic Jerry Seinfeld. In 1994, ABC developed and aired "All American Girl," based on the family stories of her comic routine. The show proved to be a failure both for the network—garnering low ratings and being lambasted by Asian Americans for perpetuating stereotypes about their community before being cancelled after a single season—and for Cho personally. In its wake, Cho admits in her 2001 memoir *I'm the One That I Want,* that she became addicted to drugs and alcohol.

But by the end of the 1990s, she had recovered, and was making her experiences with the show and her struggle for sobriety the subject of her one-woman show "I'm the One That I Want." A hit on the road, the show also became the basis for a popular concert film in 2000, as well as a best-selling recording. This success was followed up two years later by the equally well-received "Notorious Cho," a sexually explicit one-woman show about growing up in 1970s San Francisco and her own bisexuality.

In the years since, Cho has continued to perform around the country and to write, penning a second book, *I Have Chosen to Stay and Fight,* a collection of essays on politics and human rights, in 2005. The book highlighted Cho's other career, as an outspoken political activist on gay rights and other issues. Cho has won numerous awards, both for her comedy and for her activism, including the American Comedy Award for Best Female Comedian and the First Amendment Award from the American Civil Liberties Union.

James Ciment

Further Reading

Cho, Margaret. *I'm the One That I Want.* New York: Ballantine Books, 2001.
Tiger, Caroline. *Margaret Cho.* New York: Chelsea House, 2007.

Community Organizations, Korean American

Korean American community organizations are nearly as old as Korean immigration to the United

States. Since the first organized group of Koreans arrived in Hawaii in 1903, Korean immigrants have sought out meeting places and formed social, educational, and religious societies. Many of these organizations struggled with financial difficulties and sometimes attempted to merge, but their efforts at unification were rarely successful. While preserving Korean cultural traditions and language, they promoted education for children and helped maintain peace in the community. Soon, however, events in Korea—especially the occupation and annexation of the country by Japan in 1905 and 1910, respectively—transformed these fraternal societies into activist political organizations. Korea's liberation from Japan in 1945 finally brought an end to the single political preoccupation of these early organizations and resulted in a resurgence of community-minded associations. Nevertheless, despite shared interests in promoting civic, social, and cultural welfare in the Korean American community, conflicts and generational differences caused rifts among the various organizations. Members of the community found fellowship in other ethnic associations, such as Korean churches, *dong moon hoes* (Korean alumni associations), business and professional associations, and numerous social services organizations—which remain the most influential in the Korean American community today.

Political Associations

In the early Korean American community organizations, political refugees, activists, and students devoted themselves to fighting for Korea's independence from Japanese oppression. As early as 1903, the first political Korean organization in U.S. territory, Sin-Min-Hoi (New People's Society), was established in Honolulu for the purpose of resisting Japanese aggression and rebuilding Korean by regenerating national spirit at home and abroad. Although Sin-Min-Hoi disbanded by the end of 1904, more than twenty other political organizations were established within the following three years. In 1908, the various political organizations sought to unite in order to mount a more effective resistance against the Japanese oppression. The consolidated organization that emerged from this effort was the Korean National Association (KNA), founded the following year. With the headquarters in San Francisco, the KNA had more than 3,200 members and more than 130 local chapters in California, Hawaii, Mexico, Siberia, and Manchuria. With a common thread of patriotism for the homeland, these Korean Americans devoted their efforts to raising awareness and organizing politically against the invasion of their country by Japanese troops, the Eulsa Treaty of 1905 (which made Korea a protectorate of Japan), and

the disbandment of the Korean Army. In America, they lobbied for the U.S. government to differentiate between Korean and Japanese immigrants and to consult the Korean National Association, rather than Japanese authorities, on all matters concerning the Korean American community. They had success on the latter issue, as confirmed by the formal public announcement on July 2, 1913, by Secretary of State William Jennings Bryan.

During the 1920s and 1930s, as the Korean National Association grew in size and influence, the need for strong, competent, consistent leadership became increasingly evident. At the time, the three most notable Korean leaders in America were Yong-man Park, Syngman Rhee, and Chang-ho Ahn. Park helped start the Korean National Association of Hawaii, lost his leadership to Rhee, and went on to organize the Korean Independence League in 1919. As the Korean National Association of Hawaii declined under Rhee's factional leadership, he began the Dong-Ji Hoi in Honolulu in 1921 to focus on supporting the provisional government in Korea. Chang-ho Ahn, meanwhile, established the Heung Sa-Dan (Young Korean Academy) in San Francisco in 1913; its purpose was to train Korean youth by developing their minds, bodies, and traditional virtues. While each of these organizations and their leaders advocated Korean freedom and cultural values, their specific priorities and methods were strikingly different. Each man developed his own organization of followers, which inevitably resulted in disunity within the Korean American community. The result was a proliferation of smaller organizations, and with the liberation of Korea 1945, the nationalist movement among political groups in America came to an end.

The following years mark a transitional period for Korean organizations and communities in America. Despite another attempt at unification, the Korean American community remained divided by leadership, vision, and now, generation. Second- and third-generation Korean Americans had concerns that differed from those of their elders and other newly arrived immigrants. While several of the newer organizations have maintained close associations with Korean national politics—including movements for Korean "comfort" women, farmers, and reunification—many of them focus on issues particular to the Korean experience in America. Community groups are dedicated to building empowerment in the American political process; representation in government, the professions, and the media; the promotion of a unique, albeit diverse Korean American identity and community; and the defense of the rights of Korean Americans. Additionally, multiple generations of Korean Americans have found alternative means of community and fellowship in the Korean ethnic church, alumni associations, business associations, and other groups.

Church Organizations, Alumni Associations, and Others

Unlike the Chinese and Japanese, many Koreans had a strong affiliation with the Christian faith prior to their immigration to America. Most Korean immigrants had been exposed to, if not already baptized by, a Christian church. Within the first decade after their arrival in Hawaii, more than 40 percent of the total Korean population had been baptized, regarding this as a fast route to acculturation. Today, the Korean ethnic church remains one of the most important and vibrant organizations for Korean Americans, with more than 28,000 community churches in the United States. Christian churches, most of them Protestant, make up about 75 percent of Korean American religious organizations; another 10 percent are Buddhist organizations. By functioning as a meeting place for fellow immigrants, the church serves as a site for spiritual as well as ethnic fellowship. It also works to sustain the Korean language and cultural traditions while providing essential social services. It is no surprise, therefore, that the number of Korean ethnic churches in America is constantly growing. "Mega-churches" such as Young Nak Presbyterian Church and Oriental Mission Church have congregations with well over 4,000 members in Los Angeles alone, with additional branches throughout the country. However, churches are not the only significant nonpolitical organizations in the Korean American community.

The *dong moon hoe* (alumni association) is the second most popular type of ethnic association among Korean immigrants. Based on alumni circles from Korean high schools and colleges, these associations provide Koreans in America with a connection to others they knew before their emigration. Moreover, in Korean social tradition, there is an obligation for *seon-baes* (seniors) to provide general support for their *hoo-baes* (juniors), who in return must pay respect to their *seon-baes*. Such relationships provide new immigrants with a source of fellowship and a sense of security. Although their meetings are not as frequent as church meetings, the impact of alumni associations on the Korean American community is still significant.

Many of the other popular Korean American community organizations, including business associations (such as the Korean American Merchants Association, Korean American Grocers Association, Korean American Professionals Association, and Korean American Lawyers Association) and social service or nonprofit community organizations (such as the Korean Youth and Community Center, Korean American Coalition, Korean Resource Center, and Koreatown Immigrant Workers Alliance), are regional in nature. Since Koreans are geographically concentrated throughout America, their organizations do not necessarily have to be national in reach. In order to promote the general welfare of the community, regional chapters of national organizations have tended to focus their efforts at the state and local levels. This is only natural, considering that 43 percent of the Korean American population resides in California and New York and 75 percent in just ten states. Thus, while the issue of national reunification remains unresolved, Korean American organizations continue to play a large role in the lives of Koreans in America.

Nancy Josephine Park

Further Reading

Hurh, Won Moo. *The Korean Americans.* Westport, CT: Greenwood, 1998.

Kim, Hyung-Chan, ed. *The Korean Diaspora: Historical and Sociological Studies of Korean Immigration and Assimilation in North America.* Santa Barbara, CA: ABC-CLIO, 1977.

Kim, Warren Y. *Koreans in America.* Seoul, South Korea: Po Chin Chai, 1971.

Yu, Eui-Young, and Peter Choe. "Korean Population in the United States as Reflected in the Year 2000 U.S. Census." *Amerasia Journal* 29:3 (2003–2004): 2–21.

Koreagate

Koreagate takes its name from the nearly contemporaneous Watergate scandal of 1972–1974, after which the American media became fond of using the suffix "gate" to designate political scandals. The Koreagate scandal concerned attempts at influence peddling in the U.S. Congress by a wealthy South Korean businessman named Tongsun Park, who was bankrolled by the South Korean government under President Park Chung Hee.

The origins of the scandal date to 1970, when plans announced by President Richard Nixon to significantly reduce U.S. troop presence in South Korea deeply concerned President Park. In response, the Seoul government regime developed a strategy to funnel South Korean funds through the K-CIA (the South Korean national intelligence organization) into the United States, to influence Democratic members of Congress against the idea of troop withdrawal and to nurture pro–South Korean sentiment across a range of issues. The threat of deteriorating U.S.–South Korean relations became more critical after 1976, with the election of Jimmy Carter, increased talk of U.S. troop withdrawal, and heightened American concern over human rights violations in South Korea. Meanwhile, the South Korean government enlisted the services of businessman and international socialite Tongsun Park to disperse money to certain members of Congress as well as other government officials, journalists, and businesspeople. The payments began in the early 1970s and involved upward of $1 million annually—with some individuals receiving $100,000–$250,000 at a time—through mid-decade.

The U.S. Department of Justice began investigating allegations of wrongdoing in 1975, but it was not until the following year that the investigation was made public, through a story in the *Washington Post*. Soon thereafter both the U.S. Senate and House of Representatives began looking into the matter. The investigations into what had been dubbed "Koreagate" continued through 1978, with Tongsun Park himself testifying under immunity in April of that year. Although Park claimed to have paid money to thirty members of Congress, only two—Representatives Richard T. Hanna (D-CA) and Otto E. Passman (D-LA)—were ever indicted. Hanna pleaded guilty to conspiring to commit bribery by accepting nearly $250,000 from Tongsun Park and served a year in federal prison; Passman was acquitted. Three other U.S. representatives—John McFall (D-CA), Charles H. Wilson (D-CA), and Robert L.F. Sykes (D-FL)—received congressional reprimands for accepting gifts and cash in violation of congressional rules. In 1979 the Carter administration dropped all charges against Tongsun Park, bringing an end to a three-year-long investigation that served to tarnish South Korea's image in the United States as well as to further erode Americans' confidence in the integrity of their elected officials.

Daniel C. Kane

Further Reading

Boettcher, Robert. *Gifts of Deceit: Sun Myung Moon, Tongsun Park, and the Korean Scandal.* New York: Holt, Rinehart and Winston, 1980.

Lee, Manwoo, Ronald McLaurin, and Chung-in Moon. *Alliance Under Tension: The Evolution of South Korean–U.S. Relations.* Boulder, CO: Westview, 1988.

Korean American Coalition

The Korean American Coalition (KAC) is a nonprofit, nonpartisan organization whose declared mission is to facilitate the Korean American community's participation in civic, community, and legislative affairs. Founded in 1983 in Los Angeles, the KAC and its national network provide a wide range of services and programs for Korean Americans of all generations.

Through advocacy, education, empowerment, outreach, and cooperation, KAC has aimed for more than two decades to help Korean Americans overcome the many barriers they face as an ethnic minority.

In the early 1980s, a small group of Korean American activists in Los Angeles took steps to address what they saw was a serious lack of political empowerment for Korean American immigrants. On the heels of a successful voter registration drive in 1982, leaders of the registration campaign decided to continue their efforts by creating an organization that would represent the interests and needs of Los Angeles' large but insular Korean American community. This vision led to the establishment of KAC, an advocacy organization that sought not only to support Korean Americans' active participation in the broader society, but also to bridge language and cultural gaps among Korean Americans of different generations.

A crucial turning point in KAC's history and the historical experience of Korean Americans as a whole was the 1992 Los Angeles riots. Even though Korean Americans made up less than 2 percent of the population in Los Angeles at the time, Korean American businesses suffered more than 50 percent of the total property damages caused by the civil unrest. In the midst of that turmoil, KAC became a voice for the Korean American community, arranging meetings with government officials, providing relief assistance for devastated businesses, and expressing the community's concerns to local and national media. Following the riots, KAC moved toward organizational growth with the establishment of a KAC chapter in Cerritos, California, in 1993. The organization has since expanded to a national network of chapters in cities across the United States, including Anchorage, Honolulu, Denver, Chicago, Atlanta, and Washington, D.C.

Today, KAC offers an array of services and programs that range from citizenship education for immigrants to conflict mediation with neighboring ethnic communities. Promoting the civic involvement of Korean Americans remains a cornerstone of KAC's mission: More than 75 percent of Korean American voters in Southern California register through KAC registration drives and outreach campaigns. KAC is also committed to supporting leadership training for the Korean American community's next generation of leaders. The National College Leadership Conference and the Summer College Internship Program give college students opportunities to gain experience in the workplace, develop leadership skills, and participate in various team-oriented activities. Since its inception, KAC has worked to strengthen and make visible the growing Korean American community, serving as an important resource for one of the largest Asian ethnic groups in the United States.

Andrea Kwon

Further Reading

Korean American Coalition, Los Angeles chapter. http://www
.kacla.org.

Yang, Steven. "The Korean American Coalition (KAC)." In
*Community in Crisis: The Korean American Community After
the Los Angeles Civil Unrest of April 1992,* ed. George O.
Totten III and H. Eric Schockman, 261–65. Los Angeles:
University of Southern California, Center for Multiethnic
and Transnational Studies, 1994.

Korean National Association

The Korean National Association (KNA) was founded in the first decade of the twentieth century to
fight Japanese colonial policies and support the cause of
freedom in Korea. The organization promoted religious,
educational, and cultural activities in the United States,
as well as the solidarity of Koreans abroad in the struggle
for the independence of their homeland. The KNA came
to include more than 130 branches and 3,200 members
throughout the world in the years before World War II
and became a major source of resistance and political
empowerment until Japan surrendered at the end of the
war, largely by organizing Korean immigrants and lobbying allied governments.

The KNA was established by immigrant scholar
Chang-ho Ahn in San Francisco after the assassination
of Durham White Stevens, a pro-Japanese American
diplomat who had supported Japanese expansion and
criticized the Korean people, by two Korean immigrants
on March 23, 1908. The court trial of the two alleged
assassins, Chang-in Hwan and Chun-myung Un, unified
Korean immigrants in Hawaii and on the U.S. mainland
who were determined to defend the rights of these men
to fight for Korean independence. On February 1, 1909,
two Korean civic organizations—the Mutual Assistance
Society (MAS) in San Francisco (founded by Ahn in 1906)
and the United Korean Society of Hawaii (founded in
1907)—officially merged to become the KNA, with
headquarters in San Francisco. On February 10, the organization launched a weekly newspaper, the *New Korea.* In
1912, the various branches of the KNA were organized
under a governing body called the Central Congress, with
Chang-ho Ahn (who preferred his pen name, Dosan) as
president and Yong-man Park as vice president.

Critical to the political activism of the KNA was a
1913 racial incident in the agricultural community of
Hemet, California, which spurred the organization to
action. On June 27, 1913, a group of Korean workers
employed at an apricot orchard owned by an English-
man were attacked by angry citizens not wanting Asians

working in the area. The Japanese consul in Los Angeles
interceded with the U.S. government on behalf of the
Koreans, whom they considered "Japanese subjects." The
Korean community refused representation by the Japanese. Tae-whi Yi, the president of the North American
Branch of the KNA, sent a telegram to U.S. secretary
of state William Jennings Bryan requesting that the
government take an official position that the Japanese
government should not represent Koreans. Bryan, under
pressure from Japanese diplomats in Washington, D.C.,
to support Japan's control over Korea and Koreans, nevertheless ruled in the KNA's favor, issuing a statement
requesting U.S. government officials to deal with the
KNA in all matters pertaining to the Korean American
community. The decision turned the KNA into a virtual
embassy for Korean political exiles and students living
in the United States.

Over the next three decades, the KNA collected
funds from Korean American immigrants to support the
independence movement in the home country, as well as
the Korean provisional government in exile. With the
bombing of Pearl Harbor in 1941 the KNA became part
of the United Korean Committee in Los Angeles, which
spearheaded Korean American efforts to fight Japan after
1941. After supporting the Korean American community
and the political interests of the homeland through the
Korean War and its aftermath, the Korean National Association dissolved in 1988.

Philip Ahn Cuddy

Further Reading

Choy, Bong Youn. *Koreans in America.* Chicago: Nelson-Hall,
1979.

Dae, Sook Suh. *The Writings of Henry Cu Kim.* Honolulu: University of Hawai'i Press, 1987.

Gardner, Arthur Leslie. *The Korean Nationalist Movement and Ahn
Chang Ho: Advocate of Gradualism.* Honolulu: University of
Hawai'i Press, 1979.

Kim, Warren Y. *Koreans in America.* Seoul, South Korea: Po
Chin Chai, 1971.

Korean National Association. http://koreannationalassn.com.

Koreatown (Los Angeles)

Koreatown is a neighborhood in the midtown area
of Los Angeles, encompassing the core of the city's
large Korean American community. Officially designated
Koreatown by the Los Angeles City Council in 1980, it is
located in the Wilshire Center district, roughly bounded
by Arlington Avenue on the west, Melrose Avenue on

the north, Hoover Street on the east, and Pico Boulevard on the south. Twenty percent, or 40,000, of the Koreans who reside in California live in K-Town, as it is often referred to. With roughly 250,000 residents—most of them non-Koreans—it is among the most densely populated urban neighborhoods in the United States.

Although Koreans have been present in Los Angeles for a little more than a century, it was in the mid-1960s that Koreatown had its beginnings. Two events heralded its genesis. First, passage of the Immigration and Nationality Act of 1965 led to a rapid rise in Korean immigrants in the Los Angeles area, from 5,000 in 1964 to about 9,000 in 1970. Second, the state of racial and civil unrest, highlighted by the Watts uprising of 1965, left a vacuum as small businesses left the area. For the Korean immigrants, this offered opportunities for entry into the local economy. As they flowed in, Korean Americans revitalized the area and stamped it with their own cultural identity.

Korean influence in the neighborhood increased rapidly during the 1970s. Most of its businesses—including strip malls, shopping centers, liquor stores, and restaurants—became Korean-owned. Signs in Hangul, the Korean alphabet, declared the neighborhood "Koreatown" even before it was officially recognized as such. The newfound sense of a unified community was further advanced by the growth of Korean media, including newspapers, magazines, radio, and television.

In 1992, the so-called Sa-i-gu Riot—literally "4-2-9" in Korean, after the day, April 29, the riots began—marked a terrifying moment and a turning point in the history of Koreatown. Also known as the Rodney King rebellion, it was the largest riot in the city's history, leaving 53 people dead and 2,000 injured. Material damage was estimated at $800 million to $1 billion. Many of the damaged stores, more than 2,500 in all, were owned by Koreans. Indeed, Koreatown suffered greater violence and damage than any other neighborhood in the city.

While the destruction was widespread, many Korean Angelenos point to the positive outcomes of the riots. The events served to galvanize the Korean community and led to a concerted effort to improve and develop local resources, as well as to rebuild. Korean American banks, such as Benjamin Hong's Nara Bancorp, took a gamble and agreed to extend emergency loans to Koreatown business owners on what was often nothing more than a handshake. Moreover, recognizing the need for a stronger voice in government, several Korean Americans ran for and were elected to public office, including the first elected Korean American representative to Congress, Chang-jun "Jay" Kim.

As of the early 2000s, the economic renaissance of the largest Korean community outside of Korea is being financed by the local boom driven by foreign investment and an increasingly affluent immigrant population. In addition, Korean families who fled Koreatown after the 1992 riots have been returning since the mid-1990s. Some affluent Korean Americans, however, prefer to live in the nearby suburbs while maintaining their businesses in the downtown community.

By the early 2000s, Koreatown had become well-known for its many restaurants and lively nightclub scene. The district has two popular shopping centers, Koreatown Galleria and Koreatown Plaza. Most of the Korean American establishments are merchandisers, whether of textile and other dry goods, or in the food or liquor store businesses.

Higher education institutions in the area include the Southwestern Law School (founded 1911), Dongguk Royal University (1997), and World Mission University, all of which cater to many Korean American students. Public schools are part of the Los Angeles Unified School District. After-school tutoring, offered at any private school serving the community, helps preserve its character, culture, language, and traditions. A number of important Korean American organizations are based in Koreatown as well. The Korean American Coalition (1993) facilitates the community's participation in civic, legislative, and other local affairs, and encourages Korean Americans to contribute to and become an integral part of American society at large. The Korean Youth and Community Center (1975) started out as an outreach project of the Asian American Drug Abuse Program and later expanded its role and services to a broader vision of community development and capacity building; projects now include urban environmentalism, affordable housing, and neighborhood economic development. The Korean Immigrant Workers Alliance (1992) campaigns to improve working conditions and immigrant worker empowerment in various Korean ethnic industries and the living wages campaign.

Since 75 percent of Korean immigrants are Christians belonging to the Protestant and Catholic churches, religious institutions also play an important role in the community. St. Basil's Catholic Church, Young Nak Presbyterian Church, and the Oriental Mission Church are all located there, as are places of worship for members of other faiths. Among the latter are the Wilshire Boulevard Temple for the Jewish community, Islamic Center for the Muslims, and a Buddhist temple.

Rodelen Paccial

Further Reading
Abelmann, Nancy, and John Lie. *Blue Dreams: Korean Americans and the Los Angeles Riots.* Cambridge, MA: Harvard University Press, 1995.

Song, Min Hyoung. *Strange Future: Pessimism and the 1992 Los Angeles Riots.* Durham, NC: Duke University Press, 2005.

Lee, Sammy (1920–)

Diver Samuel "Sammy" Lee, the son of Korean immigrants, became the first Asian American to win an Olympic gold medal for the United States, in platform diving at the 1948 Games in London. He successfully defended his title at the 1952 Olympics in Helsinki, making him the first man to win two consecutive gold medals in diving.

Lee was born on August 1, 1920, in Fresno, California. His parents, Soon-ki and Eun-ki Chun Lee, opened a grocery store in Los Angeles, where Sammy took an interest in diving at the age of eleven. He later spoke of the summer of 1932 and watching divers at the local public swimming pool, which nonwhites were allowed to use only one day a week. Lee attended Benjamin Franklin High School in Los Angeles, where he served as the first nonwhite student council president, was chosen the school's top athlete in 1939, and graduated first in his class.

In 1942, while attending Occidental College in L.A., the 5′0″ Lee won his first national U.S. championship in both springboard and ten-meter platform diving. He gave up diving the following year to pursue a medical degree at the University of Southern California. He resumed competitive diving in 1946 and promptly recaptured the U.S. championship in springboard. He received his MD in 1947 and competed in the London Olympics the following year as Dr. Sammy Lee. In addition to his gold medal in platform diving, he won a bronze medal in the three-meter springboard event. His repeat triumph at age thirty-two in the 1952 Helsinki Games also made him the oldest diver to win an Olympic gold medal. It also earned him the prestigious 1953 James E. Sullivan Award as the nation's outstanding amateur athlete, becoming the first person of color to be accorded that honor.

Retiring from competition in 1953, Dr. Lee remained actively involved in the sport as a coach and judge while pursuing his medical career as an ear, nose, and throat specialist. He was the coach of the U.S. Olympic diving team at the 1960 Games in Rome, where Bob Webster won the gold medal in the platform event; like his mentor, Webster repeated the feat at the 1964 Games. Among the other divers whom Lee coached was the great Greg Louganis in the 1970s and 1980s. Lee was inducted into the U.S. Olympic Hall of Fame in 1990.

Justin Corfield

Further Reading

Yoo, Paula. *Sixteen Years in Sixteen Seconds: The Sammy Lee Story.* New York: Lee and Low, 2005.

Wampler, Molly Frick. *Not Without Honor: The Story of Sammy Lee.* Santa Barbara, CA: Fithian, 1987.

Literature, Korean American

Much as for other Asian ethnic groups in the United States, Korean American literature focuses heavily on the immigrant experience, the hardships of adjusting to a new culture and country, and the psychology of dislocation. Yet the literature over the years has also been distinctively shaped by the unique aspects of Korean immigration history and the complex and changing relationships between Korean Americans and their country of origin. Although Korean immigration to the United States essentially began at the turn of the twentieth century, it was not until the late 1920s and 1930s that literary works in English by Koreans first came into print and gained general circulation. U.S. immigration reform in 1965 opened the door to a new wave of émigrés from South Korea, which greatly altered the demographics of the Korea American community and influenced the literary output of ethnic Koreans correspondingly. Korean American literature has especially proliferated since the 1980s, with a growing pool of authors expanding the purview of Korean American literature to a new range of subjects and a broader readership.

Early Period

Korean American literature before the 1970s was largely the product of first-generation immigrants who came to the United States as students or political exiles. Prominent themes of their writings include the firsthand experience of immigration and the introduction of Korean culture and history. Notable examples include New Il-Han's memoir *When I Was a Boy in Korea* (1928), and Younghill Kang's *The Grass Roof* (1931). The latter title, a work of autobiographical fiction, was well received by the public and circulated both in the United States and in Europe. The sequel, *East Goes West: The Making of an Oriental Yankee* (1937), dramatizes the hopes and despairs of a young Korean trying to realize his American dream. Another important figure in the early phase of Korean American literature was Richard Eunkook Kim, who produced such novels as *The Martyred* (1965), *The Innocent* (1968) and *Lost Names: Scenes from a Korean Boyhood* (1970). *The Martyred,* which explores matters of human conscience and suffering through the story of Christian missionaries captured and executed by Communists during the Korean War, was critically acclaimed and became a best seller.

Modern Literature

Compared to such authors as Kang and Kim, Korean American writers since the great influx of immigrants no longer constitute a homogeneous group. Women writers, second-generation writers, and even third-generation writers emerged as major participants in Korean American letters, widening the scope of subject matter, theme, and audience. They have experimented with new styles, written in a variety of genres, and explored a wide array of themes and subjects while continuing to reflect on immigration and cultural adaptation begun by earlier generations. The 1980s brought a proliferation of works by Korean American writers. Theresa Hak Kyung Cha's multigenre *Dictee* (1982), an unorthodox work described as "auto-ethnography," quickly emerged as a landmark of modern Korean American literature. The author, who immigrated to America with her parents in 1962 at the age of eleven, studied at the University of California at Berkeley and received training in film theory while doing postgraduate work in Paris. Through her numerous and varied experiments in forms and media, Cha raised lingering questions of language, memory, and identification. In *Dictee,* a collage of poetry, prose, and visual art, she explores language through references to the Japanese colonial rule of Korea (during which the Korean language was banned), and by inserting other languages and visual material. Cha proved inspirational to other Korean American writers, including the poet Myung Mi Kim, whose verse collection, *Under Flag* (1991), reflects the influence of *Dictee.*

Indeed, a number of women writers emerged in the 1980s to represent the immigration experience from a female perspective. Second-generation Korean American Gloria Hahn (pen name Ronyoung Kim) published *Clay Walls* (1986), a novel set in 1940s and 1950s Los Angeles and Korea. The novel is divided into three parts, each narrated by the mother, father, and daughter. The employment of narrative perspectives across generations and gender, as well as the novel's diasporic scope, provides a unique view of Korean immigration. Mary Paik Lee's autobiography, *Quiet Odyssey: A Pioneer Korean Woman in America* (1990), recounts her family's immigration when Lee was five and the challenges they encountered in moving from Hawaii to California. *The Dreams of Two Yi-Min* (1989) is also an autobiographical narrative by a second-generation Korean American woman, Margaret K. Pai, that sheds light on early immigrant life in Hawaii

through her picture-bride mother and small-business-owner father.

Partly due to the long history of Korean immigration to Hawaii, Hawaii-born writers of Korean heritage have played a significant role in shaping the ethnic literature. Among third-generation Korean American writers from Hawaii, Willyce Kim was the first Asian Pacific lesbian to publish a collection of poetry, *Curtains of Light,* in 1971. She published two more collections of verse, *Eating Artichokes* (1972) and *Under the Rolling Sky* (1976), before turning to mystery-adventure novels in *Dancer Dawkins and the California Kid* (1985) and *Dead Heat* (1988), both set in California, where she works and lives. Gary Pak, in the award-winning short-story collection *The Watcher of Waipuna* (1992), describes moments in the lives of first- and second-generation immigrants he witnessed as the grandson of Korean immigrants. Later works are likewise set in Hawaii, including the novels *A Ricepaper Airplane* (1998) and *Children of a Fireland* (2004). Poet Cathy Song, a Chinese Korean native of Hawaii, made an acclaimed debut with the collection *Picture Bride* (1983), which earned her the prestigious Yale Series for Younger Poets. Her second collection, *Frameless Windows, Squares of Light,* came out in 1988, followed by *School Figures* (1994), *The Land of Bliss* (2001), and *Cloud Moving Hands* (2007).

Young Peoples's Literature

The late 1990s brought a proliferation of books for children and young adults by Korean American writers that represented the immigrant experience from children's perspectives or looked to Korean folk tales for their motifs and themes. Sook Nyul Choi's *Year of Impossible Goodbyes* (1991) and *Echoes of the White Giraffe* (1993), both set in Korea and containing autobiographical elements, are intended to inform young readers of what Korea was like during the years of early emigration to the United States. Linda Sue Park's *A Single Shard* (2001), set in twelfth-century Korea and modeled after a Korean folk tale, tells the story of a young apprentice potter whose character and judgment are put to the test. The book won the prestigious Newbery Medal, awarded annually to the outstanding American book for children, in 2002.

As Korean American literature grows in volume, the body of works written and published by writers of Korean descent is becoming increasingly heterogeneous in character. While still cherishing their Korean heritage and using it as a source of literary creativity, writers such as Chang-Rae Lee and Susan Choi also step outside the limitations of the "Korean American" label. While both have published novels that invoke Korean history and the immigration experience—such as Lee's *A Gesture Life*

(1999) and Choi's *The Foreign Student* (1998)—they have also published works on subjects that are not ethnically Korean in any immediate sense of the word.

The desire of the new generation of writers to be recognized and understood for the complex identities and breadth of interests and perspectives they embrace is well expressed by the wish of poet Cathy Song to be known as "a poet who happens to be Asian American."

Jeehyun Lim

Further Reading

Cheung, King-Kok, and Stan Yogi, eds. *Asian American Literature: An Annotated Bibliography.* New York: Modern Language Association of America, 1988.

Fenkl, Heinz Isu, and Walter Lew. *Kŏri: The Beacon Anthology of Korean American Fiction.* Boston: Beacon, 2002.

Kim, Elaine. *Asian American Literature: An Introduction to the Writings and Their Social Context.* Philadelphia: Temple University Press, 1982.

———. "Korean American Literature." In *An Interethnic Companion to Asian American Literature,* ed. King-Kok Cheung. Cambridge: Cambridge University Press, 1997.

Los Angeles Riots

The largest urban disturbance in America since the Civil War, the Los Angeles riots in April–May 1992 had a disproportionate impact on the city's large Korean American community, in terms of both property losses and the community's sense of belonging and security. Over several days of violence, Korean American–owned businesses in the Koreatown neighborhood and elsewhere suffered more than $400 million in damage from burning and looting, an estimated half the total property losses suffered in the city during the upheaval, known in the Korean community as *Sa-i-gu,* or April 29, after the day the rioting broke out.

The origins of the riots had little to do with the Korean American community, resulting instead from a jury's absolving of four Los Angeles police officers of charges rising from their videotaped beating of an African American motorist, Rodney King, the year before. And the rioting began far from Koreatown, in the predominantly black South Central Los Angeles area.

But Korean Americans and Korean American businesses quickly became targets of the rioters for several reasons. With entrepreneurial drive but few resources, many Korean American immigrants in the 1970s and 1980s had opened small retail businesses where they could afford to and where competition with established

A Koreatown shopkeeper sifts through the remains of his business in the aftermath of the Los Angeles riots in spring 1992. Korean businesses became targets of large-scale unprovoked violence; as many as 2,000 were destroyed. *(Jonathan Utz/AFP/Getty Images)*

businesses was less intense. This was often in underserved low-income and minority neighborhoods, including the predominantly African American South Central Los Angeles (now South Los Angeles) neighborhood.

Tensions soon rose between the Koreans and the residents of the area. Residents complained that Koreans charged high prices, treated customers rudely, and refused to hire locals to work in their businesses, preferring other Koreans instead. Korean business owners rarely spoke up, but those who did pointed out that the Koreans they hired were family members, which saved on labor expenses. Roughly one year before the riots, on March 16, 1991, Korean-black relations reached a new low when shopkeeper Soon Ja Du shot African American teenager Latasha Harlins, whom she accused of shoplifting orange juice from her store. Ja Du received no jail time for the nonfatal shooting, creating a perception among African Americans that assaults on community members were unlikely to lead to appropriate punishment for the perpetrators, a perception reinforced by the acquittal of the police officers accused of unlawfully beating King.

The mass violence that broke out on April 29 began in the South Central Los Angeles area, with rioters targeting businesses of all kinds, including those owned by Korean Americans. Very soon, the mobs—consisting of African Americans, Latinos, and whites—overwhelmed police antiriot efforts and spread across the city, with the Koreatown neighborhood, home to roughly a quarter million Korean Americans and located several miles to the north, especially targeted for attack. With television cameras rolling, Angelenos and Americans watched as armed Korean shopkeepers stood on the roofs of their businesses, warding off potential looters, the police having largely left them to their own defenses, according to reports. Ironically, shooting by shopkeepers and security patrols hastily assembled within the Korean American community were responsible for the riot's only Korean American casualty, an eighteen-year-old teenager named Edward Lee.

In the aftermath of the riots, which saw some 2,000 Korean American–owned businesses destroyed, many Korean Americans moved out of Koreatown to safer environs in the suburbs, though maintaining businesses in the commercial heart of the neighborhood, which remained quite vibrant. In 1992, the midtown area where Koreatown is located was roughly one-third Korean; by decade's end the population was down to 10 percent, though some of this shift no doubt had to do with other factors, including rising prosperity and assimilation. At the same time, Korean American civic leaders recognized that fences with the black and Latino communities needed mending. Clinics were begun to teach cultural awareness to Korean shop owners, and a number of conferences were held to discuss ways to improve Korean American–African American relations.

James Ciment

Further Reading

Abelmann, Nancy, and John Lie. *Blue Dreams: Korean Americans and the Los Angeles Riots.* Cambridge, MA: Harvard University Press, 1995.
Chang, Edward, and Jeannette Diaz-Veizades. *Ethnic Peace in the American City: Building Community in Los Angeles and Beyond.* New York: New York University Press, 1999.

Moon, Sun Myung (1920–)

The Reverend Sun Myung Moon is a Korean-born religious leader who founded a widespread but controversial denomination called the Unification Church in the 1950s and has headed the movement—whose adherents are popularly referred to as "Moonies"—ever since.

Moon was born into a family of Confucians on January 6, 1920, in the village of Sangsa-ri in what is now North Korea. The family converted to Presbyterianism when he was a boy. Moon claims that he was visited by Christ at age fifteen—on Easter Sunday, 1935—and directed to establish God's kingdom on earth. After studying religion and electrical engineering in Seoul and Tokyo, Moon returned to Korea in 1943 and began ministering independently. By 1948, he had been excommunicated by the Presbyterian Church, and not long after that he was arrested and interned in a North Korean labor camp, allegedly because the government did not approve of his religious teachings. He was released in 1950 after United Nations forces landed on the Korean Peninsula to defend the south from the Communist north.

Moon moved to Pusan in 1951 and the following year published *Divine Principle,* which outlined the doctrine and foundation of what two years later would officially become the Holy Spirit Association for the Unification of World Christianity—better known as the Unification Church. The term "unification" had particular relevance to Koreans, for whom the concept represented an ideal future. By 1957, the sect had spread throughout Korea; by 1959, missionaries were traveling to the United States. In March 1960, Moon married Hak Ja Han (his third wife), and the two became what Moon's followers call the "True Parents."

The Unification Church is funded primarily by Moon's network of factories. First established in Korea and Japan, they produce a wide a variety of items, including tea, paint, and weapons. After several visits to the United States, Moon finally moved church headquarters to Tarrytown, New York, in 1971. The new religious movement was especially popular among young people, who were drawn to the wholeness and purity they were told the church could provide. With missionaries fanning out across the country, the movement gained hundreds of members during its first year in America and thousands of adherents—associated with more than thirty church centers—by 1973.

The group was the object of suspicion virtually from the outset. The parents of some Moonies, dismayed by what they had heard or read about the movement, accused Moon of being a cult leader and his organization of brainwashing their children. The government was also suspicious. Moon's 1981 application for tax-exemption status for the Unification Church was denied, and the following year he was convicted on charges of tax evasion. He was fined $25,000 and sentenced to prison beginning in 1984, completing his eighteen-month sentence in the summer of 1985. A coalition of mainstream religious groups protested the prosecution, and the National Council of Churches called it harassment.

Although he has played a somewhat lower-key role in the United States in the years since, Moon has retained his personal influence in the international movement. He has held mass weddings—an important ritual in the Unification belief system—and conducted missionary tours throughout the world and played an active role in the movement's diverse organizations and programs. The Unification Church itself is said to have anywhere from 200,000 to millions of members worldwide, depending on which estimates are believed. Moon's commercial holdings, including the *Washington Times,* social agenda, and international political connections have also continued to proliferate. In 2005, at age eighty-five, he began a 120-city international speaking tour to launch the Universal Peace Federation. In April 2008, he appointed his youngest son, Hyung Jin Moon, as the new leader of the worldwide Unification Church and movement.

Leah Irvine

Further Reading

Barker, Eileen. *The Making of a Moonie: Choice or Brainwashing.* New York: Basil Blackwell, 1984.

Chryssides, George. *The Advent of Sun Myung Moon: The Origins, Beliefs, and Practices of the Unification Church.* New York: Palgrave Macmillan, 1991.

Horowitz, Irving Louis, ed. *Science, Sin, and Scholarship: The Politics of Reverend Moon and the Unification Church.* Cambridge, MA: MIT Press, 1978.

Tillet, Gregory. *The Lord of the Second Coming: Sun Myung Moon and the Unification Movement.* Boston: Routledge and Kegan Paul, 1984.

Paik, Nam June (1932–2006)

Korean-born artist Nam June Paik, widely regarded as the father of video art, is also known for dramatic mixed-media works and multimedia performance-art "happenings." No modern artist is more associated with, or has had a greater influence on, the use of television and video as artistic media. His prolific body of work established a new genre—and revolutionary set of principles—in modern art.

Paik was born into a wealthy manufacturing family on July 20, 1932, in Seoul, South Korea. With the outbreak of the Korean War in 1950, his family fled the country, heading first to Hong Kong, and then to Japan. After studying art and music at the University of Tokyo, Paik graduated in 1956, then moved to Germany to study classical music. Two years later, he met the American avant-garde composer John Cage, whose influence on Paik

and his work would prove enduring. Inspired by Cage's experimental compositions, Paik began to incorporate dramatic theatrical elements into his musical performances, such as toppling pianos and smashing violins on stage. Also during this period, he began participating in a Neo-Dada, Cage-influenced, sound-and-image arts group called Fluxus group, whose members included Paik's wife, Japanese artist Shigeko Kubota.

It was in the early 1960s that Paik began to recognize the possibilities of television as an art form. He purchased thirteen used television sets and learned how to distort the electronic image by manipulating sound waves, tinkering with the black-and-white controls, and changing the horizontal input. He staged the first known video art exhibit at Galerie Parnass in Wuppertal, Germany, in 1963. Later that year, he returned to Tokyo to work with the newly emerging technology of color television, using electromagnets to warp the electron flow in the cathode-ray tube and create unexpected images on screen.

Arriving in New York in 1964, Paik met long-time collaborator cellist Charlotte Moorman. In their most famous performance, titled *Cello Sonata No. 1 for Adults Only,* Moorman disrobed to the waist as she played a composition by Bach. Paik and Moorman were later arrested during a similar performance in New York City and charged with obscenity and indecent exposure. In 1965, Paik purchased Sony's first portable video camera—recorder and, as an artist-in-residence at the

Video and multimedia performance artist Nam June Paik fled Korea with his family as a teenager, after the outbreak of the Korean War in 1950. He later settled in New York City, where he evolved his innovative electronic artistry. *(Mario Ruiz/Time & Life Pictures/Getty Images)*

public television stations WGBH in Boston and WNET in New York, continued his experimentation with the electronic medium. Working with Japanese electronics engineer Shuya Abe in 1969, Paik invented the video synthesizer—a machine that generates and modifies visual images.

Paik's artistic philosophy emphasizes the humanization of technology and a desire to create a "global village"—bringing together diverse groups of people from around the world—through the medium of television art. In 1973, WNET broadcast Paik's *Global Groove,* a video montage of television clips, commercials, and music from various countries intended to facilitate global understanding through television. As a counter to George Orwell's apocalyptic vision of technology, Paik broadcast *Good Morning Mr. Orwell* on January 1, 1984, to a worldwide audience, demonstrating satellite television's potential for fostering cross-cultural exchange. For the 1988 Olympic Games in Seoul, South Korea, Paik built a tower of 1,003 video monitors and kicked off the games with another television show broadcast around the world via satellite. In 2000, the Solomon R. Guggenheim Museum in New York honored Paik with a retrospective of his work titled *The Worlds of Nam June Paik.* Paik died on January 29, 2006, in Miami Beach, Florida.

Elizabeth Mauldin

Further Reading

Decker-Phillips, Edith. *Paik Video.* Barrytown, NY: Station Hill, 1998.
Hanhardt, John G. *The Worlds of Nam June Paik.* New York: Guggenheim Museum, 2000.
Nam June Paik Studios. http://www.paikstudios.com.
Stooss, Toni, and Thomas Kellein, eds. *Nam June Paik: Video Time, Video Space.* New York: Harry N. Abrams, 1993.

Religion, Korean American

Buddhism was introduced to Korea from China in the fourth century C.E., by traders, monks, and other travelers long before European missionaries introduced Christianity during the seventeenth century. By the end of the twentieth century, however, approximately a quarter of the population of South Korea—the source of virtually all Korean immigration to the United States—was Christian, while roughly 30 percent was Buddhist. Of the remaining 45 percent of the population, most listed "no religion" in official tallies. But while Christianity represents but a minority of all South Koreans, this is not the case among the Korean

population in the United States. Since the first Korean immigrants arrived in Hawaii in 1903, Christianity has had a significant presence among Korean Americans, and the ethnic church has served as the center of the Korean community in the United States.

The Church in Early Immigrant Life

Influenced by the evangelizing work of Western missionaries in the late 1800s, many of the Koreans who immigrated to the United States prior to World War II had previous exposure to Christianity through membership in missionary-run churches. Historians estimate that as much as 40 percent of the first wave of Korean immigrants to Hawaii in the early 1900s were Christian before they arrived. Accordingly, the Korean church became a key social institution—serving as the center of education, culture, politics, and social services for the Korean community. Churches provided both religious and secular training to Korean immigrant children, including classes in traditional Korean culture and language for the American-born generation. Older Koreans received English language instruction in church-run classes. In addition to maintaining ongoing education in culture, history, and other aspects of life in the home country, the churches also fostered Korean arts by hosting concerts, dance performances, and other events. Korean churches even served as forums for political organizing among laborers and as places where members of the community could network for business and for traditional social activities such as charity and welfare services for the poor among the immigrant community.

Role of Religion After 1965

Several thousand of the roughly 7,000 Koreans in Hawaii had moved to the U.S. mainland by the 1920s, but the Korean population in both places remained relatively small until 1965, when federal immigration reform opened the doors for skilled workers and family members of persons already in the United States. With roughly 1.5 million Koreans in America as of 2007, Korea has consistently been on the list of the top ten immigrant-sending countries since the 1980s.

Like the early wave of Korean immigrants at the turn of the twentieth century, the recent waves consist of a large number of Christians. Surveys conducted in the 2000s showed that roughly 80 percent of the Korean immigrant population in the United States identified themselves as Christian; just over 90 percent of these identified themselves as Protestant and the remaining

7–8 percent as Catholic. As for the 20 percent of non-Catholics, most said they were either Buddhist or had no religious affiliation at all. Among Protestants, most Korean Americans belonged to churches affiliated with North American denominations. A majority belonged to mainstream denominations, especially Methodists and Presbyterians, though a significant minority were members of churches aligned with more evangelical organizations, such as the Southern Baptists.

Sociologists in both Korea and the United States offer a number of explanations—both practical and psychological—for the predominance of Christians among Korean émigrés to the United States. As members of a faith well represented in America, Korean Christians of various denominations were more familiar with American culture and ideas, making the idea of adjusting to life in a foreign land less daunting. They also knew that there would be a social infrastructure in place when they got there—something they could belong to and somewhere they could go every Sunday, easing the anomie of immigrant life. But there were less concrete reasons as well. Christianity, particularly in its Protestant forms, emphasizes the individual's relationship with God. And just as individuals choose salvation to ensure eternal life, so individuals choose immigration to improve their lives in this world. That is to say, Koreans who chose to give up their Buddhist and Confucian traditions likewise might be willing to leave their homeland in the name of making a better life elsewhere. Moreover, most South Koreans were familiar with American culture and the ethic of individualism through their exposure to U.S. media and the large American military presence in their country.

Once in America, Korean Christians found churches that catered to both their spiritual and secular needs. To the present day, Korean churches continue to function as the center of community life. Immigrant ethnic congregations offer members the opportunity to take on leadership positions unavailable in society at large and provide them a place where they can be respected and understood. Korean churches help immigrants preserve their language and customs, and observe the various holidays and rituals transported from the homeland. They serve as important venues of social networking, offering practical social services ranging from babysitting, to language instruction, to help in finding a job.

The various nonreligious social functions of the ethnic church—especially its entrepreneurial activities, such as sponsoring business forums—have led some in the Korean community to question the religious authenticity and commitment of churchgoers. Korean immigrant churches have also been criticized for being ethnically exclusive and detached from their surrounding communities. They are also known for breaking apart over personal and narrow theological reasons. The abundance of Korean American lay leaders and pastors in part contribute to church divisions and lead some former members to break off and move to other churches or create new churches of their own. Such divisions contribute to the profusion of Korean churches across the United States.

The Future

Influenced by economic recovery in Korea and the aftermath of the 1992 Los Angeles riots, the number of Korean immigrants declined significantly in the 1990s—from an average of 35,000 per year in the late 1980s to less than 15,000 per year by the early 2000s. The decline in immigration, combined with the growing number of U.S.-born, second-generation Korean Americans, has contributed to a cultural bifurcation within the community: more traditionally religious members of the immigrant generation versus their more secular, Americanized offspring. While the first generation currently control many of the ethnic congregations, the future of Korean Americans and religion will hinge on church participation and the level of faith among the growing number of second-generation Korean Americans.

Modes of religious participation on the part of the two generations are already unlike in several key respects. The U.S.-born second generation typically attends separate English-language services specifically tailored to the younger, more acculturated members of the community. These services, moreover, are led by Korean American pastors most often trained in the United States, and emphasize values of personal self-improvement. In contrast, older first-generation members attend Korean-language services that emphasize traditional religious values such as family and hard work. The result, in many cases, has been the splitting of some congregations into two distinct "de facto congregations."

The growing rift between the generations has been evident most of all in the outright departure of many second-generation Korean Americans from first-generation congregations. The trend has been dubbed the "silent exodus" because much of it goes unnoticed by the first generation and because the numbers are staggering. More than 80 percent of second-generation Korean Americans are said to have left their immigrant parents' ethnic churches—turning the churches of families into churches of parents.

Where second-generation Korean Americans go when they leave their parents' churches remains to be seen. Some leave the faith altogether, while others leave only temporarily. Some form their own ethnic churches for U.S.-born Korean Americans, while others turn to other Asian American or multiracial congregations. Thus far, however, second-generation Korean American Christians generally opt for separate ethnic religious institutions in which Koreans or Asians are the majority.

Rebecca Y. Kim

Further Reading

Hurh, Won Moo, and Kwang Chung Kim. "Religious Participation of Korean Immigrants in the United States." *Journal for the Scientific Study of Religion* 29 (1990): 19–34.

Jeung, Russell. "Asian American Pan-ethnic Formation and Congregational Culture." In *Religions in Asian America*, ed. Pyong Gap Min and Jung Ha Kim, 215–44. Walnut Creek, CA: Altamira, 2002.

Kim, Rebecca. "Asian American Evangelicals: Ethnic, Multiethnic, or White Campus Ministries?" *Sociology of Religion* 65:1 (Spring 2004): 19–34.

Kwon, Ho-Youn, Kwang Chung Kim, and R, Stephen Warner, eds. *Korean Americans and Their Religions: Pilgrims and Missionaries from a Different Shore.* University Park, PA: Pennsylvania State University Press, 2001.

Min, Pyong Gap. "The Structure and Social Functions of Korean Immigrant Churches in the United States." *International Migration Review* 26 (1992):1370–94.

Students, Korean American

Korea has had a long tradition of sending scholars abroad for study and cultural observation. The tradition began with a single student, Yu Giljun, who arrived in the United States in 1883 as a member of the first Korean diplomatic mission. He remained in the United States for one year to study Western civilization and the American political system at Dammer Academy in Massachusetts. A political coup in Korea the following year led three men to seek refuge in the United States, one of whom—So Chae-p'il (Philip Jaisohn)—later became the first Korean to earn a medical degree in the United States.

More students arrived in the last decade of the nineteenth century, including the children of political elites and those sponsored by American Christian organizations in Korea. But it was not until after World War II, and the end of Japan's occupation of Korea, that the number of Korean students began to grow beyond a handful. And it would not be until after the Korean War in the early 1950s that the number grew to the hundreds and then the thousands. Since the early 1950s, the growth in the number of Korean students studying in the United States has been explosive, with South Korea ranking high among all countries sending students to the United States.

Korean students in the United States can roughly be divided into three historical groups. The first period began with the first diplomatic mission to the United States in 1883 and ended with Japan's annexation of Korea in 1910. Approximately sixty to seventy Korean students arrived in the United States during this period, most of whom migrated for political reasons. Of this group, according to historian Bong-youn Choy, forty-five completed their studies (mostly at the undergraduate level); a few, such as Philip Jaisohn, Kim Kiusic, and Syngman Rhee, went on to earn doctoral degrees. Most of these students entered the United States through San Francisco, where one of the earliest Korean American communities was being formed.

The second period of Korean student immigration coincides with Japan's occupation of Korea, from 1910 to 1945. Many Korean intellectuals and patriots who had engaged in anti-Japanese activities fled to China to avoid persecution and to continue their pro-independence activities. Approximately 500 of them then migrated to the United States, either directly from China or by transmigrating via Europe. Some disembarked in California or New York with Chinese passports and proficiency in multiple East Asian languages, but many came without a passport and limited English skills. Beginning in 1919, Japan eased its restrictive emigration policy and allowed about 300 Korean students to depart for the United States with Japanese passports. During World War II, the U.S. government employed about 200 of those familiar with the Japanese language as interpreters, translators, and language instructors.

It is uncertain how many Korean students entered the United States during the first two periods (1883–1945). Few entered with Korean passports, but many entered with a Japanese or Chinese passport, especially during Korea's colonial period. Furthermore, since the United States did not recognize Korea as an independent country, Koreans could not claim their ethnicity on forms or in registries. Then during World War II, East Asian groups in the United States sought to differentiate themselves from the Japanese. Korean American leaders urged members of the community to register as Korean, rather than as Japanese subjects, under the Alien Registration Act of 1940. Earl G. Harrison, the director of U.S. alien registration, ruled that Koreans indeed had the right to register as Koreans rather than as Japanese, but the bureau itself did not systematically abide by that ruling. Regardless of the exact number, new leaders of the Korean American community and diasporic independence movement emerged from among the student population.

The third period of student life in America commenced with the end of World War II. The period from the mid-1940s to the early 1960s marked the peak of U.S. military involvement in the Korean Peninsula and of economic aid to South Korea. It also corresponded with the rapid growth of chain immigration, as students, wives of U.S. soldiers and officers, and medical professionals followed family members to settle permanently in America. With the end of World War II, the United States became the most popular destination for Koreans studying abroad. The availability of government funds, including Fulbright fellowships, and private scholarships encouraged students to pursue higher education in the United States.

In Korea, meanwhile, Park Chung Hee seized power through a coup d'état in 1961 and implemented a series of five-year economic plans that accelerated economic development. A stronger Korean economy led to a greater number of students whose funding came from personal and family sources. The number of students traveling abroad increased even more with a modification of Korean legislation in the late 1970s. Until that time, the government had required candidates for foreign study (most of whom were men) to pass a qualifying exam, to have served in the armed forces for three years, and to have completed their undergraduate education. In the late 1970s, the government abolished the qualifying exam, reduced the minimum domestic education to the completion of high school, and canceled military service as a prerequisite. As a consequence, the number of Korean students arriving in the United States increased steadily in the years that followed. Even the rise of anti-American sentiment in Korea during the mid-1980s did not dampen the desire for a degree from an American institution of higher learning.

According to the Country Locator Report by the Institute of International Education, there were more than 50,000 Korean students studying in the United States in the early 2000s. Of this number, about half were graduate students, another 40 percent were undergraduates, and about 10 percent were enrolled in nondegree programs. California was the most popular state with Korean students, followed by New York, Texas, Pennsylvania, and Illinois. The terrorist attacks of September 11, 2001, brought a decline in the number of students admitted from many countries—but not Korea. That community continued to grow.

Jane J. Cho

Further Reading

Choy, Bong-youn. *Koreans in America*. Chicago: Nelson-Hall, 1979.

Takaki, Ronald. *From the Land of Morning Calm: The Koreans in America*. New York: Chelsea House, 1994.

Treaty of Amity and Commerce (1882)

Signed in 1882 by the governments of the United States and Korea, the Treaty of Amity and Commerce established formal diplomatic relations between the two countries, marking the first time the so-called Hermit Kingdom had ever signed a formal treaty with a Western power.

The changing East Asian diplomatic situation of the mid- to late nineteenth century was key to the signing of this pathbreaking treaty. China had lost a series of conflicts with Western nations since the 1840s, and Japan was rapidly shedding its traditional culture in favor of modernization. Korean Confucian scholar-officials looked upon both China's deterioration and Japan's modernization as trends to be avoided. As a result, Korean officials sought to isolate their country from the West, hoping to maintain it as a bastion of traditional Confucian culture.

This isolationist policy, however, ran counter to the international diplomatic climate of the day. Western nations, such as the United States, hoped to open Korea's economy to trade by establishing political and economic relations. Indeed, the United States had made several attempts to establish ties between the 1840s and 1870s, but their efforts proved unfruitful because Confucian conservatives controlled the Korean government.

In the mid-1870s, however, reformist King Kojong pushed to open Korea despite strong opposition from conservative scholar-officials. In 1876, Japan used "gunboat diplomacy" to force Korea to open up to trade, and the Western powers moved quickly to capitalize on Japan's lead. In 1880, the United States sent Rear Admiral Robert W. Shufeldt to negotiate a treaty with Korea, using the good offices of Japan, but the Koreans resisted once again. The following year, Chinese statesman Li Hongzhang offered to mediate a treaty between the United States and Korea, hoping to counterbalance Japan's growing influence on the peninsula.

The United States and Korea signed the Treaty of Amity and Commerce, also known as the Shufeldt Convention, on May 22, 1882. The agreement was unequal in several respects. Korea granted the United States extraterritoriality rights—that is, U.S. citizens living in Korea would be held to U.S. rather than Korean law—as well most-favored-nation trade status. The United States also agreed not to import opium into Korea (as the Western powers had done in China). The treaty further stipulated that the United States would use its "good offices" should Korea need assistance. Many Koreans expected the United

States to intervene when Japan colonized Korea in 1910 and accused America of bad faith when it did not.

The treaty is historically significant because it was Korea's first modern agreement with a Western nation and opened the way for Korea's modernization. In later years, the Seoul government invoked the treaty to hinder Chinese encroachment on Korean sovereignty. The Treaty of Amity and Commerce was soon followed by similar pacts signed by Korea with Great Britain, France, Russia, and other Western powers.

Brandon Palmer

Further Reading

Chay, Jongsuk. *Diplomacy of Asymmetry: Korean-American Relations to 1910.* Honolulu: University of Hawai'i Press, 1990.

Deuchler, Martina. *Confucian Gentlemen and Barbarian Envoys: The Opening of Korea, 1875–1885.* Seattle: University of Washington Press, 1977.

War Brides, Korean

The phenomenon of "war brides" was an integral part of U.S.-Korean relations and Korean American life from the early 1950s to the mid-1970s. The term refers to Korean women who married American servicemen and returned with them to the United States. Because the majority of these women met and married their soldier husbands in "camptowns" adjacent to U.S. military bases during times of suspended armed conflict between North and South Korea—periods of relative peace— historian Ji-Yeon Yuh and others refer to them as "Korean military brides." They entered the United States under the War Brides Act of 1945, as later amended, which allowed the spouses and adopted children of U.S. military to immigrate legally.

During the poverty-stricken period of the 1950s through 1970s, the U.S. military presence in South Korea created a situation that made marriage to American servicemen an attractive option for Korean women. American military bases there gave rise to a large number of so-called camptowns, communities that revolved around the bases and provided entertainment for American GIs, especially bars, clubs, and brothels. The first camptown was located in Bupyong, near the west coast port city of Inchon. The number of camptowns increased significantly during the Korean War (1950–1953); among the largest were Itaeown in Seoul, Texas in Pusan, American Town in Kunsan, and Little Chicago in Tongdochon. The 1960s were the heyday of the camptowns, with as many as 30,000 prostitutes entertaining some 62,000 U.S. soldiers across South Korea. In the 1970s, the U.S. military brass and South Korean government launched the Camptown Clean-Up Campaign (also referred to as the Purification Movement) to regulate military prostitution and control venereal disease.

Most of the Korean military brides were originally camptown prostitutes. For many impoverished women in South Korea at the time, military prostitution was a last resort. In other cases, they were kidnapped and forced into becoming prostitutes. During the early years of U.S. military presence and then during the Korean War, many of the camptown prostitutes were war widows or orphans. Some were former prostitutes of the Japanese colonial period, and some—according to historian Chul-in Yoo—were victims of rape by U.S. and UN forces. Most camptown women of the 1950s, 1960s, and even 1970s had little formal education, and many were completely illiterate. Once women entered camptown prostitution, they became trapped in a system of debt bondage. First they began by borrowing money from club owners to establish themselves, and then they were forced to give their earnings to club owners.

Meanwhile, life on American military bases in Korea throughout the 1950s to 1970s was marked by strong black-white polarization. Black soldiers could not go to the bars where white soldiers socialized, and vice versa. Witnessing the discrimination toward African American soldiers, Koreans internalized the racial prejudices in American society and developed corresponding biases and stereotypes. Thus, it was common for camptown prostitutes to be socially and geographically segregated according to the color of the men they associated with. Women who associated with Caucasian soldiers were considered "higher class" than those who entertained black soldiers. A prostitute might even risk losing business from her white patrons if she entertained African American soldiers.

Once a Korean woman entered camptown prostitution, it was extremely difficult for her to marry a Korean man and return to mainstream society. Koreans referred to camptown prostitutes as "foreign princess" (*yanggongju*), a derogatory term that implied they were selling their bodies—and the traditional values of chastity and virginity—for the sake of American materialism. Virtually the only options for these women were to remain a prostitute or become a military bride. Those who married American servicemen were determined to leave South Korea for the United States, setting aside their past and starting a new life in America.

Prior to the civil rights movement of the 1950s and 1960s, many military brides dreamed of associating with and living like whites in their quest for upward mobility. Thus, upon arriving in the United States, many reproduced the same racial boundaries among themselves as those they perceived in mainstream American society. A racial and social hierarchy soon emerged among the military brides, whereby those who had married white soldiers looked down upon those who had married African American soldiers, with little interaction between the two groups.

The established Korean American community was not always hospitable to military brides—no matter whom they married—because of their past association with camptown life. Consequently, Korean military brides tended to live at the fringes of both Korean and American societies. Social outcasts in their home country and yearning for a new life, many found that American society at large was not always welcoming to Asian immigrants and even less ready to accept cross-cultural marriage.

Joseph Tse-Hei Lee

Further Reading

Moon, Katharine H.S. *Sex Among Allies: Military Prostitution in U.S-Korea Relations.* New York: Columbia University Press, 1997.

Yuh, Ji-Yeon. *Beyond the Shadow of Camptown: Korean Military Brides in America.* New York: New York University Press, 2002.

Women, Korean American

While women were among the first organized group of Koreans to arrive in America in 1903, their unique immigration history is often overlooked or else subsumed in the account of Korean male migration. In a little over a century, five main groups of Korean women have immigrated to the United States: wives of Korean immigrant workers, students, and political exiles (1903–1905); picture brides and other wives (1910–1924); war brides (1950–1970s); educated professionals (late 1960s); and wives and mothers of Korean immigrant families (post-1965). The specific experiences of each group of women depended on the time and circumstances of their arrival.

Early Immigrants

The first two groups were essentially partners of Korean immigrant men who worked as laborers on Hawaiian sugar plantations. The plantation owners recruited these men to work as strikebreakers against disgruntled Japanese laborers, who constituted a majority of the labor force. In the first wave, 637 Korean women accompanied their husbands to Hawaii. The standard wage for a ten-hour workday on the plantations was sixty-five cents for men and fifty cents for women. The plantations provided living quarters, but immigrants had to endure any conditions they were offered. Largely due to racial discrimination, manual labor was usually the only profitable occupation for these immigrants. Some women were able to find additional work as laundresses and cooks.

With the onset of the second wave of women, Korean immigrants began to venture into other areas for work and wage. Between 1910 and 1924, more than 1,100 Korean "picture brides" arrived in the United States (most in the territory of Hawaii). Because of the severely unbalanced sex ratio in the first wave of immigration (ten males to every female), marriages were arranged through the exchange of pictures of prospective brides in Korea and grooms in Hawaii. These women were generally younger and more educated than their prospective husbands, and many had experience working outside the home as teachers or nurses before emigrating. Once they arrived in Hawaii, many encouraged their husbands to leave plantation labor for better prospects on the U.S. mainland. Thus began the heavy remigration of Korean Americans from Hawaii to the mainland—primarily the West Coast—where a majority opened small family businesses or entered the professional world. Indeed, Koreans left plantation work for urban opportunities faster than any other ethnic immigrant group in Hawaii. Women worked alongside their husbands in family-owned enterprises such as grocery stores, fruit and vegetable stands, wholesale companies, boardinghouses, and tailor shops. In addition, they organized with other women and became involved in church activities or women's organizations often related to the Korean independence movement.

Between 1908 and 1919, several Korean American women's organizations were founded to sponsor religious, educational, and social programs for the general community welfare and later for the political support of the Korean homeland. The first Korean American women's organization, Hankuk Puin Hoe (Korean Woman's Association), was founded in San Francisco in 1908. Although it was officially independent, its purpose was to support church activities, facilitate Korean language education for children, and promote solidarity among Koreans. A similar organization, Taehanin Puin Hoe (Korean Women's Society), was created in Hawaii in 1913. In addition similar community activities, Taehanin Puin Hoe helped organize and perpetuate a boycott of Japanese goods after the annexation of Korea in 1910. Beginning in the late 1910s, women's organizations began to focus their attention on the movement for Korea's independence and relief programs for needy soldiers, victims, and students in Korea. Groups such as the Taehan Puin Kujehoe (Korean Women's Relief Society of Hawaii) and Taehan Yojsa Aikukdan (Korean Women's Patriotic Society), worked side by side with the Korean National Association on political activities in Korea, America, and Europe.

Mass Immigration

The last three waves of Korean women came with the general rise in immigration due to changes in U.S. law after World War II, beginning with the War Brides Act of 1945. This legislation, as amended in 1950, admitted "alien" wives and children of U.S. servicemen who had fought during the Korean War on a nonquota basis. As a result, approximately 6,400 wives of American servicemen immigrated to the States between 1950 and 1964.

The fourth wave of Korean women immigrants was largely composed of educated professionals, products of the rising opportunities for college education and professional work for women in Korea during the 1960s. Due to political and economic instability at home (resulting from the division of the Korean Peninsula and the Korean War), many of these women pursued their goals in America. At the same time, the U.S. Immigration and Nationality Act of 1965 eliminated the national-quota system, encouraged kinship chain migrations, and gave preferential immigration status to certain professional occupations—including nursing. The result was an influx of professional Korean women, many of them trained as nurses. In most cases, however, their training proved useless in the United States because professional licensing boards did not recognize it or because language barriers made it difficult to pass certification exams. Those who managed to stay in the health-care field were usually demoted to lower-level occupations. Others found jobs as operators of small businesses, garment workers, seamstresses, supermarket checkers, or waitresses.

By the early 1970s, the educated professional immigrant population became more diversified. Continuing the immigration movement of middle-class Koreans that began with the previous wave, wives and mothers of immigrant families became a part of the fifth and largest wave of Korean women immigrants. They came not so much out of necessity or survival, but in hopes of raising their standard of living by improving their family's economic and children's educational opportunities. This remains a top priority and motivation for a majority of Korean immigrants to the present day.

With the social realities of living as immigrants in the United States, Korean American women have increasingly renounced the traditional Confucian ideal of women as submissive subordinates to men, or *Hyun Mo Yang Cho*. According to this principle, women are defined primarily by their relation to men—as daughters, wives, and mothers. Included among the modern Western realities that have prompted the break from traditional gender identity are demographics, industrialization, the feminist movement, Christianization, and a high rate of self-employment. Studies have shown that women play a crucial role in starting and maintaining small Korean family businesses through their long hours of work (often unpaid), as well as in maintaining family and home life in their traditional roles as wives and mothers.

The distinctive experiences of women from the five immigrant groups have contributed to an extremely diverse and multifaceted population. The reasons for and types of Korean female migration to the United States continue to evolve, while the ratio of Korean American women to men has actually reversed: women now outnumber men by 54 to 46 percent. Another notable demographic trend is that the population of young and single Korean American women now exceeds that of Korean American men—evidence of the fact Korean women are no longer the mere accompaniments of male immigrants but independent individuals in search of their own social and economic opportunities.

Nancy Josephine Park

Further Reading

Hurh, Won Moo. *The Korean Americans.* Westport, CT: Greenwood, 1998.

Kim, Warren Y. *Koreans in America.* Seoul, South Korea: Po Chin Chai, 1971.

Yu, Eui-Young, and Earl H. Phillips, eds. *Korean Women in Transition at Home and Abroad.* Los Angeles: Center for Korean American and Korean Studies, 1987.

Yu, Eui-Young, Peter Choe, and Sang Il Han. "Korean Population in the United States, 2000: Demographic Characteristics and Socio-Economic Status." *International Journal of Korean Studies* 6:1 (Spring–Summer 2002): 71–107.

The Laotian and Hmong American Experience: History and Culture

Believed to have originally migrated from Siberia into China, the Hmong people were driven into Southeast Asia by the dominant Han Chinese during the latter half of the eighteenth century. Successive wars during the Qing dynasty (1644–1911) resulted in the displacement of Hmong throughout parts of China and the migration of communities into areas of Laos. Resettlement during the nineteenth century created Hmong communities in the highlands of Laos, where they lived in relative peace and resumed their traditional lifestyle of slash-and-burn agriculture. Viewed as an ethnic minority group by Laotians (members of the Tai ethnic group as well as indigenous Lao), the Hmong enjoyed relative peace until the Second Indochina War (late 1950s to 1975) and the Communist overthrow of the royal Lao government in 1975.

Sociopolitical and economic instability propelled Laos into turmoil, and the change in government necessitated a mass migration out of the country. Those who were able to migrate included former royal supporters, Hmong fighters and their families, and those who could claim refugee status (families wanting to flee for personal safety). The wave of refugee migration was primarily to the United States, Canada, and Australia. The United States, because of its military and diplomatic involvement in the region, gained the largest Hmong and Lao population outside Southeast Asia. According to the 2000 U.S. Census, there were a total of 350,000 Hmong and Lao—divided roughly fifty-fifty—living in the United States. However, the Hmong and Lao communities both maintain that the census figures underrepresent their population, because young respondents often select the generic "Asian" classification rather than identify themselves primarily as Hmong or Lao.

The Hmong and Lao communities of the United States retain strong cultural, social, and religious ties to their past. Religious observance, social and cultural gatherings, and strong familial ties ensure that American-born Lao and Hmong and recent refugees are able to retain their shared cultural identity. The Hmong and Lao communities are most prevalent and active in the states of California and Minnesota, where newcomers feel at home with established cultural institutions and support groups if not with actual family members. Frequently, however, migration to a new country has not been without pitfalls, and many new migrants have found it difficult to adjust to differences in language, education, and social expectations. Problems of cultural adaptation have persisted even as problems diminish as each generation becomes more Americanized.

War and Displacement

During the seventeenth century, the Hmong tribes in China fled a succession of wars and were dispersed across a vast area from Siberia to southern China. During the eighteenth century, driven from Chinese lands entirely by the expanding Han majority, the Hmong fled into the jungles of Laos. There they were able to reestablish their agricultural lifestyle and live in relative peace among ethnic Lao tribes in different parts of the country. Native Lao areas were later divided among neighboring states (mostly Thailand and Vietnam), so they are often mistaken as having a Thai heritage. Historically, however, the Lao and Hmong were able to coexist in Laos—a trend that continues in the United States today.

In 1954, Communist forces in neighboring Vietnam defeated French colonialists at the Battle of Dien Bien Phu, raising fears in the rest of Southeast Asia and the West of a Communist takeover of the entire region. Laos, during these tumultuous times, was under royal patronage (as a semiautonomous state in the French Union) and enjoyed neutral status (under the Geneva Convention) that both the United States and North Vietnam would soon exploit. In 1961, after a succession of coups radically destabilized Laos's political situation, U.S. president John F. Kennedy realized that Lao neutrality could be utilized to provide a buffer zone against the surge of Communist aggression from Vietnam. Elite U.S. forces such as the Green Berets were already operating in Laos as counterinsurgency units, but they could not compromise their positions by redeployment. Instead, it was hoped, a strategic military force could be created by joining Hmong and Lao recruits with American forces to stem the growing Communist movement in Laos by both the Pathet Lao and Vietnamese Communists.

Headed by Prince Souphanouvong, the Pathet Lao were ultimately instrumental in the fall of a free Laos and committed heinous acts of genocide against Hmong and Laotian communities that had sided with the monarchy and allies, or individuals of royal descent. The Pathet Lao encouraged raids on Lao and Hmong villages as an act of reprisal for supporting foreign forces, and concentration camps were set up in the northeastern highlands of Laos where prisoners of war and members of royalty (children included) were sent to be tortured and killed. The persecution of Lao and Hmong families triggered an exodus of refugees to the United States after the wars in Southeast Asia came to an end in the mid-1970s.

At the outset, however, the Kennedy administration envisioned that local people would be recruited to fight alongside the established Royal Army of Laos. The United States also wanted to recruit autonomous fighters who would undertake ad hoc reconnaissance missions and provide foreign forces with intelligence. All in all, Hmong and Lao recruits were expected to protect the growing areas of Laos in which Communists were running secret supply routes. The Central Intelligence Agency (CIA) actively set about recruiting the so-called Secret Army of Laos and trained Hmong and Lao recruits in all aspects of guerrilla warfare.

The recruitment of men for the secret army created a unique relationship between U.S. soldiers and Hmong and Lao fighters and their families. A relationship of interdependence became evident as the Hmong and Laotian families relied on the Americans and their allies for food, medicine, weapons, arms, and general village safety in order just to survive. Anti-Communist forces in turn depended on the newly recruited army to fight enemies that could not often be located due to lack of jungle warfare training. The U.S. military, now engaged in war on two fronts (Vietnam and Laos), depended on the fighting prowess of recruits. Even Hmong and Lao villagers were instrumental finding and nursing wounded Allied servicemen and keeping them safe until they could be returned to their units.

The Refugee Experience

The successful recruitment of both Hmong and Lao peoples continued until the withdrawal of U.S. forces from Vietnam in April 1975. The pullout of American troops marked an abrupt end to the relationship between the U.S. military and the Hmong and Lao fighters, and the immediate result was disastrous both for the former recruits and for the nation as a whole. Laos fell to the Vietnamese-controlled Pathet Lao and became a Communist nation that actively committed genocide against royalists, Lao patriots, and Hmong and Lao recruits. Chemical and biological warfare ensued against known Hmong settlements, with napalm sprayed over vast areas of Lao jungle. Reeducation camps were set up throughout Laos with the help of the Vietcong, primarily on the border with Vietnam. Inmates endured systematic torture and the climate became dangerous for all those who were against the Pathet Lao or merely perceived to be so.

The war, and the time preceding it, saw a mass reorganization of traditional Hmong and Lao settlements in Laos. The United States immediately flew out the most important recruits and their families, but more than 100,000 Hmong and Laotian soldiers and civilians were forced to flee to Thailand to escape torture and reprisals by the Lao government. Most Hmong and Lao immigrants to the United States made their way directly from refugee camps in Thailand. As second- and third-generation families settled down and became successful, they were able to help immediate family members migrate as well.

Few other countries were prepared to accept Hmong and Lao refugees, though, in any case, the United States appeared to be the first choice among those seeking asylum. This was largely due to the relationship between Laos and the United States during the years of turbulence, and later to family-based chain migration. Hmong refugees are true asylum seekers and the last remnants of Vietnam-era migration, as they are still able to prove that they are in danger in Laos.

The majority of Hmong and Lao refugees were considered uneducated by Western standards, and many were certainly in need. Thus, at least at first, most depended on government services and the help of family members and the community to help establish their new lives. Although English teachers had been available in the Thai refugee camps to teach those wanting to emigrate to the United States, the culture shock proved difficult for many.

Between 1975 and 1989, the United States placed Hmong and Lao refugees strategically throughout the country in an attempt to ensure integration into the population as a whole while maintaining the specific clan-based society of the Hmong and Lao communities. Thus, Hmong and Lao families were able to create their own enclaves as a way of ensuring adequate peer support. Religious organizations were also involved in the settlement of refugees, with churches and various

Christian groups and organizations encouraged to sponsor refugee families; many pledged to look after the new immigrants for a minimum of three months. Christian groups were especially prominent in the sponsorship and placement of refugees in small rural communities. With their strong insistence upon religious education, some Christian sponsors caused conflict among the shamanic Hmong and Buddhist Laotians. Thus, in some locations, strong shamanic and Buddhist convictions came into conflict with the pressing need to conform, assimilate, and integrate into the new environment. Church groups sometimes used religious conversion for leverage; families who readily converted often received much better support than those who refused.

The most common ailments experienced among first-generation (and occasionally second-generation) Hmong and Lao refugees were depression, schizophrenia, and post-traumatic stress disorder. The inability to converse in English and unfamiliarity with social customs, institutions, and ways of life contributed to the difficulties of adjustment for many new refugees, while a lack of support outside small communities exacerbated the sense of displacement. The most common ailment among American-born Hmong and Lao were and remain stress-related disorders. This is largely due to the pressures placed on them by immediate families in dealing with day-to-day life and bureaucracy. Younger members of the household are often called upon to assume responsibilities and make decisions normally left to the head of the family, which may prove stressful.

Population patterns for Hmong and Lao Americans are similar to those of other Asian refugee groups, with most settling down either in states with large Southeast Asian communities, such as California and Texas, or in states where there are established support networks, such as Minnesota and Wisconsin.

Adjusting to Life in America

Adjusting to life in America proved problematic for many in the Lao and Hmong refugee communities. Many were farmers, and a high percentage were considered illiterate and unskilled. High unemployment, combined with the language barrier, made it hard to integrate successfully into American society. First-generation Hmong and Lao families especially suffered culture shock, as integration into American society required them to alter deeply engrained social, economic, and political practices that were very different from the ones they now encountered. The traditional clan-based hierarchy, for example, conflicted fundamentally

with the American ethic of individualism. Likewise, the American emphasis on gender equality stood in direct opposition to the traditional roles of women and men in Lao and Hmong social practices. Indeed the differences went beyond abstract values and principles. Shamanic rituals involving animal sacrifice were illegal in the United States, forcing alterations in traditional religious practices.

Lack of previous knowledge about the United States and the tools necessary to integrate successfully—command of English, literacy, and familiarity with social mores, among others—caused great trouble for refugees used to more traditional ways and a fundamentally different social hierarchy. Thus, not only did children become less dependent upon their parents, but the dynamics of adult-child dependency shifted dramatically. Many children were able to function more successfully in American society than their parents due to their superior language skills and sheer adaptability, making parents dependent on them for day-to-day transactions. The traditional family hierarchy was thereby blurred even further.

The majority of young Lao and Hmong in American cities have at least a high school diploma, with many choosing to pursue higher education. Their peers in smaller rural towns, however, are less likely to attend university and have steady employment. This has been attributed to the lack of employment opportunities in more remote areas, as well as less extensive Hmong and Lao social networks. Most, if not all, American-born Hmong and Lao speak English as their primary language and are thoroughly integrated into American life—often at the expense of not knowing traditional customs or language. The majority of first-generation Hmong and Lao refugees, however, spoke only their native language and perhaps a few simple sentences in English (usually learned in refugee camps) before arriving in the United States. In 2000, Congress passed the Hmong Veterans' Naturalization Act, which waived English-language requirements and granted special consideration to those applying from Laos for naturalization who had served with, or worked for, special units in Laos from 1961 to 1978.

Organizations and Associations

The Hmong and Lao communities in the United States today are active in the social, cultural, and political arenas alike. Community-specific events, such as Lao New Year celebrations, beauty and singing contests, and regular social gatherings, are commonplace. Many communities provide educational support in the form of grants and scholarships to local schoolchildren. Compared to

A young member of the Hmong community talks on his cell phone at the 2004 Wisconsin State Fair. Hmong refugees have retained strong social and cultural ties while struggling to adjust to life in America. *(Darren Hauck/Stringer/Getty Images)*

the 1980s and 1990s, the early twenty-first century provides ample opportunity for Hmong and Lao representation in the immediate and extended communities. The American-born younger generation has greater and more diverse opportunities than their parents had. As assimilated American citizens with native command of English, a native understanding of the society and culture, higher education, and often professional training, they have access to the social, political, and economic infrastructure to an extent their parents and grandparents never did. By contrast, many older Hmong and Lao remain reluctant to take part in peer organizations for fear that they have been infiltrated by Lao Communists seeking out political refugees. Indeed many first-generation immigrants remain relatively anonymous and maintain close contact only with immediate, trusted family members, out of fear that those left behind in Laos might be targeted.

The biggest and most influential Hmong and Lao organizations in the United States today are the Lao Veterans of America (LVA) and the Lao Human Rights Council (LHRC). The LVA, which includes former Lao and Hmong fighters and their families, provides support to both communities across the country. The LHRC actively lobbies the U.S. government and the United Nations for humanitarian aid to the Hmong and Lao still in Laos, and acts as an information clearinghouse regarding their plight. Especially with the aid of online networking—and the growing number of Hmong and Laotian students with computer science backgrounds—Hmong and Lao organizations are able to increase their exposure within the community. Organizations and cultural centers focusing on Hmong and Lao history and arts are on the rise. The Hmong Cultural Center in Minnesota has a large national as well as local following, with a Web site that provides links on Hmong studies for anyone interested in expanding his or her social or academic interests. A number of American universities have established Lao and/or Hmong studies departments or institutes. The First International Conference on Lao Studies was held at Northern Illinois University in 2006. As an outgrowth of that event, the nonprofit Center for Lao Studies was established in San Francisco that same year. The mission of the center is "to promote and advance the field of Lao Studies in all disciplines through research, education, seminars, conferences, and cultural and study abroad exchange programs."

Samaya L.S. Chanthaphavong

Further Reading

Center for Lao Studies. http://www.laostudies.org.

Chan, Sucheng. *Hmong Means Free: Life in Laos and America.* Philadelphia: Temple University Press, 1994.

Conboy, Kenneth. *Shadow War: The CIA's Secret War in Laos.* Boulder, CO: Paladin, 1995.

Hones, Donald, and Cher Cha. *Educating New Americans: Immigrant Lives and Learning.* Philadelphia: Lawrence Erlbaum, 1999.

Lao Human Rights Council. http://www.laohumanrightscouncil .org.

Lao Veterans of America. http://www.laoveterans.com.

Miyares, Ines. *The Hmong Refugee Experience in the United States: Crossing the River.* New York: Garland, 1998.

Quincy, Keith. *Hmong: History of a People.* 2nd ed. Cheney: Eastern Washington University Press, 1995.

———. *Harvesting Pa Chay's Wheat: The Hmong and America's Secret War in Laos.* Cheney: Eastern Washington University Press, 2000.

Community Organizations, Hmong American

The Hmong American community boasts more community organizations and associations than perhaps any other Indochinese refugee group, with greater variety in mission and objective. A number of well-established organizations focus on broad economic needs and social services for members of the immigrant community, while others address more specific needs and issues, such as cultural preservation and language maintenance. Together, formal and informal groups reflect the special needs, leadership, diversity, and aspirations of the Hmong American community.

Emergence

The first wave of Hmong refugees, who came to the United States in 1975, began to organize on an informal basis soon after their arrival. The early organizations were based on traditional Hmong social institutions, such as the clan, village leadership, and other social structures. Lao Family Community, Inc., the first nonprofit Hmong American community organization, was established in 1977, and was soon found in various cities with significant Laotian American communities, especially in California and Minnesota. Its purpose was and remains to provide social services to Hmong and other refugees from Laos.

Since then, a number of formal and informal organizations have been formed to respond to the needs and issues of the Hmong American community. The Southeast Asia Resource Action Center in 2000 listed a total of forty-five Hmong Mutual Assistance Associations, exceeding the number of analogous groups representing Vietnamese Americans (thirty-nine), Lao Americans (twenty-three), and Cambodian Americans (twenty). This does not include Hmong American professional associations, political associations, and organizations based on clan membership or district of former residence in Laos. The list at the end of this article identifies Hmong American community organizations, categorized by purpose and function.

Mutual Assistance Associations

Leadership of the Hmong American community, it has been observed, has taken three forms: older, traditional leadership; middle-aged, middle-of-the-road leadership, and younger, Americanized leadership. The older, traditional leaders tend to be former government and military officers from Laos, with leadership styles like those practiced in the old country. Middle-aged, middle-of-the-road leaders tend to be bilingual and bicultural, enabling them to serve as a bridge between the Hmong and non-Hmong and between the old and young Hmong. Younger, Americanized leaders are those who are educated in the United States and have much stronger ties to their adoptive nation than to the homeland of Laos. In the decades since the first wave of immigrants in the mid-1970s, Hmong American Mutual Assistance Associations have been established by all three types community leaders, with still others founded and led by Hmong American women.

Lao Family Community, Inc., is one example of an organization founded by traditional, older leaders. Major General Vang Pao, the former commander of the Second Military Region (MRII) of Laos, founded the organization in Santa Ana, California, in 1977, after which branches were established in cities with other large Hmong American communities, such as Fresno, Merced, Stockton, and Sacramento, California, and St. Paul, Minnesota. The organization offers a variety of social and cultural services, from citizenship and resettlement programs, employment assistance, language instruction, and senior transportation to informal social gatherings and cultural activities.

The Fresno Center for New Americans is a nonprofit organization in California established in 1991 by Anthony K. Vang, a middle-aged, middle-of-the-road leader, and associates. The organization helps local immigrants from Southeast Asia and elsewhere meet critical acculturation needs, including job services, health care, education, and civic networking. It has emerged as the largest Hmong American community organization in Fresno, with an annual budget of about $2 million.

The majority of Hmong American Mutual Assistance Associations are now run by middle-aged, politically moderate leaders. Others—most founded in the 1980s—include the Wisconsin United Coalition of Mutual Assistance Associations (WUCMAA), Hmong Association of Long Beach, Hmong Association of South Carolina, Hmong United Association of Rhode Island, Hmong Community (Detroit), Hmong American Association of Oklahoma, and Hmong Association of Oregon.

The Hmong American Partnership (HAP) is among those community organizations founded by the generation of younger, Americanized leaders. The group was established in 1990 by T. Christopher Thao, the first Hmong attorney in America, and other members of the community in Minneapolis–St. Paul, Minnesota. Hmong American community organizations founded and led by women include the Hmong American Women's Association (Fresno), Women's Association of Hmong and Lao (St. Paul), Hmong Women Association of Milwaukee, and the Association for the Advancement of Hmong Women in Minnesota (Twin Cities). This last organization has an annual budget of about $1 million and provides a wide variety of services, including family counseling, translation, parenting, advocacy, and after-school programs for youth.

Political Organizations

Hmong political organizations are divided into three types. Those established in the late 1970s and 1980s were created primarily to protest and lobby against the policies of the Communist government of Laos. Examples include the United Lao National Liberation Front and the Democratic Chao Fa Party of Laos. Other organizations, such as the Laotian Multi-Ethnic Alliance, promote change and democracy in Laos through peaceful dialogue between expatriates and the Laotian Communist government. The third type includes organizations dedicated to the political advancement of Hmong Americans. Ranging from formal organizations to informal local groups, they may be Republican or Democratic in orientation; some are organized on an ad hoc basis to respond to a particular election or political event, while others are organized for long-term political education and advancement

Hmong National Organization

The Hmong National Development, Inc., is the only known Hmong national organization with a headquarters in Washington, D.C. The group was incorporated in 1992 to serve as the voice of Hmong Americans, provide networking opportunities, and hold the annual Hmong National Conference. The conference serves as a forum for young Hmong American professionals to network, disseminate information, and formulate strategies and programs to address needs and issues in the Hmong American community at large.

Other Organizations

Hmong American organizations also include a wide variety of professional associations, language and cultural centers, student associations, clan- and district-based organizations, and human right groups.

Professional and Commercial Organizations
  Minnesota Hmong Chamber of Commerce
  Hmong Minnesota Bar Association
  Hmong Business Association of California (Fresno)
  Southeast Asian American Professional Association
    (Central California)
Arts, Language, and Cultural Associations
  Center for Hmong Arts and Talent
  Hmong American Institute for Learning (HAIL)
  Hmong Language Institute
  Hmong Cultural and Resource Center
Student Groups
  Hmong Student Inter-Collegiate Coalition (HSIC)
  Hmong Student Association of CSU Sacramento
  Hmong Student Association of CSU Stanislaus
Clan-Based Organizations
  Lo Society
  Thao Universal
  Hmong Her Association
  Yang Wang Meng Association of America
District-Based Organizations
  Hmong Mong Pheng Association
  Phou Pheng Association
Human Rights Groups
  Hmong-Lao Human Right Council
  Hmong International Human Rights Watch

Hmong American community organizations remain in flux in the early twenty-first century, with some being phased out and others growing to meet the many needs of the community. While some of the clan- and district-based organizations are similar to those of the early Chinese in California, most Hmong American organizations are unique to their experience in America.

Kou Yang

Further Reading
Hein, Jeremy. *From Vietnam, Laos, and Cambodia: A Refugee Experience in the United States.* New York: Twayne, 1995.

Hmong National Development, Inc. http://www.hndinc.org.

Southeast Asian American Mutual Assistance Association Directory. Washington, DC: Southeast Asia Action Resource Center, 2000.

Yang, Kou. "Hmong Diaspora of the Post-War Period." *Asian Pacific Migration Journal* 12:3 (2003): 271–300.

Political and Social Empowerment, Hmong American

The experience of political empowerment in the Hmong American community is unique and unanticipated, given the fact that it is one of the poorest and least educated Asian immigrant groups. Yet the Hmong became the first refugee group from Indochina to have an elected public official and have gone on to make steady progress in political participation despite their unprepared background and preoccupation with acculturation needs and issues. Since the election of Choua Lee to the St. Paul, Minnesota, Board of Education in 1992, more than a dozen other Hmong Americans have been elected to public office.

Participation

When Choua Lee, a twenty-two-year-old Hmong American woman, was elected to the Board of Education of the St. Paul Public Schools, she became not only the first former Hmong refugee, but also the first former refugee from Indochina, to hold elective office in the United States. It was an achievement that many in the Hmong community regarded as highly unlikely, if not impossible, at the time. Her election thus became a turning point in the political empowerment of the Hmong American community, marking its emergence into mainstream American politics and bringing a new sense of pride and identity. For many, that event marked a transition from refugee status to full membership in society, even though about half the community still have not become citizens. Younger members of the community began calling themselves Hmong Americans and began to exercise their rights and responsibilities as full-fledged residents, if not citizens.

A few young Hmong Americans followed Lee's example and ran for office in their own right. In Wisconsin, Ya Yang ran a successful campaign for a seat on the Wausau Board of Trustees and became the first Hmong to hold elected office in the state of Wisconsin. Until 2006, Yang also served on the Board of Supervisors of Marathon County, Wisconsin. In 1993, Thai Vue won a seat in the Board of Trustees of La Cross School District, Wisconsin. In 1996, Joe Bee Xiong was elected to the City Council of Eau Claire, Wisconsin, becoming the first Hmong American to reach that level in municipal government. Lormong Lor, the second Hmong to serve on an American city council, was appointed in 1994 to fill a vacant seat in Omaha, Nebraska, and won an election in his own right two years later. In the spring of 1997, Bon Xiong, a twenty-four-year-old Hmong American, was elected to the city council of Appleton, Wisconsin. In 2001, Shwaw Vang won a seat on the Board of Trustees of Madison School District, where the majority of the Asian students are Hmong.

Political participation in the Hmong community of California seems to be growing more slowly than in Minnesota and Wisconsin. Only two Hmong Americans ran campaigns—both unsuccessful—in the state during the mid-1990s, for seats on the Fresno City Council. The first member of the community to win elective office in California was attorney Paul C. Lo, who in 2001 won a seat on the Board of Trustees of the Merced School District; he served until the expiration of his term in 2006 and chose not to seek reelection.

A highly publicized election victory came in early 2002, when Mee Moua, a Hmong American woman and an attorney, was elected to the Minnesota Senate in a special election to fill a one-year term vacancy. She thus became the first former refugee from Indochina to win election to statewide office. In November 2002, a total of five Hmong Americans ran for public office, of whom three were elected: Mee Moua was reelected to her seat in the Minnesota Senate; Cy Thao won a seat in the Minnesota State Assembly; and Anthony K. Vang was elected to the Board of Trustees of Fresno Unified School District. Anthony K. Vang, a professor of education and longtime community leader of the Fresno Hmong American community, became the second Hmong American to hold elected office in California, winning a seat on the city's board of education in 2002; he was returned for a second term in 2006.

Since Joe Bee Xiong's 1996 election to the City Council of Eau Claire, Wisconsin, two more Hmong Americans have been elected to the same body. After Bee Xiong stepped down in 2000, Neng Lee was elected to the same seat. He, in turn, was replaced by Saidang Xiong in 2002. Meanwhile, the St. Paul community has maintained Hmong representation on its board of education continuously since 1992. Choua Lee served only one term and was replaced by Neil Thao, who served two terms before stepping down. Kazoua Kong-Thao was elected in 2003 to the seat previously held by Neil Thao. By the mid-2000s, a total of eight Hmong Americans had been elected to political office in Minnesota: four school trustees, two city council members, one state senator, and one state assembly member.

Empowerment

The Hmong American community reflects two extremes of political empowerment in the early twenty-first century. At one extreme, the achievements of community members in seeking and maintaining public office have been a somewhat surprising development, given the fact that Hmong were among the least culturally, educationally, and vocationally prepared communities to offer viable candidates for elective office. At the same time, more than half of foreign-born Hmong Americans have not become naturalized U.S. citizens, held back by language and cultural barriers. Moreover, according to the 2000 U.S. Census, more than half of all Hmong Americans were under the age of eighteen, making it unlikely that the majority of the population would become active participants in the American political process, and make their voices and votes count, for some time. Finally, the political empowerment of the Hmong American community is held back by the geographic dispersal of its small population, with fewer than 200,000 people residing in forty-nine of the fifty states.

The political strength of the community appears to lie in the persuasiveness of Hmong candidates and their ability to garner votes from non-Hmong. Among those eligible to vote, another strength is the ability to swing election outcomes at the municipal and even county level. Indeed, the Hmong swing vote was a central agenda item among community leaders at the 2003 Hmong National Conference in Washington, D.C., where mobilization in local elections was recognized as a vital means of political empowerment.

While Hmong Americans have come a long way politically and socially in the decades since refugees first began arriving in the mid-1970s, political empowerment will require overcoming the many social challenges still facing the community—including the language barrier, access to jobs and education, health care, poverty, discrimination, and prejudice. To fully exercise their rights and responsibilities as citizens—indeed to be motivated to *become* citizens—they will need to be educated further about the American political system, policies and issues that directly affect them, and government institutions and programs at the national, state, and local levels.

Kou Yang

Further Reading

Yang, Kou. "Hmong Americans: Needs, Problems and Community Development." *Hmong Studies Journal* 4 (2003): 1–24.
———. "The Hmong in America: Twenty-Five Years after the U.S. Secret War in Laos." *Journal of Asian American Studies* 4:2 (2001): 165–74.
———. "Choua Eve Lee." In *Making It in America: A Sourcebook on Eminent Ethnic Americans,* 197–98. Santa Barbara, CA: ABC-Clio, 2001.

Religion, Hmong American

Hmong Americans are about equally divided between Christians—both Protestants and Catholics—and those who practice traditional folk religions, with many of the former participating in ceremonies and rituals associated with traditional faiths.

Christianity

Most Hmong Christians either were brought to their faith by missionaries—who have been active in the Hmong homeland since the late eighteenth century—or converted to Christianity in deference to the individuals and groups that brought them to the United States or helped them settle once they got here. Conversion was smoothed by the fact that traditional Hmong folk religions have few institutions to resist the process. Although many were converted by Americans, most Hmong in the United States tend to worship in congregations of their own, a result of cultural differences, linguistic issues, and de facto settlement segregation.

Among the faiths most diligent in converting Hmong have been the Baptists, Catholics—the Hmong homeland in Laos was ruled for more than a century by Catholic France—Presbyterians, members of the Church of Christ, members of the Church of Jesus Christ of Latter-day Saints (Mormons), and Jehovah's Witnesses, though precise statistics on Hmong American adherents of each faith are unavailable. Conversion to Christianity has not been easy for many Hmong, since a number of traditional marital practices—including the paying of bride price, arranged marriage, and the marriage of minors—are discouraged by Christian sects, creating divisions within Hmong families between converts and followers of traditional folk faiths. Thus, many of the Hmong who converted to Christianity as part of the process of getting into the United States did so with little conviction and have since reverted to their old traditions.

Folk Religions

Unlike the other traditional faiths of Southeast Asia, Hmong folk religion is not organized or institutionalized, as the Hmong themselves were originally politically unconnected tribal peoples dispersed across a mountainous homeland. But while there are a number of different folk traditions—known collectively as spirit cults, or *neeb*—they share certain commonalities. Followers worship spirits, some associated with hearth and home, others with nature and natural forces, and still others with ancestors.

While Hmong faiths are not institutionalized, they do have religious specialists, known as shamans, who can be either male or female. These shamans are largely self-selected, usually because the person has had a profound spiritual experience while undergoing and surviving prolonged illness or suffering. Novice shamans go through an apprenticeship with a master shaman for two to three years. During this time, the novice shaman learns magical chants (*khawv koob*), and procedures for shamanistic rites, in addition to the names and natures of all *neeb* spirits that can cause fortune or misfortune. Hmong shamanism is an oral tradition, hence variation is commonly heard from shaman to shaman. When a Hmong family needs a shaman's services, it will select one from within its own clan—one who will travel from home to home performing rituals of healing, *ua neeb*, or for calling back a lost soul, *hu plig*. But shamans are becoming increasingly rare among Hmong Americans, as a younger generation receive a Western education and become acculturated to life in their new homeland. Moreover, having placed their faith in Western medicine, many younger Hmong Americans discredit the traditional healing practices that are so much a part of the shaman's duties.

As with most faiths, the rituals of traditional Hmong folk religion are connected to major life events. Birth rituals are particularly important in Hmong communities. Hmong, for example, believe that the placenta is a kind of jacket, the finest worn over the course of one's existence. When life comes to an end, the soul must return to put on that jacket or be doomed to wander eternity naked and alone. Thus, the Hmong perform a ritual after birth in which the placenta is buried beneath the home. Naming ceremonies are critical too, with one known as the *luu plig,* or soul calling, performed on the third day of a child's life. This ritual is said to bind the baby to his or her family and to the human race as a whole. Hmong believe that newborns are nonetheless susceptible to *dab* spirits and so are dressed in intricately embroidered hats to fool the *dab* into thinking that that the baby is a flower.

Dying and death (*kev mob kev tuag*) are understood as a natural part of one's life cycle. At birth all Hmong are given a mandate that determines the length of one's life, when the soul is required to leave the physical body and reside in the ancestral realm. Funerary rituals are generally performed at the home. However, in the United States and other Western countries in which Hmong refugees have resettled, death rituals are held at funeral parlors. A proper funerary ritual is critical in the Hmong worldview, as it ensures the prosperous afterlife for the deceased on the quest toward becoming an ancestor; otherwise, the soul can become a malevolent ghost.

The most important public ceremonies are those that surround the Hmong New Year, which usually comes in December. (As the Hmong follow a lunar calendar, the date varies according to the Western calendar.) The purpose of New Year ceremonies is to banish the evil influences of the old and to beckon good fortune in the new. In the "world renewed ritual," Hmong elders hold chickens while walking circles around young trees and chanting sacred incantations; clockwise rotations exorcise accumulated bad fortune and counterclockwise rotations bring good fortune. After the rotations, the chicken, whose blood is now believed to have absorbed the bad fortune, is sacrificed ritualistically.

Cultural Clashes

Just as Christianity looks askance at certain traditional marriage customs of the Hmong, so non-Hmong neighbors find the birth and death ceremonies of the Hmong a source of confusion and even disgust. Cultural clashes have arisen between the Hmong and other communities over animal sacrifice and the burying of placentas. Medical practitioners and health officials have also tried to ban Hmong mothers from taking the placenta home with them from the delivery hospital. In addition, because spirituality is connected with illness in the Hmong tradition, there are disagreements about treatment. Epileptics, for instance, are viewed by the Hmong as being endowed with potential spiritual gifts and so while a Western doctor would view the illness as a neurological disorder, to be treated with pharmaceuticals, a Hmong would seek the assistance of a *txiv neeb,* who would recommend the sacrifice of chickens and pigs to "call back the soul," since an epileptic seizure is considered to be the result of losing one's soul. Indeed, illnesses are generally associated with accidental encounters with *dab* spirits, hence sacrifices of dogs, cats, chickens, sheep, and other animals are attempts to get the *dab* to exit the human body and enter the sacrificial animal body, thus curing the sick.

But such cultural differences may become a thing of the past, even as Hmong folk practice customs lose their meaning and become formalistic rituals only. Some younger Hmong, acculturated to Western education and science, have come to see such practices as having little meaning in their lives, in a transition common to many immigrant groups from non-Western cultures.

Jonathan H.X. Lee and James Ciment

Further Reading

Fadiman, Anne. *The Spirit Catches You and You Fall Down: A Hmong Child, Her American Doctors, and the Collision of Two Cultures.* New York: Farrar, Straus and Giroux, 1997.

Faruque, Cathleen Jo. *Migration of Hmong to the Midwestern United States.* New York: University Press of America, 2002.

Koltyk, Jo Ann. *New Pioneers in the Heartland: Hmong Life in Wisconsin.* Boston: Allyn and Bacon, 1998.

Takaki, Ronald. *Strangers from a Different Shore: A History of Asian Americans.* Rev. ed. Boston: Little, Brown, 1998.

Religion, Laotian American

Lowland Laotians, as opposed to the tribal highland Hmong, have a diverse and complicated religious profile. The majority of the population is Buddhist, though belief in this pan-Asian faith is coextensive and ritually integrated with *phe*, an indigenous Lao cult. Smaller numbers of Lao practice the Hindu faith, a tradition brought by traders and settlers from India, and Christianity—both in its Catholic and Protestant manifestations—a result of extensive missionary activity in the country since the beginning of French colonial influence in the region in the nineteenth century. Islam and Baha'i are also present, as well as the local variations of spirit cults found among the Lao Theung and Lao Sung minorities.

Buddhism, in its Theravada ("Way of the Elders") form, reached Laos from China in the eighth century C.E., introduced by Mon Buddhist monks, and was widely practiced by the fourteenth, having become the official state religion of the Kingdom of Laos until its absorption into the French colonial empire as a protectorate at the end of the nineteenth century. Buddhism remained the dominant religion of the country through the roughly seventy years of French rule, as it did under the independent royal government in the 1950s and 1960s and the Communist Pathet Lao regime that has ruled the country since 1975. Most of the Laotians who fled to the United States in the 1970s and 1980s, largely to escape Communist rule, are followers of both Theravada Buddhism and the *phe* cult.

Buddhist *Wats*

At the heart of Lao Buddhism is the *wat,* or temple, which also functions as a religious center, school, public meeting hall, and site for community rituals and elections of local leaders. It is, in short, the main conduit of Lao moral and cultural socialization. In traditional settings, all male Lao are expected to enter monastic life as a monk or novice (*vihan*) prior to marriage. This was a tradition that virtually all male Lao Loum, the majority of the Laotian population, practiced up until the 1970s. Ordination was the most important way to earn merit, or *bun,* for himself, his parents, and his community, as the monk became the receiver of alms and merit-making rituals for others. Monks renounce the material world and rely on the generosity of people's donations of food and clothing. Lao women are active in preparing and presenting offerings of food and clothing to monks, who make their morning alms round through their communities carrying an alms bowl. The greatest merit-making ritual revolves around the construction of the Buddhist temple, which features a residence quarter for monks and novices, and a main hall where the Buddha statue (*sim*) is housed.

As a result of this, Laotian refugee communities are preoccupied with the establishment of a Lao Buddhist temple, not only to fulfill their religious needs, but also to create a center for Lao socialization and the moral education of young Laotian refugees. Hence, the effort to construct a Lao Buddhist temple is a major component of Lao refugee community stories in the diaspora throughout the United States—including Fort Worth; Rockford and Springfield, Illinois; Bakersfield, California; Seattle; Des Moines; and Portland, Oregon—as well as in Australia, Canada, and France. This can be a difficult process, however, because of the scarcity of monks in America. Hence, most communities rely on elders who are familiar with Lao Buddhism, rituals, and architecture. Financial constraints also make the building of the *wat* a challenge. Thus Lao often establish what are known in the Laotian American community as "apartment temples"—that is, impromptu spiritual centers created in a respected community member's home—which can meet the immediate religious needs of the community until a formal temple can be constructed and consecrated.

Buddhist practices of the Lao, although Theravadic, are carried out differently from those among their Southeast Asians neighbors, largely because they are embedded in indigenous Lao *phe* rituals and spirit beliefs. However, all Theravada Buddhists share some common practices and beliefs, such as Buddha, dharma, and *sangha,* as well as the observance of Wesak or Visakha, the celebration of the birth, enlightenment, and final passing of the historical Buddha Siddhartha. Lao Buddhism emphasizes the ritual dimension of Buddhism, with the theological component, as well as key rituals, supplied by *phe* values and moral education.

The influence of *phe* belief is seen in the Lao concern with maintaining the integrity of the person and his or her "souls," which is the basis of health or illness. Hence, *phe* rituals such as *soukhouan* rites ("calling back the souls") are held to celebrate rites of passage (such as marriage, pregnancy, birth, ordination), to mark the start of new life paths, or to help overcome illness. In the United States, this includes beginning college or celebrating someone's homecoming after a period of extended absence. This ritual ends with a tying of cotton threads to the wrist of the officiant, the celebrant, and others participating in the ritual, connecting their souls to their bodies. If this ritual is performed for someone leaving the community, the thread bracelet is worn for at least three days and nights as a reminder of the strength of the family to boost the departed's morale and to maintain solidarity with family and community. Therefore, *phe* rituals and beliefs dominate the health and therapeutic aspect of Lao religious life, while Buddhism dominates funerary rituals and merit-making activities.

Holidays and Observances

In the United States, many traditional religious holidays are observed, even though they may be altered to fit the immigrants' new way of life. Traditional agricultural rituals performed in conjunction with merit-making rituals at the Lao temple, for example, have been changed to meet the demands of new economic pursuits. Village festivals tied to specific dates or times of the year, such as Bun Bang Fai (rocket festival), or rituals associated with the monastic communities (such as ordination and merit making) may be moved across the calendar, as Lao monks may visit a Laotian American community only occasionally, with community members forced to take advantage of the opportunities to perform religious rituals and receive dharma lessons when they can. In addition, Laotian elders in the United States have had to assume the responsibility of religious specialists in the absence of monks, and audiotaped recordings of sermons by monks have been used as substitutes for real monks during ritual occasions. On a lighter note, meanwhile, American foods (such as Cola-Cola) have been adopted into Lao offerings.

In short, Lao Buddhism, and if available, a Lao Buddhist temple, have become critical influences for cultural preservation among the first generation of Lao Americans, many of whom grow up speaking English and have become largely acculturated to the American way of life and American value systems. Thus, Lao Bud-

dhism becomes a marker of community identity as well as individual ethnic identity.

Jonathan H.X. Lee

Further Reading

Swearer, Donald K. "Buddhism in Southeast Asia." In *The Religious Traditions of Asia: Religion, History, and Culture,* ed. Joseph M. Kitagawa. New York: MacMillan, 1989.

Takaki, Ronald. *Strangers from a Different Shore: A History of Asian Americans.* Rev. ed. Boston: Little, Brown, 1998.

Van Esterik, Penny. *Taking Refuge: Lao Buddhists in North America.* Monographs in Southeast Asian Studies. Tempe: Arizona State University Press, 1992.

Women, Hmong American

Coming from a largely rural culture in which men are socially predominant and boys are expected to be the future leaders, Hmong women in America continue to play largely subservient roles within their families and local communities. They also lag behind Hmong American men in terms of educational opportunity and achievement. Nevertheless, exposure to American culture and opportunities has begun to close the gap in terms of education and has allowed a minority of Hmong women to break out of assigned gender roles and into positions of community leadership.

Gender Role and Transition

Prior to their resettlement in the United States, Hmong women were generally perceived as passive, submissive, and obedient to their husbands and fathers. In Laos, Hmong men have traditionally played the primary roles as leaders in the community and as decision makers and providers in the home, while women have generally been assigned the secondary roles of wife, mother, and farm helper. Moreover, Hmong boys are trained to be effective leaders and provided the skills to make decisions, while girls are generally not so empowered. Sociologists suggest that such gender inequality is a product of the Hmong's largely rural background and patriarchal clan system.

In America, however, Hmong women in the twenty-first century have begun to overcome some of the traditional gender inequality, becoming more assertive politically and shrinking the gap in educational and socioeconomic attainment. While some Hmong women continue to live in America clinging to old social patterns and without assimilating, others have begun to enjoy American social mores and the support of their parents and families in pursuing education and careers. Among those who do not fully benefit from life in America, a sizable number do not have access to education, employment, and general information. There have also been a few high-profile cases of domestic abuse and polygamy within the Hmong American community.

Although the practice is rapidly changing, some families continue to show more support for their sons to pursue higher education than for their daughters. The socialization of daughters to be shy, submissive, and obedient has been loosely promoted within some Hmong American families, while others have strongly embraced equality between sons and daughters. The change is a function of three decades of adapting to life in the United States and the encouragement of American education, law, and other institutions. The shift in gender roles is evident in the election of Choua Lee to the St. Paul Board of Education in 1992 and Mee Moua to the Minnesota Senate in 2002. Lee, then a twenty-two-year-old Hmong American woman, became not only the first Hmong, but also the first former refugee from Indochina to be elected to political office in the United States. Moua, a thirty-two-year-old Hmong American woman, was the first Hmong and former Indochinese refugee to hold state office.

Hmong American women have also emerged as leaders in a number of community organizations. For example, both the president and executive directors of the Hmong National Development in 2003 were Hmong American women. KaYing Yang, the former executive director of Southeast Asia Resource Action Center, likewise is a Hmong American woman. Other well-known leaders include Pakou Hang, a community leader who

A small business owner who manufactures children's clothes seeks out Hmong women in her community for employment as seamstresses. The Hmong refer to themselves as M'yeo, or "embroidery people," because of their strong tradition of textile crafts. *(James A. Sugar/National Geographic/Getty Images)*

was awarded the Hubert Humphrey Leadership Award in 2003; MayKao Hang, director of the Adult Service Division of Ramsey County, Minnesota; and Ilen Her, executive director of the Asian Pacific Minnesotan Council.

Hmong American women are also making names for themselves among the ranks of professionals. Pafoua Yang is a physician in Milwaukee, Wisconsin, and Phoua Xiong is a physician in St. Paul, Minnesota. Dia Cha, an associate professor at St. Cloud State University in Minnesota is the first Hmong American anthropologist. Za Vue is a cartoonist for Disney Films. Doualy Saykaothao is a reporter for National Public Radio, and Zoua Vang was a television anchorperson for KSEE 24 in Fresno, California. Mai Neng Moua is the editor of *Bamboo Among the Oaks* (2002), the first anthology of Hmong American writers; she also heads the Hmong American Institute for Learning. Although nearly half of Hmong American attorneys are women, only two out of eight Hmong American elected officials in 2003 were women.

Another area in which Hmong American women are making notable progress is their collective leadership in forming Hmong American women associations to provide needed services to the entire community. Among these organizations are the Hmong American Women's Association of Milwaukee, Hmong American Women's Association of Fresno, Women's Association of Hmong and Lao (St. Paul), and the Association for the Advancement of Hmong Women in Minnesota.

Gender Equality

Despite such conspicuous progress, high-achieving Hmong American women such as these remain more the exception than the rule. According to the 2000 U.S. Census, Hmong American women aged twenty-five and older continued to lag behind their male counterparts in education: 56.8 percent of Hmong American women had no formal schooling, compared to 33.5 percent of Hmong men; 34.4 percent of Hmong American men completed a high school education, compared to only 20.1 percent of women; and only 7.0 percent of Hmong American women had a college education, compared to 16.5 percent of men. Sociologists debate whether the gap in educational achievement is attributable to the fact that, in their homeland in Laos, Hmong men had more access to early education or to the perpetuation of the old cultural emphasis on education for boys rather than girls among Hmong Americans—or both.

On the positive side, the number of Hmong American female college students in 2004 reached virtual parity with Hmong American male students. Further reflecting the transition, a majority of officers in the Hmong American Student Association today are female.

All in all, gender roles in the Hmong American community have already begun to change. While many Hmong American women continue to play the role of mother, wife, cook, and family manager, many have added new roles and responsibilities as members of the workforce, both blue-collar and professional. Likewise, the role of family leader, decision maker, and provider is increasingly assigned to both genders or shared.

Kou Yang

Further Reading

"Khoua Her's Story." *Hmong Times,* November 16, 2000.

Pfeifer, Mark, and Kou Yang. *Profile of Hmong American Education Attainment.* Washington, DC: Hmong National Development, 2004.

Yang, Kou. "Choua Eve Lee." In *Making It in America: A Sourcebook on Eminent Ethnic Americans,* 197–98. Santa Barbara, CA: ABC-Clio, 2001.

The Malaysian American Experience: History and Culture

As ethnically diverse as their homeland, the relatively small number of Malaysian Americans tend to identify themselves by the ethnic group—Chinese, Malay, and, to a lesser extent, Indian—of which they are a member. At the same time, a sense of Malaysian nationalism has become a more important component of Malaysian American identity in recent years. Despite their diverse ethnic backgrounds, Malaysian Americans—of which there were an estimated 40,000 by the year 2000—share several attributes, including higher-than-average levels of education and income.

Background History— The Homeland

The diversity of the Malaysian homeland is a product of its geography. Situated astride a critical strait connecting the Indian Ocean and the South China Sea, Malaysia has long been home not only to ethnic Malays but also to large communities of Chinese and Indian merchants, most of whom settled in urban areas. Arab traders brought the Islamic faith to the region beginning in the fifteenth century, converting much of the ethnic Malay population, though most Chinese held to their native faiths of Buddhism and Taoism. European traders came to the region beginning in the sixteenth century, with the British gradually pushing out competitors and establishing a protectorate over the region in the 1880s. After a drawn-out Communist-nationalist insurgency beginning in the late 1940s, the independent Federation of Malaysia (consisting of Malaya, Singapore, Sarawak, and Sabah) was established in 1963. Two years later, the predominantly Chinese city of Singapore unilaterally separated from the federation. While the various communities of Malaysia have largely lived at peace with one another since that time, conflicts have arisen from time to time. The major issues have been Chinese Malay concerns about the role of Islam in government and Malay resentment about Chinese dominance of the national economy. As of the early 2000s, approximately two-thirds of Malaysians were of Malay background, a quarter of Chinese extraction, and the remainder largely of Indian origin.

The American Experience

Living on international sea-lanes, the Malays have long been an ocean-faring people. A handful of Malay sailors are believed to have settled in American port cities by the middle of the nineteenth century, with a tiny community coalescing in Boston. Military records indicate that four Malays served in the American Civil War, two in the Union Navy and two in its Confederate counterpart. By the early twentieth century, British Malaya, as it was then called, produced a large portion of America's tin and rubber, with some British colonials from Malaysia settling in the United States in connection with that trade. The Japanese conquest of the region in World War II sent small numbers of Malaysians, particularly of Chinese ethnic origin, to the United States. Greater numbers of Malaysians—though still just in the dozens—came to the United States (specifically, Fort Leavenworth, Kansas) to receive counterinsurgency training in the 1950s. Most of these were ethnic Malays, as the rebellion was largely a rural one where that group predominated. Some of the trainees eventually returned to the United States and settled permanently in the 1960s.

Another source of Malaysian immigrants in the 1960s were the brides of U.S. soldiers. During the Vietnam War, some GIs took their "rest and rehabilitation" leaves in that nearby Southeast Asian country. A third factor in Malaysian immigration to America has been education. Malaysia, with its English-speaking population and high-quality British-style primary and secondary educational institutions, had always sent significant numbers of graduates to British universities. But America's much larger higher-education infrastructure offered more opportunity for admission, and, beginning in the 1970s, many Malaysians began opting to attend U.S. colleges, universities, and graduate schools. When British universities began charging significantly higher fees to foreign nationals in the 1980s, even more Malaysian students were drawn to the United States—a flow that increased as Malaysia's economy grew rapidly in the closing years of the century. By the early 2000s, roughly 6,000 to 7,000 Malaysians were studying annually at American institutions of higher education. Like other student immigrant groups, many young Malaysians—recognizing the economic opportunities, enjoying the lifestyle, or having married Americans—have opted to remain in the United States after completing their schooling.

As of the early 2000s, the overall population of Malaysian Americans had climbed to more than 40,000. While there are no statistics available that break out the ethnic origins of community members, most immigration experts believe that the better-educated and more economically prosperous ethnic Chinese Malays are represented in larger numbers than their portion of the population of Malaysia itself. The largest population of Malaysian Americans live in California, with significant communities also located in New York, Texas, Illinois, Virginia, and Hawaii. Because their numbers are so small, however, the U.S. Census tends to lump Malaysian Americans into the category of "Other Asian." This makes it difficult to measure average income and education levels, though it is believed that both correspond with general Asian trends. Roughly 40 percent of members of the "Other Asian" category had bachelor's degrees or higher (compared with about 25 percent for the U.S. population as a whole), with male and female incomes of $36,000 and $30,000, respectively (compared to $37,000 and $27,000 for all Americans), according to the 2000 census.

As in their homeland, most Malaysian Americans identify and associate with their own ethnic group. Chinese Malays tend to see themselves as Chinese, practicing various Chinese faiths and celebrating the traditional holidays of the Chinese calendar, while ethnic Malays follow the Islamic calendar. Far from the centers of Islamic culture and living in an ethnically diverse country, most ethnic Malays are not as orthodox in their beliefs and practices as the Muslims of the Middle East. This is even more the case for the Westernized Malays of the diaspora, including those in the United States. Indian Malays tend to be Hindu and follow the Hindu calendar.

Despite these deep differences, Malaysian Americans have certain things in common. One is their unique version of English and the other is their eclectic cuisine, which blends the culinary traditions of China, India, and Southeast Asia—though Muslim Malays generally eschew pork and Hindu Malays beef. As with other immigrants from ethnically divided homelands, living abroad has also tended to blur some of these divisions—as well as enhance the sense of nationalism—among Malaysian Americans. Many Malaysian American university student groups, for example, hold celebrations of Malaysian culture and nationalism on August 31, the country's independence day. The Malaysia-America Society, founded in 1967 and with a membership base numbering in the hundreds, promotes Malaysian culture through a variety of community activities, festivities, and programs, including exchanges between the homeland and the United States.

Justin Corfield and James Ciment

Further Reading

Sodhy, Pamela. "Malaysia and the United States in the 1980s." *Asian Survey* 27:10 (October 1987): 1074–94.

Stewart, Ian. *The Mahathir Legacy: A Nation Divided, a Region at Risk.* Crows Nest, Australia: Allen and Unwin, 2003.

The Mongolian American Experience: History and Culture

Mongolian Americans hail from one of the most isolated, rural, and traditional countries in the world, and form one of the tiniest of Asian American communities. Largely closed off from emigration to America by their geography and a Soviet-dominated Communist government until the early 1990s, Mongolians have trickled into the United States in the years since. Because of the small size of the community, Mongolians have been forced to settle in areas where few other Mongolians live. Still, most are well educated and have achieved relative economic prosperity.

Heavily influenced by their huge neighbor to the south, Mongolians follow many Chinese customs. Most are Buddhist in religious affiliation and follow the teachings of Tibetan lamas (spiritual leaders and teachers). Proud of their history as great conquerors, Mongolian Americans try to maintain their cultural traditions, including a love for traditional song, dance, tales, and myths. Mongolian families are strong and usually extended in size. For traditional Mongolians, duty and obedience to family generally come before individual expression and identity, though this is changing among American-born Mongolian children.

Immigration History

Mongolian Americans are a relatively new community, virtually nonexistent before World War II. In the wake of that conflict came a small wave of so-called Kalmyk, or Western, Mongolians, a subgroup that had moved to Russia before that country's Communist revolution in 1917. Fleeing that upheaval, many settled in Eastern Europe. When that region fell to Communism after World War II, roughly 1,000 Kalmyks were admitted as refugees to the United States. From that time until the early 1990s, very few Mongolians were able to immigrate to the United States. With the fall of Communism in Mongolia in the early 1990s, however, the gates to the country were opened. While most Mongolians immigrated to an economically booming China, a few hundred a year made their way to the United States,

largely to improve their economic situation or to obtain higher education. According to the U.S. Census, there were approximately 3,500 Mongolian Americans in 2000.

The Kalmyks largely settled primarily in New Jersey and the Philadelphia area, aided by local refugee support organizations. Many of the Kalmyks and their children have since moved out of the region and, joined by more recent immigrants, have settled throughout the United States—from New York, Maryland, West Virginia, and Florida to Texas, New Mexico, Arizona, and California. Cities with Mongolian populations include San Francisco, Los Angeles, Chicago, New York City, and Washington, D.C.

It is difficult to characterize the economic status of the Mongolian American population with any precision. Like other Asian American groups, they enjoy higher-than-average education and income levels. There is no clear occupational pattern, however, with members of the community working variously as professionals, entrepreneurs, and skilled and unskilled laborers.

While their small numbers have made it difficult for Mongolians to establish their own neighborhoods and communities, many immigrants—coming from a rural, formerly Communist-dominated country—have had a difficult time assimilating to American life. As in the case of other immigrant groups, tensions have arisen between the immigrant generation steeped in the values of their traditional culture and the U.S.-born generation, many of whom have abandoned part or all of those values and have intermarried with non-Mongolians. The latter trend, in particular, upsets the strong Mongolian tradition of arranged marriages, as does the idea of Mongolian American women working outside the home.

Culture and Heritage

Still, many younger Mongolians are rediscovering their heritage and, along with their parents' generation, maintain a close connection with their culture, particularly its almost mystical attachment to nature. In Mongolian culture, women are largely responsible for maintaining the traditions, customs, and history of the community. Astrology—based on the Chinese calendar—plays an important role in traditional Mongolian culture. Mongolian Americans often consult astrologers and astrological charts before making key decisions in their lives, such as getting married, accepting a job, moving to a new location, or buying a house.

Weddings are perhaps the most important event in the Mongolian American community, filled with highly stylized ritual and ceremony. Preparations for the wedding, which include formal visits and gift exchanges between the two families, occur over an extended period of time, with the wedding date itself carefully chosen within the astrological calendar. Also central to the Mongolian American community are its cultural holidays, some of which are unique and some of which —such as the Lunar New Year—they share with other East Asian Americans. Among the former is Tsagaan Sar (White Month), an ancient Mongolian celebration that marks the passage from winter to spring, and the Chinggis Khan (Gengis Khan) Ceremony, held in March to commemorate the exploits of the Mongolian leader who conquered much of Asia in the twelfth and thirteenth centuries. The beginning of summer sees the commemoration of the Buddha, or Shagja-muni in Mongolian, when believers make offerings at Buddhist shrines to ward away malevolent spirits. During such ceremonies, Mongolian Americans may dress in traditional garb such as the *del*—a long, one-piece woolen gown highlighted by brightly covered collar and sash— the *gul*, or leather riding boot, and fox-skin hat, or *loovuz*. Mongolian Buddhists, like their Tibetan counterparts, generally follow the teachings of the lamas, or religious teachers. By the early 2000s, there were five Mongolian Buddhist temples in the United States, three in New Jersey, one in New York, and another in Philadelphia, each presided over by lamas and monks.

Many Mongolian Americans maintain close ties with their homeland. Working through their only national political organization, the Mongol American Association, the community seeks to foster the budding democracy and economic reform in their homeland by lobbying the U.S. government to offer aid and support. Among the most important Mongolian American activists promoting human rights in Mongolia is scholar Djab Nominov Burchinov, the author of a critical work on the history and struggle of the Kalmyk Mongolians. The main Mongolian American publication is the newsletter *Mongol Tolbo*, produced by the Mongol American Cultural Association and devoted to both cultural and political news of the homeland. Other notable Mongolian American institutions include the Kalmyk American Cultural Association, dedicated to preserving that community's unique heritage; the Mongolia Society, which publishes several scholarly journals, including *Mongolian Studies*, *Journal of the Mongolia Society*, and *Mongolia Survey*; and the U.S.-Mongolia Business Council, which promotes economic ties between the two countries.

Whether Mongolians can achieve socioeconomic success in America while preserving their cultural heritage remains a major challenge, according to community leaders. While Mongolia's rich history and culture offer inspiration, the tiny size of the community, its dispersal across the United States, and its relative youth—more than 80 percent of Mongolian Americans are under the age of thirty-five—makes it a particularly difficult one.

James Ciment

Further Reading

Baatar, Ts. "Social and Cultural Change in the Mongol-American Community." *Anthropology of East Europe Review* 17:2 (Autumn 1999).

Mongol American Cultural Association. http://www.maca-usa .org.

Rubel, Paula G. *The Kalmyk Mongols: A Study in Continuity and Change*. Bloomington: Indiana University Press, 1967.

Myanmar Americans
See The Burmese American Experience

The Nepalese American Experience: History and Culture

The history of Nepalese immigration and settlement in North America is recent in comparison to other communities that form the larger South Asian diaspora. Nepalese immigration rates into the United States have increased gradually due to changes in immigration law in the 1950s and especially due to the introduction of the Diversity Immigration Visa program (or Green Card Lottery) in 1990.

Immigration History

Permanent resident status was granted to one Nepalese in 1952 and to roughly 2,000 annually in the early 2000s. Official data from the former U.S. Immigration and Naturalization Service indicates that the number of Nepalese entering as immigrants was 56 from 1952 to 1967; 1,517 from 1968 to 1989; and 3,203 from 1990 to 1999. Nepalese immigration rates became even steeper in the first few years of the twenty-first century, increasing from 617 in 2000 to 949 in 2001 and 1,138 in 2002. By the mid-2000s, more than 2,000 Nepalese were being admitted to the United States annually. These numbers do not include legal and illegal workers, students, scholars, exchange visitors, tourists, businesspeople, international job holders, and others. The actual number of Nepalese in the United States and Canada is estimated to be more than 60,000, many of them students.

The relatively late arrival and small number of Nepalese immigrants can largely be attributed to Nepal's relative isolation from foreign influence, a condition that enabled the country to maintain a substantial degree of independence during the colonial period but also prevented economic development and social modernization in the postcolonial era. Other factors affecting immigration include the restrictive internal policies of the Nepalese government, the lack of opportunity for linguistic and cultural exchange between Nepal and the United States, and the absence of diplomatic relations between Nepal and the United States prior to 1947.

Nepalese immigration was further hampered by U.S. immigration and naturalization policies. The national origins system effectively restricted Nepalese entry into the United States prior to 1952. The McCarran-Walter Act of 1952 altered several aspects of the national origins system by eliminating exclusionary acts against Asian nationalities and instituting limits on immigration from the territorial region of the "Asia-Pacific Triangle." Although these provisions made it possible for Nepalese to enter the country, their immigration rates were restricted in favor of larger countries on the Asian continent, such as India, China, Pakistan, and South Korea. The Immigration and Nationality Act of 1965, which completely abolished the national origins system in favor of a quota and preference system based on the priority of family reunification, did not immediately bring about a dramatic increase in Nepalese immigration, as it did in other Asian immigrations, because of the small size of the initial Nepalese American community. The cycle of chain immigration and sponsorship did not begin to play an important role in shaping the Nepalese American community until the mid- to late 1990s.

The early wave of Nepalese immigrants who arrived prior to the mid-1980s consisted of highly educated professionals such as doctors, lawyers, professors, engineers, and technicians. The second-generation children of these early immigrants are now establishing families of their own. Many of the immigrants who arrived after the mid-1980s do not have the same professional qualifications as their predecessors. With increased numbers of Nepalese already in the United States, lower-skilled immigrants have been allowed in based on family connections. A higher percentage of these later immigrants are semiskilled or unskilled workers who earn subsistence wages, largely in the service industry. The number of Nepalese students more than doubled during the five-year period from 1999 to 2004, with 4,384 studying in various American universities and colleges in 2003–2004, an 18 percent increase over the previous year.

Demographics, Culture, and Community Life

Among the several ethnic and linguistic divisions within the Nepalese American community are the Bahun-Chhetri, Newar, Bhotia, and Tarai or Madhese. The Bahun-Chhetri, who come from the central hill country of Nepal, and the Newars, who come mainly from Kathmandu Valley, are the two largest groups in America, each accounting for 40–45 percent of the total. The Tarai, who come from the southern plains of Nepal, constituted the third largest group until the late 1980s, when the Bhotia from the Himalayan highlands began to immigrate in large numbers. The Bhotia now constitute about 10 percent of the total, while the Tarai account for about 5 percent. Aside from dialectical and cultural distinctions, the main difference among the different immigrant groups is that those from the more urban Kathmandu region tend to be better educated, more fluent in English, and more acculturated to modern Western society. In general, Nepalese culture bears many similarities to that of its huge neighbor to the south, India. Most Nepalese practice Hinduism, though a small minority are Buddhist. The main holidays in the Nepalese calendar are Buddhist or Hindu, while Nepalese society is divided into the traditional caste structure of Hindu India.

Despite internal ethnic divisions, the Nepalese American community—because of its small size—has worked to strengthen the importance of a common Nepalese national identity. Nepalese American community associations operate in a number of states and cities, particularly areas of high concentration such as California, Washington, D.C., New York, Boston, Atlanta, and Texas. Organizations such as the Association of Nepalese in the Americas (ANA), the Nepalese Americas Council (NAC), the America-Nepal Friendship Society, the Alliance for Democracy and Human Rights in Nepal, and the Nepalese Women's Association, among others, promote a sense of affinity across lines of division within the community.

Through its various associations, the Nepalese American community is actively engaged in the preservation of the cultural and linguistic heritage of the homeland, particularly through cultural education programs among the younger generations of the diaspora. It also maintains connections to the home country through targeted interventions in business investment, economic development, and political transformation in Nepal. The Non-Resident Nepali Association has urged the government of Nepal to formalize the legal provisions for Nepalese living abroad by constitutionally defining their status as Non-Resident Nepalis. This dual-citizenship system, which is found in various forms in Asian countries such as India, Pakistan, Bangladesh, and Sri Lanka, would enable Nepali Americans to play a larger role in the political and economic life of Nepal from their positions in the United States and other countries of settlement.

Haley Duschinski

Further Reading
Association of Nepalis in the Americas. http://www.anaonline.org.

Hedrick, Basil C., and Anne K. Hedrick. *Historical and Cultural Dictionary of Nepal.* Metuchen, NJ: Scarecrow, 1972.

Leonard, Karen Isaksen. *The South Asian Americans.* Westport, CT: Greenwood, 1997.

Shrestha, M.N., ed. *Nepalese American Perspectives.* Cincinnati, OH: Association of Nepalese in Midwest America, 1995.

Nepalese Americas Council. http://www.nepalcouncil.org.

U.S. Department of Homeland Security. *Yearbook of Immigration Statistics 2003.* Washington, DC: Government Printing Office, 2004.

The Pacific Islander American Experience: History and Culture

Pacific Islander Americans are a diverse group, with roots in dozens of island archipelagos—some independent countries, others possessions of European nations, and still others colonies, or in the case of Hawaii, a state, within the United States. Pacific Islanders fall into three basic ethnic categories: Polynesian (Hawaiians, Samoans, and Tongans being the main groups), Micronesian (Guamanians or Chamorros, Marshall Islanders, and Palauans), and Melanesians (the only significant group in America being persons from Fiji). While Pacific Islanders have been present on the U.S. mainland since the nineteenth century, major immigration and migration did not begin until after World War II. More generally, Pacific Islander Americans can be divided into two basic groups—those who have migrated or immigrated to the American mainland and those who live in Hawaii or territories belonging to the United States. The former tend to follow the acculturation patterns of other immigrants; the latter retain more of their traditional way of life.

Population and Immigration History

According to the 2000 U.S. Census, there were 398,835 persons living in the United States and its overseas territories who identified themselves as Pacific Islanders. In addition, there were 475,579 persons who identified themselves as part Pacific Islander. Of those who identified themselves as purely Pacific Islander, the largest group by far was Native Hawaiian, at 140,652, or just over one-third of the total. Behind the Hawaiians were two other groups that live on islands or island chains that were territories of the United States: Samoans, at 91,029, though a small part of this figure represents persons from the independent nation of Samoa (formerly known as Western Samoa); and Guamanians, or Chamorros, from the island of Guam, at 58,240. Of the immigrant Pacific Islander groups, the largest was that from Tonga, at 27,713. All other Pacific Islander groups

were much smaller. With the exception of Fijians, at 9,796, Marshall Islanders, at 5,479, and Palauans, at 2,228—the latter two being U.S. trust territories until the 1980s and 1990s, respectively—all single island chain Pacific Islander American groups numbered less than 1,000 persons each.

Because they come from so many different places with such different histories, it is difficult to generalize about Pacific Islander immigration history. Indeed, most Hawaiians, Samoans, and Guamanian never immigrated to America at all. Hawaii became a part of

Students of diverse backgrounds, photographed here in the 1950s, epitomize the melting pot of modern Hawaii. In addition to Native Hawaiians and whites, the population includes other Pacific Islander peoples, East and Southeast Asians, and mixed-race residents. *(B. Anthony Stewart/National Geographic/Getty Images)*

the United States through annexation in 1893; Guam was seized from Spain during the Spanish-American War in 1898, and Samoa (later American Samoa) was annexed in 1899. In addition, a number of other islands became trustees of the United States after being seized from Japan during and immediately after World War II. These included the Marshall Islands (a U.S. trust territory from 1947 to 1986); the Marianas (the Northern Marianas became a U.S. trust territory in 1947 and a U.S.-administered commonwealth in 1986; while Guam has remained a U.S. territory through the present day); and the Caroline Islands, or Micronesia (the Federated States of Micronesia were a U.S. trust territory from 1947 to 1986, while Palau was a U.S. trust territory from 1947 to 1994). Thus, when one speaks of Pacific Islander settlement in the United States, it can mean either migration or immigration or not moving at all.

Small numbers of Hawaiians and Guamanians made their way to the mainland United States (Guamanians also migrated to Hawaii) beginning in the early part of the twentieth century, though a few Pacific Islanders, usually those working in the maritime industry, had settled in U.S. ports, most notably San Francisco, in the late nineteenth century. Most of the early Pacific Islander migrants to the mainland ended up working in the agricultural fields of California and other Western states. The major influx of Pacific Islanders from islands under U.S. control came after World War II, usually among persons who worked for the American armed forces or married military personnel. Most of these settled in urban areas, largely in Hawaii or on the West Coast. Pacific Islander immigrants from non-U.S. territories began arriving in measurable numbers following the Immigration and Nationality Act of 1965, which ended national quotas and allowed for larger numbers of non-European peoples to enter the United States legally.

As of the early 2000s, of the vast majority of Pacific Islander Americans living in the fifty American states, about 75 percent live in the West (including Hawaii). In descending order, the states with the largest Pacific Islander populations were California (116,961), Hawaii (113,539), Washington (23,953), and Utah (15,145). The only non-Western state with more than 10,000 Pacific Islanders was Texas (14,434). Of metropolitan areas, Honolulu had the most Pacific Islanders, at 58,130; the Los Angeles–Long Beach metropolitan area followed with 21,007; and San Diego had 10,613. Wherever they live, Pacific Islanders represent a tiny minority, usually dispersed among the population at large, though sometimes settling near Filipino and other Asian American communities. Of major American cities, the one with the largest percentage of Pacific Islanders is Salt Lake City, Utah, at about 2 percent. The Mormon Church, headquartered in the Utah capital, actively proselytizes in the Pacific basin. Still, even in their home state, pureblood Native Hawaiians represent, at less than 7 percent, a minority of the population, though persons with mixed Hawaiian and other ancestry account for another 20 percent of the population.

Education and Economics

In terms of socioeconomic indices, different Pacific Islander groups vary widely, with those from Guam or Hawaii usually scoring better than other communities. According to the 2000 U.S. Census, adult Native Hawaiians and Guamanians, at 15.2 and 14.3 percent, respectively, were far more likely than Fijians and Tongans, at 8.8 and 8.6 percent, respectively, to have college degrees or higher, though all lagged behind the overall U.S. figure of 24.4 percent. (All figures cited here are based on the 2000 census and apply only to the fifty states, the District of Columbia, and Puerto Rico, not to U.S. territories in the Pacific, including Guam and Samoa.) Most Pacific Islanders are also proficient in English, a legacy of being under American rule or, in the case of Tongans and Fijians, British rule, for generations. Some 56.2 percent of Pacific Islanders spoke English at home, while another 29.2 percent spoke English "very well." Again, this varied among different groups, with some 83 percent of Native Hawaiians speaking English at home and just 16.3 percent of Fijians doing so, though fully three-quarters of the latter group spoke the language "very well."

Native Hawaiians and Guamanians, at 26.4 percent, were also more likely to be in managerial or professional positions than other Pacific Islanders; Fijians were their closest rivals at 19 percent. The figure for the U.S. population as a whole was just over one-third. With median household incomes of $49,680 and $49,122 respectively, Hawaiians and Guamanians stood just below the overall U.S. median of $50,046. Tongans and Fijians followed with median family incomes of just over $46,000. Poverty rates were more varied. Roughly 15 percent of Native Hawaiians fell below the official poverty line, compared to 13.7 percent of Guamanians, 20.2 percent of Samoans, and fully 38.3 percent of Marshall Islander Americans. Indeed, this tiny group lagged significantly behind all Pacific Islanders in all major socioeconomic categories.

Family, Faith, and Culture

Because they come from so many different backgrounds—and because they are divided between those who have immigrated to the United States and those who live in a territory that is now part of the United States—it is also difficult to generalize about Pacific Islander culture and lifestyle. In terms of religion, most Pacific Islanders tend to be Protestant, a legacy of decades and even centuries of missionary activity. The one major exception is Guamanians, who are largely Catholic, a legacy of being under Spanish rule for several centuries. Many Pacific Islanders, however, retain remnants of their traditional polytheistic religions in traditional music and dance. (For more information on the culture of major Pacific Islander groups, see their entries in this section.)

While most Pacific Islanders live in nuclear households, they tend to have more children than the U.S. population as a whole. While the median U.S. household has roughly 2.6 persons, the median Pacific Islander household has 3.6. Again, however, the latter figure varied significantly among subgroups, from 3.2 persons among Native Hawaiians to 5.3 among Tongan Americans. Pacific Islanders tend to be younger than Americans generally, with the median age of the former being 27.6 years and that of the latter 35.4. Within the Pacific Islander American population, the median ranged from 31.8 years among Native Hawaiians to just 23.2 among Tongan Americans. Although they tend to live in nuclear households, Pacific Islanders maintain close ties to extended kin. In some traditional cultures, for example, the mother's brother often serves as his nephews' and nieces' legal guardian rather than the father, as many Pacific Islander cultures are matrilineal, passing on family names and property through the mother's line rather than the father's. Since most Pacific Islander cultures frown on marital breakup, the percentage of divorced persons among many Pacific Islander groups run at rates less than half that of the 9.7 percent for all Americans. The exceptions are the more acculturated Hawaiians and Guamanians, whose divorce rates stood at 10.3 and 7.7 percent, respectively, in 2000.

In general, Pacific Islander Americans can be divided into two general groups—those who have immigrated or migrated to the U.S. mainland and those who continue to live in Hawaii or their U.S.-administered home islands. The former tend to resemble other immigrant groups; they tend to live in large urban areas, with older island-born parents retaining more of their native culture and their U.S.-born children being more acculturated to the American way of life. In the islands, many Pacific Islander Americans live in rural communities, where they retain more of their traditional way of life, though American culture, disseminated through mainland media and U.S.-style educational institutions, is eroding old customs.

James Ciment

Further Reading

Barkan, Elliott Robert. *Asian and Pacific Islander Migration to the United States: A Model of New Global Patterns.* Westport, CT: Greenwood, 1992.

Inkelas, Karen Kurotsuchi. *Racial Attitudes and Asian Pacific Americans: Demystifying the Model Minority.* New York: Routledge, 2006.

Okihiro, Gary Y. *Island World: A History of Hawai'i and the United States.* Berkeley: University of California Press, 2008.

Spickard, Paul, Joanne L. Rondilla, and Debbie Hippolite Wright, eds. *Pacific Diaspora: Island Peoples in the United States and Across the Pacific.* Honolulu: University of Hawai'i Press, 2002.

Pacific Islander Americans
Alphabetical Entries

Chamorros

After Native Hawaiians and Samoans, Guamanians—or Chamorros, native people of the Mariana Islands—are the largest Pacific Islander community in the United States. Chamorros are divided into two groups: those who live on the island of Guam and, to a lesser extent, those who live on the other islands of the Northern Marianas. While the Northern Marianas came under U.S. rule after World War II, Guam has been an American territory since 1898, when it was seized from Spain during the Spanish-American War. The other major groups are those who have immigrated to Hawaii and the U.S. mainland in the years since annexation. Guam is the largest and southernmost of the Mariana Islands, located about 3,400 miles (5,500 kilometers) west-southwest of the Hawaiian Islands in the Western Pacific Ocean.

Guam was first settled by peoples originating in Indonesia about 2000 B.C.E. The first European to encounter the island was Ferdinand Magellan on his pioneering around-the-globe expedition in the early 1500s. Magellan claimed the island for Spain, which used it as a provisioning stop on transpacific journeys. Much of the native population died from disease and in rebellions against Spanish rule. Seized by the United States in 1898, it was briefly occupied by the Japanese in World War II, before returning to U.S. control. Since 1950, Guamanians have been citizens of the United States; since 1973, they have had a nonvoting representative in the U.S. Congress. They pay no federal taxes and cannot vote for president.

Chamorros are a Micronesian people, related to other groups in the Marianas Islands and other archipelagos in the Western Pacific. The vast majority of Chamorros—about 85 percent—are Catholic, a legacy of Spanish rule; most of the rest are members of various Protestant denominations or the Church of Jesus Christ of Latter-day Saints (Mormons). Chamorros speak their own language, akin to other Micronesian tongues, but the vast majority are also fluent in English. According to the 2000 U.S. Census, roughly 56 percent of Chamorros in the United States speak English at home, while another roughly 28 percent said they speak it "very well."

The population of Guam is approximately 155,000 according to the 2000 census (173,000 according to a 2007 estimate); in addition, roughly 85,000 people inhabit the other islands of the Northern Marianas, of whom about one-third, or 28,000, are Chamorro by ethnicity. Some 35 percent of the population of Guam, or 55,000, is Chamorro; other major ethnic groups on the island include Filipinos, other Pacific Islanders, whites, and Asians. According to the 2000 census, there were about the same number of Chamorros living in Hawaii or on the U.S. mainland, accounting for about 15 percent of the country's overall Pacific Islander population. In addition, another 90,000 or so persons listed themselves as partially of Chamorro origin in the 2000 census. California has the largest population of Chamorros in the fifty states, followed by Hawaii and Washington State. Metropolitan areas with significant Chamorro populations include Los Angeles, San Francisco, Honolulu, Seattle, and Washington, D.C.

Chamorros have been emigrating in small numbers to Hawaii and the U.S. mainland since the beginning of the twentieth century, though large-scale immigration did not begin until after World War II. While most Chamorros have migrated to Hawaii and the United States in search of educational and economic opportunities, a significant number came to work for the military or government. (Guam is home to the largest U.S. military installation in the Western Pacific.)

Chamorros generally lag behind the American population in educational achievement, though they rank second to Native Hawaiians among Pacific Islanders. While less than 20 percent of Americans over the age of twenty-five lacked a high school diploma in 2000, the figure for Chamorros was 22.2 percent—compared to 21.7 percent for Pacific Islanders overall. In higher education, 14.3 percent of Chamorros had a college degree, compared to 24.4 percent for the U.S. population as a whole, 15.2 percent for Native Hawaiians, and 13.8 percent for Pacific Islanders overall.

Their disproportionate numbers in government employment result in relatively high levels of participation in managerial and professional positions. At 26.4 percent, Chamorros had the highest percentage of workers in that sector (tied with Native Hawaiians) among Pacific Islanders. Meanwhile, just under 50 percent of Chamorros worked in sales or service-sector jobs. At just over $49,000, Chamorro households had the second highest income of any Pacific Islander group, roughly $500 below that of Native Hawaiians and about $1,000 below that of Americans generally. Aside from Fijians, Chamorros had the lowest rate of poverty among all Pacific Islander groups; at 13.7 percent, it was just 1.3 points higher than for Americans generally.

While the Spanish tried to impose their culture on the Chamorro people, they were largely unsuccessful, other than imposing the Catholic religion. Chamorros maintained their matrilineal society, dominated by extended families and clans, and passed on their myths across generations. As a matrilineal society, Chamorros pass on family names and property through females; even among those who live off the islands, women wield great power within the family. Chamorros also maintain their traditions through formal institutions, such as the Guam Society of America, founded in Washington, D.C., in 1952.

Like other Pacific Islander groups, the Chamorros continue to maintain their traditions even as they become acculturated to life in the United States. Nevertheless, tensions between island-born parents and Hawaiian- or mainland-born children often run high in many families. In general, older Guamanians, heavily influenced by Catholicism, are socially conservative, expecting even grown-up children to defer to the decisions of their parents and their clan elders. Many younger Chamorros, educated in U.S. schools and influenced by mass media, believe that individual choice gives them the right to make their own decisions about marriage, careers, and where they live.

James Ciment

Further Reading

Guam Society of America. http://www.guamsociety.org.

Janes, Craig R. *Migration, Social Change, and Health: A Samoan Community in Urban California.* Palo Alto, CA: Stanford University Press, 2006.

Spickard, Paul, Joanne L. Rondilla, and Debbie Hippolite Wright, eds. *Pacific Diaspora: Island Peoples in the United States and Across the Pacific.* Honolulu: University of Hawai'i Press, 2002.

Hapa

The term "hapa" (meaning "half" in Hawaiian) has been used in the islands since the nineteenth century to denote an individual of mixed Hawaiian ancestry. In the roughly 230 years since contact with Westerners, intermarriage between racial and ethnic groups in Hawaii became highly prevalent and accepted, due in part to native traditions of sexual openness and the aloha tradition of tolerance. The original hapas—also called *hapa haole,* or half-foreigner/white—were the children of Hawaiian women and American or European male newcomers. Later hapas included the children of Hawaiians and imported sugar laborers, who arrived from locations worldwide. As the offspring of respected intermarriages, hapas have not been subject to the same degree of prejudice as that encountered on the U.S. mainland by mulattos and other persons of mixed ancestry. Today it is nearly impossible to identify a hapa population or interest group in Hawaii, since most hapas are integrated into the general Native Hawaiian populace. The word "hapa" has also been appropriated by mainland Asian Americans of mixed ancestry to describe themselves, much to the objection of Native Hawaiians. Nevertheless, Asian Americans of mixed ancestry, though mostly not related to Hawaii in any way, form probably the most coherent hapa identity group today.

After the arrival of British explorer James Cook in 1778, whalers and explorers began to use the islands as a provisioning stopover between Europe and the New World. Many couplings took place between the men from these ships and Hawaiian women, some becoming more permanent when men deserted their ships and decided to remain in the islands. Higher-status marriages took place as well, between Hawaiian female *ali'i* (nobles) and higher-class passengers of the ships, some of whom became close to, or advisers of, Hawaiian monarchs. The children of these marriages moved in the high circles of Hawaiian society and often formed part of the royal court. Queen Emma, the wife of King Alexander Liholiho (Kamehameha IV, crowned in 1855) was reputedly hapa, as were some of her ladies-in-waiting. Another prominent hapa figure, Robert W. Wilcox, was sent by King Kalakaua (crowned in 1874) to Italy to be educated. He later returned to become a well-known statesman in support of the indigenous monarchy.

Although hapa children and the marriages that produced them were respected by the Hawaiian monarchy, the missionaries who arrived in 1820 from the East Coast of the United States were not as accepting. When one missionary, Samuel G. Dwight, married a Hawaiian woman in the mid-nineteenth century, he was voted out of the mission by other missionaries. Despite this prejudice, the overriding positive feeling toward hapas in Hawaii, and the fact that the missionaries were dependent on the pro-hapa *ali'i* for their right to operate on the islands, prevented them from taking strong action against Hawaiian-Anglo marriages.

In 1850, the Hawaiian government passed the Masters and Servants Act, which allowed sugar plantation owners to import indentured laborers from locations worldwide. The laborers were primarily Asian men, many of whom married Hawaiian women. The rate of intermarriage was especially high among Chinese laborers, the earliest Asian group to arrive in Hawaii. Chinese culture accepted polygamy, and workers sometimes married Hawaiian women even if they had left wives behind in China. The children of these and other Asian-Hawaiian marriages also became known as hapa. Intermarriage was encouraged by the monarchy, which was concerned with the continuing devastation of the Hawaiian population by Western diseases. Polynesians and Asians were considered to be closely related racially, and some of the *ali'i* felt that intermarriage between the two groups would reinvigorate the Native Hawaiian population. As Portuguese, Japanese, Filipino, and other ethnic groups arrived throughout the nineteenth and early twentieth centuries to work on the plantations, intermarriage among all groups continued, although only those of part-Hawaiian descent were called hapa.

It is difficult to ascertain the number of hapas in Hawaii at any given time, because the nomenclature used by government organizations was inconsistent, particularly after Hawaii's annexation by the United States in 1898. At various times, hapas could be classified as part Hawaiians, Asian Hawaiians, or Anglo-Hawaiians, or recorded under the ethnicity of either parent. Attempts to record the range of ethnic and racial mixes in Hawaii in the 1940s and 1950s resulted in the creation of no fewer than 524 racial categories. To create a more manageable system, the U.S. Census Bureau created a set of rules specifically pertaining to race and ethnicity in Hawaii. All of those with mixed Hawaiian ancestry of any kind (including hapas) were designated "Part-Hawaiian." In later generations, and particularly since the Hawaiian cultural renaissance of the 1970s, individuals of mixed Hawaiian ancestry are likely to label themselves Hawaiian if given a choice. Community institutions bear out the identification of Hawaiians of mixed ancestry as Hawaiian. In the state-run Hawaii Health Survey, for example, an individual is considered Hawaiian if either parent is identified as Hawaiian. Similarly, the admissions form for the University of Hawai'i includes a category called "Hawaiian/Part Hawaiian." More concretely, according to the Hawaiian Home Lands Act (1921), half-Hawaiian ancestry is the cutoff point for being considered for inexpensive leaseholds on homestead land. As time goes by, however, true hapas, like full Hawaiians, are becoming less common. As intermarriage continues among the many groups in Hawaii, individuals are likely to be less than half of any given ancestry, including Hawaiian.

Since the 1980s, the term "hapa" has also come to be used by mixed-ancestry Asian Americans on the mainland, and many organizations, particularly on college campuses, have been formed for individuals of mixed ancestry using that term. Because Hawaii is the only state that has maintained a consistent Asian majority, some Asian Americans claim connection to it even if they do not have actual ties there. Many Hawaiians have taken offense at this co-optation of their language and a term from their history. Thus, while use of the word "hapa" outside a Hawaiian context is increasingly common, it remains controversial.

Chana Kraus-Friedberg

Further Reading

Hapa Life Magazine. http://www.hapalife.com.
Lind, Andrew W. *Hawaii's People.* Honolulu: University of Hawai'i Press, 1980.
Office of Board Services. *Native Hawaiian Data Book 2006.* Honolulu: Office of Hawaiian Affairs, 2006.

Hawaiians

Native Hawaiians, or *Kanaka Maoli,* are a Polynesian group whose ancestors arrived in present-day Hawaii from the Marquesas Islands sometime between the fourth and sixth centuries C.E. Members of this group today number approximately 400,000. Of these, about two-thirds live in the islands and another one-third on the U.S. mainland, largely in the western states of California, Nevada, and Washington.

The earliest Hawaiians brought livestock, domesticated plants, and the knowledge to exploit marine resources along with them, and their society was based on these forms of subsistence. The society was ruled by *ali'i,* or nobles, who received tribute from the *maka'ainana,* those who worked the land. In exchange, the *ali'i* protected the *maka'ainana.* This reciprocal system was disrupted by the arrival of Europeans and Euro-Americans after the landing of British explorer Captain James Cook in 1778. The influx of Western ways eventually led to the illegal ousting of the indigenous monarchy and the alienation of the Hawaiian people from their land and culture. Since the mid-1970s, a variety of Native Hawaiian groups have been publicly fighting to regain their political and cultural rights.

Traditional Hawaiian society was organized in a complex network of chiefdoms. Every island except Molokai and Lanai (included in the Maui government) was ruled by a "high" chief, or *ali'i ai moku*. Under this chief were the *ali'i ahupua'a*, each of whom ruled over an *ahupua'a* (district), and the *konohiki*, who controlled smaller divisions of land on which the *maka'ainana* worked. The *ali'i* were not seen as owning the land they controlled, but as taking care of it in exchange for its resources. Similarly, an *ali'i*'s relationship with the *maka'ainana* was seen as reciprocal. If an *ali'i* was seen as behaving without aloha (love and kindness) to his or her people, he or she would often be overthrown by the *maka'ainana* and replaced. The higher one stood in the chiefdom system, the more *mana*, or spiritual power, one had and the more equipped one was to approach the gods. It was also possible to gain or lose *mana* by one's actions, and the religious-legal *kapu* (taboo) system was designed partly to protect the *mana* of the *ali'i*. The punishment for breaking one of the *kapu* was often death. Because the *ali'i ai moku* had the most *mana*, it was his job to approach the gods, particularly Ku (god of war) and Lono (god of agriculture) on behalf of his people.

When Captain Cook landed on the island of Kauai, this system was still in place. By the early 1800s, however, Kamehameha I, a chief on the island of Hawaii, had unified the islands under one government for the first time. Additional changes were brought by the arrival of Captain Cook's expedition and the subsequent arrival of other explorers and whalers. These voyagers, in addition to trade goods, brought with them venereal diseases, which reduced the Hawaiian population by 75 percent by 1854.

Another change occurred upon the death of King Kamehameha I in 1819. At the urging of Ka'ahumanu and Kapiolani, two of his wives, Kamehameha's heir, Liholiho (Kamehameha II) declared an end to the *kapu* system. Combined with the arrival of Protestant missionaries in 1820, this signaled the end of formal Hawaiian religion.

In addition to Protestant Christianity, which was embraced by many of the *ali'i*, the missionaries also brought a written version of the previously oral Hawaiian language and the beginnings of Western-style democracy. Under the influence of missionary advisers, Kamehameha III also made Hawaii a constitutional monarchy in 1840, based on a constitution that limited his powers. Shortly thereafter, he passed the Great Mahele (1848), which made land exchangeable for fee simple and divided Hawaii into portions owned by the crown, the government, and the *ali'i*. Subsequent laws allowed *maka'ainana* to establish tenure on the land they inhabited, but the procedures were expensive, and many did not take advantage of the opportunity. Many Hawaiians were thus alienated from their land and subject to severe economic disadvantage, a situation that still exists today.

As a result of the Mahele, American families acquired large tracts of land, which they used to establish sugar plantations. Plantation owners became increasingly concerned about the need for a government that would respond to their business concerns rather than those of the Hawaiian people. Thus, a series of efforts was made to limit the power of the indigenous monarchy. In 1887, a group of powerful American businessmen forced King Kalakaua to sign the Bayonet Constitution, which limited the power of the king and allowed noncitizens to vote. In 1893, Queen Lilioukalani attempted to replace the Bayonet Constitution and restore the power of the monarchy, but she was forced, under threat from U.S. warships stationed in Honolulu, to abdicate her throne.

Despite the protests of the Hawaiian people and the efforts of President Grover Cleveland to restore Lilioukalani's rule, *haole* (white) businessmen remained in control of the new Republic of Hawaii until 1898, when they engineered Hawaii's annexation as a territory of the United States. This gave sugar planters in Hawaii increased access to the U.S. market but also placed Native Hawaiians under an increasingly restrictive government. Hawaiian traditions were continually devalued, and use of the Hawaiian language in schools was legally banned. The influx of workers from around the world to the sugar plantations ensured that Native Hawaiians became less of a majority in their homeland. In 1959, Hawaii was granted statehood.

Today, Native Hawaiians continue to be a disadvantaged group overall, struggling with poverty and associated health and education issues. In a state where the cost of living is among the highest in the United States, about 62 percent of Native Hawaiians have household incomes under $50,000. Native Hawaiian students score disproportionately low on standardized tests, largely due to the discord between the school curriculum and Hawaiian culture. The Native Hawaiian population also suffers high rates of obesity, hypertension, smoking, and alcoholism. Hawaiian activists are fighting to empower their people via Hawaiian immersion schools (which teach Hawaiian language and culture, in addition to standard school curricula) and are waging extensive legal battles to improve Hawaiian access to land and resources. Although important progress has been made, Native Hawaiians continue to face serious obstacles in their homeland today.

Chana Kraus-Friedberg

Further Reading

Buck, Elizabeth. *Paradise Remade: The Politics of Culture and History in Hawai'i*. Philadelphia: Temple University Press, 1993.

Halualani, Rona Tamiko. *In the Name of Hawaiians: Native Identities and Cultural Politics.* Minneapolis: University of Minnesota Press, 2002.

Samoan Americans

The second-largest Pacific Islander community in the United States (after Native Hawaiians), Samoan Americans are one ethnic group whose origins lie in two separate jurisdictions. The vast majority come from or live in American Samoa, a territory ceded to the United States by Germany in 1899 and formally annexed in 1900. (Like Hawaiian Americans and the Chamorro of Guam, many Samoans never immigrated to the United States but became part of it by virtue of political transfer.) A much smaller contingent of Samoans are immigrants from the independent nation of Samoa (Western Samoa until 1997), the geographically and demographically larger half of the Samoan Islands. Both jurisdictions are located in the southwestern Pacific, some 1,700 miles (2,700 kilometers) to the northeast of New Zealand. Approximately 20 percent of Samoans in Hawaii and on the U.S. mainland are foreign-born; the vast majority of these are from the independent nation of Samoa. (Unless otherwise specified, all statistics in this article are culled from 2000 census reports and pertain only to the fifty states and the District of Columbia.)

Settled by the ancestors of modern Polynesians around 500–1000 B.C.E., the Solomon Islands were first encountered by Europeans in the early eighteenth century. Disputed by various European powers in the nineteenth century, they became a protectorate of Germany in 1889. Ten years later, Berlin ceded the smaller eastern half of the archipelago, with its coveted deepwater port of Pago Pago, to the United States, while maintaining control of the larger western islands. During World War I, the latter were occupied by New Zealand, which ruled them as a trust territory until 1962, when Western Samoa became the first Polynesian state to win its independence.

Samoans are a Polynesian people, ethnically and linguistically related to Native Hawaiians, who speak their own language (though most living in American Samoa also speak English). According to the 2000 U.S. Census, about 35 percent of Samoans living in Hawaii or the U.S. mainland reported speaking English at home, while another 45 percent said they spoke the language "very well." Having come under missionary influence in the nineteenth century, the majority—about 70 percent of the population—are members of various Protestant sects, while another 20 percent are Catholic. Most of the remaining 10 percent are members of the Church of Jesus Christ of Latter-day Saints (Mormons), a result of a concerted missionary outreach by the Utah-based faith since World War II.

Population and Immigration History

According to the U.S. Census, there were just over 91,000 Samoans living in the United States in 2000, representing about 19 percent of the roughly 476,000 Pacific Islander Americans. In addition, American Samoa itself had a population of about 65,000, of which about 93 percent, or 60,000, were ethnically Samoan. Together, Samoans on the U.S. mainland and Hawaii, plus those living in American Samoa, totaled 156,000. In addition, another 40,000 or so persons on the U.S. mainland and Hawaii identified themselves as partially Samoan in the 2000 census.

With just under half of all Samoans in the fifty states, California has the largest population. Another 25 percent live in Hawaii and about 5 percent live in Utah. Cities with significant Samoan American populations include Los Angeles, Honolulu, San Francisco, Oakland, and Salt Lake City. With a population of about 12,000, the city of Pago Pago is the largest urban area in American Samoa.

As members of international ship crews, small numbers of Samoans have been settling in the United States and Hawaii since the nineteenth century. But it was only after World War II that large-scale Samoan emigration from the islands occurred, with significant numbers moving to Australia, New Zealand, and the United States. Two institutions were largely responsible for Samoan immigration to Hawaii and the United States. The first were missionary churches, which sponsored many young Samoans to come for an education. Even when they did not sponsor young immigrants, they introduced Samoans to the idea that there were educational and job opportunities in the United States. The second institution was the U.S. military, which appealed to Samoans, who have a long and proud martial tradition. Indeed, Samoans earned a reputation among military leaders for their toughness and valor during the Korean and Vietnamese conflicts. Because of their American connection, Samoans tended to migrate to the United States earlier than other Pacific Islander groups. Nearly 40 percent have been in the country since before 1980, compared to about 25 percent for Pacific Islanders overall.

Social Indices and Culture

Samoans tend to lag behind the U.S. population as a whole in terms of education. While less than 20 percent of Americans lack a high school diploma, the figure for Samoans is nearly 25 percent. At the other end of the educational scale, roughly 25 percent of Americans have college degrees or higher, compared to just over 10 percent for Samoans. At the same time, Samoans fit in with the general educational patterns for Pacific Islanders, tending to lag somewhat behind Native Hawaiians but having educational levels higher than most other Pacific Islander groups.

Partly as a result of their lower educational levels, Samoans tend to work in service-sector and blue-collar jobs. Less than 20 percent have managerial or professional positions, compared to about one-third for the U.S. population overall; the figure for Native Hawaiians is over 25 percent. Meanwhile, fully half work in service or sales positions (compared to 40 percent for Americans generally), while another 21 percent are in manufacturing or transportation (compared to less than 15 percent for Americans generally). At just over $41,000, Samoan American household incomes lag behind the population overall, at just over $50,000; Native Hawaiians had annual household incomes of just under $50,000. Samoans, at just over 20 percent, were also more likely to be living in poverty than virtually any other Pacific Islander group, for whom the average was about 18 percent; for the U.S. population as a whole, the figure was just over 12 percent. Like many Pacific Islanders, Samoans are in poorer health than the overall American population. Among the illnesses and conditions particularly common in the Samoan community are obesity and diabetes, a result of a diet rich in coconut oil, a major source of saturated fat.

Along with their intensely felt Protestant, Catholic, and Mormon faiths, the center of Samoan life is the family. While the vast majority of Samoans live in nuclear households, extended kinship networks are important, providing income and other forms of support. In addition, many Samoans living in the United States maintain connections to the traditional clan networks of the home islands. Clan leaders often step in to resolve disputes within and between families. And while missionary-inspired Christianity discouraged premarital sex, Samoan traditions—which encourage young people to experiment sexually—live on in the islands. Among Samoan communities in Hawaii and on the U.S. mainland, this has contributed to relatively high rates of HIV infection.

Like other Pacific Islander groups, the Samoan American population is divided into two general groups—those who live on their home islands and those who have immigrated to Hawaii or the U.S. mainland, usually to large urban areas. The former tend to be poorer and less educated, but more connected to their ethnic roots. Meanwhile, those who have emigrated—and particularly their Hawaiian- or mainland-born children—tend to be more acculturated to the American way of life.

James Ciment

Further Reading

Janes, Craig R. *Migration, Social Change, and Health: A Samoan Community in Urban California*. Palo Alto, CA: Stanford University Press, 2006.

Spickard, Paul, Joanne L. Rondilla, and Debbie Hippolite Wright, eds. *Pacific Diaspora: Island Peoples in the United States and Across the Pacific.* Honolulu: University of Hawai'i Press, 2002.

Tongans

Tongan immigrants to the United States and Tongan Americans constitute one of the smallest ethnic groups in the country. In 2000, according to the U.S. census, there were a total of 27,300 residents, a 70 percent increase over ten years (from 17,600 in 1990) and a 342 percent increase over twenty years (from 6,200 in 1980). In addition, there were approximately 9,000 others who identified themselves as having mixed Tongan ancestry. In the 1970s and early 1980s, the emigration rate for Tongans averaged 2 percent annually. By the mid-1980s, more than 1,900 Tongans were leaving the South Pacific kingdom each year, prompted by a shortage of land and the efforts of missionaries. As a result, according to the 1996 Tongan census, the nation's growth rate slowed from 2.3 percent to 0.3 percent annually. Today, approximately half of the estimated 216,000 Tongans in the world are living outside the archipelago; virtually every household in Tonga has at least one resident living in another country, with roughly one in four residing in the United States. Other major destinations include Australia, New Zealand, and Great Britain, which had a protectorate over the islands until granting independence in 1970.

Mormon missionaries were instrumental in promoting Tongan immigration to the United States, promising education, work visas, employment, and spouses for those of marriageable age in exchange for accepting the religion. While a small percentage of Tongan Americans continue to follow Mormonism today, the majority are Methodist.

The first Tongan immigrants to U.S. territory arrived in Laie, Hawaii, as early as 1916, with the number increasing after World War II. On the U.S. mainland, the largest settlements of Tongans are now located in California (San Francisco and Los Angeles), Utah (Provo and

Salt Lake City), Washington, and Texas. Approximately 20,000 Tongans or mixed Tongans reside in California, the majority in the Bay Area and San Mateo County; one-quarter live in Greater Los Angeles, particularly Carson, Lennox, and Hawthorne counties. Nearly 4,000 Tongans or mixed Tongans live in north Texas, specifically Tarrant County (the Hurst-Euless-Bedford region). According to the 2000 U.S. Census, 6,587 Tongans or mixed Tongans made up 3 percent of the entire Utah population (2.2 million). The Tongan population is the largest and fastest-growing Pacific Islander community in Utah.

Among immigrant cultures in the United States, Tongans have one of the highest rates of native language at home, although later-generation Tongan Americans are more fluent in English. According to the 2000 census, 46.5 percent of Tongans by race were born in the United States; of these, 40 percent could no longer hold an everyday conversation in Tongan nor have returned to visit the islands.

Tongan Islanders venerate the tradition of supporting families and communities. Even as the population has moved overseas, 75 percent of all Tongan Island households have continued to receive financial support or remittances from their kin abroad to underwrite village ceremonial and family events. In 2003, Tongans in the United States reportedly earned ten times more than Tongan Islanders. Compared to other ethnic groups in the United States, however, Tongans overseas earn relatively little—indeed, 70 percent less than the average American. Tongan Americans suffer inordinately high rates of unemployment and underemployment. Those who do work are generally employed in sales, construction, manufacturing, and transportation. In north Texas, more than 90 percent of Tongan families run family-owned landscaping businesses or are employed in the airline industry (especially manual jobs at the Dallas-Fort Worth Airport). The average income for Tongan Americans generally falls between $25,000 and $35,000 a year.

Given their economic difficulties and gradual distancing from their homeland, later generations of Tongan Americans are reducing the amount of remittances they send home. The shift from traditional values greatly concerns Tongan nationals who have moved to the United States as well as those they have left behind. They regard it as a sign of the deterioration of essential values that have long supported Tongan life and economy at home: 'ofa (love), faka'apa'apa (respect), and fuakavenga (responsibility). On the island of Oahu in Hawaii, a Tongan Village at the Polynesian Cultural Center helps preserve Tongan culture, crafts, foods, traditions, and legends. For those living and being born on the U.S.

mainland, however, Tongan identity is undergoing radical change. The trend among younger Tongan Americans is to embrace a more individualistic (American) versus a community-oriented (Tongan) mind-set. Their struggles to fit into American mainstream culture have led to identity conflicts, manifested in an upsurge in violence (including many Tongan-on-Tongan incidents), gang warfare, and teenage pregnancy. The high school dropout rate among Tongan youths is about 50 percent. Their crisis prompted at least one prominent Tongan American to action. Chris Ma'umalanga, a former professional football player, helped organize the first annual Tonga High School Conference at Cal State Dominguez Hills in 2006, to reach Tongan American parents and youths struggling with their ethnic identity and drifting into gangs and crime.

In addition to Ma'umalanga, who played for the New York Giants of the National Football League for three seasons (1994–1996), several Tongan Americans have risen to prominence in the world of sports. Alatini "Tini" Saulala was a member of the U.S. National Rugby Eagles team, which won the World Rugby Cup in 1999, and boxer Paea Wolfgramm was a silver medalist in the Super Heavyweight division at the 1996 Summer Olympics in Atlanta, Georgia, becoming the first Pacific Islander to win an Olympic medal.

The pop/R&B/dance group the Jets, which had several hit recordings during the 1980s, are children of Maikeli and Vaké Wolfgramm, who migrated to Minneapolis, Minnesota, in the late 1960s and raised seventeen children. The eight oldest siblings formed the band, which put five songs on the Top 10 charts during the 1980s.

Tonga today remains a hereditary constitutional monarchy, ruled by King George Tupou V since September 2006. Just two months before he succeeded to the throne, Crown Prince Tu'ipelehake ('Uluvalu) and his wife were killed in a car accident near San Francisco during a visit to the United States.

Gabriella Oldham

Further Reading

Barkan, Elliott Robert. *Asian and Pacific Islander Migration to the United States: A Model of New Global Patterns.* Westport, CT: Greenwood, 1992.

Lee, Helen Morton. *Tongans Overseas: Between Two Shores.* Honolulu: University of Hawai'i Press, 2003.

National Tongan American Society. http://ntasutah.org.

Spickard, Paul, Joanne L. Rondilla, and Debbie Hippolite Wright, eds. *Pacific Diaspora: Island Peoples in the United States and Across the Pacific.* Honolulu: University of Hawai'i Press, 2002.

The Pakistani American Experience: History and Culture

The second-largest group of South Asian immigrants in the United States (after Indians) and the second-largest community of immigrants from a predominantly Muslim country (after Iranian Americans), Pakistanis represent one of the oldest Asian groups in the United States, with the earliest immigrants arriving in the first years of the twentieth century. However, as in the case of most other Asian immigrant communities, the vast majority have arrived since liberalization of U.S. immigration law in the mid-1960s. As former subjects of the British Empire, Pakistani Americans tend to be more fluent in English than other Asian Americans and relatively well educated, but they lag behind many of their fellow Asian immigrants in terms of income. Generally traditional in cultural and family matters, Pakistani Americans tend to be devout in their practice of Islam and have played an important role in the development of Muslim institutions in the United States. That role has placed the community under greater government scrutiny—and caused it to face increased popular hostility—since the September 11, 2001, terrorist attacks.

Background and Immigration History

Home to one of the cradles of civilization in the Indus River Valley, Pakistan was conquered by Islamic armies in the early eighth century C.E. and fell under British rule in the nineteenth century, before winning its independence in 1947. Until 1971, the country consisted of two parts—West and East Pakistan—but the latter won its independence, as Bangladesh, in a bloody revolution in 1971. More recently, Pakistan has suffered from ongoing civil strife, particularly in the so-called tribal regions along the Afghanistan border, though the fighting has spilled over into the rest of the country in the form of terrorist attacks and government crackdowns.

The first significant immigration of Pakistanis (then part of British India) came in the early twentieth century. These were largely Punjabis and Sindhis—two

of the largest ethnic groups in the home country (many of whom also came from what is now India)—who emigrated to western Canada and then moved south of the border in search of jobs in agriculture, the timber industry, and railroad construction, particularly in California and Washington State. Many ended up buying land and becoming successful farmers of their own, while others opened small businesses. Like East Asian immigrants of the early twentieth century, however, many of these Pakistani immigrants faced white hostility, including efforts by the Asiatic Exclusion League to expel all Asian workers from the United States. With the passage of restrictive immigration legislation in the early 1920s, the flow of Pakistani immigrants to the country virtually dried up until the mid-1960s, when the Immigration and Nationality Act ended national quotas.

From that time to the early twenty-first century, the Pakistani American population has grown steadily, from roughly several thousand to just over 210,000 by 2007. Approximately 80 percent of foreign-born Pakistani Americans have arrived in the United States since 1980. The largest community of Pakistanis, some 100,000, lives in the New York City metropolitan area. Other significant populations are located in Illinois, California, Texas, and the Washington, D.C., metropolitan area. (All statistics in this article are based on the 2000 U.S. Census.)

Representing 1.5 percent of all Asian Americans—making them the tenth-largest such community—Pakistani Americans tend to be fluent in English and well educated, as most of those who move to the United States come from the middle class back home. While only 7.7 percent of Pakistani Americans spoke English at home, more than two-thirds said they spoke the language "very well." At the same time, some 54.3 percent of all Pakistani Americans had a bachelor's degrees or higher, a rate higher than that of any Asian American group other than Indian Americans, and more than double the rate for Americans generally.

The high level of educational attainment is also reflected in the job status of Pakistani Americans. Some 43.5 percent of working members of the community were in managerial or professional positions—especially in the medical and high-tech sectors—a rate nearly a third higher than that of the U.S. population overall. Despite the high level of education and professional achievement, the median household income for Pakistani Americans was just over $50,000 per year, roughly equal to that of American households generally but about 15 percent lower than that of Asian American households. The lag in income may be the result of the fact that, along with educated, middle-class immigrants, there is a significant cohort of impoverished, poorly educated Pakistani immigrants. With a reported 16.5 percent living in poverty, Pakistani Americans had the highest rate of any Asian American group other than Cambodians, Hmong, and Laotians, all of which are predominantly war refugee communities.

Culture and Community

Pakistani Americans tend to be traditional in their family arrangements, lifestyle, and culture. Many marriages are still arranged and, where they are not, parental permission to marry is still insisted upon. Family is extremely important to Pakistanis, as reflected in the fact that, other than the Hmong, members of the community were more likely—at 76 percent—to be living in two-parent households than any other Asian American group. Divorce rates are also the lowest of any significant Asian American community; with just 2.1 percent of adults having divorced, the rate was less than one-fourth that of the American population as a whole. While most Pakistani Americans lived in nuclear households, extended kinship networks remained important economically and socially.

The vast majority of Pakistani Americans practice the Islamic faith—most are Sunni, but a significant minority are Shi'a—and they tend to be among the most devout of any Muslim American group. This is reflected in the traditional, homemaker role assigned to women. With just 36.9 percent in the workforce, adult Pakistani American women were less likely to be gainfully employed than women from any other Asian American group. This appears to be changing, however, as American-born and educated Pakistani girls come of age. Indeed, religion informs much of Pakistani American life, with the local mosque serving not just as a place of worship but also as a community center, cultural center, and school where young Pakistanis are taught faith, traditional culture, and language. Most

Muslim faithful join in prayer at the Makki Masjid, a mosque in the Little Pakistan neighborhood of Brooklyn, New York. Pakistani American life is heavily informed by Muslim practice, culture, and social values. *(Mario Tama/Getty Images)*

Pakistanis perform the rituals of the faith and follow halal (the Islamic dietary code).

Like other Muslim American communities, Pakistanis faced a backlash of discrimination in the wake of September 11, including a scattering of attacks on individuals and desecrations of places of worship. Some Pakistani community leaders have complained of being singled out by law enforcement and airport security based solely on their accent, appearance, or national origin. Organizations such as the Pakistan League of America and Muslim Students Association, a pan-Islamic organization in which Pakistanis have played a leading role since its founding in 1963, have struggled to combat the stereotypes and discrimination while establishing social and cultural ties to the broader American community.

James Ciment

Further Reading

Purkayastha, Bandana. *Negotiating Ethnicity: Second-Generation South Asian Americans Traverse a Transnational World.* New Brunswick, NJ: Rutgers University Press, 2005.

Rajan, Gita, and Shailja Sharma, eds. *New Cosmopolitanisms: South Asians in the US.* Palo Alto, CA: Stanford University Press, 2006.

Shankar, Lavina Dhingra, and Rajini Srikanth, eds. *A Part, Yet Apart: South Asians in Asian America.* Philadelphia: Temple University Press, 1998.

Williams, Raymond Brady. *Religions of Immigrants from India and Pakistan: New Threads in the American Tapestry.* New York: Cambridge University Press, 1988.

Pakistani Americans
Alphabetical Entries

Pakistan League of America

The Pakistan League of America was formed in New York in 1971 to promote Pakistani culture in the United States, to help immigrants to become more acculturated to American society, and to lobby in Pakistan's interest with U.S. officials. With a membership of several thousand, the Pakistan League holds annual meetings and sponsors seminars on various topics of interest to members. It also sponsors a number of annual awards for individuals who have helped Pakistan and its people.

Immigration from Pakistan began formally after the subcontinent was granted independence and partitioned into India and East and West Pakistan in 1947. Unlike Indian immigrants, who are often viewed as having both a cultural and political identity, Pakistanis had only a political identity. Immigration was strictly limited until 1965, when the Immigration and Nationality Act lifted national quotas. Most Pakistanis in the United States were students, businessmen, or others who were not usually permanent residents.

By 1950, an antecedent organization also called the Pakistan League of America had been formed to lobby for the new nation and represent the government's positions in Washington and the American media. That year, the organization countered Indian requests for 2 million tons of wheat to avert a food shortage by revealing figures that showed adequate supplies were available from Pakistan, if only India would break its self-imposed trade embargo. Later in the 1950s, the group also protested the deportation of Pakistanis who had entered the United States illegally and were working as agricultural and factory workers.

By the early 1970s, the number of Pakistani immigrants had grown significantly, and many joined the Pakistan League of America upon arriving. As tensions between East and West Pakistan intensified, the organization itself grew divided. When East Pakistan revolted and became Bangladesh in 1971, the original Pakistan League of America collapsed as members from that region left the organization and formed a separate group.

The modern Pakistan League of America was established in 1971 by Dr. Mazhar Malik, a professor of economics and engineering, and Dr. Shafi Baizar, a physician. Malik served as its first president, and both men were determined to preserve the organization so that it could help the many immigrants from the former West Pakistan. Based in New York, the organization had members around the country. The Pakistan League of America provided a variety of services to the immigrant community. Most had settled in urban areas, though few neighborhoods were dominated by the Pakistanis. Because Pakistan had at least five ethnic groups and nine languages, immigrants generally did not form single, cohesive communities. Nevertheless, the Pakistan League offered English language classes and other forms of support for anyone seeking help in the transition to life in America.

The Pakistan League also makes annual awards to individuals who have helped either the immigrant community or Pakistanis at home. In 2007, for example, plastic surgeon Paula Moynahan received the Appreciation Award for her work among poor women and children in Pakistan, treating scars and congenital defects. The group also sponsors seminars and speakers. In August 2007, exiled Pakistani leader Benazir Bhutto spoke to a large gathering at the invitation of the league about conditions in the homeland just prior to her return from overseas. In addition, the organization maintains active links and support programs with Pakistan. In 2005, for example, when that country was hit with a devastating earthquake, the Pakistan League organized aid collection and other relief efforts.

In addition to helping immigrants and maintaining contacts with the home country, the Pakistan League of America has also become an active lobbying organization in the United States. Indeed it was one of the first such groups made up of immigrants from South Asia. Its early efforts in this regard were admittedly minimal and poorly organized, in part because U.S. policy at the time was regarded as heavily pro-Pakistan. By the 1990s, however, Indian groups had greater success in influencing American leaders, and the Pakistan League became increasingly active in building good relations between Islamabad and Washington. Leaders of the group supported General Pervez Musharraf in his support for U.S. military intervention in Afghanistan in 2001. The group reluctantly supported Musharraf's 2007 crackdown on opponents in an attempt to bring stability to Pakistan.

Tim J. Watts

Further Reading

Pakistan League of America. http://pakistanleagueofamerica.com.

Rajan, Gita, and Shailija Sharma, ed. *New Cosmopolitanisms: South Asians in the U.S.* Palo Alto, CA: Stanford University Press, 2006.

Zhou, Min, and James V. Gatewood. *Contemporary Asian America: A Multidisciplinary Reader.* New York: New York University Press, 2000.

Religion, Pakistani American

Pakistan was founded in 1947 as the homeland for Muslims in the former British colony of India. Thus, the Islamic faith has always played a critical role in the life of Pakistanis, both in their Asian homeland and among diaspora Pakistani communities, particularly in Great Britain and the United States. In the latter, several institutions have arisen to promote the faith among immigrants and to defend Pakistanis against religious discrimination, particularly in the wake of the September 11, 2001, terrorist attacks on New York and Washington, D.C.

Virtually all Pakistanis and Pakistani immigrants to the United States are Muslim. Given the centrality of Islam in the social and political lives of believers, it is not surprising to find that religious organizations have played a key role in organizing the Pakistani American community and in helping Pakistani American immigrants adjust to life in their adoptive homeland. One of the first groups to be created by the Indian and Pakistani Muslim students in the United States after 1965 was the Muslim Students Association (MSA), composed of both South Asian and Middle Eastern students. The MSA, with national headquarters in Falls Church, Virginia, began its work by providing a community in which Muslim students could maintain their religious duties and celebrate as a community. Two nationwide organizations grew out of the MSA: the Islamic Society of North America (ISNA) and the Islamic Circle of North America (ICNA). The ISNA is headquartered in Plainfield, Indiana, and serves as an umbrella organization for regional and student Muslim groups; Pakistani American Muslims remain active in ISNA and its constituent organizations. The ICNA focuses on mission work (*dawa*) and the dissemination of information about Islam. Although ICNA is not an exclusively Pakistani American organization either, it was founded by South Asian Muslim students and meetings are widely conducted in Urdu. Other Muslim organizations in America include the American Muslim Council, the Muslim Public Affairs Council, the American Muslim Alliance, and the Council on American-Islamic Relations.

Because the Muslim community (*ummah*) stresses its oneness and unity, religious organizations generally do not release statistics on the size, composition, and origin of adherents. Thus it is difficult to ascertain how many Muslims in America come from South Asia generally and how many from Pakistan in particular. Nevertheless, according to the Council on American Islamic Relations (CAIR), about one-third of Sunni mosque attendees in the United States are of South Asian descent. More Muslims—an estimated 17 percent—are believed to come from Pakistan than from any other country. Although most Pakistani Americans are Sunni Muslims, there is also a minority population of Shi'a Muslims, mostly in the Ishmaili Nizari community.

As part of the American Muslim community, Pakistani Americans grapple with the same struggles as Muslim immigrants from other parts of the world—and look to their faith to aid them in their efforts. Mosques and Islamic centers serve as venues for community and cultural events as well as prayer, especially during the two most important community celebrations in the Muslim calendar: Eid al-Fitr (end of Ramadan) and Eid al-Adha (Festival of Sacrifice). In addition, the same Islamic centers and mosques also function as sources of information, sites of social or civil services (such as language instruction and weddings), and links to the larger Muslim community in the city or region. Responding to the need to balance integration into American society with the retention of Pakistani and Muslim identities, Islamic schools are being created across the United States to educate Pakistani American children about Islam and their cultural heritage.

Pakistani American civic organizations and Muslim groups have become especially visible and vocal since the terrorist attacks of September 11, 2001. Responding to the misunderstandings of the American public about Islam, and to threats to the safety and civil liberties of American Muslims—particularly those from South Asia and the Middle East—the various organizations have mounted major campaigns to disseminate information about Islam and Muslims, to build unity within the Muslim community, and to foster relationships with other civic and interreligious organizations.

Tara G.V. Munson

Further Reading

Council on Islamic-American Relations. http://www.cair.com.

Eck, Diana L. *A New Religious America: How a "Christian Country" Has Now Become the World's Most Religiously Diverse Nation.* New York: HarperSanFrancisco, 2001.

Melendy, H. Brett. *Asians in America: Filipinos, Koreans, and East Indians.* Boston: G.K. Hall, 1977.

Muslim Students Association. http://www.msanational.org.

Williams, Raymond Brady. *Religions of Immigrants from India and Pakistan: New Threads in the American Tapestry.* New York: Cambridge University Press, 1988.

The Singaporean American
Experience: History and Culture

Numbering approximately 15,000, the Singaporean American population is among the smallest of all Asian ethnic groups in the United States. There are several reasons for this. First, the base population of Singapore, at less than 5 million, is relatively small by Asian standards. Second, because it is a former colony of Great Britain, many Singaporeans seeking to live, work, and attend school overseas choose Britain or other members of the British Commonwealth, especially nearby Australia. And finally, with the second-highest per capita income in Asia (after Japan), Singapore offers its populace abundant economic opportunities at home, diminishing the desire to move overseas.

Indeed, so small is the population of Singaporean Americans—fewer than 3,000 were naturalized between 1997 and 2006—that the U.S. Census Bureau does not even break out statistics for them, lumping them together under the category "Other Asians." Nevertheless, most students of Asian immigration agree that Singaporean Americans compare well with immigrants from other high-wage, high-educated East Asian countries, such as Japan, South Korea, and Taiwan; that is, they have educational and income levels higher than those for the U.S. population as a whole. According to the 2000 census, about 40 percent of "Other Asians" had a bachelor's degree or higher (compared with about 25 percent for the American population as a whole), and male and female incomes of $36,000 and $30,000, respectively (compared to $37,000 and $27,000 for all Americans).

Most Singaporeans are of Chinese descent. The population of the home country is more than 75 percent Chinese, with Malays and Indians making up most of the remainder. Thus, most Singaporean Americans follow basic Chinese customs and cultural practices, though the vast majority, like their counterparts back home, are very Westernized. English, for example, is spoken almost universally in Singapore. Indeed, English is the first language of roughly 25 percent of all Singaporeans, the highest proportion in Asia.

The islands that make up the city-state of Singapore, lying just off the southern tip of the Malay Peninsula, were largely uninhabited when the British established

their main trading port in Southeast Asia there in the early nineteenth century. Between its founding date in 1819 and the mid-twentieth century, Singapore grew into a major port and business center, before being occupied by the Japanese in World War II. Granted independence as part of Malaysia in 1963, Singapore broke away two years later, its largely ethnic Chinese population unwilling to live under a government dominated by Muslim Malays. Since 1965, Singapore has thrived economically under authoritarian, pro-business regimes, becoming not just a major trading port but a center of high-tech industry and finance.

Under the leadership of Prime Minister Lee Kuan Yew from 1959 (as a self-governing entity within the British Empire) through his retirement in 1990, Singapore emphasized education. But because the country lacked a well-developed higher-education infrastructure, the government sponsored its students to go abroad. Thousands attended colleges, universities, and professional and graduate schools in the United States beginning in the 1960s. While most American-educated students returned to Singapore—where some took up high positions in government and business—a few remained in the United States, establishing the core of the tiny Singaporean American community. In addition, with close military ties between the anti-Communist Lee government and Washington, D.C., many Singaporean officers trained in the United States. Although virtually all of them returned to serve in the Singaporean military, a few eventually returned to live in the United States after retirement.

In fact, most Singaporeans in the United States are not immigrants but temporary residents, either businessmen working for Singaporean firms in the United States or students attending higher educational institutions. The vast majority go back to the home country when their jobs or schooling come to an end. Of the several thousand Singaporeans who have chosen to settle in the United States since 1965, most tend to live in urban areas, largely in California, Washington, D.C., and New York City. From the 1980s, Singaporean residents in the United States have included Chinese, Malay, and Indian Singaporeans, as well as some members of Singapore's tiny Jewish and Armenian communities, though ethnic Chinese predominate.

Since the early 2000s, Singaporeans living in the United States have been allowed to vote in Singaporean elections providing they have spent two of the previous five years in Singapore, or are in the United States on government business or work for international agencies. In 2006, a few hundred voted in polling stations established in Washington, D.C., and San Francisco.

Most Singaporean Americans follow the customs and cultural patterns of the ethnic group of which they are a part. Nevertheless, as one of the most Westernized Asian groups, they tend not to be orthodox in belief and adapt easily and thoroughly to American lifestyles, aided by their near universal fluency in English. Explaining their reasons for choosing the United States over their very prosperous homeland, most Singaporean Americans cite the usual reasons: education, marriage, and jobs. Many, particularly among the younger cohort, also cite America's relative openness, a stark contrast to the highly regulated society in their homeland where freedom of the press is highly restricted, lifestyles are closely monitored, and even mildly antisocial behavior is harshly punished.

Justin Corfield and James Ciment

Further Reading

Corfield, Justin, and Robin Corfield. *Encyclopedia of Singapore.* Lanham, MD: Scarecrow, 2006.

Lee, Geok Boi, ed. *Singaporeans Exposed: Navigating the Ins and Outs of Globalisation.* Singapore: Landmark, 2001.

The Sri Lankan American Experience: History and Culture

Sri Lankan Americans constitute the smallest of the major South Asian American communities, after, in descending order, Indians, Bangladeshis, and Pakistanis. Arriving in small numbers since the 1970s, most have come seeking better economic circumstances or higher education, though a few have come as war refugees. Sri Lanka, known before 1972 as Ceylon, has been torn by civil war between the Buddhist Sinhalese majority (about 75 percent of the population) and a Tamil Hindu and Muslim minority (about 15 percent) since the early 1980s.

As in their homeland, Sri Lankan Americans are divided religiously while sharing a culture heavily influenced by their homeland's giant neighbor to the north, India. Like Asian Indian Americans, Sri Lankan Americans tend to be highly educated and enjoy a median household income above that of the U.S. population as a whole. While older members of the community, though highly acculturated, maintain many aspects of their traditional culture, younger Sri Lankan Americans tend to eschew certain restrictive aspects of life in Sri Lanka, paying little attention to caste distinctions, for example, when associating with other members of the community.

Immigration History

It is difficult to trace the history of Sri Lankan immigration to the United States before the 1970s, when U.S. immigration agencies first began differentiating them from other South Asian groups. Since Sri Lanka is an island nation with a long sea-faring tradition, it is highly likely that small numbers of Sri Lankan sailors may have settled in U.S. port cities before the middle years of the twentieth century. The year 1975, the first year in which Sri Lankans were listed separately by U.S. immigration officials, saw 432 entering the United States legally. During the 1980s, about 400 Sri Lankans entered the United States annually, rising to about 1,000 a year in the 1990s. By the 2000 U.S. Census, there were approximately 25,000 persons living in the United States who had either immigrated from Sri Lanka or were descended from ones who had. Sri Lankans tend to settle in large metropolitan areas and congregate with coreligionists. Significant Sri Lankan American communities exist in Chicago, Los Angeles, New York, Newark, Miami, and Tampa.

Sri Lanka has maintained an excellent educational system, with compulsory schooling to the age of seventeen and a well-developed college and university system. As a former British colony, the country has a large English-speaking population as well. However, the weak national economy—debilitated by decades of civil war—does not offer commensurate economic opportunities, sending many well-educated Sri Lankans abroad. While most of these settle in the United Kingdom, increasing numbers have been coming to the United States since the 1990s, where, along with Indian Americans, they have achieved notable success in the high-tech sector.

Traditions and Acculturation

Often well educated and fluent in English, even first-generation Sri Lankan Americans tend to be highly acculturated to life in the United States, especially as their small numbers make it difficult to form self-contained communities like those of larger Asian American groups. At the same time, many Sri Lankans attempt to maintain their cultural traditions by having their children attend religious classes in addition to their formal schooling and to participate in traditional cultural events and ceremonies.

Among the most important elements of Sri Lankan culture is the high value placed on education. Sri Lankan American families often perform the *akuru kiyaweema* ceremony, when a child first begins to master the alphabet. Indeed, the teaching of the alphabet to a young boy or girl is usually delegated to a respected elder and is a highly ritualized process involving a special sitting posture and clothes of a particular color on the part of the child. Courtship and marriage are likewise highly ritualized. In Sri Lanka, traditional marriages are the norm and often involve members of the same clan. While many younger Sri Lankan Americans eschew such practices, arranged marriages are still relatively common within the community, often serving to link family members living in the United States with those still residing in the home country. For the most part, the caste distinctions that dictate marriage and other social interactions in Sri Lanka hold little sway in the well-educated, highly acculturated Sri Lankan American community.

Important dates in the Sri Lankan American calendar tend to be determined by religion. Buddhists holidays include the Buddha's birthday in May, when members of the community decorate their homes with lanterns and attend temple ceremonies. Among the most widely observed Hindu Sri Lankan holidays is Deepavali, or the festival of lights, celebrated in autumn, when lamps are lit to mark the triumph of light over darkness. Muslim Sri Lankans celebrate the major Islamic holidays, most notably Ramadan, the month of fasting. The only holiday shared by all Sri Lankan Americans is a secular one, February 4, marking the country's 1948 independence from Britain.

Sri Lankans also share an artistic heritage heavily influenced by India, including the classical dance form *bharata natyam*, often performed in Sri Lankan American communities on independence day. Sri Lankan American families take great pride if any of their children become dancers, issuing *arangetram* announcements to mark the child's first performance.

Most Sri Lankan organizations in the United States resist taking sides in the sectarian conflict in their homeland. Ethnic Tamils especially avoid openly supporting the independence struggle, as the main armed group fighting for a Sri Lankan Tamil homeland—the Liberation of Tamil Eelam, better known as the Tamil Tigers—has been designated a terrorist organization by the U.S. State Department. However, the Tamil Nadu Foundation is dedicated to relieving the suffering of Tamil war refugees, while the Friends of Sri Lanka in the United States is dedicated to fighting what it calls Tamil terrorism.

Instead, the major Sri Lankan organizations in the United States, such as the Association of Sri Lankan Americans of Houston, emphasize aid programs to the home country as well the promotion of Sri Lankan culture in the United States through educational and artistic programs. Because such a large proportion of young Sri Lankans attend institutions of higher learning, many American universities have Sri Lankan student associations, which promote the national culture as well as provide services and social functions for the ethnic community.

Among all Asian American groups, Sri Lankan Americans appear to have distanced themselves farthest from their homeland. Immigrants from a poor and largely rural land, they are among the best-educated and most highly acculturated of Asian Americans. While many attempt to maintain their country's rich cultural heritage, most eschew its traditional caste distinctions and refuse to be drawn into the bloody sectarian conflict that has torn their homeland apart and resulted in the deaths of nearly 70,000 people.

James Ciment

Further Reading

Das Gupta, Monisha. *Unruly Immigrants: Rights, Activism, and Transnational South Asian Politics in the United States.* Durham, NC: Duke University Press, 2006.

Leonard, Karen Isaksen. *The South Asian Americans.* Westport, CT: Greenwood, 1997.

Rajan, Gita, and Shailja Sharma, eds. *New Cosmopolitanisms: South Asians in the US.* Palo Alto, CA: Stanford University Press, 2006.

Shankar, Lavina Dhingra, and Rajini Srikanth, eds. *A Part, Yet Apart: South Asians in Asian America.* Philadelphia: Temple University Press, 1998.

Sri Lankan American Association. http://www.slaah.org.

The Taiwanese American Experience: History and Culture

The history of the Taiwanese in America has been short compared to that of other Asian Americans, technically beginning with the Communist occupation of Mainland China in 1949 and the establishment of the Nationalist regime by refugees on the island then known as Formosa. In the relatively brief period since then, however, Taiwanese Americans have developed strong roots in the general fabric of American society. One main element of Taiwanese American identity is its evolving character, reflecting the change that has guided Taiwan's political, social, and cultural climate over the decades. Generally, the term "Taiwanese Americans" refers to naturalized citizens from Taiwan and their American-born children.

Taiwanese identity had been associated with people living on the island long before 1949, when hundreds of thousands of refugees from Communism on the mainland settled on the island at the end of the Chinese Civil War. Taiwanese aborigines, Austronesian peoples with a linguistic connection to native groups in Malaysia, the Philippines, and Indonesia, were the earliest inhabitants of the island. The majority of Taiwanese today are descendants of early Fujianese and Hakka immigrants who settled in the seventeenth and eighteenth centuries. In the 270 years preceding 1895, Taiwan and the Penghu Islands (Pescadores) were controlled by a number of successive regimes: the Dutch East India Company, the Zheng Chenggong (Koxinga) kingdom, and finally the Qing Empire. Taiwan's fifty years as a Japanese colony ended with the Japanese defeat by the Allies in 1945; four years later, the island came under the rule of the Chinese Nationalists (Kuomintang/KMT), which had ruled Mainland China until that time. Ousted in the Communist Revolution led by Mao Zedong, the KMT fled the Chinese mainland and established its government in Taiwan under the official name of the Republic of China (ROC).

During the evacuation, some 2 million refugees from the mainland—mostly KMT officials and soldiers—went over to Taiwan. This group came to monopolize political and economic power on the island after 1950, while na-tive Taiwanese were excluded. The dominant minority thus came to be known as "Mainlanders." Meanwhile, the KMT also instituted martial law on the island from 1949 to 1987, years that also saw a period of unprecedented economic growth for Taiwan. Throughout this time, the Nationalists insisted that they were the legitimate government of all of China, as well as Taiwan. Original island inhabitants, however, with a distinct history and culture, did not strongly identify with China. Thus, while Taiwanese Americans are often regarded as Chinese Americans, origins and allegiances conflict in several respects, making the identification and naming of diaspora groups a politically controversial subject.

Immigration and Settlement

When the U.S. Immigration and Nationality Act of 1965 lifted immigration quotas and opened the nation's doors to more nonwhites, large-scale Chinese immigration began almost immediately. A large proportion of those who came during the first two decades after passage of the legislation were from Taiwan, consisting of both Taiwanese Chinese and Mainland Chinese. Many held undergraduate degrees when they arrived and sought to pursue advanced degrees in American universities. While some returned to Taiwan after completing their studies, many stayed on and found employment in a market that valued their technical and scientific skills. Indeed, the prospect of greater economic opportunity and advancement in the United States represented a powerful draw even among Taiwanese who could not immediately earn as much as they did at home. Thus, while some remain employed in manual labor and the service economy, the Taiwanese American community is well represented in the class of trained American professionals.

The migration patterns of Taiwanese to the United States were largely a reflection of the relatively comfortable socioeconomic status of this group. Whereas Chinese immigrants traditionally had clustered in urban "Chinatowns," most Taiwanese Americans settled in the

Members of the Taiwanese Nationalist Party, or Kuomintang, march in the Chinese New Year parade in Washington, D.C. The Nationalist lobby has remained active and influential in U.S. politics since the establishment of the Taiwan regime in 1949. *(Alex Wong/Getty Images)*

outlying suburban areas of Los Angeles, New York, and other cities during the peak period from the late 1970s through the 1980s. Taiwanese American communities began to flourish in such areas as Monterey Park (giving rise to the nickname "Little Taipei") and throughout the San Gabriel Valley in California, as well as in Queens, New York.

As such, the Taiwanese American immigrant experience differed considerably from that of Chinese Americans. Chinatowns were Cantonese-speaking enclaves, primarily working-class, and traced their roots to the bachelor society of sojourners during the late nineteenth and early twentieth centuries. Taiwanese Americans, by contrast, were primarily Mandarin speakers, highly trained and educated, and relative newcomers to the United States. While the Los Angeles and New York metropolitan areas have drawn the most Taiwanese, sizable populations have developed as well in Texas, New Jersey, Illinois, and Washington. As many Taiwanese brought their wealth with them to the United States, they injected money into the local economy through business and real estate investments. This, in turn, helped revitalize some

suburban communities, even in the face of resistance by local, mainly white, residents.

Life in America

The general socioeconomic stability and relatively high academic achievement of Taiwanese Americans has brought the group undue attention as a "model minority"—a stereotypical term used by mainstream media to promote the success of certain immigrant groups at the expense of other minorities. Since the 1960s, the term has been used specifically in reference to the "success" of Asian Americans in the face of discrimination and marginalization, advancing a mythical premise that Asian Americans provide an example to others for socioeconomic success based on intrinsic cultural traits. As a result, the label serves to pigeonhole Taiwanese Americans and other Asian Americans in a way that promotes assimilation over the preservation of traditional values, while ignoring problems in the community and the obstacles created by mainstream society.

Much as the family—rather than the individual—

has been regarded as the basic unit of society throughout Chinese history, so it remains the central construct of the Taiwanese American community and way of life. In Taiwan itself, the traditional extended family began to disappear as the country became increasingly urbanized during the 1950s and 1960s; large, extended families were proving more difficult to maintain than they had been in the countryside. By the time Taiwanese began to immigrate in large numbers to the United States, the nuclear family had become the primary social unit. None of which is to say that extended family and cross-generational ties are not strong. It is not uncommon for grandparents who reside in Taiwan to visit their families in America for extended periods. In other cases, one or both parents return to work in Taiwan while their children remain in the United States for schooling.

Taiwanese Americans observe both standard American holidays and traditional Chinese festivals—from Christmas and Thanksgiving to the Mid-Autumn Festival and Lunar New Year. Members of the community adhere to a variety of faiths, the two largest of which are Mahayana Buddhism and Protestant Christianity. While the number of Buddhist adherents continues to grow, the increasing popularity of Christianity has been a more conspicuous phenomenon in Taiwanese American life. Whereas Protestant Christians account for only about 2 percent of the population of Taiwan, more than a quarter of the Taiwanese American population is Christian, at least in part because churches provide a social gathering place and cultural center as well as a place of worship.

Taiwanese American political and social organizations have helped represent the interests of segments of the community in American society, as well as facilitating the transition for new arrivals. Noteworthy political organizations include the World Taiwanese Congress and the Formosan Association for Public Affairs (FAPA), advocacy groups for Taiwanese independence. The latter publishes the *Taiwan Communiqué*, a bimonthly journal focusing on political issues pertaining to the homeland. Social organizations include the Taiwanese American Citizens League (TACL), a civic group that focuses on citizenship and leadership development,

and the Intercollegiate Taiwanese American Students Association (ITASA), which operates as a network for university students. In addition, there are a number of Buddhist temples and centers affiliated with Fo Kuang Shan (Buddha's Light Mountain), as well as the Buddhist Compassion Relief Tzu Chi Foundation. Both are based in Taiwan but claim strong followings in such U.S. cities as Los Angeles, Houston, San Jose, New York, San Francisco, and Honolulu.

As the Taiwanese American community has increased its role and prominence in U.S. society, a growing number of individuals have made a name for themselves in the realms of politics, business, entertainment, and science. Notables include Ang Lee, the Academy Award–winning film director; Jerry Yang, the cofounder of Yahoo! Inc.; Elaine Chao, secretary of labor in the George W. Bush administration; Iris Chang, the best-selling author of *The Rape of Nanking* (1997), which raised awareness about the massacre of Chinese civilians at the hands of Japanese soldiers in 1937; and David Ho, a prominent AIDS researcher who was *Time* magazine's 1996 Man of the Year.

Theodore Chang

Further Reading

Chen, Carolyn. "The Religious Varieties of Ethnic Pressure: A Comparison Between a Taiwanese Immigrant Buddhist Temple and an Evangelical Christian Church." In *Sociology of Religion* 63:2 (2002): 215–38.

Chen, Hsiang-shui. *Chinatown No More: Taiwan Immigrants in Contemporary New York*. Ithaca, NY: Cornell University Press, 1992.

Formosa Foundation. http://www.formosafoundation.org.

Formosan Association for Public Affairs. http://www.fapa.org.

Gu, Chien-juh. *Mental Health Among Taiwanese Americans: Gender, Immigration, and Transnational Struggles*. El Paso, TX: LFB Scholarly Publishing, 2006.

Intercollegiate Taiwanese American Students Association. http://www.itasa.org.

Ng, Franklin. *The Taiwanese Americans*. Westport, CT: Greenwood, 1998.

Taiwanese American Citizens League. http://www.tacl.org.

Taiwanese United Fund. http://www.tufusa.org.

Taiwanese Americans
Alphabetical Entries

Business and Entrepreneurship, Taiwanese American

Few in number prior to passage of the Immigration and Nationality Act of 1965, which ended national quotas, Taiwanese Americans in subsequent decades have arrived in the United States in significantly larger numbers. The Taiwanese community in America in the early twenty-first century—totaling more than 150,000 in all—is generally well educated and often backed by capital from their economically dynamic homeland. Taiwanese American entrepreneurs have prospered particularly in the high-technology sector.

In the first decades after passage of the Immigration Act, thousands of Taiwan's most promising engineering students traveled to the United States to earn postgraduate degrees at American colleges. Initially drawn by the quality of U.S. universities and discouraged by the lack of openings at Taiwan's few postgraduate programs, many were prompted to stay in America after earning their degrees by the prospect of higher salaries and greater opportunities in a more developed high-tech sector. By the 1990s, however, the most successful Taiwanese American high-tech innovators and entrepreneurs were those who had come to the United States as younger children—the so-called 1.5 generation—reflecting the fact that the ethnic community was establishing deeper roots in the country. Among the 1.5 generation are Jerry Yang, who cofounded the Web directory and portal Yahoo! in 1994, and Steve Chen, cofounder of the popular video-sharing Web site YouTube in 2005.

As the Taiwanese American community tended to settle in suburban ethnic enclaves rather than the old urban Chinatowns, many invested in shopping centers, retail, and other sectors that were enjoying great growth in suburban areas, especially in the San Gabriel Valley section of Los Angeles County. Such burgeoning ethnic enclaves—where Taiwanese, non-Taiwanese Chinese, and other Asian immigrants increasingly settled—offered opportunities for ethnically oriented consumer businesses,

especially as per capita incomes there were far higher than in urban Chinatowns. Among the most successful of entrepreneurs to take advantage of these markets was Roger Chen, founder of the Ranch 99 supermarket chain, and Alan Yu and Marvin Cheng, cofounders of Lollicup Coffee and Tea, a national chain of cafés featuring popular Asian boba teas.

Ethnic Associations

What has made for entrepreneurial success within the Taiwanese American community, say experts, is not just education, but a uniquely strong network of ethnically based professional associations. Among the most well-known are the Southern California–based Chinese American Computer Association, founded in 1981; the Silicon Valley–based Monte Jade Science and Technology Association (MJSTA), founded in 1989; and the North American Taiwanese Engineers Association (NATEA), founded in 1991 and also based in Silicon Valley. Such associations offer networking opportunities not only for individuals and corporations in the United States but also for business contacts between the United States and Taiwan.

Many of these professional associations have also become significant sources for cross-generational financing and mentoring. Older generations of Taiwanese American engineers and entrepreneurs play a key role in financing and mentoring younger generations, providing more accessible sources of financing than mainstream investors. Each professional organization, either explicitly or informally, provides first-generation Taiwanese Americans with a source of business contacts and social networks at the local community level. The associations also sponsor regular events that provide forums for sharing specialized information and knowledge.

Taiwanese American entrepreneurs also rely on less formal social networks to enhance their know-how, skills, and financial resources to start new ventures. Such connections have been of particular importance in Silicon Valley computer ventures. The most popular recruiting method for Taiwan-based firms is referral by friends and personal contacts at previous jobs—in other words, informal networks that reflect the traditional reliance on *guanxi* (personal "connections" or networks) rather than on formal advertisements.

Financing Taiwanese American Businesses

New Asian immigrants who need capital to set up businesses traditionally have had difficulty in obtaining commercial loans from mainstream American banks. In recent decades, Taiwanese immigrants have increasingly turned to their home country or ethno-banks for initiating new businesses because credit procedures are easier than in mainstream financial institutions and there are typically no language impediments. Ethnic banks are more flexible than mainstream banks in the kinds of financing arrangements they make, sometimes demanding less in the way of traditional collateral and relying more on familiarity with the borrower's background and family.

To overcome the problem of obtaining loans for capital, financial institutions were created to provide a large spectrum of services, including assistance in importing and exporting products and services from and to Taiwan. General Bank (now Cathay Bank), for example, was established by Taiwan's Wu family in the 1980s and in ten years became the largest Taiwanese American bank in Los Angeles. The initial customers were typically closely held private and family firms, small in size and lacking sufficient credit history to get financing from mainstream banks.

Meanwhile, Taiwan has also become an important source of capital for Silicon Valley start-ups—especially those started by immigrant entrepreneurs—and a number of American banks that cater to the Taiwanese American community are owned by Taiwanese shareholders. For example, FCB Taiwan California Bank, China Trust Bank (U.S.A.), and Far East National Bank (FENB) are controlled by three major financial institutions in Taiwan: First Commercial Bank in Taipei, Chinatrust Commercial Bank, and Bank SinoPac (a member of SinoPac Holdings). Far East National Bank, the first federally chartered Asian American bank, was founded in 1974; Chinatrust Bank (USA) was established in 1989; and First Commercial Bank (USA) was founded in 1997. In addition to providing financing, these banks also introduce Taiwanese American entrepreneurs to suppliers in Taiwan and then help arrange import-export deals.

Since the 1980s, another trend has emerged among Taiwanese American entrepreneurs, particularly in the high-tech sector: returning to Taiwan to invest in that country's rapidly growing computer sector. These returnees have been critical in building a dynamic technological infrastructure in their homeland, in part by building partnerships with Silicon Valley companies. At the same time, a large number of engineers began to work in both the United States and Taiwan, helping develop such venues as Hsinchu Science and Industrial Park, a major center of semiconductor manufacturing in Taiwan since 1980.

The growing integration of the Taiwanese and U.S. technological communities offers substantial benefits to both economies. Silicon Valley remains at the center of new product innovation and the development of leading-edge technologies, while Taiwan offers world-class manufacturing and access to key consumers and markets in China and Southeast Asia. The underlying social structures and institutions provided by the community of Taiwanese engineers ensure the continuous flows of information between the two regions, partially reversing the "brain drain" of top engineers from Taiwan in the early days of mass emigration from the island in the 1960s and 1970s.

Alfredo Manuel Coelho

Further Reading
Chang, Shenglin. *The Global Silicon Valley Home: Lives and Landscapes Within Taiwanese American Trans-Pacific Culture.* Palo Alto, CA: Stanford University Press, 2005.

Chee, Maria W.L. *Taiwanese American Transnational Families: Women and Kin Work.* New York: Routledge, 2005.

Hsiang-shui, Chen. *Chinatown No More: Taiwan Immigrants in Contemporary New York.* Ithaca, NY: Cornell University Press, 1992.

Ng, Franklin. *The Taiwanese Americans.* Westport, CT: Greenwood, 1998.

Tseng, Yen-Fen. "Beyond Little Taipei: Taiwanese Immigrant Businesses in Los Angeles." *International Migration Review* 29:10 (1995): 33–58.

———. "The Mobility of Entrepreneurs and Capital: Taiwanese Capital-Linked Migration." *International Migration* 38:2 (June 2000): 143–68.

Coordination Council for North American Affairs

The Coordination Council for North American Affairs (CCNAA) is the original name for Taiwan's de facto diplomatic office in the United States. (The representative U.S. body in Taipei is called the American

Institute in Taiwan, or AIT). The quasi-diplomatic relationship was established between the two countries after the United States officially recognized the Communist People's Republic of China (PRC) and withdrew formal recognition from the Nationalist Republic of China (Taiwan) on January 1, 1979. Operating as a kind of embassy, consulate, and general liaison, the CCNAA in 1994 was redesignated as the Taipei Economic and Cultural Representative Office (TECRO).

Although derecognition often relegates the subject country to enemy status, U.S.-Taiwan relations after 1978 were different from the outset. The United States had and still has close trade relations with Taiwan and, under the Taiwan Relations Act of 1979, maintains a defense and security commitment to the republic. That legislation was effectively imposed on the Jimmy Carter administration after he announced recognition of the mainland regime and the breaking of formal ties with the Kuomintang (KMT) Nationalists (a diplomatic development referred to as the "One China Policy"). Signed into law by President Carter on April 10, 1979, the statute provided for a "Taiwan Instrumentality," or essential restructuring of the relationship between the two countries. While Taiwan would not have an official ambassadorial presence in America, the legislation called for "the same number of offices and complement of personnel as were previously operated in the United States by the governing authorities on Taiwan recognized as the Republic of China prior to January 1, 1979." The new office was called the Coordination Council for North American Affairs.

The unofficial (and therefore second-class) status of the CCNAA represented a compromise between Washington and the People's Republic, which still regards Taiwan as a renegade province and has always sought to isolate it internationally. Yet while Taiwan's diplomatic presence in the United States is unofficial, it is also rather substantial in terms of personnel and institutions. Diplomatic, trade, and cultural relations were extensive from the beginning, with matters ranging from the granting of entrance and exit visas to the sale of defensive missiles being handled through the CCNAA.

By the late 1980s and early 1990s, Taiwan's isolated position in the world was beginning to change, as its formidable economy and democratization process made it more legitimate in the eyes of many nations. At the same time, the Communist PRC lost stature, especially following the Tiananmen Massacre of 1989. With the collapse of the Soviet Union in 1991 and the end of the global struggle between Communism and the West, Taiwan was able to better integrate itself into the world community and to solidify its relations with the United States. In response, the Clinton administration conducted the so-called Taiwan Policy Review in 1994. The result was a reaffirmation of the One China Policy but an adjustment in the conduct of relations with Taiwan. The CCNAA was redesignated the Taipei Economic and Cultural Representative Office, a slightly more official presence.

Taipei Representative Offices (TROs) have been established in more than thirty other countries around the world. In the United States and its territories, TECRO maintains twelve regional offices and is headed by a representative with ambassador credentials and two deputy offices. Its mission is to "promote bilateral trade, investment, culture, science and technology exchanges and cooperation, as well as better understanding," while performing many of the functions of an official ambassy or consulate, such as issuing visas. Organizationally, it includes a Political Division, a Congressional Liaison Division, a Consular Division, an Administrative Division, a Press Division, a Cultural Division, an Economic Division, a Science and Technology Division, a Defense Liaison Division, and a Defense Procurement Division— together responsible for managing the various aspects of bilateral relations between the United States and Taiwan.

Vincent K. Pollard

Further Reading

Damrosch, Lori Fisler. "The Taiwan Relations Act After Ten Years." *Journal of Asian Law* 3:2 (Fall 1989): 157–83.
Taiwan Economic and Cultural Representative Office. http://www.taiwanembassy.org/US.
Taiwan Relations Act (Public Law 96–8). *United States Code,* Title 22, Chapter 48 (1979).

Demographics, Taiwanese American

Like many other Asian immigrant groups, Taiwanese began arriving in the United States in large numbers after passage of the Immigration and Nationality Act of 1965, which ended the system of national quotas. The 2000 census identified a total of 144,795 Taiwanese in the United States, about half of whom, 75,000, were living in California. The metropolitan areas with the three largest Taiwanese Americans populations were Los Angeles–Riverside–Orange County, California, with 37,544; New York–Northern New Jersey–Long Island with 14,240; and San Francisco–Oakland–San Jose, California, with 13,448.

The socioeconomic impact of the Taiwanese American community goes beyond their relative numbers. Compared to the rest of the Chinese in America, the Taiwanese population in general is well educated and technologically skilled. As of 1990, some 60 percent of Taiwanese Americans age twenty-five years or older had a bachelor's degree, compared to about 40 percent among Chinese generally and 20 percent among all Asian Americans. Partly as a result, Taiwanese immigrants usually do not settle in urban Chinatowns, but more often reside in ethnically homogenous suburbs.

Perhaps the most significant Taiwanese American community in the United States is Monterey Park, California, the largest city in the United States with a Chinese American majority. In the 1980s and 1990s, the American public designated this new post-1965 suburban community "Little Taipei." The social and economic impact of the Taiwanese community on this suburb of Los Angeles has transformed the entire San Gabriel Valley region from a largely Anglo suburb of Los Angeles—especially such communities as Monterey Park, Alhambra, San Gabriel, and Rosemead—into a Taiwanese economic and cultural outpost in the region. There are retail shopping centers geared to the Taiwanese American community as well as businesses engaging in trade and other commercial activities with Taiwan itself. The Taiwanese government, recognizing the political and economic importance of Little Taipei, has supported two community organizations in the area: the Chinese Cultural Center II in El Monte and the Los Angeles Chinese Educational Service Center in Rosemead.

In 2000, Little Taipei experienced a demographic shift due to a surge of immigrants from Mainland China. That year, the number of immigrants from the People's Republic was estimated to be ten times greater than that from Hong Kong and six times greater than that from Taiwan. In 2002, according to U.S. federal statistics, 61,282 Mainland Chinese immigrated legally to the United States. With the People's Republic easing its restrictions on those seeking to emigrate, some 30,000 to 40,000 have moved to the United States each year since the late 1990s. Thus, the designation of Monterey Park as Little Taipei is giving way to Little Beijing or Little Shanghai.

The growing number of immigrants produced other suburban Taiwanese communities in the San Gabriel Valley as well. The second core Taiwanese settlement in the valley encompasses the cities of Walnut, Rowland Heights, West Covina, and Hacienda Heights. For instance, the total number of Chinese residents in Rowland Heights is 15,740, representing 32.4 percent of the total population of the city. Many wealthier, more established Chinese and Taiwanese Americans have moved to the northwestern region of the valley, which includes such

upscale cities as South Pasadena, San Marino, Acadia, and Temple. In 2000, for example, Chinese constituted 37.1 percent and 30.8 percent of the total populations of Acadia and Temple, respectively.

Major Chinese communities in major U.S. metropolitan areas consist of five ethnic Chinese subgroups: Mainland Chinese, Taiwanese Chinese, Hong Kong Chinese, Chinese American, and Chinese Vietnamese. Depending on the particular community, one subgroup may be dominant, or it may coexist with others. In San Francisco, for example, the Chinese community is dominated by long-standing, well-established Cantonese Chinese, while in nearby Oakland, the community is dominated by both Wah-Q and more recent Chinese Vietnamese. In the San Gabriel Valley suburbs of Los Angeles, by contrast, the Chinese community is dominated by a Taiwanese American presence, which coexists with other subgroups.

The second-largest Chinese settlement, which includes a sizable Taiwanese community, is found in New York City, which accounts for 16 percent of the Chinese in the United States (compared to 40 percent in California). Much as their counterparts in Monterey Park, Taiwanese immigrants have had an especially strong impact in the Flushing neighborhood of Queens, New York. The difference in New York is that Taiwanese and other Chinese subgroups in Flushing, Queens, coexist with thriving communities of Koreans and Indians.

The third-largest concentration of Taiwanese Americans can be found in Northern California's Silicon Valley and such suburbs as Cupertino, Milpitas, and San Jose, as well as Fremont on the east side of San Francisco Bay. Unlike the San Gabriel Valley suburbs of Los Angeles, where Taiwanese settlements are clustered in several cities, Taiwanese in Northern California are dispersed. Silicon Valley includes dozens of Chinese technology associations.

Metropolitan Washington-Baltimore (4,360) and the Seattle-Tacoma area (4,345) represent two other sizable Taiwanese American communities, with smaller enclaves across the country. With all the changes and dispersal, however, Monterey, California, remains the cultural center and primary economic outpost of overseas Taiwanese.

Joe Chung Fong

Further Reading

Lai, Eric, and Dennis Arguelles, eds. "A People of Their Own: Taiwanese Americans." In *The New Face of Asian Pacific America.* San Francisco: Asian Week, 2003.

Ng, Franklin. *The Taiwanese Americans.* Westport, CT: Greenwood, 1998.

U.S. Census Bureau. *Statistical Abstract of the United States.* 2001 and 2008 eds. Washington, DC: Government Printing Office, 2000 and 2007.

Ho, David (1952–)

Molecular biologist David Da-I Ho is one of the world's leading Acquired Immune Deficiency Syndrome (AIDS) researchers, known for championing the use of protease inhibitors in patients with the human immunodeficiency virus (HIV)—a breakthrough treatment. Ho is also the founding scientific director and chief executive officer of the Aaron Diamond AIDS research center in New York, where he is also the Irene Diamond Professor at Rockefeller University. For his achievements in fighting AIDS, *Time* magazine named Ho its Man of the Year in 1996.

Da-I Ho was born on November 3, 1952, in Taichung, Taiwan, where he spent most of his childhood with his younger brother Phillip and his mother. (Da-I means "Great One.") His father, an engineer, was in the United States earning money to bring the family to join him, which they did in 1964. The family settled in downtown Los Angeles, where David—as he was now called—mastered the English language within six months, made friends, and excelled in academics. He went on to study physics at the California Institute of Technology, graduating summa cum laude in 1974, and then switched to medicine. He earned his MD from the Harvard-MIT Division of Health Sciences and Technology in 1978, followed by clinical training in internal medicine at UCLA School of Medicine (1978–1982) and in infectious diseases at Massachusetts General Hospital (1982–1985). It was during his residency in internal medicine at Cedars-Sinai Medical Center in Los Angeles, beginning in 1981, that he came into contact with some of the first reported cases of what was later identified as AIDS.

Devoting his efforts full-time to AIDS research, Ho was among the first to propose that the disease was caused by a virus and one of the first to isolate the retrovirus. In the research community, he is recognized for explaining the dynamic nature of HIV replication in infected persons. This led Ho and his colleagues to advocate for the use of a combination antiretroviral therapy, including protease inhibitors to prevent viral replication. Such therapies resulted in major reductions in AIDS-associated mortality, especially in the developing world, beginning in the mid-1990s. Theorizing that a combination of powerful protease inhibitors with other HIV drugs would be more effective in treating full-blown AIDS, Ho devised a treatment method based on a regimen of "cocktails"—which became a therapeutic mainstay in treating HIV patients. More recently, Ho and his team have been working on an anti-AIDS vaccine.

David Ho has been combating AIDS/HIV in his capacity as an educator and institutional organizer as well. In addition to publishing hundreds of articles on his research, he serves on the scientific advisory board of the National Cancer Institute and the American Foundation for AIDS Research; heads a consortium of organizations in China and the United States to address the crisis of HIV/AIDS in China; is an honorary professor at both Peking Union Medical College and the Chinese Academy of Medical Sciences; and serves on the Board of Overseers of Harvard University and the Board of Trustees of the California Institute of Technology.

David Hou

Further Reading

Aaron Diamond AIDS Research Center. http://www.adarc.org.

Bayer, Ronald, and Gerald M. Oppenheimer. *AIDS Doctors: Voices from the Epidemic.* New York: Oxford University Press, 2000.

Chua-Eoan, Howard. "The Tao of Ho." *Time,* December 30, 1996.

Hsi Lai Temple

Hsi Lai ("Coming to the West") Temple is said to be the largest Buddhist monastery in the Western Hemisphere. Located in Hacienda Heights in California's San Gabriel Valley—which boasts the largest concentration of Chinese American communities in the United States—the temple complex is nestled in the foothills about 20 miles (36 kilometers) east of downtown Los Angeles.

Completed in 1991, Hsi Lai Temple is the first and largest overseas center of Fo Kuang Shan ("Buddhist Lights Mountain"), an order founded by Master Hsing-yun in Taiwan in 1967 and one of the largest religious orders on the island. Seeking to revitalize and promote Buddhist belief, Fo Kuang Shan—a Mahayana Chinese Buddhism monastic order—pursues its goal through "humanization, modernization, and internationalization" by establishing branch temples on foreign soil. In 1978, the order acquired land along Hacienda Boulevard that was ideal for a mountain monastery, offering panoramic views of the San Gabriel Valley. Like its mother temple in Taiwan, the new facility was to practice "Humanistic Buddhism," attracting new adherents through education, cultural activities, and charity while promoting cultural exchange between East and West.

Due to local opposition, construction of the temple did not begin until eight years later, in 1986. Residents

The Hsi Lai Temple, a Chinese Buddhist monastery in California's San Gabriel Valley, follows traditional Ming and Ching dynasty design. Originally opposed by area residents, the temple attracts a welcome tourist trade and organizes popular community events. *(Hyungwon Kang/Time & Life Pictures/Getty Images)*

feared a spike in area housing prices, traffic jams, and an influx of tourists. Local business owners worried that the temple might damage commercial trade. Some opposed the establishment of a Buddhist temple in their largely Christian neighborhood. Others responded to the temple plan on racial grounds, fearing that it was a means for the Chinese to establish a dominant position in their community. During the planning stage, monks and Buddhist nuns went door to door explaining their good intentions and the benefits they could bring to the neighborhood. They also mounted a petition drive to help secure permission to build and made a number of concessions in order to obtain the permit. There were a total of six public hearings before the plan was finally approved. The $25 million temple, funded primarily by devotees and patrons from Taiwan, the United States, Malaysia, and Hong Kong, was finally completed in November 1988.

Occupying 15 acres (6 hectares), the central structure contains the Bodhisattva Hall, Buddha Hall, Meditation Hall, Dining Hall, Tripitaka library, gift shop, museum, reception rooms, classrooms, and monastic living quarters. The architecture follows traditional Ming and Ching dynasty design, and the gardens and statuary are likewise based on those of ancient Chinese monasteries. Hsi Lai

Temple soon emerged as a primary attraction in the San Gabriel Valley, drawing tourists from throughout the United States and other countries. It has also generated business revenue for the local community. Emphasizing the importance of peace and understanding in eliminating racial and religious conflict, it organizes a host of charity activities, a New Year's prayer service, and other special events in collaboration with local Christian and Mormon churches. In addition to hosting regular services and a variety of workshops, the temple functions as a community center, social relief organization, and cultural center. It was also the original site of the University of the West, the first Buddhist-funded institution of higher learning in the United States. Founded by Hsing-yun in 1991, the university moved to nearby Rosemead in 1996.

Wei Li

Further Reading

Hsi Lai Temple. http://www.hsilai.org.

Li, Wei. "Building Ethnoburbia: The Emergence and Manifestation of the Chinese *Ethnoburb* in Los Angeles' San Gabriel Valley." *Journal of Asian American Studies* 2:1 (1999): 1–28.

Lin, Irene. "Journey to the Far West: Chinese Buddhism in America." *Amerasia Journal* 22:1 (1996): 107–32.

Lee, Ang (1954–)

The Academy Award–winning motion-picture director Ang Lee, a native of Taiwan, is one of few filmmakers to achieve success in both Asia and the West. His understanding of Western mores and filmmaking techniques, combined with his Taiwanese upbringing and knowledge of Chinese culture, has allowed his artistry to resonate with audiences in both hemispheres as perhaps no other director in cinematic history.

He was born Li An on October 23, 1954, in the town of Chaojhou in Pingtung county in southern Taiwan. Both of his parents had moved to Taiwan from Mainland China following the Communist takeover in 1949 and the establishment of the Nationalist Republic of China on Taiwan. Lee attended the prestigious Tainan First Senior High School, where his father was a former principal. To the disappointment of his father, he twice failed the annual college entrance examination, the only route to a full university education in Taiwan. Instead, Lee attended a three-year college, the Taiwan Academy of Arts (now known as National Taiwan University of Arts) in Taipei, graduating in 1975. After completing his mandatory two-year military service, Lee traveled

Taiwanese American film director Ang Lee won Academy Awards for *Crouching Tiger, Hidden Dragon* (Best Foreign Language Film, 2000), an international coproduction; and for the U.S.-made *Brokeback Mountain* (Best Director, 2005). *(Hector Mata/AFP/Getty Images)*

alone to the United States in 1978 to pursue a bachelor of fine arts degree in theater at the University of Illinois at Urbana-Champaign. After graduating the following year, he enrolled in the Tisch School of the Arts at New York University, where he received his master's degree in film production. Among his classmates at Tisch was Spike Lee, on whose acclaimed thesis film, *Joe's Bed-Stuy Barbershop: We Cut Heads* (1983), Lee worked.

After spending six years on screenplays, Lee made his directorial debut with *Pushing Hands* (1992), a comedy about the generational and cultural divides in a Taiwanese family living in a New York City suburb. The film was a critical and box-office success in Taiwan and received eight nominations at the Golden Horse Film Festival, the nation's premier cinema showcase. Lee's second film, *The Wedding Banquet* (1993), about a gay Taiwanese immigrant who stages a marriage of convenience to please his visiting parents, won the Golden Bear Award at the Berlin Film Festival and was nominated as Best Foreign Language Film at both the Golden Globes and Academy Awards. *The Wedding Banquet* collected a total of eleven Taiwanese and international awards, launching Lee into prominence. His third film, *Eat Drink Man Woman* (1994), portrays traditional values, modern relationships, and family conflicts in Taipei. It was Lee's most successful film to date, winning an Oscar nomination for Best Foreign Film, an Independent Spirit Award, and a British Academy Award.

Three successful dramas opened doors in mainstream Hollywood filmmaking, and Lee was hired by Columbia Pictures to direct an adaptation of Jane Austen's *Sense and Sensibility* (1995), his first English-language movie; the film went on to receive seven Oscar nominations, including Best Picture. His next projects, *The Ice Storm* (1997) and *Ride with the Devil* (1999), drew critical praise but underperformed at the box office. In 2000, Lee made his first Chinese-language project in years, the martial-arts fantasy *Crouching Tiger, Hidden Dragon,* which garnered ten Academy Award nominations, winning the Oscar for Best Foreign Language Film and in three technical categories. With Chinese dialogue and English subtitles, *Crouching Tiger* became the highest-grossing foreign film in a number of countries, including the United States.

In 2003, Lee returned to Hollywood to direct the comic-book adaptation *Hulk,* his first big-budget production. *Hulk* proved disappointing to both critics and audiences, however, and Lee decided to try a small-budget, low-profile independent film as his next project. Based on Annie Proulx's Pulitzer Prize–finalist short story, "Brokeback Mountain," the 2005 release showcased Lee's ability to probe the depths of the human heart. *Brokeback Mountain,* which told of the forbidden love between two Wyoming cowboys, was critically acclaimed at major international film festivals and earned Lee numerous best director and best film awards. A cultural phenomenon as well as a box-office hit, *Brokeback Mountain* was nominated for eight Oscars, including Best Picture and Best Achievement in Directing. Although it lost the former to *Crash* in a controversial upset, Lee was honored with the Oscar for directing—becoming the first Asian to win that award.

Jennifer Liu

Further Reading

Cheshire, Ellen. *Ang Lee.* North Pomfret, VT: Trafalgar Square, 2001.

Dilley, Whitney Crothers. *The Cinema of Ang Lee: The Other Side of the Screen.* London: Wallflower, 2007.

Lee, Yuan-Tseh (1936–)

Yuan-Tseh Lee (Li Yuan Zhe) is a Chinese American chemist who shared the 1986 Nobel Prize in Chemistry with Dudley R. Herschbach and John C. Polanyi for, in the words of the Nobel Prize committee, "their contributions to the dynamics of chemical elementary processes."

Yuan-Tseh Lee was born on November 29, 1936, in the city of Hsinchu, Taiwan, to Tse-Fan Lee, an artist, and Pei Tsai, an elementary schoolteacher. Lee's childhood education was interrupted during World War II when the Japanese occupied Taiwan. After the war, Lee was able to finish both elementary and high school in Hsinchu. Because of his outstanding academic record, he was accepted at the National Taiwan University in 1955 without taking the required examination. He obtained his bachelor's degree in chemistry in 1959 and began graduate studies at the National Tsinghua University, where he received an MS two years later. In 1962, Lee entered the University of California at Berkeley under chemistry professor Bruce H. Mahan, where he developed a special interest in ion-molecule reactions and the dynamics of molecular scattering. After receiving his PhD in 1965, he continued work at Mahan's laboratory as a postdoctoral fellow for a year and a half, continuing his advanced study in chemistry.

In 1967, Lee joined the research team of Harvard University chemist Dudley Herschbach, where he worked on the design of a new, highly complicated apparatus to allow a wider range of scattering studies. With Herschbach's encouragement, Lee overcame a number of technical difficulties and developed an instrument that was the first truly successful universal crossed-molecular-beam apparatus. Several levels of magnitude more sensitive than its competitors, the device revolutionized the crossed-beam study of reaction dynamics and provided a powerful tool for modern chemical research.

In 1968, Lee accepted a position as assistant professor of chemistry at the University of Chicago, where he was elevated to associate professor three years later and full professor in 1973. The following year he became a U.S. citizen and returned to California as professor of chemistry and principal investigator at the University of California's Lawrence Berkeley Laboratory. In his 1986 Nobel Prize presentation, Lee was specifically cited for his contributions in making the crossed-molecular-beam technique applicable to relatively large molecules. Lee has received many other major awards and prizes, including the Ernest Orlando Lawrence Memorial Award for Physics of the United States Energy Research and Development Agency (1981); the Peter Debye Award in Physical Chemistry (1986) of the American Chemical Society; and the National Medal of Science (1986) of the National Science Foundation.

In 1994, Lee moved back to Taiwan, renewing his citizenship and becoming president of the Academia Sinica; he devoted himself to advanced scientific research, establishing academic guidelines, and recruiting and developing scholars. He also became active in Taiwanese politics, establishing an organization to promote community empowerment and working to improve relations between the island republic and mainland China. Lee played a high-profile role in the 2000 Taiwanese presidential election, endorsing the eventual winner, Chen Shui-bian, in the last days of the campaign. In the aftermath, Lee is said to have declined the position of premier, the head of the executive branch appointed by the president.

Wenxian Zhang

Further Reading

Wasson, Tyler, and Gert H. Brieger, eds. *Nobel Prize Winners: An H.W. Wilson Biographical Dictionary.* New York: H.W. Wilson, 1987.

Zia, Helen, and Susan B. Gall, eds. *Notable Asian Americans.* New York: Gale, 1995.

Lee (Wen Ho) Case

A Taiwanese-born nuclear scientist working at the Los Alamos National Laboratory in New Mexico, Wen Ho Lee became the center of a political controversy over national security and anti-Chinese prejudice when he was arrested on December 10, 1999, for allegedly selling

American nuclear secrets to the Chinese government in Beijing.

During his imprisonment, Wen Ho Lee, a diminutive sixty-year-old Taiwan-born physicist, was confined to a jail cell measuring 13 feet by 7 feet (4 meters by 2.1 meters) with his legs shackled, his hands manacled, and the handcuffs chained to his waist. To pass time, he read books, listened to classical music, and wrote a mathematics textbook. Family members—including wife Sylvia Lee, daughter Alberta Lee, and son Chung Lee, a medical student in Ohio—were horrified at the treatment he received, and U.S. District Court judge James A. Parker called his imprisonment "draconian" and "unfair."

On September 13, 2000, Lee was released from the Santa Fe County Detention Center after nine months of this confinement. The release was a result of his pleading guilty to one count of unlawfully gathering national defense information, out of fifty-nine counts of violating national security. In exchange, Lee would cooperate with FBI agents to reveal all he knew about seven computer tapes onto which he was accused of downloading sensitive information on the design of W-88, a thermonuclear warhead built for U.S. missile submarines, and giving the information to Beijing.

The release of Lee delighted the Asian American community, which had been petitioning the federal government to free him unconditionally and drop all fifty-nine charges against him. Lee's guilty plea, however, had made him a felon. As a result, he lost the right to vote and other privileges of citizenship. Consequently, the Asian American community continued to fight for his civil rights by petitioning a presidential pardon.

The case of Wen Ho Lee has been characterized by the Asian American community as racial profiling. Wen Ho Lee was born in Nantou, Taiwan, in 1939 and graduated from National Cheng Gong University in 1963. He came to the United States in 1965 for graduate study at Texas A&M University, receiving his PhD in 1969. He became a U.S. citizen in 1974 and went to work at the Los Alamos National Laboratory in Albuquerque four years later as a contract employee of the University of California, designing weapons.

The case began in 1995 when a U.S. intelligence agent in Asia was approached by a Chinese defector with a sensational document that contained the blueprint of China's nuclear weapons program suggesting a leak from Los Alamos. In May 1996, federal investigators identified Lee as a possible spy for China, and he became the subject of an ongoing criminal investigation. An article in the New York Times revealed the case to the general public on March 6, 1999, and Lee was fired by Los Alamos two days later for breaches of workplace rules. On August 1, 1999, after five months of silence, Lee denied spying for Beijing on the television news magazine 60 Minutes. Saying that downloading classified files to unsecured computers was a common practice at Los Alamos, he claimed that he was singled out because he was an ethnic Chinese.

Upon his arrest that December, Lee was indicted on fifty-nine counts and held without bail in Santa Fe County Detention Center—even through investigators conceded that they did not have the evidence to convict him as a spy. On August 24, 2000, Judge Parker announced that Lee was eligible for bail, and on September 13, 2000, after 279 days in prison, Lee pleaded guilty to one felony count of mishandling nuclear secrets; the government dropped the fifty-eight other charges. In releasing Wen Ho Lee, Judge Parker declared that the actions of the top decision makers at the Department of Justice and Energy Department had "embarrassed our nation."

The case of Wen Ho Lee outraged the Asian American community, which felt that a great injustice had been done to Lee personally and that racial profiling and discrimination on the part of federal law enforcement was an affront to all of them. Asian American scientists expressed particular concern; indeed, the number applying for jobs at national defense and nuclear weapons labs declined dramatically after the case was reported. In the aftermath of Lee's arrest and imprisonment, national Asian American organizations passed resolutions demanding that all fifty-nine charges against Lee be dropped unconditionally, that Lee be set free and reinstated in his job with back pay, that the University of California president and secretary of energy publicly apologize to Lee and his family, and that all racial profiling and discrimination against Asian Americans be put to an end. Asian American communities in Silicon Valley, Albuquerque, Detroit, Los Angeles, New York, San Francisco, and Seattle rallied for Lee's release. Even after the case was concluded, the Asian American community continued to lobby for the full restoration of Lee's civil rights. In June 2006, he received a $1.6 million settlement from the U.S. government and several media companies in a lawsuit over the leaking of his name before criminal charges had been filed against him.

Huping Ling

Further Reading

Lee, Wen Ho, and Helen Zia. *My Country Versus Me: The First-hand Account by the Los Alamos Scientist Who Was Falsely Accused of Being a Spy.* New York: Hyperion, 2001.

Wong, Samsong. "The Wen Ho Lee Five." *AsianWeek,* August 27, 2004.

Parachute Kids

Parachute kids, also referred to as "unaccompanied minors," "little overseas students," and *xiao liu xue sheng* (in Mandarin), are Taiwanese American—and, to a lesser extent, Hong Kong and Mainland Chinese—young people, generally between the ages of eight and eighteen, who are sent by their parents to be educated in the United States. This select group of students, who attend elementary schools or high schools, are unaccompanied by their parents and typically live with relatives, with members of the community, or in boarding schools. In the case of some wealthier families, one parent may spend weeks or months with the child in the United States. Some critics of the practice contend that because the parents do not pay local taxes, the students represent a drain on public resources; others say it is wrong to separate the children from their parents, especially in a distant, alien culture. Advocates cite the generally high academic ability of parachute children, the opportunity for higher educational achievement, and their positive impact in the classroom.

The rapid growth of globalization, transnationalism, and the Taiwanese economy, coupled with escalating tensions between Taiwan and China, has resulted in tens of thousands of Taiwanese children leaving their families to come to America in the hope of a better, safer future. The first wave of parachute kids came in the 1970s, when parents feared that their sons, who were required by law to serve two years in the Taiwanese military, would have to fight in a war if China attacked Taiwan. At the time, the Nationalist government prohibited boys over the age of fifteen from leaving the country. Thus, many wealthy parents sent their sons to live abroad before they turned fifteen.

Nevertheless, it was not until the United States officially ended diplomatic relations with Taiwan in 1979 that Taiwanese parents began sending their children to America in large numbers. During the 1980s and 1990s, the rapid economic growth in the Pacific Rim and the increase in transnational commerce further boosted the parachuting phenomenon. Taiwanese parents had more financial incentives to stay in their homeland, while the rise in household income and greater social ties with people residing in the United States enabled more families to send their children abroad. As a result, the parachute kids of the 1990s came from a broader range of backgrounds and for a greater variety of reasons than those of the 1970s and early 1980s.

The current wave of parachute kids consists of children from middle- to upper-class families, who may be as young as five years old. They typically live in America with relatives, friends, "homestays" (people who rent rooms to foreign students), or siblings. A small minority live alone. Most believe that an American education and fluency in the English language will give them a competitive edge over their compatriots. Many parachute kids also come to the United States to escape the competitive and stressful educational systems and national entrance examinations at home. A smaller percentage come to escape a bad academic record or negative peer influences and to turn their life around.

The vast majority of parachute kids reside in California. During the early 1990s, school officials and state legislators began voicing their concern about the growing presence of parachute kids in California's public schools and the burden on local budgets. As a result, U.S. senator Dianne Feinstein (D-CA) convinced Congress to change immigration policies by adding an amendment to the Illegal Immigration Reform and Immigrant Responsibility Act of 1996. Under that measure, foreigners would not be granted student visas to attend public elementary schools, and foreign students who attended public school grades seven through twelve could stay for only twelve months. Since passage of the amendment, the number of new parachute kids arriving in the United States has decreased significantly. However, some private schools continue to recruit foreign students, and parachute kids with green cards are still eligible to attend public primary and secondary schools. Thus, families with sufficient resources continue to send their children to America hoping for a brighter future.

Christy Chiang-Hom

Further Reading

Lee, Cathy. "The Perils of 'Parachute Kids.'" *AsianWeek*, July 8, 1999.

Zhou, Min. "'Parachute Kids' in Southern California: The Educational Experience of Chinese Children in Transnational Families." *Educational Policy* 12:6 (1998): 682–704.

Political Empowerment, Taiwanese American

Taiwanese Americans, relative newcomers to the United States, have attained a level of political empowerment comparable to other, more established Asian American groups such as Chinese Americans and Japanese Americans. Taiwanese immigrants did not arrive in any sizable numbers until the late 1950s and migrated en masse only during the 1960s and 1970s, when political and economic factors in Taiwan and the United States led to the arrival of thousands of Taiwanese students in America for graduate education. Many of these immigrants remained in America and established families that today include a second and young third generation of Taiwanese Americans. The strong educational background of the majority of Taiwanese Americans has given them the ability to contribute economically and politically to their own communities and to life in the United States.

Political interest among Taiwanese Americans falls into two general categories: (1) issues concerning the safety and status of Taiwan, and (2) broader Asian American issues. In the second case, the issues faced by Taiwanese Americans such as affirmative action, hate crimes, and English-only laws are no different from those faced by other Asian American groups. However, Taiwanese Americans are less affected by issues of poverty, poor education, and crime and generally do not place a high priority on those issues.

Historical Context

First-generation Taiwanese Americans tend to remain emotionally and politically tied to Taiwan and have a strong interest in political and economic events associated with the motherland. For the 2004 Taiwanese elections, for example, an estimated 10,000 Taiwanese Americans—most of whom hold dual citizenship in Taiwan and the United States—returned to the island to vote for the presidential candidate of their choice. At least a part of the identification with and allegiance to the homeland is due to historical influences: older Taiwanese Americans left Taiwan during the period of Kuomintang (KMT) authoritarianism before the mid-1980s. Unaccustomed to political freedoms while living under martial law, many Taiwan-born students took advantage of their newfound freedom in America and built organizations and publications critical of the KMT regime. Because of their actions, many Taiwanese students in the United States were blacklisted and unable to return to Taiwan until democratization. Free elections in Taiwan, unknown prior to 1996, allowed Taiwanese Americans to vote their will in their motherland and, indirectly, encouraged participation in U.S. politics.

Issues and Organizations

Although there is no exact count of Taiwanese-related organizations in the United States, the 114,812 Americans who—according to the 2000 U.S. Census—identified their race and ethnicity as Taiwanese are associated with more than 100 groups that focus on legal, academic, medical, cultural, and educational issues. These organizations have greatly facilitated collective action among Taiwanese Americans on domestic issues such as bilingual 911 emergency services, housing discrimination, and English-only laws, and international issues such as dispatching aid for earthquake relief in Taiwan, medical assistance for populations infected with Severe Acute Respiratory Syndrome (SARS), and U.S. diplomatic recognition of Taiwan as a sovereign nation.

Among the oldest Taiwanese political organizations in the United States is the Formosan Association for Public Affairs (FAPA). Founded in 1982, FAPA works to promote the right of Taiwan's inhabitants to establish an independent and democratic country and advance the rights of Taiwanese communities worldwide. Based in Washington, D.C., and supported by fifty-two chapters across the United States, FAPA educates the public and policy makers on such issues as the sale of military hardware to Taiwan, foreign policy, the visitation rights of Taiwanese government officials, and Taiwan independence.

The Formosa Foundation, founded in 2002, is a Los Angeles–based nonprofit that seeks to change Taiwan's official relationship with the United States by promoting a "One China, One Taiwan" policy rather than the "One China" policy adopted in President Richard Nixon's 1972 Shanghai Communiqué. According to that document, the basis of ongoing diplomatic wrangling and domestic lobbying ever since, "the U.S. acknowledges that all Chinese on either side of the Taiwan Strait maintain there is but one China and that Taiwan is part of China."

Taiwanese Americans protest Mainland China's anti-secession law, which authorizes the use of force if Taiwan moves toward formal independence. China considers the island part of its territory; U.S. policy hedges the issue of Taiwanese sovereignty. *(Nicholas Kamm/AFP/Getty Images)*

Taiwanese American organizations and individuals have been strongly supportive, both financially and politically, of politicians who favor recognition of an independent Taiwan or affirm a strong U.S. commitment to Taiwan's security. Outspoken members of the Senate and Congressional Taiwan Caucuses have included Representative Steve Chabot (R-OH, 1995–2008); Senator Sherrod Brown (R-OH, 2007–); Representative Howard Berman (D-CA, 1983–); Representative Robert Wexler (D-FL, 1997–); and Representative Dana Rohrabacher (R-CA, 1989–). Support of these congressmen by Taiwanese Americans gives the community a powerful voice on issues surrounding Taiwan.

Community support for Taiwan's entry into the United Nations in 1993, the World Trade Organization in 2001, and the World Health Organization in 2003—especially after the outbreak of SARS on the island—was manifested in campaigns to educate and influence politicians, in public demonstrations, and in massive public relations and media efforts. In 1996, prior to Taiwan's first democratic election, the Mainland Chinese fired several missiles into the Taiwan Strait to express their displeasure. Taiwanese Americans rallied in protests at Chinese consulates, staged hunger strikes, and aggressively lobbied politicians to remind them of America's moral, strategic, and legal obligations to protect Taiwan. President Bill Clinton finally dispatched the U.S. Seventh Fleet into the Taiwan Strait to maintain peace.

Participation in American Politics

While there are no formal surveys or polls on the political affiliations of Taiwanese Americans, the first generation tend to be Republican because of the party's strong pro-Taiwan stance. Second-generation Taiwanese Americans tend to vote Democratic because of their concern with minority issues despite the fact that Democrats tend to be pro-China.

The political empowerment of Taiwanese Americans has also entailed efforts to gain recognition for a distinctive "Taiwanese" identity. To facilitate self-identification of Taiwanese Americans during the 1990 and 2000 U.S. Censuses, community groups lobbied the Census Bureau to include "Taiwanese" as a selection category for questions pertaining to race, ethnicity, and ancestry. Failing that, the Taiwanese American Citizens League (TACL) organized a nationwide campaign to urge members of the community to write in "Taiwanese" as the answer to race and ancestry questions.

One interesting consequence of active political participation among first-generation Taiwanese Americans is the recognition that careers in political, civil service, and nonprofit sectors are acceptable and desirable for their children. In contrast to other Asian American groups that eschew politics for safer careers in business, medicine, and law, many second-generation Taiwanese Americans have actively pursued careers as political staff for local, state, and federal politicians with the goal of running for public office themselves some day. Nonprofit organizations such as the Asian Pacific American Legal Center and the Orange County Asian Pacific Islander Community Alliance are staffed by many second-generation Taiwanese Americans. Several other Taiwanese American political organizations, such as the TACL and Formosa Foundation, have created political internship programs expressly for the purpose of promoting interest in political and service careers for high school and college students.

Elected Officials

First-generation Taiwanese Americans have held a number of elected and appointed offices at the local and federal levels. In 1998, Taiwan-born David Wu became the first Taiwanese American to win election to the U.S. House of Representatives, representing Oregon's First Congressional District as a Democrat. In 2001, Matthew Lin was the first minority elected to San Marino's City Council in Los Angeles County, an area with a significant Taiwanese American presence. In 2003, President George W. Bush appointed Chiling Tong as associate director of the Minority Business Development Agency and in 2004 to the Presidential Advisory Commission on Asian Americans and Pacific Islanders. Elaine Chao, the U.S. secretary of labor from 2001 to 2009, is the first Taiwanese American to serve on a presidential cabinet.

Among second-generation Taiwanese Americans, John Chiang was elected California state controller, making him the highest-ranking Taiwanese American in that state's government. In 2001, Benjamin Wu was appointed to the office of deputy undersecretary for technology in the U.S. Department of Commerce, and in 2004 he was named assistant secretary for technology policy. In New York, John Liu became the first Asian American elected to citywide office, winning a seat on the city council representing a district in Queens for the first time in 2001.

Grassroots Organizing

Taiwanese Americans have also made notable contributions on a variety issues at the local level. The city of Monterey Park, California, referred to as "Little Taipei," was transformed from an aging suburb populated mostly by white Americans in the 1970s to a community that was 65 percent Asian by 1996. In the mid-1980s, however, city councils in the San Gabriel Valley of California, including Monterey Park, began proposing "English only" ordinances in an effort to block commercial and residential development for Asian American residents and businesses. The ordinances ultimately were defeated by a coalition of groups that included several Taiwanese American organizations. On July 14, 1986, the TACL organized a demonstration of 400 people in front of Monterey Park City Hall when the city council vetoed a proposal by Taiwanese American immigrants to build an apartment complex. The TACL charged that the proposal, which had been unanimously approved by the city planning commission, was rejected for racially motivated reasons and further cited the city's adoption of a resolution instructing police to cooperate with immigration officials and promoting English as the official language of the United States. In 1991, the TACL argued for bilingual 911 emergency response operators in Monterey Park. Taiwanese Americans have supported Asian American candidates for political office and argued for equitable redistricting of areas subject to gerrymandering to dilute the influence of Asian American and minority communities.

The 2001 murder of seventeen-year old Taiwanese American Kenneth Chiu in Orange County, California, and the outcome of the trial that followed prompted the Taiwanese American community to address the issue of hate crimes. Although animus toward minorities was demonstrated during the trial of defendant Christopher Hearn, he was found not guilty by reason of insanity. Chiu's father, with support from Chinese American, Taiwanese American, and other Asian American groups, worked with Assemblywoman Judy Chu to propose and eventually pass "Kenny's Law" (Assembly Bill 2428), which mandated protective orders for victims of hate crimes and their families.

Richard T. Wang

Further Reading

Formosa Foundation. http://www.formosafoundation.org.

Formosan Association for Public Affairs. http://www.fapa.org.

Ng, Franklin. *The Taiwanese Americans.* Westport, CT: Greenwood, 1998.

Saito, Leland. *Race and Politics: Asian Americans, Latinos, and Whites in a Los Angeles Suburb.* The Asian American Experience Series. Urbana: University of Illinois Press, 1998.

Taiwanese American Citizens League. http://tacl.org/classic.

Tucker, Nancy Bernkopf. *Taiwan, Hong Kong, and the United States, 1945–1992: Uncertain Friendships.* New York: Twayne, 1994.

U.S. House of Representatives, Committee on International Relations. *U.S. Domestic Politics and the US-Taiwan-PRC Relationship.* Washington, DC: Government Printing Office, 2002.

Students, Taiwanese American

Taiwanese American students can be divided into two general categories: those who have immigrated to the United States with their families and those who come alone solely for the purpose of education. Of the latter, the majority come for postsecondary education. One reason is that the top universities in Taiwan strictly limit admissions to those who do exceptionally well on national college examination tests, limiting choices in advanced education for many others. Attending college in the United States is often considered preferable to attending a less prestigious institution in Taiwan. Younger students come for secondary education, to hone their English language skills, and to increase their chances of gaining admission to a top American university. Such students are sometimes referred to as "parachute kids," because they are dropped in to American neighborhoods while their parents remain home in Taiwan to earn a living.

According to the U.S. Census, there were a total of about 26,000 students from Taiwan studying at U.S. colleges and universities in 2005. This was a roughly 28 percent drop from the peak of 36,000 in 1995, bucking the trend in the general U.S. population toward more postsecondary students in the late decades of the twentieth century. In 1976, only 11,000 Taiwanese students were attending postsecondary institutions in the United States.

Students from Taiwan have studied a wide range of subjects, with the largest number, according to a 1998 survey—the most recent available—studying business (25 percent), engineering (15 percent), and the life sciences (6 percent). This was a significant change from 1980, when the number of undergraduate majors and doctoral candidates in business, engineering, and the life science majors were roughly equal, at 17 percent, 17 percent, and 15 percent, respectively. Some experts say this is due to the improved quality of technical and science teaching in Taiwan, leading many to stay at home to study, while American business schools are still considered superior to those in Taiwan.

Of the Taiwanese student population whose families live in the United States—about 20 percent of the Taiwanese American population was born in the United States—census data indicate that they rank among the most educated of all Asian Pacific Islander groups. As in the case of many Asian Pacific Islanders, they tend to emphasize studies in engineering, computer science, medicine, and business, though many have pursued careers in journalism, law, politics, entertainment, and a wide variety of other professional fields.

Over the decades, a sizable number of Taiwanese families have immigrated to the United States with children who have not yet completed secondary education. Thus, members of the so-called "1.5-generation" began their educations in Taiwan and completed them in U.S. schools. Indeed, many families of 1.5-generation students come specifically to pursue educational opportunities for their children, especially in preparation for college. Anecdotal evidence suggests that this trend was more common in the 1970s and 1980s than it is now, as the quality of universities in Taiwan has become more comparable to that of American universities.

Since English is a required secondary language in Taiwan, the language barrier is mitigated for 1.5-generation students. Although their choice of field and career does not differ significantly from that of American-born Taiwanese students, the age at which these students immigrate correlates with how likely they are to return to Taiwan after completion of college. Those who arrive at an older age are much more likely than younger ones to pursue careers in Taiwan. Although students who are older when they immigrate have greater difficulty finding peers with whom to socialize—especially in secondary school—they tend to find students with similar backgrounds once they reach college. Although the percentage of 1.5-generation students in the overall Taiwanese student population is not known with any precision, they definitely represent a minority.

Richard T. Wang

Further Reading

Census Profile: New York City's Taiwanese American Population. New York: Asian American Federation of New York, 2005.

Chang, M.J., J.J. Park, M.H. Lin, O.A. Poon, and D.T. Nakanishi. *Beyond Myths: The Growth and Diversity of Asian American College Freshmen, 1971–2005.* Los Angeles: Higher Education Research Institute, UCLA, 2007.

Taiwan Independence Movement

Since its founding in the 1950s, the Taiwanese independence movement—with adherents in Taiwan, Japan, Europe, and North America—has pushed a two-fold agenda: a Republic of Taiwan independent of Mainland China and run by a democratic government. Both goals have put the independence movement at odds with the long-ruling Kuomintang (KMT), or Nationalist Party, which has pushed for a unification of China and Taiwan, with itself as the island's sole ruling body.

The post–World War II Taiwan independence movement has its genesis in the so-called 228 Incident of 1947; "228" refers to February 28, when the events began. On that day, the Chinese Nationalist government, still headquartered on the mainland, brutally suppressed a protest by native Taiwanese against police brutality, resulting in a series of uprisings across the island that left more than 30,000 persons dead. The Nationalist government's suppression of the protest and its ensuing manhunt for leaders of the independence movement resulted in the imprisonment and execution of a generation of Taiwanese intellectuals who challenged the KMT's authoritarian rule. Two years later, the KMT lost the civil war on the mainland to the Chinese Communists (CCP), fled to Taiwan (Formosa), and imposed a martial-law regime on the island's native Taiwanese majority. In the wake of the 228 Incident and the relocation of the KMT, Taiwanese survivors of February 28 established dissident communities in the United States, Canada, Europe, and Japan.

In January 1956, Taiwanese graduate students in Philadelphia established an independence organization called Formosans for a Free Formosa (FFF). By 1959 the movement was expanding across the country, and the FFF was renamed United Formosans for Independence (UFI) to recruit students on other college campuses. UFI activists publicized the KMT's human rights abuses and called for the establishment of a democratic and independent Taiwan. In 1970, with the UFI and Taiwan independence activists in Japan sharing a common vision for Taiwan's nationhood, they joined together to form the World United Formosans for Independence (WUFI).

In 1982, WUFI helped found the Formosan Association for Public Affairs (FAPA), a nonprofit organization that recruited and trained volunteers to lobby U.S. politicians regarding human rights abuses on the island and to pressure the KMT to release political prisoners in Taiwan. The WUFI and FAPA also monitored the implementation of U.S. defense commitments based on terms of the Taiwan Relations Act of 1979 (which established quasi-diplomatic relations and guaranteed the island's security after the United States officially recognized the Communist People's Republic). Formosan Clubs in far-flung international locations, the World Federation of Taiwanese Associations, and other overseas organizations also worked to promote an independent and democratic Taiwan.

In September 1986, the democratic opposition to the KMT in Taiwan established the Democratic Progressive Party (DPP), which remained illegal for five years in the island's one-party system. The DPP was founded for the immediate purpose of contesting the legislative elections of 1986, in which it won a total of twenty-three seats. Despite the legalization of the party in 1991 and the gradual democratization of the island during the course of the 1990s, many WUFI members in the United States were targeted for prosecution and harassment by the KMT government. In 1992, several WUFI leaders decided to transfer the organization's headquarters back to Taiwan; upon their return, they were promptly arrested and charged with sedition. Under diplomatic pressure from the United States and political pressure within Taiwan, the KMT eventually discontinued its blacklist of WUFI members and released the prisoners.

Upon their release, some WUFI members joined the pro-independence DPP and began urging the KMT government to apply for Taiwanese membership in the United Nations. Because the mainland government considers Taiwan a renegade province of China, it has repeatedly blocked international recognition of the island regime. In the presidential election of 2000, the DPP replaced the KMT as Taiwan's ruling party. Since then, the DPP government has worked with FAPA and WUFI to promote international support for Taiwanese self-determination. Members of those organizations and others in the United States have continued to write letters to the White House and members of Congress to urge support for Taiwan's de facto independence and the peaceful coexistence of Taiwan and Mainland China.

Doris T. Chang

Further Reading

Cohen, Marc J. *Taiwan at the Crossroads.* Washington, DC: Asia Resource Center, 1991.

Formosan Association for Public Affairs. http://www.fapa.org.

Yang, Jerry (1968–)

Internet entrepreneur Jerry Yang is the cocreator of the Yahoo! search engine and the cofounder and former CEO of Yahoo! Inc., with former graduate school classmate David Filo. The search engine, Web portal, and service provider founded by Yang and Filo in April 1994—and incorporated as Yahoo! Inc. the following year—helped fuel the global Internet revolution and became one of the most visited Web sites in the world.

Taipei native Jerry Yang, who came to America at age ten with no knowledge of English, went on to earn undergraduate and graduate engineering degrees from Stanford University. With classmate Dave Filo, he cofounded the Yahoo! Web portal in 1994. *(Paul J. Richards/AFP/Getty Images)*

The success of Yahoo! has made Yang one of the 100 richest men in the world, according to *Forbes* magazine, and a legendary figure in Silicon Valley.

Jerry Yang was born on November 6, 1968, in Taipei, Taiwan. He immigrated to America with his parents at the age of ten and grew up in San Jose, California, then as now a center of the American computer technology industry. Speaking virtually no English, Yang quickly immersed himself in the culture and language of his adoptive land. A bright student with prodigious energy, Yang quickly mastered the English language, graduated from public high school in San Jose, and gained acceptance to nearby Stanford University. Earning both his bachelor's and master's degrees, Yang studied electrical engineering at Stanford and then entered the PhD program. With fellow graduate student Dave Filo, he created an early Web site directory called "Jerry's Guide to the World Wide Web," which they realized had commercial potential as an Internet navigation system. They renamed the directory Yahoo! in April 1994 and incorporated it in March 1995. Both Yang and Filo left Stanford, taking indefinite leaves of absences from the PhD program.

A key member of Yahoo!'s executive management team since the company's founding—with the unofficial title of "Chief Yahoo"—Yang was named CEO by the board of directors in June 2007. The company foundered during his tenure, undergoing a declining share of the Internet search market, shrinking stock value, and two rounds of layoffs. After Yang refused a takeover bid by Microsoft and saw the value of Yahoo! stock drop even further, the company announced in November 2008 that he would be stepping down as CEO—and reverting to the titular role of Chief Yahoo.

Jerry Yang has ridden the success of his company to become one of the world's richest men, estimated to be worth more than $2 billion. An active philanthropist with his wife, Akiko Yamazaki, he has contributed considerable money and time in support of various Bay Area arts and education organizations with an Asian American focus. Among these are the Asian Art Museum of San Francisco and the East Asian Library at the University of California, Berkeley. Yang is a major donor to the Asia Pacific Fund and a member of its board of directors; with his wife, he has also helped manage and cochair the billion-dollar endowment of the Campaign for Undergraduate Education at their alma mater, Stanford University.

David Hou

Further Reading

Sherman, Josepha. *Jerry Yang and David Filo: Chief Yahoos of Yahoo!* Brookfield, CT: Twenty-First Century, 2001.

Weston, Michael R. *Jerry Yang and David Filo: The Founders of Yahoo!* New York: Rosen, 2007.

The Thai American Experience:

History and Culture

On Sunday, August 16, 1829, when the American sailing ship *Sachem* arrived and docked at Long Wharf in Boston Harbor, among its cargo of sugar, sapan wood, gamboge, buffalo horns, leopard skins, and tin were the first Thais ever to set foot on American soil—the so-called "Siamese twins," Chang and Eng. While these human curiosities entered the country at a time and a place in American history better known for mass immigration from Ireland, the majority of Thai immigrants did not arrive until much later. The earliest real movement of Thais to the United States began in the 1950s, when a few thousand arrived to pursue their studies, primarily in the fields of medicine and education. Still, it was not until the deployment of U.S. troops to Southeast Asia during the 1960s and early 1970s that the first significant wave of Thai migration took place. A second, larger wave came in the 1980s and early 1990s, followed by a leveling off in the years thereafter. By 2007, the total population of Thais in the United States stood at nearly 200,000.

Although a significant portion of Thai émigrés have settled in the Middle East and the Asian-Pacific region to take advantage of growing economies and booming labor markets, the United States—especially the greater metropolitan area of Los Angeles—claims the largest concentration of Thais living permanently abroad.

Unlike refugees from Southeast Asia who entered the United States seeking asylum as a consequence of the war in Vietnam, Thais generally did not come to America in search of political freedom. More often they sought higher education, specialized training, and job opportunities. Some came as spouses of U.S. military personnel and civilians.

Immigrants Admitted to the United States from Thailand, 1969–2005	
Dates	Immigrants
1969–1972	10,093
1973	5,943
1974	4,956
1975	4,217
1976	6,923
1977	3,945
1978	3,574
1979	3,194
1980	4,115
1981	4,799
1982	5,568
1983	5,875
1984	4,885
1985	5,239
1986	6,204
1987	6,733
1988	6,888
1989	9,332
1990	8,914
1991	7,397
1992	7,090
1993	6,654
1994	5,489
1995	5,136
1996	4,310
1997	3,094
1998	3,102
1999	2,381
2000	3,785
2001	4,291
2002	4,175
2003	3,158
2004	4,900
2005	5,500
Total	181,859

Note: Figures are rounded.

Source: U.S. Census Bureau.

Missionary Legacy

Beginning in 1831 and for nearly a century thereafter, hundreds of American missionaries sought the peaceful conversion of the Thais (then known as the Siamese) to Christianity. Although their failure in this effort is well-known—even today, only a tiny minority of Thais have embraced Christianity—the work of American missionaries in education and medicine made significant contributions to advancing the Kingdom of Siam along the path to becoming the modern nation-state that Thailand is today. Within the course of a century, largely Protestant missionaries had established ten hospitals throughout the kingdom, two leper asylums, and

561

a nursing school in the northern city of Chiang Mai. Some even served the royal palace in the official capacity of "consulting physicians," providing medical treatment to the king and others in the court. The close relationships forged between American missionaries and the Siamese impelled generations of Thais, from commoners to elites, to journey to the United States. Nai Thianhee Sarasin, a student of the missionaries and one of their few converts to Christianity, studied medicine at New York University in the mid-nineteenth century and became the first Thai to receive a medical degree from the United States. The first Thai woman to study nursing and midwifery in America was Esther Pradepasena, who was also the first Thai woman to convert to Christianity. She returned to Siam in 1859 to work as a teacher, nurse, and midwife. Arriving in 1916, Prince Mahidol (also known as Prince Songkhla), one of the founders of public health and medical education in Siam, spent some of his most productive years in the United States studying medicine at Harvard University in Cambridge, Massachusetts. There, he met and eventually married another Thai student, Sangwan Talapat (Thailand's beloved Princess Mother, also known as Somdej Phra Sri Nakarintara), who was pursuing a course in nursing at Simmons College in Boston and a degree in public health at the Massachusetts Institute of Technology (MIT). In 1919, Prince Mahidol established the Siamese Alliance, the first Thai fraternal association in America, to provide a social and recreational link for Thai students. On December 5, 1927, while the royal couple was residing in Massachusetts, Prince Bhumibol Adulyadej (the current ruler) was born. Prince Bhumibol ascended to the throne in 1946 and was officially crowned King Rama IX of the Chakri Dynasty in 1950. The longest-reigning king in Thai history, he is also the world's only monarch born in the United States.

U.S.-Thai Relations

Long-standing positive diplomatic relations between the two nations have also contributed to the presence of Thais in the United States. The Treaty of Amity and Commerce, establishing diplomatic relations in 1833, was the first ever forged between the United States and an Asian nation. A second treaty, signed in 1856, initiated full diplomatic relations between the two countries, with the establishment of U.S. consular services in Bangkok. In 1884, His Royal Highness Prince Nares Warariddhi, younger brother of the much-revered King Chulalongkorn (Rama V), met with President Chester Arthur in Washington, D.C., becoming the first Thai

minister to present his credentials to a U.S. president. But it was King Chulalongkorn, who, throughout his reign, demonstrated a particularly keen interest in America and actively promoted his kingdom and culture in the United States. Although he never visited the United States, he sent Thai musical instruments to the Smithsonian Institution in Washington, D.C., and encouraged Siam's participation in three world exhibitions—the Centennial International Exhibition at Philadelphia in 1876, the World's Columbian Exposition in Chicago in 1893, and the Louisiana Purchase Exposition in St. Louis, Missouri, in 1894.

The first Thai monarch to set foot on U.S. soil was King Vajiravudh (Rama VI), still crown prince at the time of his visit in 1902. It was on this trip, while visiting Santa Cruz, California, that His Royal Highness famously granted the name "Siam Makut Rajakumar" (Crown Prince of Siam) to a giant redwood tree measuring 275 feet (84 meters) high and 45 feet (13.7 meters) around the trunk. Every Thai monarch since (there have been three) has visited the United States.

Free Thai Movement

On December 8, 1941, within hours of Japan's attack on U.S. naval facilities at Pearl Harbor, Hawaii, Japanese troops invaded Thailand and compelled the government, by threat of force, to declare war on Great Britain and the United States. M.R. Seni Pramoj, the Thai minister in Washington, signaled his protest by refusing to deliver the declaration of war to President Franklin Roosevelt. Minister Pramoj was joined by a group of Thai students in the United States who ignored a repatriation order. Together, they formed a resistance movement, Seri Thai (Free Thai), to provide voluntary military support to the Allies and persuade their compatriots in Thailand to join forces in resisting the Japanese. Since the U.S. government had frozen all Thai assets following Thailand's declaration of war, the Free Thai movement's first task was to convince the United States to release Thai funds. After five months of negotiations, the U.S. government recognized the independent status of the Free Thai legation. Following the release of funds, two groups from the Free Thai movement returned to Thailand through various clandestine means and established an intelligence operation to monitor Japanese troop movements and assist the Allies in airlifting military and medical supplies into Thailand. At the same time, leaders of the Free Thai movement in Washington convinced the U.S. House of Representatives Foreign Affairs Committee that the Free Thai movement enjoyed broad support within Thailand and that the alliance with the Japanese had been enforced against the will of the Thai people. At the end of the war, on September 2, 1945, members of the Free Thai movement became the first Asians in U.S. history to receive the Presidential Medal of Freedom, the nation's highest civilian award.

The Vietnam War and First Wave of Migration

During the latter part of the twentieth century, tens of thousands of Thais entered the United States as a result of bilateral military relations, educational cultural exchange programs, and specialized government and civilian training efforts. Prior to the 1970s, however, few Thais established U.S. residency or were naturalized as citizens. The majority of Thais who remained in the country—especially those who earned coveted American university credentials—returned to Thailand to secure positions in civil society. In 1965, two unrelated events triggered a dramatic change in this pattern. President Lyndon Johnson's decision to send U.S. combat troops into South Vietnam was followed, several months later, by the passage into law of the landmark Hart-Celler Immigration and Nationality Act, which reversed a 1924 law that had effectively banned all immigration from Asia. These two decisions stimulated the first wave of Thai migration to America, with 42,845 admitted over the course of a ten-year period (1969–1979). These were not refugees. At the height of the war in Southeast Asia, with more than 50,000 U.S. troops stationed in Thailand, the new group of immigrants that emerged in the late 1960s and increased throughout the 1970s was composed largely of Thais married to U.S. military personnel. This new flow of immigration coincided with the appearance of a small cadre of Thai professionals, including physicians, nurses, engineers, technicians, architects, accountants, and others who worked in some capacity with the American government or in American business circles during the war in Vietnam.

"Robin Hoods"—Second Wave of Migration

The first wave of Thai immigrants subsided by the late 1970s. A new and much larger flow of Thai nationals—more than 100,000—arrived during the 1980s and 1990s. While students, skilled professionals, and immediate relatives (spouses, children, and parents) of U.S. citizens continued to enter the country as before,

it was during this period that a new type of Thai immigrant emerged. These were individuals who had come to America if not to escape the collapsing local economies of rural Thailand, then with the hope of finding a new means of revitalizing their family's prospects in the homeland. Many of these individuals, predominately Thai women, entered the country through a complicated patchwork of schemes to evade or circumvent U.S. immigration laws. These undocumented workers found that they were in high demand as restaurant workers, parking attendants, janitors, gas station attendants, and convenience store clerks. A few were lured into garment factories or "sweatshops," where they performed cheap labor. This group of undocumented workers is sometimes referred to as the "Robin Hoods." The term is neither derogatory nor romantic; it reflects the simple fact that immigration redistributes wealth. The Robin Hood of popular mythology, by taking from the rich to give to the poor, embodies an ethic of social justice that is easily mapped onto the Thai immigrant experience, particularly in the case of undocumented workers who land jobs that pay "under the table." Those in this group who marry their American "fans"—the Thai term for a lover or spouse—find the quickest route to naturalization and socioeconomic mobility. By wiring a portion of their untaxed cash income back to Thailand each month, or by marrying an American who can help provide financial support and stability to their family, these individuals are, in effect, transferring wealth from "rich" America to "poor" Thailand.

Prominent Thai Americans

The two best-known Asians in nineteenth-century America were the "Siamese twins" Chang and Eng Bunker (1811–1874) from Thailand. They were the first Asians in American history to become naturalized U.S. citizens, the first Asians to vote in the United States, and the first to marry white Americans. Lesser known is George "Yod" Dupont (1844–1900), a Thai who journeyed to America to fight for the Union Army in the Civil War and was later naturalized as a U.S. citizen. In the late twentieth century, multiracial Thai American athletes such as golfer Tiger Woods and Boston Red Sox center fielder Johnny Damon (in 2004, the first Thai American to become a World Series champion) became new national and worldwide record holders. Ajarn Surachai "Chai" Sirisute introduced Americans to Muay Thai (kick boxing), the prestigious national sport and martial art of Thailand. The award-winning composer, author, and media personality Somtow Sucharitkul is best known in late-twentieth-century America for his gothic horror and science fiction novels. Vibul Wonprasat founded the Thai Gallery in Marina del Rey, California, and is the artistic director of the Thai Community Arts and Cultural Center in Los Angeles. His 1991 mural "East Meets West" outside the Bangkok Market on Melrose Avenue (the first Thai market in the United States) presents an optimistic depiction of Asian immigration to the city. In West Hollywood, visual artist Kamol Tassananchalee transforms stories from *nangyai,* or shadow puppet plays. San Francisco–based Thai painters Surachai Promsuntisiti, Srimongkol Darawali, Veerakeat TongPaiBoon, and Panom Suwannart have also made significant contributions to contemporary art. Hollywood fashion designer Tom Mark, who was born in Lampang, Thailand, to a seamstress mother and lumberjack father, operates a trendy Los Angeles boutique catering to movie and television stars. The plays of Khamolpat "Prince" Gomolvilas, including *Big Hunk o' Burnin' Love* (1997), *Seat Belts and Big Fat Buddhas* (1999), *The Theory of Everything* (2000), *Debunking Love* (2000), and *Bee* (2001), have been produced in theaters across the United States. Thai immigrants are also fighting in U.S. military operations. Corporal Kemaphoom "Ahn" Chanawongse, for instance, was killed in action during the U.S. occupation of Iraq; on April 28, 2003, a month after his unit was ambushed outside Nasiriyah, he was honored in the first-ever Thai Buddhist ceremony held at Arlington National Cemetery.

Culture

Apart from the achievements and contributions of prominent individuals, immigrant Thais and Thai Americans are actively engineering new social, cultural, and religious institutions in the United States. Excluding Thai Robin Hoods and other undocumented workers, many of the Thais residing in America are professionals with undergraduate degrees who have helped advance their careers, especially in the medical, nursing, and civil engineering fields. Most Thais, regardless of their legal status or educational background, share a strong entrepreneurial spirit characteristic of all U.S. immigrants, who, in every decennial census from 1880 to 2000, were more likely to be self-employed than natives. While a great number of Thais are restaurateurs or work in other areas of the food-service industry, the broader community is also employed in a wide variety of fields. One indicator of the diversity among self-employed Thais can be found in the listings published by Thai Yellow Pages U.S.A., an online gateway to Thai businesses and

agencies. Although restaurants outnumber other listings by far, this bilingual Web site also lists businesses that are run by or employ Thais in more than eighty other commercial categories. The top fifteen categories after restaurants are: automobile (sales/repairs/accessories), real estate, physicians, video stores, jewelry and watch shops, accountants, dentists, attorneys, language schools, food retailers and grocery stores, import and export businesses, insurance agents, massage therapists, travel agencies, fortune tellers, and construction.

In California, a total of nineteen Thai newspapers and magazines, some of which are bilingual or multilingual, publish either daily, weekly, biweekly, monthly, bimonthly, or online. The *Asian Pacific News, Inter-Thai Pacific Rim, Khao Sod USA, Khao Thai, Mahachon, Matiseree, Muang Thai, New Chiab, New Chumchon, Peaceful Thai, Prachachon USA, Reach Out, Santiparp, Sereechai, Siam Chronicle, Siam Media, Thai L.A., Thai Times USA,* and *TV Parade* all report on local events as well as news from Thailand. Bangkok papers such as *Thai Rath, Siam Rath, Matichon,* the *Daily News,* the *Nation,* and the *Bangkok Post* are readily available in local Thai markets. Thais in Los Angeles can also listen to local radio broadcasts of Thai music and news on Pimjai Radio KALI-1430 AM.

Interracial Families

While Asian immigrants are historically less likely to outmarry because the first generation is more closely tied to a traditional culture that does not sanction outmarriage, Thais are nonetheless outmarrying at surprisingly high levels—from 25 percent to more than 30 percent. Since 1843, when Siamese twins Chang and Eng Bunker became the first Asian Americans to outmarry, Thai immigrants have established a long history of intermarriage between Asians and non-Asians. Today, with the increasingly heterogeneous nature of the Thai community, the number of interfaith, interethnic, or interracial families corresponds with a growing demographic trend in the United States, whereby at least 5 percent of all marriages are mixed (nearly a quarter of them in California). Families such as these have made California the nation's leader in children born to parents of different races. The most prominent example of this transformation in traditional ethnic categories is golfer Tiger Woods, born in Cypress, California, in 1975. Sometimes referred to as the "Great Black Hope" of golf, Woods is actually among the generation of offspring produced in the first wave of Thai immigration to the United States. His father, Earl Woods, served as an officer in the U.S. Army during the war in Vietnam. His mother, Kultida, is a native of Thailand who worked on the U.S. Army base in Bangkok where Earl Woods was stationed.

Cuisine

Since the 1980s, Thai cuisine has enjoyed increasing popularity in the United States. Putachat, the first Thai restaurant in Los Angeles, opened in 1968 on Vermont Avenue at Eighth Street in Hollywood. What began as a modest food shop with a few tables changed ownership a year later and was renamed Arunee Thai. Soon, restaurateurs such as Surabon Mekapongsatorn began opening Thai restaurants throughout the Los Angeles area. In 1971, Bangkok Market—the first food store in Los Angeles devoted principally to Thai products—opened in Hollywood. By the 1980s, Thai food was enjoying increasing popularity throughout the United States, perceived as an attractive and healthy alternative to other types of cuisine. The result was a dramatic rate of growth in the number of Thai restaurants. In Southern California, the number of Thai restaurants went from 200 in 1990 to more than 600 by the mid-2000s.

By the mid-2000s, there were more than 900 Thai restaurants across California and 3,000 nationwide, feeding more than 2 million Americans per week. With awareness and appreciation of ethnic cuisines at an all-time high, Thai restaurants can now be found in all but three U.S. states (the Dakotas and Wyoming). The rapid growth in the popularity of Thai food has corresponded with a culinary trend that began in the 1980s, in which Asian foods have become elements of mainstream cuisine in America. The Los Angeles–based entrepreneurial chef and restaurateur Wolfgang Puck, for instance, infused his Continental menus with Asian influences, offering gourmet wood-fired "Thai Chicken pizza" and "ObaChine Pad Thai pasta." Even the quintessentially American *Betty Crocker Cookbook* now features recipes for "Thai Chicken."

Religion

Just as Thais have altered the culinary map of the United States, so, too, have they contributed to the transformation of America's religious geography. Since the late 1960s, the flow of migration from Thailand—a predominately Theravada Buddhist country—has coincided with a cultural turn toward Buddhism as an alternative to mainstream religion in America. Thais found an America receptive to the addition of a Buddhist *wat* (temple) to a dynamic architectural mix in which church steeples were joined in the nation's skylines by Muslim minarets, onion-domed Sikh *gurdwaras,* and towering Hindu temples and shrine complexes. The establishment of Wat Thai of Los Angeles in 1972 (officially dedicated by Thailand's king in 1979)—the first Thai temple in America—inspired Thais elsewhere to build their own temples. By the end of the decade, Thais had established five additional *wats* to serve the communities of Washington, D.C. (1974), New York (1975), Denver (1976), Chicago (1976), and San Francisco (1979). Over the course of the next two decades, as the flow of Thai immigrants increased and spread across the country, a need for more *wats* became evident. Accordingly, the number of Thai temples went from forty in 1990 to ninety-three *wats* in twenty-nine states in the early 2000s. The Council of Thai Bhikkhus, an umbrella organization of monks charged with overseeing all of the Thai temples in the United States, was established in 1977.

In its American context, the Thai *wat* is not only a religious center of spiritual significance charged with the duty of propagating the Buddha-*dhamma* (the pivotal doctrines, laws, insights, and teachings of the historical Buddha), but also the preeminent site of Thai culture in its most luxuriant and institutionalized form. Here, through the elaborate staging of ritual and ceremony, custom and tradition, traditional Thai culture is performed, displayed, generated, accrued, spent, and reinvested in the community. This is most evident in the annual holidays and festivals joyously celebrated at the *wat* when the laity and monks take refuge in the "triple gem": the Buddha, or teacher of compassion and wisdom; the *dhamma*, his teaching; and the *sangha,* or community. During these times, food is offered to the monks, children and young adults perform classical Thai music

Thai Americans, 2000

Top Ten States	Total Population	Thai Restaurants	Thai *Wats* (Temples)
California	46,868	920	25
Texas	9,918	135	9
Florida	8,618	232	5
New York	8,158	122	3
Illinois	7,231	161	6
Washington	5,527	204	4
Virginia	5,406	72	3
Nevada	4,220	35	2
Maryland	3,782	40	2
Georgia	3,090	60	3
U.S. Total	150,283	2,840	90

Source: U.S. Census Bureau.

to accompany live performances of royal court drama and folk dance, Thai food is prepared onsite and sold to benefit the temple, and monks give "dharma talks" or brief sermons and lead families in ritual chants to transfer merit to the laity. Meanwhile, adults offer essential and sundry necessities to the monks as well as financial gifts to support the temple.

In the 1990s, the first Buddhist temples in the Thai forest meditation tradition were led by white abbots. Thanissaro Bhikkhu, a white American monk born as Geoffrey DeGraff, was ordained and practiced meditation for fourteen years in Thailand, after which he returned to the United States to assume leadership of Metta Forest Monastery. Located in the mountains outside San Diego, California, this temple attracts Thais, Laotians, and white Americans. Ajahn Amaro, a British monastic who was ordained as a monk in Thailand by the renowned Thai meditation master Ajahn Chah, helped start Abhaya-giri, a forest monastery in Redwood Valley, California, founded and led by white monastics and attended by both Americans and Asians.

A small fraction of the Thai community, only about 2–3 percent, is Christian. There are just over thirty Thai Christian church communities in America, the majority of which are based in Southern California and, to a lesser extent, Texas. An even smaller number of Thai immigrants—less than half of 1 percent—are Muslim. In 1993, the first Thai mosque in the United States, Masjid Al-Fatiha, was established northeast of Los Angeles in the predominately Hispanic town of Azusa, California. Under the leadership of Hajj Rahamed Phyome, the mosque, which began in neighboring Monrovia with about 100 Thai Muslim families, gathers up to 350 people each week for *jumuah* (Friday prayer).

Civic Engagement—Cultural Festivals and Thai Associations

Since the late 1990s, Thais have become increasingly active in bringing Thai culture into the streets and centers of urban America through the staging of summer festivals and parades. In addition to Thai food booths and hands-on cooking demonstrations, these festivals often feature parades with elaborate floats, an entertainment stage to showcase folk and classical forms of Thai music and dance, Muay Thai kick boxing, and a Miss Thai beauty contest. Exhibitors display traditional fruit and vegetable carving, Thai umbrella and Khon mask painting, weaving, gifts, and handicrafts. Traditional forms of Thai massage are also made available. Such

events not only generate cultural pride but are part of a concerted effort to matriculate younger generations of Thais into the performative language of Thai customs and tradition.

At the same time, these festivals broaden the appeal and accessibility of Thai culture to the American mainstream. Many of these events are part of a nationwide initiative sponsored in large part by the Tourism Authority of Thailand and Thailand's Department of Skill Development and Ministry of Labour. Tens of thousands of people come to the larger festivals, which include the Thai Community Arts and Cultural Center's annual Thai Cultural Day in Southern California's Thai Town and the biennial Thai Food Festival in Northern California, organized by the national Thai Restaurant Association in Sunnyvale. Similar festivals are held in Washington, D.C., Chicago, New York, and Phoenix. Through the Houston-based Thai American Chamber of Commerce, Thais have participated in the Asian Pacific American Heritage Association's Heritage Parade and Festival, the Houston Dragon Boat Festival, and Lunar New Year celebrations. Thais in Southern California have also been involved in Pan-Asian cultural celebrations such as the Asian and Pacific Islanders Festival in San Fernando Valley and have entered award-winning floats in the annual Tournament of Roses Parade in Pasadena, California.

Beyond the pageantry and pomp of festivals, vibrant new forms of civic engagement have emerged in recent years, including professional associations and nonprofit social service organizations. One of the first of these organizations to incorporate was the Washington, D.C.–based Thai-American Association (formerly the Friends of Thailand), founded in 1973 to foster and strengthen friendly relations between Thailand and the United States. The Association of Thai Professionals in America and Canada, a Texas-based network founded in 1991, actively promotes the advancement of scientific knowledge, technology, and education in Thailand. While this organization is made up mostly of first-generation Thai immigrants, a second group, the San Francisco–based Thai American Young Professionals Association, seeks to enhance the social status and professional advancement of second-generation Thais, born in America, through the creation of a nationwide network with affiliates in Los Angeles and Chicago.

Community volunteers, leaders, and activists have also begun to focus awareness on issues directly affecting Thais both at home and abroad. The New York–based collective ThaiLinks sponsors activist-oriented art exhibits and public lectures and is the lead organizer for the biennial Thai Film Festival. Thai Health and Information Services (THAIS) in Hollywood serves low-income women, youth, seniors, and other disadvantaged Thais in need of social services by providing health education, outreach, job and lifestyle training, and access to social services. THAIS was the first Thai organization to direct outreach specifically toward the lesbian, gay, bisexual, transgender, intersexual, queer, and questioning community (LGBTIQ).

The Thai Community Development Center (Thai CDC) was launched in 1994 with the goal of improving the standard of living and quality of life for Thais vulnerable to substandard housing and labor conditions or lacking access to basic health services, education, quality housing, and employment opportunities. The Thai CDC is part of a consortium of five Asian Pacific Islander communities assisting small and largely immigrant businesses in Los Angeles.

The plight of sweatshop workers became an early concern of the Thai CDC when federal and state officials raided a small apartment complex in El Monte, California, in 1995. The raid uncovered seventy-two undocumented Thai garment workers—mostly women who had entered the country illegally—fenced in by razor wire and forced to work under slavery-like conditions seventeen hours a day for a $1.60 an hour. The case provoked a brief crisis of civic identity that divided the Thai community across generational lines, as older community leaders were bypassed by a newer and younger generation of social activists (such as the executive director of the Thai CDC, Chanchanit Martorell, then twenty-seven years old). In response to the incident, the Thai consul general in Los Angeles enlisted the assistance of the Thai Muslim Association under the leadership of Hajj Rahamed Phyome, which posted bail and arranged shelter for sixteen of the El Monte workers. The Thai CDC worked closely with the Asian Pacific American Legal Center of Southern California and other public-interest groups on behalf of the workers, who received more than $4 million in compensation for their injuries. The successful outcome of the El Monte case resulted in broad-based improvements in the lives of garment workers throughout the industry. While the ordeal temporarily opened a generational rift that divided Thais, it also provided the first significant opening for effective organizing, advocacy, and coalition building with other Asian Americans and therefore stands as an important touchstone for the Thai community.

Future Prospects

The generally positive reception of Thais in America is especially notable because Asians immigrants and their offspring have historically experienced severe racial prejudice and discrimination. Why Thais have not encountered the same degree of discrimination, prejudice, and inequality experienced by other Asian Americans, and why fewer have been targeted as victims of hate crimes even as the number of anti-Asian hate crimes remain at their highest levels, remain largely unanswered questions. Thais have not yet figured prominently in the extant histories, chronologies, anthologies, or major works of reference in the field of Asian American studies.

Nevertheless, Thai contributions to the history of Asians in America and to American culture in general over the last two centuries have not been insignificant and can be attributed to at least five factors. First, the long history of cordial relations between Thailand and the United States provides an important framework for considering the context in which Thais migrated to America. Another factor may be the diverse demographic profile of Thai immigrants, along with the broad territorial dispersion of Thais across the United States. Unlike other Asian immigrant communities, Thais have never been forced to live and work in isolated inner-city ghettos as a matter of survival. A third possibility is related to the fact that the majority of Thais emigrated to the United States after the passage of landmark immigration and civil rights legislation in the 1960s, thus benefiting from constitutional guarantees unavailable to immigrants of previous eras. Antidiscrimination and affirmative-action legislation helped create a cultural climate more tolerant of ethnic diversity. A fourth factor relates to the incorporation of Thais and their rich cultural heritage into the American mainstream through intermarriage, new cuisines, and a cultural turn toward Buddhism. Finally, in recent years, Thais have demonstrated a high degree of civic engagement and a willingness to share and celebrate their culture with others. The staging of festivals and parades, along with the creation, in 1999, of Thai Town in East Hollywood, are healthy manifestations of cultural pride and entrepreneurial zeal. Together, these five factors have played a crucial role in the success of Thais in America and should continue to serve the community well into the future.

Todd LeRoy Perreira

Further Reading

Bhongbhibhat, Vimol, Bruce Reynolds, Sukhon Polpatpicharn, and Beatrice Camp, eds. *The Eagle and the Elephant: Thai-American Relations Since 1833.* Golden Jubilee Edition. Bangkok: United States Information Service, 1997.

Cadge, Wendy. *Heartwood: The First Generation of Theravada Buddhism in America.* Morality and Society Series. Chicago: University of Chicago Press, 2004.

Perreira, Todd LeRoy. "Sasana Sakon and the New Asian American: Intermarriage and Identity at a Thai Buddhist Temple in Silicon Valley." In *Asian American Religions: The Making and Remaking of Borders and Boundaries* (Race, Religion, and Ethnicity), ed. Tony Carnes and Fenggang Yang. New York: New York University Press, 2004.

Su, Julie. "El Monte Thai Garment Workers: Slave Sweatshops." In *No Sweat: Fashion, Free Trade, and the Rights of Garment Workers*, ed. Andrew Ross. New York: Verso, 1997.

Thai American Young Professionals Association. http://www.taypa.org/.

Thai Buddhist Temples in the U.S. http://www.thaiembdc.org/thaicommu/AssoMedia/temples.aspx.

Thai Community Development Center (Thai CDC). http://thaicdchome.org/cms.

Thai Health and Information Services (THAIS). http://www.thaihealth.org.

Thai Yellow Pages. http://www.thaiyellowpagesusa.com.

Thongthiraj, Rahpee. "Unveiling the Face of Invisibility: Exploring the Thai American Experience." In *The New Face of Asian Pacific America: Numbers, Diversity and Change in the 21st Century,* ed. Eric Lai and Dennis Arguelles. San Francisco: AsianWeek, SF, with UCLA's Asian American Studies Center Press, 2003.

Thai Americans
Alphabetical Entries

Bunker, Chang and Eng (1811–1874)

Famously known as the "Siamese twins," Chang and Eng were born conjoined at the sternum on May 11, 1811, in the Kingdom of Siam (later Thailand). They were "discovered" by a British merchant who arranged a partnership with an American trader to exhibit the eighteen-year-old boys as "curiosities" on a two-and-a-half-year tour of the United States and Great Britain. Their arrival at Boston Harbor on August 16, 1829, marks the first known entry of Thais into the United States.

The public exhibition of Chang and Eng was received enthusiastically before overflow crowds in Boston, New York, and Philadelphia; their subsequent tour to London was equally successful. Upon fulfilling their contractual obligations and declaring their independence, they capitalized on their celebrity status and expanded their tours throughout North America and Europe. Wherever they traveled, they were the constant subject of medical examinations and newspaper articles, becoming the most studied and documented Asians of the nineteenth century.

After a decade of tours, the twins retired from show business to settle in Wilkesboro, North Carolina. Welcomed by a resolution passed by the state legislature declaring them honorary citizens, the twins officially became naturalized U.S. citizens on October 12, 1839. They were the first known Asians to do so in American history. As citizens, they exercised their right to participate in all elections, becoming the first Asian Americans to cast votes.

In 1843, they legally adopted the surname "Bunker" and married the sisters Adelaide and Sarah Anne Yates—the first known case in U.S. history of Asian Americans outmarrying. Between them, Chang and Eng fathered twenty-one children and had more than 2,000 descendants.

Having retired from public life, Chang and Eng moved to Surry County, North Carolina, where they acquired several hundred acres of property for farming. At the outbreak of the Civil War in 1861, they had thirty-three slaves between them, including "house slaves" and "field slaves," whom they were compelled to free or retain on salary following the war. They died in North Carolina within hours of each other at age sixty-two on January 17, 1874. A plaster cast made of their bodies remains on public display to this day at the Mütter Museum in Philadelphia.

The Siamese twins have been the subject of the work of many artists, writers, and playwrights, including Edward Bulwer-Lytton, Gilbert Abbott à Beckett, Mark Twain, William Linn Keese, and Darin Strauss. Ekachai Uekrongtham's 1997 *Chang and Eng—The Musical* is Singapore's longest-running musical and the first English-language musical to be staged in China. In 1994, Thai officials dedicated a bronze statue of Chang and Eng in their native province, Samut Songkhram. In 2001, the twin bridges over Stewart's Creek in North Carolina were dedicated as the Eng and Chang Bunker Memorial Bridge. North Carolina's Visitors Center and Museum of Regional History at Mount Airy maintain permanent exhibits about the twins. The Bunker papers are housed at the Southern Historical Collection, University of North Carolina, Chapel Hill.

Todd LeRoy Perreira

Further Reading

Pingree, Allison. "America's 'United Siamese Brothers': Chang and Eng and Nineteenth-Century Ideologies of Democracy and Domesticity." In *Monster Theory: Reading Culture,* ed. Jeffrey Jerome Cohen. Minneapolis: University of Minnesota Press, 1996.

Quigley, Christine. *Conjoined Twins: An Historical, Biological and Ethical Issues Encyclopedia.* Jefferson, NC: McFarland, 2003.

Wallace, Irving, and Amy Wallace. *The Two.* New York: Simon and Schuster, 1978.

Woods, Tiger (1975–)

Eldrick "Tiger" Woods—among the generation of offspring produced by the first wave of Thai immigration to the United States—is widely regarded the greatest professional golfer of his era and one of the world's best-known athletes. Since his emergence in the late 1990s, the California native has been the sport's top-ranked player and greatest money winner on a perennial basis. Of multiracial background, he has given a new face to a sport dominated by white mainstream Americans and is credited with generating new interest in golf among minorities and young people.

Woods was born on December 30, 1975, in Cypress, California to Earl and Kultida Woods. He is one-quarter Chinese and one-quarter Thai on his mother's side, and one-quarter African on his father's side. Woods's father began teaching him to play golf at the age of two, even before he could walk. As a child, Woods appeared on television and in a variety of publications because of his remarkable golfing abilities, including a legendary appearance on *The Mike Douglas Show* in 1978.

Throughout the 1980s, Woods dominated youth golfing events, including three U.S. Junior Amateur Championships (1991–1993). He entered Stanford University in 1994, majoring in economics and winning ten collegiate events, including the NCAA title in 1996. In the meantime, he had also won the U.S. Amateur Championship three times (1994–1996). After two years at Stanford, Woods turned professional full-time in August 1996 and signed endorsement deals with Nike and Titleist worth more than $60 million.

In April 1997, Woods won his first professional major tournament, the Masters, by a record margin of twelve strokes; in addition, he was the youngest player to win that prestigious event and the first winner of African or Asian descent. Despite suffering some slumps (in relative terms) due to periodic adjustments in his swing technique, Woods dominated professional golf throughout the 1990s and early 2000s, compiling a list of records, accomplishments, and honors almost too long to cite. On June 15, 1997, he became the youngest player ever to reach number one in the world rankings and has held or flirted with the top spot ever

since. Among his records are most Professional Golf Association (PGA) player of the year awards; most years leading the PGA in prize money; and most years leading the PGA in lowest average score. As of 2008 (much of which he missed due to injury), Woods was chasing the most cherished record in the sport—Jack Nicklaus's eighteen career victories in major tournaments; Woods had fourteen.

Over the course of his career, Tiger Woods has also established a variety of charity projects for youth and minorities, with the goal of empowering young people to achieve their personal goals. In 1996, Woods and his father established the Tiger Woods Foundation, which runs golf clinics, the Tiger Woods Learning Center, and character development programs for disadvantaged youth. The foundation has raised more than $30 million for grants, scholarships, and a variety of programs, which have served an estimated 10 million children.

The issue of Woods's race has been controversial in some circles. Woods himself embraces his mixed-race background, refusing to be labeled as simply an "African American" and pointing out his mother's Asian identity. Many in the media, however, have continued to refer to him as an African American and write stories about his relationship with his father while ignoring his mother. This has made it more difficult for both the Thai American and Chinese American communities to claim Woods as an icon of their own, though he certainly is a hero to many Asian Americans. Regardless, Woods's success in professional golf and image in mainstream culture are respected by people from virtually every background.

Silas Chamberlin

Further Reading

Callahan, Tom. *In Search of Tiger Woods: A Journey Through Golf with Tiger Woods.* New York: Three Rivers, 2004.

Londino, Lawrence. *Tiger Woods: A Biography.* Westport, CT: Greenwood, 2005.

The Tibetan American Experience: History and Culture

A relatively tiny immigrant group in the United States, Tibetan Americans have had an outsized influence. As a result of their unique spiritual traditions and their compelling story as refugees of a repressive Chinese Communist government—their homeland has been occupied by Beijing since 1950—Tibetan Americans have drawn the U.S. public at large to their cause and have made Tibetan rituals and art an important component of the American cultural mosaic.

Immigration History

An ancient people with a tradition and culture of their own, the Tibetans have been ruled by the Chinese through much of their modern history, other than a roughly forty-year hiatus during the early twentieth century, when the country was independent. While information on Tibetans coming to America in the nineteenth and early twentieth centuries is scarce—they were listed under the general rubric of "Other Asians" in immigration statistics—it can be safely assumed that, given its small population and isolated and landlocked mountain setting, Tibet sent very few of its people to the United States until the latter half of the twentieth century.

In 1950, one year after their own Communist revolution, the Mainland Chinese sent their army into Tibet, reconquering the Himalayan kingdom. Ten years later, the Tibetans, following their spiritual and political leader, the Dalai Lama, rose in rebellion against Chinese rule. The struggle cost the lives of nearly 90,000 people and sent some 80,000 refugees out of the country. The vast majority settled in Bhutan, Nepal, and the Himalayan region of India. All together, it is estimated that Chinese Communist rule in Tibet is responsible for more than 1 million Tibetan deaths, mostly from disease, hunger, and other indirect consequences of the occupation.

Statistics on Tibetan immigrants to the United States in the late twentieth and early twenty-first century are also difficult to come by since, as citizens of China, they are generally not counted separately by U.S. immigration or census officials. Nevertheless, it is estimated that several thousand made their way into the United States, largely as refugees, through the early 1990s, when about 1,000 Tibetans were granted special visas under the Immigration Act of 1990. By the early 2000s, it was estimated that approximately 10,000 persons of Tibetan or mixed-Tibetan ancestry were living in the United States.

Tibetans have settled in clusters throughout the United States, usually where refugee support groups have provided aid—including in the metropolitan areas of New York City, Boston, Minneapolis, and Washington, D.C., along with college towns such as Berkeley, California, and Ithaca, New York. Another significant community can be found in Colorado, where a number of anti-Communist Tibetan guerrillas were trained by the Central Intelligence Agency in the 1950s and 1960s. But the largest concentration of Tibetan Americans—about 40 percent of the total population—is located in the Los Angeles area.

Society and Culture

The Chinese occupation of Tibet has been harsh on that land's people. Both the Tibetan government-in-exile in India and international observers have criticized the Beijing regime for attempting to crush Tibetan culture by underfunding Tibetan education and settling large numbers of Han, or ethnic Chinese people, in the province. Because fewer than half of Tibetan children attend primary school, many Tibetans who have fled to the United States are poorly educated. Most work in menial service occupations, the main exceptions being monks who are supported by the Tibetan American community or Buddhist organizations in the United States. In some rural areas, particularly in the Great Lakes region and Colorado, small numbers of Tibetans have found work as laborers on dairy and other kinds of farms.

As a largely nomadic people in their homeland, Tibetans migrated to pastures in large family clans. And while Tibetans in the United States usually live in nuclear families, the clan tradition lives on. Refugees place great

Pro-Tibetan human rights activists march across the Golden Gate Bridge in San Francisco to protest the 2008 Olympic Games in Beijing. The "Free Tibet" campaign has energized the refugee community since the Communist occupation in 1950. *(David Paul Morris/Stringer/Getty Images)*

emphasis on family reunification, using up much of their savings and free time to bring even distant family members to join them. Traditionally, Tibetan women have enjoyed near-equal status with men in the secular sphere, long being permitted to own their own land and businesses. Indeed, Tibetan women once enjoyed the privilege of having more than one husband.

The region's distinctive Buddhist traditions play an outsized role in Tibetan life, both in the homeland (despite Chinese suppression) and in exile communities abroad. Prior to 1950, Tibet was a theocracy, ruled by the Dalai Lama and other monks. For the first three decades of Chinese rule, however, religion was driven underground, as Communists destroyed thousands of monasteries at the center of cultural, religious, and political life in Tibet and displaced nearly half a million monks and nuns. While the Chinese have eased up on such repression since the 1980s, the Dalai Lama remains in exile, where he leads a global crusade to expose Beijing's campaign to extinguish Tibetan culture. For Tibetan Americans, then, Buddhism serves not only as a connection to their ancient traditions but also as a forum for the struggle against Chinese rule in their homeland. Tibetans, alongside non-Tibetan American Buddhists, drawn to the faith by its austere mysticism, ancient rituals, and spiritual scholarship, devote much money and time to supporting the monks and nuns who keep those spiritual traditions alive in the United States.

Much of Tibetan culture revolves around religion as well, most notably its mandala works, in which concentric rings of elaborate religious imagery are rendered in colored sand by monks and then ritualistically destroyed, so as to convey the impermanence of the material world and the eternity of the spiritual. Religious music, including vocal chanting accompanied by long copper horns, known as *rag-dung*, is also an important part of Tibetan cultural life.

For such a small immigrant group, Tibetans maintain a strong and vibrant political presence in the United States. Support comes from the Dalai Lama's government-in-exile and the non-Tibetan Buddhist population of the United States, including several influential figures in the Hollywood entertainment community. While the ultimate aim of Tibetan political activists is an independent homeland, most work on a daily basis to expose to the American people China's efforts to suppress Tibetan culture, and to persuade the U.S. government to pressure Beijing to change its policies.

Perhaps the most important of the Tibetan political support groups is the Washington-based International Campaign for Tibet (ICT), founded in 1987. In addition, there are a number of support groups, including the Tibet Fund, founded in New York in 1981, whose aim is to help the Tibetan refugee communities of India and Nepal. While there are no national Tibetan American civic groups, a number of local organizations help Tibetan refugees adjust to life in the United States by providing social services. Most prominent among these is the Los Angeles Friends of Tibet Association, founded in 1991.

Most Tibetan media in America is a product of the various groups fighting for Tibetan rights. Both the ICT and the Seattle-based Tibetan Rights Campaign publish newsletters on events in Tibet. The former produces two bimonthlies—the *Tibet Environment and Development Newsletter* and *Tibet Press Watch*; the latter puts out the monthly *Tibet Monitor*.

As the Beijing government continues to promote mass migration into Tibet by the ethnic Han as a means of subordinating the province to Chinese rule, Tibetan culture—both secular and religious—remains under siege in its homeland. Tibetan communities in the diaspora, including those in the United States, have made keeping that culture alive and exerting pressure on the Chinese government a key component of civic, political, and social activities.

James Ciment

Further Reading

Nowak, Margaret. *Tibetan Refugees: Youth and the New Generation of Meaning.* New Brunswick, NJ: Rutgers University Press, 1984.

Wright, Alison. *The Spirit of Tibet: Portrait of a Culture in Exile.* Ithaca, NY: Snow Lion, 1998.

The Vietnamese American Experience: History and Culture

Perhaps more than any other Asian American immigrant group—with the possible exception of Filipinos, whose homeland was a U.S. colony for fifty years—the Vietnamese American community has been heavily shaped by U.S. foreign policy. The first large contingent of Vietnamese came to the United States in the wake of the overthrow of South Vietnam by the Communists in 1975, after more than a decade of American efforts to prevent that outcome. In the years since, America has become the most important overseas destination for Vietnamese. In Orange County, California, the center of Vietnamese American life, and other locations, the Vietnamese have thrived, opening businesses, building communities, and establishing civic and cultural institutions, all the while nurturing a hard-line anti-Communism, a legacy of decades of armed struggle in their homeland.

Immigration History

Prior to the mid-1960s, when reform legislation ended national quotas for immigrant entry, there were almost no Vietnamese living in the United States. That law—the Immigration and Nationality Act of 1965—and, more important, growing U.S. military involvement in Vietnam around the same time brought small numbers of Vietnamese to America, largely students, businesspersons, government officials, a few war refugees, and others with the financial means and ability to leave their country. As of the beginning of 1975, there were fewer than 15,000 Vietnamese living in the United States.

After a decade of conflict, America began withdrawing its troops from Vietnam in the early 1970s, a process largely completed by early 1973. Without U.S. troops, South Vietnam was soon overwhelmed by Communist forces, both insurgents from within the country and the North Vietnamese army from without. In April 1975, Communist troops entered the South Vietnamese capital of Saigon and promptly renamed it Ho Chi Minh City, after the late Vietnamese nationalist leader. As America hurriedly withdrew its diplomatic personnel and remain-

ing military advisers from the country, thousands of Vietnamese who had worked for the South Vietnamese regime or American forces scrambled to get out; these people feared reprisals by the victorious Communists against whom they had been struggling. Media images portrayed chaos as Vietnamese clung to the skids of helicopters carrying Americans out of the embassy compound in Saigon. The tragedy surrounding the U.S. exit was compounded by ignominy when an army transport airlifting orphans out of the country crashed, killing nearly 150 persons. Less than two weeks after the fall of Saigon, President Gerald Ford authorized an emergency quota of 130,000 places for refugees from the wars of Southeast Asia (Cambodia and Laos had recently fallen to the Communists as well); 125,000 of the places went to Vietnamese.

Six official camps were set up in different parts of the United States to disperse the 125,000 refugees. Politicians feared a nativist backlash if too many Vietnamese were settled in any one community. Southern California, with about one-quarter of the 125,000 newcomers, be-

Messages of gratitude are left at the Vietnam War Memorial near the Little Saigon area of Westminster, California, to mark the thirtieth anniversary of the fall of Saigon in April 1975. Little Saigon is said to be the largest Vietnamese community outside Vietnam. *(David McNew/Getty Images)*

came home to the largest group of this first large-scale Vietnamese immigration.

The number of Vietnamese immigrants dropped off dramatically in 1976 and 1977, to just a few thousand per year, largely because Vietnam itself was now stable and its government had largely closed off the borders. In 1978 and 1979, however, war returned to Southeast Asia, first in the form of a Vietnamese invasion of neighboring Cambodia, where a genocidal regime had murdered more than a million of its own citizens, and then in a brief but bloody war between old enemies, China and Vietnam. Hundreds of thousands of Vietnamese left the country, fleeing harsh economic times and Communist repression.

With various refugee support societies pressuring the U.S. government to admit more Vietnamese into the country, the number of immigrants rose to nearly 50,000 in 1979 and more than 300,000 from 1980 to 1981. Many made their escape aboard rickety, hastily constructed vessels—earning them the sobriquet "boat people." Many died in storm-tossed waters or at the hands of pirates in the South China Sea. This second and much larger wave of Vietnamese immigration, which continued in smaller numbers through the early and middle 1980s, generally settled where Vietnamese communities had already sprung up, both in South California and, to a smaller extent, coastal Texas. Whereas by 1980 the Vietnamese American population had grown to about 245,000, by 1990 the number reached nearly 615,000, including some 8,000 Amerasian children, the offspring of U.S. GIs and Vietnamese women who faced discrimination and ostracism in their home country.

While Vietnam was largely at peace in the 1990s and undergoing rapid economic development by the latter half of the decade, immigrants from that country continued to pour into the United States, largely under provisions of immigration law that allowed for family reunification. Indeed, of foreign-born Vietnamese, according to the 2000 U.S. Census, nearly half had come into the country since 1990, raising the total Vietnamese American population in 2000 to 1,110,207; another 100,000 or so identified themselves as partly Vietnamese. Of these, about 40 percent—or 440,000—were living in California, including about 135,000 in the Orange County cities of Garden Grove and Westminster, the heart of so-called Little Saigon. Another 135,000, or about 12 percent, lived in Texas. Other states with significant Vietnamese communities have included Louisiana, Pennsylvania, Massachusetts, Illinois, Minnesota, Washington, Florida, and Virginia. Aside from Greater Los Angeles–Orange County, metropolitan areas with Vietnamese neighborhoods, or Little Saigons, of their own include the San Francisco Bay Area, Houston, Dallas–Fort Worth, Seattle, and Washington, D.C.

Education and Economics

Like other immigrant groups from Southeast Asia—notably Cambodians, Laotians, and the Hmong—Vietnamese Americans tend to lag behind other Asian American groups in terms of education and income. Among Southeast Asian groups, however, they rank second to highest, bested only by the relatively small Thai American community. According to the 2000 U.S. Census, 61.9 percent of Vietnamese Americans had a high school diploma or higher, compared with 80.4 percent for the Asian American community and for the U.S. population as a whole. (Unless otherwise noted, all figures in this section come from the 2000 U.S. Census.) Similarly, only 19.4 percent of Vietnamese Americans had a college degree or higher, compared to 44.1 percent among all Asian Americans and 24.4 percent for the total U.S. population. The difference is even more stark given the relatively high rate of English language proficiency among Vietnamese Americans. Whereas about 30 percent of Vietnamese Americans reported that they did not speak English "well," the figure for Asian Americans generally was near 40 percent.

In terms of income, Vietnamese also lag behind other Asian immigrant groups. With a median household income of just over $47,000 annually, Vietnamese Americans earned less than Asians Americans generally by more than $12,000, or about 25 percent, and less than the overall U.S. population by about $3,000, or 6 percent. Nevertheless, as the Vietnamese have settled into American life over the years, their income levels have risen significantly. The median household income of $47,000 in 2000 represented a nearly 30 percent increase in inflation-adjusted terms from 1990 ($27,000, or about $36,500 in 2000 dollars). Likewise, their poverty rate fell from 23.7 percent in 1990 to just 16 percent a decade later. One socioeconomic measure in which Vietnamese Americans fell within the overall Asian average was home ownership, with about 53 percent of Vietnamese Americans and Asian Americans generally living in owner-occupied housing. Both groups lagged significantly behind the overall U.S. figure of about two-thirds. Unlike native-born Americans, immigrants from Asia generally do not inherit homes from their parents; largely urban and suburban, coastal-dwelling Asian Americans also tend to live in higher-priced housing markets than the average American.

Sociologists offer several reasons why the Vietnamese

tend to lag behind other Asian American groups in education and income. First, the Vietnamese are a relatively new community compared with the Chinese, Filipinos, and Japanese. Indeed, like income, educational levels have also risen as the community has become better established in the United States. In 1990, just 12.2 percent of adult Vietnamese Americans had college degrees or higher; by 2000, the figure had climbed by more than half to 19.4 percent. Second, among other relatively new groups, they come from a poorer country than do Koreans or Taiwanese; Vietnam's per capita annual income in the early 2000s was about $3,500; the figure for both South Korea and Taiwan was closer to $25,000. Finally, and perhaps most important, a much broader cross-section of the Vietnamese population has immigrated to America than that of other major non–Southeast Asian groups, with the possible exception of the Chinese. While professionals are predominant in the ranks of Asian Indian and Filipino immigrants, and middle-class entrepreneurs are prevalent among Koreans, Vietnamese immigrants, many of whom are refugees, come from all walks of life—from farmers to workers to professionals. Thus, whereas nearly 60 percent of Asian Indian Americans and nearly 40 percent of Filipinos and Koreans are in professional or managerial positions, the figure for Vietnamese is just over one-fourth; this was still significantly higher than the roughly 15 percent for other Southeast Asian groups.

Family and Faith

Most Vietnamese Americans live in nuclear households. According to the 2000 census, 64 percent lived in two-parent households, either with or without children. This was slightly above the overall figure for Asian Americans (61.8 percent) but significantly above that for Americans generally (52.5 percent). The average Vietnamese household size was 3.7 persons, again somewhat higher than that for Asian Americans generally (3.1) and significantly higher than that for the U.S. population as a whole (2.5).

While many Vietnamese Americans live in nuclear households, they also tend to define immediate family much more broadly and to retain closer ties than Americans generally do. For example, Vietnamese Americans are more likely to settle near other family members. Children typically are expected to set up households within easy visiting distance of their parents, and extended family get-togethers are commonplace. In addition, respected members of the extended family, usually elders, are more likely to be involved in decision making and problem solving pertaining to their kin than American families

are. Family closeness extends to marriage as well. Just 4.1 percent of adult Vietnamese Americans in 2000 had been divorced, about the same as the rate among Asian Americans generally (4.2 percent), but less than half the rate for the U.S. population as a whole (9.7).

As in the case of other immigrant groups, however, there is a generational split among Vietnamese Americans between the more traditional-minded immigrant generation and their American-born or raised children. Traditional Vietnamese, for example, expect children to obey their parents unquestioningly, while the U.S.-born children, raised in a culture that values individualism, often chafe at such restrictions. Similarly, the directness of U.S.-born children in addressing their parents and other adults sometimes strikes more traditionally oriented Vietnamese—raised in a culture that places a premium on politeness and indirectness in speech—as rude and disrespectful. Dating behavior likewise raises intergenerational issues. In Vietnam and in the rules of propriety among traditionalists, young women rarely go out with men unchaperoned. When U.S.-born daughters insist on this typical American privilege, conflict is often the result.

Another arena of cultural adjustment is gender roles. In Vietnam, male children traditionally have been valued more than females, because they can pass on the family name and are expected to take care of the parents when they age. In allocating scarce family resources, for example, emphasis is traditionally given to the education of the male children. In the United States, however, two factors have served to break down this value system. First, resources are more plentiful in the United States, making it possible to educate all children in the family; the Vietnamese, who place great value on education, tend to encourage both sons and daughters to seek out higher education. Second, with Social Security benefits and a high savings rate, parents no longer need their sons to take care of them financially in old age—or, at least, not as much as they did in Vietnam. Still, for all of the equality in education, many U.S.-born Vietnamese women complain that their husbands and fathers expect them to settle down as housewives when they get married, whether they are educated or not.

Vietnam is primarily a Buddhist country, though with a small Catholic minority, a legacy of a century of French colonial rule. (As a Communist country, Vietnam is officially secular. According to the government, more than 80 percent of the people practice no religion.) Because the French colonialists favored Catholics, they tended to become the best-educated and most well-off segment of society in the 1940s and 1950s. When the Communists took over, Catholics were most likely to have the resources and motivation—many feared persecution by the Communists—to leave. Thus, more than 30 percent of Vietnamese Americans are Catholic, compared to only 6.7 percent in the homeland today. Vietnamese Buddhists follow the Mahayana tradition, prevalent in much of East Asia, and many are heavily influenced by the Buddhist philosophy known in Vietnamese as *tien* (referred to in the West by the Japanese term "zen"). *Tien* emphasizes enlightenment through meditation and introspection rather than faith and devotion. Because *tien* de-emphasizes worship, temples are relatively rare in Vietnamese American communities, and usually focus on providing social services. Still, the Vietnamese *tien* master Thich Nhat Hanh is widely revered among Vietnamese Americans and has a following among non-Asian Americans as well.

Society and Politics

Because the Vietnamese community is relatively new and because so many members of that community have come to the United States as refugees, most of its civic organizations have been dedicated to helping newcomers adjust to life in their new country. Many of the organizations are Pan–Southeast Asian, aiding refugees from Cambodia and Laos as well as Vietnam. Among the most important of these is the San Francisco–based Southeast Asian Refugee Resettlement Center, established in the 1970s to provide social services for newly arrived refugees from Cambodia, Laos, and Vietnam. The Vietnamese American Cultural and Social Council, located in San Jose, California, offers many of the same health, education, and social services for Vietnamese only. The Vietnamese American Chamber of Commerce, headquartered in Westminster, California, the commercial heart of Little Saigon, provides advice and networking opportunities to the many small Vietnamese entrepreneurs and merchants there.

One organization with a unique history is the Vietnamese Fishermen Association of America (VFAA), located in Oakland, California. With a long coastline, Vietnam has long been home to a thriving fishing and shrimping industry. Thus, when refugees began pouring into the United States in the late 1970s, many headed to the rich fish and shrimp grounds of Texas and Louisiana. As poor newcomers, they were willing to sell their catch for less than American fishermen, who came to regard the Vietnamese as unfair competitors. In the early 1980s, the tensions turned violent when members of the Ku Klux Klan began issuing threats against Vietnamese American fishermen on the Gulf Coast of Texas and burning several of their boats. In response, Vietnamese American fishermen organized the VFAA to defend their interests by lobbying government agencies for protection. The effort was largely effective, and tensions gradually died down. By the early 2000s, Vietnamese Americans had come to control up to two-thirds of America's shrimping industry.

Like other relatively recent Asian immigrant groups, the Vietnamese have tended to avoid mainstream American politics, though groups such as the Massachusetts-based Vietnamese American Civic Organization works to increase voter registration among naturalized citizens of the community. Since the 1990s, Vietnamese Americans in the Little Saigon area of Orange County, California, have become more active in local politics. In 1992, civic leader Tony Lam was elected to the city council of Westminster, becoming the first Vietnamese American to win elective office. Since then, Lam has been joined by several others on the municipal councils of Westminster and nearby Garden Grove. In 2007, Janet Nguyen was elected to the Orange County Board of Supervisors, becoming the highest elected Vietnamese American official in the United States. Meanwhile, Viet Dinh was appointed by President George W. Bush in 2001 to serve as assistant attorney general, in which capacity he became one of the principal authors of the USA Patriot Act.

One area in which Vietnamese differ from other Asian immigrant groups is their involvement in the politics of the homeland. As refugees from a Communist government, Vietnamese Americans tend to be strongly anti-Communist, holding frequent protests against the human rights record of the Hanoi regime and organizing demonstrations whenever Vietnamese officials visit the United States. Indeed, the Vietnamese American community, particularly in Orange County, vigorously protested U.S. normalization of relations with Vietnam in the 1990s.

The intense interest in the politics of Vietnam has turned into intolerance on some occasions. In 1999, for example, when an Orange County video store owner displayed a picture of Communist leader Ho Chi Minh in his shop, along with the national flag of Vietnam (most Vietnamese Americans insist on flying the flag of now-defunct South Vietnam), more than 15,000 protesters held an all-night vigil. When the shop owner refused to take down either the photo or the flag, he was assaulted by angry members of the community.

Not surprisingly, perhaps, the Vietnamese tend to be conservative in American politics. Of all Asian American groups, the Vietnamese are the only one whose voter registration leans heavily Republican. Among the Vietnamese Americans of Orange County, in fact, some 55 percent are registered Republicans and just 22 percent Democrats. Nevertheless, as in the case of Cuban Americans in South Florida, the strong anti-Communism of the immigrant generation is being increasingly offset by the views of their U.S.-born or raised children, who have little or no direct experience of what the family lost in fleeing the homeland.

Arts and Culture

The Vietnamese American community is divided into two subgroups: the vast majority are ethnic Vietnamese, and a small but significant minority are ethnic Chinese. The latter, Chinese-Vietnamese, are disproportionately represented in the Vietnamese American community for two reasons. First, many were entrepreneurs who lost their businesses and decided to flee when the Communists took over. Others fled during the 1979 border war between China and Vietnam, when they faced persecution by the government and ordinary citizens. While Chinese Vietnamese tended to be highly acculturated to Vietnamese life—many could trace their ancestry in Vietnam many generations—they clung to their own language, speaking Cantonese at home (the language of South China, from which most of the Chinese Vietnamese originally hailed) and Vietnamese in public. They also preserved some of their own cuisine and clothing styles.

At the same time, the Chinese Vietnamese and ethnic Vietnamese shared many cultural practices. Both celebrated Lunar New Year, known as Tet in Vietnam, in February. The most important holiday of the year, Tet is a time to shoot off fireworks, offer gifts, and honor the ancestors through Buddhist and other rituals. The Chinese Vietnamese and ethnic Vietnamese also share the mid-autumn festival known as *trung thu,* during which people exchange sticky-rice moon cakes and hang lights around their homes and businesses. Because many Vietnamese live in areas dominated by their own ethnic group, many of these events are still widely celebrated in America, with observances crossing generational lines. However, because Vietnam itself is controlled by a despised Communist regime, most Vietnamese Americans do not celebrate the civic holidays of their homeland. In support of their ideals, the U.S. Congress in 1994 designated May 11 as Vietnam Human Rights Day.

Vietnamese American arts and literature are only beginning to come into their own, especially among the so-called 1.5 generation—those born in Vietnam but raised in the United States. Many of the writers of this group focus on the traditional immigrant theme of intergenerational conflict between old-country parents and acculturated children. Critical works in this vein include Lan Cao's semiautobiographical novel *Monkey Bridge* (1997) and Quang X. Pham's memoir *A Sense of Duty: My Father, My American Journey* (2005). Perhaps the most acclaimed work by a Vietnamese American author, Andrew Lam's award-winning collection of essays, *Perfume Dreams: Reflections on the Vietnamese Diaspora* (2005), examines the meaning of the Vietnam War to Vietnamese both in the home country and in America. In the arts generally, the Vietnamese American Cultural Organization in New York City works to promote Vietnamese culture with concerts and dance performances across the United States.

The Vietnamese American community is served by a thriving media. While local papers exist wherever there is a Little Saigon, national newspapers include *Nguoi Viet* and *Vien Dong,* both published in Orange County. Specialized media include *Across the Sea,* a semiannual magazine based in Berkeley, California, and aimed at the sizable Vietnamese American student population; the monthly Catholic magazine *Gia Dinh Moi,* published in San Jose; *Khang Chien,* a San Jose–based monthly magazine covering events in Vietnam; and the literary magazine *Van Huoc,* based in Orange County.

Like other Southeast Asian immigrant groups, Vietnamese Americans stand out from other Asian American communities. While sharing the same strong entrepreneurial drive and dedication to education, they lag somewhat in terms of household income and the number of those holding college degrees. They are catching up fast in both areas, however, and have long passed the U.S. population as a whole in terms of educational achievement. What makes their experience most significant, however, is their status as refugees of war and Communism. While some Koreans and Chinese came to the United States as political refugees, those who did remain a small minority within their community; the relatively tiny Cambodian American community is also composed of refugees fleeing war and Communist persecution. Vietnamese Americans, on the other hand, are by far the largest group to have been strongly shaped by this experience, a fact reflected in intense political feelings largely unknown in other Asian American communities.

James Ciment

Further Reading

Caplan, Nathan, John K. Whitmore, and Marcella H. Choy. *The Boat People and Achievement in America: A Study of Family Life, Hard Work, and Cultural Values.* Ann Arbor: University of Michigan Press, 1989.

Do, Hien Duc. *The Vietnamese Americans.* Westport, CT: Greenwood, 1999.

Freeman, James M. *Changing Identities: Vietnamese Americans, 1975–1995*. Boston: Allyn and Bacon, 1995.

———. *Hearts of Sorrow: Vietnamese-American Lives*. Palo Alto, CA: Stanford University Press, 1989.

Kibria, Nazli. *Family Tightrope: The Changing Lives of Vietnamese Americans*. Princeton, NJ: Princeton University Press, 1993.

Lam, Andrew. *Perfume Dreams: Reflections on the Vietnamese Diaspora*. Berkeley, CA: Heyday, 2005.

Rutledge, Paul James. *The Vietnamese Experience in America*. Bloomington: Indiana University Press, 1992.

Vietnamese American Chamber of Commerce. http://www.vacoc.com.

Vietnamese Americans
Alphabetical Entries

"Boat People"

The term "boat people" refers to the vast wave of refugees who fled Vietnam in the late 1970s to escape political persecution and economic want. Because the Communist regime prohibited most people from emigrating, the refugees escaped the country on small boats, sailing into the stormy and pirate-infested waters of the South China Sea, with the goal of reaching non-Communist countries that would provide them refuge. Most hoped ultimately to settle in the United States and, to a lesser extent, such other Western countries as Australia and France.

When Saigon fell to Communist forces in April 1975, more than 100,000 Vietnamese were airlifted out of the country by American military forces or made their way in small boats to U.S. Navy ships in the South China Sea. The first wave of refugees consisted mostly of educated professionals with ties to the former Vietnamese government or to the U.S. armed forces. In the year after this initial wave of refugees, few Vietnamese attempted to leave the country. As the new Communist government began implementing social and economic reforms, however, a large number of Vietnamese began to flee the country in small boats in 1978. This second wave of Vietnamese refugees is often referred to as the "boat people," though the term has also been used in reference to refugees from other nations, such as Cubans and Haitians, who also fled their countries by boat.

In an attempt to rebuild a nation laid waste by years of war, the new Communist regime began a series of economic reforms that had a particularly harsh impact on ethnic Chinese merchants whose families had lived in Vietnam for generations. Fueled by both economic concerns and anti-Chinese sentiment, authorities dis-

A group of second-wave Vietnamese "boat people"—refugees who fled the country in the late 1970s, after the new Communist regime began implementing social and economic reforms—awaits transport at a government dockyard in Hong Kong. *(M. Fresco/Stringer/Hulton Archive/Getty Images)*

possessed ethnic Chinese of their property and goods, limited their freedoms, and rationed their food, among other restrictions. As a result of these new policies, many ethnic Chinese, as well as others unwilling to endure harsh life under the new regime, fled the country. By July 1979, nearly 1 million Vietnamese, a significant portion of them ethnic Chinese, managed to escape by boat. Of these, according to the United Nations, about 200,000 made it to Hong Kong, 250,000 to Malaysia, and 160,000 to Thailand; a an estimated quarter million died at sea. Of those who survived, roughly half a million ended up settling in the United States.

Because the Vietnamese government did not allow people to leave the country, those who wished to leave had to sneak away secretly or bribe authorities. Those who were caught were imprisoned and punished as traitors. Escapees climbed into small fishing boats and attempted to reach Hong Kong, Thailand, Malaysia, or Indonesia. The passage across the South China Sea was perilous not only because of the hazards of crossing the ocean in such small craft, but also because of pirates who preyed on them. Many Thai fisherman who encountered these small craft plundered their occupants for their valuables and supplies, often raping the women and killing indiscriminately. Historians estimate that at least 10 percent of people who fled Vietnam by boat did not survive the journey; some estimates run as high as 70 percent.

Especially controversial was the practice by Malaysian and Thai officials, overwhelmed by the influx of refugees, of towing back out to sea many of the desperate people who attempted to come to shore. This practice subsided as the international community worked to establish refugee camps in these countries and guaranteed that the refugees would be resettled in third countries. In 1979, the United Nations High Commissioner for Refugees (UNHCR) succeeded in establishing the Orderly Departure Program with the Hanoi regime. Under the agreement, Vietnam would permit certain people to emigrate directly to countries such as the United States and Canada without having to make the dangerous sea journey. While the program effectively decreased boat departures for several years, the number of boat people surged again in the 1980s as the result of an administrative backlog in the program. In the 1990s, attempts to leave Vietnam by boat decreased significantly as departures were regularized through other channels.

Timothy J. Randazzo

Further Reading

Chan, Sucheng. *Asian Americans: An Interpretive History.* New York: Twayne, 1991.

Freeman, James M. *Changing Identities: Vietnamese Americans, 1975–1995.* Boston: Allyn and Bacon, 1995.

Robinson, W. Courtland. *Terms of Refuge: The Indochinese Exodus and the International Response.* New York: Zed Books, 1998.

Bui, Tony (1973–)

Born on September 14, 1973, in Saigon (now Ho Chi Minh City) and raised in Sunnyvale, California, Tony Bui is known primarily for his work as director and coproducer of the award-winning independent film *Three Seasons (Ba Mùa,* 1999). The first full-length Hollywood movie filmed in Vietnam since the end of the war in 1975, *Three Seasons* swept up Best Film awards at festivals around the world. For many Vietnamese Americans, Bui's success and the film itself highlighted the experience of those who were born in the United States or arrived as children, and who have sought to maintain their native cultural identity while finding a place in an alien society and culture.

Like thousands of others, Bui and his family fled Vietnam shortly before the fall of Saigon to Communist forces in the spring of 1975. Bui was two. The rest of the family included his father, who had served in the South Vietnamese Air Force, his mother, an older brother, and a younger sister. After arriving in America, the family was processed at Fort Chaffee, Arkansas, one of four primary U.S. military locations set up to receive Vietnamese refugees in 1975. A family in Chico, California, agreed to sponsor the Bui family, which soon moved to San Francisco, where there was a large Asian population, and eventually settled in the Bay Area suburb of Sunnyvale.

After working in several businesses, Bui's father was laid off and decided to open a chain of video rental stores. The exposure to movies sparked the boy's interest in cinema, and he began shooting his own films with a Super-8 home-movie camera. He went on to pursue a degree in film at Loyola Marymount University in Los Angeles, in 1994. It was during his time in college, at age nineteen, that Bui made his first visit back to Vietnam. He made several more trips to his home country in succeeding years before making his first short film (and senior thesis), *Yellow Lotus,* shot in Vietnam.

After writing the initial screenplay for *Three Seasons/Ba Mùa,* Bui went about seeking financing and eventually was granted a $2 million budget from October films, a division of Universal Studios. In addition to directing the film, Bui served as coproducer with his brother, Timothy Linh Bui. Starring Harvey Keitel and Don Duong, a famous actor in Vietnam, the film follows three primary story lines about life in Ho Chi Minh City. One is about an American who searches for a daughter he fathered during the Vietnam War. A second details the story of a cyclo (small motorized rickshaw) driver who gives a ride to a call girl and falls in love with her. The third chronicles the life of a woman who harvests lotuses for a reclusive poet and helps revive his passion. Also a portrayal of urban Vietnamese culture undergoing Westernization, the film addresses such themes as the changing hopes and hardships of youth culture, prostitution, working-class life, and coming to terms with the Vietnam War. Debuting at the Sundance Film Festival in 1999, *Three Seasons* became the first release to win both the Grand Jury Prize and Audience Award at the event.

In 2001, the Bui brothers coproduced their second film, *Green Dragon,* which focused on Camp Pendleton near San Diego, California, during the mass exodus from Vietnam and the resettlement of refugees in the United States. The film depicts the lives of Vietnamese and Americans during the fall of Saigon and the adjustment of refugees to life away from home. In addition to pursuing new film projects, Bui has taught directing at Loyola Marymount University and served on the board of directors of Film Independent, an internationally acclaimed Los Angeles–based organization supporting and promoting indie films.

Vu H. Pham

Further Reading

Arellano, Gustavo. "Freedom Free Little Saigon." *OC Weekly* 10:10 (2004).

Blackwelder, Rob. "Return of the Native." Interview. San Francisco, March 11, 1999. http://splicedwire.com/features/tonybui.html.

Bui, Tony. Personal correspondence with the author, June 2007.

Nguyen Vu Viet-Huong. "Tony Bui." In *25 Vietnamese Americans in 25 Years: 1975–2000.* San Jose, CA: New Horizon, 2000.

Wilkinson, Kelly. "In the Director's Studio: Tony Bui Talks about *Three Seasons*—and His Early Years in Sunnyvale." *The Sun,* March 31, 1999.

Business and Entrepreneurship, Vietnamese American

Despite being one of the poorer cohorts of Asian Americans—a legacy of their initial status as refugees from war and Communism—Vietnamese Americans have done surprisingly well as entrepreneurs, largely in retail, food services, the service sector, and extractive (fishing) industries. Vietnamese Americans have been drawn to these forms of entrepreneurialism for a number of reasons. For one thing, many of these businesses require little capital to get started and those who own them do not necessarily need to speak English well. In addition, operating a small private business, which often requires long hours, fits into the traditional work ethic of the Vietnamese culture. Finally, with large and close-knit families, Vietnamese business owners have access to low-paid or even no-wage workers for their enterprises.

Prior to 1975 and the fall of South Vietnam to Communism, there were fewer than 15,000 Vietnamese in America, mostly students and refugees from the war. Between 1975 and 1985, approximately 500,000 Vietnamese fled their country, many with little more than the clothes on their backs, having spent what savings they had buying their way out of Vietnam and into the South China Sea on rickety ships. By 1990, the Vietnamese American population stood at just over 600,000, and by 2007 there were an estimated 1.6 million persons of Vietnamese descent living in the United States.

From the beginning, a significant minority of Vietnamese gravitated toward business ownership, roughly at the same rate as other major Asian American groups but far behind that of Korean Americans. As early as 1987, the U.S. Census counted nearly 26,000 Vietnamese-owned businesses nationwide, up nearly 400 percent from just five years earlier. Most were small, single-employee firms. Altogether, the 26,000 enterprises employed just over 13,000 persons. About 45 percent of the firms were located in California—many in the burgeoning Little Saigon community of Orange County—and another 20 percent in Texas, largely along the Gulf Coast and in the Houston area. By 1990, about 10 percent of working Vietnamese Americans were self-employed; by 2000, the figure had risen slightly to just under 11 percent. One reason for the slow growth is that many American-born Vietnamese were shunning the long hours and often low-status work that comes with small business ownership. Better educated and much more proficient in English, they preferred to work for large American firms or the government. Thus, while 11.2 percent of Vietnamese-raised persons were self-employed, the figure dropped to just 7.9 percent among American-raised Vietnamese.

According to a 2006 U.S. Census study (with statistics for 2002), there were just over 147,000 Vietnamese-owned businesses in the United States, or roughly 13.3 percent of all Asian American–owned enterprises (while Vietnamese represented just over 10 percent of the overall Asian American population); sales and receipts totaled about $15.5 billion. With about 50,000, California ranked first among the states in Vietnamese American–owned businesses, followed by Texas with just over

24,000 and Florida and Georgia, each with just over 7,000 businesses. The Los Angeles metropolitan area had the largest concentration of Vietnamese-owned firms, with more than 30,000—many of them in the Little Saigon communities of Westminster and Garden Grove, Orange County. The San Francisco Bay Area had about 14,000, many located in San Jose, another large Vietnamese American population center. Outside California, the largest concentrations were in Houston, with nearly 12,000 businesses, and Atlanta, with 6,000.

The vast majority of Vietnamese American businesses in 2002—about 122,000, or more than 80 percent—had no paid employees. Of the roughly 25,000 that did have paid employees, the number averaged about five, with an annual payroll of about $2.8 billion. Like other Asian American groups, Vietnamese were largely involved in retail (about 14,300 firms); professional, technical, and scientific services (8,500); health care (8,500); real estate and property rental (5,700); and construction (4,400). Unique among Asian American groups was Vietnamese American ownership of firms dealing in extractive industries (4,100). The latter figure largely consisted of owners of fishing and shrimping boats on the Gulf Coast of Texas and Louisiana, with Vietnamese Americans pulling in anywhere between 45 and 85 percent of the shrimp in America, depending on the season.

A number of factors have drawn Vietnamese Americans to entrepreneurship. With many lacking skills and command of the English language, small business ownership offered a faster path to social and economic mobility than unskilled or semiskilled labor. Vietnamese culture, like that of many Asian Americans, puts a high value on both hard work and family cohesion. Many Vietnamese American firms survive because they can tap into low-wage and no-wage family help. In addition, the fact that Vietnamese tended to settle in close-knit communities, often in working-class neighborhoods, opened up opportunities to provide the unique goods and services demanded by their countrymen. Many Vietnamese opened businesses in decaying inner-city Chinatowns after many of the original inhabitants had moved to Chinese-dominated or mixed-ethnic suburbs, as was the case of the Chinatown in Los Angeles. Finally, a significant number of Vietnamese immigrants have been Chinese-Vietnamese, that is, ethnically Chinese people who have lived in Vietnam for generations. Many were business owners in Vietnam, chased out when the Communists nationalized much of the country's economy. These Chinese Vietnamese brought more capital with them than other Vietnamese and, of course, came to America with the necessary entrepreneurial skills and the ability to tap credit lines from well-established Chinese American banks. One of the most successful of Vietnamese

American businesses is the Chinese-Vietnamese-owned Shun Fat chain of supermarkets in California and Nevada, founded in the 1980s.

Not all Vietnamese American businesses have been geared strictly to the Vietnamese American community. One popular service-sector business is nail salons. According to a study conducted by a Vietnamese-language newspaper in the early 2000s, more than one-third of nail salons in America were owned by Vietnamese, including about 80 percent of those in California. And while most Vietnamese restaurant owners cater to diners from their own community, the exotic cuisine has become increasingly popular with non-Asians as well.

As in the case of other Asian American groups, the profile of Vietnamese American businesses is changing as the population becomes more Americanized. While fewer American-born Vietnamese are choosing self-employment, those who do usually shun the long hours of small retail establishments, using their education and fluency in English to start up professional and high-end service-sector businesses, such as medicine, law, real estate, and insurance. Most of these cater to the expanding Vietnamese American community but, increasingly, other Asians and non-Asians as well.

James Ciment

Further Reading

Leba, John Kong. *The Vietnamese Entrepreneurs in the U.S.A.: The First Decade.* Houston, TX: Zieleks, 1985.

Mai, Jesse. "Vietnamese-American Entrepreneurship." *Kaufman Center for Entrepreneurial Leadership Clearinghouse on Entrepreneurship Education Digest* 4:2 (July 2004).

Park, Lisa Sun-Hee. *Consuming Citizenship: Children of Asian Immigrant Entrepreneurs.* Palo Alto, CA: Stanford University Press, 2005.

U.S. Census. *Asian-Owned Firms: 2002.* Washington, DC: U.S. Department of Commerce, August 2006.

Vietnamese American Chamber of Commerce. http://www.vacoc.com.

Lam, Tony (1937–)

The first Vietnamese American to be elected to public office—a seat on the city council of Westminster, California, in 1992—Tony Lam was born Lam Quang in the city of Haiphong, then part of French Indochina, in 1937. One of eight children, he grew up in a prosperous household. His father was chief accountant for a French company in Vietnam, and his mother owned 150 acres (60 hectares) of land in Thanh Hoa Province.

Following the victory of Communist-nationalist Viet Minh forces over the French colonialists in 1954, Vietnam was divided into a Communist north and a non-Communist south. Like hundreds of thousands of others in the north, Lam's family fled south, as the Communists seized their property and Lam's father lost his job as the company he worked for closed down its North Vietnamese operations.

After leaving high school, Lam joined the South Vietnamese Navy and then took a job with an American construction company. During the 1960s, he went to work for the United States Agency for International Development (USAID), helping coordinate its counterinsurgency, anti-Communist programs. In 1966, he formed a company with his brother that helped supply construction materials and services to the U.S. military and government in South Vietnam.

With the fall of South Vietnam to the North Vietnamese Army and Communist insurgents in 1975, Lam saw his property seized and was forced to flee the country. As a wealthy businessman who had worked with the U.S. military, he was likely to have been placed in reeducation camp or even prison, where he would have been forced into indoctrination programs and hard labor, as were thousands of people like him.

Along with more than 100,000 other refugees, Lam was evacuated with the last U.S. forces in South Vietnam, and sent to refugee camps in Guam and Camp Pendleton, California. His leadership abilities were soon recognized by authorities, and he was made a camp director at Pendleton, before being resettled in Florida. Like many South Vietnamese refugees scattered around the country, Lam soon migrated to Orange County, California, a conservative bastion that was emerging as the home to thousands of ardently anti-Communist South Vietnamese refugees. Lam worked in a variety of low-paying jobs at first, including gas station attendant and grocery store clerk, before becoming an insurance salesman and then manager for a local defense company. He later opened a restaurant called Vien Dong in the north Orange County city of Westminster, then emerging as the heart of what was coming to be called "Little Saigon."

During the late 1970s and 1980s, Lam was instrumental in creating key civic institutions in the Vietnamese American community, becoming secretary of the Vietnamese-dominated Lions Club of Westminster and first vice president of the Vietnamese Chamber of Commerce. He was a leading figure in organizing the annual Tet festivities (Vietnamese Lunar New Year holiday) in Orange County; the two organizations he officered also helped provide social and language services to the community.

In November 1992, Lam made history by running successfully for a seat on the Westminster city council. Although the city was becoming heavily Vietnamese, only about 2,000 members of that community were eligible to vote. Lam garnered some 6,500 votes by putting together a coalition of whites, Latinos, and Vietnamese Americans and winning the endorsements of the mayor and police to defeat two fellow Vietnamese American candidates, Jimmy Tong and Margie Rice. Appealing to the broader community, Lam took a moderate position and eschewed the often bitter anti-Communist politics that dominated Vietnamese American life. In 1999, he took the advice of city attorneys and refused to join or endorse Vietnamese protests against a local video store who displayed pictures of former Communist leader Ho Chi Minh and the Communist Vietnamese flag in his window. Many members of the community were outraged at Lam, burning him in effigy and boycotting his restaurant. There were even calls for his resignation. Lam continued to resist the appeals but decided not run for reelection in 2002.

Vu H. Pham

Further Reading

Lien, Pei-te. *The Making of Asian America Through Political Participation.* Philadelphia: Temple University Press, 2001.

Nakanishi, Don T. "Beyond Electoral Politics: Renewing a Search for a Paradigm of Asian Pacific American Politics." In *Asian Americans and Politics: Perspectives, Experiences, Prospects,* ed. Gordon H. Chang. Palo Alto, CA: Stanford University Press, 2001.

Nguyen, Tram Quynh Quang. "Tony Lam." In *25 Vietnamese Americans in 25 Years: 1975–2000.* San Jose, CA: New Horizon, 2000.

Literature, Vietnamese American

Vietnamese American literature may be divided into two general categories: relatively early autobiographical memoirs, which struggle with the traumas of postwar experiences and the transition to America; and more varied work beginning in the 1990s, which explores a variety of literary genres and themes unique to the so-called 1.5 generation (those who immigrated during childhood). Much of Vietnamese American literature can be characterized by its exploration of several common themes: an ongoing focus on the exile, immigration, and assimilation entailed in the struggle to settle in America; the psychological working through of problems of memory, trauma, and historical loss and reconstruction; and an emphasis on the family and communality.

Vietnam War

Notable works of early Vietnamese American writing attempt to understand, explain, and come to terms with the Vietnam War: themes of battle, torture, and post-traumatic stress dominate. Many of these texts bear witness to the forced labor and interrogations of Communist reeducation camps, among them Nguyen Ngoc Ngan's *The Will of Heaven: A Story of One Vietnamese and the End of His World* (1982), Truong Nhu Tan's *Vietcong Memoir* (1985), Doan Van Toai's *The Vietnamese Gulag* (1986), and Tran Tri Vu's *Lost Years: My 1,632 Days in Vietnamese Reeducation Camps* (1988).

In the mid-1980s, memoirs written by women began to appear, broadening the range of published Vietnamese American experience beyond the battlefield. These female writers focused on narrating cultural changes rather than military experiences, documenting and describing prewar civilian experience, postwar American cultural colonization, and experiences of immigration to America. In tracing the transition from war to peace, Le Ly Hayslip's first memoir, *When Heaven and Earth Changed Places* (1989), was a best seller that sought to soothe postwar feelings of guilt with its themes of forgiveness and reconciliation, providing a mediating description of the war from both Viet Cong and American perspectives. Hayslip's second memoir, *Child of War, Woman of Peace* (1993), traces her immigration to America and her business success on its shores, telling a story that resonates with other tales of immigrant accomplishment. Mai Holter's *While I Am Here* (1993) and Nguyen Van Vu's *At Home in America* (1979) also deal with adjustments to American life, focusing on transitions to capitalism and conversions to Christianity. Other notable texts of this period include Anna Kim-Lan McCauley's *Miles from Home* (1984), Nguyen Thi Thu-Lam's *Fallen Leaves* (1989), and Nguyen Thi Tuyet Mai's *The Rubber Tree* (1994).

Until the 1990s, Vietnamese American literature consisted almost entirely of memoirs, with few exceptions, such as Tran Van Dinh's *No Passenger on the River* (1965). Although many contemporary writers continue to write autobiographies or include autobiographical elements in their texts, Vietnamese American literature since the 1990s has challenged, complicated, and expanded this genre. Rather than offering up straightforward chronicles of the immigrant experience, these new writers more insistently interrogate their identities and their complicated allegiances and ancestries.

Family Themes

Like other Asian American texts, Vietnamese American literature since the 1990s has focused on the family as a venue and source of confrontation, revealing a generational conflict between mothers and fathers who want to maintain cultural ethnicity and the children who want freedom to be more "American." Notable writers of the 1990s include Trinh Thi Minh-Ha, Andrew Pham, Lan Cao, and Bao Nihn. Splicing prewar flashbacks of Vietnam with present-day survivor's guilt, Andrew Pham's *Catfish and Mandala* (1999) tells the story of his dramatic bicycle journey from San Francisco to his former home in Hanoi. Lan Cao's *Monkey Bridge* (1997) depicts the struggles of a young Vietnamese girl and her mother as they adjust to American culture. As Cao's text links mother and daughter in a web of shared history, culture, affect and grief, and physical blood, bone, and body, the narrative complicates and questions the limits, wholeness, and consistency of identities through collapsed timelines and confused temporal frameworks, oscillating back and forth between Vietnam and Virginia. Barbara Tran's edited volume *Watermark: Vietnamese American Poetry and Prose* (1998) collects contemporary works by the 1.5 generation and provides a representative overview of the literature from the late 1980s and early to mid-1990s.

As Vietnamese American literature enters the twenty-first century, one perceives a continued sense of transition in cultural and individual identity. Recent literature reflects a growing range of new thematic interests (sexuality, Western culture, urban and pop culture) and stylistically innovative exploration of abiding themes. While the literature remains preoccupied with lost chapters of personal and genealogical history, it renders, imagines, and reconstructs this history in newly inventive ways. In works such as Monique Truong's novel *The Book of Salt* (2003), which imagines the life of the Vietnamese cook of Alice B. Toklas and Gertrude Stein, stylistic experimentation abounds—especially techniques of nonchronological storytelling, rupture, and fragmentation, which are vividly realized as structural complements to themes of historical and personal loss and alienation. Other works that bring contemporary stylistics to bear on the past include Barbara Tran's poetry collection *In the Mynah Bird's Own Words* (2002), which imagines the lives of relatives in Vietnam; poet Truong Tran's 2002 collection, *Dust and Conscience,* which explores the work of memory; Kien Nguyen's *The Tapestries* (2004), an intricately plotted novel about a boy who tries to reclaim his family's royal legacy in Vietnam; Linh Dinh's short stories and poems that explore sexuality and American alienation

(*Fake House*, 2004; *Drunkard Boxing*, 1998; *Blood and Soap*, 2004); Dao Strom's *Grass Roof, Tin Roof* (2003), which traces a Vietnamese family's bumpy path to immigration and assimilation in California; Aimee Phan's *We Should Never Meet: Stories* (2005); and Thi Diem Thuy Le's *The Gangster We Are All Looking For* (2003), a stark, elliptical story of a Vietnamese family adjusting to life in California while wrestling with their own haunted past and troubled relationships. Another work that handles themes new to Vietnamese American literature is Kien Nguyen's 2003 memoir, *The Unwanted*, which deals centrally with an issue new to straightforward representation: the author's ostracism in postwar Vietnam due to his biracial heritage (his father was an American).

In focusing less directly on the aftermath of war, contemporary Vietnamese American writers turn more frequently to the ongoing, multigenerational struggle of cross-cultural transition and articulate how issues of ethnicity, sexuality, class, and gender are thought of differently by the 1.5 generation.

Lisa Hinrichsen

Further Reading

Christopher, Renny. *The Vietnam War/The American War: Images and Representations in Euro-American and Vietnamese Exile Narratives.* Amherst: University of Massachusetts Press, 1995.

Linh, Dinh, ed. *Night, Again: Contemporary Fiction from Vietnam.* New York: Seven Stories, 1996.

Minh Ha, Trinh. *Woman, Native, Other: Writing Postcoloniality and Feminism.* Bloomington: Indiana University Press, 1989.

Tran, Barbara, ed. *Watermark: Vietnamese American Poetry and Prose.* New York: Asian American Writers' Workshop, 1998.

Truong, Monique. "Vietnamese American Literature." In *An Interethnic Companion to Asian American Literature,* ed. King-Kok Cheung, 219–46. New York: Cambridge University Press, 1997.

Little Saigon (Orange County, California)

The popular name for a section of northern Orange County inhabited by the largest Vietnamese community outside Vietnam itself, Little Saigon is the vibrant center of Vietnamese business, politics, and media in America. (Vietnamese communities in other U.S. metropolitan areas, such as San Jose and Houston, also go by the name of Little Saigon.) Originally established by refugees from the Communist takeover of South Vietnam in 1975, the community is home today to about 75,000 Vietnamese Americans.

The origins of Little Saigon go back to the end of the Vietnam War, when many middle-class Vietnamese, particularly those who had worked for the South Vietnamese government or the U.S. armed forces, fled the victorious Communists. The American government accepted tens of thousands of the refugees and, after housing them for several years in temporary camps at U.S. military bases in Arkansas, California, and Florida, attempted to disperse them throughout the country to avoid the creation of what some officials feared would be an impoverished and isolated "ethnic ghetto."

In 1978, several businessmen who had been housed at Camp Pendleton Marine Base in nearby San Diego County set up stores and restaurants in Westminster, then a depressed, lower-middle-class suburb of Los Angeles. That same year saw the establishment of *Nguoi Viet Daily News,* the first Vietnamese American daily newspaper. Like earlier businesses, the paper was based on Bolsa Avenue, which soon became the commercial heart of Little Saigon. With the much larger wave of refugees pouring out of Vietnam in the 1970s and early 1980s, the so-called boat people exodus, came large numbers of regular Vietnamese, including many ethnic Chinese Vietnamese who had seen their successful businesses nationalized by the Communists.

The new wave of immigrants swelled Little Saigon's population, and the confines of the community soon spread to nearby Garden Grove and a few other cities. By the early 2000s, about 30 percent of Westminster's population of 90,000 and 20 percent of Garden Grove's 165,000-strong population were Vietnamese American.

Little Saigon has a thriving economy, with some 3,500 businesses owned by Vietnamese and other Asian Americans. Bolsa Avenue is lined with shopping centers, including the 250-store Asian Mall, and small office buildings housing stores, cafés, bakeries, restaurants, and banks, as well as insurance, real estate, and law offices, that largely cater to the Vietnamese American community. The restaurants, with their exotic and spicy cuisines, have become increasingly popular with non-Asian customers as well. Little Saigon is also home to much of the Vietnamese American media, with both the *Nguoi Viet* and *Vien Dong* Vietnamese-language newspapers located there, as well as the studios of Little Saigon TV, Little Saigon Radio, and Bolsa Radio. The community has also gained notoriety as the base of various Vietnamese American criminal gangs, some of which run drug rings and extortion rackets that prey on legitimate Vietnamese merchants.

The community is known as well for its conservative politics, a legacy of the fact that many of the residents were forced to flee a Communist government in their home country. Little Saigon and its media fought against the normalization of Vietnamese-American relations in the 1990s, and large protests are organized whenever high-ranking Vietnamese government officials visit the United States. In addition, members of the community who have sought rapprochement with the homeland's government have been attacked in the media and have had their businesses picketed; some have even met with violence. Those who study the community point out that, as in the case of Cubans in Miami, anti-Communist politics are not nearly as strident among the American-born generation as with their elders. At the same time, Vietnamese Americans are beginning to make their impact felt in local politics. In 1992, a community leader named Tony Lam won a seat on the Westminster City Council, becoming the first Vietnamese-born person to win elective office in the United States. By the early 2000s, several Vietnamese served on the city councils of both Westminster and Garden Grove. In 2007, a Vietnamese-born doctor named Janet Nguyen joined the Orange County Board of Supervisors, becoming the highest-elected Vietnamese American official in the United States.

James Ciment

Further Reading

Do, Hien Duc. *The Vietnamese Americans*. Westport, CT: Greenwood, 1999.

Eljera, Bert. "Big Plans for Little Saigon." *AsianWeek*, May 17–23, 1996.

Rutledge, Paul James. *The Vietnamese Experience in America*. Bloomington: Indiana University Press, 1992.

Politics and Political Empowerment, Vietnamese American

Vietnamese American politics is very much a product of the tortured recent history of Vietnam itself. Shaped by war and the ideological struggle between capitalism and Communism, the Vietnamese American community holds strong political opinions both about the home country's government and about the relationship expatriate Vietnamese should have with their homeland and its government. In this, Vietnamese Americans bear a greater similarity to Cuban Americans, also exiles from a Communist land, than to other Asian groups. At the same time, Vietnamese Americans have shared the reluctance of some Asian Americans to become involved in American electoral politics, a reticence that is gradually giving way to more involvement as the community matures. Vietnamese Americans, particularly in the fishing and shrimping industries of the Gulf Coast, have also had to organize to fight attacks on their community from xenophobic whites.

Anti-Communism

In the mid-1950s, after years of fighting against French imperialists, Vietnam won its independence but was divided into a pro-Western southern half and a Communist northern half. From the early 1960s until 1975, the two sides—as well as Communist insurgents in the south—fought a bitter war over the future of the country. While North Vietnam was aided by Communist China and Russia, mostly in the form of weapons, South Vietnam was backed by the United States, with both soldiers—more than 500,000 by 1968—and weaponry. As the war ground on, it became more unpopular in the United States, leading to a gradual withdrawal of American troops in the early 1970s and the expansion of the South Vietnamese Army. Thousands of South Vietnamese worked for the Americans or in high positions in the military and in government. When South Vietnam fell to the Communists in 1975, more than 125,000 of these people, fearing political retribution, fled the country, largely to the United States. In the late 1970s and early 1980s, they were joined by several hundred thousand more refugees, fleeing Communist oppression. Many members of the entrepreneurial class, especially among ethnic Chinese, also fled after their businesses were nationalized by the Communists.

The exodus produced great bitterness among the Vietnamese American community, at Communism generally and the Communist government of a now unified Vietnam in particular. Like South Florida's expatriate Cuban Americans, with their anti-Communist politics, members of the Vietnamese community in Southern California, the largest in America, have focused on relations between the United States and Vietnam. But while anti-Communist Cuban Americans have effectively blocked any significant warming between Havana and Washington, Vietnamese Americans have watched in frustration as the United States and Vietnam have grown steadily closer. In the 1980s, the two countries cooperated on the issue of finding the remains of American soldiers missing in action, and then followed with the termination of the U.S. trade embargo in 1994, normalization of relations in 1995, a visit by President Bill Clinton to Vietnam in 2000, and a visit by Vietnam's prime minister to America in 2005. At every step of the way, Vietnamese Americans organized protests and lobbying campaigns to block closer U.S. ties with the Hanoi regime.

Anti-Communist sentiment erupted in the Vietnamese community of Westminster, California, after a video store owner hung a portrait of Vietnamese Communist leader Ho Chi Minh in his shop window in 1999. He refused to take it down and was attacked by a mob. *(David McNew/Getty Images)*

In their intense antipathy to Communism and the Vietnamese government, some Vietnamese Americans, particularly in the Little Saigon neighborhood of Orange County, have shown intolerance and an unwillingness to brook dissent within the community. Vietnamese Americans who express a willingness to find common ground with the government in Hanoi are routinely attacked in the community's lively press and media, which rarely print or broadcast dissenting opinions. Vietnamese American businesses that have established trade relations with Vietnam have been boycotted and protested. In perhaps the best-known outbreak of community wrath, Truong Van Tran, a video-shop owner in Little Saigon, faced huge protests in 1999 after hanging a picture of Vietnamese Communist leader Ho Chi Minh and the Vietnamese national flag in his store window. (Vietnamese Americans insist on flying the flag of the former South Vietnam, which can be seen on lampposts and businesses throughout Little Saigon.) When the mall owner asked him to take it down, he refused. The issue went to federal court, which ruled that Tran had the right to hang the picture and flag as part of his First Amendment rights. Upon returning to his store after the ruling, however, Tran was physically attacked by a mob of several hundred protesters. That same year, an exhibit called "A Winding River" at the Bowers Museum of Cultural Art in nearby Santa Ana was met with pickets and protests because some Vietnamese Americans claimed it was displaying art with a Communist message. Of course, not all anti-Vietnam actions are based on intolerance. In 1999 as well, a physician named Nguyen Dan Que organized a meeting of former political prisoners of the Vietnamese government in Washington,

D.C., followed the next year by the establishment of a Movement for Human Rights in Vietnam by American-born or American-raised Vietnamese Americans.

Electoral Politics

The Republican Party, perceived as being tougher on the Communist government of Vietnam, has won the allegiance of most Vietnamese who participate in American electoral politics. In this respect, Vietnamese generally differ from other Asian American groups, who tend to lean Democratic. In Orange County, more than half of Vietnamese affiliated with a party are registered as Republicans, while less than one-quarter register as Democrats. Among Vietnamese nationwide in 2004, polls found that about three out of four voted for Republican George W. Bush over his Democratic challenger, Senator John Kerry, in the presidential election. Although allegiance to the GOP has been eroding in the second generation of immigrants, a poll in the run-up to the 2008 presidential race indicated that about two-thirds of Vietnamese Americans favored Republican candidate John McCain over Democrat Barack Obama.

While differing in voter registration, Vietnamese Americans long resembled other Asian Americans in their general indifference to American politics—aside from the issue of Washington's relations with Hanoi. The lack of interest has been changing in recent years, however, as the Vietnamese community becomes more Americanized and as more American-born or American-raised Vietnamese come of political age. The Vietnamese American Voters' Association, a loose confederation of local civic groups, is active in many communities, helping Vietnamese Americans gain U.S. citizenship and teaching them about participation in the American electoral system. Like many immigrant groups, Vietnamese Americans have entered politics first at the local level. A civic leader named Tony Lam was elected to the city council of Westminster, in the heart of Orange County's Little Saigon, in 1992, becoming the first Vietnamese American to win elective office. Since then, several others have joined him there and on the council of nearby Garden Grove. In 2007, Orange County voters elected Janet Nguyen to the board of supervisors, making her the highest elected Vietnamese American official in the country. Less successful was Republican congressional candidate Tan Nguyen, who lost his bid for a seat from Orange County in 2006 after it was revealed that he had sent threatening letters to registered Latino voters, warning that they might be deported if they were in the country illegally and tried to vote.

A major breakthrough came in December 2008 with the election of Anh "Joseph" Cao, a former Vietnamese refugee, as a U.S. congressman from Louisiana. As a boy,

Cao was separated from his father, a South Vietnamese army officer who was sent to prison camp, and loaded by his mother onto a U.S. military transport plane during the fall of Saigon in 1975. Raised by an uncle in Houston, Cao went on to earn degrees in physics, philosophy, and finally law; during this time he also trained to become a Jesuit priest, but left the order in 1996. A longtime independent, he converted to the Republican Party for his run for Congress—which made him the first Vietnamese American to be elected to national office in the United States.

Despite such progress in the electoral arena, Vietnamese immigrants in some local communities—such as the Gulf Coast of Texas—have been forced to fight for their civil rights and stand up to racist attacks. Upon arriving in the United States, many Vietnamese took up their old profession of fishing and shrimping on the Gulf Coast, an environment much like that of coastal Vietnam. Poor but ambitious, they were often willing to sell their catches at prices that undercut those of native-born Americans. The latter complained of unfair competition, drawing in the Ku Klux Klan, which issued threats against the Vietnamese and burned several of their boats in the early 1980s. In response, the community organized the Vietnamese Fishermen Association of America (VFAA) to fight for their rights. The VFAA lobbied state and federal officials to crack down on the Klan and met with great success. It also worked with the Southern Poverty Law Center, an antiracism group, to get the courts to issue an injunction forcing the Texas Emergency Reserve, a violent anti-Vietnamese fisherman group with connections to the Klan, to disband. The court also ordered a halt to all paramilitary activity by the Klan.

Vietnamese American politics, according to political scientists, are likely to change significantly in coming years. American-born and American-raised Vietnamese have little or no memory of Communist oppression and are unlikely to hold the same strong anti-Communist politics as their parents. As Vietnam continues to transform itself into a market economy and, if it continues to experience the rapid economic growth of recent years, many younger Vietnamese Americans may put politics aside in the interest of making money investing in or trading with Vietnam. At the same time, younger Vietnamese, who are more familiar with American culture and politics than their parents, are more likely to become involved in the political process. Given their numbers—just over 1.6 million by 2008—and the fact that they tend to be concentrated in a few large communities around the country, the election of one of their own to national office in 2008 seems likely to signal a new chapter in Vietnamese American political participation.

James Ciment

Further Reading

Do, Hien Duc. *The Vietnamese Americans.* Westport, CT: Greenwood, 1999.

Freeman, James M. *Changing Identities: Vietnamese Americans, 1975–1995.* Boston: Allyn and Bacon, 1995.

Lam, Andrew. *Perfume Dreams: Reflections on the Vietnamese Diaspora.* Berkeley, CA: Heyday, 2005.

Rutledge, Paul James. *The Vietnamese Experience in America.* Bloomington: Indiana University Press, 1992.

Refugee Act (1980)

In response to increasing numbers of Southeast Asians and other refugees being resettled in the country, the United States in 1980 passed a comprehensive refugee law designed to bring the domestic definition of a refugee into line with the definition adopted by the United Nations more than a decade earlier. The Refugee Act of 1980 defined a refugee as a person who is unable or unwilling to return to his or her country "because of persecution or a well-founded fear of persecution on account of race, religion, nationality, membership in a particular social group, or political opinion." While written to deal with political refugees from around the world, the legislation was inspired by the mass exodus of Vietnamese, and other Southeast Asians, following the collapse of South Vietnam and Cambodia to Communist forces in the spring of 1975.

The legislation provided the first regular and systematic procedure for the admission of refugees to the United States. While the Immigration and Nationality Act of 1965 had included limited provisions for the admission of refugees fleeing Communism or the Middle East, its annual quota of 17,400 was inadequate to address the growing number of refugees fleeing Southeast Asia and other parts of the' world in the 1970s. Prior to 1980, most refugees were admitted on an ad hoc basis under the "parole" authority, an element of immigration law that allowed the U.S. attorney general to temporarily admit individuals into the country for humanitarian reasons or for reasons "strictly in the public interest." However, the parole power was originally designed to admit individuals on an emergency, case-by-case basis, not to admit large numbers of refugees.

By 1980, the United States had admitted more than 2 million refugees under various special legislation and procedures. Of these, about 400,000 were from Southeast Asia and more than 700,000 were from Cuba. Many others were admitted from countries in Eastern Europe. In 1980 alone, the United States admitted 166,700 refugees from Southeast Asia. It became clear that the refugee provisions of the 1965 Immigration Act were inadequate, resulting in the passage of the new legislation.

The Refugee Act of 1980 raised the number of annual refugee admissions to 50,000, with provisions allowing the president, upon consultation with Congress, to increase the number when needed. The act also established a system of Voluntary Agencies (VOLAGs) to provide social services such as English-language instruction, job training, health services, and other basic support for refugees resettled in the United States. Refugees were also made eligible for a limited amount of cash assistance and medical benefits. Though many of the benefits made available to refugees were curtailed in the years following their initial implementation, the legislation provided an invaluable economic safety net for early groups of Vietnamese and other refugees.

The number of Vietnamese refugees admitted under the Refugee Act of 1980 gradually decreased during the course of the decade, partly as a result of humanitarian pressure on the Vietnamese government to address causes of emigration. In the mid-1980s, an average of 22,000 Vietnamese refugees were being admitted each year; by 1988, the number had dropped to 17,626. Today, the majority of Vietnamese and other Southeast Asians who enter the United States are admitted under regular immigration provisions, such as family reunification, rather than as refugees.

Timothy J. Randazzo

Further Reading

Daniels, Roger, and Otis L. Graham. *Debating American Immigration, 1882–Present.* New York: Rowman and Littlefield, 2001.

Hing, Bill Ong. *Making and Remaking Asian America Through Immigration Policy, 1850–1990.* Palo Alto, CA: Stanford University Press, 1993.

Musalo, Karen, Jennifer Moore, and Richard A. Boswell. *Refugee Law and Policy: A Comparative International Approach.* 2nd ed. Durham, NC: Carolina Academic, 2002.

Religion, Vietnamese American

The religious and spiritual life of the Vietnamese and Vietnamese American people has been shaped by several of the world's major faiths: Confucianism (Khong giao or Nho), Daoism (Lao giao or Laõo), Buddhism (Phat giao or Thích), Protestantism, and Catholicism. Over the centuries, Confucianism, Daoism, Buddhism, and popular Chinese folk traditions have merged with ancient Vietnamese animism to form what is collectively known as Tam Giao (Three Religions—Nho-Thích-Laõo). Sometimes referred to as "Vietnamese Buddhism," Tam Giao is more appropriately termed "Vietnamese popular religion." Prior to the arrival of Chinese rule in the second century B.C.E., ancestral veneration profoundly influenced the religious life of the Vietnamese people.

Confucianism was introduced in Vietnam as early as the first century C.E., during Chinese rule. Confucian ethics and values have deeply penetrated the Vietnamese family structure and its emphasis on ancestral veneration and remembrance, which reinforces the Confucian virtue of filial piety. Hence, it is no surprise that the family altar is considered the cosmic center and most honored place in a Vietnamese household. Daoism was also introduced into Vietnam during Chinese rule, but remained largely marginal within the Tam Giao tradition. Nevertheless, its influence is clear in forms of divination, fortune-telling, and ritual performance. The predominant religion of Vietnam is Buddhism. Vietnamese Buddhism—a combination of Chan (Zen), Pure Land, Tiantai, and popular Vajrayana—is the main tradition for the majority of Vietnamese people.

Christianity has also exerted an enduring influence on Vietnamese spirituality, with its emphasis on divine grace and the afterlife. Vietnam today has the highest percentage of Catholics in Asia outside the Philippines, an estimated 8–10 percent of the population. Portuguese, Spanish, and French missionaries introduced Christianity into Vietnam during the second half of the sixteenth century, but practice of the faith was later banned. Despite the proscription, Catholic missionaries evangelized in Vietnam from the sixteenth century on. Catholicism continued to spread during the French colonial era, which helps explain why some 30-40 percent of Vietnamese refugees in America today are Roman Catholic.

In addition, several relatively new Vietnamese religions have been transplanted to the Vietnamese American community, most notably, Cao Daism and Hoa Hao Buddhism. The emergence of the Cao Dai movement in 1962 was also associated with French colonialism, blending Western spiritism and séances with Chinese-style divination. Cao Dai represents a cornucopia of belief systems, incorporating elements of Buddhism, Confucianism, Daoism, Protestantism, Catholicism, Hinduism, and Islam with the thinking of various secular personalities—the French poet and writer Victor Hugo; the exiled founder of the People's Republic of China, Sun Yat-sen; British Prime Minister Winston Churchill; and a Vietnamese diviner named Trang Trinh.

Hoa Hao, a reform Vietnamese Buddhist sect of the

Theravada tradition, was founded in 1930 in An Giang Province. This is the religion and system of ritual practice that many Vietnamese refugees have brought with them to America, helping them adjust to relocation and establish solidarity and a network of support to begin their new life.

In the United States as in the home country, many Vietnamese practice ancestral veneration by building a family altar in the home as a sacred place for the ritual veneration and commemoration of ancestors. This belief and ritual is based on a particular understanding of the "soul" in at least two iterations. The *am*-soul is dense and clings to the body after death; as such, it is believed to remain at the gravesite after burial. The *duong*-soul is understood as less dense, less malevolent, and attended by better auspice; it may be encountered around the home and family altar. Daily ritual offerings are performed at the home altar for the *duong*-soul. Special foods are prepared during the fifteenth and sixteenth of each lunar month and during Tet Nguyen Dan (Vietnamese Lunar New Year) for the *duong*-souls on the ancestral altar.

As in other Southeast Asian Buddhist communities (such as the Khmer American and Thai American), the faith plays a central role in the moral and social education of Vietnamese American youth. Hence, Vietnamese temples in both Vietnam and the United States are not only venues of meditation and spiritual communion, but also places where traditional and cultural values are preserved and transmitted. When the first wave of Vietnamese refugees arrived in the United States in 1975, they soon established a distinctive Buddhist community. Twenty years later, there were more than 160 Vietnamese Buddhist temples and centers in North America.

By contrast with Buddhist temples in Vietnam, few in the United States have permanent resident monks or nuns. The economic necessity for monks to work outside the temple is one of a number of factors that have altered the relationship between the laity and the monk. This, in turn, has modified the function of the Vietnamese Buddhist temple in the United States. Smaller temples, many of which operate from private rural residences known as "home temples," are used primarily in the performance of rituals, especially funerals (an important rite of passage in ancestral veneration). Larger temples, typically located in larger communities, also function as cultural centers and language schools. Congregations transplanted from Vietnam would invite a monk to come and build a temple; otherwise, they would build the temple and then recruit a monk.

Since the primary use of Vietnamese Buddhist temples is in the performance of rituals, many members of the community visit them only when an occasion arises, such as a funeral. Memorial services are still often held for family members and relatives who died during the Vietnam War. This is possible because the spirit of the deceased is believed to remain part of the family, having accompanied it on the migration to the United States. Some older Vietnamese Americans find the prospect of death stressful because they fear that their spirits and memories will not be accorded proper traditional veneration by their Americanized children.

Orange County, California, is home to the largest Vietnamese community in the United States and has come to be known as "Little Saigon." There and elsewhere across America where Vietnamese Americans reside, small "home temples" can be found. Given the adaptability of the community and its religious beliefs—which have withstood centuries of colonial rule and outside influence—spiritual belief and practice will provide a unique, evolving, and enduring source of strength for new Vietnamese immigrants and their descendants building a life in America.

Jonathan H.X. Lee

Further Reading

Crawford, Ann. *Customs and Culture of Vietnam*. Rutland, VT: Charles E. Tuttle, 1966.

Do, Hien Duc. *The Vietnamese Americans*. Westport, CT: Greenwood, 1999.

Eck, Diana L. *A New Religious America: How a "Christian Country" Has Now Become the World's Most Religiously Diverse Nation*. New York: HarperSanFrancisco, 2001.

Henkin, Alan B., and Liem Thanh Nguyen. *Between Two Cultures: The Vietnamese in America*. Saratoga, CA: Century Twenty One, 1981.

Women, Vietnamese American

The immigration experience of Vietnamese American women differs from that of many other groups, Asian or otherwise. The vast majority of Vietnamese were refugees, either fleeing the Communist takeover of the southern part of their country in the mid-1970s or escaping the repression that followed the takeover in the latter half of that decade and the early part of the next. Because most refugees fled as families, the Vietnamese American community did not undergo the usual period of gender imbalance, with far more males coming first, followed by their wives later. Indeed, of the nearly 1 million Vietnamese refugees who came into the United States in the last quarter of the twentieth century, roughly half were female.

This immigration pattern is reflected in the numbers. According to the 1990 U.S. Census, the first to take in the full scope of the refugee population, the Vietnamese had the largest households of any Asian group, other than their fellow war refugees from other Southeast Asian countries. At 4.4 persons, the average Vietnamese household was about 15 percent larger than the American norm. By 2000, the figure had fallen to 3.7 persons per household, closer to the American average but still higher than that of any other major Asian group from outside Southeast Asia. And, according to the 2000 census, at 64 percent, the rate of Vietnamese households headed by two parents was higher than for any other major Asian group except Indians, and about 25 percent higher than for the American norm.

As in other immigrant groups, older Vietnamese women have had a more difficult time adjusting to American life than younger women. Cultural and linguistic barriers are harder to overcome. Moreover, many Vietnamese males, particularly in the first group of refugees, had worked for the U.S. armed forces or government during the Vietnam War. Thus, they had a stronger command of English and were more attuned to American cultural nuances than their female co-refugees. However, many Vietnamese males have had a more difficult time adjusting economically. Although some had advanced degrees and skills, many found that these were not accepted or recognized by American employers. Low-skilled and unskilled women were able to get work that did not require good English skills, such as custodial work, more easily. Vietnamese families had the highest rate of any major Asian group (21.3), other than Filipinos, with more than one household member in the workforce. According to the 2000 census, nearly 60 percent of Vietnamese women over the age of sixteen were in the labor force. But reflecting the skill differential, Vietnamese males in 2000 earned roughly one-third more than their female counterparts in the labor force.

Vietnamese women have also experienced problems at home. With many husbands out of work or forced to rely on their wives to support the family, tensions have arisen, often leading to domestic violence. In fact, numerous studies have found that domestic abuse among Vietnamese refugees exceeds that for most other non-refugee Asian groups and for the American population as a whole. Compounding problems for women has been the breakdown of the traditional Vietnamese household, which was patriarchal but often multigenerational. And, if other adult family members were not present in the household, they usually lived nearby, particularly for those Vietnamese living in villages. The disruption of the refugee process broke down such family and household structures, so that most Vietnamese had to adjust to the

reality that they would be forced to form more nuclear families in their new homes in the United States. This created problems for women. The husband still expected to exert control over the family but the wife was deprived of other counterbalancing authority figures to turn to. Moreover, most Vietnamese women were not willing or able, due to cultural reticence or an inability to speak English, to seek outside help from authorities.

As is often the case with immigrant populations, some of these problems are easing as new, American-born or American-raised generations come of age and start their own families. Gone are some of the patriarchal assumptions of the old country, as well as the cultural reticence and linguistic barriers preventing women from seeking outside help in cases of domestic abuse.

Younger Vietnamese American women are also far better educated than their mothers as a rule. Indeed, some studies have shown that they excel against their male counterparts, making Vietnamese women part of an American sociocultural phenomenon of recent decades that transcends ethnicity. But factors specific to the Vietnamese community may also play a role. As with other Asians, Vietnamese place a high value on education and hold to the Confucian ideal that every member of the family plays a specific role, with women expected to be helpmates to their husbands. In America, that means the woman should be well educated to find a well-educated, high-income husband.

As in the case of other immigrant groups, increasing acculturation brings a greater break from the cultural norms of the old country. Younger Vietnamese women are moving into skilled positions in greater numbers, with a few achieving success unattainable in their mother's generation. Several Vietnamese women novelists, including Monique Truong (author of *The Book of Salt*, 2003), Duong Van Mai Elliott (*The Sacred Willow*, 1999), and Mong-Lan (*Song of the Cicadas*, 2001), have achieved recognition in the world of letters for works dealing with the generational and gender issues within Vietnamese refugee families.

James Ciment and Tim J. Watts

Further Reading

Do, Hien Duc. *The Vietnamese Americans.* Westport, CT: Greenwood, 1999.
Freeman, James M. *Hearts of Sorrow: Vietnamese-American Lives.* Palo Alto, CA: Stanford University Press, 1989.
Kibria, Nazli. *Family Tightrope: The Changing Lives of Vietnamese Americans.* Princeton, NJ: Princeton University Press, 1993.
Zinn, Maxine Baca, and Bonnie Thornton Dill. *Women of Color in U.S. Society.* Philadelphia: Temple University Press, 1994.

Chronology

1784   The *Empress of China* becomes the first U.S. merchant ship to arrive in China, inaugurating trade between the two countries.

1790   The U.S. Congress passes the Naturalization Act, restricting naturalized citizenship to white persons only; the law bars naturalized citizenship for Asian immigrants until the mid-twentieth century.

1818   The first Chinese students to attend a U.S. institution of higher education enroll at the Foreign Mission School in Cornwall, Connecticut.

1829   The Siamese twins Chang and Eng are the first Thais to arrive in the United States; they are granted citizenship in 1839.

1848   Gold is discovered in California, leading to the immigration of tens of thousands of Chinese in the late 1840s and 1850s.

1852   The first Chinese contract laborers enter the United States.

Chinese immigrants found America's first Buddhist temple in San Francisco.

The first Chinese secret society, or tong, is founded in San Francisco.

1854   Yung Wing graduates from Yale College, becoming the first person of Chinese ancestry to graduate from a U.S. institution of higher learning.

The Convention of Kanagawa is signed between the Japanese government and Commodore Matthew Perry, establishing formal relations between the two countries; Perry is representing the United States on his second expedition to open up Japan to the outside world.

1856   The *Chinese Daily News* is launched in Sacramento, California, becoming the first Chinese-language daily newspaper in the world.

1858   Joseph Heco, a stranded Japanese fisherman and translator for Commodore Matthew Perry on his pioneering visit to Japan in 1854, becomes the first person of Japanese ancestry to gain U.S. citizenship.

1859   San Francisco opens the Chinese School, America's first public school for Asian immigrants.

1862   Chinese American businessmen in San Francisco found the Chinese Six Companies, later the Chinese Consolidated Benevolent Association, an umbrella organization for various mutual aid societies.

1863   The first Chinese Americans are hired by the Central Pacific to lay track on the transcontinental railroad; by the time the project is finished in 1869, more than 9,000 will be hired.

1868   The governments of the United States and Imperial China sign the Burlingame Treaty, guaranteeing fair treatment and residency rights for each other's immigrants; the treaty will be abrogated as a result of the Chinese Exclusion Act of 1882.

    The first Japanese plantation workers arrive in Hawaii, lured to what was then an independent kingdom by an American businessman there.

1869   The first significant contingent of Japanese immigrants to the U.S. mainland arrive in California and form the first Japanese American settlement, in the gold country of the Sierra Nevada foothills.

1871   Rioting in Los Angeles leads to the deaths of twenty-one Chinese at the hands of white mobs.

1873   San Francisco passes the Laundry Ordinance, shutting down Chinese-owned laundries in the city; the U.S. Supreme Court overturns the law as unconstitutional in *Yick Ho v. Hopkins*, the first time it rules in favor of the rights of Asian American immigrants.

1875   Congress passes the Page Act, requiring potential Chinese immigrants to win approval of U.S. consul representatives before immigrating to the United States; the act represents the first legislation aimed at restricting Chinese immigration.

    White Californians found the Native Sons of the Golden West as a fraternal society aimed at preserving the state's gold rush heritage; by the early twentieth century, the Native Sons had become one of the most influential anti-Asian immigrant organizations in the country.

1876   The San Francisco municipal government enacts the Queue Ordinance, banning Chinese men from wearing their characteristic queues, or long pigtails.

1880   California becomes the first state to include Asian Americans under its anti-miscegenation statutes.

    Whites riot in Denver, Colorado, killing one Chinese and leaving much of the city's Chinatown neighborhood in ruins.

1882   Congress passes the first Chinese Exclusion Act, banning the immigration of Chinese laborers for ten years; the law is extended in 1892 and 1902.

    The United States and Korea sign the Treaty of Amity and Commerce, establishing diplomatic relations between the two countries.

1883   Yu Giljun becomes the first Korean to study in the United States when he enrolls at the Dammer Academy in Massachusetts.

1885   Twenty-eight Chinese laborers are killed by white miners in the town of Rock Springs, Wyoming.

1885	Local government officials order the expulsion of Chinese from the Puget Sound region of Washington Territory, resulting in gun battles over the next two years between Chinese, whites, and police.
1888	Congress amends the Chinese Exclusion Act of 1882 to include all persons from China, with a limited number of exemptions for students and teachers; it also passes legislation preventing Chinese who return to their home country on visits to return to the United States.
1893	American planters and businessmen seize control of Hawaii from Queen Liliuokalani, the last native ruler of an independent Hawaii.
1895	In response to anti-Chinese discrimination and to promote opportunity within the Chinese American community, the predecessor organization of the Chinese American Citizens Alliance is founded in San Francisco.
1898	The California Supreme Court rules in the case of *Tape v. Hurley* that Chinese children are permitted to attend public schools in their neighborhoods if there are no schools set up specifically for them.
	With Hawaii's annexation by the United States in 1898, thousands of Japanese and other Asian workers there migrate to the continental United States.
	The United States gains possession of the Philippines and Guam as a result of the Spanish-American War.
	Congress passes the Pensionado Act to train Filipino students at U.S. colleges and universities.
1899	Part of the Samoan island chain is annexed by the United States, eventually becoming the territory of American Samoa.
1900	Mainland labor recruiters begin bringing Japanese agricultural workers from Hawaii to California and the West Coast.
1901	The U.S. Navy begins to recruit Filipino sailors, of whom some 6,000 will serve in World War I.
1902	Congress passes the Geary Act, making the Chinese Exclusion Act "permanent."
1903	Federal legislation establishes an "Asiatic barred zone," prohibiting immigration from British India (including Burma), French Indochina, and parts of the Middle East, Central Asia, Oceania, and Russia's Far East.
	The Japanese Mexican Labor Association is founded in Oxnard, California, becoming the first farmworkers union in California.
	The first organized group of Korean laborers arrives in Hawaii. Some of them found Sin-Min-Hoi, dedicated to fighting Japanese imperialism in their home country; it is the first organization of Koreans in the United States.
	Filipino students with U.S. government scholarships, known as *pensionados*, begin to study at American universities.
1905	White labor leaders in San Francisco found the Asiatic Exclusion League, aimed at preventing immigration from Japan, Korea, and later India.

1906 A massive earthquake and fire level Chinatown in San Francisco, the largest Chinese enclave in the United States.

The San Francisco school board attempts to segregate Asians from white students through the creation of the Oriental School.

The first Filipino laborers arrive in Hawaii to work on sugar plantations.

1907 The first large contingent of Indian immigrants enters the United States; coming via British Columbia, they settle in California's Sacramento River Valley.

The Hawaiian Sugar Planters Association begins to recruit unskilled workers from the Philippines.

1907–1908 President Theodore Roosevelt negotiates and signs the Gentlemen's Agreement with the government of Japan, an informal understanding that the latter will severely restrict its citizens from immigrating to the United States.

1910 The Angel Island Immigration Station is opened in San Francisco Bay, largely to process immigrants from Asia; the station will remain in operation until it is partially destroyed by fire in 1940.

1912 Sikh immigrants found their first temple the United States, located in Stockton, California.

The first U.S. branch of the Khalsa Diwan (Free Divine) Society, the first social and political organization of Asian Indians in North America—founded in Vancouver, British Columbia, in 1906—is established in Stockton, California.

1913 The California legislature passes the Alien Land Law, restricting and/or prohibiting the lease or sale of land to "aliens ineligible for citizenship"; the measure primarily affects Asian Americans.

The Ghadr Party, or Hindi Association of the Pacific Coast, is launched by Indian immigrants in Astoria, Oregon; the party pushes for Indian independence from Britain.

1915 Chinese farmers and merchants found the predominantly Chinese American community of Locke, California, the largest nonurban Asian American town in the continental United States.

1916 The first Tongans of modern times arrive in Hawaii.

1919 The Filipino Federation of Labor, America's first Filipino labor union, is founded by sugar workers in Hawaii.

1920 California voters pass a referendum further restricting the leasing of land to Asian aliens in the United States, closing loopholes in the 1913 Alien Land Law that permitted Asian immigrants to own land under the names of their native-born children; eleven other states pass similar laws between 1917 and World War II.

Bengali guru Paramahansa Yogananda arrives in the United States and lectures on yoga, helping introduce that discipline and Indian spirituality to Americans.

1920   White Californians organize the Japanese Exclusion League to advocate a ban on Japanese immigration into the United States.

1922   Congress passes the Cable Act, nullifying the citizenship of all U.S.-born women who marry someone ineligible for citizenship; the law primarily affects Asian Americans.

The U.S. Supreme Court rules in *Takao Ozawa v. United States* that Japanese immigrants are not eligible for citizenship.

1923   In *United States v. Bhagat Singh Sind*, the U.S. Supreme Court rules that immigrants from India are not "free white persons," and therefore not eligible for citizenship under the Naturalization Act of 1790.

1924   The omnibus National Origins Act, which includes the Asian Exclusion Act, establishes strict national quotas for immigration, limiting newcomers from Asian countries and colonial possessions, among others, to token numbers.

A gun battle between striking Filipino sugar plantation workers and police in Hanapepe, Hawaii, results in the deaths of sixteen Filipino workers and four police officers.

1925   The Chinese Hospital, the first in the United States devoted to the health needs of Chinese immigrants, is founded in San Francisco.

The Filipino Federation of America, a leading mutual aid society, is founded in Los Angeles, California.

1927   In the case of *Farrington v. Tokushige*, the U.S. Supreme Court rules that efforts to close private Japanese-language schools are unconstitutional.

1929   The Japanese American Citizens League, the leading advocacy organization for Japanese Americans, is founded in California.

White mobs, angered by interracial mingling between Filipino men and white women at local dance halls, attack Filipinos in Watsonville, California, leading to dozens of injuries and the death of one Filipino.

1934   The Tydings-McDuffie Act provides limited self-government for the U.S. colony of the Philippines, setting it on the road to independence; the measure also sets strict limits on the number of Filipinos entering the United States.

1935   The Filipino Repatriation Act is passed by Congress and signed into law; the measure helps Filipinos residing in the United States return to their native islands.

1937   In response to Japan's invasion of China, Chinese Americans establish the China War Relief Association of America in San Francisco to coordinate aid to their homeland.

The Bank of Canton, the first Chinese American–owned bank, opens in San Francisco.

1941   On December 7, military forces of imperial Japan attack the U.S. naval base at Pearl Harbor, Hawaii, triggering a declaration of war against Tokyo and U.S. entry into World War II.

1942   In response to the Japanese attack on Pearl Harbor, President Franklin Roosevelt issues Executive Order 9066, calling for the incarceration of more than 120,000 West Coast Japanese Americans in "internment camps" for the duration of World War II.

An armed confrontation between internees and guards at the Manzanar, California, over informants results in the deaths of two Japanese American inmates; it is the worst incident of violence in any wartime internment camp for Japanese Americans.

1943   Congress repeals the Chinese Exclusion Act of 1882, though still limiting Chinese immigration to about 100 persons per year.

The U.S. government organizes the 442nd Regimental Combat Team and 100th Infantry Battalion of Japanese American soldiers; the two units see action in Italy.

Japanese American Ikuko "Iva" Toguri, better known as "Tokyo Rose," begins her English-language propaganda broadcasts from Tokyo aimed at U.S. servicemen. In 1949, she receives a ten-year federal prison sentence for treason; released in 1955, she is granted a pardon in 1977.

1943–1944   In three *coram nobis* ("error before us") cases—*Gordon Hirabayashi v. United States* (1943), *Yasui v. United States* (1943), and *Fred Korematsu v. United States* (1944)—the U.S. Supreme Court upholds wartime laws and rules requiring Japanese Americans to obey curfews or turn themselves over to authorities for incarceration, per Executive Order 9066 in 1942.

1944   In a rare wartime ruling, the U.S. Supreme Court declares in *Ex parte Endo* that the federal government could not incarcerate a Japanese American woman whose loyalty it had already conceded.

The Heart Mountain Fair Play Committee is established at the Japanese American relocation center of the same name in Wyoming to resist U.S. efforts to draft Japanese Americans for service in the military. Arrested for conspiring to violate the Selective Service Act, several leaders of the committee are granted pardons in 1946.

1944–1945   U.S. forces seize much of Micronesia from the Japanese, establishing a protectorate that will continue into the 1990s and, in the case of the Northern Marianas, to the present day.

1946   The United States grants independence to its colony of the Philippines.

With passage of the Filipino Naturalization Act, or Luce-Celler Act, the U.S. Congress grants naturalization rights to immigrants from India and the newly independent Philippines.

1947   Congress passes the War Brides Act, permitting U.S. military personnel to marry and bring into the United States brides from Japan, China, the Philippines, and Korea, exempting them from the national quotas of the Immigration Act of 1924. Several thousand women enter the country under the law.

1947   California removes segregation clauses from the its education code, allowing for the integration of Asian and non-Asian students in public schools.

1948   In the case of *Oyama v. California*, the Supreme Court declares California's Alien Land Law of 1913 unconstitutional under the Fourteenth Amendment's "equal protection" clause.

Congress passes the Displaced Persons Act, accelerating the immigration of World War II refugees; following the Communist takeover of China the following year, the act is used to allow in thousands of refugees fleeing the new Communist regime in Mainland China.

The Evacuation Claims Act, aimed at providing compensation to Japanese Americans for financial losses suffered during their incarceration in World War II, is passed by Congress and signed into law by President Harry Truman.

Korean American Sammy Lee becomes the first Asian American to win an Olympic gold medal, in platform diving at the London Games.

1949   After more than twenty years of warfare, Communist forces emerge victorious in Mainland China; the United States refuses to recognize the new Communist government, backing Nationalist forces on Taiwan instead.

1950   The United States leads an international military force to turn back a North Korean invasion of South Korea; the war continues through 1953.

Communist China invades Tibet, sending tens of thousands of refugees to India, Nepal, and other countries; several thousand eventually settle in the United States.

1951   Chinese-born immigrant Wang An founds Wang Laboratories, which will become one of the country's leading early computer hardware and software companies.

1952   The Immigration and Nationality Act, better known as the McCarran-Walter Act, reverses earlier laws that banned Asian immigrants from gaining U.S. citizenship.

1953   Though aimed at European refugees of World War II and Communism, the Refugee Relief Act allows some 2,000 Chinese and 3,000 other Asian refugees to enter the United States.

1954   In the landmark *Brown v. Board of Education* decision, the U.S. Supreme Court declares racially segregated public schools unconstitutional; while aimed primarily at African American students, the ruling affects Asian students as well.

1956   The Immigration and Naturalization Services launches its Confession Program, allowing Chinese immigrants who came into the country under false pretenses to regularize their status and put them on the road to citizenship.

Democrat Dalip Singh Saund of California becomes the first Asian American elected to U.S. Congress.

1957   Tsung-dao Lee and Chen Ning Yang become the first Asian Americans to win a Nobel Prize, in physics.

1959   Hawaii is admitted to the Union as the fiftieth state. With its large Asian American population, it becomes the first state with a nonwhite majority; its representative, Daniel Inouye, becomes the first Japanese American to serve in the U.S. Congress.

The American Federation of Labor creates the Agricultural Workers Organizing Committee to organize Filipino grape pickers in California.

1963   President John F. Kennedy establishes the Chinese Refugee Relief Committee, to aid persons fleeing Communist China; he appoints Anna Chenault to head the committee, the first Chinese American to serve in a high-level White House position.

1965   The United States begins sending combat troops to defend the South Vietnamese government against indigenous Communist forces backed by North Vietnam. Direct American involvement in the war continues until 1973; South Vietnam falls to Communist forces in 1975, ending near continuous warfare in the country since the late 1940s.

President Lyndon Johnson signs into law the Immigration and Nationality Act, ending the small national quotas established under the Immigration Act of 1924. Emphasizing family reunion, education, and job skills as criteria for immigration, the law opens the possibility of immigration to millions of Asian immigrants over the subsequent decades.

The East West Players, a leading showcase for Asian American theater, is founded in the Little Tokyo neighborhood of Los Angeles.

Japanese American Patsy Mink of Hawaii becomes the first Asian American woman, and the first nonwhite woman, to serve in the U.S. Congress.

1966   Sociologist William Peterson coins the term "model minority" to describe Asian Americans as an educationally and economically successful ethnic minority. Many Asian Americans would come to resent the term, saying it allowed non-Asian Americans to overlook the problems and prejudice facing many Asian Americans.

1967   In *Loving v. Virginia*, the U.S. Supreme Court declares the antimiscegenation laws of Virginia and thirty-seven other states unconstitutional, allowing for interracial marriages between, among others, Asians and non-Asians.

1968   The federal Bilingual Education Act mandates and funds bilingual education for non-English-speaking students.

1970   In pursuit of Vietnamese Communist sanctuaries, the United States launches an invasion of neighboring Cambodia.

1971   The first advocacy group for Pakistani Americans, the Pakistan League of America, is founded in New York City.

1972   President Richard Nixon visits the Communist People's Republic of China, beginning a rapprochement between Washington and Beijing.

1974   The Asian American Dance Theatre is founded in New York City.

1974   The U.S. Supreme Court rules in the precedent-setting case of *Lau v. Nichols* that San Francisco must provide bilingual education to its Chinese American students.

1975   The fall of Cambodia, Laos, and South Vietnam to Communist forces leads to a mass exodus of Vietnamese, Hmong, and, later, Cambodian refugees to the United States.

The Khmer Rouge seize power in Cambodia, leading to four years of genocide that results in the deaths of up to one-third of the country's population and sends tens of thousands of refugees abroad, many eventually settling in the United States.

Chinese American assemblywoman March Fong Eu is elected California's secretary of state, becoming the first Asian American to hold statewide office anywhere in the United States.

1976   Chinese immigrant Charles Wang cofounds Computer Associates International, which later becomes one of the nation's largest software firms.

1978   The first so-called boat people, seagoing refugees from the Communist government of Vietnam, set sail. Over the next several years, more than a million Vietnamese refugees will leave the country, though not all by sea; about half ultimately settle in the United States.

1979   The United States and the Communist People's Republic of China normalize relations; Washington shifts diplomatic recognition from Taiwan to Mainland China, though it maintains its commitment to defense of the former.

Vietnam invades Cambodia, putting to an end the genocidal Khmer Rouge regime and setting off a vast wave of refugees to the United States and other Western countries.

1980   Congress passes the Refugee Act, bringing the U.S. definition of refugees into line with that of the United Nations; the law will help pave the way for the entry of hundreds of thousands of Southeast Asians fleeing Communist regimes in Cambodia, Laos, and Vietnam.

The Los Angeles City Council declares part of the Mid-City neighborhood Koreatown, reflecting its importance as the largest Korean community outside Asia.

Los Angeles–area activists found Asian/Pacific Lesbians and Gays, the first advocacy organization for gay and lesbian Asian American and Pacific Islanders.

1982   Chinese American immigrant Vincent Chin is murdered by two unemployed autoworkers in Detroit who mistake him for Japanese; resentment against Japanese imported cars, which are perceived to be undermining the U.S. car industry and causing job losses, had been running high in the Motor City. The minimum sentence received by the perpetrators, three years' probation and a $3,000 fine, outrages the Asian American community.

The Vietnam Veterans Memorial, designed by Chinese American artist Maya Ying Lin, opens on the National Mall in Washington, D.C.

The American Association of Physicians of Indian Origin is founded in Dearborn, Michigan.

1983   The Korean American Coalition, a nonprofit, nonpartisan organization whose mission is to facilitate the Korean American community's participation in civic, community, and legislative affairs, is founded in Los Angeles.

1984   Taiwanese immigrant Roger Chen launches the 99 Ranch Market supermarket chain, the largest U.S. retail chain dedicated to Asian Americans.

Indian businesspersons in the San Francisco Bay Area found the Indo American Bank, the first lending institution formed specifically to aid the Indian American community.

1987   Asian American activists found the Washington-based National Network Against Anti-Asian Violence, partially in response to the 1982 racially motivated murder of Chinese American immigrant Vincent Chin.

1988   President Ronald Reagan signs the Civil Liberties Act, offering a formal apology and $20,000 in reparations to Japanese American survivors of incarceration during World War II.

1989   Playwright David Henry Hwang becomes the first Asian American to win a Tony Award for Best Play, for his drama *M. Butterfly.*

1990   Chinese-born Chang-lin Tang becomes chancellor of the University of California, Berkeley; he is the first Asian American to head a major university in the United States.

Chinese American Vera Wang, one of America's premier wedding gown designers, opens her first design salon in New York.

1992   The Los Angeles riots result in some $350 million in damages to Korean American–owned businesses, though only one Korean American is killed in the violence.

Choua Lee becomes the first Hmong American elected to public office when she wins a seat on the St. Paul, Minnesota, Board of Education.

Tony Lam is elected to the city council of Westminster, California—the heart of Orange County's "Little Saigon" community—becoming the first Vietnamese American elected to public office.

1993   Asian American lawyers and others found the National Asian Pacific American Legal Consortium in Washington, D.C., to protect the civil and legal rights of the Asian American and Pacific Islander communities.

President Bill Clinton selects Japanese American congressman Norman Mineta of California as his secretary of commerce; Mineta becomes the first Asian American to serve in a presidential cabinet.

1994   The American Broadcasting Company (ABC) begins airing the first regularly scheduled program—*All-American Girl,* starring Korean American comedian Margaret Cho—to feature a primarily Asian American cast; the show proves unsuccessful and is taken off the air the following year.

Taiwanese-born immigrant Jerry Yang cofounds the Web portal and Internet search engine Yahoo! in Silicon Valley.

1996   Democrat Gary Locke of Washington is elected as the first Asian American state governor in U.S. history.

    Time magazine chooses Taiwan-born immigrant David Ho as its Person of the Year for research that led to successful drug therapies for persons with HIV/AIDS.

1997   Golfer Tiger Woods becomes the first person of Asian background, and the youngest player ever, to win the prestigious Masters Tournament.

1998   California voters pass Proposition 227, requiring English-only instruction in public schools, with a one-year immersion course in English for non-English speakers.

1999   U.S. authorities arrest Wen Ho Lee, a Taiwanese-born nuclear physicist working at the Los Alamos National Laboratory, for allegedly selling U.S. nuclear secrets to the People's Republic of China. Lee is released from jail a year later after pleading guilty to a single count of unlawfully gathering national defense information.

    Street protests against a video-store owner who displayed portraits of a Vietnamese Communist leader in his shop window roils the Little Saigon neighborhood of Orange County, California, attesting to the community's intense anti-Communist politics.

2000   For the first time, the U.S. Census allows people to register as members of more than one race. Statistics gathered in the decennial census show that some 7.3 percent of Asian Americans consider themselves multiracial.

    The U.S. Census Bureau counts 10,171,820 persons of Asian and Pacific Islander background living in the United States, as well as another 1,687,626 of mixed Asian and other race background; the former figure is up from 202,970 in 1970.

2001   Taiwanese-born immigrant Elaine Chao is appointed secretary of labor by President George W. Bush, becoming the first Chinese American and the first Asian American woman to serve in a presidential cabinet.

2005   Chinese American Steve Chen cofounds the Internet video file-sharing Web site YouTube.

2009   President Barack Obama appoints Chinese Americans Stephen Chu, a Nobel Prize–winning physicist, and former Washington State governor Gary Locke as secretary of energy and secretary of commerce, respectively.

Bibliography

Books and Articles

Aaseng, Nathan. *The Inventors: Nobel Prizes in Chemistry, Physics, and Medicine.* Minneapolis, MN: Lerner, 1988.

Abelmann, Nancy, and John Lie. *Blue Dreams: Korean Americans and the Los Angeles Riots.* Cambridge, MA: Harvard University Press, 1995.

Abraham, Margaret. *Speaking the Unspeakable: Marital Violence Among South Asian Women in the United States.* New Brunswick, NJ: Rutgers University Press, 2000.

Adachi, Ken. *The Enemy That Never Was: A History of Japanese Canadians.* Toronto: McClelland and Stewart, 1991.

Adams, Bella. *Amy Tan.* Manchester, UK: Manchester University Press, 2005.

Adler, Susan Matoba. *Mothering, Education, and Ethnicity: The Transformation of Japanese American Culture.* New York: Garland, 1998.

Aguilar-San Juan, Karin, ed. *The State of Asian America: Activism and Resistance in the 1990s.* Boston: South End, 1994.

Ahn, Hyeon-Hyo, and Jang-Pyo Hong. "The Evolution of Korean Ethnic Banks in California." *Journal of Regional Studies* (Korea) 7:2 (2001): 97–120.

Alam, Fakrul. *Bharati Mukherjee.* New York: Twayne, 1996.

Alba, Richard, and Victor Nee. *Remaking the American Mainstream: Assimilation and Contemporary Immigration.* Cambridge, MA: Harvard University Press, 2003.

Alejandro, Reynaldo. *The Philippine Cookbook.* New York: Perigee Books, 1985.

Allen, James P. "Recent Immigration from the Philippines and Filipino Communities in the United States." *Geographical Review* 67:2 (1977): 195–208.

Allen, James Paul, and Eugene Turner, eds. *The Ethnic Quilt: Population Diversity in Southern California.* Northridge: California State University, Northridge, The Center for Geographical Studies, 1997.

Amar, Estrella Ravelo, and Willi Red Buhay. *Images of Filipinos in Chicago.* Chicago: Tempus, 2001.

Anderson, Gerald H., ed. *Studies in Philippine Church History.* Ithaca, NY: Cornell University Press, 1969.

Anderson, Wanni W., and Robert G. Lee. *Displacements and Diasporas: Asians in the Americas.* New Brunswick, NJ: Rutgers University Press, 2005.

Andrei, Mercedes Tira. "Historic 'Little Manila' Imperiled." *Filipino Reporter* 30:28 (July 3, 2003): 24.

Angelo, Michael. *The Sikh Diaspora: Tradition and Change in an Immigrant Community.* New York: Garland, 1997.

Apostolos-Cappadona, Diane, and Bruce Altshuler, eds. *Isamu Noguchi: Essays and Conversations.* New York: Harry Abrams/Isamu Noguchi Foundation, 1994.

Appadurai, Arjun. *Modernity at Large: Cultural Dimensions of Globalization.* Minneapolis: University of Minnesota Press, 1996.

Aranas, Jennifer. *The Filipino-American Kitchen: Traditional Recipes, Contemporary Flavors.* New York: Tuttle, 2006.

Arellano, Gustavo. "Freedom Free Little Saigon." *OC Weekly* 10:10 (2004).

Asato, Noriko. *Teaching Mikadoism: The Attack on Japanese Language Schools in Hawaii, California, and Washington, 1919–1927.* Honolulu: University of Hawai'i Press, 2006.

Ashton, Dore. *Noguchi East and West.* New York: Alfred A. Knopf, 1992.

Asian American Almanac: A Reference Work on Asians in the United States. Detroit: Gale Research, 1995.

Asian American Studies. *Chinese America: History and Perspectives.* San Francisco: Chinese Historical Society of America/San Francisco State University, 1990.

Asian American Studies Center, University of California, Los Angeles. *National Asian Pacific American Political Almanac.* 12th ed. Los Angeles: UCLA Asian American Studies Center and the Asian Pacific American Institute for Congressional Studies, 2007.

Asian and Pacific Islander American Health Forum (APIAHF). "Health Briefs: Cambodians (Khmer), Hmong, Samoans, Filipinos, South Asians, Vietnamese, Japanese, Koreans, Chinese and Others." 2003.

Asian Women United of California, ed. *Making Waves: An Anthology of Writings by and About Asian American Women.* Boston: Beacon, 1989.

Aspillera, Paraluman S. *Basic Tagalog for Foreigners and Non-Tagalogs.* Rev. 2d ed. Rutland, VT: Tuttle, 2007.

Assar, Nandini Narain. "Indian-American Success Story of 'Potel'-Motels: Immigration, Traditions, Community, and Gender." *Current Research on Occupations and Professions* 10 (1998): 67–86.

Association of Asian/Pacific American Artists. *Inside Moves. AAPAA Newsletter.* Los Angeles, June 1979.

Attanas, John. *Yo-Yo Ma: A Life in Music.* Evanston, IL: J.G. Burke, 2003.

Attinasi, John J. "English Only for California Children and the Aftermath of Proposition 227." *Education* 119 (December 1998): 263–84.

Au, Kathryn Hu-pei. "Participation Structures in a Reading Lesson with Hawaiian Children: Analysis of a Culturally Appropriate Instructional Event." *Anthropology and Education Quarterly* 11:2 (1980): 91–115.

Austin, Allan W. "Eastward Pioneers: Japanese American Resettlement During World War II and the Contested Meaning of Exile and Incarceration." *Journal of American Ethnic History* 26:2 (2007): 58–84.

———. *From Concentration Camp to Campus: Japanese American Students and World War II.* Urbana: University of Illinois Press, 2004.

Azuma, Eiichiro. *Between Two Empires: Race, History, and Transnationalism in Japanese America.* Cary, NC: Oxford University Press, 2005.

Baatar, Ts. "Social and Cultural Change in the Mongol-American Community." *Anthropology of East Europe Review* 17:2 (Autumn 1999).

Bailey, Benjamin. "Communication of Respect in Interethnic Service Encounters." *Language in Society* 26:3 (1997): 327–56.

Bain, David Haward. *Empire Express: Building the First Transcontinental Railroad.* New York: Viking, 1999.

Balagopal, Padmini, ed. *Indian and Pakistani Food Practices, Customs, and Holidays.* Alexandria, VA: American Dietetic Association, 1996.

Baluja, Kaari Flagstad. *Gender Roles at Home and Abroad: The Adaptation of Bangladeshi Immigrants.* New York: LFB Scholarly, 2003.

Bao, Xiaolan. *Holding Up More than Half the Sky: Chinese Women Garment Workers in New York City, 1948–92.* Urbana: University of Illinois Press, 2001.

Barde, Robert Eric. *Immigration at the Golden Gate: Passengers, Ships, Exclusion, and Angel Island.* Westport, CT: Praeger, 2008.

Barkan, Elliott Robert. *Asian and Pacific Islander Migration to the United States: A Model of New Global Patterns.* Westport, CT: Greenwood, 1992.

———. *Making It in America: A Sourcebook on Eminent Ethnic Americans,* 197–98. Santa Barbara, CA: ABC-Clio, 2001.

Barker, Eileen. *The Making of a Moonie: Choice or Brainwashing.* New York: Basil Blackwell, 1984.

Barlow, William, and Peter Shapiro. *An End to Silence: The San Francisco State College Student Movement in the '60s.* New York: Pegasus, 1971.

Bartell, Karen Hulene. *Fine Filipino Food.* New York: Hippocrene Books, 2003.

Bates, Timothy. *Race, Self-Employment, and Upward Mobility: An Illusive American Dream.* Baltimore: Johns Hopkins University Press, 1997.

Bayer, Ronald, and Gerald M. Oppenheimer. *AIDS Doctors: Voices from the Epidemic.* New York: Oxford University Press, 2000.

Beechert, Edward D. *Working in Hawaii: A Labor History.* Honolulu: University of Hawai'i Press, 1985.

Bennitt, Mark, ed. *History of the Louisiana Purchase Exposition.* New York: Arno, 1976.

Bernstein, Nina. "Immigrant Entrepreneurs Shape a New Economy." *New York Times,* February 6, 2007.

Besa, Amy, and Romy Dorotan. *Memories of Philippine Kitchens: Stories and Recipes from Far and Near.* New York: Stewart, Tabori and Chang, 2006.

Bhatia, Sunil. *American Karma: Race, Culture, and Identity in the Indian Diaspora.* New York: New York University Press, 2007.

Bhongbhibhat, Vimol, Bruce Reynolds, Sukhon Polpatpicharn, and Beatrice Camp, eds. *The Eagle and the Elephant: Thai-American Relations Since 1833.* Golden Jubilee Edition. Bangkok: United States Information Service, 1997.

Bishoff, Tonya, and Jo Rankin, eds. *Seeds from a Silent Tree: An Anthology by Korean Adoptees.* Glendale, CA: Pandal, 1997.

Blackwelder, Rob. "Return of the Native." Interview. San Francisco, March 11, 1999. http://splicedwire.com/features/tonybui.html.

Bladholm, Linda. *The Indian Grocery Store Demystified.* Los Angeles: Renaissance Books, 1999.

Bloom, Harold, ed. *Amy Tan.* Philadelphia: Chelsea House, 2000.

———, ed. *Asian-American Writers.* Philadelphia: Chelsea House, 1999.

Blum, Daniel C. *A Pictorial History of the Silent Screen.* New York: G.P. Putnam, 1953.

Boettcher, Robert. *Gifts of Deceit: Sun Myung Moon, Tongsun Park, and the Korean Scandal.* New York: Holt, Rinehart and Winston, 1980.

Bogardus, Emory S. "Filipino Repatriation." *Sociology and Social Research* 31 (September–October 1936): 67–71.

Bonacich, Edna, and John Modell. *The Economic Basis of Ethnic Solidarity: Small Business in the Japanese American Community.* Berkeley: University of California Press, 1980.

Bond, Michael Harris, ed. *Handbook of Chinese Psychology.* London: Oxford University Press, 1996.

Bonner, Arthur. *Alas! What Brought Thee Hither? The Chinese in New York, 1800–1950.* Madison, NJ: Fairleigh Dickinson University Press, 1997.

Bonus, Rick. "Homeland Memories and Media." *Locating Filipino Americans.* Philadelphia: Temple University Press, 2000.

———. *Locating Filipino Americans: Ethnicity and the Cultural Politics of Space.* Philadelphia: Temple University Press, 2000.

Bookspan, Martin, and Ross Yockey. *Zubin: The Zubin Mehta Story.* New York: Harper and Row, 1978.

Borja-Mamaril, Concordia R., and Tyrone Lim. *Filipino Americans: Pioneers to the Present.* Portland, OR: Filipino American National Historical Society, 2000.

Borjas, George J., and Richard B. Freeman, eds. *Immigration and the Work Force: Economic Consequences for the United States and Source Areas.* Chicago: University of Chicago Press, 1992.

Bornstein, Marc H., ed. *Handbook of Parenting.* 2nd ed. Mahwah, NJ: Lawrence Erlbaum, 2002.

Bose, Sudhindra. *Fifteen Years in America.* New York: Arno, 1974 [1920].

Brians, Paul. *Modern South Asian Literature in English.* Westport, CT: Greenwood, 2003.

Brislin, Tom. "Weep into Silence/Cries of Rage: Bitter Divisions in Hawaii's Japanese Press." *Journalism and Communication Monographs* 154 (1995): 1–29.

Brousse, Michel, and David Matsumoto. *Judo in the U.S.: A Century of Dedication.* Berkeley, CA: North Atlantic Books, 2005.

Brown, Emily C. *Har Dayal: Hindu Revolutionary and Rationalist.* Tucson: University of Arizona Press, 1975.

Brown, Giles. "The Hindu Conspiracy, 1914–1917." *Pacific Historical Review* 17:3 (August 1948).

Brush, Barbara L. "'Exchangees' or Employees? The Exchange Visitor Program and Foreign Nurse Immigration to the United States, 1945–2000." *Nursing History Review* 1 (1993): 171–80.

Buaken, Manuel. *I Have Lived with the American People.* Caldwell, ID: Caxton Printers, 1948.

Buck, Elizabeth. *Paradise Remade: The Politics of Culture and History in Hawai'i.* Philadelphia: Temple University Press, 1993.

Buddhist Churches of America. *Buddhist Churches of America.* 2 vols. Chicago: Nobart, 1974.

———. *2006 Annual Report.* San Francisco: Buddhist Churches of America, 2007.

Buenaventura, Ronald S. "San Diego's *Manongs* of the 1920s and '30s." *Filipino American National Historical Society Journal* 5 (1998): 31.

Bulosan, Carlos. *America Is in the Heart: A Personal History.* Reprint ed. Seattle: University of Washington Press, 1973.

———. *The Laughter of My Father.* New York: Harcourt, Brace, 1944.

Burke, Marie Louise. *Swami Vivekananda in the West: New Discoveries.* 4th ed. 6 vols. Calcutta: Advaita Ashrama, 1983.

Byrd, Martha. *Chennault: Giving Wings to the Tiger.* Tuscaloosa: University of Alabama Press, 2003.

Cabarloc, Ron. "Filipina Garment Workers in Los Angeles." *Filipino American National Historical Society Journal* 4 (1996): 52.

Cadge, Wendy. *Heartwood: The First Generation of Theravada Buddhism in America.* Morality and Society Series. Chicago: University of Chicago Press, 2004.

Cady, John F. *The United States and Burma.* Cambridge, MA: Harvard University Press, 1976.

Cahn, Steven M., ed. *The Affirmative Action Debate.* New York: Routledge, 1995.

Callahan, Tom. *In Search of Tiger Woods: A Journey Through Golf with Tiger Woods.* New York: Three Rivers, 2004.

Campbell, Sid, and Greglon Yimm Lee. *The Dragon and the Tiger: The Birth of Bruce Lee's Jeet Kune Do, The Oakland Years.* Vol. 1. Berkeley, CA: Frog, 2003.

Cannell, Michael. *I.M. Pei: Mandarin of Modernism.* Westminster, MD: Random House, 1995.

Canniff, Julie G. *Cambodian Refugees' Pathways to Success: Developing a Bi-Cultural Identity.* New York: LFB Scholarly, 2001.

Caplan, Nathan, John K. Whitmore, and Marcella H. Choy. *The Boat People and Achievement in America: A Study of Family Life, Hard Work, and Cultural Values.* Ann Arbor: University of Michigan Press, 1989.

Carlsen, Clifford. "First Indo-American Bank Seeks Merger to Add Capital, Earnings." *San Francisco Business Times* 8 (March 22, 1991).

Carnes, Tony, and Fenggang Yang, eds. *Asian American Religions: The Making and Remaking of Borders and Boundaries.* New York: New York University Press, 2004.

Carreon, Sonia D. "Occupational Decisions of Selected Filipina Immigrants in a Midwestern City." *Filipino American National Historical Society Journal* 3 (1994): 44–48.

Catapusan, Benicio T. "Filipino Intermarriage Problems in the United States." *Sociology and Social Research* 22 (January 1938): 265–72.

Ceniza Choy, Catherine. *Empire of Care: Nursing and Migration in Filipino American History.* Durham, NC: Duke University Press, 2003.

Census Profile: New York City's Taiwanese American Population. New York: Asian American Federation of New York, 2005.

"Center for Philippine Studies in Hawaii." *Heritage* 7:2 (June 1993): 21.

Chai, May-lee. *Glamorous Asians: Short Stories and Essays.* Indianapolis, IN: University of Indianapolis Press, 2004.

Chai, Winberg. "The Taiwan Factor in U.S.-China Relations." *Asian Affairs: An American Review* 29:3 (Fall 2002): 131–47.

Chan, Kenyon S. "Rethinking the Asian American Studies Project: Bridging the Divide Between 'Campus' and 'Community.'" *Journal of Asian American Studies* 3:1 (2000): 17–36.

Chan, Moly Sam. *Khmer Court Dance: A Comprehensive Study of Movements, Gestures, and Postures as Applied Technique.* Newington, CT: Khmer Studies Institute, 1987.

Chan, Sucheng. "Asian American Historiography." *Pacific Historical Review* 65 (1996): 363–99.

———. *Asian Americans: An Interpretive History.* New York: Twayne, 1991.

———. *Asian Californians.* San Francisco: MTL/Boyd and Fraser, 1991.

———. *This Bittersweet Soil: The Chinese in California Agriculture, 1860–1910.* Berkeley: University of California Press, 1986.

———. *Hmong Means Free: Life in Laos and America.* Philadelphia: Temple University Press, 1994.

———. *Survivors: Cambodian Refugees in the United States.* Urbana: University of Illinois Press, 2004.

Chan, Sucheng, ed. *Entry Denied: Exclusion and the Chinese Community in America, 1882–1943.* Philadelphia: Temple University Press, 1994.

———, ed. *Remapping Asian American History.* Walnut Creek, CA: AltaMira, 2003.

Chan, Sucheng, Douglas Henry Daniels, Mario T. Garcia, and Terry P. Wilson, eds. *Peoples of Color in the American West.* New York: Houghton Mifflin, 1994.

Chandrasekhar, S., ed. *From India to America: A Brief History of Immigration; Problems of Discrimination; Admission and Assimilation.* La Jolla, CA: Population Review, 1982.

Chang, Edward, and Jeannette Diaz-Veizades. *Ethnic Peace in the American City: Building Community in Los Angeles and Beyond.* New York: New York University Press, 1999.

Chang, Gordon. "We Almost Wept: Professor Yamato Ichihashi was a Respected Scholar and Member of the Stanford Community, but That Wasn't Enough to Spare Him the Humiliation of Internment." *Stanford Today,* November–December 1996.

Chang, Gordon H., ed. *Asian Americans and Politics: Perspectives, Experiences, Prospects.* Washington, DC: Woodrow Wilson Center Press, 2001.

Chang, Iris. *The Chinese in America: A Narrative History.* New York: Viking, 2003.

Chang, M.J., J.J. Park, M.H. Lin, O.A. Poon, and D.T. Na-kanishi. *Beyond Myths: The Growth and Diversity of Asian American College Freshmen, 1971–2005.* Los Angeles: Higher Education Research Institute, UCLA, 2007.

Chang, Mitchell J. "Expansion and Its Discontents: The Formation of the Asian American Studies Programs in the 1990s." *Journal of Asian American Studies* 2:2 (1999): 181–206.

Chang, Shenglin. *The Global Silicon Valley Home: Lives and Landscapes Within Taiwanese American Trans-Pacific Culture.* Palo Alto, CA: Stanford University Press, 2005.

"Chang-lin Tien (1935–2002): A Chancellor's Extraordinary Legacy." *Forefront* (Spring 2005): 4–5.

Chavez, Lydia. *The Color Bind: California's Battle to End Affirmative Action.* Berkeley: University of California Press, 1998.

Chay, Jongsuk. *Diplomacy of Asymmetry: Korean-American Relations to 1910.* Honolulu: University of Hawai'i Press, 1990.

Cheah, Joseph. "Cultural Identity and Burmese American Buddhists." *Joseph Cheah Peace Review* 14:4 (2002): 415–19.

Chee, Maria W.L. *Taiwanese American Transnational Families: Women and Kin Work.* New York: Routledge, 2005.

Chen, C., and H.W. Stevenson. "Motivation and Mathematics Achievement: A Comparative Study of Asian-American, Caucasian-American, and East Asian High School Students." *Child Development* 66:4 (1995): 1215–34.

Chen, Carolyn. "The Religious Varieties of Ethnic Pressure: A Comparison Between a Taiwanese Immigrant Buddhist Temple and an Evangelical Christian Church." *Sociology of Religion* 63:2 (2002): 215–38.

Chen, Hsiang-Shui. *Chinatown No More: Taiwan Immigrants in Contemporary New York.* Ithaca, NY: Cornell University Press, 1992.

Chen, Jack. *The Chinese of America.* San Francisco: Harper and Row, 1980.

Chen, Shehong. *Being Chinese, Becoming Chinese American.* Urbana: University of Illinois Press, 2002.

Chen, Yong. *Chinese San Francisco 1850–1943: A Trans-Pacific Community.* Stanford, CA: Stanford University Press, 2000, 192–94.

Chennault, Anna. *A Thousand Springs: The Biography of a Marriage.* New York: Paul S. Ericksson, 1962.

———. *The Education of Anna.* New York: Times Books, 1980.

Cheshire, Ellen. *Ang Lee.* North Pomfret, VT: Trafalgar Square, 2001.

Cheung, King-Kok. *An Interethnic Companion to Asian American Literature.* New York: Cambridge University Press, 1997.

Cheung, King-Kok, and Stan Yogi, eds. *Asian American Literature: An Annotated Bibliography.* New York: Modern Language Association of America, 1988.

Chi, Tsung. *East Asian Americans and Political Participation: A Reference Handbook.* Santa Barbara, CA: ABC-CLIO, 2005.

Chin, Frank, Jeffery Chan, Lawson Inada, and Shawn Wong, eds. *Aiiieeeee! An Anthology of Asian-American Writers.* Washington, DC: Howard University Press, 1974.

Chin, Ko-lin. *Chinese Subculture and Criminality: Non-traditional Crime Groups in America.* New York: Greenwood, 1990.

———. *Smuggled Chinese: Clandestine Immigration to the United States.* Philadelphia: Temple University Press, 1999.

"China Lobbies Operate for Both Sides in the United States." *China and U.S. Far Eastern Policy 1945–1966.* Washington, DC: Congressional Quarterly Series, 1967, 23–28.

Chinn, Thomas W. *Bridging the Pacific: San Francisco Chinatown and Its People.* San Francisco: Chinese Historical Society of America, 1989.

Cho, Margaret. *I'm the One That I Want.* New York: Ballantine Books, 2001.

Chotiner, Isaac. "Interview with Jhumpa Lahiri." *The Atlantic,* March 18, 2008.

Chow, May. "Denver Investor Buys APA-Owned Examiner." *AsianWeek* (February 27, 2004).

———. "First Ever Filipino American Historic Site Dedicated in Stockton." *Asian Week,* November 1–November 7, 2002.

Choy, Bong Youn. *Koreans in America.* Chicago: Nelson-Hall, 1979.

Choy, Catherine Ceniza. *Empire of Care: Nursing and Migration in Filipino American History.* Durham, NC: Duke University Press, 2003.

Christgau, John. *"Enemies": World War II Alien Internment.* Ames: Iowa State University Press, 1985.

Christopher, Renny. *The Vietnam War/The American War: Images and Representations in Euro-American and Vietnamese Exile Narratives.* Amherst: University of Massachusetts Press, 1995.

Chryssides, George. *The Advent of Sun Myung Moon: The Origins, Beliefs, and Practices of the Unification Church.* New York: Palgrave Macmillan, 1991.

Chu, Lenora. "Beauty Contest Loses Luster: The History of the Miss Chinatown U.S.A. Pageant." *AsianWeek* 21:24 (February 10, 2000).

Chu, Samuel, ed. *Madame Chiang Kai-shek and Her China.* Norwalk, CT: EastBridge, 2004.

Chua-Eoan, Howard. "The Tao of Ho." *Time,* December 30, 1996.

Chu-Chang, Mae, and Victor Rodriguez. *Asian- and Pacific-American Perspectives in Bilingual Education: Comparative Research.* New York: Teachers College Press, 1983.

Chun, Gloria Heyung. *Of Orphans and Warriors: Inventing Chinese American Culture and Identity.* New Brunswick, NJ: Rutgers University Press, 2000.

Chung, Angie Y. *Legacies of Struggle: Conflict and Cooperation in Korean American Politics.* Palo Alto, CA: Stanford University Press, 2007.

Chung, Rita Chi-Ying. "Psychosocial Adjustment of Cambodian Refugee Women: Implications for Mental Health Counseling." *Journal of Mental Health Counseling* 23:2 (April 2001).

Cimmarusti, Rocco A. "Exploring Aspects of Filipino-American Families." *Journal of Marital and Family Therapy* 22:2 (April 1996): 205–17.

Civil Rights Act of 1964, Sec. 601. *United States Statute at Large* 78. Washington, DC: Government Printing Office, 1964.

Clark, Blake. "G.J. Shows That East and West Can Meet." *Reader's Digest* 51 (December 1947): 73–77.

Clarke, Colin, Ceri Peach, and Steven Vertovec, eds. *South Asians Overseas: Migration and Ethnicity.* Cambridge: Cambridge University Press, 1990.

Clouse Robert. *Bruce Lee: The Biography.* Burbank, CA: Unique, 1988.

Cohen, Daniel. "The Fall of the House of Wang." *Business Month* 135:2 (February 1990): 22–29.

Cohen, Jeffrey Jerome, ed. *Monster Theory: Reading Culture.* Minneapolis: University of Minnesota Press, 1996.

Cohen, Marc J. *Taiwan at the Crossroads.* Washington, DC: Asia Resource Center, 1991.

Collignon, Francine F., Makna Men, and Serei Tan. "Finding Ways In: Community-Based Perspectives on Southeast Asian Family Involvement with Schools in a New England State." *Journal of Education for Students Placed at Risk* 6 (2001): 27–44.

Comas-Diaz, Lillian, and Beverly Greene, eds. *Women of Color: Integrating Ethnic and Gender Identities in Psychotherapy.* New York: Guilford, 1994.

Commission on Wartime Relocation and Internment of Civilians. *Personal Justice Denied.* Washington, DC: Government Printing Office, 1982.

Conboy, Kenneth. *Shadow War: The CIA's Secret War in Laos.* Boulder, CO: Paladin, 1995.

Conrat, Maisie. *Executive Order 9066: The Internment of 110,000 Japanese Americans.* Los Angeles: University of California Press, 1992.

Conroy, Hilary, and T. Scott Miyakawa, eds. *East Across the Pacific: Historical and Sociological Studies of Japanese Immigration and Assimilation.* Santa Barbara, CA: American Bibliographic Center, 1962.

Coolidge, Mary. *Chinese Immigration.* New York: Henry Holt, 1909.

Cooper, Patricia. *Once a Cigar Maker: Men, Women, and Work Culture in American Cigar Factories, 1900–1919.* Urbana: University of Illinois Press, 1987.

Cordova, Dorothy Laigo. *A Study of the Problems of Asian Health Professionals.* Seattle: Demonstration Project for Asian Americans, 1975.

Cordova, Fred. *Filipinos, Forgotten Asian Americans: A Pictorial Essay 1763–circa 1963.* Demonstration Project for Asian Americans. Dubuque, IA: Kendell/Hunt, 1983.

Corfield, Justin, and Robin Corfield. *Encyclopedia of Singapore.* Lanham, MD: Scarecrow, 2006.

Cornford, Daniel, ed. *Working People of California.* Berkeley: University of California Press, 1995.

Council for Native Hawaiian Advancement. *A Tribute to Senator Daniel Kahikina Akaka and His Life's Work.* Honolulu, HI, 2003.

Cox, Susan Soon-Keum. *Voices from Another Place: A Collection of Works from a Generation Born in Korea and Adopted to Other Countries.* St. Paul, MN: Yeong and Yeong, 1999.

Cranston, Sylvia. *HPB: The Extraordinary Life and Influence of Helen Blavatsky, Founder of the Modern Theosophical Movement.* New York: G.P. Putnam, 1993.

Crawford, Ann. *Customs and Culture of Vietnam.* Rutland, VT: Charles E. Tuttle, 1966.

Crawford, James. *Bilingual Education: History, Politics, Theory and Practice.* 3rd ed. Los Angeles: Bilingual Educational Services, 1995.

Criddle, Joan D., and Teeda Butt Mam. *To Destroy You Is No Loss: The Odyssey of a Cambodian Family.* New York: Atlantic Monthly, 1987.

Cropp, Fritz, Cynthia M. Frisby, and Dean Mills, eds. *Journalism Across Cultures.* Ames: Iowa State Press, 2003.

Cropper, William H. *Great Physicists: The Life and Times of Leading Physicists from Galileo to Hawking.* New York: Oxford University Press, 2001.

Crost, Lyn. *Honor by Fire: Japanese Americans at War in Europe and the Pacific.* Novato, CA: Presidio, 1994.

Crouchett, Lorraine Jacobs. *Filipinos in California: From the Days of the Galleons to the Present.* El Cerritos, CA: Downey Place, 1982.

Cwiertka, Katarzyna, and Boudewijn Walraven, eds. *Asian Food: The Global and the Local.* Honolulu: University of Hawai'i Press, 2001.

Dae, Sook Suh. *The Writings of Henry Cu Kim.* Honolulu: University of Hawai'i Press, 1987.

Daley, William. *The Chinese Americans.* New York: Chelsea House, 1987.

Damrosch, Lori Fisler. "The Taiwan Relations Act After Ten Years." *Journal of Asian Law* 3:2 (Fall 1989): 157–83.

Daniels, Roger. *Asian America: Chinese and Japanese in the United States Since 1850.* Seattle: University of Washington Press, 1988.

———. *Concentration Camps, North America: Japanese in the United States and Canada During World War II.* Malabar, FL: Robert E. Krieger, 1981, 1993.

———. *Concentration Camps U.S.A.: Japanese Americans and World War II.* New York: Holt, Rinehart, and Winston, 1971.

———. *History of Indian Immigration to the United States: An Interpretative Essay.* New York: Asia Society, 1989.

———. "No Lamps Were Lit for Them: Angel Island and the Historiography of Asian American Immigration." *Journal of American Ethnic History* 17 (1997): 3–18.

———. *The Politics of Prejudice: The Anti-Japanese Movement in California and the Struggle for Japanese Exclusion.* 2nd ed. Berkeley: University of California Press, 1977.

———. *Prisoners Without Trial: Japanese Americans in World War II.* New York: Hill and Wang, 1993.

Daniels, Roger, ed. *Anti-Chinese Violence in North America.* New York: Arno, 1978.

Daniels, Roger, and Otis L. Graham. *Debating American Immigration, 1882–Present.* New York: Rowman and Littlefield, 2001.

Daniels, Roger, Sandra C. Taylor, Harry H.L. Kitano, and Leonard J. Arrington. *Japanese Americans: From Relocation to Redress.* Seattle: University of Washington Press, 1992.

Dannen, Fredric. "Revenge of the Green Dragons." *New Yorker,* November 16, 1992, 76–99.

Das, Gurcharan. *India Unbound.* New Delhi: Penguin Books, 2002.

Das Gupta, Monisha. *Unruly Immigrants: Rights, Activism, and Transnational South Asian Politics in the United States.* Durham, NC: Duke University Press, 2006.

DasGupta, Shamita Das, ed. *A Patchwork Shawl: Chronicles of South Asian Women in America*. New Brunswick, NJ: Rutgers University Press, 1998.

Davé, Shilpa, Leilani Nishime, Tasha G. Oren, and Robert G. Lee. *East Main Street: Asian American Popular Culture*. New York: New York University Press, 2005.

David, Stephen. "Sisters to the Rescue." *India Today International,* February 2, 2004, 35–37.

Davidson, Sue. *A Heart in Politics: Jeannette Rankin and Patsy T. Mink*. Seattle: Seal, 1994.

De Courtivron, Isabelle. *Lives in Translation: Bilingual Writers on Identity and Creativity*. New York: Palgrave Macmillan, 2003.

Decker-Phillips, Edith. *Paik Video*. Barrytown, NY: Station Hill, 1998.

DeJong, Gordon F., Brenda Davis Root, and Ricardo G. Abad. "Family Reunification and Philippine Migration to the United States: The Immigrants' Perspective." *International Migration Review* 20:3 (1986): 598–611.

Demonstration Project for Asian Americans. *An Analysis of Problems of Asian Wives of U.S. Servicemen*. Seattle, WA: Sil Dong Kim, Demonstration Project for Asian Americans, 1975.

———. *Final Evaluation Report*. Los Angeles, CA, January 15, 1972.

———. *Newsletter, The Forgotten Asian Americans: Filipinos and Koreans* (May 1981). Seattle, WA.

———. *Newsletter, The Forgotten Asian Americans: Filipinos and Koreans* (September 1982). Seattle, WA.

Deol, G.S. *The Role of the Ghadar Party in the National Movement*. Delhi, India: Sterling, 1969.

DePaul, Kim, and Dith Pran, *Children of Cambodia's Killing Fields: Memoirs by Survivors*. New Haven, CT: Yale University Press, 1997.

Desmond, Jane. "Asian American Dance Theatre, at Cornell University." *BRIDGE: An Asian American Perspective* (Summer 1978): 58.

Deuchler, Martina. *Confucian Gentlemen and Barbarian Envoys: The Opening of Korea, 1875–1885*. Seattle: University of Washington Press, 1977.

DeWitt, Howard A. *Violence in the Fields: California Filipino Farm Labor Unionization During the Great Depression*. Saratoga, CA: Century Twenty One, 1980.

Dilley, Whitney Crothers. *The Cinema of Ang Lee: The Other Side of the Screen*. London: Wallflower, 2007.

Dillon, Richard H. *The Hatchet Men: The Story of the Tong Wars in San Francisco's Chinatown*. New York: Coward-McCann, 1962.

Dirlik, Arif, ed. *Chinese on the American Frontier*. Lanham, MD: Rowman and Littlefield, 2001.

Dirlik, A., ed. *What Is in a Rim? Critical Perspectives on the Pacific Region Idea*. Boulder, CO: Westview, 1992.

Dizon, Nicolas C. *The "Master" vs. Juan de la Cruz*. Honolulu, HI: Mercantile, 1931.

Do, Hien Duc. *The Vietnamese Americans*. Westport, CT: Greenwood, 1999.

Doi, Takeo. *The Anatomy of Dependence*. New York: Kodansha, 1973.

Dong, Selena. "'Too Many Asians': The Challenge of Fighting Discrimination Against Asian-Americans and Preserving Affirmative Action." *Stanford Law Review* 47 (May 1995): 1027–57.

Draeger, Donn F., and Robert W. Smith. *Asian Fighting Arts*. New York: Berkeley, 1974.

Dudley, William, ed. *Asian Americans: Opposing Viewpoints*. San Diego, CA: Greenhaven, 1997.

Dusselier, Jane. "Does Food Make Place? Food Protests in Japanese American Concentration Camps." *Food and Foodways* 10 (2002): 137–65.

Duus, Masayo. *Tokyo Rose: Orphan of the Pacific*. New York: Harper and Row, 1979.

Dwyer, Lance Cardozo. "Larry Itliong, Labor Leader, Honored." *Philippine News,* April 4, 2006.

Dymski, Gary A., and Wei Li. "Financial Globalization and Cross-Border Co-Movements of Money and Population: Foreign Bank Offices in Los Angeles." *Environment and Planning A* 36:2 (2004): 213–40.

Eberhard, Wolfram. *Chinese Festivals*. New York: Henry Shuman, 1952.

Ebihara, May, Carol A. Mortland, and Judy Ledgerwood, eds. *Cambodian Culture Since 1975: Homeland and Exile*. Ithaca, NY: Cornell University Press, 1994.

Eck, Diana L. *Darsán: Seeing the Divine Image in India*. New York: Columbia University Press, 1996.

———. *A New Religious American: How a "Christian Country" Has Become the World's Most Religiously Diverse Nation*. San Francisco: HarperSanFrancisco, 2001.

Edwards, Jerome E. *Pat McCarran: Political Boss of Nevada*. Reno: University of Nevada Press, 1982.

Ekspong, Gösta. *Nobel Lectures in Physics, 1996–2000*. Stockholm: Stockholm University, 2003.

Eljera, Bert. "Big Plans for Little Saigon." *AsianWeek,* May 17–23, 1996.

Eng, Alvin, ed. *Tokens? Asian American Experience on Stage*. New York: Asian American Writers' Workshop, 1999.

Eng, David L., and Alice Y. Hom, eds. *Q&A: Queer in Asian America*. Philadelphia: Temple University Press, 1998.

España-Maram, Linda. *Creating Masculinity in Los Angeles's Little Manila: Working-Class Filipinos and Popular Culture, 1920s–1950s*. New York: Columbia University Press, 2006.

Espiritu, Yen Le. *Asian American Panethnicity: Bridging Institutions and Identities*. Philadelphia: Temple University Press, 1992.

———. *Filipino American Lives*. Philadelphia: Temple University Press, 1995.

———. *Home Bound: Filipino American Lives Across Cultures, Communities, and Countries*. Berkeley: University of California Press, 2003.

Evangelista, Susan. *Carlos Bulosan and His Poetry: A Biography and Anthology*. Seattle: University of Washington Press, 1985.

Evans, Karin. *The Lost Daughters of China: Abandoned Girls, Their Journey to America, and the Search for a Missing Past*. New York: J.P. Tarcher, 2000.

Fabros, Alex S., Jr. "When Hilario Met Sally." *Filipinas* (February 1995): 50–52, 58.

Fadiman, Anne. *The Spirit Catches You and You Fall Down: A Hmong Child, Her American Doctors, and the Collision of Two Cultures*. New York: Farrar, Straus and Giroux, 1997.

Fanning, Branwell, and William Wong. *Angel Island*. Charleston, SC: Arcadia, 2006.

Faruque, Cathleen Jo. *Migration of Hmong to the Midwestern United States.* New York: University Press of America, 2002.

Feinberg, Rosa Castro. *Bilingual Education: A Reference Handbook.* Santa Barbara, CA: ABC-CLIO, 2002.

Feng, Peter. "In Search of Asian American Cinema." *Cineaste* 35:4 (Winter–Spring 1995): 88–118.

———. "The State of Asian American Cinema: In Search of Community." *Cineaste* 24:4 (1999): 20–24.

Feng, Peter X., ed. *Screening Asian Americans.* Piscataway, NJ: Rutgers University Press, 2002.

Fenkl, Heinz Isu, and Walter Lew. *Kŏri: The Beacon Anthology of Korean American Fiction.* Boston: Beacon, 2002.

Fenton, John Y. *Transplanting Religious Traditions: Asian Indians in America.* New York: Praeger, 1988.

Fessler, Loren W., ed. *Chinese in America: Stereotyped Past, Changing Present.* New York: Vantage, 1983.

The Filipino American Experience in Hawai'i (Social Process in Hawaii). Honolulu: University of Hawai'i at Manoa, 1991.

Fisher, Maxine P. *The Indians of New York City: A Study of Immigrants from India.* Columbia: South Asian Books, 1980.

Fitzgerald, Stephen. *China and the Overseas Chinese: A Study of Peking's Changing Policy, 1949–1970.* New York: Cambridge University Press, 1972.

Fong, Colleen, and Judy Yung. "In Search of the Right Spouse: Interracial Marriage Among Chinese and Japanese Americans." *Amerasia Journal* 21:3 (Winter 1995–1996): 77–98.

Fong, Eric, ed. *Chinese Ethnic Economy: Global and Local Perspectives.* London: Routledge, 2007.

Fong, Timothy. *The Contemporary Asian American Experience: Beyond the Model Minority.* 3rd ed. Upper Saddle River, NJ: Prentice Hall, 2008.

Ford, Daniel. *Flying Tigers: Claire Chennault and the American Volunteer Group.* Washington, DC: Smithsonian Institution, 1991.

Foster, Nellie. "Legal Status of Filipino Intermarriages in California." *Sociology and Social Research* 16:5 (May 1932): 441–54.

Fox, Timothy J., and Duane R. Sneddeker. *From the Palaces to the Pike: Visions of the 1904 World's Fair.* St. Louis: Missouri Historical Society, 1997.

Francia, Luis, and Eric Gamalinda, eds. *Flippin': Filipinos on America.* New York: Asian American Writers' Workshop, 1996.

Fraser, Thomas G. "Germany and Indian Revolution, 1914–1918." *Journal of Contemporary History* 12 (1977): 255–72.

Frazier, John W., and Florence M. Margai, eds. *Multi-cultural Geographies: The Changing Racial/Ethnic Patterns of the United States.* Binghamton, NY: Global Academic, 2003.

Freeman, James M. *Changing Identities: Vietnamese Americans, 1975–1995.* Boston: Allyn and Bacon, 1995.

———. *Hearts of Sorrow: Vietnamese-American Lives.* Palo Alto, CA: Stanford University Press, 1989.

Friday, Chris. *Organizing Asian American Labor: The Pacific Coast Canned Salmon Industry, 1870–1942.* Philadelphia: Temple University Press, 1994.

Fugita, Stephen S., and David J. O'Brien. *Japanese American Ethnicity: The Persistence of Community.* Seattle: University of Washington Press, 1991.

Fujioka, J.M. "Abating Stereotypical Attitudes: Views on Career Paths of an Asian American Comedian." *Career Development Quarterly* 39 (March 1991): 337–40.

Fukei, Budd. *The Japanese American Story.* Minneapolis, MN: Dillon, 1976.

Fukuda, Keiko. *Born for the Mat: A Kodokan kata Textbook for Women.* San Francisco: N.p., 1973.

Furst, Al, and Xiaoge Xiong. "Pay Back the Past: In Memory of An Wang." *Electronic Business* 16:8 (April 30, 1990): 31.

Garcia Coll, Cynthia T., Daisuke Akiba, Natalia Palacios, Benjamin Bailey, Rebecca Silver, Lisa DiMartino, and Cindy Chin. "Parental Participation in Their Children's Education: Lessons from Three Immigrant Groups." *Parenting: Science and Practice* 2 (2002): 303–24.

Gardiner, C. Harvey. *The Japanese and Peru: 1873–1973.* Albuquerque: University of New Mexico Press, 1975.

———. *Pawns in a Triangle of Hate: The Peruvian Japanese in the United States.* Seattle: University of Washington Press, 1981.

Gardner, Arthur Leslie. *The Korean Nationalist Movement and Ahn Chang Ho: Advocate of Gradualism.* Honolulu: University of Hawai'i Press, 1979.

Garrett, Jessie A., and Ronald C. Larson, eds. *Camp and Community: Manzanar and the Owens Valley.* Fullerton: California State University, Japanese American Oral History Project, 1977.

Gee, Emma, ed. *COUNTERPOINT: Perspectives on Asian America.* Los Angeles: UCLA Asian American Studies Center, 1976.

Gee, Harvey. "Why Did Asian Americans Vote Against the 1996 California Civil Rights Initiative?" *Loyola Journal of Public Interest Law* (Spring 2001): 1–52.

Geertz, Clifford. *The Rotating Credit Association: An Instrument for Development.* Cambridge, MA: Center for International Studies, 1956.

Gillenkirk, Jeff, and James Motlow. *Bitter Melon: Stories from the Last Rural Chinese Town in America.* Seattle: University of Washington Press, 1987.

Glenn, Evelyn Nakano. *Unequal Freedom: How Race and Gender Shaped American Citizenship and Labor.* Cambridge, MA: Harvard University Press, 2002.

Goh Pei Ki and Fu Chunjiang. *Origins of Chinese Festivals.* Singapore: Asiapac Books, 2001.

Gong, Eng Ying, and Bruce Grant. *Tong War! The First Complete History of the Tongs in America.* New York: N.L. Brown, 1930.

Gonzales, Juan L., Jr. "Asian Indian Immigration Patterns: The Origins of the Sikh Community in California." *International Migration Review* 20:1 (Spring 1986).

Gordon, Milton M. *Assimilation in American Life.* New York: Oxford University Press, 1964.

Green, Thomas A., ed. *Martial Arts of the World: An Encyclopedia.* Santa Barbara, CA: ABC-CLIO, 2002.

Green, Thomas A., and Joseph Svinth, eds. *Martial Arts in the Modern World.* Westport, CT: Praeger, 2003.

Grodzins, Morton. *Americans Betrayed: Politics and the Japanese American Evacuation.* Chicago: University of Chicago Press, 1949.

Gu, Chien-juh. *Mental Health Among Taiwanese Americans: Gender, Immigration, and Transnational Struggles.* El Paso, TX: LFB Scholarly Publishing, 2006.

Gudykunst, William B. *Asian American Ethnicity and Communication.* Thousand Oaks, CA: Sage, 2001.

Guest, Kenneth J. *God in Chinatown: Religion and Survival in New York's Evolving Immigrant Community.* New York: New York University Press, 2003.

Guillermo, Emil. *Amok: Essays from an Asian American Perspective.* San Francisco: AsianWeek Books, 1999.

Guimary, Donald L. "Filipino-American Newspapers: A Never-Ending Study." *Filipino American National Historical Society Journal* 3 (1994): 52–54.

Gupta, S.P.K., and Edgar L. Milford. *In Quest of Panacea: Successes and Failures of Yellapragada SubbaRow.* Nanuet, NY: Evelyn, 1987.

Gupta, Sangeeta R., ed. *Emerging Voices: South Asian American Women Redefine Self, Family, and Community.* Walnut Creek, CA: AltaMira, 1999.

Gyory, Andrew. *Closing the Gate: Race, Politics, and the Chinese Exclusion Act.* Chapel Hill: University of North Carolina Press, 1998.

Habal, Estella. *San Francisco's International Hotel: Mobilizing the Filipino-American Community in the Anti-Eviction Movement.* Philadelphia: Temple University Press, 2007.

Hagedorn, Jessica. *Dogeaters.* New York: Pantheon Books, 1990.

Hagedorn, Jessica, ed. *Charlie Chan Is Dead: An Anthology of Contemporary Asian American Fiction.* New York: Penguin Books, 1993.

Haines, David, and Karen Rosenblum, ed. *Illegal Immigration in America: A Reference Handbook.* Westport, CT: Greenwood, 1999.

Hall, Patricia Wong, and Victor Hwang, eds. *Anti-Asian Violence in North America: Asian American and Asian Canadian Reflections on Hate, Healing, and Resistance.* New York: Rowman and Littlefield, 2001.

Halloran, Richard. *Sparky: Warrior, Peacemaker, Poet, Patriot: A Portrait of Senator Spark M. Matsunaga.* Honolulu: Watermark, 2002.

Halseth, James A., and Bruce Glasrud, eds. *The Northwest Mosaic: Minority Conflicts in Pacific Northwest History.* Boulder, CO: Pruett, 1977.

Halualani, Rona Tamiko. *In the Name of Hawaiians: Native Identities and Cultural Politics.* Minneapolis: University of Minnesota Press, 2002.

Hamamoto, Darrell, and Sandra Liu, eds. *Countervisions: Asian American Film Criticism.* Philadelphia: Temple University Press, 2000.

Haney-López, Ian F. *White by Law: The Legal Construction of Race.* New York: New York University Press, 1996.

Hanhardt, John G. *The Worlds of Nam June Paik.* New York: Guggenheim Museum, 2000.

Hansen, Arthur. "James Matsumoto Omura: An Interview." *Amerasia Journal* 13:2 (1986–1987): 99–113.

Harper Ann C. "The Iglesia ni Cristo and Evangelical Christianity." *Journal of Asian Mission* 3:1 (2001): 101–19.

Harris, Paul W. "A Checkered Life: Yung Wing's American Education." *American Journal of Chinese Studies* (April 1994): 87–107.

Harrison, Charles H. *Growing a Global Village: Making History at Seabrook Farms.* New York: Holmes and Meier, 2003.

Hart, Donn V. *Compadrinazgo: Ritual Kinship in the Philippines.* DeKalb: Northern Illinois University Press, 1977.

Harth, Erica. *Last Witnesses: Reflections on the Wartime Incarceration of Japanese Americans.* New York: Palgrave MacMillan, 2001.

Hasday, Judy L. *Kristi Yamaguchi.* New York: Chelsea House, 2007.

Hasegawa, Yoshino Tajiri, and Keith Boettcher, eds. *Success Through Perseverance: Japanese-Americans in the San Joaquin Valley.* Fresno, CA: Japanese-American Project, San Joaquin Valley Library System, 1980.

Hata, Don, and Nadine Hata. "George Shima: "The Potato King of California." *Journal of the West* (January 1986): 55–63.

Hatamiya, Leslie T. *Righting a Wrong: Japanese Americans and the Passage of the Civil Liberties Act of 1988.* Palo Alto, CA: Stanford University Press, 1993.

Hawkins, John. "Politics, Education, and Language Policy: The Case of Japanese Language Schools in Hawaii." *Amerasia* 5:1 (1978): 39–56.

Hayashi, Bruce Masaru. *Democratizing the Enemy: The Japanese American Internment.* Princeton, NJ: Princeton University Press, 2004.

Heco, Joseph. *Narrative of a Japanese.* Ed. James Murdoch. San Francisco: Japanese Publishing Association, 1950.

Hedrick, Basil C., and Anne K. Hedrick. *Historical and Cultural Dictionary of Nepal.* Metuchen, NJ: Scarecrow, 1972.

Hein, Jeremy. *Ethnic Origins: The Adaptation of Cambodian and Hmong Refugees in Four American Cities.* New York: Russell Sage Foundation, 2006.

———. *Ethnic Origins: History, Politics, Culture, and Adaptation of Cambodian and Hmong Refugees in Four American Cities.* New York: Russell Sage Foundation, 2006.

———. *From Vietnam, Laos, and Cambodia: A Refugee Experience in the United States.* New York: Twayne, 1995.

Helweg, Arthur W. *Strangers in a Not-So-Strange Land: Indian American Immigrants in the Global Age.* Belmont, CA: Wadsworth, 2004.

Helweg, Arthur W., and Usha M. Helweg. *An Immigrant Success Story: East Indians in America.* Philadelphia: University of Pennsylvania Press, 1990.

Henkin, Alan B., and Liem Thanh Nguyen. *Between Two Cultures: The Vietnamese in America.* Saratoga, CA: Century Twenty One, 1981.

Herskoovitz, Jon. "U.S. Hotel Dreams and Barons Born in India." *India Bulletin* 15 (May 2004).

Hill, David Lee "Tex." *"Tex" Hill: Flying Tiger.* Spartanburg, SC: Altman Printing, 2003.

Hing, Bill Ong. *Making and Remaking Asian America Through Immigration Policy 1850–1990.* Palo Alto, CA: Stanford University Press, 1993.

Hirabayashi, Lane Ryo, Akemi Kikumura-Yano, and James A. Hirabayashi, eds. *New Worlds, New Lives: Globalization and People of Japanese Descent in the Americas and from Latin America in Japan.* Palo Alto, CA: Stanford University Press, 2002.

Hirabayashi v. United States 320 U.S. 81 (1943).

Hirobe, Izumi. *Japanese Pride, American Prejudice: Modifying the Exclusion Clause of the 1924 Immigration Act.* Palo Alto, CA: Stanford University Press, 2001.

Hirschman, Charles, and Morrison G. Wong. "The Extraordinary Educational Attainment of Asian Americans: A Search for Historical Evidence and Explanations." *Social Forces* 65:1 (September 1986): 1–27.

Hirschman, Charles, Philip Kasinitz, and Josh DeWind, eds. *The Handbook of International Migration: The American Experience.* New York: Russell Sage Foundation, 1999.

"Historic Ads." *Filipino American National Historical Society Journal* 4 (1996): 68–70.

Hodges, Graham Russell. *Anna May Wong: From Laundryman's Daughter to Hollywood Legend.* New York: Palgrave Macmillan, 2004.

Holliday, J.S. *The World Rushed In: The California Gold Rush Experience.* Norman: University of Oklahoma Press, 2002.

Holmes, T. Michael. *The Specter of Communism in Hawaii.* Honolulu: University of Hawai'i Press, 1994.

Hom, Marlon K. *Songs of Gold Mountain: Cantonese Folksongs on the American Experience.* Berkeley: University of California Press, 1987.

Hom, Sharon K., ed. *Chinese Women Traversing Diaspora: Memoirs, Essays, and Poetry.* New York: Garland, 1983.

Hones, Donald, and Cher Cha. *Educating New Americans: Immigrant Lives and Learning.* Philadelphia: Lawrence Erlbaum, 1999.

hooks, bell. *Reel to Real: Race, Sex and Class at the Movies.* New York: Routledge, 1996.

Hoover, Karl. "The Hindu Conspiracy in California, 1913–1918." *German Studies Review* 8:2 (May 1985).

Hopkins, MaryCarol. *Braving a New World: Cambodian (Khmer) Refugees in an American City.* Westport, CT: Bergin and Garvey, 1996.

Horowitz, Irving Louis, ed. *Science, Sin, and Scholarship: The Politics of Reverend Moon and the Unification Church.* Cambridge, MA: MIT Press, 1978.

Hosokawa, Bill. *JACL in Quest of Justice.* New York: William Morrow, 1982.

———. *Nisei: The Quiet Americans.* New York: William Morrow, 1969.

Houston, Jeanne Wakatsuki, and James D. Houston. *Farewell to Manzanar: A True Story of Japanese American Experience During and After the World War II Internment.* Boston: Houghton Mifflin, 2002.

Howe, Kenneth. "Indo-Americans Form New Bank to Serve a Growing Community." *San Francisco Business Times* 6 (February 23, 1987).

Howe, Russell Warren. *The Hunt for "Tokyo Rose."* Lanham, MD: Madison Books, 1990.

Hsiang-shui, Chen. *Chinatown No More: Taiwan Immigrants in Contemporary New York.* Ithaca, NY: Cornell University Press, 1992.

Hsu, Hsuan L. "Personality, Race, and Geopolitics in Joseph Heco's Narrative of a Japanese." *Biography* 29:2 (Spring 2006): 273–306.

Hsu, Hua. "Ethnic Media Grows Up." *Colorline* 5:3 (Fall 2002): 7–9.

Hsu, Madeline Yuan-yin. *Dreaming of Gold, Dreaming of Home: Transnationalism and Migration Between the United States and South China, 1882–1943.* Palo Alto, CA: Stanford University Press, 2000.

Hurh, Won Moo, and Kwang Chung Kim. "Religious Participation of Korean Immigrants in the United States." *Journal for the Scientific Study of Religion* 29 (1990): 19–34.

Hurh, Won Moo. *The Korean Americans.* Westport, CT: Greenwood, 1998.

Hurst, G. Cameron, III. *Armed Martial Arts of Japan: Swordsmanship and Archery.* New Haven, CT: Yale University Press, 1998.

Huston, Peter. *Tongs, Gangs, and Triads: Chinese Crime Groups in North America.* Boulder, CO: Paladin, 1995.

Hutchinson, Edward P. *Legislative History of American Immigration Policy, 1798–1965.* Philadelphia: University of Pennsylvania Press, 1981.

Hwang, Sean-Shong, Rogelio Saenz, and Benigno E. Aguirre. "Structural and Assimilationist Explanations of Asian American Intermarriage." *Journal of Marriage and the Family* 59 (1997): 758–72.

Ichioka, Yuji. "*Amerika Nadeshiko*: Japanese Immigrant Women in the United States, 1900–1924." *Pacific Historical Review* 49:2 (May 1980): 339–57.

———. "'Attorney for the Defense': Yamato Ichihashi and Japanese Immigration." *Pacific Historical Review* 55:2 (May 1986): 192–225.

———. *Before Internment: Essays in Prewar Japanese American History.* Ed. Gordon H. Chang and Eiichiro Azuma. Stanford, CA: Stanford University Press, 2006.

———. "A Historian by Happenstance." *Amerasia* 26:1 (2000): 32–53.

———. *The Issei: The World of the First Generation Japanese Immigrants, 1885–1924.* New York: Free Press, 1988.

———. "Japanese Associations and the Japanese Government: A Special Relationship, 1906–1926." *Pacific Historical Review* 46 (1977): 409–37.

Inkelas, Karen Kurotsuchi. "Diversity's Missing Minority: Asian Pacific American Undergraduates' Attitudes Toward Affirmative Action." *Journal of Higher Education* 74:6 (November–December 2003): 601–40.

Inkelas, Karen Kurotsuchi. *Racial Attitudes and Asian Pacific Americans: Demystifying the Model Minority.* New York: Routledge, 2006.

Inouye, Daniel K., with Lawrence Elliott. *Journey to Washington.* Englewood Cliffs, NJ: Prentice-Hall, 1967.

Irons, Peter. *Justice at War.* New York: Oxford University Press, 1983; Berkeley: University of California Press, 1993.

———, ed. *Justice Delayed: The Record of the Japanese American Internment Cases.* Middletown, CT: Wesleyan University Press, 1989.

Irwin, Wallace. *Letters of a Japanese Schoolboy.* Reprint ed. Upper Saddle River, NJ: Literature House, 1969.

Isaac, Allan Punzalan. *American Tropics: Articulating Filipino America.* Minneapolis: University of Minnesota Press, 2006.

Ishi, Tomoji. "Class Conflict, the State and Linkage: The International Migration of Nurses from the Philippines." *Berkeley Journal of Sociology* 32 (1987): 281–312.

Iwamoto, Gary. "Rise and Fall of an Empire." *International Examiner,* August 17–September 7, 2005, 16.

Iwata, Masakazu. *Planted in Good Soil: A History of the Issei in United States Agriculture.* New York: Peter Lang, 1992.

Jackson, Carl T. *Vedanta for the West: The Ramakrishna Movement in the United States.* Bloomington: Indiana University Press, 1994.

Jaffrey, Madhur. *An Invitation to Indian Cooking.* New York: Alfred A. Knopf, 1973.

Janes, Craig R. *Migration, Social Change, and Health: A Samoan Community in Urban California.* Palo Alto, CA: Stanford University Press, 2006.

Japanese American Curriculum Project. "Keisaburo Koda." *Japanese American Journey: The Story of a People.* Ed. Florence M. Hongo. San Mateo, CA: JACP, 1985.

Japanese American Historical Society of Southern California. *Nanka Nikkei Voices: Little Tokyo, Changing Times, Changing Faces.* Vol. 3. Los Angeles: Japanese American Historical Society of Southern California, 2004.

Jensen, Joan M. *Passage from India: Asian Indian Immigrants in North America.* New Haven, CT: Yale University Press, 1988.

Jo, Moon H. *Korean Immigrants and the Challenge of Adjustment.* Westport, CT: Greenwood, 1999.

Johnson, Douglas P. "Individual Strength, United Voice—Theme of AAHOA Convention." *India Tribune,* May 1, 2004.

Johnson, K. Paul. *Initiates of Theosophical Masters.* Albany: State University of New York, 1995.

Joshi, Khyati Y. *New Roots in America's Sacred Ground: Religion, Race, and Ethnicity in Indian America.* New Brunswick, NJ: Rutgers University Press, 2006.

Journal of Asian American Studies. Baltimore: Johns Hopkins University Press for the Association of Asian American Studies, 1997–present.

Kachi, Teruko Okada. *The Treaty of 1911 and the Immigration and Alien Land Law Issued Between the United States and Japan, 1911–1913.* New York: Arno, 1978.

Kafka, Phillipa. *On the Outside Looking In(dian): Indian Women Writers at Home and Abroad.* New York: P. Lang, 2003.

Kalita, S. Mitra. *Suburban Sahibs: Three Immigrant Families and Their Passage from India to America.* Piscataway, NJ: Rutgers University Press, 2003.

Kamath, M.V. *The United States and India, 1776–1976.* Washington, DC: Indian Embassy, 1976.

Kang, K. Connie. "Harry Kitano, 76; UCLA Professor, Expert on Race Relations." *Los Angeles Times,* October 24, 2002.

———. "Yuji Ichioka, 66; Led Way in Studying Lives of Asian Americans." *Los Angeles Times,* September 7, 2002.

Karagueuzian, Dikran. *Blow It Up! The Black Student Revolt at San Francisco State College and the Emergence of Dr. Hayakawa.* Boston: Gambit, 1971.

Kashima, Tetsuden. *Judgment Without Trial: Japanese American Imprisonment During World War II.* Seattle: University of Washington Press, 2003.

Kaur, Tejinder. "Cultural Dilemmas and Displacements of Immigrants in Jhumpa Lahiri's *The Namesake.*" *Journal of Indian Writing in English* 32:2 (2004): 34–44.

Kennedy, Randall. *Interracial Intimacies: Sex, Marriage, Identity, and Adoption.* New York: Pantheon, 2003.

Kerber, Linda. *No Constitutional Rights to Be Ladies: Women and the Obligations of Citizenship.* New York: Hill and Wang, 1998.

Kerkvliet, Melinda Tria. *Unbending Cane: Pablo Manlapit, a Filipino Labor Leader in Hawai'i.* Honolulu: Office of Multicultural Student Services, University of Hawai'i at Manoa, 2002.

Kessler, Lauren. "Fettered Freedoms: The Journalism of World War II Japanese Internment Camps." *Journalism History* 15 (1988): 60–69.

Khandelwal, Madhulika S. *Becoming American, Being Indian: An Immigrant Community in New York City.* Ithaca, NY: Cornell University Press, 2002.

"Khoua Her's Story." *Hmong Times,* November 16, 2000.

Kibria, Nazli. *Becoming Asian American: Second-Generation Chinese and Korean American Identities.* Baltimore: Johns Hopkins University Press, 2002.

———. *Family Tightrope: The Changing Lives of Vietnamese Americans.* Princeton, NJ: Princeton University Press, 1993.

Kim, Elaine. *Asian American Literature: An Introduction to the Writings and Their Social Context.* Philadelphia: Temple University Press, 1982.

Kim, Hyung-Chan, ed. *Asian Americans and Congress: A Documentary History.* Westport, CT: Greenwood, 1996.

———, ed. *Dictionary of Asian American History.* New York: Greenwood, 1986.

———, ed. *Distinguished Asian Americans: A Biographical Dictionary.* Westport, CT: Greenwood, 1999, 97.

———, ed. *The Korean Diaspora: Historical and Sociological Studies of Korean Immigration and Assimilation in North America.* Santa Barbara, CA: ABC-CLIO, 1977.

Kim, Hyung-Chan, and Cynthia C. Mejia, eds. *The Filipinos in America, 1898–1974: A Chronology and Fact Book.* Dobbs Ferry, NY: Oceana, 1976.

Kim, Rebecca. "Asian American Evangelicals: Ethnic, Multiethnic, or White Campus Ministries?" *Sociology of Religion* 65:1 (Spring 2004): 19–34.

Kim, Thomas P. *The Racial Logic of Politics: Asian Americans and Party Competition.* Philadelphia: Temple University Press, 2007.

Kim, Warren Y. *Koreans in America.* Seoul, South Korea: Po Chin Chai, 1971.

Kimball, Richard C., and Barney Noel. *Native Sons of the Golden West.* Charleston, SC: Arcadia, 2005.

Kimura, Yukiko. *Issei: Japanese Immigrants in Hawaii.* Honolulu: University of Hawai'i Press, 1988.

King, Haitung, and Frances B. Locke. "Chinese in the United States: A Century of Occupational Transition." *International Migration Review* 14:1 (1980): 15–42.

Kitagawa, Joseph M., ed. *The Religious Traditions of Asia: Religion, History, and Culture.* New York: MacMillan, 1989.

Kitano, Harry H.L. *Japanese Americans: The Evolution of a Subculture.* Englewood Cliffs, NJ: Prentice Hall, 1969, 1976.

———. *Race Relations.* Englewood Cliffs, NJ: Prentice Hall, 1974.

Kitano, Harry H.L., and Roger Daniels. *American Racism: Exploration of the Nature of Prejudice.* Englewood Cliffs, NJ: Prentice-Hall, 1970.

———. *Asian Americans: Emerging Minorities.* 3rd ed. Upper Saddle River, NJ: Prentice Hall, 2001.

———. *Generations and Identity: The Japanese American.* Needham Heights, MA: Ginn, 1993.

Kitano, Harry H.L., and S. Sue. "The Model Minorities." *Journal of Social Issues* 29:2 (1973).

Kittler, Pamela Goyan, and Kathrun P. Sucher. *Food and Culture.* 4th ed. Belmont, CA: Wadsworth/Thomson Learning, 2004.

Kiyama, Henry. *The Four Immigrants Manga: A Japanese Experience in San Francisco, 1904–1924.* Trans. and ed. Frederik L. Schodt. Berkeley, CA: Stone Bridge, 1999.

Kiyota, Minoru, and Linda Klepinger Keenan. *Beyond Loyalty: The Story of a Kibei.* Honolulu: University of Hawai'i Press, 1997.

Klatzkin, Amy, ed. *A Passage to the Heart: Writings from Families with Children from China.* St. Paul, MN: Yeong and Yeong, 2001.

Knippling, Alpana Sharma. *New Immigrant Literatures in the United States: A Sourcebook to Our Multicultural Literary Heritage.* Westport, CT: Greenwood, 1996.

Koehn, Peter H., and Xiao-huang Yin, eds. *The Expanding Roles of Chinese Americans in U.S.-China Relations: Transnational Networks and Trans-Pacific Interactions.* Armonk, NY: M.E. Sharpe, 2002.

Koestler-Grack, Rachel A. *Michelle Kwan.* New York: Chelsea House, 2007.

Koltyk, Jo Ann. *New Pioneers in the Heartland: Hmong Life in Wisconsin.* Boston: Allyn and Bacon, 1998.

Kondo, Dorinne. *About Face: Performing Race in Fashion and Theater.* New York: Routledge, 1997.

Korematsu v. United States 323 U.S. 214 (1944).

Koshy, Susan. "Category Crisis: South Asian Americans and Questions of Race and Ethnicity." *Diaspora* 7:2 (1998): 285–320.

Kotani, Roland. *The Japanese in Hawaii: A Century of Struggle.* Honolulu: Hawaii Hochi, 1985.

Kramer, Eric Mark, ed. *The Emerging Monoculture: Assimilation and the "Model Minority."* Westport, CT: Praeger, 2003.

Krohn, Katherine. *Vera Wang.* Minneapolis, MN: Twenty-first Century Books, 2007.

Kumar, Amitava. *Bombay, London, New York.* New York: Routledge, 2002.

Kurahashi, Yuko. *Asian American Culture on Stage: The History of the East West Players.* New York: Garland, 1999.

Kuramitsu, Kristine C. "Internment and Identity in Japanese American Art." *American Quarterly* 47:4 (December 1995): 619–58.

Kurashige, Lon. *Japanese American Celebration and Conflict: A History of Ethnic Identity and Festival, 1934–1990.* Berkeley: University of California Press, 2002.

Kurien, Prema. "Religion, Ethnicity and Politics: Hindu and Muslim Indian Immigrants in the United States." *Ethnic and Racial Studies* 24:2 (2001): 263–93.

Kwan, Michelle. *Michelle Kwan: Heart of a Champion, an Autobiography.* New York: Scholastic, 1997.

Kwon, Ho-Youn, Kwang Chung Kim, and R. Stephen Warner, eds. *Korean Americans and Their Religions: Pilgrims and Missionaries from a Different Shore.* University Park: Pennsylvania State University Press, 2001.

Kwong, Peter. *Chinatown, N.Y.: Labor and Politics, 1930–1950.* New York: New Press, 2001.

———. *Forbidden Workers: Illegal Chinese Immigrants and American Labor.* New York: New Press, 1997.

Kwong, Peter. *The New Chinatown.* Rev. ed. New York: Hill and Wang, 1996.

Kwong, Peter, and Dusanka Misocevic. *Chinese America: The Untold Story of America's Oldest New Community.* New York: New Press, 2005.

La Duke, Betty. "On the Right Road: The Life of Mine Okubo." *Art Education* 40:3 (May 1987): 42–48.

LaBrack, Bruce, and Karen Leonard. "Conflict and Compatibility in Punjabi-Mexican Immigrant Families in Rural California, 1915–1965." *Journal of Marriage and the Family* 46:3 (August 1984): 527–37.

Laderman, Gary, and Luis D. Leon. *Religion and American Cultures: An Encyclopedia of Traditions, Diversity, and Popular Expressions.* Santa Barbara, CA: ABC-CLIO, 2003.

LaFeber, Walter. *The Clash: A History of U.S.–Japan Relations.* New York: W.W. Norton, 1997.

Lai, Eric, and Dennis Arguelles, eds. *The New Face of Asian Pacific America: Numbers, Diversity and Change in the 21st Century.* San Francisco: AsianWeek, 2003.

Lai, Him Mark. *Becoming Chinese American: A History of Communities and Institutions.* Walnut Creek, CA: AltaMira, 2004.

———. "The Historical Development of the Chinese Consolidated Benevolent Association/Huiguan System." *Chinese America, History and Perspectives* 1 (1987): 13–51.

———. "Roles Played by Chinese in America During China's Resistance to Japanese Aggression and During World War II." *Chinese America: History and Perspective* 11 (1997): 75–128.

———. "To Bring Forth a New China, to Build a Better America: The Chinese Marxist Left in America to the 1960's." *History and Perspectives.* San Francisco: Chinese Historical Society of America, 1992.

Lai, James S., Wendy Tam Cho, Thomas Kim, and Okiyoshi Takeda. "Asian Pacific American Campaigns, Elections and Elected Officials." *PS: Political Science & Politics* 3 (2001): 611–17.

Lai, Jim Mark. "Retention of the Chinese Heritage." *Chinese America: History & Perspectives* (2000): 10–27.

Lam, Andrew. *Perfume Dreams: Reflections on the Vietnamese Diaspora.* Berkeley, CA: Heyday, 2005.

Lau, Estelle T. *Paper Families: Identity, Immigration Administration, and Chinese Exclusion.* Durham, NC: Duke University Press, 2006.

Lawler, Andrew. "Asian-American Scientists: Silent No Longer: 'Model Minority' Mobilizes." *American Association for the Advancement of Science* 290:5494 (November 2000): 1072–77.

Leba, John Kong. *The Vietnamese Entrepreneurs in the U.S.A.: The First Decade.* Houston, TX: Zieleks, 1985.

Lee, Anthony W. *Picturing Chinatown: Art and Orientalism in San Francisco.* Berkeley: University of California Press, 2001.

Lee, Bobbie. "Commodore Stockton: 100 Years of Struggle." *AsianWeek* 11:17 (December 1989): 14.

Lee, Cathy. "The Perils of 'Parachute Kids.'" *AsianWeek,* July 8, 1999.

Lee, Douglas W. "The Overseas Chinese Affairs Commission and the Politics of Patriotism in Chinese America in the Nanking Era, 1928–1945." *Annals of the Chinese Historical Society of the Pacific Northwest 1984.* Bellingham: Western Washington University Press, 1984.

Lee, Erika. *At America's Gates: Chinese Immigration During the Exclusion Era, 1882–1943*. Chapel Hill: University of North Carolina Press, 2003.

Lee, Geok Boi, ed. *Singaporeans Exposed: Navigating the Ins and Outs of Globalisation*. Singapore: Landmark, 2001.

Lee, Helen Morton. *Tongans Overseas: Between Two Shores*. Honolulu: University of Hawai'i Press, 2003.

Lee, Joann. *Asian American Actors: Oral Histories of Stage, Screen and Television*. Jefferson, NC: McFarland, 2000.

Lee, Jonathan H.X. *Auburn's Joss House: Preserving the Past for the Future (The Auburn Chinese Ling Ying Association House)*. Auburn, CA: Auburn Joss House Museum and Chinese History Center, 2004.

———. *Hanford's Taoist Temple and Museum (#12 China Alley): The Preservation of a Chinese-American Treasure*. Foreword by Vivian-Lee Nyitray. Hanford, CA: Hanford Taoist Temple Preservation Society, 2004.

———. *The Temple of Kwan Tai: California Historic Landmark No. 927—Celebrating Community and Diversity*. Mendocino, CA: Temple of Kwan Tai, 2004.

Lee, Josephine. *Performing Asian America: Race and Ethnicity on the Contemporary Stage*. Philadelphia: Temple University Press, 1997.

Lee, Lee C., and Nolan W.S. Zane, eds. *Handbook of Asian American Psychology*. Thousand Oaks, CA: Sage, 1998.

Lee, Linda. *The Bruce Lee Story*. Burbank, CA: Ohara, 1989.

Lee, Manwoo, Ronald McLaurin, and Chung-in Moon. *Alliance Under Tension: The Evolution of South Korean–U.S. Relations*. Boulder, CO: Westview, 1988.

Lee, Rachel C. *The Americas of Asian American Literature: Gendered Fictions of Nation and Transnation*. Princeton, NJ: Princeton University Press, 1999.

Lee, Robert G. *Orientals: Asian Americans in Popular Culture*. Philadelphia: Temple University Press, 1999.

Lee, Rose Hum. *The Chinese in the United States of America*. Hong Kong: Hong Kong University Press, 1960.

———. "The Decline of Chinatowns in the United States." *American Journal of Sociology* 54 (March 1949): 422–32.

Lee, Sharon, and Keiko Yamanaka. "Patterns of Asian American Intermarriage and Marital Assimilation." *Journal of Comparative Family Studies* 21 (1990): 287–305.

Lee, Sharon, and Marilyn Fernandez. "Trends in Asian American Racial/Ethnic Intermarriage: A Comparison of 1980 and 1990 Census Data." *Sociological Perspectives* 41 (1998): 323–42.

Lee, Wen Ho, and Helen Zia. *My Country Versus Me: The Firsthand Account by the Los Alamos Scientist Who Was Falsely Accused of Being a Spy*. New York: Hyperion, 2001.

LeMay, Michael C. *From Open Door to Dutch Door: An Analysis of U.S. Immigration Policy Since 1820*. New York: Praeger, 1987.

Leonard, Karen Isaken. "Historical Constructions of Ethnicity: Research on Punjabi Immigrants in California." *Journal of American Ethnic History* 12:4 (Summer 1993): 3–27.

———. *Making Ethnic Choices: California's Punjabi Mexican Americans*. Philadelphia: Temple University Press, 1992.

———. *The South Asian Americans*. Westport, CT: Greenwood, 1997.

Leonard, Kevin Allen. "'Is This What We Fought For?' Japanese Americans and Racism in California, the Impact of World War II." *Western Historical Quarterly* 21:4 (November 1990): 463–82.

Leong, Russell, ed. *Moving the Image: Independent Asian Pacific American Media Arts*. Los Angeles: UCLA Asian American Studies Center Press, 1991.

Leventhal, Frances. "Commodore Stockton Elementary: S.F. Chinatown School Faces New Challenges." *AsianWeek* 10:31 (March 1989): 24.

Levine, Daniel. "First Indo-American Bank Changes Moniker, Seeks Broader Clientele." *San Francisco Business Times* 10 (August 4, 1995).

Levinson, David, and Melvin Ember, eds. *American Immigrant Cultures: Builders of a Nation*. New York: Macmillan Reference USA, 1997.

Levithan, David. *You Are Here This Is Now: The Best Young Writers and Artists in America*. New York: Push, 2002.

Li, Laura Tyson. *Madame Chiang Kai-shek: China's Eternal First Lady*. New York: Atlantic Monthly, 2006.

Li, Peter S. "Ethnic Businesses Among Chinese in the U.S." *Journal of Ethnic Studies* 4:3 (1976): 35–41.

Li, Wei. "Anatomy of a New Ethnic Settlement: The Chinese Ethnoburb in Los Angeles." *Urban Studies* 35:3 (1998): 479–501.

———. "Building Ethnoburbia: The Emergence and Manifestation of the Chinese *Ethnoburb* in Los Angeles' San Gabriel Valley." *Journal of Asian American Studies* 2:1 (1999): 1–28.

———. "Los Angeles' Chinese Ethnoburb: From Ethnic Service Center to Global Economy Outpost." *Urban Geography* 19:6 (1998): 502–17.

Li, Wei, Gary A. Dymski, Yu Zhou, Maria Chee, and Carolyn Aldana. "Chinese American Banking and Community Development in Los Angeles County." *Annals of Association of American Geographers* 92:4 (2002): 777–96.

Lien, Pei-te. *The Making of Asian America Through Political Participation*. Philadelphia: Temple University Press, 2001.

———. "Transforming Patterns of Contemporary Asian American Community Politics." *Asian American Policy Review* 4 (2002): 59–73.

Lien, Pei-te, Christian Collet, Janelle Wong, and S. Karthick Ramakrishnan. "Asian Pacific-American Public Opinion and Political Participation." *PS: Political Science & Politics* 3 (2001): 611–17.

Light, Ivan H. *Ethnic Enterprise in America: Business and Welfare Among Chinese, Japanese, and Blacks*. Berkeley: University of California Press, 1972.

———. "From Vice District to Tourist Attraction: The Moral Career of American Chinatowns, 1880–1940." *Pacific Historical Review* 43 (1974): 367–94.

Light, Ivan, and Parminder Bhachu. *Immigration and Entrepreneurship: Culture, Capital and Ethnic Networks*. New Brunswick, NJ: Transaction, 1993.

Light, Ivan, and Steven J. Gold. *Ethnic Economies*. San Diego, CA: Academic, 2000.

Lim, Genny, ed. *The Chinese American Experience*. San Francisco: Chinese Culture Foundation, 1980.

Lim, Shirley, and Amy Ling. *Reading the Literatures of Asian America*. Philadelphia: Temple University Press, 1992.

Lin, Irene. "Journey to the Far West: Chinese Buddhism in America." *Amerasia Journal* 22:1 (1996): 107–32.

Lin, Maya Ying. *Boundaries*. New York: Simon and Schuster, 2000.

Lind, Andrew W. *Hawaii's People*. Honolulu: University of Hawai'i Press, 1980.

Ling, Huping. *Chinese St. Louis: From Enclave to Cultural Community*. Philadelphia, PA: Temple University Press, 2004.

———. *Surviving on the Gold Mountain: A History of Chinese American Women and Their Lives*. Albany: State University of New York Press, 1998.

———. *Voices of the Heart: Asian American Women on Immigration, Work, and Family*. Kirksville, MO: Truman State University Press, 2007.

———, ed. *Asian America: Forming New Community, Expanding Boundaries*. Piscataway, NJ: Rutgers University Press, 2009.

———, ed. *Emerging Voices: Experiences of Underrepresented Asian Americans*. Piscataway, NJ: Rutgers University Press, 2008.

Linh, Dinh, ed. *Night, Again: Contemporary Fiction from Vietnam*. New York: Seven Stories, 1996.

Little, John, ed. *Jeet Kune Do: Bruce Lee's Commentaries on the Martial Way*. Boston: C.E. Tuttle, 1997.

———, ed. *Letters of the Dragon: An Anthology of Bruce Lee's Correspondence with Family, Friends and Fans, 1958–1973*. Boston: C.E. Tuttle, 1998.

———, ed. *Words of the Dragon: Interviews 1958–1973*. Boston: C.E. Tuttle, 1997.

Little Manila: Filipinos in California's Heartland. Documentary film. Written and produced by Marissa Aroy. 2007.

Liu, C.S., and S.-T. Yau, eds. *Chen Ning Yang: A Great Physicist of the Twentieth Century*. Cambridge, MA: International, 1995.

Liu, Eric. *The Accidental Asian: Notes of a Native Speaker*. New York: Vintage, 1999.

Liu, John M., Paul M. Ong, and Carolyn Rosenstein. "Dual Chain Migration: Post-1965 Filipino Immigration to the United States." *International Migration Review* 25:3 (1991): 487–513.

Liu, Miles Xian, ed. *Asian American Playwrights: A Bio-Bibliographical Critical Sourcebook*. Westport, CT: Greenwood, 2002.

Lo, Adrienne, and Angela Reyes, eds. "Relationality: Discursive Constructions of Asian Pacific American Identities." Special issue, *Pragmatics* 14:2–3 (2004).

Lo, Karl, and H. Mark Lai. *Chinese Newspapers Published in North America, 1854–1975*. Washington, DC: Center for Chinese Research Materials, Association of Research Libraries, 1977.

Lobb, Nancy. *Sixteen Extraordinary Asian Americans*. Portland, ME: J. Weston Walch, 1998.

Lobo, Arun Peter, and Joseph J. Salvo. "Changing U.S. Immigration Law and the Occupational Selectivity of Asian Immigrants." *International Migration Review* 32:3 (1998): 737–60.

Londino, Lawrence. *Tiger Woods: A Biography*. Westport, CT: Greenwood, 2005.

Long, Patrick Du Phuoc, and Laura Ricard. *The Dream Shattered: Vietnamese Gangs in America*. Boston: Northeastern University Press, 1996.

Lotchin, Roger W., ed. *The Way We Really Were: The Golden State in the Second Great War*. Urbana: University of Illinois Press, 2000.

Lott, Juanita Tamayo. *Common Destiny: Filipino American Generations*. Lanham, MD: Rowman and Littlefield, 2006.

Louie, Steve, and Glenn Omatsu. *Asian Americans: The Movement and the Moment*. Los Angeles: UCLA Asian American Studies Center Press, 2001.

Louie, Vivian S. *Compelled to Excel: Immigration, Education, and Opportunity Among Chinese Americans*. Palo Alto, CA: Stanford University Press, 2004.

Low, Victor. *The Unimpressible Race: A Century of Educational Struggle by the Chinese in San Francisco*. San Francisco: East/West, 1982.

Lowe, Lisa. *Immigrant Acts: On Asian American Cultural Politics*. Durham, NC: Duke University Press, 1996.

Lu, Jiaxi, ed. *Biographies of Contemporary Chinese Scientists*. Beijing: Science Publisher, 1992.

Lye, Colleen. *America's Asia: Racial Form and American Literature, 1893–1945*. Princeton, NJ: Princeton University Press, 2005.

Ma, L. Eve Armentrout. *Revolutionaries, Monarchists, and Chinatowns: Chinese Politics in the Americas and the 1911 Revolution*. Honolulu: University of Hawai'i Press, 1990.

Ma, Laurence J.C., and Carolyn Cartier, eds. *The Chinese Diaspora: Space, Place, Mobility, and Identity*. New York: Rowman and Littlefield, 2003.

Ma, Marina, and John A. Rallo. *My Son, Yo-Yo*. Hong Kong: Chinese University Press, 1995.

Ma, Sheng-Mei. *The Deathly Embrace: Orientalism and Asian American Identity*. Minneapolis: University of Minnesota Press, 2000.

Magill, Frank N., ed. *The Nobel Prize Winners, Physics*. Pasadena, CA: Salem, 1989.

Mai, Jesse. "Vietnamese-American Entrepreneurship." *Kaufman Center for Entrepreneurial Leadership Clearinghouse on Entrepreneurship Education Digest* 4:2 (July 2004).

Maira, Sunaina. *Desis in the House: Indian American Youth Culture in New York City*. Philadelphia: Temple University Press, 2002.

Maki, Mitchell T., Harry H.L. Kitano, and S. Megan Berthold, eds. *Achieving the Impossible Dream: How Japanese Americans Obtained Redress*. Chicago: University of Illinois Press, 1999.

Manlapit, Pablo. *Filipinos Fight for Justice: Case of the Filipino Laborers in the Big Strike of 1920, Territory of Hawaii*. Honolulu, HI: Kumalae, 1933.

Mansfield-Richardson, Virginia. *Asian Americans and the Mass Media: A Content Analysis of Twenty United States' Newspapers and a Survey of Asian American Journalists*. New York: Garland, 2000.

Mariani, John. *America Eats Out: An Illustrated History of Restaurants, Taverns, Coffee Shops, Speakeasies, and Other Establishments That Have Fed Us for 350 Years*. New York: Lebhar-Friedman, 1999.

Mark, Diane M.L., and Ginger Chih. *A Place Called Chinese America*. Dubuque, IA: Kendall/Hunt, 1993.

Marshall, Grant N., Terry L. Schell, Marc N. Elliott, S. Megan Berthold, and Ci-Ah Chun. "Mental Health of Cambodian Refugees Two Decades After Resettlement in the United

States." *Journal of the American Medical Association* 294:5 (August 3, 2005).

Masaoka, Mike, with Bill Hosokawa. *They Call Me Moses Masaoka: An American Saga.* New York: William Morrow, 1987.

Mathur, L.P. *Indian Revolutionary Movement in the United States of America.* New Delhi: S. Chand, 1970.

Matsumoto, Valerie J. *Farming the Home Place: A Japanese American Community in California, 1919–1982.* Ithaca, NY: Cornell University Press, 1993.

Matsumoto, Valerie J., and Blake Allmendinger, eds. *Over the Edge: Remapping the American West.* Berkeley: University of California Press, 1999.

Matsunaga, Spark M. *The Mars Project: Journeys Beyond the Cold War.* New York: Hill and Wang, 1986.

Matsunaga, Spark M., and Ping Chen. *Rulemakers of the House.* Urbana: University of Illinois Press, 1978.

McCaye, Milton. "U.S. Congressman from Asia." *Saturday Evening Post,* August 2, 1958.

McClain, Charles. *In Search of Equality: The Chinese Struggle Against Discrimination in Nineteenth Century America.* Berkeley: University of California Press, 1994, 1996.

McClain, Charles, ed. *Asian Indians, Filipinos, Other Asian Communities and the Law.* New York: Garland, 1994.

———, ed. *Chinese Immigrants and American Law.* New York: Garland, 1994.

McCunn, Ruthanne Lum. *Chinese American Portraits: Personal Histories 1828–1988.* San Francisco: Chronicle Books, 1988.

———. *Thousand Pieces of Gold: A Biographical Novel.* Boston: Beacon, 1981.

McEwen, Marylu K., Corinne Maekawa Kodama, Alvin N. Alvarez, Sunny Lee, and Christopher T.H. Liang, eds. "Working with Asian American College Students." *New Directions for Student Services.* No. 97. San Francisco: Jossey-Bass, 2002.

McGowen, Tom. *Go for Broke: Japanese Americans in World War II.* New York: F. Watts, 1995.

McGrayne, Sharon Bertsch. *Nobel Prize Women in Science: Their Lives, Struggles and Momentous Discoveries.* Washington, DC: Joseph Henry, 2001.

McKee, Delber L. *Chinese Exclusion Versus the Open Door Policy, 1900–1906: Clashes Over China Policy in the Roosevelt Era.* Detroit, MI: Wayne State University Press, 1977.

McKeown, Adam. "Transnational Chinese Families and Chinese Exclusion, 1875–1943." *Journal of American Ethnic History* 18:2 (Winter 1999): 73–110.

Melendy, Brett. *Asians in America: Filipinos, Koreans, and East Indians.* Boston: Twayne, 1977.

Melendy, H. Brett. "Filipinos in the United States." *Pacific Historical Review* 43:4 (1974): 520–47.

Mendoza-Denton, Norma, and Melissa Iwai. "'They Speak More Caucasian': Generational Differences in the Speech of Japanese-Americans." *Proceedings of the First Annual Symposium About Language and Society—Austin* 33 (1993): 58–67.

Miller, Davis. *The Tao of Bruce Lee: A Martial Arts Memoir.* New York: Harmony Books, 2000.

Miller, James, ed. *Chinese Religions in Contemporary Societies.* Santa Barbara, CA: ABC-CLIO, 2006.

Miller, Sally M. *The Ethnic Press in the United States: A Histori-*

cal Analysis and Handbook. Westport, CT: Greenwood, 1987.

Millis, Harry Alvin. *The Japanese Problem in the United States.* New York: Arno, 1978 [1915].

Min, Pyong Gap. *Caught in the Middle: Korean Merchants in America's Multiethnic Cities.* Berkeley: University of California Press, 1996.

———. "The Structure and Social Functions of Korean Immigrant Churches in the United States." *International Migration Review* 26 (1992):1370–94.

Min, Pyong Gap, ed. *Asian Americans: Contemporary Trends and Issues.* Thousand Oaks, CA: Sage, 1995.

Min, Pyong Gap, and Jung Ha Kim. *Religions in Asian America: Building Faith Communities.* Walnut Creek, CA: AltaMira, 2002.

Minh Ha, Trinh. *Woman, Native, Other: Writing Postcoloniality and Feminism.* Bloomington: Indiana University Press, 1989.

Miyares, Ines. *The Hmong Refugee Experience in the United States: Crossing the River.* New York: Garland, 1998.

Monush, Barry. *The Encyclopedia of Hollywood Film Actors: From the Silent Era to 1965.* New York: Applause, 2003.

Moon, Katharine H.S. *Sex Among Allies: Military Prostitution in U.S-Korea Relations.* New York: Columbia University Press, 1997.

Moon, Krystyn. *Yellowface: Creating the Chinese in American Music and Performance, 1850s–1920s.* Piscataway, NJ: Rutgers University Press, 2005.

Moore, Gloria Jean. *The Anglo-Indian Vision.* Melbourne, Australia: AE, 1986.

Moran, Jeffrey. "Chinese Labor for the New South." *Southern Studies* 3:4 (1992): 277–304.

Moran, Rachel F. *Interracial Intimacy: The Regulation of Race and Romance.* Chicago: University of Chicago Press, 2001.

Moreno, Barry. *Encyclopedia of Ellis Island.* Westport, CT: Greenwood, 2004.

Morimoto, Toyotomi. *Japanese Americans and Cultural Continuity: Maintaining Language and Heritage.* New York: Garland, 1997.

Moriyama, Alan Takeo. *Imingaisha: Japanese Emigration Companies and Hawaii 1894–1908.* Honolulu: University of Hawai'i Press, 1985.

Moss, Philip, and Chris Tilly. *Stories Employers Tell: Race, Skill, and Hiring in America.* New York: Russell Sage Foundation, 2003.

Muller, Eric L. *Free to Die for Their Country: The Story of the Japanese American Draft Resisters in World War II.* Chicago: University of Chicago Press, 2001.

Muñoz, Romeo S. *Filipino Americans: Journey from Invisibility to Empowerment.* Chicago: Nyala, 2002.

Murase, Ichiro Mike. *Little Tokyo: One Hundred Years in Pictures.* Los Angeles: Visual Communications / Asian American Studies Central, 1983.

Musalo, Karen, Jennifer Moore, and Richard A. Boswell. *Refugee Law and Policy: A Comparative International Approach.* 2nd ed. Durham, NC: Carolina Academic, 2002.

Nair, Mira. *So Far from India.* Mirabai Films: 1982.

Nakamaki, Hirochika. *Japanese Religions at Home and Abroad: Anthropological Perspectives.* New York: RoutledgeCurzon, 2003.

Nakanishi, Don T., and James S. Lai, eds. *Asian American Politics: Law, Participation, and Policy.* Lanham, MD: Rowman and Littlefield, 2003.

Nakanishi, Don T., and Tina Yamano Nishida, eds. *The Asian American Educational Experience: A Source Book for Teachers and Students.* New York: Routledge, 1995.

Narasimham, Raji, and S.P.K. Gupta. *Yellapragada SubbaRow, a Life in Quest of Panacea: An Album in Words and Pictures.* New Delhi: Vigyan Prasar, 2003.

Nash, Phil Tajitsu. "In Memorium." *Amerasia* 25:1 (1999): iv–viii.

National Asian Pacific American Legal Consortium (NAPALC). "Audit of Violence Against Asian Pacific Americans. Remembering: A Ten-Year Retrospective." Washington, DC: NAPALC, 2002.

Nee, Victor G., and Brett de Bary Nee. *Longtime Californ': A Documentary Study of an American Chinatown.* Palo Alto, CA: Stanford University Press, 1986.

Nelson, Emmanuel S., ed. *Bharati Mukherjee: Critical Perspectives.* New York: Garland, 1993.

———, ed. *Reworlding: The Literature of the Indian Diaspora.* Westport, CT: Greenwood, 1992.

Ng, Franklin. *The Taiwanese Americans.* Westport, CT: Greenwood, 1998.

Ng, Franklin, ed. *Asian American Family Life and Community.* New York: Garland, 1998.

Ng, Wendy. *Japanese American Internment During World War II: A History and Reference Guide.* Westport, CT: Greenwood, 2002.

Ngai, Mae. *Impossible Subjects: Illegal Aliens and the Making of Modern America.* Princeton, NJ: Princeton University Press, 2004.

———. "Legacies of Exclusion: Illegal Chinese Immigration During the Cold War Years." *Journal of American Ethnic History* 18:1 (Fall 1998): 3–33.

Nicolosi, Ann Marie. "We Do Not Want Our Girls to Marry Foreigners: Gender, Race, and American Citizenship." *NWSA Journal* 13:3 (Fall 2001): 1–21.

Niedzwiecki, Max, and T.C. Duong. *Southeast Asian American Statistical Profile.* Washington, DC: Southeast Asia Resource Action Center (SEARAC), 2004.

Niiya, Brian, ed. *Encyclopedia of Japanese American History, Updated Edition: An A-to-Z Reference from 1868 to the Present.* New York: Facts on File, 2001.

———, ed. *Japanese American History: An A-to-Z Reference from 1868 to the Present.* New York: Facts on File, 1993.

———, ed. *More Than a Game: Sport in the Japanese American Community.* Los Angeles: Japanese American National Museum, 2000.

Noda, Kesa. *Yamato Colony: 1906–1960 Livingston, California.* Livingston, CA: Livingston-Merced JACL Chapter, 1981.

Noguchi, Isamu. *Isamu Noguchi: A Sculptor's World.* New York: Harper and Row, 1968.

Norell, Irene. *Literature of the Filipino-American in the United States: A Selective and Annotated Bibliography.* San Francisco: R and E Research Associates, 1976.

Nowak, Margaret. *Tibetan Refugees: Youth and the New Generation of Meaning.* New Brunswick, NJ: Rutgers University Press, 1984.

Noyes, Henry. *China Born: Adventures of a Maverick Bookman.* San Francisco: China Books and Periodicals, 1989.

Oades, Riz A. *Beyond the Mask: Untold Stories of U.S. Navy Filipinos.* National City, CA: KCS, 2005.

Oaks, Robert F. "Golden Gate Castaway: Joseph Heco and San Francisco, 1851–1859." *California History* 82:2 (Spring 2004): 38–65.

O'Brien, David J., and Stephen S. Fugita. *The Japanese American Experience.* Bloomington: Indiana University Press, 1991.

O'Connell, Joseph T., ed. *Sikh History and Religion in the Twentieth Century* Toronto: Centre for South Asian Studies, University of Toronto, 1988.

Office of Board Services. *Native Hawaiian Data Book 2006.* Honolulu: Office of Hawaiian Affairs, 2006.

O'Hearn, Claudine, ed. *Half and Half: Writers on Growing Up Biracial and Bicultural.* New York: Pantheon, 1998.

Okamura, Jonathan Y. *Imagining the Filipino American Diaspora: Transnational Relations, Identities, and Communities.* New York: Garland, 1998.

Okamura, Jonathan, ed. *The Japanese American Historical Experience in Hawaii.* Dubuque, IA: Kendall/Hunt, 2001.

Okihiro, Gary Y. *Cane Fires: The Anti-Japanese Movement in Hawaii 1865–1945.* Philadelphia: Temple University Press, 1991.

———. *Island World: A History of Hawai'i and the United States.* Berkeley: University of California Press, 2008.

———. *Margins and Mainstreams: Asians in American History and Culture.* Seattle: University of Washington Press, 1994.

———. *Storied Lives: Japanese American Students and World War II.* Seattle: University of Washington Press, 1999.

Okihiro, Gary, ed. *Privileging Positions: The Sites of Asian American Studies.* Pullman: Washington State University Press, 1995.

Okihiro, Gary Y., John M. Liu, Arthur A. Hansen, and Shirley Hune, eds. *Reflections on Shattered Windows: Promises and Prospects for Asian American Studies,* Pullman: Washington State University Press, 1988.

Ong, Aihwa. *Buddha Is Hiding: Refugees, Citizenship, the New America.* Berkeley: University of California Press, 2003.

———. *Flexible Citizenship: The Cultural Logics of Transnationality.* Ed. O. Aihwa. Durham, NC: Duke University Press, 1999.

Ong, Paul, Edna Bonacich, and Lucie Cheng, eds. *The New Asian Immigration in Los Angeles and Global Restructuring.* Philadelphia: Temple University Press, 1994.

Osajima, Keith. "Pedagogical Considerations in Asian American Studies." *Journal of Asian American Studies* 1:3 (1998): 269–92.

Pan, Erica Y.Z. *The Impact of the 1906 Earthquake on San Francisco's Chinatown.* New York: Peter Lang, 1995.

Pan, Lynn. *Sons of the Yellow Emperor: A History of the Chinese Diaspora.* New York: Kodansha International, 1994.

———, ed. *The Encyclopedia of the Chinese Overseas.* Cambridge, MA: Harvard University Press, 1999.

Park, Lisa Sun-Hee. *Consuming Citizenship: Children of Asian Immigrant Entrepreneurs.* Palo Alto, CA: Stanford University Press, 2005.

Pascoe, Peggy. *Relations of Rescue: The Search for Female Moral Authority in the American West, 1874–1939.* New York: Oxford University Press, 1990.

Patterson, Tom. "Triumph and Tragedy of Dalip Saund." *California Historian* (June 1992).

Pecson, Evaristo Casiano. *Those Who Serve.* Stockton, CA: Muldowney, 1945.

Peffer, George Anthony. *If They Don't Bring Their Women Here: Chinese Female Immigration Before Exclusion.* Champagne: University of Illinois Press, 1999.

Peterson, William. *Japanese Americans: Oppression and Success.* New York: Random House, 1971.

———. "Success Story, Japanese-American Style." *New York Times Magazine,* January 9, 1966, 20–43.

Pfaelzer, Jean. *Driven Out: The Forgotten War Against Chinese Americans.* New York: Random House, 2007.

Pfeifer, Mark, and Kou Yang. *Profile of Hmong American Education Attainment.* Washington, DC: Hmong National Development, 2004.

Pido, Antonio J.A. *The Pilipinos in America: Macro/Micro Dimensions of Immigration and Integration.* New York: Center for Migration Studies, 1985.

Pilapil, Virgilio R. "Remains, Remnants of the Early Filipino Settlements in Southeastern Louisiana." *Filipino American National Historical Society Journal* 4 (1996): 37–41.

Posadas, Barbara M. *The Filipino Americans.* Westport, CT: Greenwood, 1999.

Prasad, Leela, ed. *Live Like the Banyan Tree: Images of the Indian American Experience.* Philadelphia: Balch Institute for Ethnic Studies, 1999.

Prasad, Leela, and David H. Wells. *Live Like the Banyan Tree: Images of the Indian American Experience.* Philadelphia: Balch Institute for Ethnic Studies, 1999.

Puri, Harish. *Ghadar Movement: Ideology, Organisation, and Strategy.* 2nd ed. Amritsar, India: Guru Nanak Dev University, 1993.

Purkayastha, Bandana. *Negotiating Ethnicity: Second-Generation South Asian Americans Traverse a Transnational World.* New Brunswick, NJ: Rutgers University Press, 2005.

Quigley, Christine. *Conjoined Twins: An Historical, Biological and Ethical Issues Encyclopedia.* Jefferson, NC: McFarland, 2003.

Quincy, Keith. *Harvesting Pa Chay's Wheat: The Hmong and America's Secret War in Laos.* Cheney: Eastern Washington University Press, 2000.

———. *Hmong: History of a People.* 2nd ed. Cheney: Eastern Washington University Press, 1995.

———. "Racial Violence Against Asian Americans." *Harvard Law Review* 106 (1993): 1926–43.

Rajan, Gita, and Shailija Sharma, ed. *New Cosmopolitanisms: South Asians in the U.S.* Palo Alto, CA: Stanford University Press, 2006.

Rajghatta, Chidanand. "The Billionaires." *Indian Express North American Edition,* September 29, 2000.

Ramakrishnan, S. Karthick, and Thomas J. Espenshade. "Immigrant Incorporation and Political Participation in the United States." *International Migration Review* 3 (2001): 870–95.

Rangaswamy, Padma. *Indian Americans.* New York: Chelsea, 2007.

———. *Namasté America: Indian Immigrants in an American Metropolis.* University Park: Pennsylvania State University Press, 2000.

Ratti, Rakesh, ed. *A Lotus of Another Color: An Unfolding of the South Asian Gay and Lesbian Experience.* Boston: Alyson, 1993.

Rehnquist, William H. *All the Laws but One: Civil Liberties in Wartime.* New York: Alfred A. Knopf, 1998.

Reimers, David. *Other Immigrants: The Global Origins of the American People.* New York: New York University Press, 2005.

Reinecke, John E. *The Filipino Piecemeal Sugar Strike of 1924–1925.* Honolulu: University of Hawai'i Press, 1996.

———. *A Man Must Stand Up: The Autobiography of a Gentle Activist.* Honolulu: University of Hawai'i Press, 1993.

Revilla, Linda, et al., eds. *Bearing Dreams, Shaping Visions: Asian Pacific American Perspectives.* Pullman: Washington State University Press, 1993.

Reyes, Angela. *Language, Identity, and Stereotype Among Southeast Asian American Youth: The Other Asian.* Mahwah, NJ: Lawrence Erlbaum Associates, 2006.

Reyes, Angela, and Adrienne Lo, eds. *Beyond Yellow English: Toward a Linguistic Anthropology of Asian Pacific America.* New York: Oxford University Press, 2008.

Reyum Institute of Arts and Culture. *Cultures of Independence: An Introduction to Cambodian Arts and Culture in the 1950s and 1960s.* Phnom Penh, Cambodia: Reyum, 2001.

Rich, Mari, ed. *Nobel Prize Winners, 1997–2001, Supplement: An H.W. Wilson Biographical Dictionary.* New York: H.W. Wilson, 2002.

"The Rise and Fall of the American China Lobby." *China: U.S. Policy Since 1945.* Washington, DC: Congressional Quarterly Series, 1980: 6–7, 46–47.

Roberts, J.A.G. *China to Chinatown: Chinese Food in the West.* London: Reaktion Books, 2002.

Robinson, Greg. *By Order of the President: FDR and the Internment of Japanese Americans.* Cambridge, MA: Harvard University, 2001.

Robinson, Katy. *A Single Square Picture: A Korean Adoptee's Search for Her Roots.* New York: Berkley, 2002.

Robinson, W. Courtland. *Terms of Refuge: The Indochinese Exodus and the International Response.* New York: Zed Books, 1998.

Robison, Greg, and Elena Tajima Creef, eds. *Miné Okubo: Following Her Own Road.* Seattle: University of Washington Press, 2007.

Romano, Octavio. "Larry Dulay Itliong: Our Forgotten Hero." *A Report from the TQS Research Center.* Berkeley, CA: TQS, 1999.

Root, Maria P.P. *Filipino Americans: Transformation and Identity.* Thousand Oaks, CA: Sage, 1997.

———. *Love's Revolution: Racial Intermarriage.* Philadelphia: Temple University Press, 1996.

Rosinsky, Natalie. *Amy Tan: Author and Storyteller.* Minneapolis, MN: Compass Point Books, 2006.

Ross, Andrew, ed. *No Sweat: Fashion, Free Trade, and the Rights of Garment Workers.* New York: Verso, 1997.

Rossell, Christine H., and Keith Baker. "The Educational Effectiveness of Bilingual Education." *Research in the Teaching of English* 30 (February 1996): 7–74.

Rothestein, Richard. "Bilingual Education." *Phi Delta Kappan* 79 (May 1998): 672–78.

Rubel, Paula G. *The Kalmyk Mongols: A Study in Continuity and Change.* Bloomington: Indiana University Press, 1967.

Rudrappa, Sharmila. *Ethnic Routes to Becoming American: Indian Immigrants and the Cultures of Citizenship.* New Brunswick, NJ: Rutgers University Press, 2004.

Rumbaut, Rub'en G., and Alejandro Portes, eds. *Ethnicities: Children of Immigrants in America.* Berkeley: University of California Press, 2001.

Rutledge, Paul James. *The Vietnamese Experiences in America.* Bloomington: Indiana University Press, 1992.

Saito, Leland. *Race and Politics: Asian Americans, Latinos, and Whites in a Los Angeles Suburb.* The Asian American Experience Series. Urbana: University of Illinois Press, 1998.

Salter, Christopher L. *San Francisco's Chinatown: How Chinese a Town?* San Francisco: R and E Associates, 1978.

Salyer, Lucy E. *Laws Harsh as Tigers: Chinese Immigrants and the Shaping of Modern Immigration Law.* Chapel Hill: University of North Carolina Press, 1995.

Sam, Sam-Ang, and Moly Sam Chan. *Khmer Folk Dance.* Newington, CT: Khmer Studies Institute, 1987.

San Juan, Epifanio, Jr. *From Exile to Diaspora: Versions of the Filipino Experience in the United States.* Boulder, CO: Westview, 1998.

———. "Fillipino Immigrants in the United States." *Philippine Studies* 48:1 (2000): 121–25.

Sanders, Jimy, Victor Nee, and Scott Sernau. "Asian Immigrants' Reliance on Social Ties in a Multiethnic Labor Market." *Social Forces* 81 (2002): 281–314.

Sandmeyer, Elmer Clarence. *The Anti-Chinese Movement in California.* Chicago: University of Illinois Press, 1991.

Saran, Paramatma, and Edwin Eames, eds. *The New Ethnics. Asian Indians in the United States.* New York: Praeger, 1980.

Saul, Eric, and Don Denevi. *The Great San Francisco Earthquake and Fire, 1906.* Millbrae, CA: Celestial Arts, 1981.

Saund, Dalip Singh. *Congressman from India.* New York: Dutton, 1960.

Savage, Jeff. *Kristi Yamaguchi: Pure Gold.* New York: Maxwell Macmillan, 1993.

Sawada, Miziko. "After the Camps: Seabrook Farms, New Jersey, and the Resettlement of Japanese Americans, 1944–47." *Amerasia Journal* 13:2 (1986–1987): 117–36.

Saxton, Alexander. "The Army of Canton in the High Sierra." *Pacific Historical Review* 35:2 (May 1966): 141–52.

———. *The Indispensable Enemy: Labor and the Anti-Chinese Movement in California.* Berkeley: University of California Press: 1971.

Scharlin, Craig, and Lilia V. Villanueva. *Philip Vera Cruz: A Personal History of Filipino Immigrants and the Farmworkers Movement.* Seattle: University of Washington Press, 2000.

Schiff, Judith Ann. "When East Met West." *Yale Alumni Magazine,* November–December 2004.

Schmit, Peter. "A Federal Appeals Court Upholds California Measure Barring Racial Preferences." *Chronicle of Higher Education,* April 18, 1997, 28–29.

Scott, Robert Lee, Jr. *Flying Tigers: Chennault of China.* New York: Doubleday, 1959.

Seager, Richard Hughes. *Buddhism in America.* New York: Columbia University Press, 1999.

Sear, Katherine. "Raised on American Streets, Cambodian Youths Face Deportation." *Pacific News Service,* August 11, 2004.

The Second Coming of Christ: The Resurrection of the Christ Within You. Los Angeles: Self-Realization Fellowship, 2004.

Seshadri P., and L. Ramakrishnan. "Queering Gender: Transliberation and Our Lesbigay Movements." *Trikone Magazine,* July 1999, 6–8, 18.

Shah, Nayan. *Contagious Divides: Epidemics and Race in San Francisco's Chinatown.* Berkeley: University of California Press, 2001.

Shah, Purvi. "Interpreter of Maladies." *Amerasia Journal* 27:2 (2001): 183–86.

Shankar, Lavina Dhingra, and Rajini Srikanth, eds. *A Part, Yet Apart: South Asians in Asian America.* Philadelphia: Temple University Press, 1998.

Sherman, Josepha. *Jerry Yang and David Filo: Chief Yahoos of Yahoo!* Brookfield, CT: Twenty-First Century, 2001.

Shimabukuro, Robert Sadamu. *Born in Seattle: The Campaign for Japanese American Redress.* Seattle: University of Washington Press, 2001.

Shimakawa, Karen. *National Abjection: The Asian American Body Onstage.* Durham, NC: Duke University Press, 2002.

Shinagawa, Larry Hajime, and Gin Yong Pang. "Asian American Panethnicity and Intermarriage." *Amerasian Journal* 22 (1996): 127–52.

Shrestha, M.N., ed. *Nepalese American Perspectives.* Cincinnati, OH: Association of Nepalese in Midwest America, 1995.

Shridharani, Krishnalal. *The Mahatma and the World.* New York: Duell, Sloan and Pearce, 1946.

———. *My India, My America.* New York: Duell, Sloan and Pearce, 1941.

Sibley, Mulford Quickert, ed. *The Quiet Battle: Writings on the Theory and Practice of Non-Violent Resistance.* Garden City, NY: Doubleday, 1963.

Simon, Charnan. *Midori: Brilliant Violinist.* Chicago: Children's Press, 1993.

Simpson, Caroline Chung. *An Absent Presence: Japanese Americans in Postwar American Culture, 1945–1960.* Durham, NC: Duke University Press, 2001.

Sing, Bill, ed. *Asian Pacific Americans: A Handbook on How to Cover and Portray Our Nation's Fastest Growing Minority Group.* Los Angeles: National Conference of Christians and Jews, 1989.

Singh, Bhai Jodh, and Teja Singh. *The Message of the Sikh Faith.* Stockton, CA: Pacific Coast Khalsa Diwan Society, 1929.

Singha, Bhagata. *Canadian Sikhs Through a Century, 1897–1997.* Delhi: Gyan Sagar, 2001.

Siu, Paul C.P. *The Chinese Laundryman: A Study of Social Isolation.* New York: New York University Press, 1987.

Skandera-Trombley, Laura, ed. *Critical Essays on Maxine Hong Kingston.* New York: G.K. Hall, 1998.

Skenazy, Paul, and Tera Martin, eds. *Conversations with Maxine Hong Kingston.* Jackson: University Press of Mississippi, 1998.

Smedvig, Caroline, ed. *Seiji: An Intimate Portrait of Seiji Ozawa.* Boston: Houghton Mifflin, 1998.

Smelser, Neil J., William Julius Wilson, and Faith Mitchell, eds. *America Becoming: Racial Trends and Their Consequences.* Washington, DC: National Academy, 2001.

Smith, Peter C. "The Social Demography of Filipino Migrations Abroad." *International Migration Review* 10:3 (1976): 307–53.

Smith, Timothy B. *Practicing Multiculturalism: Internalizing and Affirming Diversity in Counseling and Psychology.* Boston: Allyn and Bacon, 2004.

Smith-Hefner, Nancy J. *Khmer American: Identity and Moral Education in a Diasporic Community.* Berkeley: University of California Press, 1999.

Sodhy, Pamela. "Malaysia and the United States in the 1980s." *Asian Survey* 27:10 (October 1987): 1074–94.

Song, Annie. *U.S. Senator Daniel Akaka: A Man of Public Service, Education and Love.* Organization of Chinese Americans, Washington, DC, Chapter.

Song, Min Hyoung. *Strange Future: Pessimism and the 1992 Los Angeles Riots.* Durham, NC: Duke University Press, 2005.

Song, Miri. *Choosing Ethnic Identity.* Cambridge, MA: Blackwell, 2003.

South Asian Public Health Association. "A Brown Paper: The Health of South Asians in the United States." July 2002.

Southeast Asia Resource Action Center. *Directory of Southeast Asian American Community-Based Organizations 2004: Mutual Assistance Associations (MAAs) and Religious Organizations Providing Social Services.* Washington, DC: Southeast Asia Resource Action Center, 2004.

Southeast Asian American Mutual Assistance Association Directory. Washington, DC: Southeast Asia Action Resource Center, 2000.

Spickard, Paul R. *Japanese Americans: The Formation and Transformations of an Ethnic Group.* New York: Twayne, 1996.

Spickard, Paul, Joanne L. Rondilla, and Debbie Hippolite Wright, eds. *Pacific Diaspora: Island Peoples in the United States and Across the Pacific.* Honolulu: University of Hawai'i Press, 2002.

Stepanchuk, Carol, and Charles Wong. *Mooncakes and Hungry Ghosts: Festivals of China.* San Francisco: China Books and Periodicals, 1992.

Stewart, Ian. *The Mahathir Legacy: A Nation Divided, a Region at Risk.* Crows Nest, Australia: Allen and Unwin, 2003.

Stone, Amy. *Maya Lin.* Chicago: Raintree, 2003.

Stooss, Toni, and Thomas Kellein, eds. *Nam June Paik: Video Time, Video Space.* New York: Harry N. Abrams, 1993.

Strauss, Anselm L. "Strain and Harmony in American-Japanese War-Bride Marriages." *Marriage and Family Living* 16:2 (May 1954): 99–106.

Street, Douglas. *David Henry Hwang.* Boise, ID: Boise State University, 1989.

Sue, Stanley, and Nathaniel Wagner, eds. *Asian Americans: Psychological Perspectives.* Ben Lomond, CA: Science and Behavior Books, 1973.

Sung, Betty Lee. *Chinese American Intermarriage.* New York: Center for Migration Studies, 1990.

———. *Mountain of Gold: The Story of the Chinese in America.* New York: MacMillan, 1967.

Suzuki, Bob H. "Education and the Socialization of Asian Americans: A Revisionist Analysis of the 'Model Minority' Thesis." *Amerasia Journal* 4 (1977): 23–51.

Svinth, Joseph R. *Getting a Grip: Judo in the Nikkei Communities of the Pacific Northwest 1900–1950.* Ontario: Electronic Journals of Martial Arts and Sciences, 2003.

Szalay, Lorand B., and Jean A. Bryson. *Filipinos in the Navy: Service, Interpersonal Relations and Cultural Adaptation.* Washington, DC: American Institutes for Research, 1977.

Taguma, Kenji G. "National Redress Activist, Author Michi Weglyn Dies." *Nichi Bei Times,* April 27, 1999.

Taiwan Relations Act (Public Law 96–8). *United States Code,* Title 22, Chapter 48 (1979).

Takahashi, Jere. *Nisei/Sansei: Shifting Japanese American Identities and Politics.* Philadelphia: Temple University Press, 1997.

Takaki, Ronald. *Double Victory: A Multicultural History of America in World War II.* Boston: Little, Brown, 2000.

———. *Ethnic Islands: The Emergence of Urban Chinese America.* New York: Chelsea House, 1994.

———. *From the Land of Morning Calm: The Koreans in America.* New York: Chelsea House, 1994.

———. *A History of Asian Americans: Strangers from a Different Shore.* Boston: Little, Brown, 1989.

———. *India in the West: South Asians in America.* New York: Chelsea House, 1995.

———. *Pau Hana: Plantation Life and Labor in Hawaii 1835–1920.* Honolulu: University of Hawai'i Press, 1983.

———. *Strangers at the Gates Again: Asian American Immigration After 1965.* New York: Chelsea House, 1995.

———. *Strangers from a Different Shore: A History of Asian Americans.* Boston: Little, Brown, 1989.

———. *Strangers from a Different Shore: A History of Asian Americans.* Rev. ed. Boston: Little, Brown, 1998.

Takeda, Okiyoshi. "One Year After the Sit-in: Asian American Students' Identities and Their Support for Asian American Studies." *Journal of Asian American Studies* 4:2 (2001): 147–64.

Takenaka, Ayumi. "The Japanese in Peru: History of Immigration, Settlement, and Racialization." *Latin American Perspectives* 31:3 (May 2004): 77–98.

Takezawa, Yasuko I. *Breaking the Silence: Redress and Japanese American Ethnicity.* Ithaca, NY: Cornell University Press, 1995.

Tamura, Linda. *The Hood River Issei: An Oral History of Japanese Settlers in Oregon's Hood River Valley.* Chicago: University of Illinois Press, 1993.

Taylor, Anne. *Annie Besant: A Biography.* New York: Oxford University Press, 1992.

Taylor, Quintard. "Blacks and Asians in a White City: Japanese Americans and African Americans in Seattle, 1890–1940." *Western Historical Quarterly* 22:4 (November 1991): 401–29.

Tchen, John Kuo Wei. *New York Before Chinatown: Orientalism and the Shaping of American Culture, 1776–1882.* Baltimore: Johns Hopkins University Press, 1999.

Thomas, Gordon, and Max Morgan Witts. *The San Francisco Earthquake.* New York: Stein and Day, 1971.

Thompson, Laurence. *Chinese Religion: An Introduction.* Belmont, CA: Wadsworth, 1989.

Thousand Pieces of Gold. Produced and directed by Nancy Kelly. 105 min. American House Theatrical Films, 1991.

Tiger, Caroline. *Margaret Cho*. New York: Chelsea House, 2007.

Tillet, Gregory. *The Lord of the Second Coming: Sun Myung Moon and the Unification Movement*. Boston: Routledge and Kegan Paul, 1984.

Tiongson, Antonio T., Jr., Edgardo V. Gutierrez, and Ricardo V. Gutierrez, eds. *Positively No Filipinos Allowed: Building Communities and Discourse*. Philadelphia: Temple University Press, 2006.

Todd, Anne M. *Vera Wang*. New York: Chelsea House, 2007.

Tolention, Roland B. "Identity and Difference in 'Filipino/a American' Media Arts." *Amerasia Journal* 23:2 (1997): 137–61.

Tong, Benson. *The Chinese Americans*. Rev. ed. Boulder: University Press of Colorado, 2003.

Torgersen, Gordon M. *A Ten Talent Christian from India: The Story of Yellapragada Subbarow*. New York: American Baptist Foreign Mission Society, 1952.

Totten, George O., III, and H. Eric Schockman, eds. *Community in Crisis: The Korean American Community After the Los Angeles Civil Unrest of April 1992*. Los Angeles: University of Southern California, Center for Multiethnic and Transnational Studies, 1994.

Tran, Barbara, ed. *Watermark: Vietnamese American Poetry and Prose*. New York: Asian American Writers' Workshop, 1998.

"A Tribute to Mine Okubo." *Amerasia Journal* 30:2 (2004).

Trout, Polly. *Eastern Seeds, Western Soil: Three Gurus in America*. Mountain View, CA: Mayfield, 2000.

Tsai, Shih-shan Henry. *The Chinese Experience in America*. Bloomington: Indiana University Press, 1986.

———. *China and Overseas Chinese in the United States, 1868–1911*. Fayetteville: University of Arkansas Press, 1983.

Tseng, Yen-Fen. "Beyond Little Taipei: Taiwanese Immigrant Businesses in Los Angeles." *International Migration Review* 29:10 (1995): 33–58.

———. "The Mobility of Entrepreneurs and Capital: Taiwanese Capital-Linked Migration." *International Migration* 38:2 (June 2000): 143–68.

Tsuchida, Nobuya, ed. *Asian and Pacific American Experiences: Women's Perspectives*. Minneapolis: University of Minnesota, 1982.

Tuchman, Barbara W. *Stillwell and the American Experience in China, 1911–1945*. New York: Macmillan, 1970.

Tuck, Donald R. *Buddhist Churches of America: Jodo Shinshu*. Lewiston, NY: Edwin Mellen, 1987.

Tucker, Nancy Bernkopf. *Taiwan, Hong Kong, and the United States, 1945–1992: Uncertain Friendships*. New York: Twayne, 1994.

Tweed, Thomas A., and Stephen Prothero, eds. *Asian Religions in America: A Documentary History*. New York: Oxford University Press, 1999.

25 Vietnamese Americans in 25 Years: 1975–2000. San Jose, CA: New Horizon, 2000.

Uchida, Yoshiko. *Desert Exile: The Uprooting of a Japanese American Family*. Seattle: University of Washington Press, 1982.

———. *The Invisible Thread: An Autobiography*. New York: Beech Tree Paperback, 1995.

Ung, Loung. *First They Killed My Father: A Daughter of Cambodia Remembers*. Sydney, Australia: HarperCollins, 2000.

———. *Lucky Child: A Daughter of Cambodia Reunites with the Sister She Left Behind*. New York: HarperCollins, 2005.

United States. Works Projects Administration (California). *The Story of Japanese Farming in California*. San Francisco: R and E Research Associates, 1971 [1957].

United States v. Bhagat Singh Thind, 261 U.S. 204 (1923).

United States v. Sakharam Ganesh Pandit, 273 U.S. 759 (1927).

Unterburger, Amy L., ed. *Who's Who Among Asian Americans*. Detroit: Gale Research, 1994.

Urofsky, Melvin I. *100 Americans Making Constitutional History: A Biographical History*. Washington, DC: Congressional Quarterly, 2004.

U.S. Census Bureau. "The American Community—Asians: 2004." *American Community Survey Reports*, 2007.

———. *Asian-Owned Firms: 2002*. Washington, DC: U.S. Department of Commerce, August 2006.

———. "The Asian Population: 2000." Report C2K-BR/01–16, February 2002.

———. Census 2000, Summary File 3 and 4.

———. *Displaced Person's Act of 1948*. 80th Cong., 2nd sess., 1948.

———. *Statistical Abstract of the United States*. 2001 and 2008 eds. Washington, DC: Government Printing Office, 2000 and 2007.

———. "Voting and Registration in the Election of November 2004." Report P20–542, March 2007.

———. *We the People: Asians in the United States, Census 2000 Special Reports*. December 2004.

———. *Asian-Owned Firms: 2002*. Washington, DC: U.S. Department of Commerce, August 2006.

U.S. Commission on Civil Rights. *Civil Rights Issues Facing Asian Americans in the 1990s*. Washington, DC: Government Printing Office, 1992.

U.S. Department of Education, National Center for Education Statistics. *Profile of Undergraduates in U.S. Postsecondary Institutions: 1999–2000*. Washington, DC, 2002.

U.S. Department of Homeland Security. *Yearbook of Immigration Statistics, 2002*. Washington, DC: Government Printing Office, 2003.

U.S. Government Accountability Office. *Report to the Committee on Banking, Housing, and Urban Affairs, U.S. Senate: International Remittances: Different Estimation Methodologies Produce Different Results*. Washington, DC: Government Printing Office, 2004.

———. *Report to the Committee on Banking, Housing, and Urban Affairs, U.S. Senate: International Remittances: Information on Products, Costs, and Consumer Disclosures*. Washington, DC: Government Printing Office, 2004.

U.S. House of Representatives, Committee on International Relations. *U.S. Domestic Politics and the US-Taiwan-PRC Relationship*. Washington, DC: Government Printing Office, 2002.

Vallangca, Caridad Concepcion, and Jody Bytheway Larson, eds. The Second Wave: Pinay & Pinoy (1945–1960). San Francisco: Strawberry Hill, 1987.

Van Esterik, Penny. *Taking Refuge: Lao Buddhists in North America*. Monographs in Southeast Asian Studies. Tempe: Arizona State University Press, 1992.

van Naerssen, Ton, Ernst Spaan, and Annelies Zoomers, eds. *Global Migration and Development.* New York: Routledge, 2008.

Varadarajan, Tunku. "A Patel Motel Cartel?" *New York Times Magazine,* July 4, 1999, 36–39.

Verma, K.D. *The Indian Imagination: Critical Essays on Indian Writing in English.* New York: St. Martin's, 2000.

Võ, Linda Trinh, and Rick Bonus, eds. *Contemporary Asian American Communities: Intersections and Divergences.* Philadelphia: Temple University Press, 2002.

Volpp, Leti. "American Mestizo: Filipinos and Antimiscegenation Laws in California." *U.C. Davis Law Review* 33 (2000): 795–835.

Wallace, Irving, and Amy Wallace. *The Two.* New York: Simon and Schuster, 1978.

Wampler, Molly Frick. *Not Without Honor: The Story of Sammy Lee.* Santa Barbara, CA: Fithian, 1987.

Wang, An, and Eugene Linden. *Lessons: An Autobiography.* Reading, MA: Addison-Wesley, 1986.

Wang, Emma. "Retrospectives of Chinese American Banks." *Chinese International Daily,* section C, "Southern California Economy," April 28–May 3, 1994.

Wang, Ling-chi. "Structure of Dual Domination: Toward a Paradigm for the Study of the Chinese Diaspora in the U.S." *Amerasia Journal* 21:1–2 (1995): 149–70.

Wang, Ling-chi, and Gungwu Wang, eds. *The Chinese Diaspora: Selected Essays,* vol. 1. Singapore: Times Academic, 1998.

Wang, Xueying, ed. *A View from Within: A Case Study of Chinese Heritage Community Language Schools.* Washington, DC: National Foreign Language Center, 1997.

"The Wang Clan Cornered." *Economist,* May 23, 2002.

War Relocation Authority, U.S. Department of Interior. *WRA: A Story of Human Conservation.* Washington, DC: Government Printing Office, 1946.

Warner, R. Stephen, and Judith G. Wittner. *Gatherings in Diaspora: Religious Communities and the New Immigration.* Philadelphia: Temple University Press, 1998.

Wasson, Tyler, and Gert H. Brieger, eds. *Nobel Prize Winners: An H.W. Wilson Biographical Dictionary.* New York: H.W. Wilson, 1987.

Waters, Tony, and Lawrence E. Cohen. *Laotians in the Criminal Justice System.* Berkeley: California Policy Seminar, 1993.

Wayne M. Collins Papers, BANC MSS 78/177 c, Bancroft Library, University of California, Berkeley.

Weber, Robert L. *Pioneers of Science: Nobel Prize Winners in Physics.* Philadelphia: A. Hilger, 1988.

Wegars, Priscilla. *Polly Bemis: A Chinese American Pioneer.* Cambridge, MA: Backeddy Books, 2003.

Weglyn, Michi. *Years of Infamy: The Untold Story of America's Concentration Camps.* New York: William Morrow, 1976.

Wei Min She (Organization for the People) Labor Committee. *Chinese Working People in America: A Pictorial History.* San Francisco: United Front, 1974.

Wei, Li, ed. *From Urban Enclave to Ethnic Suburb: New Asian Communities in Pacific Rim Countries.* Honolulu: University of Hawai'i Press, 2006: 74–94.

Wei, William. *The Asian American Movement.* Philadelphia: Temple University Press, 1993.

Wepman, Dennis. *Immigration: From the Founding of Virginia to the Closing of Ellis Island.* New York: Facts on File, 2002.

Wertheimer, Andrew B. "Admitting Nebraska's Nisei: Japanese American Students at the University of Nebraska, 1942–1945." *Nebraska History* 83 (Summer 2002): 52–78.

Weston, Michael R. *Jerry Yang and David Filo: The Founders of Yahoo!* New York: Rosen, 2007.

Wilkinson, Kelly. "In the Director's Studio: Tony Bui Talks about *Three Seasons*—and His Early Years in Sunnyvale." *The Sun,* March 31, 1999.

Williams, Raymond Brady. *Religions of Immigrants from India and Pakistan: New Threads in the American Tapestry.* New York: Cambridge University Press, 1988.

Williams-León, Teresa, Cynthia L. Nakashima, eds. *The Sum of Our Parts: Mixed-Heritage Asian Americans.* Philadelphia: Temple University Press, 2001.

Wilson, Ernest. *Diversity and U.S. Foreign Policy: A Reader.* New York: Routledge, 2004.

Wilson, Patrick A., and Hirokazu Yoshikawa. "Experiences of and Responses to Social Discrimination Among Asian and Pacific Islander Gay Men: Their Relationship to HIV Risk." *AIDS Education and Prevention* 16 (2004): 68–83.

Wilson, Robert A., and Bill Hosokawa. *East to America: A History of the Japanese in the United States.* New York: William Morrow, 1980.

Wing, Rick L. *Northern Shaolin Style: Shaolin Number 5 Martial Skill.* San Francisco: Jing Association, 2005.

Wing, Yung. *My Life in China and America,* 1909. Reprint ed. New York: Arno, 1978.

Winters, Loretta I., and Herman DeBose. *New Faces in a Changing America: Multiracial Identity in the 21st Century.* Thousand Oaks, CA: Sage, 2003.

Wiseman, Carter. *I.M. Pei: A Profile in American Architecture.* New York: Harry N. Abrams, 1990.

Wolf, Diane L. "Family Secrets: Transnational Struggles Among Children of Filipino Immigrants." *Sociological Perspectives* 40:3 (1997): 457–82.

Women of South Asian Decent Collective, ed. *Our Feet Walk the Sky.* San Francisco: Aunt Lute, 1993.

Wong, Bernard. *Ethnicity and Entrepreneurship: The New Chinese Immigrants in the San Francisco Bay Area.* Needham Heights, MA: Allyn and Bacon, 1998.

———. *Patronage, Brokerage, Entrepreneurship, and the Chinese Community of New York.* New York: AMS, 1988.

Wong, Deborah. *Speak It Louder: Asian Americans Making Music.* New York: Routledge, 2004.

Wong, Doc-Fai, and Jane Hallander. *Choy Li Fut Kung-fu.* Burbank, CA: Unique, 1989.

Wong, Jade Snow. *Fifth Chinese Daughter.* Seattle: University of Washington Press, 1989.

———. *No Chinese Stranger.* New York: Harper and Row, 1975.

Wong, K. Scott. *Americans First: Chinese Americans and the Second World War.* Cambridge, MA: Harvard University Press, 2005.

Wong, K. Scott, and Sucheng Chan, eds. *Changing America: Constructing Chinese American Identities During the Exclusion Era.* Philadelphia: Temple University Press, 1998.

Wong, Samsong. "The Wen Ho Lee Five." *AsianWeek,* August 27, 2004.

Wong, William. *Yellow Journalist: Dispatches from Asian America.* Philadelphia: Temple University Press, 2001.

Woo, Deborah. *Glass Ceilings and Asian Americans: The New Face of Workplace Barriers.* Walnut Creek, CA: AltaMira, 2002.

Woo, S.B. "Political Clout and Equal Opportunity." *Asian American Policy Review* 10 (2002): 48–50.

Woodbridge, Sally B., and John W. Woodbridge. *San Francisco Architecture: The Illustrated Guide to over 1,000 of the Best Buildings, Parks, and Public Artworks in the Bay Area.* San Francisco: Chronicle Books, 1992.

Woodrum, Eric. "An Assessment of Japanese American Assimilation, Pluralism, and Subordination." *American Journal of Sociology* 87:1 (July 1981): 161.

Worthy, Edmund H. "Yung Wing in America." *Pacific Historical Review* (August 1965): 265–87.

Wright, Alison. *The Spirit of Tibet: Portrait of a Culture in Exile.* Ithaca, NY: Snow Lion, 1998.

Wright, Evan. 1999. "Dance with a Stranger." *LA Weekly,* January 22, 1999.

Wu, Diana Ting Liu. *Asian Pacific Americans in the Workplace.* Walnut Creek, CA: AltaMira, 1997.

Wynne, Robert E. *Reaction to the Chinese in the Pacific Northwest and British Columbia, 1850–1910.* New York: Arno, 1978.

Xieng v. People's National Bank of Washington, 120 Wn.2d 512, 844 (P.2d 389 1993).

Xing, Jun. *Asian America Through the Lens: History, Representations, and Identity.* Walnut Creek, CA: AltaMira, 1998.

Yang, Fenggang. *Chinese Christians in America: Conversion, Assimilation, and Adhesive Identities.* University Park: Pennsylvania State University Press, 1999.

Yang, Kou. "Hmong Americans: Needs, Problems and Community Development." *Hmong Studies Journal* 4 (2003): 1–24.

———. "Hmong Diaspora of the Post-War Period." *Asian Pacific Migration Journal* 12:3 (2003): 271–300.

———. "The Hmong in America: Twenty-Five Years after the U.S. Secret War in Laos." *Journal of Asian American Studies* 4:2 (2001): 165–74.

Yasui v. United States 320 U.S. 115 (1943).

Yee, Alfred. *Shopping at Giant Foods: Chinese American Supermarkets in Northern California.* Seattle: University of Washington Press, 2003.

Yeh, Chiou-ling. "'In the Traditions of China and in the Freedom of America': The Making of San Francisco's Chinese New Year Festivals." *American Quarterly* 56:2 (2004): 395–420.

Yin, Xiao-huang. *Chinese American Literature Since the 1850s.* Urbana: University of Illinois Press, 2000.

Yip, Alethea. "Time Out for Chancellor Tien." *AsianWeek* (July 4–10, 1997).

Yogananda, Paramahansa. *Autobiography of a Yogi.* Los Angeles: Self-Realization Fellowship, 1993.

Yoneda, Karl. *Ganbatte: Sixty-Year Struggle of a Kibei Worker.* Los Angeles: Asian American Studies Center, 1983.

Yoo, David. "Captivating Memories: Museology, Concentration Camps, and Japanese American History." *American Quarterly* 48:4 (1996): 680–99.

———. *Growing Up Nisei: Race, Generation, and Culture Among Japanese Americans of California, 1924–49.* Urbana: University of Illinois Press, 2000.

———. "'Read All About It': Race, Generation and the Japanese American Press, 1925–1941." *Amerasia Journal* 19 (1993): 69–92.

Yoo, David K., ed. *New Spiritual Homes: Religion and Asian Americans.* Honolulu: University of Hawai'i Press, 1999.

Yoo, David, and Ruth H. Chung, eds. *Religion and Spirituality in Korean America.* Urbana: University of Illinois Press, 2008.

Yoo, Paula. *Sixteen Years in Sixteen Seconds: The Sammy Lee Story.* New York: Lee and Low, 2005.

Yoshioka, Marianne R., Quynh Dang, Nanda Shewmangal, Carmen Chan, and Rev. Cheng Imm Tan. Asian Family Violence Report: A Study of the Cambodian, Chinese, Korean, South Asian, and Vietnamese Communities in Massachusetts. Boston: Asian Task Force Against Domestic Violence, 2000.

Yount, Lisa. *Asian-American Scientists.* New York: Facts on File, 1998.

Yu, Eui-Young, and Earl H. Phillips, eds. *Korean Women in Transition at Home and Abroad.* Los Angeles: Center for Korean American and Korean Studies, 1987.

Yu, Eui-Young, and Peter Choe. "Korean Population in the United States as Reflected in the Year 2000 U.S. Census." *Amerasia Journal* 29:3 (2003–2004): 2–21.

Yu, Eui-Young, Peter Choe, and Sang Il Han. "Korean Population in the United States, 2000: Demographic Characteristics and Socio-Economic Status." *International Journal of Korean Studies* 6:1 (Spring–Summer 2002): 71–107.

Yu, Henry. *Thinking Orientals: Migration, Contact, and Exoticism in Modern America.* New York: Oxford University Press, 2001.

Yu, Renqiu. *To Save China, To Save Ourselves: The Chinese Hand Laundry Alliance of New York.* Philadelphia: Temple University Press, 1992.

Yuh, Ji-Yeon. *Beyond the Shadow of Camptown: Korean Military Brides in America.* New York: New York University Press, 2002.

Yung, Eleanor. "Madhouse." *BRIDGE: An Asian American Perspective* (Summer 1978): 35–36.

Yung, Judy. *Unbound Feet: A Social History of Chinese Women in San Francisco.* Berkeley: University of California Press, 1995.

Zamora, Maria C. *Nation, Race & History in Asian American Literature: Re-membering the Body.* New York: Peter Lang, 2008.

Zarni, ed. *Burmese Political Exiles, Their Thoughts and Actions: A Reflection.* Washington, DC: Free Burma Coalition, 2007.

Zelasko, Nancy, and Beth Antunez. *If Your Child Learns in Two Languages: A Parent's Guide for Improving Educational Opportunities for Children Acquiring English as a Second Language.* Washington, DC: National Clearinghouse for Bilingual Education, 2000.

Zhan, Lin, ed. *Asian Americans: Vulnerable Populations, Model Interventions, and Clarifying Agendas.* Boston: Jones and Bartlett, 2003.

Zhao, Xiaojian. *Remaking Chinese America: Immigration, Family, and Community, 1940–1965.* New Brunswick, NJ: Rutgers University Press, 2002.

Zhou, Min. *Chinatown: The Socioeconomic Potential of an Urban Enclave.* Philadelphia: Temple University Press, 1992.

———. "'Parachute Kids' in Southern California: The Educational Experience of Chinese Children in Transnational Families." *Educational Policy* 12:6 (1998): 682–704.

Zhou, Min, and James V. Gatewood, eds. *Contemporary Asian America.* New York: New York University Press, 2000.

Zhou, Min, and James V. Gatewood. *Contemporary Asian America: A Multidisciplinary Reader.* New York: New York University Press, 2000.

Zhow, Mei, and Cai Guoxuan. "Chinese Language Media in the United States: Immigration and Assimilation in American Life." *Qualitative Sociology* 25:3 (Fall 2002): 419–40.

Zhu, Liping. *A Chinaman's Chance: The Chinese on the Rocky Mountain Mining Frontier.* Niwot: University Press of Colorado, 1997.

Zia, Helen. *Asian American Dreams: The Emergence of an American People.* New York: Farrar, Straus and Giroux, 2000.

Zia, Helen, and Susan B. Gall, eds. *Notable Asian Americans.* New York: Gale, 1995.

Zinn, Maxine Baca, and Bonnie Thornton Dill. *Women of Color in U.S. Society.* Philadelphia: Temple University Press, 1994.

Web Sites

Aaron Diamond AIDS Research Center. http://www.adarc.org.

American Physicians of Indian Origins. http://www.aapiusa.org.

Angel Island Immigration Station. http://www.angelisland.org/immigr02.html.

Angkor Dance Troupe. http://www.angkordance.org.

Asian American Hotel Owners Association. http://www.aahoa.com.

Asian American Journalists Association. http://www.aaja.org.

Asian Law Caucus. http://www.asianlawcaucus.org.

Asian/Pacific Gays and Friends. http://www.apgf.org.

AsianWeek. http://www.asianweek.com.

Association for Asian American Studies. http://www.aaastudies.org.

Association for Asian Studies. http://www.aasianst.org.

Association of Indians in America. http://www.aiausa.org.

Association of Korean Political Studies. http://www.akps.org.

Association of Nepalis in the Americas. http://www.anaonline.org.

Azine: Asian American Movement Ezine. http://apimovement.com/.

Buddhist Churches of America. http://buddhistchurchesofamerica.org.

Cambodian American League of Lowell. http://www.cambodianamerican.net/html/sitemap.htm#about.

Cambodian American National Council. http://www.cancweb.org.

Cambodian Living Arts. http://www.cambodianlivingarts.org.

Cambodian Mutual Assistance Association. http://www.cmaalowell.org.

Cambodian-American Heritage, Inc. http://www.cambodianheritage.org.

Cameron House. http://www.cameronhouse.org.

Center for Lao Studies. http://www.laostudies.org.

Center for Philippine Studies, University of Hawai'i at Manoa. http://www.hawaii.edu/cps.

China Books and Periodicals, Inc. http://www.chinabooks.com.

Chinese American Citizens Alliance. http://www.cacanational.org.

Chinese Hospital. http://www.chinesehospital-sf.org.

Chinese Restaurant News. http://www.c-r-n.com.

Council on Islamic-American Relations. http://www.cair.com.

Dillon S. Myer Papers (1934–1966). Including correspondence, memoranda, meeting minutes, newspaper clippings, reports, and speeches. Harry S. Truman Library and Museum, Independence, Missouri. http://www.trumanlibrary.org/hstpaper/myers.htm.

Discover Nikkei. http://www.discovernikkei.org/en.

Edison Uno Papers Web site. Online Archive of California. http://www.oac.cdlib.org/findaid/ark:/13030/ft9t1nb4jd.

Education Data Partnership. Fiscal, Demographic, and Performance Data on California's K–12 Schools. http://www.ed-data.k12.ca.us.

80–20 Initiative. http://www.80–20initiative.net.

Filipinas. http://www.filipinasmag.com.

Filipino American National Historical Society. http://www.fanhs-national.org.

Filipino National Historical Society. http://www.fanhs-national.org.

Formosa Foundation. http://www.formosafoundation.org.

Formosan Association for Public Affairs. http://www.fapa.org.

Gay Asian Pacific Support Network. http://www.gapsn.org.

Guam Society of America. http://www.guamsociety.org.

Hapa Life Magazine. http://www.hapalife.com.

Hmong National Development, Inc. http://www.hndinc.org.

Hsi Lai Temple. http://www.hsilai.org.

Intercollegiate Taiwanese American Students Association. http://www.itasa.org.

Japanese American Citizens League. http://www.jacl.org.

Japanese American National Museum. http://www.janm.org.

Khalsa Diwan Society in Vancouver. http://www.sikhpioneers.com.

Khmer Freedom Committee, Committee Against Anti-Asian Violence (CAAAV). http://www.caaav.org.

Koda Farms. http://www.kodafarms.com.

Korean American Coalition, Los Angeles chapter. http://www.kacla.org.

Korean American Historical Society. http://www.kahs.org.

Korean National Association. http://koreannationalassn.com.

Lao Human Rights Council. http://www.laohumanrightscouncil.org.

Lao Veterans of America. http://www.laoveterans.com.

Little Manila Foundation. http://www.littlemanila.net.

Locke, California. http://www.locketown.com.

Manilatown Heritage Foundation. http://www.manilatown .org.

Midori Official Web site. http://www.gotomidori.com.

Mongol American Cultural Association. http://www .maca-usa.org.

Muslim Students Association. http://www.msanational.org.

Nam June Paik Studios. http://www.paikstudios.com.

National Asian American Telecommunications Association. http://www.naatanet.org.

National Association of Filipino American Associations (NaF-FAA). http://www.naffaa.org.

National Council of Associations of Chinese Language Schools. http://www.ncacls.org.

National Federation of Filipino American Associations (NaF-FAA). http://www.naffaa.org.

National Tongan American Society. http://ntasutah.org.

Native Sons of the Golden West. http://www.nsgw.org.

Nepalese Americas Council. http://www.nepalcouncil.org.

Noguchi Museum. http://www.noguchi.org.

Organization of Chinese Americans. http://www.ocanational .org.

Overseas Compatriot Affairs Commission. http://www.ocac .gov.tw.

Pacific Citizen Web site. http://www.pacificcitizen.org.

Pakistan League of America. http://pakistanleagueofamerica .com.

"Papers of Sudhindra Bose." Special Collections Department, University of Iowa Libraries. http://www.lib.uiowa.edu/ spec-coll/archives/guides/RG99.0147.htm.

Sarah Chang Official Website. http://sarahchang.com.

Secondary School Chinese Language Center. http://www .princeton.edu/ssclc.

Self-Realization Fellowship. http://www.yogananda-srf.org.

Society for Indonesian Americans. http://www.sianews.org.

South Asian Journalists Association. http://www.saja.org.

Sri Lankan American Association. http://www.slaah.org.

Taiwan Economic and Cultural Representative Office. http:// www.taiwanembassy.org/US.

Taiwanese American Citizens League. http://www.tacl.org.

Taiwanese United Fund. http://www.tufusa.org.

Thai American Young Professionals Association. http://www .taypa.org/.

Thai Buddhist Temples in the U.S. http://www.thaiembdc .org/thaicommu/AssoMedia/temples.aspx.

Thai Community Development Center (Thai CDC). http:// thaicdchome.org/cms.

Thai Health and Information Services (THAIS). http://www .thaihealth.org.

Thai Yellow Pages. http://www.thaiyellowpagesusa.com.

Theosophical Society. http://www.theosociety.org.

United Cambodian Community. http://ucclb.org/welcome.

Unrau, Harlan D. "The Evacuation and Relocation of Persons of Japanese Ancestry During World War II: A Historical Study of the Manzanar Relocation Center." National Park Service, 1996. http://www.nps.gov/archive/manz/ hrs/hrst.htm.

U.S. Census Bureau. http://www.census.gov.

U.S. House of Representatives biography. http://bioguide .congress.gov/scripts/biodisplay.pl?index=M000794.

U.S. India Political Action Committee. http://www.usinpac .com.

Vietnamese American Chamber of Commerce. http://www .vacoc.com.

Index

Italic page numbers indicate illustrations. Page numbers followed by *c* denote entries in the chronology.

Khmer Rouge (*continued*)
  Cambodian American literature, 1:107, 108
  Cambodian American music and dance, 1:109
  Cambodian American political and social empowerment, 1:112
  Cambodian American religion, 1:114
  Cambodian American women, 1:116
  deportation of Cambodians, 1:104
Khmer Society of Fresno (California), 1:103
khmoc lan, 1:116
Khorana, Har Gobind, 1:83; 2:315, 325
Khosana, 1:99
Khosla, Vinod, 2:321
Kibei, 2:417, 427–428
Kibei Citizens Council of San Francisco, 2:428
kick boxing, 2:563
Kight, Morris, 1:48
kiken, 2:394
The Killing Fields (film), 1:99, 107, 108
Kim, Chang-jun "Jay," 2:478, 489
Kim, Elaine, 1:203
Kim, In-kon, 2:483
Kim, Myung Mi, 2:491
Kim, Richard Eunkook, 2:490
Kim, Ronyoung, 2:491
Kim, Sil Dong, 1:44
Kim, Willyce, 2:491
Kim-Gibson, Dai Sil, 1:69
Kimoto, Denichi "Jack," 2:408
King, Rodney, 1:17, 30; 2:489, 492
The King and His Friends (Aruego), 1:261
The King and I (musical), 1:84
Kingston, Maxine Hong, 1:123, 193–194, 204, *204,* 235
kinship migrations, 2:501
kinship networks, 1:86, 93–94, 254, 267
Kissinger Commission, 2:416
kitanai, 2:394
Kitano, Harry H.L., 2:428–429
kitsui, 2:394
Kiusic, Kim, 2:497
Kiyama, Henry, 2:461
Klemperer, Otto, 2:344
KMT. *See* Kuomintang Party
KNA. *See* Korean National Association
Knights of Labor, 1:129
Knowland, William F., 1:165
Knox, Frank, 2:469
Kobo, Duane, 1:45
Koda, Keisaburo, 2:387, 422, 429–430
Kohlberg, Alfred, 1:141
Kojong (king of Korea), 2:498
Kokoku Shokumin Emigration Company, 2:397, 398
Kondo, Alan, 1:45
Kong-Thao, Kazoua, 2:510
konohiki, 2:529
Korea, 2:498–499, 594c
Koreagate, 2:486–487
Korean American Adoptee Adoptive Family Network, 1:7
Korean American Coalition (KAC), 2:487, 489, 602c

Korean American Historical Society, 1:44
Korean Americans, 1:2; 2:475–502, 595c
  AKPS, 2:480
  Amerasians and multiracial Asian Americans, 1:14
  anti-Asian violence, 1:17
  assimilation and acculturation, 1:33
  Association of Korean Political Studies, 2:480
  bilingual education, 1:38
  business and entrepreneurship, 2:480–483
  Chang, Sarah, 2:483
  Cho, Margaret, 2:484
  DPAA, 1:43
  history and culture, 2:475–479
  KAC, 2:487
  KNA, 2:488
  Koreagate, 2:486–487
  Korean American Coalition, 2:487
  Korean National Association, 2:488
  Koreatown (Los Angeles), 2:488–489
  Lee, Sammy, 2:490
  literature, 2:490–492
  Los Angeles riots, 2:492–493
  Moon, Sun Myung, 2:493–494
  music and musicians, 1:67
  Paik, Nam June, 2:494–495
  religion, 1:79; 2:495–497
  students, 2:497–498
  transnationalism, 1:87
  Treaty of Amity and Commerce, 2:498–499
  war brides, 1:90; 2:499–500
  women, 2:500–501
Korean Cultural Center (Los Angeles), 2:478
Korean ethnic church, 2:486
Korean Immigrant Workers Alliance, 2:489
Korean independence, 2:488
Korean Independence League, 2:485
Korean National Association (KNA), 2:485, 488
Korean Political Science Association (KPSA), 2:480
Korean Produce Association of New York, 2:477
Korean Provisional Government, 2:488
Korean War, 2:599c
  China Lobby, 1:141
  Chinese American community politics, 1:164, 165
  Korean American women, 2:501
  Korean war brides, 2:499
  transnationalism, 1:86
Korean Youth and Community Center (Los Angeles), 2:489
Koreatown (Los Angeles), 2:476, 488–489, 492–493, 601c
Korematsu, Fred, 2:374, 376, 377
  coram nobis cases, 2:391, 392
  CWRIC, 2:391
  Japanese American exile/incarceration, World War II, 2:403
  Korematsu v. United States, 2:430
  redress movement, 2:455

Korematsu v. United States, 2:374, 391–392, 398, 412, 430, 598c
Koyu, Masuyama, 2:386
KPSA (Korean Political Science Association), 2:480
Kriyananda, Swami, 2:359
kriya yoga, 2:358, 359
Kubota, Guntaro, 2:410
Ku Klux Klan, 1:52; 2:576, 588
kulintang, 1:67
Kumiai, 2:424
kumpang, 1:262
kundiman, 1:67
kung fu, 1:207–209
Kung Yu Club, 1:164
Kuno, Yoshisaburo, 2:414
Kuomintang (KMT) Party, 1:121
  CCBA, 1:155–156
  CCNAA, 2:546
  in Chinatowns (general), 1:194–195
  in Chinatown (New York City), 1:145, 146
  in Chinatown (San Francisco), 1:149
  Chinese American community politics, 1:163–166
  Chinese American press, 1:219, 220
  Taiwanese Americans, 2:541
  Taiwan independence movement, 2:557, 558
Kurtines, William, 1:71
Kusatsu, Clyde, 1:42
kuya, 1:253
Kwan, Florence Chinn, 1:244
Kwan, Michelle, 1:124, 195–196, 210, 212
Kwan, Nancy, 1:183
kyes (credit societies), 2:477, 482
kyudo, 2:438

LAAPIS (Los Angeles Asian Pacific Islander Sisters), 1:48
Labor, U.S. Department of, 1:8, 123; 2:603c
labor and employment
  Asian Americans (general), 1:3, 57–60, *58*
    alien land law movement, 1:11
    Asian American movement, 1:25
    transnationalism, 1:86
    undocumented immigration, 1:88–89
  Cambodian Americans, 1:113, 116, 117
  Chamorros, 2:526–527
  Chinese Americans, 1:120, 123, 196–198, *197*
    Burlingame Treaty, 1:133–134
    business and entrepreneurship, 1:135
    Chinatowns on the Western Frontier, 1:153
    Chinese Exclusion Act, 1:156
    contract labor, 1:168
    family life, 1:179
    garment factories, 1:186
    railroads, 1:221–222
    restaurants and cuisine, 1:227
    women, 1:245